Ginsberg

Beat Poet

Barry Miles

BOOKS

2 4 6 8 10 9 7 5 3 1

This edition published in 2010 by Virgin Books, an imprint of Ebury Publishing
A Random House Group Company

A fully revised and updated edition was published by Virgin Publishing Ltd in 2000

First published in Great Britain by Viking in 1989

Copyright © Barry Miles, 1989, 2000, 2010

Barry Miles has asserted his right under the Copyright, Designs and Patents Act
1988 to be identified as the author of this work

The Random House Group Limited Reg. No. 954009

Addresses for companies within the Random House Group can be found at
www.randomhouse.co.uk

A CIP catalogue record for this book is available from the British Library

The Random House Group Limited supports The Forest Stewardship Council
[FSC], the leading international forest certification organisation. All our titles that
are printed on Greenpeace-approved FSC-certified paper carry the FSC logo.
Our paper procurement policy can be found at www.rbooks.co.uk/environment

Mixed Sources
Product group from well-managed
forests and other controlled sources
www.fsc.org Cert no. TT-COC-2139
© 1996 Forest Stewardship Council

Typeset by TW Typesetting, Plymouth, Devon
Printed in the UK by CPI Bookmarque, Croydon, CR0 4TD

ISBN 9780753522523

To buy books by your favourite authors and register for offers visit
www.rbooks.co.uk

GINSBERG

Barry Miles is a bestselling author of numerous biographies and cultural histories of the Beat Generation luminaries, The Beatles, the sixties movements and its musicians. He lives in London.

Also by Barry Miles

William Burroughs: El Hombre Invisible
Jack Kerouac: King of the Beats
Paul McCartney: Many Years From Now
The Beat Hotel: Ginsberg, Burroughs and Corso in Paris,
   1957–1963
In the Sixties
Frank Zappa: The Biography
Hippie
Charles Bukowski
Pink Floyd: The Early Years
Peace, 50 Years of Protest
The British Invasion
London Calling: A Countercultural History of London Since 1945

[ed] Allen Ginsberg: Howl, Original Draft Facsimile Edition
[ed] William Burroughs: Naked Lunch, the Restored Text
   (with James Grauerholz)
[ed] Beat Collection

Contents

Preface

More than a decade after the deaths of Allen Ginsberg and William Burroughs, interest in the Beat Generation continues to grow. In America the Beat Generation is known as the first home-grown literary movement (in that the Lost Generation of Hemingway, Stein, Scott-Fitzgerald and company is associated more with Paris than with the USA). The Beats have become a favoured area for literary studies and are perfect material for this: they were colourful, a little bohemian, exponents of sexual freedom and experimental drug-taking, and they wanted to change society. They are also safe – the original New York group are all dead: Gregory Corso can no longer throw up over your shoes, Herbert Huncke will no longer relieve you of your wallet and even Allen Ginsberg will not startle the literature students by blurting out his most intimate sexual fantasies. A whole new generation of professors has grown up to teach the Beat Generation canon, with the number of critical studies on their work now far exceeding the number of books the Beats themselves published in their lifetimes. As Ginsberg put it, humorously, in the introduction to my biography of William Burroughs: 'Who has the time to read such big biographies? Certainly such readers are very specialised creatures in Midwestern libraries appreciatively washing their hands and smoking a little hash before opening up these dreadful tomes.' But Ginsberg very much encouraged such 'specialised creatures' and even in his lifetime a small cottage industry had grown up around him to publish his journals, letters and essays.

Of Ginsberg's own 'dreadful tomes', his *Indian Journals* was the first to appear, published by City Lights Books in 1970, followed in 1974 by *Allen Verbatim: Lectures on Poetry* edited by Gordon Ball, who followed this with *Journals Early Fifties, Early Sixties*, published by Grove in 1977. Creative Arts in Berkeley published

As Ever: The Collected Correspondence of Allen Ginsberg and Neal Cassady that same year and more letters followed in 1980 with *Straight Heart's Delight: Love Poems and Selected Letters*, a celebration of Ginsberg's relationship with Peter Orlovsky. When I was working on this biography with him, we took time out for me to edit a variorum edition of the manuscript of *Howl*, based very much on *The Waste Land*, as edited by Valerie Eliot. Called *Howl: Original Draft Facsimile, Transcript, and Variant Versions, Fully Annotated by Author, with Contemporaneous Correspondence, Account of First Public Reading, Legal Skirmishes, Precursor Texts and Bibliography*, it was published in 1986. A 50th-anniversary edition came out in 2006 to commemorate the half century of the publication of the poem, by which time there were six other books about *Howl* in print, substantiating Ginsberg's belief in the importance of the poem and confirming his prescience in deciding to fully document the poem in his lifetime.

After his death the Ginsberg cottage industry stepped up its output: first came *Death and Fame: Poems 1993–1997*, published by HarperCollins in 1999 and edited by his old friend Peter Hale, who had worked in Ginsberg's office during the final years of Ginsberg's life. Then began the collections: *Deliberate Prose: Selected Essays 1952–1995* in 2000; *Spontaneous Mind: Selected Interviews: 1958–1996* in 2001; *Family Business: Selected Letters between a Father and Son* in 2001; *The Book of Martyrdom and Artifice: First Journals and Poems 1937–1952* in 2006 and in that same year *Collected Poems 1947–1997*, which was now expanded to include everything published since 1980. 2008 saw *The Letters of Allen Ginsberg* and a year later *The Selected Letters of Allen Ginsberg and Gary Snyder*, closely followed by *Jack Kerouac and Allen Ginsberg: the Letters*. Unfortunately, William Burroughs threw away all of his correspondence until the late sixties, when he was shown that it could be valuable; however, Ginsberg kept his letters from Burroughs, and a selection was published in 1978. Allen and I had begun to compile the contents list for a book of his letters back in 1986, when he estimated that there must be more than 60,000 letters and postcards out there. The Ginsberg Estate still has plenty to do.

This biography was not the first book on Ginsberg's life, that was Jane Kramer's 1970 portrait, *Paterfamilias: Allen Ginsberg in America*, expanded from her *New Yorker* magazine profile and in

1972 Eric Mottram published a thoughtful essay, *Allen Ginsberg in the Sixties*. The book in your hands was, however, the first full-length biography. I was fortunate to have had unique access. Ginsberg and I had been friends since 1965 and I had heard many of the stories many times over. I knew the surviving members of his family: his father, stepmother, brother and several of his surviving aunts as well as most of the main characters in his life: Carl Solomon, William Burroughs, Gregory Corso, Lawrence Ferlinghetti; sadly, I never met Kerouac. I interviewed Ginsberg extensively and he went over the final manuscript twice, making hundreds of suggestions, many of which I incorporated.

There have been and will be more biographies and more PhDs; new books on the Beat Generation appear all the time and as new letters come to light and more personal memoirs are published a fuller picture of their intellectual achievement will be given. Mine is almost the last generation to have known the principals. The next generation of scholars will have to rely on published sources and library research. Given their distance from their subjects, their approach will likely be more critical – a good thing. Allen did not like my treatment of his interest in Tibetan Buddhism in this book, but it was mild compared to the opinions of many of his contemporaries. His publisher Lawrence Ferlinghetti, for instance, told David Meltzer in *San Francisco Beat: Talking With the Poets*, 'I think Buddhist practice really harmed his poetry,' and said 'I thought there was a shocking deterioration in his poetry'. This is an opinion I share, though I was never quite so blunt about it when discussing the matter with Ginsberg himself. But to the general public, he was known for his great early poems, as a media personality and as a teacher.

Evidence of widespread interest in Ginsberg came with the 50th anniversary of the publication of *Howl*. The Great Salt Lake Book Festival staged a re-enactment of the Six Gallery reading (when the poem was first read aloud) and Litquake, the annual San Francisco literary festival, also staged their own reading. There were events in New York City and Chicago and the University of Leeds celebrated the event with 'Howl for Now', a reading and discussions, a series of musical responses to the poem, dramatic monologues, and an art exhibition. Camille Paglia even said Ginsberg should have been awarded the Nobel Prize for Literature: 'Through his influence on Bob Dylan (who in turn influenced the

Beatles), Ginsberg revolutionised rock lyrics and directly affected the thinking of several generations of young people around the world. For this alone, he deserved the Nobel Prize – which continues to be awarded to safe, standard, derivative, politely leftish, literary humanitarians.'

More than a decade after his death, all of Ginsberg's major books remain in print, as do many of his recordings, musical compositions and his documentary-film appearances. He left behind a huge body of work but perhaps his most enduring legacy was to challenge the sterile, conformist, consumerist, cold-war viewpoint of America. He took centre stage in the sixties counter-culture ('flower power', which he is said to have named) to propose instead greater self-awareness, a pro-sexual, anti-war, anti-consumerist, ecologically sound approach to life. He fought against communist bureaucracies and the deadly power of big corporations, he campaigned tirelessly against censorship in all its forms but, despite periods of depression when he thought the world was doomed, he always had an ultimate goal in sight. He proclaimed his vision of utoian society in *Howl*: 'Holy the Fifth International' but he also lamented 'the fifth international of workers, entrepreneurs, peasants and indigenous communities of the world has not yet assembled to propose survival norms in an era of imperial private and state-monopoly capital's near-absolute and potentially suicidal power.'

Allen was very fond of Percy Bysshe Shelley's line: 'Poets are the unacknowledged legislators of the world', which he believed and often quoted. This belief gave him the authority to correspond with Bertrand Russell about nuclear disarmament, to telephone Henry Kissinger – and get through – to talk about the war in Vietnam and to challenge the head of the CIA to disprove Ginsberg's assertion that the CIA was involved in shipping opium from the Golden Triangle. It enabled him to declare, in his poem 'Wichita Vortex Sutra': I lift my voice aloud,/Make Mantra of American language now,/I here declare the end of the War!

Ginsberg took seriously his role as a poet and helped shape American public opinion throughout the second half of the twentieth century. For many, he was the conscience of post-war America.

Barry Miles, London, 2010.

1 Childhood, Paterson

The empty pond where I played, I will see it no more. The old house I cried to leave, the cats I cried to die. Childhood, the dresses I put on in front of the mirror. Those dreams of a magic spell, white haired Norman . . . the tree in the empty lot, the meadow and the grass. The secret pathway through the woods.

On 9 November 1993, Allen Ginsberg arrived in Paris, Gare de L'Est, a balding, distinguished-looking, 63-year-old gentleman with a neatly trimmed beard, stepping from his first-class compartment on the Munich–Paris express: 'a senior poet in state, with hotel room waiting, old confrere Jean-Jacques Lebel and taxi at station this afternoon.' He was in Paris to attend the French première of Jerry Aronson's film *The Life and Times of Allen Ginsberg*, for the relaunch of new editions of *Howl* and *Kaddish* by Editions Christian Bourgeois with new photographic covers by Ginsberg himself, and to be made a Chevalier des Arts et Lettres by the French government.

He had been inducted into the American Academy of Arts and Letters in 1974, something which gave him tremendous satisfaction and which he regarded with great seriousness and not a little pride. On one of his many reading trips to Paris, he had asked Jean-Jacques Lebel if he could get him the medal of a Chevalier des Arts et Lettres, knowing that Lebel was a good friend of Jack Lang, the Minister of Culture. Jean-Jacques Lebel thought his motive was 'trying to put forever the Beat Generation poets on the intellectual and cultural map. He was very proud to be part of the American Academy of Letters, he was very proud when Bill Burroughs was introduced there. He struggled for years to make that happen and it was important for him, the official stuff.' Lebel consulted with the Ministry and they agreed. But political intent rarely runs smoothly; there was a change in government and it was a right-wing minister of culture, Jacques Toulon, who pinned the ribbon on Ginsberg's breast that rainy evening in November.

The ceremony took place in the Palais Royal, Cardinal Richelieu's magnificent seventeenth-century residence, the east wing of which now accommodates the Ministry of Culture. Jacques Toulon had asked Lebel to help him with his speech. Though he represented a very different political viewpoint, he had read Ginsberg's books when he was young, and had a great deal of respect for him. He made a very moving speech, saying that Ginsberg deserved the medal despite any cultural conflict between their two countries, who were then in dispute over the General Agreement on Trade and Tariffs (GATT), a very touchy subject in France. He told the assembled audience of Ginsberg's friends and collegues that, along with American Beat writers like Gregory Corso and William Burroughs, Ginsberg had lived in France, and taken something from French culture and repaid the debt by leaving his imprint on a generation of French intellectuals. Ginsberg was told that the award was for 'admiration for genuine US culture, for enriching not impoverishing poetry in France'.

As Toulon spoke, Jean-Jacques Lebel whispered a translation of his speech into Ginsberg's ear, hardly able to believe it was happening: 'Here was the French State giving a medal to a poet who is openly gay, anti-war and a great mind. Then Allen said, "I will say a few words of thanks." And I thought, "Jesus Christ! What's he going to do?"' This was exactly the time when Chirac was testing French nuclear bombs in the Pacific to world-wide opprobrium and Allen naturally brought this up, saying, 'You can imagine I disagree highly with that.' Lebel recalled, 'He was telling a member of the French Government that he's against something the government is doing, and these are the very guys who are giving him the medal. That's typical of Allen, he just had to speak his mind. He could not censor himself, that's why we loved him so much.'

But this was also the week when a vocal, somewhat heated campaign was launched to establish quotas to protect European film and television programme makers from being swamped by American imports. Jean-Luc Godard and others presented an argument for fifty per cent minimum European programming to the European Parliament and the media was filled with the debate.

Ginsberg had read about it and continued his speech, saying, 'As much as I disagree with your government when they explode nuclear bombs in the Pacific or anywhere else, I want to go on record to say that I agree with you one hundred per cent in resisting Hollywood and American schlock TV. And I absolutely support the revolt of European film-makers against Hollywood. Hollywood has destroyed America . . .' and the audience applauded. He told them – as Jean-Jacques Lebel had suggested – that he represented 'The Other Americans' and that he was himself banned from daytime television by American censorship laws. If the Americans wanted a free market of goods, he would like to remind them that they should also have a 'free market in ideas, without censorship'. Here he stumbled and couldn't remember the French for 'indecent'. He hesitated and Lebel suggested 'obscenity'. He settled on 'blue words', dirty words; the words he was forbidden to use before midnight on American radio and television.

After Allen's speech, over drinks, the minister came up and said in good humour, 'I didn't like the first part of your speech, but your second part was fantastic!' The outspokenness of the American poet was picked up by the press: that Allen Ginsberg had not mouthed the usual platitudes but had used a state occasion to make his opinion known to the French minister of culture, an important figure. Afterwards they were taken to an expensive little Japanese restaurant near the Ministry. As they were eating their sushi, Ginsberg turned to Lebel and asked him, 'Well, did I say the right thing?'

He and Lebel walked home together to the Left Bank, crossing the Seine to more familiar territory. Ginsberg dropped Lebel off at his door on Blvd Raspail and continued a couple more blocks to his hotel on rue Chomel, where he washed his underwear – socks and pants, ready for another day.

This was a classic Allen Ginsberg occasion. He looked a respectable professor, but his sober suit and tie were bought very inexpensively at a Lower East Side thrift shop. He was respectful, rejoicing in the recognition that the award made to the literary movement he was largely instrumental in founding. Resourceful, he was also prepared to turn the occasion to his own ends, taking every opportunity to use his fame to broadcast unpopular or critical views. A messenger, he passionately believed in ending nuclear weapons testing, and this was one of his own hard-fought campaigns; but here he also lent his support to the fight against dubbed American soap operas and action films, not because he understood the arguments, but because he trusted the judgement of the people making them. He also knew it would curry favour, it was an easy point. Mischievous, he enjoyed the notoriety of bucking authority, deflating pomposity and hypocrisy, and getting his name in the papers. The world's most famous poet, ultimately grounded in reality, going home to wash his underwear.

Ginsberg had a Russian–Jewish background. His mother Naomi was from Nevel, a small town on the main road between Saint Petersburg and Odessa, about 120 kilometres north of Vitebsk in the middle of the Jewish Pale of Settlement. Her father, Mendel Livergant (his name was shortened to Morris Levy at Ellis Island), sold American Singer sewing machines to the peasantry; this was the family business.

The Livergants were educated men, who spoke Russian as well as Yiddish. In those days a sign of emancipation, whether Socialist or Zionist, was to shave off the traditional Jewish beard and to wear a Western suit rather than the shapeless clothes of thick brown linen woven at home. This Mendel did, but in other respects the country ways prevailed and both he and his brother, Isser, married their first cousins, the Bruks sisters from nearby Orsa.

Mendel's wife, Judith, gave birth to four children, Eleanor, Naomi, Max and Sam. She and Mendel were both sympathetic to the anti-czarist revolutionary movement, so in 1904, when it seemed as if Mendel would be drafted to fight for the czar in the Russo–Japanese War, the whole family moved to Vitebsk to stay with Isser's family while Mendel and Isser joined the flow of emigrants to the United States.

Isser and Fanny's house in Vitebsk was a two-room wooden cabin. Judith and her four children squeezed in alongside Fanny and her seven children and for the next year the two sisters brought up the eleven children, waiting for Mendel and Isser to raise enough money for boat tickets so their families could join them in America. Naomi grew up speaking Yiddish. She learned to play the mandolin Russian-style and later told her children stories of seeing Cossacks riding through the town in carriages.

Vitebsk was a city of low, crudely built wooden buildings dominated by the shining domes of the Greek Orthodox Church. It was illegal to build synagogues higher than the churches. The unpaved streets were ankle-deep in dust in summer, mud in winter. Goats, chickens, geese, ducks, cows, cats and dogs wandered everywhere. The painter Marc Chagall moved to Vitebsk when he was young and his paintings of wooden houses, rabbis and violin players floating over the rooftops reflect the town as it was when Naomi lived there. There was no Jewish ghetto since Jews made up over a third of the population and owned more than a quarter of the town's businesses.

It was the second-largest city of the province and a centre for the revolutionary ideas that spread into the Pale from Germany. Many of the Jews became Communists whereas further south, in the Ukraine, the revolutionary tendency was towards Socialism or Zionism, a division that was mirrored in the political opinions of Louis and Naomi Ginsberg when they met, years later, in Newark, New Jersey. The Vitebsk of Naomi Livergant no longer exists. It was destroyed completely by the Nazis, and after the war the Russians rebuilt it as the main industrial centre for the area.

In 1905, the year of the first pogrom in the Northern Pale, the two families left for the New World, Mendel's family heading for New York City and Isser's for Winnipeg. Mendel had settled on Orchard Street near Rivington Street, in the heart of the old Jewish section of Manhattan, where he had opened a candy store. Ginsberg described it in 'Kaddish': 'first home-made sodas of the century, hand-churned ice cream in backroom on musty brown floor boards . . .' It was here that Naomi ate 'the first poisonous tomatoes of America'; she later told Allen that Eastern European immigrants thought tomatoes were poisonous. The family then moved to Newark, New Jersey, away from the slums and tenements of the Lower East Side. There Naomi went to Barringer High School and, in 1912, met Louis Ginsberg. They were both seventeen.

Louis Ginsberg's father Pinkus (Peter), who came from Lvov, Galicia, near the present Czechoslovakian border, was orphaned when young. He moved to Pinsk, a small industrial town about half-way between Kiev and Warsaw, but in view of the increasing political unrest in Russia, he decided that his prospects would be better if he joined the growing stream of emigrants to the United States. He made the crossing sometime in the 1880s and headed for Newark, New Jersey, where he had relatives. There he met Rebecca Schechtman. Rebecca's parents had come to the United States from the Ukraine in the 1870s, when she was very young. They settled into the growing Jewish community in Newark, where her father, Yossel, was able to make a living as a piece goods dealer and played an active role in the local synagogue.

Pinkus and Rebecca married and in 1895, their first child, Louis, was born. Peter was thirty-two and Rebecca twenty-six. Their family grew, and Louis was soon followed by Abraham, Rose, Clara and finally, in 1912, by Hannah. Pinkus worked a twelve-hour day at a hat factory. Louis remembered taking his packed lunch to him there: 'It was a room full of steam. He was standing on the wooden platform. He had on only a pair of pants and was completely wet, and I couldn't see him because of the steam. I was horrified.' He was eventually fired for his role in a famous strike and, after other jobs, he and Rebecca set themselves up in business, paying three hundred dollars for the horse, wagon and goodwill of The West Side Laundry Company. The goodwill was not worth much, because the former owner immediately started a new company and poached back many of his old customers. However, the Ginsbergs had many friends and relatives, and for fifteen years they made a reasonable living washing clothes and stretching curtains.

At home, Louis grew up with the Socialist viewpoint of his parents, both members of the Yiddish Arbeiter Ring (Workmen's Circle). Pinkus took Louis to lectures by Eugene Victor Debs, a founder of the IWW and the Socialist presidential candidate from 1900 to 1920, and Louis quickly embraced his ideas. 'He was magnificent,' he later said. 'All the ironies of the capitalist system came blazing forth. He was a brilliant man.' Louis was so impressed that he named his first son after Debs.

Naomi, meanwhile, was a Communist. Her sister Eleanor, who was five years older, was a Party cell member. Naomi felt torn between Louis' Socialism and the position of her family, but eventually she sided with her sister and joined the Party. Louis' family were disgusted, particularly his mother Rebecca, who used to browbeat Naomi whenever she visited. The two women never got along.

The division between Socialists and Communists, always enormous, was exacerbated when war broke out in Europe. The Communists were in favour of the USA entering the war and the Socialists against it, with Debs coming out strongly in favour of pacifism. Despite their political differences Naomi and Louis continued to see each other. Both graduated from high school in 1914 and Louis went on to Rutgers, while Naomi attended Normal School to train as a grammar school teacher. Her specialty became teaching educationally disadvantaged children, and she was very good at it: 'teaching school, laughing with idiots, the backward classes – her Russian specialty', Ginsberg wrote in 'Kaddish', and he went on to describe her students: 'morons with dreamy lips, great eyes, thin feet & sticky fingers, swaybacked, rachitic –'

When the United States entered the Great War, Louis was drafted but was classified 4F because of his poor eyesight, and so avoided the conflict.

Naomi's mother, Judith, died in 1918, a victim of the influenza epidemic that swept Europe and the States after the war. Not long after, in 1919, Naomi had her first nervous breakdown. She was teaching school in Woodbine, New Jersey, where she developed a hypersensitivity to light and sound. She had to stay home from school and lie in a darkened room for three weeks. She knew something was seriously wrong with her but no one was able to diagnose it. After she recovered she refused to discuss it.

Naomi and Louis decided to marry. Both his parents were opposed to the marriage. Rebecca especially did not like Naomi, partly because of her political opinions, partly because Rebecca was a strong, domineering woman and Naomi stood up to her. They argued constantly. After Naomi's strange illness, Rebecca was even more convinced that Naomi was not a suitable match for her eldest son. But Louis insisted he loved her, and he and Naomi were married in Woodbine, in 1919. They settled in Newark, near his parents. They made an attractive couple: Naomi lithe, energetic and with a good figure; Louis thin, dapper, with small round eyeglasses and his hair brushed back. Both were socially concerned, determined to make the world a better place.

Louis had begun to write poetry in high school and had his first poem published in the Barringer year book. In 1920, when he was 25, Louis wrote 'Roots', which was to be the major poem on which his reputation as a poet rested. He and Naomi joined the Poetry Society of America, a meeting place for lyric poets, and they would go to readings in Greenwich Village with the poet Maxwell Bodenheim, with whom Naomi later claimed to have had a brief affair. Free love and a break with Victorian morality were vital aspects of emerging feminism, although in the United States at that time the 'new women' were more or less concentrated in Greenwich Village. Vegetarianism and nudism were other parts of the ethos of modernity, and Louis and Naomi spent at least one vacation at a Marxist nudist camp in upstate New York.

In the early 1920s, Louis was friendly with Lola Ridge, who ran the New York office of *Broom*, Alfred Kreymborg and Harold Loeb's literary magazine. Thursday afternoon was open house in the basement of Margaret Loeb's house on East Ninth Street. In *Being Geniuses Together*, Lola Ridge's assistant, Kay Boyle, remembered: 'I passed cups and plates to Marianne Moore ... John Dos Passos, who uneasily toasted the revolution in tea, and to Elinor Wylie ...; I served them in silent awe: Jean Toomer, Waldo Frank, Babette Deutsch, Mary Heaton Vorse, Gorham Munson, Laura Benét, Edwin Arlington Robinson, Louis Ginsberg, Glenway Wescott, Monroe Wheeler, and countless others, listening while they read aloud their work, listening, listening, my critical faculties wholly numbed, believing that not one dispensable word could be spoken here.'

Louis and Naomi also knew Joe Gould, then a protégé of Ezra Pound, and the anthologist Louis Untermeyer, who included Louis' work in his *Modern American and British Poetry*, *Modern American Poetry: A Critical Anthology* and other collections. Later, in the 1930s, Kreymborg published Louis' poems in *The Others*. Louis contributed to all the literary magazines of the day, including Max Eastman's *The New Masses* which, although it was the cultural organ of the Communist Party, published such non-Communists as Hemingway, Dos Passos, Mann, Cowley and Anderson. *The New Masses* awarded Louis an important poetry prize. But the biggest event was always when he had a poem printed in the *New York Times* magazine. Then, particularly if it was a full page, everyone in the family would carry a clipping to show friends and neighbours.

Louis was a lyric poet of the Elinor Wylie–A.E. Housman mode and maintained that verse should rhyme. To him, free verse was anathema, and he simply didn't understand it. He was content to remain in the literary backwater of The Poetry Society, although when Naomi's sister, Eleanor, accused him of being a 'bourgeois poet' he strongly resented it. Louis Untermeyer told him, 'You have the lyric touch,' and as John Hall Wheelock said on the dust wrapper of Louis' first book, 'There is no other poet working in quite the same field that Louis Ginsberg has made so unmistakably his own.'

Between 1921, when their son Eugene was born, and 1926, Louis and Naomi moved three times, finally settling at 163 Quitman Street, in Newark, a few doors from Louis' parents. Their marriage seems to have been happy then, although the political tensions between them continued to rankle. On 3 June 1926, at 2 a.m., Naomi gave birth to her second son, in Beth Israel Hospital. He was named Irwin Allen Ginsberg after his great-grandfather, S'rul Avrum Ginsberg.

In 1929, Naomi underwent very serious pancreas surgery, during which she nearly died and which left her abdomen badly scarred. The family moved in with Eleanor and her husband, Max, in the central Bronx, near Jerome Avenue, so that Eleanor could nurse her sister and look after the children. Ginsberg had vague early memories of these days in the Bronx, images which appeared in his poem 'White Shroud'.

After some six months in the Bronx, the Ginsbergs moved to Paterson, New Jersey, where Louis taught English at Central High School. Naomi was not with them when they moved. She had had another and much more severe nervous breakdown and was recuperating at the Bloomingdale Sanitorium, near Tarrytown, New York. Again light and sound hurt her, and she was disorientated and confused. Some of Ginsberg's earliest recollections were of visiting Naomi at Bloomingdale; dim memories of a big green lawn with croquet mallets, the patients dressed in white.

The apartment at 83 Fair Street, Paterson, was in a run-down Jewish neighbourhood of shabby apartment buildings, wood-frame houses, warehouses, small workshops and produce markets. Bridge Street, a block away, led down to the Passaic River where the warehouses and factories gave way to slums, and black people lived in old wood-frame houses, their porches heavy with laundry hanging out over the dirty water. A Bell Telephone building was constructed on the corner next door shortly after the Ginsbergs moved in. Allen remembered playing marbles on the sandy ground in front of it. There was an alley running between the Telephone building and Allen's apartment house and he was always scared of ghosts there. This common enough fear of the shadowy figure, or boogeyman, gave rise to the image of the 'shrouded stranger' that was to occur in many of his early poems.

Although they lived close to downtown Paterson, the neighbourhood still retained some links with its pastoral past. A half block along Fair Street toward Bridge Street was an old wooden house that had once been a farm. Two old ladies lived there and allowed Allen and his friends to play in the barn in the back which still had stalls with half-doors for horses.

Across the street was an orthodox synagogue and on the corner with Bridge Street was a pharmacy/cigar/candy store run by Mrs Abrams and her husband. Louis was very friendly with Mrs Abrams and Eugene and Allen once pieced together the torn-up fragments of a passionate letter from Louis to her which they found in a wastebasket. They were smart enough not to show it to Naomi who had by then returned from the sanatorium.

83 Fair Street had a long hall with the rooms leading off it. It was rented unfurnished but Louis and Naomi's mahogany wedding furniture soon filled it. They had lace curtains, a red lacquer Chinese chair and a floor-standing wind-up victrola. They owned 'The March of the Tin Soldiers' and songs by Caruso which Allen played continuously when he was old enough to operate the machine. There was great excitement when Louis brought home a radio. It was housed in a tall, fat, mahogany cabinet and was given pride of place on the sideboard. Once Louis read his poems on the local station, and the whole family gathered round to hear his voice come over the air.

Allen attended kindergarten a block and a half away, at P.S. 1. Since Naomi was still in the sanatorium, a family friend took him to school on his first day. Allen, terrified of being left alone, yelled and screamed so insistently that his father had to be called to take him home. Louis' life was difficult. He was devoted to Naomi, and the tragedy of her madness weighed heavily upon him. To pay for her care in the private sanatorium, he had to borrow heavily from the Credit Union, a worrying burden during the Depression, and he had two growing boys to care for. He found solace in his poetry and had a great deal published. Family and friends helped him with the boys, and each weekend he would take them to a family get-together in Newark.

Louis arranged for a neighbour to provide lunch for Allen and his elder brother, Eugene, on school days, and in the evenings Louis would either bring something home from the deli or take them out to eat, usually to the S&Z on River Street, just down from the poultry market where chickens were slaughtered. There they would have borscht, 'rye bread delicious tender chicken giblets in pale gravy', or Allen's favourite, Chicken Fricassee.

Later, in his notebooks, Allen referred to eating at the S&Z, out in the grown-up world with his father and brother, as one of his 'first experiences of reality'. The S&Z also influenced his taste in food. Throughout his life he preferred inexpensive Eastern European cooking to all other and was more comfortable eating borscht, kasha and blintzes at the Kiev Ukrainian restaurant on Second Avenue than dining at the Four Seasons.

Allen played with his best friend, Danny Feitlowitz, who lived next door, and with the boys and girls who lived upstairs. The boys all dressed in long stockings and woollen knickers. A few doors away was the bridge where the Erie Railroad crossed the street. The railroad ran on a cinder embankment which cut through the backyards. Beyond the railroad tracks was a huge redbrick silk factory, one of Paterson's major industries, and they could hear its constant rattle at home in the apartment. Spools of defective silk and the cardboard cones that silk was wound on were thrown out and littered the area. The kids would take them from the factory garbage and use them as playthings before leaving them lying in the street. Allen and his friends ran wild through the backyards, along the railroad embankment and explored the pond behind the silk factory where the boys bathed naked and dared each other to walk the retaining wall to the twenty-foot drop of the spillway:

The bathing pool hidden/ behind the silk factory/ fed by its drainage pipes;/ all the pictures we carry in our mind.

Naomi returned from the sanatorium not long after they moved into Fair Street. Allen's most vivid early memory was of a fire in his bedroom. Playing with matches he ignited a rattan wastebasket that Naomi had made in an occupational therapy workshop. She was asleep in another room, tended by her nurse, and when Allen was unable to stamp out the flames, the apartment filled with smoke. Fire engines were called and Louis was summoned from school. Allen denied everything.

Another memory, which recurs in his journals and dream records, was of an incident from 1931, when Allen was five. Louis sent him down to the corner candy store, where the big boys hung out, to buy a stamp and mail a letter. Allen bought the stamp but stuck it on the lower left side of the letter instead of the top right. No one had shown him how to do it. Everyone in the store laughed, and he felt such shame and humiliation that the incident remained one of the most persistent memories of early childhood.

The family spent two summers at Camp Nicht-Gedeiget ('No-worry'), run by the Communist Party, near Monroe Lake in upstate New York. A beautiful wooded place, it had cabins and a few dormitories, and there was singing round the campfire in the evening. There were salamanders and fish in the streams. It was idyllic for the city kids, used to playing in the street.

Allen wrote of those those halcyon days in 'Kaddish':

> Holy mother, now you smile on your love, your world is born anew, children run naked in the field spotted with dandelions, they eat in the plum tree grove at the end of the meadow and find a cabin where a white-haired negro teaches them the mystery of his rainbarrel –

Louis would come out and visit on weekends, but for him the camp was not so idyllic. In the mess hall there were big paintings of bloated capitalists and, such was the rift between the Communists and the Socialists in the 1930s, there were also paintings of evil Socialists with their hands dripping with blood. This was the time of the Moscow purges and the camp even had its own mock tribunal. Someone had made an improper remark to a woman who was bathing in the nude, and this minor domestic incident resulted in a full-scale trial before a big crowd gathered in front of the mess hall.

As Naomi recovered from her breakdown, she became active again in the local branch of the Communist Party, which met in a room over Esther Abramson's brother's pharmacy on Bridge Street. The group itself was quite small, five or ten members, but there was a large crowd for public meetings if someone famous, such as William Z. Foster, spoke. For a time Naomi was the branch secretary. Louis felt this threatened his job as a school-teacher and objected further on political grounds since he was a Socialist of the Eugene Debs-Norman Thomas school. Neverthe-less, Naomi would sometimes take the boys with her to meetings, and the first songs Allen learned as a child were 'The Red Flag' and the union song 'On The Line'.

In his poem 'America', he wrote: 'America when I was seven momma took me to Communist Cell meetings they sold us garbanzos a handful per ticket a ticket costs a nickel and the speeches were free everybody was angelic and sentimental about the workers it was all so sincere you have no idea what a good thing the party was in 1835 Scott Nearing was a grand old man a real mensch Mother Bloor the Silk-strikers' Ewig-Weibliche made me cry I once saw the Yiddish orator Israel Amter plain. Everybody must have been a spy.'

In 1934, when Allen was eight, the family moved to 155 Haledon Avenue where they had the whole house: two floors, a front porch and a big backyard with a chicken coop. The two brothers shared a bed. Allen always wanted to cuddle up, but Eugene kicked and pushed him back to his side of the bed. Allen later commented, 'Gene must have been sick and embarrassed at me hugging at him, pleading for physical love when we slept together as children.' The brothers were close at Haledon Avenue, but they argued constantly and Eugene teased Allen mercilessly.

The shared experience of Depression-era America was the radio and Allen grew up listening to *Flash Gordon*, *Mandrake the Magician*, the *Amos 'n' Andy Show* and *The Shadow*. At the end of the weekly *Eddie Cantor Show*, the comedian sang, 'I love to spend this hour with you, as friend to friend. I'm sorry it's through.' Allen recalled later, 'It was a really sad Jewish moment that was the high point of the week, I guess because he was Jewish and a national comedian, and everybody in the family identified with him.' Louis and Naomi, as Socialists, raised their children with no religion. Allen was not bar-mitzvahed and was not taught Hebrew. His parents spoke to Rebecca, Yossel and the other family elders in Yiddish, because that was the only language they knew, but at home they always spoke in English. In her old age,

Rebecca decided to learn English which she eventually spoke with a very thick accent. She became very patriotic and it was a matter of some amusement around the house that whenever she tried to say 'God Bless America!' it came out as 'God Blast America!'

Allen had difficulty at his new school. He was required to memorise his multiplication tables which, though he was to develop a remarkable memory for long passages of poetry, he was unable to do. He was very self-conscious at school and felt like an outsider. He would suddenly awake from sleep into the silent world of Haledon Avenue at night. The reflected lights of a passing bus would swing across the ceiling of his room as he lay thinking, in awe of the immensity of the universe. He would consider the inconceivable distances to the nearest stars and ponder the problems of infinity and the end of space. He was lonely.

Once, in an attempt to ingratiate himself with his schoolmates, he bought six baby chicks, placed them in the old chicken coop in his backyard, and invited the local kids to come and help refurbish the coop. The children took tiles from the next door neighbour's garage roof to repair the coop. After the next rainstorm Doctor Mahler, the dentist who lived next door, appeared at the door with his son Donald, one of Allen's friends, absolutely furious that Allen had wrecked his garage roof.

Doctor Mahler was a family friend. He and Louis stood talking on the stoop for an hour, and Allen was summoned to admit his guilt. Shamefully, it appeared to his brother that Allen had been trying to buy friendship. In the 1976 poem 'Drive All Blames Into One', he told the story in complete detail: 'I had six baby chicks I paid for so I could attract/ my grammar school boyfriends to play with me in my backyard . . . I'm mad at my boyfriends/ for stealing that slate I took all the blame . . .' That night Allen had a dream that the boys caught him on the street corner by the candy store: 'They got me bent over with my pants down and spanked my behind I was ashamed/ I was red faced my self was naked I got hot I had a hard on.'

A similar image of humiliation occurred in an erotic fantasy from the same year. Allen had a pre-adolescent crush on a boy named Earl, the blond-haired leader of the local gang. Once Allen spent a whole afternoon on Earl's front steps, fantasising how great it would be to have a magic spell that empowered him to do anything he wished: have millions of dollars, a white horse, a castle with a dungeon. Allen thrilled to the idea of the dungeon. Years later, in Saigon, he recalled his childhood fantasy: 'I inspect my naked victims/ chained upside down/ my fingertips thrill approval on their thighs/ white hairless cheeks I may kiss all I want/ at my mercy/ on the racks./ I pass with my strong attendants/ I am myself naked/ bending down with my buttocks out/ for their smacks of approval.'

Excited by thoughts of Earl, Allen stood behind the porch rail outside his house and pulled down his pants to expose himself to the passing motorists. No one noticed him. 'dreamy Earl/ you Prince of Paterson . . ./ first dream that made me take down my pants/ urgently to show the cars/ auto trucks/ rolling down avenue hill,' he wrote in 'Understand That This Is a Dream.' These images of humiliation found their most famous form in Ginsberg's notorious poem of 1968, 'Please Master':

> please master order me down on the floor . . .
> Master drive down till it hurts me the softness the
> Softness please master make love to my ass, give body to
> center, & fuck me for good like a girl . . .

Despite the images of punishment, Allen was disciplined rarely as a child. Though Louis would sometimes slap him, Ginsberg recalled, 'There was a lot of screaming, but Louis actually was very gentle and it was more wounded pride than wounded body.'

Naomi and Louis had frequent arguments, usually about money. When Naomi went into Bloomingdale Sanitorium, Louis had borrowed money to pay for her care and eventually owed about $3600, almost his entire annual income as a teacher. He eventually consolidated the debt with the Teachers' Credit Union, but it was still a great worry to him. During the Depression, teachers' wages were reduced, making things even worse. Naomi felt guilty about the debt and managed to convince herself that Louis had in fact given the money to his mother. Louis' family blamed Naomi for the debt, and it became a perpetual cause of familial bitterness.

Another cause of unrest in the Ginsberg home was Naomi's nudism. Louis upbraided his wife for parading naked in front of the boys, while he respected her belief in naturism (unfortunately, she had gained a good deal of weight from the medication she took and had terrible scars across her belly from her surgery). Naomi sometimes used her nudism to annoy Louis. He could never bring anyone home without telephoning first, and then she would argue vociferously for her right to be 'natural'. To Ginsberg, in retrospect, her nudism was more neurotic exhibitionism than a genuine belief in naturism. He said it did not bother him except when it upset Louis.

After her treatment in Bloomingdale, Naomi's mental health had remained stable for a number of years, and life was relatively normal. But in 1935, she suffered a relapse and the same symptoms reappeared: light pained her greatly and she lay in a darkened room in the house as the doctors ran tests. They gave her sedatives but were unable to diagnose her illness. After two months of agony, she came out of it and once again appeared to have recovered.

The illness returned a few months later in a much more severe form. Naomi paraded around the house naked, singing to herself. She began to display the classic symptoms of what is now known as paranoid schizophrenia: she heard voices, made grandiose statements and displayed exaggerated suspicion. On one level her thinking and behaviour remained clear and ordered: she had no problems with her everyday work of cooking, cleaning and bringing up the children, all of which made it almost impossible for Allen and Eugene to know when they could believe the things she said.

Louis came in for a great deal of hectoring. Naomi was convinced that he and his mother were plotting against her and that her mother-in-law was trying to kill her. As her voices and paranoia grew worse, Louis consulted her family in the Bronx and all the family friends, before he eventually made the painful decision to commit her. This time Louis simply could not afford to send Naomi back to Bloomingdale, so she was admitted to Greystone, a state hospital near Morristown, New Jersey.

It was quite different from the private sanatorium, where the patients had been treated with respect and their conditions referred to as 'nervous breakdowns'. Greystone was huge and had little therapy available other than insulin shock, Metrozol and electroshock treatments. Naomi was given a complete course of forty insulin shock treatments which succeeded in diminishing her fantasies. Though she was severely traumatised, Louis felt he had no alternative but to trust the doctors.

Most weekends, Louis brought his sons to visit. The trip took two to three hours each way on an old rattletrap bus, and Allen was frequently car-sick. They rode past small towns and farms before they reached the big grey hospital, a landscape recalled with nostalgia in Ginsberg's poems 'Garden State' and 'Kaddish'.

Upon arrival, they walked down a seemingly endless corridor, past innumerable wards filled beyond capacity with patients. 'It stank, sour smell of wards, disinfectant, vomit, piss, people incontinent,' Ginsberg said. 'I remember walking down the wards, there were all these old people, and middle-aged people lined up, crooning to themselves, singing, talking to themselves, snapping their fingers, shadow boxing, usually in sloppy ill-fitting clothes. Some of them had been left there for years by their families.'

In the visiting room there were bars on the windows, large institutional tables and long polished wooden benches like church pews. Naomi would be waiting at one of them, among the other patients receiving visitors. Haggard, she sat with her hands folded on the table, nodding her head, tearfully telling her family of her trials. She was convinced that wires had been planted in her head and that the doctors had shoved sharp sticks down her back. She was terrified of the shock treatment. She heard voices and complained about poison gas. She thought that the doctors were trying to kill her and begged Louis to take her home.

Sometimes the boys would go alone, taking with them a boiled chicken and some fruit. Naomi would tell them that Louis was plotting against her and they must help get her out. Allen found release for his sadness at the movies, sitting alone in the darkness of the Fabian Theater.

Allen and Eugene always looked forward to summer. Usually the extended family rented a house on the Jersey shore at Belmar. Each year they took a different place one or two blocks from the beach. There would be Allen's Aunt Rose and her husband Sam with their children Claire and Joel; his Aunt Clara with her husband Henry and children Patricia and Joanna; his Aunt Hannah (Honey) and his grandmother, Buba, so it was a full house, particularly at weekends when the men came down. The cousins would be at the beach by nine.

Asbury Park was a few miles away to the north and on Sunday mornings the children would be given a few dimes to take the rides at the Playland Amusement Park. They would bump into each other on the dodgems and scream with delight. They sometimes went to the Mayfair movie house in Asbury Park but most evenings were spent with the family sitting out on the porch, talking and slapping at mosquitoes.

All the cousins slept in one big room, or sometimes two or three to a room. On weekends there were sometimes so many people that meals had to be taken in shifts. On one occasion, the children were given their food at a different time and they picketed the house because they were not allowed to eat with the grown-ups. Another time they objected to the quality of the food. A note in Ginsberg's journal in July 1958 reads:

'Aunt Rose, do you remember/ Belmar, the time we kids/ at the vast breast of the dinner table/ screamed & screamed we didn't like Jewish meat?'

Naomi never liked the summers at Belmar, because she and Buba didn't get along. She would have preferred Camp Nicht-Gedeiget or another country setting. When she returned home in 1936, Naomi got her way and they spent the summer in Woodstock, New York, which in those days was an artists' colony. Various people that Louis and Naomi knew from the Poetry Society lived there. They rented a barn converted into a summer cottage by a stream in the woods, about five blocks from the village centre. Naomi won a contest at the Village Fair for the most beautiful home-made dress. Allen, who was ten years old, remembers it as an idyllic vacation. Naomi was balanced and there were very few fights and arguments.

That same year the family moved to a six-room apartment two blocks down the hill, at 72 Haledon Avenue. In the kitchen was an old fashioned black coal-fired stove where Naomi made borscht and chicken soup. To keep healthy, she bought prune juice from Felicia Kormreich's nature food shop on Main Street. Allen was transferred from P.S.17, which he had now settled into, to P.S. 12, where he felt estranged. There, a schoolyard bully, much taller than Allen, taunted him with anti-Semitic remarks. Approaching to hit Allen, he was stopped by a volley of long words. In his essay 'My Son the Poet', Louis Ginsberg recalled the event: 'He wondered what Allen meant, and in his wonderment the bully forgot his punitive intent and asked Allen what he had said. They began to talk and the threat was over. I believe that my son then felt the power of words.' It was a skill that Allen would use later in life to engage Hell's Angels in conversation or to calm antagonistic judges.

But he wasn't always so lucky. There was a black boy named Joe who constantly taunted him, eventually provoking a fight – ten-year-old Allen's first – in which both were knocked down in front of their classmates. The contest was declared a draw, but Allen came home weeping to Naomi. After this, the two boys became good friends and played together in Allen's backyard. When the landlord, who lived on the ground floor, objected, saying he didn't want Negroes around, both Naomi and Louis, believing fervently in integration and equality, sprang to the boy's defence.

Many of the neighbours were anti-Semitic. In 'Garden State', composed in 1979, Ginsberg wrote:

I was afraid to talk to anyone
in Paterson, lest my sensitivity
to sex, music, the universe, be discovered &
I be laughed at, hit by colored boys.

'Mr Professor' said the Dutchman
on Haledon Ave. 'Stinky Jew' said
my friend black Joe, kinky haired.
Oldsmobiles past by in front of my eyeglasses.

By now, Allen had acquired braces to straighten his teeth and eyeglasses to correct his vision. 'Oh what beautiful eyes! What a shame to put on glasses,' Naomi said, as Allen was examined by short, German-accented Lotte Lindner, the optician. He was almost a teenager when sex became an issue in his life. One day, walking home from school along Haledon Avenue, he innocently told a girl, 'My, what a big bust you have!' Her face red with anger, she hit him and broke his glasses, then chased him all the way home. Far from sympathising, Eugene and Louis told him that it was his own fault. 'Did you mean to insult her?' they asked. Allen did not understand what he had done wrong.

One day his friend Morton said, 'When I see girls in school, sometimes I want to rush right out and grab hold of them. Don't you feel that way?'

'I don't feel that way, no,' said Allen. Later, Allen and Morton and two other boys went into the bathroom in Morton's house.

Morton sat on the toilet seat and one of the boys knelt in front of him and kissed his penis. 'The amazing thing was that he didn't seem to be self-conscious about it,' Ginsberg recalled. 'Wasn't apparently afraid of what we'd think – that he was queer – being of an age when it was all new – and mysterious and forbidden.' Another time, during their play, a gang of children surrounded Morton and pulled his pants down. 'I stood aside, not helping him for fear of getting my own pants pulled down,' Ginsberg wrote later, 'but enjoying Morton's humiliation and baring, the baring of his privates. This last phrase is particularly exciting to me – as perhaps my whole character is exhibitionistic and evidenced by 155 Haledon Ave fantasy and action on porch – slipping down pants for short time to traffic (unseen) – and dream of that time of getting turned over and spread by boys of my gang whom I feared.'

In 1937 Louis moved the family to 288 Graham Avenue, an ivy-covered apartment building on the corner of Broadway in down-town Paterson. Naomi began to get sick again – less than a year after she was discharged from Greystone – and was often in such bad shape that Allen had to stay home from school to look after her. Naomi would try to get him to side with her in her delusional obsession that Louis' mother, whom the family always called Buba, was the head of a spy network and was out to get her. Much of her paranoia focused on Louis' debt, the money that had paid for Naomi's first hospitalisation. Naomi claimed Louis had given it to Buba. Allen, not yet eleven, was placed in a hopelessly confusing position between his two parents.

Naomi delighted in taunting Louis with allusions to her affair with Maxwell Bodenheim and did everything possible to cause him grief, but he refused to commit her again. Allen could not talk to anyone about the storm of emotions aroused by his mother's illness. Having just changed schools, he had no close friends who would understand and his brother, at sixteen, busied himself with his own group of friends. Allen's diary from June 1937 is chilling in its casual depiction of an emotionally shattering event. Three weeks after his eleventh birthday, he wrote:

> June 19: My mother thinks she is going to die and is not so good . . . My brother is to graduate from high school soon, and will go to Montclair Teachers' College.

June 21: . . . My mother is worse today.

June 22: I stayed home to mind my mother. I got a haircut and two pairs of shoes and heard the 'Louis–Braddock' fight over the radio. Louis won and is now champion of the world.

June 23: My brother graduated from high school today and we had a party. The party broke up about 12 o'clock at night. We had an excellent time and my brother (for once) kissed my aunts goodbye. I stayed home from school to take care of my mother.

June 24: I stayed home from school again only today I went to high school and saw my father teach. My mother locked herself in the bathroom early in the morning and my father had to break the glass to get in. She also went back to the sanatorium. I saw a newsreel of the Louis–Braddock fight, also *Dangerous Number* and another picture in the movies. I also developed a sty below my eye.'

As Louis Ginsberg later described the incident, Naomi, in a state of suicidal depression, had locked herself in the bathroom, refusing to come out. 'Could hear her cough in tears at sink,' Allen wrote in 'Kaddish'. When Louis finally broke the glass panel to open the door, she was standing with blood oozing from both wrists. 'They were surface cuts,' Louis said, 'so I bandaged them and then put her to bed. The boys stood there, shivering in their night clothes, panic in their eyes. "What traumas," I thought, "might sink into them and burrow into their psyches."' The next morning, an ambulance arrived for Naomi, and Louis took Allen to work with him so that he could watch over him. Every hospitalisation was a complete tragedy for Allen. 'For years Allen could not understand why his mother had deserted them,' Louis said.

Naomi's illness gave Allen an enormous empathy and tolerance for madness, neurosis and psychosis. In his 1980 poem 'After Whitman And Reznikoff', he wrote:

That round faced woman, she owns the street with her three
     big dogs,
screeches at me, waddling with her bag across Avenue B
Grabbing my crotch, 'Why don't you talk to me?'
baring her teeth in a smile, loud voice like a taxi horn,
'Big Jerk . . . you think you're famous?' – reminds me of my
     mother.

According to his secretary, Bob Rosenthal, Ginsberg would go through the day's mail and, before dealing with letters from academics and friends, instead read, with obvious relish and not a little anguish, one written in coloured crayon on sixteen pages of torn notebook paper.

With Naomi again in the hospital, Louis reorganised the apartment. Eugene had his parents' old bedroom in the back, and Allen slept with his father in the front bedroom, where Louis had his big desk. Allen would lie in bed, dozing, while Louis graded English papers and wrote poems under a metal-shaded lamp. At night, Allen would snuggle up against Louis: 'I was getting hard-ons, rubbing up against his leg, just pressing close and holding on to him as I couldn't with my mother or brother. And we neither acknowledged it.' He was not conscious of anything unusual in this intimate relationship with his father, until he looked back on it.

As a baby, Allen had three good years of Naomi's sanity before she was taken away to Bloomingdale. Then, devastated by his mother's frequent absences at the hospital, he began to make constant demands of affection and love from other members of the family. 'I must have been a sexpest to the whole family,' he recalled, 'even when sleeping with Louis. Gene was the only one who rebuked me, but without shame or guilt, just elastic rejection of elastic demand.'

During his adolescent years, Allen avoided fears and unhappiness as he had in his childhood, by hiding out at the movies. In March 1938, he recorded in his diary: 'Movies afford me great pleasure and are about the only relief from boredom which seems to hang around me like a shadow.' He saw Fredric March's award-winning performance in *Dr Jekyll and Mr Hyde*, and at the hero's transformation to a hairy beast in the park, Allen ran from the theatre and stood trembling outside, filled with 'a nightmare vision of my own future'. He wept copiously at a film that ended with the police taking a convict away to jail while his sad, sick dog ran vainly after the police car alone; and when the *Invisible Man* was hunted down in the snow and died, pitifully transformed back to visibility, Allen wept for his soul.

With Eugene commuting each day to Montclair State Teachers' College and Naomi still in hospital, Louis became active in the

New Jersey Chaucer Guild and the Manuscript Club. In 1937, he borrowed two thousand dollars to finance the publication of his first collection of poems, *The Everlasting Minute*, which consolidated his reputation as a poet. One of his poet friends loaned him a privately printed edition of *Fanny Hill* with coloured illustrations which he kept hidden among his poetry manuscripts in his desk. Allen borrowed it to read in private. He recalled, 'A day later my father, panicked, asked if I had the book – his friend, a sophisticated Frenchman, Maurice Levitt, had loaned it to him and had come to get it back. I gave it over, heart-struck . . . My father and I never discussed the theft.'

One night Louis got a telephone call at 3 a.m. and fainted on the kitchen floor. The wife of a doctor or pharmacist he was having an affair with told him her husband had found out. Gene and Allen found him on the floor and were terrified as he shook off his sleepy shock and went back to bed. The idea that his father had a life secret from them disturbed Allen enormously: 'I remember a strange feeling of prickles and alien universe and never trusted him again, and couldn't speak to him about his unknown secret life a mystery.'

When the family moved to Graham Avenue, Allen had transferred to P.S. 6, and he graduated on 27 June 1939. In his yearbook, he named Poe his favourite author, *Dr Dolittle* his favourite book and swimming his favourite sport. He gave as his motto: 'Do what you want to when you want to.'

Louis and the boys spent the summer at the shore in Belmar with the Ginsberg clan. On Labor Day weekend, September 1939, all of them were sitting around a large wooden table in their rented house when they heard that Germany had invaded Poland.

That Fall, Louis brought Naomi home on the bus after three years in Greystone. She was nervous and shaky, standing in the doorway of an apartment she barely remembered, looking down the dark hall as her two sons rushed to greet her. The excitement proved too much for her, and she retired to the back bedroom to rest. After a while Allen followed to keep her company. He told the story in 'Kaddish':

> She went to the bedroom to lie down in bed and ruminate,
> or nap, hide – I went in with her, not leave her by herself –
> lay in bed next to her – shades pulled, dusky, late afternoon

– Louis in front room at desk, waiting – perhaps boiling chicken for supper –
'Don't be afraid of me because I'm just coming back home from the mental hospital – I'm your mother –'
Poor love, lost – a fear – I lay there – Said, 'I love you Naomi,' – stiff, next to her arm. I would have cried, was this the comfortless lone reunion? – Nervous, and she got up soon.

Naomi's arguments with Louis resumed. She took the Party line on the war with Finland in the winter of 1939 and supported the USSR, so infuriating the family that even Allen would point to the map on his bedroom wall and yell, 'But look, Mama, Russia's this big and Finland's so small. It can't be. It can't be!' Nevertheless, Ginsberg remembered this as a relatively happy time, and home life was mostly tranquil. They went to the New York World's Fair in June 1940 and to Belmar that summer. Every day, Allen devoured the *New York Times*. He had compiled huge files of news clippings on Hitler and Mussolini and had been very emotional about the Spanish Civil War: 'Lots of righteous wrath and self-righteousness,' he later described it. Allen wanted the United States to join the war and was indignant about the isolationists. He and Eugene spent a lot of time at the campaign headquarters of Irving Abramson, a local CIO official who was running for Congress from the Eighth District of New Jersey. His opponent, Gordon Canfield, charged Abramson with being a 'red,' which unleashed a letter-writing campaign from the young Ginsberg.
Through Irving Abramson, Louis met Leo Perlis, the publisher of the short-lived Paterson Press. Louis wrote some poems for the paper and Naomi had children's stories published every two weeks, small parables of friendship and fellowship in which Allen and Eugene often figured. As Allen referred to them in 'Kaddish':

Naomi reading patiently, story out of a Communist fairy book – Tale of the Sudden Sweetness of The Dictator – Forgiveness of Warlocks – Armies Kissing – Deathsheads Around the Green Table – The King & The Workers – Paterson Press printed them up in the 30's till she went mad, or they folded, both.

Allen had gone on to Central High School in Paterson, where on 9 and 10 May 1940, he took part in the annual school show, *All*

Central Night. He was in the chorus and acted in several sketches, but the high spot of the evening was clearly 'Ballet Loose' which featured Allen as the premiere danseuse, with six of his schoolboy friends as ballerinas, all in tutus. Forty years later, he wrote in his journal: 'Basil Battaglia, my old Central High School mate and chum who once kissed me in excitement the night of the high school play. I did the ballerina in tutu, bumping my ass at the football players in elephant costumes or drag, too, 1940 Central High School auditorium – I was thirteen that year hardly cognisant of my sex but sensitive to love and affection.'

At Central High he continued to excel in English, and took an interest in the school magazine, the *Spectator*, where his first two pieces appeared in print in the Easter 1941 issue. One was a piece of schoolboy humour called 'On Homework in General', the other an interview with Canada Lee, the star of the Broadway production *Native Son*.

Sunday was the best day of the week at Graham Avenue. The *New York Times* was spread across the floor, and everyone would dip into it. Sometimes Louis would walk to and fro, quoting from Milton as they read. Later, when Allen was a well-known poet, Louis was led to ask, 'Is he a poet by nature or nurture? I think both.'

The more settled home life seemed to help Allen at school, and he became gregarious and popular with his schoolmates. He debated about Hitler in class and was very knowledgeable on political matters. Looking back, Ginsberg described himself: 'Big eyeglasses and a thin face with buck teeth, going to an orthodontist to have them fixed. A kind of mental ghoul, totally disconnected from any reality, existing in a world of newspapers and aesthetics: Beethoven, Leadbelly, Ma Rainey and Bessie Smith.' He had crushes on other boys, in particular one muscular young man who did a lot of weight lifting and exercises.

Across the street from the Ginsbergs' apartment house was a church and a funeral home, surrounded by a thick hedge. Ginsberg later described walking home from seeing movies at the Fabian Theater and passing the hedges with their mysterious shadows, 'and my heart would ache and I would go into some kind of swoon thinking how mysterious the universe was and how lonely I was in it'. The dark hedges were associated with his preoccupation with the end of space. 'I kept trying to figure out what's infinity. At the end of infinity there must be a wall, maybe made of rubber.' But even this flexible solution to the problem was inadequate, because something would have to be at the other side of the rubber wall.

The church was rebuilt and the hedges uprooted in the early 1950s, but their image lived on for Ginsberg as a symbol of adolescent wonder and mystery. It inspired a number of later works: 'Graham Avenue, the ugly church/ nice steeple, cock atop/ hedges – where I walked as a kid/ hedges of melancholy/ came home from the movies/ Fred Astaire dancing/ on black mirrors.'

It seems that a bureaucratic mix-up had sent Allen to the wrong school, so in September 1941, he was moved from Central to East Side High. Yet again he had to start over again and adjust to a classroom full of children who already knew the ropes. Allen's knowledge of politics, his appalling jokes (which he collected in a special notebook) and his poetry, which he read aloud in English class, all helped him to be quickly assimilated as a member of the Class of '43. He became president of both the Debating Society and the Dramatic Society. He got to know Millie Peller, falsely known as 'the class whore', and walked to school each day with 'affectionate, cute, pretty bright-eyed' Marilyn Kass.

It was Allen's English teacher, Frances Durbin, who first introduced him to Walt Whitman. He has described how one afternoon she 'read aloud verses from Walt Whitman's *Song of Myself* in so enthusiastic and joyous a voice, so confident and lifted with laughter, that I immediately understood "I wear my hat indoors as well as out . . . I find fat no sweeter than that which sticks to my own bones" forever, and still remember her black-dressed bulk seated squat behind an English class desk, her embroidered collar, her voice powerful and high, lilting Whitman's very words and shafts of sunlight through school windows that looked down on green grass.'

That year Eugene decided he had chosen the wrong vocation and wanted to be a lawyer, not a teacher. He went to study law in Newark where he took a small furnished room and worked as an elevator operator to pay his way through college.

In the winter of 1941, symptoms of Naomi's madness began to reappear. She accused Louis of poisoning her soup: Buba had bought the poison with money that Louis had given her. Allen would drink the soup and say, 'Look, Mama, it's not poisoned, see?' but to no avail. Allen again stayed home from school to look after her on her bad days, and one night she had some kind of seizure. Ginsberg described it in harrowing detail in 'Kaddish':

> One night, sudden attack – her noise in the bathroom – like croaking up her soul – convulsions and red vomit coming out of her mouth – diarrhea water exploding from her behind – on all fours in front of the toilet – urine running between her legs – left retching on the tile floor smeared with her black feces – unfainted –

Allen and Louis rushed to her aid and, holding her by the shoulders, tried to calm and comfort her. The attack was a mystery and seemed more like an epileptic seizure than a symptom of mental illness. Louis was always convinced that there was some chemical or biological explanation for Naomi's illness, but the doctors found nothing. (In September 1992, researchers at Johns Hopkins University announced that they had identified a gene in human chromosome 13 which significantly increased the risk of someone developing schizophrenia.)

One day in the winter of 1941, Allen stayed home from school with her, sat her down and demanded to know exactly what it was she was fearful of. She reiterated her problems: Buba had paid the doctors at Greystone to give her fifty insulin shocks so that she would grow fat; they put poison in her food and had inserted three big sticks down her back. She sat stiffly in the chair. Allen, trying hard to understand, felt her shoulder where she said it hurt. According to his later account, she told him there were wires in the ceiling listening to every word she said and reporting them back to President Roosevelt.

'They're listening to everything we say,' said Naomi. 'I don't want to put you in danger.'

'Who?' asked Allen, but Naomi wouldn't say. Allen gave her a pad of paper and she scribbled the name of Allen's grandmother. 'The wires are in this ceiling,' she told him. 'I could hear the crackling when you gave me the pencil. They knew it.' Exasperated, Allen took the broom from under the bed and began thumping on the ceiling around the cracked paint by the light fixture to prove that there were no wires, but Naomi insisted that they were inside the ceiling, embedded there and attached to the inside of her head. She said she could hear them talking. They were calling her names, saying she was a bad woman, a whore, and ordering their agent to kill her.

Then the voices told her that the agent was outside in the street. She jumped up and rushed to the window, closely followed by Allen. Across the street was the church, with its mysterious hedges. A few people were waiting on the corner for a bus. One of them looked a little like a banker and wore a smart hat. 'That's him,' said Naomi. 'He's the one.' She threw open the window and yelled, 'Go away, you rotten thing!' before Allen could drag her back inside.

Naomi claimed she was ill and in need of a rest. She wanted to go to Lakewood, New Jersey, to a rest home. She had been there before and liked it. Allen said he couldn't take her to Lakewood unless her doctor approved. She insisted, so he phoned Doctor Hans Wassing and explained the situation. Perhaps Wassing believed he was talking to someone older or thought Allen was Eugene, because he unaccountably agreed. Allen wanted to call Louis, but Naomi persuaded him not to, saying it would disturb his work, and in any case Louis was one of the people plotting against her. Allen did not know what to do, but since the doctor had authorised it, he helped Naomi pack her suitcase, and they left.

'It was kind of dumb,' he said later. 'I was a prisoner in the house. I was smaller than she was and she was intimidating me to do this. She was splitting my mind because I didn't know if she was right or not. She said she was being persecuted and it didn't make sense but she was so insistent about it.'

Naomi refused to go down in the elevator in case the elevator man informed them that they were escaping, so they walked down the stairs and into the street. Naomi held the collar of her large worn fur coat high to her nose as a gas mask against poison germs sprayed by Louis' mother in the downtown streets. A boy carrying his schoolbag came down the street towards them. Attracted by Naomi's furtive manner, he stared at them, then yelled, 'Where are you going lady? To death?' then he ran away, laughing. Allen shuddered.

At the bus terminal Allen bundled Naomi on to the Newark bus and asked the driver if the bus continued on to Lakewood. The driver told Allen that they would have to change at Newark. Naomi immediately backed off the bus, whispering loudly to

Allen, 'We can't go on this bus. He's not going to Newark, can't you see? The bus is empty. He's going to kidnap us.' She decided that they would go to Manhattan and take a Greyhound to Lakewood from there. At Times Square they had to wait two hours for a bus while Naomi fretted about 'invisible bugs'. The ride itself lasted three terrible hours, while Allen tried to stop her from making a scene. She argued with him, grew paranoid of the couple in the front seat who were fortunately asleep, and looked surreptitiously at the other riders over the top of her turned-up coat collar like a 'classical cartoon of a spy' as Ginsberg later described it.

He recollected the ride in a beautiful passage of 'Kaddish':

> . . . me tagging along, hoping it would end in a quiet room in a Victorian house by a lake. Ride 3 hours thru tunnels past all American industry, Bayonne preparing for World War II, tanks, gas fields, soda factories, diners, locomotive round-house fortresses – into piney woods New Jersey Indians – calm towns – long roads thru sandy tree fields –

It was late afternoon when they arrived in Lakewood. They straggled down the street, a large lady in a fur coat, peering anxiously over her shoulder, followed by a skinny youth, who looked younger than his age, dragging a large valise. They reached the address and the door was opened by an old man and a woman wearing white coats. Allen stood in the hallway and asked their rates while Naomi hid behind the door. Everything went well until Naomi came rushing out and demanded, 'I'm weak, my blood spoiled by electricity. Can you give me a blood transfusion?'

'I'm sorry,' said the woman, quickly ushering them out. 'This place is for people who want rest and don't need continuous care.' The long, quiet streets of Lakewood were filled with rest homes, but everywhere they went they received the same treatment. At last Allen yelled at Naomi, 'You won't get anyplace if you keep talking like that!' and they were able to find her a place. Allen gave the attendant a week's rent, but as the woman turned aside to write him a receipt, Naomi began whispering urgently in Allen's ear. He clamped his hand over her mouth.

They trooped up the stairs to an old attic room with stained wallpaper but there were lace curtains and a hand-crafted rug on the floor. 'Don't you dare say anything to them about your blood transfusion,' warned Allen. 'They'll kick you out. It's only a quiet rest home. Go lie down and rest. You're safe here. I'll go home and tell Louis.'

This provoked a strong reaction from Naomi. 'No don't tell Louis where I am . . . He'll send spies to watch me. He might poison me. The only reason he lets me live is he used to love me. His mother wanted me dead years ago.' Allen pushed her down on the bed and told her to be quiet, fearful that if the attendant heard them arguing they might be thrown out. He calmed her and then left to take the long bus ride back to Paterson: 'laid my head back in the last seat, depressed,' he wrote in 'Kaddish', 'the worst yet to come? Abandoning her, rode in torpor –'

It was late when Allen arrived back at Graham Avenue, and Louis was waiting anxiously in the living room. He was horrified to hear what Allen had done and deeply worried by what he knew would happen next. The inevitable telephone call came at 2 a.m. Naomi had gone mad. She had run down the hallways barefoot, banging on all the doors, scaring all the old ladies in their rooms. Then she had barricaded herself under the bed with her suitcase and was screaming about Mussolini, Hitler, poison germs and calling out, 'Help! Louis! Buba! Fascists! Death!' The frightened attendants demanded that Louis take her away at once, but since he had no car, there was no way he could get there until morning. He took the 6.30 a.m. bus to Newark and went from there to Lakewood.

All the attendants gathered on the porch as Naomi and Louis left the rest home; the old ladies peered from behind fluttering curtains. Naomi claimed there was a nail in her shoe and walked with one shoe in her hand, limping along as Louis pulled her by the arm. It was only two blocks to the bus station and Louis insisted that she could walk, but when a cab pulled up they took it. As Louis was paying, Naomi emerged from the cab and ran off, dropping her suitcase on the sidewalk. Louis snatched up the suitcase with one hand and caught Naomi with the other as she struggled into a pharmacy, yelling. The next bus to New York did not leave for two hours.

Naomi began to harangue the druggist, demanding a blood transfusion. Her voice rose as she became excited. Louis had no idea what to do and hovered near her, trying to calm her, asking her to please be quiet because she was attracting a crowd. Louis was humiliated. Naomi was triumphant. The bus finally arrived but the driver refused to allow her aboard. In desperation, Louis telephoned Greystone Hospital. 'Bring her here, Mr. Ginsberg,' they said, as Naomi stood sniffing the air for germs.

Ginsberg used the scene, as told to him that night by his father, as a central passage in 'Kaddish': 'Naomi sweating, bulge-eyed, fat, the dress unbuttoned at one side – hair over brow, her stocking hanging evilly on her legs – screaming for a blood transfusion – one righteous hand upraised – a shoe in it – barefoot in the pharmacy.'

Louis had to pay $35 for an ambulance to come from Red Bank to fetch her. The idea of returning Naomi to Greystone was so abhorrent that he took her instead to Hillgreen, a private rest home in Passaic. There the admissions doctor would not take her without a signed form from the county physician. He gave Naomi a sedative, but she and Louis had to wait in the ambulance until 6 p.m. for the forms to arrive by special messenger. Naomi was in Hillgreen for a week, but her condition was too serious for them to handle, and Louis reluctantly agreed to transfer her to Greystone, where she was to remain for the next two years.

Louis returned home exhausted. Eugene had no telephone and, visiting the next day, asked where Naomi was. 'We had to send her back to the hospital,' explained Louis. Allen described Eugene's reaction in 'Kaddish': '– his face perplexed, so young, then eyes with tears – then crept weeping all over his face – "What for?" wail vibrating in his cheekbones, eyes closed up, high voice – Eugene's face of pain.'

That June, Allen turned sixteen. In Belmar, he watched the stars 'from the Jersey shore all through one pitifully lonely summer night'. He continued his letter writing against the isolationists and spent hours listening to music: opera and Gershwin and modern composers such as Aaron Copland and Eric Coates. In October, Eugene went into the army and after basic training was sent to Great Britain where he remained for the duration of the war. Allen enrolled with Civilian Defense and spent some of his evenings on patrol duty with two women wardens. From November 1942 until the following February, he worked after school as a page in the Paterson Public Library, putting away books fifteen hours a week for thirteen cents an hour. He had earlier discovered Kraft-Ebbing's *Psychopathia Sexualis*, 'which I perused for half an hour underneath a hallway light in my doctor uncle's mahogany glass-front bookcase – and discovered with joy case histories like mine.' At the library he now sneaked into the office of the librarian and looked up 'homosexuality' in Kraft-Ebbing. 'Am I a homosexual?' he asked himself, seeking an explanation for the crushes he was always getting on other boys.

He liked one boy in particular. Paul Roth was a half-year ahead of Allen and got a scholarship to Columbia University. In 'Kaddish', he was described as 'my high school mind hero, jewish boy who became a doctor later – then silent neat kid.' Recalling his crush, Ginsberg said, 'I was totally in love, I spent all the time I could with him, but in a very shy way.' Roth had no idea of Allen's feelings, though Allen sometimes hinted at them; on one occasion, he remarked that Roth's handwriting in a letter to him from Columbia was erotic. Roth's reply was typewritten.

Allen was determined to follow his hero and applied to Columbia. On his way to New York to take the entrance examination, he stood on the prow of the Hoboken ferry in the cold air and made a solemn vow that if he got into Columbia to be with Paul Roth, he would devote his life to helping the working class. This was a serious vow, not just the by-product of a schoolboy crush. It gave direction to Ginsberg's activities over the years, and he used it as a benchmark whenever he was confused by a choice of courses of action. Curiously, when Ginsberg actually got to Columbia, he saw Roth rarely.

2 A Columbia Education. The Origins of the Beat Generation

When shall we go, over there by the shores and mountains, to salute the birth of new work, the new wisdom, the flight of tyrants, and of demons, the end of superstition, to adore . . . the first ones! . . . Christmas on Earth?

Arthur Rimbaud

It was snowing when Allen entered the Union Theological Seminary a few days before Christmas, 1943. He climbed the stairs to his seventh-floor room and looked down the long wooden corridor. Most of the students had gone home for the holidays, and the transoms above the doors were dark, except for one at the far end, where a new boy had moved in. From behind this door came the sound of a clarinet and strings, playing a work that Allen was unfamiliar with. He was intrigued and knocked on the door. It was answered by 'the most angelic looking kid I ever saw, with blond hair, pale and "hollow of cheek as though he drank the wind and took a mess of shadows for his meat",' Ginsberg said later, quoting Yeats.

'I heard the music,' explained Allen.

'Did you like it?' asked Lucien Carr.

'I thought it might be the Brahms Clarinet Quintet,' ventured Allen.

Carr seemed surprised and pleased, 'Well, well! A little oasis in this wasteland.' He invited Allen in. On his walls were prints of The Bohemian Girl by Franz Hals, Rousseau's Sleeping Gypsy and a Cezanne landscape. The crowded bookcase held copies of Flaubert, Rimbaud's *Une Saison en Enfer* and a criticism of Toulouse-Lautrec, all in French. Allen also noticed *Jude the Obscure* and a worn copy of Spinoza's *Ethics*. Lucien produced glasses and a bottle of burgundy and they began to talk.

Allen had arrived at Columbia University in September. He had book knowledge of many areas but had no real experience of life; he had not travelled or had any kind of relationship outside his family. The only thing he knew a lot about was madness, which gave him a natural affinity with eccentrics and the rejects of society, but did not prepare him for the outside world. His parents had each demanded that he accept their version of reality – diametrically opposed readings of the world: 'I was putting on a stiff upper lip and trying to fulfill the obligations I thought were demanded of me, taking over my father's role of taking care of my mother ... and having to be the recipient of her confessions and emotions but of a delusional nature. And that confused me, I didn't think I was confused but really I had a kind of split mind, of who I was supposed to trust. It left me in a kind of neutral limbo.'

Since Allen was unable to trust anyone completely, and his parents were unable to provide what he called 'empowerment or reassurance, that I was a nice man and could go out in the world', Allen had little self-esteem. He was ill-equipped to leave home.

At Columbia, he enrolled in a pre-law course, intending to become a labour lawyer to fulfill his vow made on the ferry. A scholarship boy, he was in awe of the confident, sophisticated Ivy League types he saw in the corridors, but was determined to fit in.

The Columbia halls of residence had been taken over by wartime V–12 naval cadets who needed ninety days of college to become officers, and the university found off-campus housing for its new students. When Allen arrived, he was given rooms with two other students, Jerry Rauch and Arthur Lazarus, in a large apartment at 50 Morningside Drive, half a block from the campus; by December, Allen and his two room-mates had been moved to the Union Theological Seminary, at 122nd Street and Broadway, which was filled with Columbia students displaced by the cadets.

The Columbia English department was in those days one of the most famous and influential in the country. Allen's required courses were taught by such professors as Lionel Trilling, Mark Van Doren and Raymond Weaver: Lionel Trilling was an elegant and learned literary critic, who, as Ginsberg later described him, 'in a sense tried to revive the humanistic solidarity and good manners of mid-nineteenth century England. Mahogany Mathew Arnold.' It was Trilling's 1939 book on Matthew Arnold that established his reputation. Trilling was more concerned with a respect for boundaries than breaking down barriers. Always looking for 'the best kind of truth', his class was filled with naval cadets, who would sit in the back and sleep, so Trilling concentrated his energy on the three or four students who paid attention. Among them were Allen, Herbert Gold, the future novelist, and Lucien Carr, who described Trilling as having pale blue, milky eyes that made him look blind. Carr was very impressed by Trilling and thought, 'This is the blind Homer teaching here.'

Mark Van Doren was the literary editor of *The Nation* and a distinguished critic and poet. He received the Pulitzer prize for his *Collected Poems* in 1940.

Raymond Weaver, who shared an office with Van Doren, was the author of the first biography of Herman Melville, *Herman Melville, Mariner and Mystic*. In the course of his research, he had discovered the manuscript of *Billy Budd* in a trunk in Melville's house on 23rd Street. 'I mean, the man who discovered posthumous manuscripts of Melville. That's really a professor!' Allen said later. He was flattered and inspired to be studying with men who had heretofore been only names in the *New York Times* and for his first year at Columbia he was a model student.

The amount of required reading during his first semester was prodigious. Allen made his way through Aeschylus, Herodotus, Thucydides, Sophocles, Aristotle, Euripides, Aristophanes, Plato, Virgil, Tacitus and the Book of Job. By November he had moved on to Zola, Dante, Rabelais, Machiavelli, Montaigne and Shakespeare. Despite this enormous workload, he also found time to tentatively explore New York City, going to his first Japanese restaurant (still open, despite the war), visiting the museums and walking the streets. He often went to the Metropolitan Opera, usually with Naomi, who had been released from Greystone earlier that year and was now living in the city.

Though Naomi had recovered sufficiently to be allowed home, she was still convinced that Buba was persecuting her and that Louis had given Buba all his money. It was not long before their life degenerated into one continuous argument. Despite his deep and abiding love for Naomi, the twenty-two years of their marriage had finally exhausted Louis. His love was not reciprocated; the companionship, trust and friendship had long gone,

destroyed by Naomi's paranoia and delusions. She remained
fixated on Louis' debt and the idea that Buba was plotting against
her. Naomi was often abusive, and the arguments were so
acrimonious that they sometimes ended with her moving to a local
rooming house for a few days. One time, Allen followed her and
she made him swear to keep her address a secret from Buba and
Louis.

When Allen moved to the city, Naomi was left with an empty
nest. This enabled her to make the final break from Louis, and
Louis let her go. He had done his duty and held the marriage
together as best he could until his children left home. Naomi
moved to New York, where she stayed with her sister Eleanor in
the Bronx and took a job addressing envelopes at the Workmen's
Circle. The nature of Naomi's illness was such that to most people
she appeared to be a normal, cheerful, strong-willed, self-confident
woman in her late forties. It was only when her delusions
intensified and she began to hear voices that her behaviour become
noticeably aberrant. Through Eleanor she met Doctor Leon Luria
who, like herself, was a Communist. He was the official doctor for
the National Maritime Union and had an office on West 18th
Street, near the NMU hall. Luria, whom Ginsberg described as a
'bald and pudgy old doll', was attracted to her and offered her a
job as his receptionist. It was not long before he became her lover
and she moved in with him.

The break between Louis and Naomi had been coming for a
long time, so Allen was not surprised. He continued to see them
both and frequently visited his father in Paterson or attended the
opera or a concert with him in New York, as well as visiting
Naomi and her new lover. Louis had grown used to living without
his wife and over the long years of her confinement had developed
friendships with a number of women, though Allen and Eugene
never knew how intimate these friendships were.

Soon after they met, Lucien Carr invited Allen to accompany
him to Greenwich Village to meet some of his friends. Allen had
not yet been to the Village and wrote excitedly to Eugene,
'Saturday I plan to go down to Greenwich Village with a friend of
mine who claims to be an "intellectual" (that has a musty flavour,
hasn't it?) and knows queer and interesting people there. I plan to
get drunk Saturday evening, if I can. I'll tell you the issue.'

* * *

Lucien Carr was born in New York City but his father, Russell, left his wife and child when Lucien was but five years old to go west, where he worked as a sheep herder in Wyoming. Lucien's mother, Marion, divorced him and returned to her home town of St Louis. Lucien's grandfather Benjamin Gratz was a jute and hemp magnate and also owned a department store; the Gratz family were wealthy, influential members of St Louis society, and Lucien was sent to the best private school, the John Burroughs School, which he attended until he was sixteen. Lucien's father died in Denver, where he was working as a bank clerk.

Lucien was born on 1 March 1925, which made him only fifteen months older than Ginsberg, but there was a world of difference between them. A precocious, feckless teenager, he had been expelled from Phillips–Andover and sent to a special school for difficult children, then to summer school at Bowdoin College, Maine. He spent two semesters at the academically rigorous University of Chicago, then dropped out to bum around for six months; he was admitted to Columbia in the fall. Since he had already done his preliminary reading of the classics with Elder Olson at Chicago, he was able to take it easy at Columbia and read poetry and listen to music while his fellow students sweated over Thucydides.

Most of his problems at his previous schools had been caused by a tall, thin, red-haired, bearded fellow with a large nose, named David Kammerer, who had run a once-a-week play group at John Burroughs. Kammerer, who was sixteen years older than Lucien, came from the same social background as Carr: his father was a partner in Von Schenk and Kammerer, consulting engineers. David had attended John Burroughs as a child and was at that time an English instructor at Washington University. Kammerer had become captivated by Lucien's beauty which reminded him of an *apache* he met on the rue de Lappe during a trip to Paris with his friend William Burroughs; he had become obsessed with this boy and transferred his obsession to Lucien, following him from school to school. Now he was in New York where he had taken a job washing dishes. Lucien dealt with Kammerer's attentions by forming an uneasy platonic friendship in which he had the upper hand, always telling Kammerer what to do and when he could see him. Kammerer would obey meekly. It was an unhealthy relationship, but Lucien saw no alternative to it and would clearly have preferred to be left alone.

Were it not for the sexual pressure, Carr would have undoubtably been proud to count the older man among his friends; he was witty, urbane and a fund of knowledge. Kammerer's best friend, William Burroughs, described him as 'always very funny, the veritable life of the party, and completely without any middle class morality. No conventional behaviour at all. He was very witty, very charming.'

Lucien took Allen to visit Kammerer, who lived at 48 Morton Street, just off Seventh Avenue. The street was littered with garbage cans and piles of dirty snow, but for Allen it was an enchanting experience: 'It was an uncharted, historic no-man's land wilderness to me, particularly entrancing as I was a closet queen and had not come out yet, so, going down to the Village where all the fairies were, but in disguise, with a beautiful friend, it was both romantically glorious and at the same time completely repressed, frightening and frustrating.' Allen had already fallen under Lucien's spell, mesmerised by the boy's intense slanted blue eyes, his tangled yellow hair and his air of world-weariness.

Kammerer was asleep when they arrived, and Allen noticed a heavily pencilled inscription, 'Lu – Dave,' written on the wall above his pillow, where a tear in the wallpaper revealed a patch of plaster. The three of them headed out, treading carefully over the narrow icy sidewalk to George's Bar on Seventh Avenue; 'Ginsberg in Wonderland' joked Lucien, and it was true. George's was the first bar Allen ever entered; a small triangular room packed with bohemians sheltering from the wintery streets.

On another excursion, a day or two later, Kammerer had another new arrival from St Louis visiting when they arrived. This was Kammerer's friend William Seward Burroughs, who lived just around the corner at 69 Bedford Street. At thirty, Burroughs seemed awfully old to Allen who was only seventeen. '[To me] anyone over twenty-two was superannuated,' Ginsberg said later, 'and Burroughs already seemed to have the "ashen grey of an age-old cheek." ' He was tall and thin, with wispy, sandy-coloured hair and thin lips, which he pursed in a nervous tic. He wore steel-rimmed eyeglasses and sat draped over a low settee by the fireplace.

Kammerer had a studio apartment on the ground floor with French windows looking out over a garden. A lesbian named Ruth Louise McMann lived upstairs, and Bill liked her because, in his words, she was 'straightforward, manly, and reliable'. These were the first words Ginsberg could remember hearing Burroughs speak.

Allen squatted on an upturned log, which served as the coffee table, and listened to Lucien and Burroughs talk. Lucien told the story of how, a few days earlier, he had drunkenly provoked a fight between Kammerer and a gay portrait painter he knew, which had demolished most of the painter's Greenwich Village studio. Lucien had bitten off part of the painter's earlobe and sunk his teeth into Kammerer's shoulder. Burroughs deplored the whole situation, saying, 'In the words of the immortal bard, " 'tis too starved a subject for my sword." ' Allen was amazed. It was the first time he had heard anyone casually quote an appropriate line of Shakespeare to voice an opinion.

Allen and Lucien swiftly developed a rapport. While Lucien mocked Allen's lack of worldly knowledge, Allen timorously criticised Lucien's degeneracy. Carr had this impression of the seventeen-year-old Allen: 'Naive, he was incredibly naive! He was just an eager young Jewish kid from Paterson who wanted to know everything about books and writers and art and painting, who knew nothing about the serious things in life such as wenching and drinking!'

Allen and Lucien spent most of their time together talking about literature, challenging each other to spell difficult words and trying to score intellectual points. To Allen, Lucien's little tests and arguments were often illuminating. In one typical bantering exchange, Allen used the quote 'milk of human kindness' in something he said (he had just read *Macbeth*). Lucien asked him to spell it. Allen was slightly put out at such an obvious spelling question, but Lucien showed him what he meant. They were standing at the urinal of the Minetta Tavern, and Lucien borrowed Allen's pen, then wrote on the wall 'Human-kindness' and 'Humankind-ness'. 'Macbeth is filled with the milk of humankind-ness,' Lucien concluded.

'That still sticks in my mind,' Ginsberg said, 'It was a distinction I'd never thought about, and was ultimately a real thing, between an idealist notion of human kindness and humankind-ness, an odd little verbal thing that I hadn't examined, as if I had a portion of my unexamined life. I guess the word Lucien used at that time was "jejeune".'

In October 1943, Allen began his first journal. On the front of it, he wrote carefully: 'Being The Notebook of Allen Ginsberg;

Now From the Cracked and Bleeding Heart, Triumphantly I Fashion Art.' It was the first of several hundreds of journals and notebooks he was to fill, a practice he retained throughout his life. An early entry was from an old popular song Lucien liked to sing, headed 'Carr's Melody':

'Violate me/ in violent times/ the vilest way that you know/ Ruin me/ Ravage me/ Utterly savage me/ On me no mercy bestow.'

When Allen first met him, Lucien had a girlfriend called Donna Leonard whom he had known in Chicago; but he soon encountered Céline Young, a dreamy Barnard girl who could never decide whether she preferred intellectuals or football players. She and Lucien became inseparable, constantly kissing and holding hands, to the envy and disgust of David Kammerer, who disparaged her as a 'bourgeois kitten'.

Lucien and Céline, with Allen and David Kammerer tagging along, could often be found sharing a booth at the West End Bar, just across Broadway from the Columbia campus. They were a distinctive group: Allen, with his thick horn-rimmed glasses, played the intellectual. Lucien, nonchalant, sporting a red bandanna, was the acknowledged leader. Céline, beside him, sensual and witty, mirrored Lucien with her long golden hair. Kammerer, for his part, focussed solely on Lucien, as the group sat drinking Pernod, imagining themselves drinking absinthe in *fin de siècle* Paris.

Allen's late-night conversations with Lucien continued through the Christmas break. Allen noted in his journal, 'Know these words and you speak the Carr language: fruit, phallus, clitoris, cacoethes, feces, foetus, womb, Rimbaud.' Rimbaud had come as a revelation to Ginsberg: 'The poet becomes a *seer* through a long, immense, and reasoned *derangement of all the senses*. All shapes of love, suffering, madness. He searches himself, he exhausts all poisons in himself, to keep only the quintessences. Ineffable torture where he needs all his faith, all his superhuman strength, where he becomes among all men the great patient, the great criminal, the great accursed one – and the supreme Scholar! For he reaches the *unknown*!'

Though immediately attracted, Allen still had doubts about *la vie de bohème* to which he was being introduced. It held no place for the suffering masses to whom he had sworn to devote his life and in whose service he was studying to be a labour lawyer. Lucien openly ridiculed Allen's plans as naive and one day, after the latest argument on the subject, Lucien stopped outside a rough looking bar on 125th Street and pointed out that Allen would feel uncomfortable and embarrassed if he even went in there among the working men. 'You want to be a labour lawyer?' he asked. 'You've never worked a single day in your life!' Allen was reluctantly forced to agree.

Allen remained loyal to the West End Bar, with its mixture of seamen, navel cadets and locals. Its proximity to the Columbia campus drew a large contingent of college kids, one of whom was Edie Parker, a birdlike, ebullient young woman from Grosse Pointe, Michigan. She and Lucien soon became good friends. Edie and her room-mate, a journalism student named Joan Vollmer, lived nearby on West 118th Street, and Lucien began to use their apartment as a place to escape from David Kammerer. Before long he brought Céline with him, sleeping with her on the couch in the living room.

Edie's boyfriend was a young seaman, an ex-Columbia football player called Jack Kerouac. He was away at sea when Edie first got to know Lucien, but soon returned. When Edie pointed Lucien out across the bar, Kerouac's response was, 'Looks to me like a mischievous little prick,' but he could see why Edie found him attractive. They became immediate friends and Lucien soon began to show up in class drunk or sleepless after an all-night session with Jack. Once Lucien put Jack in an empty barrel and rolled him down the sidewalks of Upper Broadway; another night, they sat drunkenly in a puddle during a rainstorm and tipped ink over each other's heads, singing at the tops of their voices.

Lucien enjoyed his talks with Jack about art and literature and, thinking that Allen would like to meet Kerouac, he gave him the address. Allen arrived one afternoon, probably in late May, 1944. Kerouac described their meeting in *Vanity of Duluoz*: 'I was sitting in Edie's apartment one day when the door opened and in walks this spindly Jewish kid with horn-rimmed glasses and tremendous ears sticking out, seventeen years old, burning black eyes, a strangely deep voice.'

Jack was sitting at the dining table having a mid-afternoon breakfast of bacon and eggs. He offered Allen a beer. Nervous and a little confused, he replied, 'No, no. Discretion is the better part of valour.' Kerouac's narrative continues: ' "Aw where's my food" I yelled at Edie, because that's precisely all I had on my mind at the moment he walked in. Turns out it took years for Irwin to get over a certain fear of the "brooding football artist yelling for his supper in big daddy chair" or some such.'

Jack Kerouac was four years older than Ginsberg. Born 12 March 1922, he was raised in Lowell, Massachusetts, a mill town where his father owned a small print shop. The Kerouacs were part of a large community of French Canadians who had immigrated to Lowell from Québéc, and Jack grew up speaking *joual*, the French of the Canucks, with English as his second language. Throughout his life he always spoke to his mother in patois, rather than English.

His mother, Gabrielle, a devout Catholic, sent Jack to a strict parochial school, which did little to boost his self-confidence. The death of his older brother, Gerard, after two years of suffering with rheumatic fever, wounded him deeply. Jack was four when Gerard died, and as an adult had no memory of him except for one occasion when Gerard slapped his face. Throughout his childhood, Gerard was always held up by his mother and the nuns as an unattainable model of saintly perfection. From parochial school Jack went to Lowell High, where he became a football hero. He was offered a football scholarship to Columbia, but first he spent a year at Horace Mann Prep to bring him up to the University's academic standards.

Once at Columbia, he fought with the coach, and finally flunked out after injuring his leg. In December 1942, he joined the navy but he did not fit in and feigned insanity to get a discharge. In the summer of 1943, he joined the merchant marine and crossed the U-boat infested Atlantic to Liverpool on an ammunition boat. When Allen met him, Jack was still working as a merchant seaman. Ginsberg later recalled: 'I remember being awed by him because I'd never met a big jock who was sensitive and intelligent about poetry.' Allen thought Jack was physically beautiful and admired his 'sturdy peasant build'. He liked his brooding Québécois moodiness and described him as 'Extraordinarily sensitive, very intelligent, very shrewd and very compassionate most of all. Compassionate toward the awkward kid. He was gruff but inquisitive.' He looked like the stereotypical gay sex object, 'The football player with a golden heart.' Allen instantly fell in love with Jack, just as he had with Lucien. Soon after they met, Allen and Jack took a walk together, and Allen was amazed and pleased at Kerouac's interest in him. They traversed the Columbia campus and got into a long conversation about the nature of phantoms and ghosts and, as Ginsberg described it, 'the tearfullness of our own ghost presence'.

Allen told Jack how he would stand in the shadow of the mysterious hedges on Graham Avenue and wonder how big space was and where the universe ended. Jack told Allen how he would stand in the backyard of his parents' house at night when everyone in the neighbourhood was eating supper, and feel that everyone was a ghost, eating ghost food. Like Allen, he often looked at the stars and pondered the size of the universe. It was the first time Allen opened up and talked about such delicate subjective experiences; the conversation was quite different from the intellectual banter that characterised his talks with Lucien. Kerouac was curious and interested in what Allen was saying. 'Gee, that's the way I think a lot too,' he would say, 'I have thoughts like that all the time.'

Their walk had taken them to the Union Theological Seminary; they stood on the corner of West 122nd Street and Broadway and looked down the hill to the grey spread of Harlem. Allen was moving out of the seminary and still had a few things to collect. He and Jack had discussed their admiration for Lucien so there was a mutual understanding when Allen pointed out the door where he first heard the Brahms Trio six months earlier.

Allen collected the few books and belongings that he had come for and, as he turned from the dormitory suite, he bowed to it, made a gesture of farewell and said, 'Goodbye door.' He continued down the stairs, saying goodbye to each step as he went. He bade farewell to the seventh-floor landing, the sixth-floor landing and all the rest, like a poem, all the way down. Kerouac was struck by this: 'Ah, I do that when I say goodbye to a place.' They had a long, excited conversation about the recognition of each of the stairs as the final stair and Allen's realisation of the changes in himself since he first climbed them six months before.

'That struck him as an awareness of a soul in space and time, which was his nature,' Ginsberg said later. Jack asked him if he knew any other people with the same awareness.

Was it awareness? Was it poetry? They decided that everyone had it who was in any way conscious or sensitive. 'Everyone has the same soul. We're all here together at once in the same place, temporarily, with a totally poignant tearful awareness that we're together,' they decided. This recognition became the basis of their deep and lasting understanding of each other.

Allen was moving to the Warren Hall Residence Club, a small hotel on West 115th Street, where Lucien Carr now lived. He took a room on Lucien's floor, and was delighted with his accommodation. For eight dollars a week he had a small room with a bed, sink, closet and hot plate. There was a telephone, connected to the lobby switchboard. He finally felt that he was out in the world.

It was a period of long, idealistic conversations. Allen and Lucien spent weeks, for example, arguing over a definition of art. Allen's position was that art had to be social and serve some purpose. Lucien maintained that art was 'self-ultimate'. The argument centred on the questions: 'If someone carved a walking stick, was that art?' and, 'If he carved it and it was put on the moon and nobody ever saw it, would that be art? Did art need an audience in order to exist?' They asked Kerouac his opinion, but he didn't have one. Finally, they put the question to Burroughs.

'That's the stupidest question I ever heard of,' Burroughs roared. 'It depends how you want to define the word "art." ' When Bill was in Chicago he had taken a week-long course with Count Korzybski, the founder of the theory of general semantics. Bill explained to Allen and Lucien that a word is not the thing it represents but whatever you use it to mean. 'Words don't have a built-in definition. If you want to define this as art, then you define it as art. If you don't want to use that word for that situation then you don't. But to argue whether the thing is art or not is obviously a confusion in terms.' Ginsberg later recalled the occasion: 'I laughed ever since on the naïveté of the discussion. Hung on words. Young kids. It was so embarrassing. It was a relief to hear such iconoclastic sense.' This role of teacher was one Ginsberg designated to Burroughs for the rest of his life, often deferring to his superior judgement when faced with conflicting opinions.

Long nights of conversation took place in the West End Bar, frequently degenerating into bouts of competitive drinking for Jack and Lucien. It was during this period that they came up with the idea of 'The New Vision'; the genesis of the philosophy of the Beat Generation.

Lucien Carr remembered, 'In those years at Columbia we really did have something going. It was a rebellious group, I suppose, of which there are many on campuses, but it was one that really was dedicated to a "New Vision". It's practically impossible to define. Maybe it was a term we just sold ourselves. It was trying to look at the world in a new light, trying to look at the world in a way that gave it some meaning. Trying to find values ... that were valid. And it was through literature that all this was supposed to be done. And it was through Jack and Allen, principally, that it was going to be done.'

'The New Vision', as defined in Ginsberg's journal, reveals that Allen was soon converted to Lucien's viewpoint: 'Since art is merely and ultimately self-expressive, we conclude that the fullest art, the most individual, uninfluenced, unrepressed, uninhibited expression of art is true expression and the true art.'

As the summer of 1944 wore on, David Kammerer became more and more obsessed with Lucien. Burroughs tried to convince him to go away, find another boy, go to sea, go to South America or even back to Saint Louis, but to no avail. Burroughs recalled: 'I told him, "This is silly, this is awful. It's also completely selfish, you're not really interested in him, you're interested in some idea of him that you have. And what you're trying to do is not at all to his advantage." Which it sure wasn't. He just couldn't see it. He said, "Oh well, it's my obsession."'

Kammerer also grew more antagonistic towards Céline Young. On one occasion, Kammerer and Burroughs called at Edie's apartment and, entering quietly, found everbody asleep. Lucien and Céline were curled up together on the couch. Kammerer commented, 'Doesn't he look pale, as though he were being sucked dry by a vampire.'

Another time, Kammerer climbed the fire escape behind Warren Hall and slipped in through Lucien's window, left open in the hot summer night. He stood over the sleeping boy, watching him silently in the moonlight for a half hour or so. As he climbed back over the fence, he was stopped at gunpoint by the hotel guard and questioned. The police were called and Lucien was roused to identify his visitor.

At 6 a.m. in the morning of 14 August 1944, Jack was awakened by someone shaking his arm. It was so hot that he and Edie were sleeping in the living room, hoping to catch a breeze through the open window. 'I got rid of the old man,' whispered Lucien, and Jack knew that David Kammerer was dead. Jack sent Edie to the kitchen to make breakfast while he and Lucien talked.

Kammerer's unrelenting pressure had begun to unnerve Lucien and he had again been considering ways to escape. He and Jack had recently seen Jean Renoir's *Grand Illusion* and had come up with the idea of imitating the escaped prisoners and fleeing to Paris. They envisioned signing on as seamen, jumping ship in Le Havre and walking to Paris in order to be there for the Liberation. At the union hall they found that a liberty ship, the *Robert Hayes*, was about to sail for France with supplies for the Second Front. At the Brooklyn Navy Yard, they found the crew swarming down the gang-plank. 'Don't go on that ship,' they warned. 'The mate is a fascist son of a bitch!' Lucien and Jack boarded the deserted ship, chose bunks and made themselves a meal. Then they encountered the mate, a huge red-headed brutish-looking man, who demanded to know who they were. Explaining they were able-bodied seamen, they told him they didn't want to sign on for France until they had made a trial run to Albany, where the ship was taking on supplies. 'You didn't sign on?' asked the mate. They weathered his abuse, packed up their things, and returned dejected and embarrassed to Manhattan, where they endured a ribbing from Edie and Céline.

They went to the West End to relieve their sorrows, but Jack left at midnight in order to get a good night's sleep before trying for another ship the next day. As he walked through the Columbia campus, he ran into David Kammerer who, as usual, wanted to know where Lucien was. Jack said he had left him at the West End with Allen and a group of other friends. Lucien was drunk, having had dinner with his mother who had now moved to New York. When the West End closed at 3 a.m., Lucien and Kammerer went to nearby Riverside Park with a bottle and sat arguing and drinking, looking out over the Hudson in the hot, humid summer night. Lucien's attempt to escape to France had brought matters to a head, and Kammerer delivered a furious drunken tirade, saying he loved Lucien and couldn't live without him. He threatened to harm Céline and said he would kill Lucien and himself if he couldn't have Lucien. He lunged at Lucien, attempting to give him a blow job. Lucien was no match for the heavier, stronger man, but in the ensuing struggle, Lucien was able to open his boy scout pocket knife. He stabbed Kammerer twice through the heart, killing him. Terrified, his first concern being disposal of the body, he tied Kammerer's hands and feet with his shoelaces. Then, tearing the dead man's shirt into strips, he anchored rocks to the body, which he awkwardly rolled down the bank and into the water.

Lucien went straight to Burroughs, waking him at dawn. 'I'll get the hot seat,' Lucien said.

'Don't be absurd,' said Burroughs. He advised Lucien to tell his family, get a good lawyer and turn himself in. To overcome his fear, Lucien summoned up a trace of his old bravado. He offered Bill a blood-stained pack of Lucky Strikes, saying, 'Have the last cigarette.'

'So this is how Dave Kammerer ends,' Burroughs thought. Kammerer had been one of his oldest friends. Calm and efficient as always, Bill lent Lucien five dollars and sent him on his way. He shredded the pack of Lucky Strikes into tiny pieces and flushed them down the toilet. Lucien went back uptown to tell Jack.

He and Jack took a walk. Lucien still had the murder weapon, and with Jack acting as lookout, Lucien dropped the bloody knife down a sewer grating near 125th Street. In Morningside Park, Jack pretended to urinate to distract any passersby, while Lucien buried Kammerer's glasses.

They ate hot dogs in Times Square, had a few beers, saw Zoltán Korda's *The Four Feathers* and visited the Museum of Modern Art. With visions of 'frying' in the electric chair at Sing Sing, Lucien was gathering his courage. He visited his psychiatrist on Park Avenue and borrowed some money, then went to an aunt who lived in Manhattan. She put him in touch with the family lawyers. Lucien turned himself in on 16 August in the presence of his lawyer. At first, the police did not believe his story, but that same day the coastguard found Kammerer's body floating off 108th Street. Lucien was booked for murder, taken to the Tombs, Manhattan's jail, and held without bail. Under the front-page headline 'Columbia Student Kills Friend and Sinks Body in Hudson River', the *New York Times* reported: 'The fantastic story of a homicide, first revealed to the authorities by the voluntary confession of a nineteen-year-old Columbia sophomore, was converted yesterday from a nightmarish fantasy into a horrible reality by the discovery of the bound and stabbed body of the victim in the murky waters of the Hudson River.' Lucien showed the police where he had buried Kammerer's glasses, and the *Daily News* ran a photograph of him pointing into the place in the river where he had dumped the body.

Burroughs and Kerouac were arrested as material witnesses. Bill's father bailed him out at once, and he left for Saint Louis. Jack was not so fortunate. When he called his father to ask for bail money, Leo Kerouac roared, 'No Kerouac ever got involved in a murder – you can go to hell!' Jack was forced to turn to Edie for help. Edie was due to inherit money, but her grandfather's will had not yet gone through probate, and her family lawyers would put up the $2,500 only if she was married to Jack. She and Jack had discussed marriage, and had already taken the required blood tests. Jack had felt that she was pressuring him into it. However, seen from the viewpoint of the Bronx County Jail, where he was being held, it now seemed a more agreeable proposition. Wedding plans were quickly made.

A few days after Lucien's arraignment, Allen and Edie went down to Kammerer's room on Morton Street. 'Lu – Dave', was no longer there. The landlord had already repainted the room, ready to rent it to someone new. Ginsberg wrote to Jack in jail, saying, 'The sorrows of yesteryear seemed to have been cooled by equally white paint.'

Jack and Edie married on 22 August 1944, the day Paris was liberated from the Nazis. Jack was taken from his cell by a plainclothes man, who drove him to City Hall and acted as Best Man; Céline was the Maid of Honor. The detective bought them all drinks at a local bar, then escorted Jack back to his cell to wait for his bail money to arrive, which it did a few days later. As soon as he was freed, Jack left town with his new wife, to live with her mother in Grosse Pointe.

Lucien, meanwhile, remained on the eighth floor of the Tombs, awaiting trial. He appeared in court on 24 August and was indicted for second-degree murder. He pleaded guilty to second degree manslaughter and his plea was accepted. The issue of whether or not Lucien was a homosexual would play a large part in his trial. Céline, Edie and Allen were all interviewed by the district attorney, and their assurances of his heterosexuality helped establish his case.

Lucien was found guilty, but his sentence depended very much upon an autobiography that his probation officer had him write for submission to the judge. 'Had Lucien felt less pride in having Dave dog his footsteps he might have gotten rid of Kammerer in a socially acceptable manner,' Céline wrote Jack. She said that Lucien's probation officer was worried that Lucien's values were all intellectual ones: 'If he persists in the idea that he has done a messianic service by ridding the world of Dave, he is becoming too presumptuous a judge. When he loses that pride in doing away with Dave, then I hope he is let out immediately. I know he is very remorseful at times.'

Lucienwas sentenced to an indefinite period in Elmira Reformatory in upstate New York, and his friends and family were told that with good behaviour he would be free within eighteen months. A few days later, Ginsberg wrote to Eugene: 'I got a long letter from Carr, who is somewhat sobered up from the decadent philosophic nihilism that used to be his attitude. He is reflective, more guilt, I suppose, and beginning to transvalue his attitudes and surrender to mores. After a long discussion of *Jude the Obscure*, Tolstoy, and Spinoza, he concludes, "as for prison life, I can't say I enjoy the discipline of steel bars, however it is a negative discipline and one can learn much under duress, esp in a society where one's confreres are all in the same boat. Amazingly strong animal – man."'

Allen had been horrified by Kammerer's death and was awed to be involved in such momentous events. He did his best to help Lucien in his interview with the D.A., met with Lucien's mother and attended to his minor affairs at Columbia. Céline Young and Allen were clearly sources of strength to each other during this difficult time. They were both teenagers, their newly constructed world in ruins. Their friends had all left town, and they were left to console each other over their loss. Ginsberg described her to Eugene: 'Carr's girl, but I have taken her over now, in a small way, for the duration. She looks like Rossetti's Bless'd Damozel and writes very good short stories.'

Though the summer break was a short one because of Columbia's accelerated wartime programme, most of Allen's other college friends had left the city. A week after Kammerer's death, Allen walked into the West End and found no one he knew. That summer's big hit, the Mills Brothers crooning 'You Only Hurt The One You Love', was playing on the jukebox – 'That mawkish, accurate, melancholy air,' as he described it in his journal. He had a beer and returned to his room. Under the heading 'Like All Sad People, I Am A Poet', he wrote, just a little theatrically, 'And now, this curtain has been rung down! Everything I have loved of the past year has fled into the past. My world is no longer the same.'

This was true. Allen felt distanced from conventional society; the New Vision he shared with Jack, Lucien and Burroughs was accentuated by the distorted news coverage and familial misgivings surrounding the death of Kammerer. The members of the inchoate Beat Generation experienced the inner workings of the law first-hand as Lucien's fate was decided by strangers in a faceless system of wheeler-dealer lawyers; they saw Columbia scrambling to defend its reputation and their families' overriding concern for respectability. It was all a great contrast to the actual human tragedy and confusion of the event itself and their youthful desire to rid the world of hypocrisy by revealing the tearful sensitivity and awareness that Allen and Jack recognised in themselves and their friends. Allen found himself unable to share the fashionable concerns of the wealthy Ivy League boys who had roomed on his corridor at the Union Theological Seminary, though even if he had aspirations in this direction, he could never have entered their world of sophistracted debauchery; he simply did not have the money.

Allen's crowd were all outsiders: Burroughs, the Harvard educated intellectual with a private income, who was fascinated by the low-life and by the behaviour of criminals; Kerouac, who had been discharged from the US Navy for being of 'indifferent character' and saw himself as a writer with no responsibilities to anyone but himself; Lucien Carr, with an arrogant disdain for authority, wandering from one school to another, confident of his own intelligence. Allen saw him as a romantic character in the French bohemian style, an image that was only enhanced by the death of Kammerer. All three were older than Allen and considerably more experienced. All three were essentially slumming, looking for their education in the street rather than the classroom. Though he stood alone in the summer of 1944 and thought that his bohemian world had been destroyed, the principal players would soon return, and their powerful influence would eventually win Allen over completely.

Jack felt completely out of place in Edie's high-society world in Grosse Pointe, and early in October, when he had earned enough money inspecting ball bearings at the Fruehauf truck plant to pay back the bail bond, he returned to New York City leaving Edie in Grosse Pointe. Shortly afterwards Jack shipped out on the *Robert Treat Paine*, but he was clearly ill-suited to life at sea. He got on very badly with the bosun and jumped ship at Norfolk, Virginia, rather than make the crossing to Naples with a man he felt sure was going to rape him. Jack returned to New York so dejected that he didn't even tell his parents where he was. This time he stayed with Allen at Warren Hall until he was able to get a room of his own.

It was during this period, after many nights of frank discussion, that Allen came out of the closet and told Jack he was homosexual. He believed Jack's tolerance gave him 'permission' to open up and talk about it. 'I knew he was going to accept my soul with all its throbbings and sweetness and worries and dark woes and sorrows and heartaches and joys and glees and mad understandings of mortality, 'cause that was the same thing he had,' said Ginsberg in 1972.

It was the middle of the night, but they were still lying awake, Jack in Allen's bed and Allen on the mattress on the floor, when Allen very timidly said, 'Jack, you know I'm really in love with Lucien. And I'm really in love with you. And I really want to sleep with you.'

Jack gave a long-drawn-out groan. 'He suddenly saw this great chasm of moral perplexity opening up in front of him for the rest of our lives,' Ginsberg said. 'I remember his groan. It wasn't rejection. It was a groan of dismay. But he didn't want to make it with me. It wasn't for about half a year.'

A room came up on the sixth floor of Warren Hall, and Jack settled down to write. In keeping with his sombre mood, he lit a candle, cut his finger and wrote 'Blood' on a small calling card which he then labelled 'The Blood of the Poet' and attached to the wall to remind himself he was a serious writer. Kerouac burned most of his output so that his art would not appear to be done for ulterior motives, and each day he would smile to himself as the candle consumed his labours. Allen recorded in his journal, 'Jeez, Kerouac is neurotic.'

That November he began work on a novel for a creative writing course taught by Professor Harrison Steeds, chairman of the

English department, taking the events of August as his subject for a romantic and awkward *roman à clef*. Shortly after he handed in a preliminary chapter, he received a letter from the Assistant Dean of Columbia, Nicholas McKnight, who asked him not to choose that subject; a matter of College policy was involved. Allen went to see McKnight and was told that his novel was 'smutty' and his friend Kerouac was a 'lout'. The university did not want any more unfavourable publicity as a result of the Kammerer affair. Ginsberg later said that Columbia's instruction for him to stop writing his novel marked his first real shock of disillusionment with the university. It was his first encounter with official censorship, something he would battle against throughout his life.

Burroughs arrived back from St Louis, and quickly put a stop to Jack's morbid candle-burning and dripping blood. 'My God, Jack,' Bill cried in horror. 'Stop this nonsense and let's go and have a drink.'

Jack had not written to Edie for two months, but as the holiday season approached, he decided that his wife should be with him, and Edie came to New York to spend Christmas. They got on well together and decided to give their marriage another try. Edie had written asking Allen to send her a book list in exchange for which she would keep their 'secret' – that Allen had jumped naked, with a full erection, into her bed one evening.

Early in September 1944, Edie's old room-mate Joan Vollmer returned to the city; she had missed all the excitement of the summer because she was away at her parents' place in Loudonville, New York, having a baby. Her husband, Paul Adams, from whom she was separated, was stationed with the army in Tennessee. She took a huge apartment on 115th Street together with a friend, Ruth Clark, who was pregnant and married to a merchant marine. She resumed an affair with John Kingsland, a sixteen-year-old Columbia student who had lived across the hall from Ginsberg at the Theological Seminary, and he moved into one of the spare rooms. Shortly after this, Ruth Clark went to join her husband where he was stationed and Joan and Kingsland found themselves with a hefty rent bill. Joan took a morning job in a nursery school and Kingsland arranged to have all his classes in the afternoon, so he could stay home with Joan's daughter Julie. The situation was saved by Jack and Edie's reconciliation that December. His room at Warren Hall was tiny, so he and Edie moved in with Joan.

Jack's return had unfortunate repercussions on Allen's status at Columbia. Johnny, the bartender at the West End, reported to the Dean's office that Allen was staying there until the 3 a.m. closing time, drinking with Kerouac. Dean McKnight asked Allen's father to come in for a conference. Even though Allen read all his assigned books and had straight A grades, McKnight thought he was not benefiting fully from his experience at Columbia. He was very stern and Louis left his office in tears. Since Allen was at Columbia on a scholarship they had power over him and were prepared to use it.

Allen moved into Livingston Hall, on the campus, and it was through his room-mate, Bill Lancaster, that Louis learned that his son was a poet. Louis of course knew that Allen had written poetry at High School but hadn't realised that he continued to take it seriously. When Louis questioned him about it, Allen explained that he didn't think Louis would want yet another poet in the family. At that time it was Eugene who was the most visible poet. He often had poems in the *New York Times* and on one memorable occasion he was in both the *Times* and the *Sun* on the same day. Louis had quipped to a friend that Allen was the only one in the family who didn't write and thus the only one who was 'normal'. Now he told Allen, 'If you write poetry, I want you to do so only because you have an inner compulsion, because you feel you must write, and because you can't help but write poetry.'

In fact it was only at the beginning of 1945 that Allen wrote his first serious poems. He kept a list of completed writings in his journal: 'Jan-Feb: Started real poems – First poems of genius?' There were four poems listed, 'He Who Walks Within The Womb', 'I Have Been Unleashed', 'This Stormy Foundation Bursts Upon The Air' and 'Now In This Park, By This Lakeside'.

Allen and Jack spent the early months of 1945 attempting to define their idea of 'The New Vision', a notion of unity of being taken mostly from William Butler Yeats's *A Vision*. He and Kerouac were deeply influenced by the Romantic poets, particularly Baudelaire's 'Invitation to the Voyage' and Rimbaud's 'Drunken Boat'. Inspired by these nautical themes, Ginsberg wrote his first long poem, and called it 'The Last Voyage'; its fifteen pages of rhymed couplets were later dismissed by Ginsberg as 'jejeune rhymed doggerel'. In addition to his college curriculum, he was reading biographies of Verlaine, Baudelaire, Rimbaud, Cocteau and Shelley as well as the works of Coleridge, Fitzgerald and the Marquis de Sade. He steeped himself in tales of *la vie de bohème* and began to fashion himself after the classic image of the poet, complete with Lucien's red kerchief. When he delivered a paper to Trilling's English Romantics class comparing the early Shelley with Rimbaud, Trilling gave it serious consideration, just as he did Allen's early efforts at poetry.

Allen and Jack were both intrigued by the enigmatic character of William Burroughs and they decided to pay him a visit to 'investigate the state of his soul' since, as a result of many hours of intense conversation, they both felt that they had a very definite and precise understanding of the nature of their own souls.

Bill now lived in a small, but rather grand apartment in one of the big buildings on Riverside Drive, overlooking the Hudson, which had been loaned to him by an ex-Harvard friend. Bill showed them his library. Most of the books they had never heard of. Bill explained that he had a scientific approach to reading, which was both functional and pragmatic: 'I read each book for a special purpose,' he told them. 'For instance, I read Chas Jackson's *Lost Weekend* to see what alcoholism is like. I read for information.' He told them he read Rimbaud for his description of the derangement of the senses, and both Rimbaud and St John Perse for 'the foreign perfume, the juxtaposition of strange experience and the images of cities glittering in the distance.' Burroughs particularly liked the T.S. Eliot translation of St John Perse's *Anabas* which had a dry, St Louis edge to it that he could appreciate.

Bill had books of parlour tricks, card games and formulas, boxing, ju-jitsu, an Egyptian grammar, Kovoor Behanan's *Yoga, A Scientific Evaluation*, a volume on hypnoanalysis and Abrahamson's *Crime and the Human Mind*, but the literature and poetry were what particularly interested Ginsberg. It was here that he and Jack discovered Kafka's *The Castle*, Cocteau's *Opium*, Louis-Ferdinand Céline's *Journey to the End of the Night*, Baudelaire's *Poesies* and Blake's poems. Blake was not much studied in the United States at that time but Burroughs thought him a 'perfect poet'.

There was a copy of the works of Shakespeare with marked passages; Burroughs was much given to quoting from him. Also on his shelves were a Louis Untermeyer anthology, *The Oxbow*

Incident by Walter van Tilburg Clark, *Nightwood* by Djuna Barnes, *Folded Leaf* by William Maxwell, Gogol's *Dead Souls* and Nabokov on Gogol, Melville's *Moby Dick* and *Maiden Voyage* by Denton Welch, who came to be Burroughs's favourite author, plus a number of John O'Hara novels and a collection of Raymond Chandler and other crime writers.

Burroughs's library was to have an enormous impact on both Allen and Jack. Allen even went so far as to note down a list of titles on a yellow pad. When they left, Burroughs gave them each a gift. Jack received a copy of Oswald Spengler's *Decline of the West*, and Bill gave Allen an old red cloth-bound Liveright edition of Hart Crane's *Collected Poems*. Allen had never heard of Hart Crane but he was later to be one of the lesser influences on Ginsberg's 'Howl'.

Burroughs had a curiously sinister reputation, even in those days, and Allen and Jack associated him with images of Berlin and Vienna before the war and the high camp culture of Proust and Gide. He was courteous and dignified, and they both came away with the image of Gainsborough's 'Blue Boy', Burroughs as a perfect gentleman but very shy and sensitive. 'Delicacy and melancholy, fragility and vulnerability, sweet and sad like a little boy,' was how Ginsberg remembered him.

Bill's grandfather, William Seward Burroughs, had invented the adding machine and founded the company that became the giant Burroughs corporation. A great inventor, he was a poor financier, and he was swindled out of most of the shares in the new corporation that bore his name. Bill's parents, Mortimer and Laura Lee Burroughs, lived a comfortable middle-class life in St Louis, with a cook, maid and gardener, and a nanny to look after their two boys. Their youngest, William Seward Burroughs II, was born in 1914. As a child, he would go duck-hunting with his brother Mortimer, his father, and the chairman of the First National Bank. Bill became a good shot and his consummate interest in guns later became a major theme in his writing.

He attended a number of expensive private schools including John Burroughs School (named after the naturalist, no relation) and studied English Literature at Harvard. He graduated in 1936, then studied medicine in Vienna for six months before the rise of the Nazis led him to return to the States. At Harvard he did postgraduate work in anthropology then worked a year in New

York as a copywriter for a small advertising agency. In 1942, after America had entered the war, he was drafted into the army, but was soon released; in 1940, he had spent a month in Bellevue and Payne-Whitney after cutting off the last joint of the little finger of his left hand with poultry shears in order to impress a boyfriend. When his psychiatric papers came to light, he was given a civilian disability discharge. Burroughs had various wartime jobs: he worked as a private detective and for a year as an exterminator in Chicago. When Allen first met him, in December 1943, he was working as a bartender in the Village. With his Harvard background and his obvious intelligence, Burroughs could easily have found better-paid employment. He took dead-end jobs more for the experience than for the money, because he always had the security of the two-hundred dollar monthly allowance sent him by his parents from the profits of an exclusive garden-supply and gift shop that they ran.

Allen came increasingly under the influence of Burroughs, much to Louis Ginsberg's dismay. 'He's dangerous,' wrote Louis, 'not because he rationalises but because his end product of thought and attitude results, eventually, if carried out in action, in danger and disharmony and chaos ... I disagree with you – but definitely – that an immoralist can confirm "enduring human values" ... You're all "wet" Allen. You simply have little experience in life. Where is your former, fine, zeal for a liberal progressive, democratic society? Your sophistry – for that is what it is – is a series of half-truths, verbal cleverness, and dangerous ideas expressed in specious and dextrous verbiage.' As an afterthought, below his signature, Louis added, 'What about a psychiatrist?'

On 16 March Kerouac paid Burroughs a visit at his new room off Columbus Circle, over Riorden's, a local bar. They had a long conversation, in the course of which Burroughs told Jack bluntly that he would never free himself from his mother unless he made a proper break with her instead of running home every time he had a problem. Bill said, 'The trouble with you is you're just tied to your mother's apron strings and you are going in a wide circle around her now, but it's going to get a narrower and narrower circle and sooner or later you are going to be right in there, unable to move away from your mother. That's your fate, that's your Faustian destiny.'

This chilling prophecy disturbed Jack so much that he went uptown to Livingston Hall to talk about it with Allen. Struck by Burroughs' words, Jack acknowledged that he was too closely tied to his mother, and that he had internalised many of her ideas. Allen was impressed by Burroughs's insight. Edie had moved back to Grosse Pointe, and Jack had been spending a lot of time in Queens with his parents in the last month, but Allen hadn't connected it with Jack's growing separation from Edie and his inability to commit himself to their relationship.

It got so late that Allen suggested that Jack stay over. Jack, of course, knew Allen's feelings toward him, but they slept chastely clad in their underwear. Allen was still a virgin and, though he was in love with Jack, he was afraid to touch him. At 8 a.m. they were awakened by the assistant dean of student-faculty relationships, who came bursting into the room.

Allen had been conducting a private war with the Irishwoman who cleaned his room. To draw her attention to the film of dirt on the windowpane, he had traced on the glass the words 'Butler has no balls' (a reference to Nicholas Murray Butler, President of Columbia University). He suspected that the cleaning woman was anti-Semitic, so he also wrote an eye-catching, 'Fuck the Jews' and drew a skull and crossbones beneath it. The graffiti caught her attention, but instead of cleaning them off she had reported them to Dean Furman.

Furman had been one of Kerouac's football coaches at Columbia, so they knew each other, but Jack didn't stay to talk. He leapt from the bed and ran to Bill Lancaster's empty bed in the next room, pulling the covers up over his face and leaving Allen to face the situation alone.

Allen was made to wipe the offending words from the window, but he knew that Furman was thinking the worst. An hour later, when Allen went downstairs, he found two notes in his box. One charged him $2.35 for entertaining an unauthorised guest overnight. The other, from Dean McKnight, informed him that he was suspended and suggested that he spend the weekend with his father, 'since the privilege of residence at Livingstone has been withdrawn from you'. Allen was forbidden to attend classes and told to abstain from all student activities. On the same day, McKnight wrote to Louis. The circumstances of Allen's suspension could not be reported in a letter, he said, but the two principal elements were obscene writings on his window and giving over-night housing to a person who was not a member of the college and whose presence on the campus was unwelcome.

On Monday morning, Allen put on his best clothes and necktie and went to see McKnight. Kerouac had gone home to his mother, so he wasn't available to substantiate Allen's story. The dean ushered Allen in and invited him to sit down. He stared grimly across the desk and said, 'Mister Ginsberg. I hope you understand the *enormity* of what you have done!'

Allen thought of a scene near the beginning of Céline's *Journey to the End of the Night*. The narrator is standing in the middle of a World War I battlefield, with bombs bursting and bullets flying about him, and realises that he is surrounded by dangerous madmen. 'Had something extraordinary then come over these people? Something which I didn't feel at all? I must have failed to notice it,' wrote Céline. 'In this sort of business there's nothing for it; the only thing to do is to shove out of it.'

Allen looked up at the dean, remembered Céline and knew that the only way out was to humour him. 'Oh I do sir! I do! I do!' he said. 'If you can only tell me what I can do to make up for this. . .'

The punishment seemed unnecessarily severe for such a minor offence, and it seemed likely that other, unspoken factors must have contributed to the decision to suspend him. Bill Lancaster proved to be a stalwart friend and went to McKnight. 'I understand there has been some difficulty,' he said, 'and I'd like to clear up the situation. I understand there are allegations of homosexuality. Is that what's at issue, when Kerouac and Ginsberg slept together?'

'No, no, no, no! Nobody said anything about it!' protested the Dean. 'Nobody has mentioned it. Nobody brought up the subject! I'm not accusing anybody of anything at all!'

But Allen's room-mate continued to press his point, 'Well, I can assure you that nothing of the sort went on, because the door was open and I was there all night and they're old friends and they just slept like college boys sleep.'

Allen sought Trilling's advice. When Trilling arrived in McKnight's office to discuss the incident, McKnight was too embarrassed to quote the graffiti to the first Jew to penetrate the English faculty at Columbia, so he wrote the offending words on a piece of paper and passed it across the desk. Trilling and his wife were utterly unable to see that Allen was simply goading the anti-Semitic Irish cleaner, and years later Diane Trilling was still using the incident as an example of Ginsberg's 'Jewish self-hatred'.

Mark Van Doren, who had often given Allen advice on his poetry, also petitioned on his behalf, but in the end, McKnight decided that Allen was not to return to Columbia until he had worked at a job for year and had seen a psychiatrist, who would submit in a letter that Allen was now mature enough to be a responsible member of the academic community. Allen told the story later, 'So I was kicked out of Columbia, but the thing that rang in my ears, was "Mister Ginsberg. I hope you realise the enormity of what you've done!" because actually I hadn't done anything. I wanted to. I lay there longing all night!'

3 A Street Education

*Everybody is going to fall apart, disintegrate, all character
structures based on tradition and uprightness and so-called
morality will slowly rot away, people will get the hives right
in their hearts, great crabs will cling to their brains . . .*
                    Levinsky [Ginsberg] in *The Town And The City*
                                             by Jack Kerouac

Allen moved straight into Joan Vollmer's sunny, well-decorated apartment at 419 West 115th Street, where he shared a bedroom with Hal Chase, a blond Columbia anthropology student from Denver, whom Allen was immediately attracted to. Joan and Kingsland had found him through an ad in the *Columbia Spectator*, the college paper. Jack still had a room with Edie, and Joan, her daughter Julie and Kingsland had the remaining bedrooms. Joan cooked simple, healthy meals, and they all contributed to the eighty-dollar rent and food costs. Apartment 62 was in the rear on the top floor, a steep climb with no elevator. There was a large living room, with big windows, and the rooms led off a long narrow hall. There was a huge white tile bath, in which Joan liked to read the newspapers. If anyone wanted to talk to her, they had to perch on the edge of the tub.

They made a young, attractive group. Joan had already graduated from Barnard, she was twenty-one and possessed a formidable intelligence. If anyone was late with a school paper she would write it in an hour or two. She wrote one in the manner of a Dryden poem for Kingsland's course with Joseph Woods Krutch on Dryden and Eighteenth-century English Literature that Krutch liked. According to Hal Chase, 'She had Kerouac totally terrified with her verbal control.' She was thin, with a heart-shaped face, small turned-up nose, soft brown dewy eyes, often with a small bandanna holding back her brown hair. She was pigeon-toed and was described by Edie Parker as having 'thick legs and nice boobs, very feminine. She never did anything in a hurry.' Kingsland was four years her junior and tried to disguise his baby fat by wearing three-piece suits.

Edie looked like Barbara Stanwyck, particularly in the mouth; a forties Hollywood ideal of a 'glamorous broad' in her wide shoulder-pads and high heels. She had a fondness for tight sweaters which emphasised her large breasts and always had two or three V–12 cadets in tow, all waiting to light her cigarette, whenever Jack was not around.

Allen enjoyed the company and talked endlessly with Joan and Jack. Edie was not much taken with Allen: 'Allen was unattractive, and when he talked he got all excited and he kind of drooled, he lisped.' He was still a teenager, thrilled to be out in the big wide world. He took a job as a welder at the Brooklyn Navy Yard, working for Eastern Gas and Fuel, the general agents of the US War Shipping Administration. It was heavy work, but the money was good, and he stuck it till the end of April. Then he worked as a dish-washer and at the Gotham Book Mart for a few weeks, but Frances Steloff fired him because he was too bemused and timid to do the job efficiently.

Allen's swift and unexpected suspension from Columbia cast him into limbo, with no plans and no idea when he would be permitted to resume his studies. In the course of his two years at Columbia he had grown up. He now knew his sexual inclination, though it was still a closely guarded secret. He knew that he wanted to write; he and Jack intended to write the New Vision into existence. He had arrived at Columbia friendless. Now, though only eighteen, he was a member of an adult group and had a number of close friends who gave him a level of emotional security he had not previously enjoyed. He loved them with a fierce loyalty, while deep down he still felt unloved and alone: the trauma of his childhood was lodged in his unconscious.

As long as he attended Columbia, his *nostalgie de la boue* was held in check by the authority of the English department and its celebrated professors. Now that he was out on his own, he looked for new teachers, and turned naturally to William Burroughs. Together they explored the carnival world of Times Square, of petty thieves and hoodlums, hustlers and prostitutes, cheap bars and rooming houses. Burroughs was engaged in a systematic study of the Eighth Avenue bars and Allen joined him, dividing the bars into nine categories to investigate. Burroughs was fascinated by criminals and sought out various underworld characters, mostly petty thieves. He explored their world even when it required breaking the law, usually by acting as an accessory or a receiver of stolen goods. He struck up a friendship with a small-time hoodlum called Bob Brandenberg, who had come to New York with the desperate desire to be a mobster but in the meantime worked as a soda jerk in a drugstore at 112th Street and Amsterdam. Bill liked to sit in the drugstore listening to Bob's stories about the underworld. One winter afternoon, Bill leaned across the counter conspiratorially and asked if Bob knew where he could unload a tommygun and some boxes of morphine syrettes. Bob could only think of his two room-mates: Herbert Huncke and Phil White. They had just returned from six months at sea, where they tried unsucessfully to kick a junk habit.

He took Bill to meet them at their apartment, on Henry Street beneath the Brooklyn Bridge.

Herbert Huncke, a small man with an oval face, a weary expression and huge, heavily lidded chelonian eyes, reacted to Bill's presence with extreme paranoia. He stepped into the next room with Bob and told him he thought that Bill might be a plainclothes man, possibly even FBI. If Bob didn't ask him to leave, then he, Huncke, would. Just then, in the other room he heard Phil White say, 'What's that you said, Bill? You have morphine syrettes?'

Bill explained that there had been a drugstore stickup and that one of the men involved, a friend of his, had taken a gross of half grain morphine syrettes after cleaning out the register. Bill was trying to shift the goods. Huncke rapidly joined Bill and Phil at the living room table. Bill went on to explain that he wanted to sell all but one or two of the syrettes, which he wanted to try out himself. 'Do you know this stuff?' he asked, 'Do you know how it is taken?'

Burroughs recalled the event: 'I was alone when I shot up the first time with the morphine syrettes. It was sort of scary; you have a feeling of moving just off the ground at great speed, past warehouses or something, then suddenly you'll wake up. I was sick, something makes you start. I do remember being in a neon lit cocktail lounge and the waitress came in with a skull on a tray. 'What are you doing here? I didn't order no fuckin' skull! Take it back!' I didn't have the syrettes with me when I met Phil, and he came around the next day. Huncke wasn't even there. It's all described very precisely in *Junky*.'

Bill saw a lot of Phil during the winter of 1944–45. After a couple of months he developed a small drug habit. One day Bill took Kerouac down to Henry Street to score some morphine from Phil White, and the door to the apartment was opened by a tall, thin young woman with red hair. Vickie Russell was Bob's girlfriend and was the only one at home. There were no drugs in the house, but with Bill paying the cab fares, she was prepared to see if she could find something in Times Square for them.

She was speeding on a Benzedrine high and showed them how to crack open a nasal inhaler and extract the concertina strip of Benzedrine inside. The inhalers were available anywhere for ninety-eight cents and each one contained eight folds of blotting paper impregnated with the drug. One and half strips could get a person extremely high, and two strips would last eighteen hours. The strips were rolled into balls and washed down with a cup of coffee. They were hard to swallow, and the taste was very unpleasant. Jack took too much the first time and thought he had overdosed but Vickie looked after him and they wound up spending the night together at Bill's apartment.

Jack introduced Benzedrine to 115th Street, and soon Vickie herself started to visit. Jack liked taking it to write, because it enabled him to handle many complicated thoughts simultaneously, but the person in the house who most appreciated the Benzedrine was Joan, and soon she was using it every day.

Jack's reconciliation with Edie had not lasted long, and she moved out of 115th Street early in 1945. Jack spent more and more time at his parents' house at Ozone Park, Queens, where his father, Leo, was slowly dying of cancer. When Jack was in town, he stayed at 115th Street where he and Allen spent much time discussing the New Vision. Allen later described it as a matter of seeing 'everybody lost in a dream world of their own making. That was the basis of the Beat Generation. That was the primary perception. The idea of transience of phenomemon – the poignant Kewpie-doll dearness of personages vanishing in time. Not a morbid interest in death but the realisation of the mortal turn ... it's the sigh of mortality that Jack had.'

Allen was still a virgin, his love for Jack unrequited. He discussed his sexual orientation with both Jack and Bill, but it remained hypothetical. Finally, he felt driven to sleep with just *anyone*. He went to the MacDougal Street Bar, a gay bar in the Village, and allowed himself to be picked up by a greying, forty-year old sailor. He took Allen to a room in the Seamen's Institute where he made Allen blow him. 'He abused me, I thought, because he didn't entertain me, he didn't reciprocate and was a bit brutal,' Ginsberg recalled. Bill told Allen, 'The guy didn't treat you right.' Allen felt the whole experience was inauthentic.

The next time was better. Allen had gone with Bill to the Museum of Modern Art, where he met a young student of his own age and went home with him. 'I wasn't much taken with him emotionally, it was just a relief to have somebody physical,' Ginsberg remembered. They spent a weekend together but quickly lost interest in each other.

Then, finally, Allen had his first sexual experience with Kerouac. They were walking by the waterfront where the elevated West Side Highway passed Christopher Street. The area beneath it was used as a truck park and would later became the centre of the New York gay scene. They stopped between two trucks and jacked each other off. 'I don't know why there should be some erotic spirit of a place,' Ginsberg commented. 'I think it was just the industrial isolation, and we were horny.' However, the next time they walked through that area, they did it again, and it was not long before Kerouac allowed Allen to blow him. Allen fell completely in love.

Memorial Day came, and everyone left for the summer. Allen found himself in the empty 115th Street apartment alone and broke. At that time, the easiest way to make quick money was to go to sea as Kerouac and Huncke had done, so Allen enrolled in the US Martime Service which was the fastest route to the coveted Seaman's Union card. On 1 August 1945, he presented himself at the US Maritime Service Training Station in Sheepshead Bay, Brooklyn, and became Irwin Allen Ginsberg 4514-24594. His home for the next three-and-a-half months was Bunk 6, Compartment H-44, Section 408. Ginsberg was in the Navy. When he showed up in the city in his crisp uniform, short hair and sailor's hat on his first leave, Céline hardly recognised him.

He buffed floors, washed dishes and was sometimes on night watch. He soon understood that the idea was to put in the hours at work or at classes but not to get anything done. Bored, he taught himself how to box a compass and to name the parts of a ship. Allen also learned how to swear. 'It's sort of juvenile and overdone, but I got in the groove quick,' he told Eugene. His letter was filled with swear words, and he ended it, affectionately, 'you old peckerhead!'

Allen was caught reading Hart Crane, and the navy mailman who delivered a postcard from Kerouac remarked suspiciously that it was in French, but Allen was accepted completely as 'one of the boys' and they tended to come to him for advice and sympathy since, at nineteen, he was the oldest in his section.

'The boys here are all overgrown or warped adolescents, all screaming neurotics,' he told Jack. Manhattan Beach was nearby, and on weekends he swam and lazed there in the sun. He found that he was quite enjoying himself.

But Allen was not cut out for the military life. He came down with a cold. He half-masochistically presented himself at the sick bay, only to be laughed at and told that he was goldbricking. He threw up in a toilet that was out of bounds to him and got into trouble; he had a nosebleed; and finally, the day after he reported sick, someone took his temperature. By this time he had developed pneumonia and was sent straight to a comfortable bunk in the sick bay, where he passed his time reading *The Way of All Flesh*, *The Bridge of San Luis Rey* and *War and Peace*. He decided he preferred Dostoyevsky to Tolstoy.

From his sick bed, Allen wrote long, ruminative love letters to Kerouac. After a tentative comparison of Jack and Lucien to Tadzio, the beautiful boy in Thomas Mann's *Death in Venice*, and himself, even more tentatively, to Aschenbach, the self-conscious writer obsessed with the beautiful boy, Allen asked, 'What am I? What do I seek? Self-aggrandisement, as you describe it, is a superficial description of what my motives are, and my purposes. If I over-reach myself for love, it is because I crave it so much and have known so little of it. Love is perhaps opiate, but I know it to be creative as well.'

He went on, 'Well, these last years have been the nearest to fulfilment of my desires, and with full feeling I thank you for the gift. You were right, I suppose in keeping your distance. I was too intent on self-fulfillment, and rather crude about it, with all my harlequinade and conscious manipulation of your pity. I overtaxed my own patience and strength even more than I did yours, possibly. You behaved like a gentleman, though I think that you did take me too seriously, assign too much symbolic value to my motion and friction.'

Jack replied asking Allen not to be so sophomoric and moribund in his criticisms and pleading for a little more finesse and, if possible, a dash of humour. Sometimes Jack experienced Allen's articulate affection as emotional pressure and tried to distance himself, but he always came back. Jack was finding life difficult. He was working on three novels simultaneously, keeping a large diary and reading prodigiously; but he was living at home, and his mother was working in a shoe factory in order to support him. His dying father clearly thought Jack would never make anything of his life.

Jack was also upset by his homosexual tendencies; as well as fooling around with Allen, he had spent an evening drinking with Bill and some of Bill's friends, ending up as a participant in a drunken homosexual orgy, which he regretted the next day. 'It automatically repels me,' he told Allen, 'thereby causing a great deal of remorse and disgust.' However, it was also during this time that Jack went with Bill and Allen to the Everard Turkish Baths, where a group of French sailors blew him. 'I think he just dug the idea of a bunch of French sailors,' Ginsberg said, 'He was quite sociable and happy . . . He was very gay about it.'

Until then, Jack only allowed Allen to blow him and did not reciprocate. 'I was pulling him in different directions that were unnatural to him and difficult,' Allen said. 'He was bending and stretching quite a bit to accommodate my emotions. That's why I've always loved him, because I was able to completely unburden myself and express my deepest feelings and he could relate to them. Reject them, hear them out, reciprocate sometimes, actually go to bed with me sometimes, rarely. Get drunk with me, walk around, being there, hearing me through and giving me a reaction to bounce off against. So I was more intimate with him about my feelings than anybody on earth. I bared myself to him and he was able to take it.'

The letters continued back and forth, charting Kerouac's periods of closeness and distance. He claimed that the quality of his friendship for Allen was much purer than Allen's was for him, and that he was wasting his friendship on 'a little self-aggrandising weasel'. But then, in another letter, he said he had grown fond of Allen again.

In November 1945, Allen graduated from MSTS and was released from active duty, having earned $103.79 in defence of his country. He used his new Seaman's Union card to ship out that same day, working as a messman on the Kearny-to-Norfolk run. Next, he joined a coal-carrying barge which made its way slowly down the coast to unload at New Orleans, where he smoked marijuana for the first time with some Puerto Rican sailors in a brothel.

After Labor Day, the various inhabitants of 115th Street had drifted back to the city. Those actually sharing the rent were Joan, Hal Chase, Allen and Bill. Jack was now living with his parents but stopped over two or three nights each week.

Allen and Jack had decided that Bill Burroughs and Joan Vollmer would make a great couple. They were both older than Jack and Allen, both witty and well-read. They had the same kind of sardonic intellectual sophistication. Bill and Joan hit it off right away. Burroughs remembered Joan: 'She was a very extraordinary woman and we got talking, exchanging ideas. She was the smartest person around, certainly as smart as Allen, in many ways smarter, because Allen still has decided limits to his thinking, and she didn't. So that was the basis of the attraction – an intellectual, not the usual talks about nothing. She had a sense of humour and it was more humour my style.'

Bill moved into Jack and Edie's old room, 'It was sort of a communal set up and I liked the people. I had to move anyway, my lease had expired. So I moved up there. My relationship with Joan became physical later.' Though Burroughs was primarily a homosexual, they had an active sex life. Joan once told him, 'You're supposed to be a faggot. You're as good as a pimp in bed.'

Hal Chase recalls that the physical side of their relationship was largely Joan's idea: 'Life in the apartment was a psychodrama. Joan was after Bill. There was a power struggle. Was she gonna get him? He had one room and she had another, and pretty soon she started going to his room . . . . the struggle between Joan and Bill seemed to be life-and-death. Joan was scornful of Bill. She'd describe in detail how he'd be all set to make love, and then he'd get a cramp in his foot.'

'It was a year of evil decadence,' said Kerouac in *Vanity of Duluoz*. Joan had a huge double bed with an oriental drape over it where up to six people could sprawl, taking Benzedrine, morphine, and talking for days on end in an amphetamine haze. Jack took so much Benzedrine that his health began to suffer. His hair began to fall out (a symptom of excessive amphetamine use), and he looked pale and drawn. One day Vickie Russell applied pancake make-up to his face before she would go on the subway with him. Bill's day-to-day presence changed the atmosphere of the apartment. He began conducting his experiments; the drug intake rose rapidly and conversations centered on the idea of expanding individual awareness.

Throughout one summer night, which came to be known to Beat Generation scholars as 'The Night of the Wolfeans and the Non-Wolfeans' (after Thomas Wolfe), Allen lay in one bed with Hal, and Bill and Jack were in another. On the Wolfean side were the heterosexual all-American boys; Jack Kerouac and Hal Chase. On the other side, the non-Wolfeans, Burroughs and Ginsberg, held forth, 'the sinister European fairies . . . who didn't believe in the wide open, dewy-eyed lyrical America' of the Wolfeans but who were always trying to go to bed with them, nonetheless, as Ginsberg later summed it up. 'Homosexuality was one of the attributes of non-Wolfeans, and among other things, intellectuality and fear of the body and manipulativeness and Jewishness. International concern rather than appreciation of America and homeyness and family and normal values.'

Allen got very upset by the conversation that night. They were all coming down from a Benzedrine high and had the usual experience of exhaustion, depression and dissociation from the world. Allen began to talk openly about how it felt to be a non-Wolfean. He used the image of a curtain of cellophane that separated him from his friends and from reality itself.

'I was trying urgently to break through and explain once and for all what I felt like, so as to appeal to them and win their sympathy and make them hug me and sleep with me . . . I remember it being a reference point between us for many years. We came to try and define our roles and relationships, not intentionally, just to poetically find some image of how we were related . . . If I had been the only non-Wolfean I would have felt like a jerk, but with Burroughs as one of them, I felt there was some dignity and possibility in the situation despite our deficiency in earthiness.'

The experience of that night stayed with him always and even in India, years later, he recorded in his journals: 'Talking about transparent waterfalls of cellophane – pure synthetic abstraction making me groan with desire to be kissed on the mouth and held close to the breast of the fair boy's body I desired then and there, but it wasn't done, so I talked all night, explaining my delicate condition as hurt-voiced as I felt in my crying throat and sad warm eighteen-year-old breast.'

That fall the household began to play a complicated game of charades, inspired by Burroughs's attempts to psychoanalyse Allen and Jack. Burroughs had been in analysis for many years, first with Doctor Louis Federn, an old-time Viennese analyst who had been analyzed by Freud himself, and now with Dr Leo Walberg, who used hypnosis to reach the different layers of the patient's personality. With Bill, he was able to find many different personality layers.

The top layer was Burroughs, the distinguished scion of an old St Louis family. Below that was a nervous, possibly lesbian, English governess with a prissy, self-conscious, simpering personality. Below her was Old Luke, the tobacco farmer, who just sat in his rocking chair on his front porch with his shotgun over his knees, watching the catfish come down the river. Old Luke had the personality of a psychotic Southern sheriff. Beneath them all was an implacable, silent Chinaman, sitting starving, skull-headed, on the banks of the Yangtse, with no ideals, no beliefs and no words, the ultimate Burroughs persona.

Bill liked to play out these characters in a form of charades that he called 'routines'. As an English governess he was very prim, always rapping people on the knuckles and serving tea, shrieking in a high voice, 'My dear, you're just in time for tea. Don't say those dirty words in front of everybody!'

He could become quite terrifying as the old southern sharecropper. He would slowly build his monologue, 'See that catfish comin' down the river? Well, it's just one catfish after another going down. I jest sit an' watch 'em all day long. Once in a while I get out my fishing tackle and I catch me a catfish. *Ever gut a catfish?*' he would yell, and go completely mad with bloodlust to gut a catfish in a truly psychopathic manner, while they all cracked up.

In Allen's favourite routine, he played The Well Groomed Hungarian, while Jack would put on his father's old straw hat, which he had brought for the purpose, and play the innocent American bumpkin in Paris. Bill would don a wig and a woman's skirt and become a lesbian countess who acted as the shill for the Hungarian's art gallery. The countess brought naive Wolfean American tourists to buy the phony family masterpieces that Allen had supposedly taken with him when he fled Hungary during the war. Allen would rub his hands together and affect a thick middle-European accent, 'Ah, my young man, you vant to buy some culture?'

'Aw gee, fellers,' said Jack. 'I cain't. I gotta girl. I have a date with my girl at the coffeehouse you got out there.'

'You want to stay away from those, Jack,' warned Burroughs. 'Those ladies got poison juices. Your cock falls off if you do that. Sometimes they got teeth up there.'

Many years later, Bill recalled his role. 'I was playing, er-hum, an Edith Sitwell part. I got in drag and I looked like some sinister old lesbian.'

Hal Chase played the role of the brash but innocent mountaineering Denver boy, Child of the Rainbow, 'with pretty blond golden hair and good physique, an Indian hawk-nose and American boy State Fair fresh manners', as Ginsberg described him later. 'Routines', as Burroughs called them, played a major part in his later writings.

Burroughs's lay analysis continued until June 1946. Allen and Jack each spent an hour at a time free-associating. Bill sat in a straight-backed chair like a proper Freudian analyst, while they lay on the couch. Allen found the sessions effective. He began to bare frail, sensitive, private fears. One day he suddenly burst into tears and wailed, 'Nobody loves me!' Bill sat impassively in the chair, friendly but impersonal, listening and commenting.

'It was kind of a breakthrough for me, a realisation of my actual feelings,' Ginsberg said. 'Painful feelings I didn't want to admit to at that age, nineteen.' These revelations, presumably connected with his mother's apparent withdrawal of love, left him naked and defenceless, and though Bill was not trained to help Allen to deal with them, he found the experience valuable. In a letter to Burroughs written from Sheepshead Bay, Allen discussed their latest session:

'Sunday nite was the first time I'd really been completely disintegrated and confused under analysis; it was not so much that "resistance" was overcome, but that before my analysis I sensed that I could not regain my wits and perspective until I had set the specific paranoia in my mind straight, and, possibly, had "confessed" it by way of grace.' He went on to say the analysis 'illustrated what I have dimly known, I feel more guilty and inferior by reason of faggishness than intellectualisations will admit is proper.'

Bill's recollection was that there were only about ten sessions: 'He unburdened himself to me to no purpose at all. There were various traumatic events, but on the whole nothing of much significance. "Nobody loves me, nobody loves me, nobody loves me!" Now I felt, even at the time, that this was sheer histrionics. Sheer histrionics. It just didn't ring true and it didn't mean anything.' There were probably more sessions than this, and all the household was involved. Edie remembered that she and Joan would write down their dreams and Bill would analyse them. Hal Chase also recalled, 'Bill would come back from his analyst and try to analyse us.'

It was a very creative period for Ginsberg and Kerouac, as inspired by Burroughs, the teacher. Virtually everything they did was motivated by their concern for investigating, and exploring the nature of consciousness. 'The whole point of smoking grass or taking peyote was as a probe,' Ginsberg recalled, 'an examination of what is the alteration of consciousness caused by amphetamine, or morphine, or marijuana, or heroin, or peyote, or mescaline. At least that was my terminology then. Examination, like William James' experiments with nitrous oxide, very much in mind.' It was a very scientific investigation; Ginsberg and Burroughs looked into hypnotism and made a few experiments together with cards, since they both had an interest in telepathy. They explored the sinister, the criminal and the forbidden. They rejected the conformist, consumerist society of America in the late 1940s but were not thinking in terms of rebelling against it. The Beat Generation began with personal exploration. 'It wasn't a political or social rebellion,' Ginsberg said. 'Everybody had some form of break in their consciousness, or an experience, or a taste of a larger consciousness, or satori.' They had all read Spengler's *Decline of the West* and took it for granted that civilisation was collapsing around them. The atomic bomb had just been dropped on Japan and that, to them, was proof enough. The early Beats had no hope of trying to change society.

Herbert Huncke began dropping by with some regularity till, in the end, he was there most days, sometimes staying over. At first, Huncke, as a junkie and thief, felt his new friends were patronising him. Joan was the exception. 'She was in all probability one of the most charming and intelligent women I've ever met,' he said. 'I think I fell sort of in love with her in a funny way. At one time I think she loved me in return.' Huncke was surprised to discover that she and Burroughs had a sexual relationship.

Huncke's insecurity was completely unfounded. The group was charmed and fascinated by him. He was very well known on 42nd Street, having been a male hustler there for about four years, so when Doctor Alfred Kinsey came to New York to conduct interviews for his massive study of the sexual habits of Americans, it was Huncke he approached when his research led him to the floating population of Times Square. Huncke introduced Kinsey to the whores, pimps, hustlers and thieves of the neighborhood. Allen, Jack and Bill all did interviews for the Kinsey Report as well. When the distinguished doctor asked Allen, 'Did you ever "brown" anybody?' Allen did not know what he meant.

Another person who began to come around was Bill Garver, an old prison friend of Huncke's, whom Bill liked, possibly because they had similar backgrounds. Garver was the son of an Ohio banker who was paid one hundred dollars a month to stay away from Ohio. He was tall and gaunt with sunken eyes, greying hair and loose features. It was only when he spoke that he betrayed his educated background. Garver supported a junk habit by stealing overcoats. He would sit in a cafeteria, nursing a cup of coffee until the coast was clear, then go to the coat-rack and take the best coat there. He stole two or three a day and had to travel all over the city to pawn them without anyone becoming too suspicious. Allen found him interesting and would sometimes go to Horn & Hardart and watch him at work.

Allen entered 1946 looking much as Kerouac described him in *The Town and the City*, written that year: wearing a belted raincoat, a paisley scarf and dark-rimmed glasses, smoking cigarettes through a red cigarette holder and carrying the works of Auden and Rimbaud under his arm. In the book Allen is called Leon Levinsky: 'Levinsky was an eager, intense, sharply intelligent boy of Russian–Jewish parentage who rushed around New York in a perpetual sweat of emotional activity, back and forth in the streets from friend to friend, room to room, apartment to apartment. He "knew everyone" and "knew everything", was always bearing tidings and messages from "the others", full of catastrophe. He brimmed and flooded over day and night with a thousand different thoughts and conversations and small horrors, delights, perplexities, deities, discoveries, ecstasies, fears. He stared gog-eyed at the world and was full of musings, lip-pursings, subway broodings – all of which rushed forth in torrents of complex conversation whenever he confronted someone.' Forty years later he was doing the same thing – on a global scale.

This was Jack's idealised description of the persona that Ginsberg presented to the world; that of the moody, brooding intellectual. Allen was always attracted to beautiful youths, particularly those with great practical skills. He thought of himself as clumsy and unattractive, and in his love relationships he sought to overcome this by offering to share his scholarship. He did this with Kerouac, but Kerouac saw beyond to the anxious youth inside. It is a measure of Kerouac's friendship that he was prepared to so completely accept Allen's public face.

Allen was in constant correspondence with his father, on whom he tested most of his new ideas; not surprisingly, Louis often disagreed. Louis had the usual ambitions for his son; he wanted him to get ahead in the world. He wanted Allen to become a labour lawyer – a thoroughly satisfactory way of combining socialist ideals and upward mobility. He was clearly concerned about Burroughs' influence. As far back as January 1945, Louis had used his parental authority to caution Allen against Bill: 'Frankly, I shall be disappointed in you if you persist in your intimate relation with him.'

Louis, with the best intentions, was trying to steer Allen away from the madness and confusion of his youth, but for Allen, to reject madness meant to reject his mother. Naomi was the biggest influence on his life, and the great appeal of the bohemian lifestyle that Burroughs and Carr had introduced to him was its acceptance and approval of madness, since it gave Allen a framework within which he was able to accept her. Louis felt responsible for the trauma of Allen's childhood, and his overriding concern was for Allen's happiness.

Twenty-year-old Allen was now pulled in two directions. On the one hand was Columbia, and the ambition of his father. At the polar opposite was Rimbaud, poetry and madness; drugs, criminals and the underworld.

Allen had no intention of losing touch with any of his family. He loved the warmth and security of family life and always remained close to his relatives. He saw a lot of Naomi, and now that he was living in New York City he was able to see more of his aunt Eleanor and uncle Max. Often he would spend Sunday at their house in the Bronx, eating a long relaxed meal of lox and bagels, reading the papers, listening to music on WQXR or playing Rosa Ponselle records on the phonograph.

Eugene was accepted into NYU Law School, and Naomi proposed that he come and live with her. He moved to New York at the beginning of 1946 and slept on the couch in Doctor Luria's office. Naomi and Doctor Luria lived across the street, but their relationship was becoming strained. Shortly after Eugene moved to New York, they broke up. Naomi found a furnished room in a brownstone on the West Side, and she and Eugene moved into it. It was a large room, crowded with furniture, with two windows overlooking the backyard. Eugene took jobs at Macy's and Schraffts and spent the rest of the time studying his law books, getting only six hours' sleep a night. Allen would often visit.

Naomi took to reading the Bible and told Allen, 'I will think nothing but beautiful thoughts.' In a long passage in 'Kaddish' Ginsberg describes how, on one of his visits, Naomi told him that she had seen God:

> He was a lonely old man with a white beard.
>
> I cooked supper for him. I made him a nice supper – lentil soup, vegetables, bread and butter – miltz – he sat down at the table and ate, he was sad.
>
> I told him, 'Look at all those fightings and killings down there, what's the matter? Why don't you put a stop to it?'
>
> 'I try,' he said – That's all he could do, he looked tired. He's a bachelor so long, and he likes lentil soup.
>
> Serving me meanwhile, a plate of cold fish – chopped raw cabbage dript with tapwater – smelly tomatoes – week-old health food – grated beets and carrots with leaky juice, warm – more and more disconsolate food – I can't eat it for nausea sometimes – the Charity of her hands stinking with Manhat-

tan, madness, desire to please me, cold undercooked fish –
pale red near the bones. Her smells – and oft naked in the
room, so that I stare ahead, or turn a book ignoring her.

To Louis' great relief, Allen applied for re-admission to Columbia
and, after some delay, a clearly uncomfortable Nicholas McKnight
replied, to say that it was a difficult question for him to decide. He
asked Allen to provide him with the professional opinion of a
psychiatrist.

Allen contacted Hans Wassing, Naomi's old doctor, who signed
the letter Allen wrote himself. The letter stressed Allen's emotional
stability and even said, 'I have noticed as well, that he takes good
care of his personal appearance and shows adequate attention to the
various necessary amenities of social intercourse. In my opinion,
there is no question, that at present time he is psychologically pretty
much as sound as they come.' McKnight was satisfied, and Ginsberg
was enrolled for the September 1946 term. Allen was glad to be
returning to his studies. He genuinely wanted to complete his course
before going off into the world and realised the practical necessity
of the degree. He was also getting fed up with short-term jobs, the
most recent of which had been checking coats in a night-club.

The apartment at 115th Street began to fall apart. Bill had a
morphine habit and was forging prescriptions for drugs. Edie was
left a property in Brooklyn by a doctor and she had piles of his
prescription pads all over the apartment; they used them as
notepads. Bill's various Times Square hoodlum friends began to
use the place to stash stolen goods and hide their guns. Allen, Jack,
Joan and Bill were all taking a lot of drugs; Joan, now completely
addicted to Benzedrine, was using the entire contents of an inhaler
in one day.

Joan claimed to have very acute hearing and said she could hear
the old Irish couple talking in the apartment below. The others
believed her reports of their conversations, chiefly quarrels over
petty things and over the old man's sexual demands. Joan said they
often referred to Joan as a whore and the others as dope fiends and
debated whether they should tell the police about the goings-on
upstairs.

One evening, Joan reported there was a bad quarrel in progress
below. The man was threatening to stab his wife. Joan insisted they
do something to stop it, so Jack and Allen ran downstairs and

thumped loudly on the door. No one answered. There was no one at home. The whole five months of Joan's reported conversations had been auditory hallucinations caused by the amphetamine.

Joan displayed other symptoms of amphetamine psychosis. She and Huncke, who was also a heavy user, would spend hours talking about spores that they saw coming out of their skin. This was in keeping with the theory of radioactive disease Joan and Huncke had evolved: atomic testing was causing mutation and skin cancers, which would eventually affect everyone but which could be seen most clearly among the inhabitants of Times Square. Under the bright neon and brilliantly lit all-night cafeterias, the diseased skins and other effects of molecular breakdown were immediately apparent.

Allen, mystified and intrigued by their hallucinations, was apparently oblivious to the disintegration of his friends. Phil White and Huncke took advantage of the situation and spent more and more time at the apartment, bringing in stolen goods, then spiriting them away a few days later. Sometimes they would borrow Bill's gun or blackjack to commit a robbery, and other times Phil stored his gun there.

Phil talked Bill into forging scripts from Doctor Grico. They had already filled other legitimate scripts from Doctor Grico, but when the inspectors checked, they discovered they were not in the same handwriting. Bill had been cashing scripts in his own name. Bill was arrested at the apartment for obtaining narcotics by fraudulent means, and yet again his father flew into town to post bail.

In the two months between his arrest and his appearance in court, Bill remained in New York, moving around the city from one cheap rooming house to another, selling heroin with Bill Garver, keeping enough back to take care of his heroin habit. Unlike most dealers, Bill was punctual and gave a good deal; sixteen per cent pure, better than anyone else in the city. In June 1946, Bill's case finally came up; since he was a first offender, the judge gave him a four-month suspended sentence and sent him home to St Louis with his father for the summer.

Allen was shocked and worried by Bill's arrest, but it didn't make him change his life-style. It was as if Allen was purposely rejecting his father's bourgeois values by letting his own life go to pieces. Joan reacted to Bill's arrest by taking more Benzedrine. Hal Chase was planning on living at a Columbia Hall of Residence and had already moved out and gone back to Denver for the summer. When he heard of the arrest he broke off relations with all of them except Jack. Thus the division between the Wolfeans and the non-Wolfeans began to be played out.

Huncke took over Chase's old room and Phil White moved in. After Bill's arrest Joan's behaviour became more and more erratic. In the tape recordings that Kerouac made of conversations with Neal Cassady, transcribed in *Visions of Cody*, he described the state of 115th Street at that time; he dropped by to see what was happening and found Joan out of her mind on Benzedrine. 'She came in and she immediately stripped. I said "Joan, what are you doing?" She said, "Who are you, strange man, get out of this house," standing there.'

Jack tried to remind her who he was, then Joan complained to Huncke that Jack was trying to rape her, but Huncke just lay in bed saying, 'Well ba-by, I don't know what to *do*,' and 'Well, I'm all hung up baby, I . . .' In the end she went into Huncke's room to talk about it and closed the door. It was obvious from the way things were going that the apartment was doomed, but Allen didn't seem to notice; he sat typing a ten-page amphetamine-inspired introduction to his epic poem 'Death In Violence', as the place collapsed around him. '. . . who scribbled all night rocking and rolling over lofty incantations which in the yellow morning were stanzas of gibberish,' he later wrote in 'Howl', remembering the period.

Huncke was the next to be arrested and was sent to the Bronx Jail for possession of drugs. It was only a matter of days before Joan cracked and was taken to Bellevue Hospital suffering from acute amphetamine psychosis; she was the first female case they had on record and was kept there for ten days. Allen closed down the apartment. He went to stay with his father in Paterson until the Columbia term started on 20 September.

Allen got a room with an Irish family at West 92nd Street, and prepared to become a student again. He had not lost touch with Columbia. Even though officially suspended, he had somehow remained the assistant editor of the *Columbia Review* and had poems, stories and book reviews published in all four issues for 1946. He had been in correspondence and had meetings with Trilling, who encouraged him with his poetry, and he was still in contact with Weaver and Van Doren. However, Allen was no longer in awe of his professors. He had begun to realise that they were old-fashioned and closed to new ideas: Pound's mature work was dismissed, William Carlos Williams was raw and immature and Walt Whitman nothing but a provincial bumpkin.

Although he seemed to be fulfilling his father's expectations, Allen returned to campus in a daze: his attempt at psychoanalysis with Burroughs had revealed a deep pit of loneliness and lack of love; he was frustrated and confused sexually; he had no idea what he wanted to do after graduation; and he had not yet resolved his relationship with Naomi. Part of him wanted to be like Trilling, but when he was with Trilling, it was Burroughs's ideas that they argued about, particularly when Allen tried to argue the subtle effects of marijuana.

Bill's life had taken a new direction. While in St Louis, he had run into his old friend Kells Elvins, and he went into business with him as a citrus farmer in the Rio Grande Valley of East Texas. With Bill away, Joan had a light affair with a petty crook named Whitey but when Bill heard she was in Bellevue he flew to New York and took her back to Pharr, Texas, with him, accompanied by three-year-old Julie.

Lucien was released from jail that fall, having served just over two years. He returned to New York and his old friends, and one evening he asked Allen about his sex life. Allen told him he was 'queer'. Lucien was surprised: 'So *that's* the set up!' Suddenly Allen's attitude towards him during 1943–44 made sense. 'I had no idea that Allen was into homosexuality when I left New York,' Carr said. 'I thought he was just a shy little boy. I don't think anybody, myself, Kerouac, was aware of it anymore than just hero worship.' When he found out he was saddened. 'I remember thinking at the time that this is not the way to go, this is a lonely, sorry life, Allen, pull yourself together man.' At the time, Allen wrote, 'The conversation was sort of a memorial landmark, after all these years, but I can't feel very historic about it.' He thought Lucien's understanding of homosexuality was 'technically naïve'.

Jack had invited Hal Chase and other friends for Thanksgiving at his parents' home, but would not invite Allen because his mother disapproved of their friendship. Allen, understandably upset, thought that Jack should stand up to his mother. Kerouac was spending most of his time in Ozone Park, working on *The*

Town and the City. Huncke was still in the Bronx jail, and Allen felt lonely. His journal entry for 25 November read: 'Things going ill; poetry stopped, reading desultory, neurasthenic sleeping, lone-liness, splenetic moods, boredom, fear, vanity.' He overcame his self-pity by pursuing a relentless social life. He ran frantically from one apartment to another, from bar to bar, assignation to assignation, sleeping only when overcome by exhaustion. He was kept going, in large part, by pentaphon, an opium derivative, which gave him feelings of elation and confidence.

One evening, he and a friend, Walter Adams, went to see *Blithe Spirit* and afterwards shot some pentaphon. Allen fumbled his vein shot and got blood everywhere. 'I then set out to hypnotise him, and did poorly to be sure,' recorded Ginsberg. At the end of that session Allen took two goofballs (Nembutals) to put himself to sleep and slept for fourteen hours. At 2 a.m. he prepared to face the night with the aid of a strip of Benzedrine washed down with whisky, four vitamin B tablets, and some of Jerry Rauch's fish oil capsules. He noted, 'Much pleased with the benny, real zest in me now!'

The first time Allen got really high on marijuana was with Walter Adams. They were in Adams's car and got lost on Allen's block. Eventually they parked the car, then went to a corner coffee shop. Allen ordered a huge black-and-white ice cream sundae. 'Then halfway through I realised the whole place was swaying back and forth, and the lights were dazzling. The sky was infinitely extensive and spacious, the plate glass windows of the restaurant showed people walking back and forth with their dogs, smiling and chattering or weeping. And it was a grand moment of synchronicity; everything was joyful and gay, and it was the first and only ice cream sundae I've enjoyed in my life; everything else has been anticlimax.'

One of the people on Allen's rounds was Vickie Russell, who had returned to New York and taken a tiny penthouse on West 89th Street. When Huncke got out of jail in December 1946, he went to stay with her there. 'Met Vickie again,' Allen noted in his journal. 'She's unattached and as attractive as any woman I know. Too bad I'm not ripe for one such as her.'

Naomi stopped working for Dr Luria and became a salad girl at a Horn & Hardart Automat, where she worked for about a year.

Her mental health began to deteriorate and she picked irrational arguments with Eugene. She walked around the apartment naked, her silhouette visible to the neighbours. Her nudity disturbed Eugene, and her arguments disrupted his studies, so finally he moved out.

Allen was also distressed by her nudity, and there was one incident, described in 'Kaddish', which he often cited as reinforcing his homosexuality. He had gone to visit her in her room:

> One time I thought she was trying to make me come lay her – flirting to herself at sink – lay back on huge bed that filled most of the room, dress up round her hips, big slash of hair, scars of operations, pancreas, belly wounds, abortions, appendix, stitching of incisions pulling down in the fat like hideous thick zippers – ragged long lips between her legs – What, even, smell of asshole? I was cold – later revolted a little, not much – seemed perhaps a good idea to try – know the Monster of the Beginning Womb – Perhaps – that way. Would she care?

Shortly after this, Naomi saw Hitler's moustache in the sink, and became convinced that Dr Luria was in on Buba's plot to poison her. Her sister Eleanor, in the Bronx, took her in.

There was a new arrival in the city in the fall of 1946: a twenty-year-old friend of Hal Chase's from Denver. Neal Cassady came to New York with his seventeen-year-old wife, LuAnne. He and Allen met briefly at the West End, but it wasn't until 10 January 1947 that they met again. Allen was visiting Vickie Russell when Jack Kerouac arrived with Cassady. Kerouac described their meeting in *On the Road*, Ginsberg as Carlo Marx, Cassady as Dean Moriarty: 'Two keen minds that they are, they took to each other at the drop of a hat. Two piercing eyes glanced into two piercing eyes – the holy con-man with the shining mind, and the sorrowful poetic con-man with the dark mind that is Carlo Marx. From that moment on I saw very little of Dean, and I was a little sorry too. Their energies met head-on, I was a lout compared, I couldn't keep up with them.'

Neal was neatly dressed, muscular and athletic with a broken Roman nose and a wide, clear-eyed Western smile. He looked a lot like Kerouac. He could, according to Kerouac, run one hundred yards in ten seconds, pass a football seventy yards, do fifty chin-ups in a row, broad jump twenty-three feet and masturbate six times a day.

Cassady had grown up in the long-lost world of pool halls and lunch carts, back alleys and freight yards echoing with the sound of steam locomotives. He was his mother's sixth child and his father's first and was born in Salt Lake City, in 1926, while his parents were driving from Des Moines to start a new life in Hollywood. His father, Neal Cassady Senior, opened a barber shop at Hollywood and Vine but the shop failed because of his drinking problem and they moved to Denver, Colorado, when young Neal was two.

He was six years old when his parents split up, and he went with his father to live in a series of flophouse hotels in Denver, finishing up in the Metropolitan, where they shared a room with a legless beggar known as Shorty. Neal and his father slept together on a dirty bed with no sheets, and in the morning the six-year-old would get himself off to school while his father slept off the previous drunken night. Neal quickly became street-wise. His first appearance in Juvenile Hall occurred when his father was arrested for drunkenness as the two hitchhiked to California to pick fruit. Neal was seven. He stole his first car when he was fourteen and by the time he was twenty-one he estimated that he had stolen over five hundred. He always took them for fun, never to sell or break up for parts, though sometimes he would change their appearance and keep them for a few weeks. He was arrested numerous times for auto theft and had done six stretches in the reformatory.

Neal's tremendous energy and enthusiasm, in addition to his physical beauty, attracted both Allen and Jack to him. He was another sensitive football player. For Allen, it was like meeting another Kerouac. His conversations with Neal, in fact, were much like his early talks with Jack, exchanging the secrets and the fantasies of their youth: 'What our actual fantasies had been as children, and later on, up to the present ... We were really interested in what was going on inside, without regard to whether it was practical or real, but more interested in the charm and the absurdity that everybody was having such an amazingly naive secret life.'

Neal was staying with the cousin of Jack's friend, Alan Temko, in Harlem. Allen and Jack walked him home, but by then it was too late for Kerouac to get back to Ozone Park or for Allen to walk back to 92nd Street so it was suggested that they should spend the night and all have breakfast together in the morning. The problem was, there were only two beds. Jack slept in the double bed with their host, Temko's cousin, and Allen and Neal took the cot. Allen lay with his back to Neal, balancing on the edge of the narrow bed, careful to keep his distance. But Neal stretched out his arm and pulled Allen to him, murmuring, 'Draw near me.' Allen lay trembling. They tentatively caressed each other and pulled off their shorts. A detailed description of what happened appeared in Ginsberg's poem 'Many Loves':

> I lay with my hair intermixed with his, he asking me 'What shall we do now?'
> – And confessed, years later, he thinking I was not a queer at first, to please me & serve me, to blow me and make me come, maybe or if I were queer, that's what I'd likely want of a dumb bastard like him.
> But I made my first mistake, and made him then and there my master, and bowed my head, and holding his buttock
> Took up his hard-on and held it, feeling it throb and pressing my own at his knee & breathing showed him I needed him, cock, for my dreams of insatiety & lone love.

Neal had been working at the New Yorker Hotel on 34th Street, spending two nights a week studying writing with Jack out at Ozone Park, and the rest of his time in bed with LuAnne in Bayonne, New Jersey, where they had found a cheap room. When Allen came on the scene, Neal reorganised his schedule to spend two nights with Allen at 92nd Street as well. Though LuAnne didn't know they were sleeping together, she recognised that she was getting a raw deal and returned to Denver within a week.

The new relationship with Neal had a profound effect on Allen. After their night together in Harlem, they spent the next two nights, 'staring into each other's eyes, finding out whether or not we bugged each other and what the limits were', as Ginsberg puts it. Their love affair developed rapidly and two weeks later Allen described in his journal what had happened to him after two whirlwind days with Neal. The entry for 21 January 1947 reads, 'Having spent a wild weekend in sexual drama with Cassady, I am left washed up on the shore of my "despair" again. It is after such like pleasure that I get full knowledge of what I have closed myself off from . . .'

Allen was aware of the potential problems of his growing entanglement with Neal but felt that Neal was 'carefully considerate of all emotional angles and will do no wrong. I trust him.' One reason he was not prepared to examine the advisability of getting involved with a married man was the possibility of good sex. Allen had had little sexual experience, all of it homosexual, most of it unsatisfactory, and was finally having a good time with Neal. He approached the matter of sex with Neal with his characteristic thoroughness and made a list:

> February 23rd, I will try to think on those sexual positions with Cassady which would please me. Try his laying me again. Try breast to breast position. Try 69 again, coming both at once. Try sitting on his chest and making him blow me. Try laying his mouth, French kissing, etc . . . Make him give me a trip around the world. Try (this requires real passion) browning him. Also a good massage. Laying his anus. Laying him backward thighs – kneeling and blowing, both ways. Wrestling – Whipping? Have I guts? Trip around the world, complete, winding up with blow job. No. I want some real hip sex. What is it?

According to Ginsberg, Neal regarded sex as 'a sort of joyful yoga, and transformed it into a spiritual social thing as well as a matter of esthetic prowess . . . an ultimate exchange of soul', a view which is in sharp contrast to that of many of Neal's women who described him as a sexual sadist.

Writing in his journal in September 1989, Allen looked back fondly at those early days with Neal: 'I remember late at night on 92nd Street and Amsterdam, 1946. Neal Cassady came and stayed over, we played music on tiny radio in the tiny furnished room I lived in . . . Neal had come to visit, it was maybe 2 a.m., we were naked, making love, I was going down on him, he lay on the bed, arms folded behind his head, naked and small lamp beside bed, bebop or rhythm & blues a little too loud on radio. The old man husband of the house, an Irish alcoholic knocked and suddenly opened the door, looked in, saw the scene, said, "Your radio's too loud" and vanished, startled, closing the door. Nor did I hear a complaint the next day – discovered in the malefic act – bare naked, sucking Neal's naked cock – and yet the haggard Catholic heterosexual said nothing.'

Allen's talks with Neal reached great depths of insight, yet, frank as they were, they never seemed so convincing afterwards and Allen began to feel that he had learned all he could from Neal. 'I think he *does* no longer excite me, I've almost used him up in a way,' he wrote on 2 March. He felt that he had 'loved him as much as I can, to no end, except final loss of real feeling and love, and want no more of him.'

Neal was due to return to Denver on 4 March 1947. Jack had been irritated by Allen's abduction of his new friend, but they had a long, sober talk the night before Neal left and achieved a rapprochement. Together they saw Neal off on the bus to Denver. Neal was wearing a new thrift-shop three-piece suit and carrying a stolen portable typewriter, determined to make use of Kerouac's lessons on how to write. Allen said goodbye with no tears and then walked home. He felt empty but was comforted by the arrangement he had made to spend the summer with Neal in Denver when the Columbia term ended.

He initially worried about paying for the trip, since he was still trying to live on the fifteen-dollar weekly allowance his father gave him, but shortly afterwards Allen won the first prize of $110 for his long poem 'Death In Violence' in the bi-annual George Edward Woodberry contest at Columbia, a welcome surprise. Later in the year, he was to win second prize in the Columbia Philolexion Society contest with his poem 'A Lover's Garden', which was published in the August 1947 issue of the *Columbia Review*. This good news appeared in the Newark press and was dutifully clipped by all the relatives to show their neighbours. Allen's slight ambivalence toward Neal was dispelled by a series of breathless letters from Cassady, saying, 'I need you now more than ever . . . every day I miss you more and more . . .' and 'Let us then find true awareness by realising that each of us is depending on the other for fulfillment.' Allen began to look forward to the summer.

Allen's plan to visit Neal underwent numerous modifications, beginning with Neal's confession that he disliked homosexual sex, and continuing with his suggestion that he and Allen should live with a girl. Neal wrote, 'I really don't know how much I can be satisfied to love you, I mean bodily, you know I, somehow, dislike pricks & men & before you, had consciously forced myself to be homosexual, now, I'm not sure whether with you I was not just forcing myself unconsciously, that is to say, and falsity on my part was all physical, in fact, any disturbance in our affair was because of this. You meant so much to me, I now feel I was forcing a desire for you bodily as a compensation to you for all you were giving me.'

Allen did not want to hear this at all, and from the force of Allen's replies, Neal obviously thought that his insistence that their relationship be entirely platonic would severely damage it, so he put off the day of reckoning with hints and suggestions that something might be worked out. Ginsberg ignored Neal's disinclination to homosexual sex and clearly thought that he would be able to talk him back into bed.

In July, Allen gave up his room on 92nd Street and took the exhausting two-thousand-mile Greyhound trip to Denver. Neal met him at the terminal and took him to the Colburn Hotel on Grant Street, where he had reserved a two-dollar room for him. Neal was living there with Carolyn Robinson, a Bennington graduate who was studying fine arts at the University of Denver. Carolyn had white-golden hair wound in braids around her head and wore a blue dress. She was obviously in love with Neal and Allen immediately sensed trouble.

Allen's money soon ran out, and Bill Burroughs sent him ten dollars to tide him over until he got a job. He was forced to move into Carolyn and Neal's room in the hotel. Sleeping there was a nightmare for him, because he could of course hear them making love and all their whispered endearments. A terse note in his journal reads, 'Colburn Hotel Apt. Such terrible nights.' It was not long before relations between Allen and Carolyn became strained. Unaware of Allen's sexual relationship with Neal, she had not considered that the cause of the tension might be intense jealousy, but she knew something was wrong.

On one occasion, Allen got her to do a drawing of Neal posing in the nude. The idea was presented as an objective, artistic exercise, but Carolyn was embarrassed as Neal posed like a Greek statue while Allen sat watching from the window. Allen tried his best not to antagonise her and was sometimes able to be helpful. When she had to give an oral report, Allen coached her and edited her notes.

Her talk was met with a stunned silence, as Carolyn stood terrified before her art professors. Then they all rushed to congratulate her on the best performance the department had ever known.

Neal was driving a shuttle bus for the May Company department store, and Allen got a night job there, pushing a vacuum cleaner across the block-square second-floor sales area for twenty dollars a week. He moved to a damp three-room basement, sublet from friends of Neal. It was in a red-brick rooming house on Grant Street not far from the Colburn Hotel. The walls oozed water and he had a small bed, a chair and a candle. The small altar he built completed the impression of a monk's cell. Pigeons nested outside his window, and he awoke each day to their flapping and cooing.

Neal worked out a complicated schedule for himself that involved seeing his three great loves, Carolyn, LuAnne and Allen, and a few other girls on the side. He and LuAnne had decided to get a divorce but, unknown to Carolyn, were still sleeping together. He would leave LuAnne's bed at 1 a.m. and go over to the Colburn. From there he went to see Allen, who had returned home from his night shift, and they would talk until 6 a.m.

The conversation was intense, a serious attempt, occasionally fuelled by Benzedrine, to understand each other fully by analysing every word and gesture. Sexually their relationship was not going well, as Neal had warned. The more Allen pressed him, claiming that this 'sacramental' side to their relationship was of vital importance in understanding each other, the more Neal withdrew. Neal was in the early days of his affair with Carolyn, and it was a fresh, exciting sexual relationship. He became more and more reluctant to leave her bed in order to spend the night fending off Allen's advances. He began to miss his meetings with Allen for days in a row, while Allen spent anxious nights waiting, unable to concentrate on anything but Neal's treachery. Some nights, he wept steadily for hours. He filled page after page of his big red journal with self-pitying prose about Neal and his own attempts to reach a 'state of peace'. Allen's only reason for being in Denver was to be with Neal. Allen had become obsessed with him and his rejection hurt deeply.

The entry for 28 July revealed the depths of his despair. 'My anxiety about the situation reached a peak of dragged hysteria at eight o'clock this evening. All last evening at work and this evening even more so, I have been developing, quite out of my control, hallucinations about the telephone. The vacuum cleaner has a high singing pitch and I began last night, awaiting Neal's call, to confuse it with the dull ringing of the telephone. It reached such a point tonight, combined with an emotional exhaustion and an intellectual despair, that I was completely paralysed for minutes on end, stopping work turning off the motor, listening, half-hearing the phone. I had a vivid auditory sensation several times, that in the confusion, it really was the phone, and dropped my work, and ran over to the phone, and found it dead and silent. At one point I could not continue work and collapsed in a chair.'

But, unhappy as he was, Allen was not rendered totally immobile by the situation. On hearing of the birth of Bill and Joan's baby on 21 July, he set out to write a birthday ode. It took him six days, working late at night on Benzedrine. Like much of his work in this period, it was an epic in many sections, written in highly artificial rhymed verse. The section on be-bop began: 'The saxophone thy mind had guessed/ He knows the Devil hides in thee;/ Fly hence, I warn thee, Stranger, lest/ The saxophone shall injure thee.'

He also wrote an entire sequence of poems that he called, collectively, 'The Denver Doldrums', but the best thing to come out of his Denver sojourn was a prose sketch, written on 23 August, his last day in Denver. Using Kerouac's 'sketching' style, he described a bricklayer across the street. William Carlos Williams later suggested the poetic possibilities of his journal prose, and Allen altered the punctuation, creating 'The Bricklayer's Lunch Hour', one of his most successful early poems.

After a lot of intense talking, Allen persuaded Neal to accompany him to Texas to visit Bill and Joan. Neal finally told Carolyn about the plan and explained that he felt an obligation to try to be homosexual for Allen. She understood but said, 'If that's the way it is, I don't want you. It's as simple as that. If you want Allen or something else, then go for it.' Neal had little idea what he really wanted, and even Allen realised that his hero was not as organised as he had originally thought. He noted, 'Neal strikes me sometimes as being even more simpleminded and confused than myself, except that may be the goofballs.'

Carolyn made arrangements to go to California the next day to stay with friends, and took her things to the house of a teacher friend, where she spent the night, leaving Neal the Colburn room.

The next morning, she returned to say a final goodbye to Neal. She opened the door and found him in bed, with Allen on one side and LuAnne on the other. She rushed out.

Neal was trying an impossible balancing act. Carolyn wanted him in San Francisco, LuAnne wanted him to stay in Denver and Allen wanted to go with him to Texas. Neal had heard a lot about Bill and Joan from both Jack and Allen, and wanted to meet them. He and Allen had always planned to go to Texas together after the summer so in this instance, Allen won.

Bill had left Elvins in charge of the citrus plantation and taken a farm outside New Waverly, fifty miles north of Houston, where he planted marijuana as a cash crop. The fields were set among oak and persimmon, several miles from the nearest road. The land sloped away from the cabin to a bayou filled with Spanish moss, thick tropical vines and vegetation.

The farmstead consisted of a few sheds, a collapsing barn and a weathered silver-grey cabin which had two enormous rooms, now divided into four. Bill constructed a stand to hold a seven-hundred-gallon tank, which collected rainwater from the corrugated iron roof. He had ninety-seven acres, but the land was not suitable for anything other than subsistence farming or growing pot. He tried planting opium poppies, but it didn't work out.

Bill enjoyed his role as the country squire. He cut wood, fenced in the property, and walked around with his guns, followed by a small hound dog. The sound of gunfire echoing through the forest was so common that local people asked if gangsters lived down there. Bill invited Huncke to come and join them, which he did, and for seven months Joan and Julie, Bill and Huncke lived happily together.

Bill was still addicted to morphine and Joan, despite being pregnant when they arrived, had doubled her Benzedrine habit to more than two inhalers a day. They soon cleaned out all the nearby towns of inhalers and had to make periodic runs to Houston, where Huncke made a contact who would sell them a gross every few weeks. He was also able to score there for pot and paregoric, which contained opium, so the farm was well stocked. They also cleaned all the local towns out of rum, tequila and gin and had to drive twenty-five miles to the big liquor store in Conroe to stock up.

Conroe was where William Burroughs, Jr. was born. They had made no arrangements. At 3 a.m., Joan knocked on Bill's door and said it was time to go to the hospital. They climbed into the Jeep and drove off into the night. The next day she was back with her baby.

At 10.30 each morning, Bill would emerge from his room, wearing a suit and tie, ready to go and get the mail and local papers, which he would then sit on the porch and read. Joan looked after Julie and little Billie and cleaned the cabin, but she spent much of her time obsessively sweeping lizards off the tree in the yard. The moment she turned away, they would climb back. Huncke's job was to fetch firewood for the outdoor grill and cook the steaks. He also wound up the record player on the porch and changed the needle from time to time, to play Billie Holiday records and the Viennese waltzes that Bill loved.

As Allen hitch-hiked toward Texas with Neal, the Rockies became a huge stage drop to the drama going on between them. It was a long, slow journey from Denver to Houston across the flat, unrelieved plains of Oklahoma and Texas, and they didn't get many rides. At one point in Oklahoma they found themselves at a crossroads at dusk with no traffic in sight. They were in the middle of a deep conversation, and at Allen's instigation, they knelt in the road and made a solemn vow to own and accept each other's bodies and souls, and to help each other into heaven. 'To accomplish a transfer of heart, and vow to stick with each other and be spiritual lovers, if not physical,' Ginsberg explained. 'He was going to teach me body and practical things, and I was going to teach him everything I knew intellectually and spiritually. Not that I knew anything.'

It is a story told often in Ginsberg's writing. There is an account, written shortly after the event, in an unpublished short story called *The Monster of Dakar*, which captured the feeling of what happened: 'He loved me, a big hustler, we kneeled together on the road in Oklahoma, in the middle of a four way cross of dirt roads, on an endless plane, at night fall. I hadn't imagined such a place or such an eternal vow: fidelity, union, seraphic insight, sights of America, everything I could imagine. He accepted it all, just a poor lost soul, an orphan in fact, looking for a father seraph and I was looking for a seraphic boy.'

It occured again, in poetry, in 'The Green Automobile':

The windshield's full of tears
rain wets our naked breasts
we kneel together in the shade
amid the traffic of night in paradise.

Ginsberg later remembered it as a poignant moment, 'although, by hindsight, I realise he was obviously just being nice to me, humouring me.'

They arrived in New Waverly on 30 August 1947. Allen wrote, 'When we got here, I expecting this happy holiday of God-given sexuality, where was the royal couch?' Huncke was still trying to build it. Huncke thought that Allen and Neal might like to have his room, since he slept out on the screened porch. Huncke's bed would not hold two people but there were some unused army cots and boards around. 'I conceived of getting these sideboards together in some kind of bed situation,' explained Huncke. 'The only place to work was dead in front of the cabin, everybody could see me working with that fucking bed . . . I did work on it because I figured I had a practical idea. Unfortunately while I was working on it, they arrived.'

Neal refused to help, so Allen and Huncke struggled with the beds. Huncke had taken one of the headboards off and they eventually got the other one off, so at least the bed was level on the ground. The bed sagged in the middle and was very uncomfortable, as well as dangerous since scorpions could reach it. 'I was absolutely outraged with Burroughs for not having the sense to get a decent bed or make provision,' Ginsberg remembered. 'We didn't make out much, and that was the whole point of it. We were gonna go down there and I was finally gonna get satisfied for the first time.' The tragic saga of the bed entered Beat legend as told by Cassady in Kerouac's *Visions of Cody* and by Huncke in *The Evening Sun Turned Crimson*.

Otherwise it was a pleasant visit. Neal busied himself putting up fenceposts. It was quiet, and there was plenty of time for long talks with Bill, Joan and Huncke. Ginsberg's strongest memory is of sitting on the porch in the evenings, talking by the light of the kerosene lamps, while little Julie ran around barefoot and Coleman Hawkins' 'Low Flame' played on the Victrola.

Two days after they arrived, Allen finally accepted the fact that Neal was not interested in men. He wrote, 'The sacramental honeymoon is over. I have a drag against turning my mind to a practical, non-romantic set of arrangements a propos Cassady. Since it has at last penetrated my mind and become obvious to me that, without angling, he means what he says when he says he can't make use of me sexually, it requires turn of mind.'

It wasn't just Allen's physical demands that turned Neal off; it was the emotional ones as well. Neal told Kerouac, 'I got so I couldn't stand Allen to even touch me, you know, see, only touch me. It was terrible. And man, I'd never been that way, you know, but, man, he was all opening up and I was all . . .' Yet despite Neal's constant warning that 'It means nothing', Allen wrote quite seriously in his journal: 'I am wondering what will happen to Neal if I really withdraw my active queer love and leave him alone emotionally.'

Neal insisted they split up; there was no other way. As a consolation, he promised one final night together in Houston. Allen had decided to try and ship out from Houston on a boat to New York, to make some money for the fall semester. Neal was going to stay on and help with the marijuana harvest, then drive Bill back to New York. Allen extracted a promise from Neal that in New York, he and Allen would have another try at living together.

The night at the Brazos Hotel was a disaster. Allen, Huncke and Neal drove into Houston, and Huncke went immediately in search of his drug connections. While Allen went to the NMU Hall to look for a ship, Neal got high on Nembutals. He picked up a girl in the Jeep and drove back to the hotel. Just as he approached it, the barbituates hit him. He managed to steer the car into the no-parking zone in front of the hotel and stop it by hitting the curb. The girl, who had just been released from a mental institution, dragged him up the stairs to his room. 'And she went to bed with me and I tried to screw her and everything and I managed to finally even though I was high . . .' but then Allen came back and was furious. The evening was destroyed. Allen felt betrayed, his fantasy once again shattered. And Neal was too high to do anything, even if he had wanted to.

Luckily Allen had found himself a ship, a collier going to Africa. The trip was twenty days out, ten in port at Dakar and twenty days coming back. It meant that he would miss the start of the Columbia term, but nonetheless he took it. He wrote to Louis to reassure him that he really did intend to return to school, but not until January 1948, and that the money from the voyage would help him get psychoanalysed. 'I can't think really of going back to school and spending money on it till I have the psychoanalysis which I need much more.'

The trip to Africa was uneventful. Dakar, once a major departure point for Africans being taken into slavery to America, was the colonial headquarters of French West Africa and had the atmosphere of a French provincial town. A boy whom Allen employed to help him on board ship showed him the bamboo shacks in the poor part of town, so he got some sense of Africa on his shore leave. He also smoked a lot of African marijuana. The best thing to come out of the experience was a short story called *The Monster of Dakar*, an account of life aboard ship and the author's unsuccessful efforts to find a boy in port.

Neal finished the harvest and then drove Bill and the marijuana back to New York. Bill immediately set about selling it then drove the Jeep on to St Louis to see his parents. Neal had nowhere to stay. He hung around the city for a week, hoping to hear from Allen, then left for California. Allen arrived a few days later, expecting a rendezvous, but all he found was a brief note saying that Neal had gone to marry Carolyn. Allen, stunned, wrote sadly to Neal, 'I suppose I must say goodbye then. I don't know how.'

Allen ran around New York, visiting his old friends, but his real desire was to be alone. He rented a small furnished room on West 27th Street and sat there, taking Benzedrine and writing rhyming couplets. One early morning at four-thirty, after writing a poem called 'The Creation of the World', he finally wrote a long sad letter to Neal, letting out his true feelings. 'I have protected myself, armoured, since I arrived, from grief or too much self pity and as a result I saw my mind turn more than ever . . . into isolation and phoney goodness.' He confessed to Neal, what Neal must have known all along, that his primary interest in him was sexual. 'I must admit that I have known more or less consciously that all the "purity" of my love, its "generosity" and "honour" was, though on its own level true, not at all my deeper intention toward you, which was and is simply a direct lover's.'

In cramped, pinched, unhappy handwriting, he begged Neal to come back to him, 'I am lonely, Neal, alone, and always I am frightened. I need someone to love and kiss me and sleep with me

. . . I have been miserable without you because I had depended on you to take care of me for love of me, and now that you have altogether rejected me, what can I do, what can I do?' He continued in the same vein, growing more maudlin and self-pitying with each page. Neal did not reply.

Allen's difficulties were compounded by Huncke, who stopped by one day and stole Allen's phonograph and pawned it. He wrote, enclosing a pawnshop ticket and saying, somewhat prophetically, in his curiously formal manner, 'I presume you have spoken of my pilfering to others – although it fails to bother me, it will place you in the role of being the proverbial sucker if you forgive me and continue allowing me parasitical advantages from my contact with you.'

Allen was also concerned about his mother. After she had moved in with her sister, her state of mind had improved a bit and she even enrolled in the painting class at the Bronx Adult High School. There she painted Russian brides, saints with lugubrious faces and the elevated trains running over the rooftops of the Bronx. There is a portrait of Allen from this period, naïve but expressive. But then her symptoms began to return, stronger than ever. She got up at 6 a.m. to listen on the radio for spies. She thought she saw Buba on the fire escape with a bag of poison germs. She got angry and kicked Eleanor, who was already weak from a rheumatic heart. After that it was obvious that she could no longer stay. Her cousins Max and Edie Frohman, whom she had known since they were all children in Russia, lived in the same building and they agreed to take her in.

Naomi woke Edie at midnight to tell her she was a spy and that Eleanor was a rat. Edie worked all day as a union organiser, and in the end she could no longer take the strain of having Naomi there. She telephoned Allen and he went to see her. In 'Kaddish', Allen wrote that Naomi's symptoms were worse than ever. She sang, she raged at Buba and Louis, complained of spies, Hitler and the three big sticks down her back. Exasperated, Allen pushed her against the door and yelled, 'Don't kick Eleanor!'

Naomi stared at him with contempt. 'Eleanor is the worst spy!' she said, 'She's taking orders!'

'No wires in the room!' yelled Allen, 'You've been away from Louis for years already. Grandma's too old to walk!' But it was impossible. She had lost all contact with reality. While she raved at him about Eleanor being a spy, Allen called the police. The knock at the door when they arrived scared her and she ran to the bathroom to hide from the spies.

She was sent to Pilgrim State, an enormous mental hospital in Islip, Long Island. Allen, Eugene and Louis all received pathetic, heart-rending letters from her, asking to be released. 'How I want you to know that I want to get out and cook for you and laugh and sing the rest of my life,' she wrote Allen. But added, 'They found kerosene in my system in this hospital. These things make me delirious.' She got worse and on 14 November 1947, Allen received a letter from the senior director of the hospital, telling him that in the opinion of the doctors, Naomi's medical condition was serious enough to warrant a prefrontal lobotomy. She was hitting her head against the wall with such fury, working herself into paroxysms of fear, that the doctors felt she was likely to have a stroke unless she was stopped. Louis had divorced Naomi when she was living with Dr Luria so it fell to her sons to assume legal responsibility for her. Allen signed the forms.

Allen began to think that he was going crazy himself. He wrote Kerouac: 'If you want to know my true nature, I am at the moment one of those people who goes around showing his cock to juvenile delinquents.' This was the winter when Allen became 'more actively queer', trying to drown out the memory of Neal by haunting the gay bars in Greenwich Village and Times Square and on 72nd Street. It was while he was living at West 27th Street that he was sometimes able to persuade Kerouac to have sex: 'I remember one particular time, he was high on Benzedrine and so extremely horny, as you get with Benzedrine, but at the same time he couldn't come for a long long while. One time there, he blew me.'

Ginsberg returned to Columbia and spent the winter of 1947–48 in a frenzy of activity, working at a part time job, staying out late drinking and carousing, sometimes staying up all night on Benzedrine or morphine, writing poetry and playing records. He was aware that he was avoiding coming to terms with the facts about his situation but was hoping that a course of psychoanalysis would overcome his indecision. It had seemed to Allen that Reichian analysis would be the most suitable for his case, so he wrote to Wilhelm Reich, asking for his recommendation of a suitable doctor: 'My main psychic difficulty, as far as I know, is the usual oedipal entanglement. I have been a homosexual for as long as I can remember, and have had a limited number of homosexual affairs, both temporary and protracted. They have been unsatisfactory to me, and I have always approached love affairs with a sort of self-contradictory, conscious masochism ... I have had long periods of depression, guilt feelings – disguised mostly as a sort of Kafkian sordidness of sense of self – melancholy, and the whole gamut I suppose.'

He described his amateur analysis with Burroughs, 'The inevitable and unfortunate effect was that it left me washed up on the shores of my neurosis with a number of my defences broken, but, centrally unchanged, with nothing to replace the lost armour.' Reich's assistant replied with a list of three doctors recommended by Reich. Allen chose Doctor Allan Cott, who was based in Newark. Allen could combine the visits with seeing his father. He began the twice weekly sessions as soon as he returned from his trip to Dakar.

It was impossible to discuss his analysis realistically with Louis without revealing that he was homosexual so, after careful consideration, he told him. The occasion is described in Ginsberg's poem, 'Don't Grow Old':

A look startled his face, 'You mean you like to take men's penises in your mouth?'
Equally startled, 'No, no,' I lied, 'that isn't what it means.'

'I got very embarrassed,' Ginsberg said later, 'and said, 'It means I can't be sexually aroused by women.' I put it into the traditional Jewish family terminology. I have the sense that he was reluctant to acknowledge that I was seriously disturbed and needed something as sophisticated as psychotherapy, because that put me more into the category of my mother – it meant trouble!'

The Reichian 'vegetotherapeutic' system identifies repressed energies with 'frozen' muscles and releases this blocked energy through body massage, including massage around the eyes and jaws. 'It was really remarkable,' Ginsberg said, 'I felt this strange buzzing from disturbing the mouth area.' As an orthodox Reichian, Cott would have had as his goal restoring Allen to his proper heterosexual genital potency, something that Burroughs, among others, was deeply critical of. 'Frankly I don't trust that kind of genital Reichian ... Feller say, when a man gets too straight he's just a god damned prick,' Burroughs wrote. But Cott clearly released some deep-seated unconscious material, because in 1960, writing about his experiences with the mind-altering drug ayahuasca, Ginsberg said: 'A few times in psychoanalysis – with the Reichian Cott – got to same depth of *significance* which was hard to bear, and drove me off.'

Cott objected strenuously to Allen's smoking marijuana; he thought it might lead to a psychotic episode. He gave him an ultimatum, but Allen continued to smoke. Cott was true to his word, and after some three months he terminated Allen's therapy.

Allen was not smoking marijuana for kicks. 'Our original use was for aesthetic study, aesthetic perception, deepening it. I was somewhat disappointed later on, when the counterculture developed the use of grass for party purposes rather than for study purposes. I always thought that was the wrong direction.' Though it seems unlikely that Allen's use of pot was always so high-minded, he was certainly employing it to heighten his perception of art. He was writing a paper on Cézanne for Professor Meyer Schapiro at Columbia, and would smoke a joint, then go to the basement of the Museum of Modern Art and look at Cézanne's watercolours. He became interested in the way that the artist juxtaposed two colours, so that the eye gave a little jolt passing from one colour to the next. 'I got a strange shuddering impression looking at his canvases, partly the effect when someone pulls a Venetian blind, reverses the Venetian – there's a sudden shift, a flashing that you see in Cézanne canvases.'

Ginsberg later characterised this shift as 'eyeball kicks', and the last part of 'Howl I' contains a specific homage to Cézanne's method, which so influenced his own work: 'Who dreamt and made incarnate gaps in Time & Space through images juxtaposed . . . jumping with sensation of Pater Omnipotens Aeterne Deus.' (The Latin quotes a letter from Paul Cézanne to Émile Bernard.) A major element of Ginsberg's compositional technique was to be an attempt to find the equivalent in words of Cézanne's gaps, a choice of words that would create a gap between them, 'which the mind would fill with the sensation of existence'. Ginsberg's favourite example is a phrase from 'Howl': 'Hydrogen jukebox'.

By February 1948, Allen was living in a small room at 536 West 114th Street, facing the Columbia campus. That Spring, with Mark Van Doren's encouragement, he assembled a book of poems called

The Denver Doldrums. He was still deeply depressed by the failure of his affair with Neal and was sleeping longer hours to avoid confronting his problems. A letter from Neal announced his marriage to Carolyn on 1 April. Disgusted, Allen wrote, 'Now, I suppose I should congratulate you on your marriage. So O.K. Pops, everything you do is great. The idea of you with a child and a settled centre of affection – shit.'

Neal replied angrily, telling Allen that he was 'way, way, way off base'. He opened by saying, 'You and I are now farther apart than ever. Only with effort can I recall you.' He was going through a psychotic period himself and felt nothing for anyone, including his wife and child. He said he was only interested in one thing, and that was women, primarily whores. He concluded, 'Let's stop corresponding – I'm not the N.C. you knew. I'm not N.C. anymore. I more closely resemble Baudelaire.'

The weather improved, and Kerouac began to come into the city more frequently. He finished *The Town and the City* and gave Allen the manuscript to read. Allen was bowled over. 'It is very great,' he wrote Neal. He perceived in Jack's book that 'all the turmoil and frenzy of the last years had somehow been justified – because I saw expressed in his novel a peace and knowledge and solidarity and, say, a whole creation, a true and eternal world – my world – finally given a permanent form. So I also felt my own failure as an artist to conclude a large, and, if not mature, at least complete and internally perfect work.'

With Neal gone, Allen's gaze returned to Jack. Allen invited him out to his father's house in Paterson for a Passover Seder, but as they parted afterward at the 125th Street subway turnstile, Allen, frustrated by his intense desire, lost his composure and demanded that Jack hit him. Jack thought he had gone mad. Ginsberg later commented, 'I wanted attention from him, *any* kind of attention!' Allen was losing control.

College ended in May, and Allen sublet an apartment from a friend, Russell Durgin, a theology student who was recuperating from tuberculosis. Allen owed Trilling a term paper, he had a gym requirement which he had neglected, and he also lacked credits in math and science, which were giving him a lot of trouble, particularly organic chemistry, since he found it almost impossible to memorise chemical formulas in his fragmented state of mind.

The apartment was at 321 East 121st Street, in East Harlem. It was light and airy, with views out over the rooftops, and far enough away from Columbia and the West End Bar scene to allow Allen to concentrate on his work. He went to a class in the morning and worked part-time as a file clerk. He idled around the house reading Durgin's books, which were kept neatly stacked in orange crates. These, and their owner, were later enshrined in 'Howl': 'Who coughed on the sixth floor of Harlem crowned with flame under a tubercular sky surrounded by orange crates of theology.' Allen dipped into Marvell, Saint Teresa of Avila, Plotinus, Martin Luther and others. He was also reading a lot of William Blake and Saint John of the Cross, and was in a distinctly mystical mood.

The apartment was too out of the way for anyone to drop in, and Allen had no telephone. Meetings had to be arranged by letter or by calling him at work. He took long exploratory walks in Harlem and wondered what to do with his life.

The summer heat was on. Allen lay on his bed by the open window, reading William Blake. The book was open to the poem 'Ah! Sun-flower', from *Songs of Innocence and Experience*. Allen had his pants open and was absent-mindedly masturbating while he read; he had just come, when he heard a deep, ancient voice, reading the poem aloud. He immediately knew, without thinking, that it was the voice of Blake himself, coming to him across the vault of time. The voice was prophetic, tender; it didn't seem to be coming from his head, in fact it seemed to be in the room, but no one was there. He described it: 'The peculiar quality of the voice was something unforgettable because it was like God had a human voice, with all the infinite tenderness and mortal gravity of a living Creator speaking to his son.'

Ah, Sunflower, weary of time,
    Who countest the steps of the sun,
Seeking after that sweet golden clime
    Where the traveller's journey is done;

Where the youth pined away with desire,
    And the pale virgin shrouded in snow,
Arise from their graves and aspire
    Where my Sunflower wishes to go!

He suddenly had a deep understanding of the meaning of the poem and realised that *he* was the sunflower. Simultaneous with the auditory vision, came a heightened visual perception: the afternoon sunlight through the window took on an extraordinary clarity. The sky was ancient, the gateway to infinity, the same deep blue universe seen by Blake himself, and Allen knew this was the 'sweet golden clime' itself. He was already in it. 'I suddenly realised that this existence was *it*!' he said, 'This was the moment I was born for. This initiation, this consciousness of being alive unto myself. The spirit of the universe was what I was born to realise.'

Silhouetted against the bright living light of the sky he saw the grimy rooftops of Harlem. It was the first time he had looked carefully at the pressed metal cornices with their ornamental consoles and entablatures; he understood what human intelligence had gone into their creation, five decades before, so that they could stand there 'like buttresses in eternity!'

Everywhere he noticed evidence of a living hand, even in the arrangement of bricks, and he was aware that each brick had been placed there by someone, that people had built the entire vast city, placing each stone and manufacturing each cornice and window-frame.

'My body suddenly felt *light* ... it was a sudden awakening into a totally deeper real universe than I'd been existing in.' He looked further, to the clouds; they seemed signals of something vaster and more far-reaching than a workman's hand. He caught an understanding of the billions of years that the sea had been evaporating and forming into clouds, each one unique in shape, and of the vast complexity of nature. 'I was sitting in the middle of an entire planetary solar system ...! I had the impression of the entire universe as poetry filled with light and intelligence and communication and signals. Kind of like the top of my head coming off, letting in the rest of the universe connected to my own brain.'

A few minutes later, the sensations began again, this time with the voice reading Blake's 'The Sick Rose'.

O Rose, thou art sick!
  The invisible worm,
That flies in the night,
  In the howling storm,

Has found out thy bed
  Of crimson joy,
And his dark secret love
  Does thy life destroy.

'I experienced "The Sick Rose", with the voice of Blake reading it, as something that applied to the whole universe, and at the same time the inevitable beauty of doom ... it was very beautiful and very awesome ... as if Blake had penetrated the very secret core of the *entire* universe and had come forth with some little magic formula statement in rhyme and rhythm that, if properly heard in the inner inner ear, would deliver you beyond the universe,' Ginsberg said.

The third and final poem that brought on the sensations was 'The Little Girl Lost', with its hypnotic repeated refrain:

Do father, mother weep?
Where can Lyca sleep?

How can Lyca sleep
if her mother weep?

If her heart does ache,
Then let Lyca wake;
If my mother sleep,
Lyca shall not weep.

'I suddenly realised that Lyca was me, or Lyca was the self,' Ginsberg said. He understood that 'If her heart does ache,/ Then let Lyca wake' was meant to wake up to the same realisation he had just experienced, 'the total consciousness of the complete universe. Which is what Blake was talking about ... a breakthrough from ordinary quotidian consciousness into consciousness that was really seeing all of heaven in a flower.'

He felt he must tell someone about his experience, and in a state of extreme elation, he crawled out on to the fire-escape and tapped on the next door window, 'I've seen God!' Allen cried, startling the two young women inside. They slammed the window shut in his face. He crawled back to his apartment and began experimenting to see if he could reach the deeper levels of meaning in other texts. He found amazing images of horses in Plato's *Phaedrus*, dipped into St John Perse, picked up Plotinus, but found him very difficult to interpret. 'I immediately doubled my thinking process, quadrupled, and I was able to read almost any text and see all sorts of divine significance in it.'

He wondered if he was able to retrieve the sensation at will, without the aid of Blake. He went into his kitchen. 'I started moving around and sort of shaking with my body and dancing up and down on the floor and saying, "Dance! dance! dance! dance! spirit! spirit! spirit! dance!" and suddenly I felt like Faust, calling up the devil. And then it started coming over me, this big . . . creepy feeling, cryptozoid or monozoidal, so I got all scared and quit.'

The sense of supra-consciousness returned to him a few days later in the Columbia University bookstore. He was standing in the poetry section, leafing through a volume of Blake, reading 'The Human Abstract' from *Songs of Experience*. 'I was in the eternal place *once more*, and I looked around at everybody's faces, and I saw all these wild animals!'

The familiar bookstore clerk had a long thin face. Allen had not paid him much attention when he entered the store but now saw that he looked like a giraffe. As Allen studied the man's long nose, 'I suddenly saw like a great tormented soul . . . I realised that *he* knew also, just like I knew. And that everybody in the bookstore knew, and that they were all hiding it! They all had the consciousness, it was like a great *un*conscious that was running between all of us that everybody *was* completely conscious, but that the fixed expressions people have, the habitual expressions, the manners, the mode of talk, are all masks hiding this consciousness. Because almost at that moment it seemed that it would be too terrible if we communicated to each other on a level of total consciousness and awareness each of the other.

'The complete death awareness that everybody has continuously with them all the time, [was] all of a sudden revealed to me at once in the faces of the people, and they all looked like horrible grotesque masks, grotesque because *hiding* the knowledge from each other. Having a habitual conduct and forms to prescribe, forms to fulfill. Roles to play. But the main insight I had at that time was that everybody knew.'

It was an experience, a vision of himself and the world, that affected him deeply, but though many societies have respected and revered those who have visions, in post-war New York City there was no one Allen could talk with. One of the first people he called was Allan Cott, his ex-analyst. 'It happened,' said Allen, 'I had some kind of breakthrough or psychotic experience.'

'I'm afraid any discussion would have no value,' said Cott and hung up.

Allen went out to Paterson to tell his father, but his wild talk about almost being swallowed by 'God' only scared Louis and made him worry even more that Allen had the same fatal flaw that had driven Naomi mad. Louis was a confirmed agnostic and they finished up arguing about God. Everyone around Columbia at that time was reading Santayana, William James's *Varieties of Religious Experience*, Buber, Donne, and books of Christian mysticism, and that was the only terminology that Allen had to discuss his spiritual experience. Many of his friends advised him to see a psychiatrist, others just backed away. 'I got very splenetic, angry and irritable, thinking that other people were resisting acknowledging what they themselves knew,' he said. When Allen ran into the English department saying, 'I just saw the light!' Mark Van Doren was the only professor who was sympathetic and asked him what he meant. Trilling and the others thought that Allen had finally gone over the edge.

Ginsberg was staggered by the experience and said that his immediate thought was: 'Now that I've seen this heaven on earth, I will never forget it. I will never stop considering it the centre of my life, which is now changed into a new world. I'll never be able to go back, and that's great. From now on, I'm chosen, blessed, sacred, poet, and this is my sunflower, my new mind. I'll be faithful the rest of my life, and I'll never deny it and I'll never renounce it.'

As the weeks passed, the vision faded. Allen kept trying to catalyse it by staring at cornices or trees or reading Blake intensely. He looked to Blake for instruction on how to regain his visionary awareness. In the 'Rossetti Manuscript' he found the lines: 'To find the Western Path,/ Right thro' the Gates of Wrath/ I urge my way . . .' 'I thought "the path" was through the Gates of Wrath; Fear and Wrath, and Terror,' Ginsberg said. 'Cultivate the terror, get right into it, right into death. I said, "Die, go mad, drop dead." So I thought for many years that my obligation was to annihilate my ordinary consciousness and expand my mystic consciousness.'

Thus he ultimately began a series of experiments with mind-altering drugs, which would continue for fifteen years. He took every powerful hallucinogen he could find, from laughing gas to mescaline; he sniffed ether and shot heroin. He disappeared into the upper reaches of the Amazon to take ayahuasca with the Indian witch-doctors and smoked hashish all night with naked saddhus in the burning grounds on the banks of the Ganges. He virtually ignored everyday life in his concentrated effort to widen his consciousness. A little over a decade later, he discovered LSD, which did approximate the sensation of eternity but, 'on acid, most of the time, I also got the horror trip, because I was trying so hard to get back to that eternity that I'd seen before; so everytime I got high, when the first doubt came that I might not see "Eternity" . . . or the fear came that I might get eaten alive by "God," then the trip immediately turned into a hell.'

He did not get free from the desire to recreate his visionary experience until 1963, when he was living in India and met Dudjum Rinpoche, the head of the Nyingma, the oldest of the various sects of Tibetan Buddhism, who, after Allen had presented him with his history of visions and drug experiences, advised him to stop clinging to the vision; to give it up. 'If you see anything horrible, don't cling to it,' he told Allen. 'If you see anything beautiful, don't cling to it.' Allen had filled his head with so much thought about the vision that he had cut himself off from direct perception. 'The remarkable thing is that I stupefied myself from 1948 to 1963. A long time. That's fifteen years preoccupied with one single thought.'

Ginsberg never did renounce his Blake vision; even in 1986, he described it as 'The only really genuine experience I feel I've had, something that seemed like a complete absorption of all my senses into something totally authentic as an experience.'

He immediately tried to put the experience into words. There were eight poems in his early collection, *The Gates of Wrath*, that attempted to do this. 'Vision 1948' reads:

I shudder with intelligence and I
   Wake in the deep light
And hear vast machinery
   Decending without sound,
Intolerable to me, too bright,
   And shaken by the sight
The eye goes blind before the world goes round.

Many unpublished manuscripts also recalled the vision: 'I stared into the sun and saw my city as it was: as real as a dream it rose on the horizon'; and over the years, he referred to it several times in his journals, including a 111-line poem about it, called 'One Day', written in 1961:

> That day I heard Blake's voice
> I say I heard Blake's voice . . .

Other references were short and occurred among travel descriptions such as an early draft of 'Siesta in Xbalba' written in 1954 in Usumascinta, Mexico:

> I think in 1948: sitting in my apartment,
>   my eyes opened for an hour
> seeing in dreadful ecstasy
>   the buildings rotting
> Under the wide eternal sky.

Louis was, of course, tremendously concerned. First Allen revealed that he was a homosexual; now he had seen God. His father was fearful of what might come next. But however worried and critical Louis may have been, he and Allen were still able to talk openly, and Allen was able to confide such intimate problems as his fixation on Neal. Louis' advice on this subject came in a two word letter in July, 1948: 'Dear Allen, Exorcise Neal. Louis.' They obviously discussed the matter further, because in October, over a year since Allen had last seen Neal, Louis wrote, 'So, take my advice now, put a tourniquet knot around your affection for N.; tone your letters down properly.'

Meantime, Neal was begging Allen's forgiveness and trying to become friends again. After a long reconciliatory letter at the beginning of August 1948, he wrote on 20 August to say that if he and Carolyn had a son, he would name him Allen Jack Cassady. 'I anticipate him always signing his name thus: Allen J. Cassady,' wrote Neal.

By September, Neal's letters had grown positively flirtatious, and he wrote, 'I love all sex – yes all, all sex. Anyway I can get it. I need it, want it, shall have it – now. I wanta fuck – in despair I cry out, "Allen, Allen, will you let me splatter my come at you?" '

Allen replied, humourously, 'Fuck you, N.C. Next time you write send me some come so I'll know you're sincere.'

Allen got a job as a copy boy at Associated Press Radio News Service in Rockefeller Center, working the midnight–8 a.m. shift. His last weeks in Harlem were not pleasant ones, as he wrote Jack. 'Huncke moved in, yakked at me irritably for a week and a half, ate my food, took my last nickel and walked off with my last suits, a jacket, Russell's winter clothes (suits, coats, etc.) and twenty or thirty expensive books (hundreds of dollars worth of books) full of theological notes.' Since he was the one who had allowed Huncke to stay in Durgin's apartment Allen felt morally obliged to pay for everything. Huncke wrote Durgin to say that he would pay him back but many of the books were irreplacable, as were Durgin's annotations.

Naîvely Allen wrote to Huncke, asking if he really intended to pay back the money. He mentioned the incident in a letter to Burroughs, who replied with a warning: 'It seems very doubtful to me that Huncke will ever make any attempt to pay Durgin. I think that any policy of appeasement in that direction will be disastrous and can only lead to further imprudence and impositions.' As was so often the case, Burroughs was right on all counts.

Among Ginsberg's new friends was Ed Stringham, a Greenwich Village literary type who worked at *The New Yorker*. Ginsberg, Stringham and a young poet named Alan Ansen began a chain novel, writing a chapter each, which is as far as it got. Ansen had inherited the family home in Woodmere, Long Island, where he lived in some splendour. Allen, Jack and other friends would go out for weekends to listen to Wagner, bringing with them girls, boys and grass.

Another new friend was a young, hard-drinking ex-Harvard Italian lawyer named Bill Cannastra whose exploits included lying down in front of the advancing traffic on an avenue crossing, and dancing drunkenly along the parapet on the roof of his building. Through another young writer, Alan Harrington, whom Allen and Jack called 'the faun', Allen met the writer John Clellon Holmes whom Harrington brought to Allen's Fourth of July party in Harlem. Holmes was the same age as Allen and, like Jack, he came from Massachusetts. He and Jack immediately took to each other and Jack began to spend a lot of time at Holmes's apartment on Lexington Avenue at 56th Street. Allen would often visit them there, and they would all stay up late, listening to Symphony Sid, the 'all night, all frantic one', who played six hours of non-stop bebop, 'at your request and in our groove', every night on WMCA. Allen even sent for a membership card in the Symphony Sid 'Bop' Club, in recognition of the hours he spent listening to Lenny Tristano, Lester Young, Ben Webster, Charlie Parker and all the other greats of 1940s bebop.

Allen's friend Walter Adams departed for France, leaving Allen his $14.95-a-month, three-room, cold water flat at 1401 York Avenue. In those days Lenox Hill was a drab neighbourhood of cheap saloons, stables, thrift shops and tenement blocks. It was October when Allen moved in with his orange crates of books. The bed, a gift from Kerouac, was the one his father had died in.

In December, Neal abandoned Carolyn and their three-month-old daughter in San Francisco and arrived in New York with his ex-wife LuAnne, having used all his and Carolyn's savings to buy a brand new maroon 1949 Hudson. They were accompanied by Neal's friend Al Hinkle, whose new wife, Helen, had been jettisoned along the way, when she ran out of money. The purpose of the trip was to collect Jack and drive him back to San Francisco, where he intended to stay for three days before returning to New York. It was one of the pointless trips later celebrated by Kerouac in *On the Road*.

Allen took a few days off from Associated Press to drive around town with them and go to all the New Year parties, but during most of their stay he was still working the night shift. Neal and LuAnne slept in his bed, and he joined them there when he got in. Al Hinkle slept on the couch. Since they were all broke, Neal sent LuAnne out to work. Meanwhile, Neal, Al and Jack sat up all night drinking, taking Benzedrine and smoking pot. When she returned, after a long day as a waitress in a Radio City coffee-shop, LuAnne was expected to clean the apartment and cook the men their food. Jack was hanging around all the time so she had to buy food for him as well. Allen bought his own.

Huncke was in the Riker's Island jail on a sixty-day rap for possession of marijuana. Allen wrote to him to propose that he get a job and leave the world of petty crime; Allen would let him stay with him until he was set up and able to plan the future. The letter never reached Huncke, and, fearful of Allen's anger over the theft of his typewriter and clothes and Durgin's books, he did not contact Allen when he was let out at the beginning of February 1949. The first person he moved in with attempted to kill him.

Huncke was ordered out of Times Square by the police, who nicknamed him the 'Creep', and judged him unworthy to hang around its seedy streets because of his total indifference to anyone's plight but his own. He wandered homeless and coatless in the February cold and snow, until he finally presented himself at Allen's door at eight o'clock one morning, in the last stages of exhaustion. His feet were blistered and bleeding, and he was almost suicidally depressed. He had been living on Benzedrine, coffee and donuts for weeks, bought by pawning the few things he had been able to steal at the Port Authority bus terminal.

Allen bathed and dressed Huncke's bleeding feet and gave him food. After a little conversation, Huncke fell back on the couch and slept. Huncke's arrival became a line in Ginsberg's 'Howl': 'who walked all night with their shoes full of blood on the snowbank docks waiting for a door in the East River to open to a room full of steamheat and opium.'

Huncke spent most of the next two weeks sleeping. Allen wrote in his journal, 'Huncke has been in bed on a couch in the living room for two weeks with the shades drawn. The most depressing thing is to get up to go to work, and wake him, and see him lift up his head, staring blankly, dumb, biting his lips, for half-an-hour at a time.'

Gradually Huncke began to come to life, and Allen told him the content of the letter he wrote him in prison. Huncke listened carefully and seemed to agree. Allen felt that if he demonstrated sufficient interest in Huncke's welfare, and showed him that someone cared, then 'perhaps the spark of life would catch'. As he recovered, Huncke began to make his presence known in the apartment, moving the furniture around until it was to his taste and burning incense.

Allen, meanwhile, was feeling a strong need to be more financially independent of Louis. He was earning $31.75 a week at Associated Press but with Huncke living off him, he found that it didn't last out the week. Allen would work himself into a rage at Huncke's dependency and vow to get rid of him, but that only brought on guilt because he felt that the desire for financial stability came from a neurotic fear of flux and change, so he kept quiet and set out to enjoy Huncke's presence, planning to send him away when he could do it with a clear conscience. 'And so my house and my belongings, wearily, painfully, anxiously, became his,' Allen recorded. 'He wore my suits, socks, shirts, even took over my bed, so that I sometimes, rather than selfishly claim possession, took over the couch to sleep on – sometimes.'

Allen remembered Burroughs's warning of what would happen if he took Huncke in again, and recognised that under Huncke's veneer of misery and impotence, there was a calculating mind that would exploit Allen's every weakness. After the first two weeks, Allen gave Huncke a week's ultimatum to decide on his offer to find him a job and see that he kept it. However, Huncke conjured up a huge boil on his leg, which incapacitated him for another two weeks, during which time it was impossible for Allen to throw him out. Allen began to see him as 'an actual damned soul living already in hell, aware of it, powerless to help himself and powerless to be aided'. Burroughs liked Huncke for what he was, a scheming petty criminal, whereas Allen had an idealised view of the criminal underworld and saw Huncke as one of Genet's criminal-saints.

Throughout this time, Allen was being warned by his father, Eugene, Lucien Carr and Jack (who had returned from California) to get rid of Huncke. They saw him as a parasite, living off Allen and distracting him from any real creative activity. Louis was convinced that Huncke had some blackmail hold over Allen; he could see no other reason for their friendship. Eugene was also concerned for Allen's mental state. At one point he went to visit Allen, bringing with him an attractive young woman from teachers' training college; 'Allen immediately embarrassed me by urinating in the sink, so I was ashamed to ask her out again.'

One day when Allen returned from work, Huncke told him that Vickie Russell and her boyfriend Little Jack Melody had visited. Allen had not seen Vickie for a year or so, and he knew Little Jack only by reputation, since, until recently, he had been in a federal prison for robbing a safe. Little Jack had helped Vickie kick a junk habit by taking her out to his family home in Long Island.

At the beginning of March, Vickie and Little Jack visited Allen. Vickie was just as striking as ever – 'a six feet marijuana smoking redhead,' as the New York *Daily News* was to call her. Allen had been expecting Little Jack to be a big gangster type, but he was a half-bald, elfin, twenty-six-year-old Sicilian–American with 'doe-like gentility and interest and sympathy with things and people around him,' as Allen described him at the time. He and Allen got on well, and over the next few days Vickie and Little Jack spent a lot of time visiting, bringing marijuana with them, and getting involved in long conversations about Cézanne, Spengler and the nature of the universe. Little Jack often got pet ideas of a vaguely cosmic nature, which he found it difficult to express, and it became somehow embarrassing to disagree or not to show the appropriate amount of enthusiam for what he was trying to say.

Towards the end of March 1949, Allen had a recurrence of a bronchial illness which had bothered him on and off for about a year, so it was Huncke's turn to nurse Allen as he spent a few days in bed. Seeing that Allen had no music in the house (because Huncke had stolen the phonograph from his previous apartment), Little Jack brought over his phonograph and some of Vickie's jazz records including a set of Billie Holiday songs. There were other gifts, mostly books and food. They spent most nights at the apartment. Towards dawn Little Jack and Vickie usually went to sleep in Allen's bed. When Allen returned from work in the morning he would sleep on the couch, or on the floor if Huncke was on the couch. He worried about his inability to keep control of even his own bed but continued to say nothing.

Little Jack began to move in small items of furniture, including a painting he had done of Vickie which made her look surprisingly savage. By this time there was a great deal of marijuana about the place; they smoked it in an opium pipe that was kept on the mantel. Little Jack and Vickie were feeling very much at home.

Kerouac was a regular visitor, and he and Allen spent hours walking around the city streets, discussing their work. Jack had revised *The Town and the City*, and it was through Allen that he found a publisher. Allen had pressured Mark Van Doren into reading the manuscript and set up a meeting between him and Jack. Van Doren was impressed and recommended the book to Robert Giroux at Harcourt Brace; it was accepted on his word. Jack received an advance of one thousand dollars against royalties and was overjoyed. Allen was pleased for him, but also envious and depressed.

Virtually all of Allen's poetry at that time was dense and abstract. But Kerouac understood and liked it and was genuinely convinced that it was the work of genius. At parties and to new acquaintances, he and Allen promoted each other's work tirelessly. They were so close throughout this time that their conversation became quite hermetic, their numerous references to each other's work and to shared mystical understandings like a secret language that none of their friends could penetrate. Not all of Allen's work was filled with dense mysticism; in the spring of 1949 he started the poem:

I love the Lord on high
I wish he'd pull my daisy

to which Kerouac wrote the refrain:

Pull my daisy,
Tip my cup,
All my doors are open.

This collaboration grew in length and was the first thing Ginsberg would publish outside of college and the local New Jersey papers.

While Allen was in bed sick, he and Huncke had long talks. Huncke advised Allen to get out of his menial job at Associated Press and plan for the future. The irony in this role reversal was not lost on either of them, but Allen realised that Huncke was right. He decided that teaching would give him enough money to be psychoanalysed and enough time to write. Allen wrote to Lionel Trilling who had once offered to help him get an instructorship at Cooper Union.

Having decided to leave Associated Press, he took up an invitation from Bill and Joan to spend the summer in New Orleans. He was concerned about the apartment, which he would need when he returned in the fall. However, he did not want to return and find Huncke still there. Little Jack had spoken to him about needing an apartment to 'operate out of', but Allen had purposely not taken the hint and decided to let Eugene have it for the summer. There was a serious flaw with the New Orleans trip. Allen had no savings and there were unpaid bills.

By now Allen was quite weary of Huncke's sponging, and there was constant tension between them, but even though he told Huncke how futile he thought their parasitical relationship was and how withdrawn from him he felt, he stopped short of telling Huncke to go, so of course Huncke stayed.

Little Jack and Vickie relieved the situation a little by suggesting that Huncke join forces with them on various projects, and Huncke again brought up the subject of Allen subletting the apartment to Little Jack. Allen didn't want to, but Jack offered to do up the place, pay off all the bills, and give Allen the fifty dollars he needed to get to New Orleans. Allen accepted. In fact, they had already practically moved in. Little Jack and Vickie already used Allen's bedroom and Vickie had brought over clothes and makeup. Several weeks before, Little Jack and Huncke had cleaned up the apartment and rearranged the furniture. Allen had not minded; the old arrangement was what he found when he moved in. The housekeeping and changing of the sheets was already done by Vickie, and Huncke was in charge of dishwashing.

Allen's possessions were gradually moved into a bureau drawer in the living room. He did not supervise this job, either, for Huncke, ever since he moved in, had been wearing Allen's clothes, and Allen was never sure where to find his personal belongings. Huncke had even appropriated a few drawers in Allen's desk in which to keep his own papers and trinkets. Allen's journal reveals his attitude at the time: 'Didn't bother much about it. It saved me the trouble of thinking for myself on "small" matters.'

He was weary and complained that it was almost impossible to write in the chaos of the apartment. although many of the poems in *Empty Mirror* and *The Gates of Wrath*, such as 'The Shrouded Stranger' and 'Psalm I' date from this period. While he ruminated about 'ghosts that stood in blood,' Huncke and Vickie heisted automobiles. One evening, in early April, Little Jack, Vickie and Huncke asked Allen if he'd like to come along on a job. He said yes. He was interested in seeing the gang in operation, just as he had previously watched Garver at work stealing coats at Horn and Hardart; he wanted no share of the spoils.

They cruised around midtown, stopping at one point for Huncke and Vickie to break into a car and steal a woman's coat. Next, they found a row of likely-looking cars. They parked around the corner and asked Allen if he would like to come and act as 'lookout'. He declined, and after a while they returned, empty-handed. He later wrote, 'My feelings at the time were mixed. I had gone along with them on the ride, not knowing how I would react or what would happen. I thought, possibily, I might take part in a car haul. But I did not, when the opportunity arose, from a clammy feeling of fear and desire not to get involved in the actual operation. We had discussed my feelings in the car. They (especially Little Jack) were quick to defer and even sympathise with my desire to keep my "cherry" as we referred to it.'

The apartment gradually filled with stolen goods. One morning he came home to find two huge sacks of rolls and bread in the kitchen. He ate some rolls and gave a loaf to the old woman who lived next door. He was surprised to find an enormous cigarette machine standing in the kitchen, covered with a blanket. It stood there for several days, until Allen demanded that they get rid of it; Little Jack and Huncke broke it up and disposed of it.

On Easter Sunday 1949, Allen watched the Fifth Avenue parade with Lucien Carr, then he went home to sleep before going to work. He spent Monday with his father and returned to the city on Tuesday to find a letter waiting from Bill Burroughs and another from Joan. Bill had been arrested for possession of narcotics and his house searched. Among the items seized by the police were letters from Allen discussing the possibility of selling pot in New York. As the letter showed, and as Bill had told the police, the deal never went through, and Bill was sure that the FBI would not bother Allen, but just to make sure, Bill suggested that Allen keep his apartment clean. Huncke had opened the letter and shown it to Little Jack and Vickie. They discussed the matter and reassured Allen that if the police came looking for drugs, they would not notice the stolen goods. Nonetheless, Allen grew more and more anxious and felt a growing sense of doom. He knew he was being used but felt incapable of doing anything about it.

That evening Little Jack and Vickie pulled another robbery, arriving home at about 9 p.m. Allen helped them carry the loot, mostly clothes, up from the car, then went to find Lucien, who was working for UPI as a news reporter. Lucien was seeing an analyst and had been writing short stories. He had been released from Elmira on parole, and his freedom was dependent on his leading a blameless life. Although he still saw his old friends, like Allen, he could not afford to be associated with anything illegal. Lucien's shift ended at ten-thirty that evening, and he and Allen walked and talked all night. Allen showed Lucien Bill's letter, which provoked from Lucien a serious lecture, rebuking Allen for letting Little Jack,

Vickie and Huncke walk all over him. Carr remembered, 'I told him, you better watch yourself, because these are a bunch of thieves you are dealing with here and when the cops come down on them, they're gonna come down on you.' He asked if Allen had disposed of his papers, journals, letters from Neal, Burroughs, or any others that could possibly contain be incriminating. Allen admitted that he had intended to do so but had not; he felt ashamed.

For a long time, Lucien had asked him never to mention him, in even the most innocent of ways, in his correspondence and journals. Allen had ignored his warnings and kept Burroughs up to date on Lucien's activities and health, and these letters were all now in the hands of the New Orleans police. Although there was nothing incriminating in them – Lucien was living an exemplary life – he was angry at Allen for endangering him. He was also horrified to find that, even as they were walking around the city, Allen was 'tempting fate' by leaving his journals and papers all over the house. Allen resolved to take care of the matter as soon as he got home. He returned at 6 a.m. Little Jack and Vickie were in his bed, Huncke was on the couch, so Allen slept on the floor.

Allen sorted through his papers, taking out all the most sensitive material. He put about one hundred of his letters in a manilla envelope along with unsorted, obscene autobiographical or confessional prose fragments that he did not want to get into the wrong hands. Then he returned the envelope to the drawer, intending to take it to Eugene's room and hide it among a pile of old legal documents. Allen no longer felt secure about storing things in Paterson; the year before, Louis had started to read through his old homosexual love letters and writings.

Allen spent the next several hours assembling his poetry for a book, and he bound it all up together to take with him to work that night. In the evening, while Allen slept, Little Jack, Vickie and Huncke pulled another robbery, returning to the house at about nine and waking Allen to help them unload the car. There were lamps, clothes, radios, cameras and piles of pornographic books. The name written in them was that of a high-ranking policeman; it was his Jackson Heights home they had just robbed.

That evening, Allen stopped off at John Clellon Holmes's place looking for Kerouac; he was there. Allen had still not disposed of his incriminating papers and asked Jack if he was planning to stop by York Avenue later that night to see Huncke, because if he did, Allen would like him to take his journals and correspondence home with him to the safety of Ozone Park. Jack had not planned to visit Huncke and pointed out that since the New Orleans police also had his letters to Bill, his address was no safer than Allen's. 'Yes, it's true,' said Allen, disappointed at Jack's unwillingness to take the problem off his hands. Jack added, 'Besides, if you really wanted to get them out of the house, you would have done so already yourself.'

Allen felt such a twinge of remorse and anxiety at his inability to deal with the matter that he dropped the subject, after agreeing that his behaviour had been confused. He later wrote, 'But this agreement did not make amends for my lack of action. I felt even more the pressure of reality – a real world in which for some desperate reason of vanity or fear, I was manoeuvring myself and everyone I knew, into some immediate catastrophe.'

He got home from work just after nine the next morning, 22 April. Allen pointed out to Little Jack that when he agreed to sublet the apartment, he had not intended for it to be used as a centre for burglaries. He asked them to clear all the stolen property out of the place. Little Jack agreed to remove everything by the next day. In fact, he had already planned to take the stolen clothes out to an Italian friend on Long Island that morning. Allen still had all of his letters and journals in his desk and asked if he could come along for the ride and be dropped off at Eugene's on the way back. That way he would be home by 2 p.m. and get for some sleep before going to work at midnight. They loaded the car and Allen sat in the back with the stolen clothes.

At twelve-thirty they were driving along Northern Boulevard in Queens, Allen was telling them about his trip to Dakar; Jack missed his turn and got off the highway to turn back. A patrol car signalled them to stop. They pulled over, and the policeman parked his car and began walking towards them. Jack was driving the wrong way up a one-way street. Patrolman McClancy pulled out his pad to write up a citation. Little Jack panicked. He was out on parole and forbidden to drive, so he couldn't show his licence. Besides, he was driving a stolen car.

In a squeal of tires, he backed up, then U-turned, burning rubber, and sped off down Forty-third Avenue. The officer leapt back into his car with his partner and gave chase, siren blaring, and, according to one newspaper report, he fired at the fleeing car with his revolver.

'We have to outrun them,' yelled Little Jack. 'We'll have to abandon the car.' Vickie began to protest about leaving all the stolen goods. 'Fuck the clothes!' yelled Jack, 'We have to abandon the whole mess.' By this time they were travelling so fast that Allen was too frightened to even look round to see if the police were on their tail. He sat, surrounded by stolen clothes, wondering if he should throw the manilla envelope of letters out of the window. 'Lord God of Israel, Isaac and Abraham,' he called out, quoting from 'The Messiah.'

At first he had assumed that the seriousness of the situation was mostly to do with Jack's parole violation, then it quickly dawned on him that he was in serious trouble. 'I began more clearly to see that the great horror had begun to descend at last,' he wrote later.

After four blocks, Little Jack struck the curb attempting to make a turn. Allen felt the car begin to turn over. He somehow relaxed himself enough to roll with it. His glasses flew off, the stolen clothes and manuscripts tumbled around him in the car as it rolled over twice and came to rest upside down.

The next thing he heard was Little Jack's asking if everyone was all right and urging them to get out and run. The doors were all open, and Allen rolled out into the street. He stumbled about, looking for his glasses and papers among the heaps of clothes and broken glass, but all he could find was one unimportant journal from 1943–44. 'I remember the horror of the scramble after them,' he wrote. 'And the sickening feeling of failure when I saw everything upside down and confused, including myself.'

Incredibly, Allen escaped and was able to make his way back to the apartment. Then Vickie arrived and announced that Little Jack had been arrested. She and Huncke were planning an escape when the police knocked on the door and arrested all three of them. They had found the address in the papers left behind in the overturned car. Allen was kept behind bars at the Long Island House of Detention until his father got him out on bail.

4 The Subterraneans

We are healed of a suffering only by experiencing it to the full.
Marcel Proust, *The Sweet Cheat Gone*

Allen sat on a chair in the sixth floor ward of the Columbia Presbyterian Psychiatric Institute, waiting to be shown his bed. He was joined by a tall, overweight Jewish boy in thick glasses, with a towel wrapped round his head. The young man was still shaky and recovering his composure after an insulin shock treatment (patients were revived from the deep coma produced by insulin shock with intravenous injections of glucose). Seeing Allen, he inquired amicably, 'Who are you?'

'I'm Myshkin,' Allen replied. (Myshkin was the saintly character in Dostoyevsky's *The Idiot*.)

'I'm Kirilov,' came the reply. (Kirilov was the demonic nihilist in *The Possessed*.) Allen felt an immediate rapport with this new acquaintance, whose name was Carl Solomon, and began to tell him about his vision of William Blake. Afterwards Allen wrote Jack, 'It is very embarrassing, in a mad house, to do this. He accepted me as if I were another nutty ignu, saying at the same time, with a tone of conspiratorial glee, "O well, you're new here. Just wait awhile and you'll meet some of the other (repentant) mystics."'

Carl, two years younger than Allen, was born in the Bronx on 30 March 1928. Something of a prodigy, he had graduated at age fifteen from Townshend Harris High School for the gifted, then gone to City College, where he joined the youth branch of the Communist Party. When he was seventeen he entered the US Maritime Service and began to alternate a term in college with one at sea. In 1947, he jumped ship in France, joined the French Communist Party and moved in with a Pigalle prostitute called Odette Belmaure. In Paris he became deeply involved with the

European avant garde. He had read Artaud's essay on Van Gogh, 'Le Suicide de la Société', and one hot night in July he saw Artaud himself do a terrifying performance of 'Ci-Gît', trembling and screaming at the top of his lungs, an experience that had a profound effect on Carl's life.

Back in New York, he left City College for the more arts-oriented Brooklyn College and moved to Greenwich Village where he hung out with Trotskyists and Reichians. When he heard that Wallace Markfield was to lecture on 'Stéphane Mallarmé and Alienation' in a hall near the Brooklyn College campus, he and two friends, Leni Grubes and Ronnie Gold, decided to stage a Dadaist event. They bought potato salad at a delicatessen and threw it at the astonished lecturer, an event which Ginsberg later immortalised, with some poetic licence, in 'Howl': 'Who threw potato salad at CCNY lecturers on Dadaism ...'

Carl later commented, 'I gave Allen an apocryphal history of my adventures and pseudo-intellectual deeds of daring. He meticulously took notes of everything I said (I thought at the time that he suffered from "the writer's disease", imagined that he was a great writer). Later, when I decided to give up the flesh and become a professional lunatic-saint, he published all of this data, compounded partly of truth, but for the most raving self-justification, crypto-bohemian boasting à la Rimbaud, effeminate prancing, and esoteric aphorisms plagiarised from Kierkegaard and others – in the form of "Howl". Thus he enshrined falsehood as truth and raving as common sense for future generations to ponder over and be misled.'

'Howl For Carl Solomon' did contain many images taken from Carl's life story, though most of them were transformed or universalised. Carl had become interested in Gide's idea of 'le crime gratuit' – gratuitous crime, and committed one in his own small way. He stole a peanut butter sandwich from the Brooklyn College cafeteria and showed it to a policeman. He was sent to a psychiatrist. He was in a very negative mood and as his twenty-first birthday approached, he and Ronnie Gold began to talk a lot about the validity of suicide. Finally, on his birthday, Carl presented himself at the Psychiatric Institute, demanding a lobotomy; a symbolic suicide – or to be 'suicided' as Artaud put it. This too was enshrined in 'Howl': '. . . and subsequently presented themselves on the granite steps of the madhouse with shaven heads and harlequin speech of suicide, demanding instantaneous lobotomy.' He was admitted.

Allen's tenure at the Psychiatric Institute was the result of the combined forces of Columbia University, Lionel Trilling and his father. After his arrest he was forbidden to have any contact with Huncke, Little Jack or Vickie. Trilling took him to see Professor Herbert Wechsler at Columbia Law School, who told him to voluntarily commit himself to a mental hospital and plead guilty, and he would then get off. Trilling recommended a psychiatrist, Doctor Fagin, who said that in his opinion, for the immediate future, Allen was too sick to do anything except go to a psychiatric hospital. He was sicker than he or anyone knew, Fagin told Allen darkly. Allen breathed a sigh of relief. He told Jack, 'I have manoeuvred myself to a position I have always fancied the most proper and true for me ... I really believe, or want to believe, really I am nuts, otherwise I'll never be sane.' He described his position as quite serious, 'I've gotten so hung up on myself now it isn't funny anymore. I stop in the middle of conversations, laughing shrilly – stare at people with perfect sobriety and remorse, and then go on cackling away.'

Van Doren told Allen that he had to choose between criminals and society. 'If you do believe that Huncke is some sort of criminal saint or illuminated being, then you have to follow through with your choice and maybe even go to jail for your beliefs, although some of us here have been thinking that it might be a good thing for you to hear the clank of iron.' Allen asked if there was a middle choice and Van Doren insisted there was not. He said that Allen had exaggerated and romanticised Huncke. This was certainly the view of Allen's lawyer who met Huncke and described him as a 'filthy stinking mess. One look at him and you can tell he's no good.' Meyer Schapiro was the only one at Columbia with a more open and sympathetic attitude. He invited Allen over, and they had a long talk about spiritual matters and vagrancy. Schapiro recounted that he had been arrested and put in jail for being a 'stateless bum' in Europe as a young traveller, which made Allen feel a little better.

Louis had remarried; his new wife was an attractive, vivacious younger woman named Edith. She was from Paterson and they were house hunting together in order to start their new life in a new home. Allen lived quietly at home with them and heard no news of the case until the beginning of June, when he was told that he had been cleared by the grand jury but that the other three were to go to court. Allen had not known that Doctor Allan Cott, Mark Van Doren, Lionel and Diana Trilling and Dean Carmen would all attend the hearing and testify on his behalf. He wrote Jack, 'I don't know any details. But I must say that's mightily cricket of them all. I was really worried last month . . . I feel grateful . . . That's what Van Doren means by society I suppose, people getting together to keep each other out of trouble (or away from tragedy) till they get an inkling of what they're getting into.' His legal costs were one thousand dollars, which were paid by Louis and Eugene. It was arranged that he would go to Columbia Presbyterian Psychiatric Institute on 168th Street but would continue to spend his days in Paterson until a bed became vacant.

Most of his news from the outside world came through Kerouac, who was very supportive through this difficult time. He kept up a stream of letters discussing poetry, his new novel (*Doctor Sax*) and the latest gossip, using pseudonyms for their friends – e.g. Huk for Huncke, Dennison for Burroughs – because Louis was now opening Allen's mail.

In addition to his remarriage, Louis' life had been changed by Naomi's release that spring from Pilgrim State. Although recovered sufficiently to be discharged, she was not well enough to look after herself or get a job, so she moved back in with Eleanor, becoming a financial drain on Louis, Eleanor and Eugene. Allen was all the more guilt-ridden about his own financial imposition on Louis and Eugene. He felt close to his mother, particularly now that he was officially 'mad' like her, and his sympathy was shown in a journal entry from that period: 'That night at Eleanor's, I suddenly became angry at Eleanor, and inwardly sickly at my brother because they so patronised and baffled and fogged the natural exuberance and innocent perception of Naomi; however, Naomi too started compulsively blindly questioning me in repeated monotones, about my travels, which she's half forgotten, till I became weary of all . . . I feel I could half start a conspiracy of the insane with her, underground – but she goes blank and mechanical often.'

Two and a half months after his arrest, the day after his birthday, Allen entered the Psychiatric Institute. The previous day, he wrote reflectively in his journal, 'I have been wrathful all my life, angry against my father and all others. My wrath must end.

All my images now are of heaven. I dream of incomprehensible love and belief. I think always that I am about to put an end to my life, only now there is no worry as to how I will do it, as last summer after the vision. In the hospital I hope to be cured. My images tell me that the hours of truth are at hand. I am not going to die, I am going to live anew. My thought has been peaceful all week. I have been reading *The Possessed*. My devils have been cast out.' The entry is strikingly similar to Naomi's saying, 'I shall think nothing but beautiful thoughts.'

Another birthday journal entry revealed the extent of his feeling of isolation, 'Tonite all is well . . . what a terrible future. I am 23, the year of the iron birthday, the gate of darkness. I am ill. I have become spiritually or practically impotent in my madness this last month. I suddenly realised that my head is severed from my body, I realised it a few nights ago.' This sad passage was later transcribed almost verbatim to become the second poem in his collection *Empty Mirror*.

There had been a bureaucratic mix-up, and on 6 June he recorded, 'Back home. Hitch in madhouse venture.' The hitch was only temporary, however, and on 29 June 1949, he was installed in the sixth floor ward of the P.I., overlooking the Hudson River. Jack, who was in Denver for the summer, wrote encouragingly, 'I admire you for delivering yourself to an actual bughouse. It shows your interest in things and people. Be careful while convincing the docs you're nuts not to convince yourself (you see, I know you well.)'

Allen spent a lot of time sunning himself on the roof, looking out at the George Washington Bridge and the boats ploughing up the Hudson. Under the influence of the doctors, he began to question the significance of his Blake vision, and wrote Kerouac, 'The people here see more visions in one day that I do in a year.' The P.I. was doing its work. Having convinced Allen that he was sick, he was now encouraged to reject madness and return to the fold. In so doing, he inadvertently drew away from Naomi. He ended the same letter to Kerouac by saying, 'I am beginning to hate my mother.'

For Allen to be 'cured' he also had to reject Burroughs. Bill made this easier for him by launching into one of his tirades against liberals. Bill had been appalled that Allen had allowed himself to be told what to do by his father and the Columbia establishment instead of fighting the case himself. He wrote Kerouac, 'If I was in Al's place I would say, "Go ahead and place your charges, if any." His present position is insufferable. Imagine being herded around by a lot of old women like Louis Ginsberg and Van Doren. Besides I don't see why Van Doren puts in his two cents' worth. Sniveling old liberal fruit.'

Kerouac reported Bill's views to Allen, who replied sadly, 'I have discovered that I have no feelings, just thoughts, borrowed thought taken from someone I admire because he seems to have feeling.' Allen began to question his whole relationship with Bill, and in particular all the findings resulting from his year of amateur analysis with him; 'O Bleak Bill,' Allen wrote Jack. 'He is afraid that I will find out that he is crazy, that his analysis of me was a tragic farce – not an absurd farce, but a tragic real one – that he has led me astray.'

For the next seven months Allen tried hard to get back to 'reality', but it was not as easy as he thought. He was given no drugs and had need of shock therapy. He saw a psychiatrist two or three times a week, and during his stay there had four different doctors, all of whom thought their job was to make Allen conform and fit into a *Saturday Evening Post* view of society, with a wife and an ordinary job. But Allen said he wanted life to be 'a sweet humane surprise'. When he looked at himself he saw a miracle, and thought others should see miracles in themselves as well, but the doctors didn't understand. 'Do you still think you are superior to other people and different?' they asked. Finally, to please them, he said no, but the lie upset him. 'I think if I had argued a lot I could have got myself into a lot of trouble,' he said later.

Allen tried to cooperate and get some good out of his hospital-isation; he even thought that perhaps the doctors had some secret knowledge. He kept expecting miracles to happen in return for agreeing and conforming, but they were raw young interns, who were unable to find the underlying causes of his anxiety or his real feelings and needs. They discouraged all talk of visions, and most displays of individuality by their patients were dismissed as 'ward nuttiness'. One time, as a joke, Allen and Carl began banging on the piano and yelling as if they were crazy, and the doctors came running in horror: the 'catatonic piano' in 'Howl'.

Allen quickly adapted to the routine. There was a time to shave (after which all the razors were locked up), a time to eat and a time to sleep. He was allowed out daily from four until seven in the evening and from 4 p.m. on Friday until Sunday night, provided someone took responsibility for him, so his social life was not too disrupted. Jack returned to New York from Denver in late August with Neal, and Allen spent most weekends with them. Neal had again abandoned Carolyn, who was now pregnant with their second child and demanding child support for their first. Neal took a job parking cars and moved in with a girl called Diana Hansen, whom he also made pregnant. Since she was the only one with an apartment, she found herself playing host to both Allen and Jack most weekends, with one of them taking the spare bed and the other sleeping in the armchair.

Carl introduced Allen to the work of Jean Genet, Henri Michaux and Antonin Artaud, writers whose works were later cited by Ginsberg as influences on the composition of 'Howl'. Carl bought an under-the-counter copy of Jean Genet's *Our Lady of the Flowers* at the Gotham Book Mart and smuggled it into the P.I., and he showed Allen the April 1949 issue of *Partisan Review* which contained a long article about Genet. He also had a copy of *Tiger's Eye* containing Artaud's article on Van Gogh and the Samuel Putnam anthology *The European Caravan* which contained Artaud's 'To Be Done With The Judgement Of God'. All this work impressed Allen enormously and, to an extent, counter-balanced the efforts of the doctors to turn him into a well-adjusted American.

Allen reciprocated by telling Carl all about Kerouac, Cassady and Burroughs. They spent their afternoons sitting in the day room, arguing over Walt Whitman and what it meant to be a poet. When Carl first met Allen, he called him a 'dopey daffodil', a reference to Wordsworth, because Allen saw the poet as a 'sensitive soul', whereas Carl preferred Artaud's concept of the poet as a brute. After reading Genet and Artaud, Allen began to come round to Carl's point of view.

As the months went by, the doctors at the P.I. convinced Allen that his only hope was to return to Paterson, get a job, find a girl and try to fit into society. Allen recognised that there was a tremendous gulf between him and ordinary people, and after eight months of treatment he believed the doctors when they said that once he closed this gulf, he would be cured. He was told that he would be released in February 1950, and he set about trying to get a job in Paterson.

He applied to local newspapers, but to no avail. His luck in finding a girl was no better. He wrote Kerouac, 'I wish I could meet a really gone sweet girl who could love me, but I guess a really gone sweet girl is too much to expect. Why is everything so hard?' At this time Kerouac was the only person that Allen could really open up to, and he responded as a true friend. On 13 January 1950, Jack wrote to him at the P.I. to tell him that he admired him loved him and considered him a great man. Such valuable friendship helped Allen to bolster his shattered ego and take charge of his life again.

On 27 February, Allen left the P.I. and moved in with his father and stepmother at their new home at 416 East 34th Street, Paterson. He had his own room, and there was a big, dry attic where he could store all of his papers and books. There was no need for Allen to hide his manuscripts any more; there were hardly any secrets left. Besides, he was now a heterosexual, albeit a virgin one. The doctors at the P.I. had cured him, or at least convinced him to give heterosexuality a try for his own good. His doctor had met with Allen, Edith and Louis to talk things over, then Allen left the room. Edith later told him that the doctor had said, 'He is partly homosexual. If you really want to have a close relation with your son, you have to accept that, even to the point of receiving his lovers in your home, and if you really want a close relation, of allowing them to stay over.' Ginsberg later said, 'This did a world of good, because my father believed in authority, and if that was the word, it relieved him of the necessity to come down hard and worry and be scandalised.' But it would be quite a while before the time came to test their tolerance, because for the next five years, Allen was to have a series of apparently satisfactory heterosexual relationships. As he wrote to Jack on the day he was released, 'A turning point has been reached in that I am no longer going to have homosexual affairs: my will is free enough now to put this in writing in a final statement.'

Although to the people of Paterson, Louis Ginsberg was their most famous poet, largely through his weekly column of puns in the local press, their city was also under scrutiny from a quite different artistic eye, that of the poet William Carlos Williams, writing from nearby Rutherford. Starting in 1946, he had been publishing his epic poem *Paterson*, a mixture of poetry and prose, quotations from newspapers and letters, idiomatic fragments of everyday American speech and chunks of stodgy local history. Book three of *Paterson* was published in 1949. Williams led a double life. An overworked local doctor, making house calls, delivering babies, prescribing medicines to his mostly impoverished patients, he was also the prolific author of plays and stories, poems and essays. Ezra Pound was an old friend of his; they met at the University of Pennsylvania in 1902, and although Williams travelled to Paris and met all the leading lights of modernism, he preferred the obscurity of Rutherford, where he lived and worked throughout his life.

On 28 March 1950, Williams gave a reading at the Guggenheim Museum in New York. Allen attended and afterwards ran backstage to meet Williams, but he changed his mind and waved to him instead. Two days later he wrote Williams a long letter:

'Dear Doctor,' he said. 'In spite of the grey secrecy of time and my own self-shuttering doubts in these youthful rainy days, I would like to make my presence in Paterson known to you, and hope you will welcome this from me, an unknown young poet, to you, an unknown old poet, who live in the same rusty county of the world. Not only do I inscribe this missive somewhat in the style of those courteous sages of yore who recognised one another across the generations as brotherly children of the muses (whose names they well knew) but also as fellow citizenly Chinamen of the same province, whose gastanks, junkyards, fens of the alley, millways, funeral parlors, river-visions – aye! the falls itself – are images white-woven in their very beards . . .

'I envision for myself some kind of new speech – different at least from what I have been writing down – in that it has to be a clear statement of fact about misery (and not misery itself), and splendour if there is any out of the subjective wanderings through Paterson. This place is as I say my natural habitat by memory, and I am not following in your traces to be poetic: though I know you will be pleased to realise that at least one actual citizen of your community has inherited your experience in his struggle to love and know his own world-city, through your work, which is an accomplishment you almost cannot have hoped to achieve.'

He enclosed nine poems, the best of his total output, including 'Ode To Sunset', which he spent many months writing at the P.I., and a recent 'Ode To Judgement'. The sixty-six-year-old Williams was amazed and delighted to receive such a letter, which must have seemed a response to his work from the streets of Paterson. The combination of the arrogance of youth and obvious poetic vision charmed him so much that he included the entire letter, and a subsequent one, in Part Four of *Paterson*. He was less delighted with Ginsberg's poetry. He replied, saying that the poems were not very good; 'In this mode, perfection is basic,' he wrote, referring to rhymed verse, and Allen's poems were imperfect. Allen later said, 'I took this to mean that there was very little concrete detail in them, it was all a sort of refining of the imagery of roses and light and mystical references – rehashing of it over again. I'd thought maybe if I could concentrate all my mind's focus into these few symbols and juggle them round a couple of times, make some crystal-like perfect symbolic statement that would turn other people on and catalyze the same vision in them. But it didn't work.'

Williams, as an imagist, believed 'No ideas but in things', a basic rule that, when he finally applied it, totally transformed Ginsberg's poetry. Williams wanted to 'Get form without deforming the language', and by language he meant everyday American speech, not the carefully pronounced British diction of formal poetry. In *I Wanted to Write a Poem*, Williams explained, 'The rhythmical construction of a poem was determined for me by the language as it is spoken. Word of mouth language, not classical English.' Allen had to get rid of his 'thee's and 'thou's before his work would be acceptable to the doctor.

Allen's uncle Leo got him a job as a reporter on a labour newspaper, the *Labor Herald*, the official journal of the New Jersey AFL. The paper was published in Newark, so Allen had to rise early to make the fifteen-mile trip to work each day, but in other respects the job was ideal, combining his ill-defined desire to become a labour leader and his vocation as a writer. He became more involved with life in Paterson, walking the streets, investigating the area around River Street, near where he grew up, with the same determination that he explored the bars on Eighth Avenue in Manhattan five years before. He wrote Williams, 'Do you know this part of Paterson? I have seen so many things – negroes, gypsies, an incoherent bartender in a taproom overhanging the river, filled with gas, ready to explode, the window facing the river painted over so that people can't see it. I wonder if you have seen River Street most of all, because that really is at the heart of what is to be known.'

Allen still went to the city every weekend to attend parties or just hang out at the San Remo. The San Remo bar, at the northwest corner of Bleecker and MacDougal streets, was the centre of the bohemian life of Greenwich Village throughout the late 1940s and early 1950s. Among its regulars were James Agee, Larry Rivers, Paul Goodman, John Cage, Merce Cunningham, Chester Kallman, Harold Norse and virtually everybody associated with Judith Malina and Julian Beck's newly launched Living Theater.

Allen's crowd included Carl Solomon, Lucien Carr, Jack Kerouac, the young poet Philip Lamantia and Bill Cannastra. Russell Durgin also turned up there, though they saw less of him after he got married that June. Alan Ansen was a regular whenever he was in town, and John Kingsland was often seen in the company of an attractive young woman called Dusty Moreland. Allen had had his eye on her before he went to the P.I., and now that he was looking for a girl, he paid her special attention. Allen referred to the people at the San Remo as the 'subterraneans', a name that Jack later used for his book about them. In it he gave Allen credit: 'The subterraneans is a name invented by Adam Moorad [Ginsberg's name in the book] who is a poet and friend of mine who said, "They are hip without being slick, they are intelligent without being corny, they are intellectual as hell and know all about Pound without being pretentious or talking too much about it, they are very quiet, they are very Christlike." ' Even if the quote sounds more like Kerouac's voice, the sobriquet at least was Ginsberg's.

Another term for this group had already been coined, but it had been all but forgotten. 'Beat Generation' was a phrase discovered by Jack Kerouac and John Clellon Holmes in the fall of 1949, while Allen was in the P.I. Their accounts differ as to what occurred:

'We were talking about the Lost Generation and what this generation would be called,' said Kerouac, 'and we thought of various names and I said, "Ah, this is really a Beat Generation!" – and he leaped up and said, "You've got it!" – see, just like that.'

Holmes said, 'Jack and I never talked about the Lost Generation particularly. You see, when Jack used that phrase, we certainly didn't say "That's it! That's it!" and make a big issue out of it.'

Either way, three years went by before anyone used it again, and it was only when Holmes's book *Go* was published by Scribners in 1952, with the line: 'You know, everyone I know is kind of furtive, kind of beat . . . a sort of revolution of the soul, I guess you'd call it,' that the *New York Times* grabbed hold of the catchy phrase and asked him to write an article about it. Holmes's piece, 'This Is The Beat Generation', appeared 16 November 1952, and the Beats were defined as a public phenomenon, long after the fact. The word itself came to them from Huncke, who had been using it long before he met any of them to describe the condition he was usually in – beat.

Another of the subterraneans at the San Remo was Jay Landesman, the editor of a magazine called *Neurotica*, dealing with existentialism and popular culture. Notable in the spring 1950 issue were Carl Solomon's powerful 'Report From The Asylum – Afterthoughts Of A Shock Patient', which he published under the name of Carl Goy, and four verses from Ginsberg's 'Pull My Daisy', published as 'Song: Fie My Fum'. Allen wrote to Jack, 'I went down on my knees (practically; took me days to recover from the fury) to Landesman to get him to publish "Pull My Daisy". He finally agreed but I had to chop the poem down to half its size so he could squeeze it in; it still looks good.' It was Ginsberg's first appearance in a commercial magazine.

At the end of May, Allen's life entered a new phase, and he wrote excitedly to Jack from Provincetown, Massachusetts, 'If you are in any ennui or doldrums, lift up your heart, there IS something new under the sun. I have started into a new season, choosing women as my theme. I love Helen Parker, and she loves me, as far as the feeble efforts to understanding of three days spent with her in Provincetown can discover. Many of my fears and dun rags fell from me after the first night I slept with her, when we understood that we wanted each other and began a love affair, with all the trimmings of eros and memory and nearly impossible transportation problems.'

In his 1955 poem 'Transcription Of Organ Music', Ginsberg wrote: 'I remember when I first got laid, H.P. graciously took my cherry, I sat on the docks of Provincetown, age 23, joyful, elevated in hope with the Father, the door to the womb was open to admit me if I wished to enter.'

Allen's new life as a heterosexual got off to a wonderful beginning with Helen Parker. She had impeccable literary credentials; older than Allen, she had been a close friend of John Dos Passos, and through him had met Ernest Hemingway and other luminaries. Allen entertained her in his best Well-Groomed Hungarian manner, and played the 'mad hipster with cosmic vibrations', but also, to his delight, he was able to just be himself and talk seriously and intimately, without recourse to irony, about a wide gamut of subjects from obscure metaphysics to everyday problems. 'Then we screw, and I am all man and full of love,' he told Jack. 'The first days after I lost my cherry – does everybody feel like that? I wandered around in the most benign and courteous stupour of delight at the perfection of nature; I felt the ease and relief of knowledge that all the maddening walls of heaven were finally down, that all my aching corridors were travelled out of, that all my queerness was camp, unnecessary, morbid, so lacking in completion and sharing of love as to be almost as bad as impotence and celibacy, which it practically was anyway. And the fantasies I began having about all sorts of girls, for the first time freely and with the knowledge that they were satisfyable. Ah, Jack, I always said that I would be a great lover some day. I am. I am at last.'

Allen asked Jack, who was staying with Neal in an apartment next door to Bill and Joan in Mexico City, to 'tell me what weary, skeptical comments Bill comes on with.' Bill had written him a month before, on 1 May, saying, 'I am more than a little dubious of a program to overcome queerness by "attentive work like studying for a job". I think you will find it is not as simple as that.' But for once Bill was wrong. Allen's heterosexual bliss was quite genuine. A picture of the continuing efforts of Allen's P. I. analyst to keep him on the straight path emerges from Bill's letters. Bill wrote, 'I simply do not recognise such an entity as a "neurotic heter with strong queer leanings". For the Cris sake do you actually think that laying a woman makes some one heter? I have been laying women for the past fifteen years and haven't heard any complaints from the women either.' (Here Joan annotated Bill's letter with the word, 'Correct!') Bill continued, 'What does that prove except I was hard up at the time? Laying a woman, so far as I'm concerned is O.K. if I can't score for a boy.'

'As for this normal man of yours who isn't sexually mature until he is thirty,' Bill continued, 'I don't buy him. I say he will never be mature, which I can say about ninety per cent of US males. And another thing, I am dubious of these slow changes. *Any basic change is sudden*. Like me getting off junk. I suspect this slow change routine is an analyst alibi . . .' But Allen's affair continued. Helen wrote him in July, 'How I miss you – you boy of repressed delight!'

There were some practical problems: she had two children, young boys aged five and ten who needed a father, something that Allen felt sure he could not be. Helen suggested that they set up home in Cape Cod and Allen stay at home and write while she went to work. She also tempted him with the idea of spending the winter in Key West, but Allen's need to continue seeing his analyst and his desire to become financially stable precluded this.

In the middle of May, Neal returned to New York from Mexico City where he claimed to have gone to get a cheap divorce from Carolyn – no papers were ever produced. Neal and Diana Hansen were already estranged but were getting married to legitimise her forthcoming child. Neal had lost his job parking cars but had been offered a job with Southern Pacific Railroad, and in typical Cassady fashion, two hours after getting married, he set out for California using his railroad pass; he promised to save money and return as soon as he could. His new wife was left with the uncomfortable suspicion that he was going back to Carolyn and the kids, which of course was true.

At the end of September, Allen received a nasty blow to his pride when he was fired from his job on the *Labor Herald* for incompetence. He was very conscious of his lack of aptitude in practical things, so he decided to rectify this with manual labour. He got a job in a Paterson ribbon factory, at the very good pay of $1.25 an hour. His function was to pick up all the broken threads and tie them back into the loom. He became so self-conscious and stricken with anxiety that he found it impossible to tie the tiny threads at all. He told Neal, 'my eyes unfocussed, I would daydream, I lost track of how to do the simplest things and wandered around embarrassedly trying to fit in.' They fired him after two and a half weeks. 'Truly the real world is my downfall,' he complained to Neal.

The logistical difficulties involved in getting to Provincetown meant that Allen was unable to see Helen Parker as often as he would have liked, and in the meantime he began going with a girl in New York called Rayanne. He told Neal that she was 'sharp, a real NY "on the town" pro type.' He called up Jack to tell him to come over and meet Rayanne but Jack said, 'I only fuck girls and learn from men, so why should I come up?' Allen, annoyed by his misogyny, wrote him a poison-pen letter saying 'That's why you're so dumb!' Eventually Allen dropped her and she had a short affair with Jack, who only went with a woman if she had previously been the lover of one of his male friends.

That summer of 1950, Allen saw a lot of Bill Cannastra, who lived in a loft three doors down from Lucien Carr on 21st Street. Cannastra was a regular at the San Remo, and both he and Lucien gave a lot of parties. Though his sexual preference was for men, Bill was living with a young woman called Joan Haverty, who regarded him as something of a father figure. They played pranks together, creeping down fire escapes and peering into people's apartments. Cannastra, fond of spying on people, had drilled peep-holes in his bathroom wall so that he could watch his guests. He was a heavy drinker, 'who . . . danced on broken wineglasses barefoot, smashed phonograph records of nostalgic European 1930s German jazz finished the whiskey and threw up groaning into the bloody toilet . . .' ('Howl').

One night in October, Bill Cannastra and a group of friends on the town ran out of money, and around midnight Cannastra decided they should take the subway to go and borrow some from Lucien. As they reached the Bleecker Street station someone mentioned the Bleecker Tavern. The train began to pull out of the station and Bill, as a joke, leapt up and lunged at the open window, as if he were going to the bar. He misjudged his leap and found himself hanging too far out of the window. The others rushed to pull him back as he struggled to regain his balance, but his coat ripped away in their hands. The train gathered speed and he began to scream for help. As the train entered the tunnel, he ducked his head to avoid the pillars. There was a thud, and he was torn from their hands, out of the window and on to the roadbed where he was dragged for fifty-five feet before the train stopped. He was rushed to Columbus Hospital but died on the way.

Joan Haverty now became the subject of much attention. With Lucien's encouragement, Allen began leaving notes, arranging meetings and showing interest in her; however, when he finally made his move to sleep with her, he failed by being overbearing and impatient with her 'sentimental enshrinement of Cannastra's image'.

Kerouac had better luck. He had returned from Mexico City and was living at his mother's house in Queens, where he was working on a new book. He moved in with Joan, then they surprised all their friends by getting married. The wedding was one month after Cannastra's death; Allen and Lucien were the best men.

Allen wrote to Neal the next day, describing Joan as 'a tall dumb darkhaired girl just made for Jack. Not dumb really, since she's "sensitive" and troubled.' Joan was only twenty years old (Jack was twenty-seven) and didn't know what she was getting into by marrying Kerouac. The marriage was doomed from the start. Joan was forbidden to hold any views that differed from Jack's and was not allowed to accompany him when he went out with his buddies. One of Jack's reasons for getting married was to find someone to look after his mother, and it was not long before he insisted that they move in with her in Queens. Joan had to hand over her wage check each week to Jack's mother, who treated her as little more than a slave. Joan quickly realised that she was being used, and took a downstairs brownstone studio apartment on West 20th Street and told Jack he could move in with her if he wanted to; otherwise she would live alone. He moved in, and it was in that apartment, in April 1951, that he wrote the first draft of *On the Road* while Joan continued to provide for them.

Allen's romance with Helen Parker floundered and that fall she left him for the folk singer Ramblin' Jack Elliott. Allen's next affair was with a girl called Mardine, whom he eventually left for her room-mate. Dusty Moreland was a beautiful young woman who had come to New York from Wyoming to study painting. She had an oval face, with dark hair, slanting eyebrows, large eyes and full lips. Allen had known her for several years, and she appeared to be the 'really gone sweet girl' he was looking for. Allen began to spend his nights with her instead of returning home to Paterson. Their love making was so exuberant that Allen developed a case of Peyronie's Syndrome, which distorts the penis in its erect stage. Scar tissue caused by internal bleeding does not have the flexibility normally found in the penis, and as a result Allen went through life with a pronounced bend in his erect member.

One day that winter of 1950, Allen stopped off for a drink at the Pony Stable, a lesbian bar on 3rd Street at Sixth Avenue. There, at a table, sat a twenty-year-old boy with dark brows, tousled black hair and bright flashing eyes. Allen was immediately attracted to his classic Italian features and youthful energy. The boy had a thick sheaf of poems with him, and announced that he was a poet, but unlike many of the self-proclaimed poets of Greenwich Village, he had his work professionally typed, which immediately made Allen take him more seriously. He read the poems and was surprised to find that the poems were good. One in particular stuck in his mind; it began: 'The stone world came to me, and said Flesh gives you an hour's life.'

The boy's name was Gregory Corso, and the images of classical antiquity that filled his poems had been acquired in jail, where he spent many of his teenage years. The old-timers there told him, 'Don't serve time, let it serve you,' and he took this good advice and embarked on a course of self-improvement. Not knowing where to begin his studies, he started at the beginning with the history of Greece and Rome, and by the time he was released he had a thorough grounding in classical culture.

Corso never knew his mother, who was from the mountains of Lombardy and may have taken the boat back there shortly after his birth. He was born above the funeral parlour across the street from the San Remo, in what was then part of Little Italy. He had lived with eight sets of foster parents in different parts of the city until he was about ten years old; then his father took him, thinking, incorrectly as it happened, that to have a child would keep him out of the war. His father went into the navy, and Gregory lived on the streets.

On one occasion when he was twelve years old, he was so hungry that he kicked in the window of a restaurant; caught on his way out, he was sent to The Tombs. Fortunately he was streetwise enough to avoid being raped, and he learned fast from the other prisoners. He was released a year later, with no money and nowhere to go. After walking the streets, he broke a window at a youth centre to get in and sleep. Discovered by a nightwatchman, he was sent straight back to the Tombs. There he fell ill and was transferred to Bellevue, which, during wartime, was overcrowded and understaffed. One day in the dining room, he flicked a piece of bread and hit one of the mental patients in the eye, and in the uproar that followed he was put in a straitjacket and carried out. He spent the rest of his time at Bellevue on the fourth floor with the seriously mentally ill. By the time he got back on the streets he was fifteen and very tough.

After pulling off several robberies, Gregory was caught again, and the judge gave him three years. He was in Clinton Prison in Dannemora, up by the Canadian border, from 1947 until 1950. He got out of jail just before his twentieth birthday, and shortly afterwards he met Allen.

Gregory and Allen discussed poetry that night and told each other their life stories. Finally, Gregory told Allen about a fantasy e had. Gregory had a furnished attic room on West 12th Street, and from his window he could see everything that went on in the fourth-floor apartment of a girl who lived across the street. Every night Gregory would masturbate while watching her take a bath, use the toilet, undress and make love to her boyfriend. He told Allen he dreamed of crossing the street, knocking on her door, and introducing himself. As Gregory told the story, Allen realised, with growing amazement, that the girl was Dusty Moreland, who lived on West 12th Street, and that the boyfriend was himself. 'You want me to introduce you?' Allen said, 'I have magical powers!' And the next day he took him round to meet her.

'My first lay when I got out of prison,' Gregory later recalled.

Over the Christmas break, Dusty went back to Wyoming to see her family, and Allen resumed his affair with Mardine. He saw a lot of different girls, and the rumours began to spread. Bill wrote to him on the first of the year, 'Lucien tells me you are a virtual satyr – a mythological Greek creature characterised by insatiable lust I mean, not Jean Paul Satre [sic] the existentialist – Well stick with it and no backsliding.'

That December, Allen took a job as a market researcher with National Opinion Research Center, asking members of the public their feelings about the Korean War. In May 1951, he moved on to Doherty, Clifford and Shenfield, a market research company on the fifty-second floor of the Empire State Building. He spent his days worrying about toothpaste. Ipana Toothpaste was about to launch a million-dollar advertising campaign. But first they had to decide whether to put their million behind the slogan 'Ipana makes your teeth sparkle', or 'Ipana makes your teeth glamorous'. Tens of thousands of dollars were spent on a research project to test people's reactions to these slogans, and Allen sat in his office drawing a graph of all the answers and writing a report. The entire project was designed to find out just which words and images would convey a particular idea; useful work for a poet.

Allen had been employed as a freelance, and when summer came, he found himself broke and out of work. He lost weight and was having dreams in which he became a giant blue skeleton, starving to death on the city streets. Lucien had planned to go to Mexico City that August to attend the wedding of a friend who worked for U.P.I. He invited Allen to join him. They planned to stay with Burroughs. Having failed as a pot farmer and been arrested for indecent behaviour in Texas, then for possession of drugs in New Orleans, Bill had taken his family to Mexico City.

They drove in Lucien's old Chevrolet, with Lucien's little dog in the back and a goodly supply of bottles in the front. In Texas they encountered a terrible heatwave, which caused the car's thermometer to explode. That June, Bill had taken a tiny apartment at 210 Orizaba Street, near the centre of Mexico City and the university, but when Allen and Lucien arrived, they found that Bill was away in Ecuador with Lewis Marker, looking for land.

Joan and Lucien immediately paired off in a protracted drinking contest, while Allen looked around the city. Joan's fine features had been eroded since Allen and Lucien had first met her seven years before. She had caught polio when she and Bill were living in Texas, but she'd refused to see a doctor. 'I have polio,' she said, 'I'll have polio.' The disease withered her leg, and she walked with a limp. Benzedrine had blackened her teeth, and alcohol had ravaged her good looks. She was drinking two bottles of tequila a day, trying to take care of her son Billy, who was now five, and her daughter, Julie, who was seven. 'Julie's getting really pretty,' Allen told Joan. 'She's gonna be some competition for you!'

'Ah, I'm out of the running,' Joan replied.

Allen had been making small talk, but Joan meant what she said. Still only in her twenties, she had more or less given up. She was an alcoholic, stuck in a Mexico City slum, with two children, a Benzedrine habit and a boyfriend who was away on a trip with *his* boyfriend. When Bill had a boy he had no use for women. Her prospects did not look good, although Bill took his family financial responsibilities very seriously.

Lucien got very drunk at the wedding. After driving the bride and groom to the airport, he was arrested when he ran into a few cars while trying to get the Chevrolet out of the airport parking lot. He spent the night in jail with a large drunken Indian.

Joan had a pot connection in Guadalajara and suggested a trip there. Lucien and Joan sat in the front, passing the Quinebra gin bottle. Allen, Julie and little Billy cowered, terrified in the back, as Lucien skidded around the hairpin bends on the mountain roads, while Joan yelled, 'How fast can this heap go?' Much of the time Lucien was too drunk to drive, so Joan would take over. Lucien lay on the floor pushing down on the gas pedal, while she steered and used her one good leg on the brake as they screamed around corners. The two of them enjoyed themselves enormously. Ginsberg's memory of the trip is of 'great kicks and torment of continual threat of death'. He thought Joan was trying deliberately to get them all killed.

Their car got stuck in an attempt to ford a river, and the Mexicans who appeared out of the night to help them stole Allen's pants; he had taken them off so that they wouldn't get wet while he helped push. Lucien couldn't stop laughing. The trip wasn't all terror and alcoholic frenzy; they had magnificent views of jungle-covered mountains and the Pacific. They spent some time in Mazatlán. On the trip back, they saw the active volcano Paricutin and drove onto its lava field at night. The car kept falling into crevices, and Lucien used the jack to get it out. Joan urged him on: 'Go on! Go on! Let's get to the volcano!' Molten lava and rock shot into the air. A mile from the rim, the smoking rocks showered all around them. Allen was vastly relieved when they got back to the city.

They dropped Joan and the kids off in Mexico City and prepared to leave. Lucien and Joan had become very close; in fact, Billy had bitten Lucien in the leg for paying too much attention to his mother. Joan looked so mournful when they left that Lucien was of half a mind to stay. 'There was something, in a wistful way, tremendously compelling about Joan,' Lucien said. 'She was very very bright and very exciting, very much in command of the various tight situations she got into. She was in command of everything but herself!'

They began the long drive back to New York City, and had reached Galveston, Texas, when the car broke down. Lucien had to return to work, so he flew on to New York, leaving Allen with the car and the dog, arranging to fly back in a week to collect Allen and the repaired car. Allen rented a little shack overlooking the Gulf of Mexico. He spent his time swimming, sitting on the beach and walking around Galveston. He did a lot of sleeping.

On 7 September he read in the evening paper, 'An American tourist trying to imitate William Tell killed his wife while attempting to shoot a glass of champagne from her head with a pistol, police said today. Police arrested William Seward Burroughs, 37, of St Louis, Mo, last night after his wife Joan, 27, died in hospital of a bullet wound in her forehead received an hour earlier.'

Allen, completely shaken, wrote to Neal that night: 'My imagination of the scene and psyches in Mexico is too limited to comprehend the vast misery and absurdity and sense of dream that must exist in Bill's mind now.'

5 On the Road to California

It is the poet, Allen Ginsberg, who has gone, in his own body, through the horrifying experiences described from life in these pages . . . Say what you will, he proves to us, in spite of the most debasing experiences that life can offer a man, the spirit of love survives to ennoble our lives if we have the wit and the courage and the faith – and the art! to persist.

William Carlos Williams, introduction to 'Howl'

Allen spent the next two and a half years in New York City, during which time, under the influence of William Carlos Williams, he made radical changes in his writing style, adopting the open form, with syllable count and variable breath-stop length for verse measurement, that enabled him to write 'Howl'. His life was much more under his control; as a freelance market researcher, he had a reliable and undemanding way of making money that gave him the time he needed to write and enough cash to enjoy a full social life in the bohemian circles of Greenwich Village, where he was still meeting the characters who would populate the poem.

In the fall of 1951, Allen was again staying on and off in Lucien Carr's spare bed, but at the beginning of December, he found himself a dark eighteen-dollar-a-month two-room attic apartment, lit by skylights, at 346 West 15th Street. He furnished it very simply with a table, a chair and a bed, and a radio on which he would play classical music late at night until the neighbours beat on the wall. Some evenings Allen would sit on the small stoop, watching the stars 'roll over the walls of the warehouse' across the street – he lived across from the giant Port Authority warehouse. He wrote a number of good poems about the place including one dedicated to Alan Ansen called 'Cockroach At My Door'. 'Walking Home At Night', which he included in his early collection *Empty*

Mirror, ended, 'Remembering/ my attic I reached/ my hands to my head and hissed/ "Oh God how horrible!" '

A huge combination New Year and wedding party celebrated the arrival of 1952 and the marriage of Lucien Carr and Francesca Van Hartz. Allen had immersed himself in a frenzy of social activity during the holidays. Dusty was visiting in Wyoming, and Allen saw a number of girls from Barnard College. When Dusty returned, she was accompanied by her mother, and together they set up an apartment in the Village. Allen told Neal, 'I dream of marrying her but don't have the force or money, and we don't love each other. We are great tired friends now. We talk a lot, sleep once in a while, but never screw.' Allen asked her to marry him, but she turned him down. Allen wrote Neal that he was tired of sex.

He was also feeling guilty about it; that January he wrote Neal that he had seduced young Gregory Corso and worried about the re-emergence of his gay leanings for weeks afterwards. Gregory travelled to the coast almost immediately afterwards and Allen did not see him before he left. Corso denied that the seduction ever took place: 'That Ginzie, he'll say anything.' But he confirmed that he and Ginsberg had become good friends before his departure for San Francisco.

Allen missed Jack and Neal, but when Jack wrote and suggested that he join them in San Francisco, Allen explained that he did not want to interrupt his analysis. He was even able to resist Neal's tempting offer, 'Why don't you come out here? Nice place if one likes it. Be brakie and make lots money. Or write in attic and make love to wife and me.' However, the idea was planted, and Allen did eventually take him up on it, with the predictable disastrous results.

Allen saw some of his old criminal friends again but with more detachment than before, having opted to join 'society'. Huncke was still in jail, but Little Jack had managed to fake insanity and only served one year. Bill Garver, the overcoat thief, told Allen that Phil ('The Sailor') White, Burroughs's old friend, had hanged himself. Phil had been held in the Tombs on three separate charges and had tried to get out by informing on an old heroin dealer he knew. The dealer was caught and sent to Riker's Island, but the police reneged on their deal with Phil and dropped only two of the charges against him. There was a third, non-narcotics charge, which would have put him on Riker's too. Phil knew what they did to stool-pigeons on the Island, so he took the only way out.

Garver told Allen, 'I never thought he had much character, but what else could he do? He was washed up as a junkie in New York.' Burroughs was astonished when Allen told him the news. 'I was sincerely shocked to hear about Phil,' he wrote Allen. 'He was so uncompromising and puritanical about stool-pigeons. He used to say, "I can't understand how a pigeon can live with himself." I guess Phil couldn't after what he did.' It was only after White's death that the facts began to emerge about him. Phil White was a psychotic killer; fuelled by a mixture of Tuinols and heroin, he would get into murderous rages, walking into a store and shooting before anyone had time to sound the alarm. He hit liquor stores and fur shops and killed one man because he didn't have enough money on him. 'He was quite a guy,' said Huncke later.

In addition to Dusty, and Lucien and Cessa Carr, Allen's friends at that time included his ex-Columbia classmates Richard Howard, John Hollander and Hollander's wife, Ann; his old friend from the Psychiatric Institute, Carl Solomon, and his wife Olive; and Alan Ansen, all of whom he saw about once a week. He was also in close touch with Eugene, Louis and Edith. He had made many new friends at the San Remo, and wrote Neal: 'I love a great new group of subterraneans.' It was one of these, Bill Keck, who gave him his first peyote, in April 1952. Allen stayed overnight in Paterson and got up early to take it. He swallowed three buttons, gagging on the bitter metallic taste. Nauseated, he lay down on the bed and the sickness passed, though he continued to feel empty-headed. He noticed the beautiful pattern on the pillowcase and the intense colour of the cherry blossoms in the garden. Taking his notebook with him, he went out to sit under the cherry tree. 'Heavens the universe is in order,' he wrote. It was a beautiful day, with a few puffy clouds floating peacefully across a deep-blue sky. A bee dropped on to the open page of his journal, and butterflies and flies danced by his head. He began to think of space as a solid form between him and the clouds. He could hear the neighbours going about their Sunday morning chores, clanking garbage pails.

He recorded all his observations in his journal. Everything took on a super-real quality. Looking at a rock, he began to think about its great age and how it would outlast him. He went into the house and talked to his relatives in the kitchen, but all the time wanted to get back to the rock. 'I have been going around grinning idiotically at people,' he wrote, back under the cherry tree, 'almost afraid they'll ask, "What's the matter with you this minute?" but they seem to me also – so strange in their momentary consciousness.' He settled into his seat and wrote, 'Rock. Serried and worn by years, so old, a huge stone tear. I can't even see you under your shroud of dirt. A bird just shat on me! It must have been on purpose.' Louis came to the back door and looked out. 'Imagine being in the literal presence of one's own father,' wrote Allen, clearly moved by seeing Louis standing there.

Some laundry fell from the washing line and a voice from the house called out, 'Please Allen, will you hang that up?' Then he heard Louis say, 'He's busy with himself.' Allen wondered if he was attracting too much attention to himself, just sitting in the backyard writing. He decided that probably only William Carlos Williams and himself, in a radius of fifty miles, could see the world in such terrible detail and were so conscious of the open sky and the solidity of the transparent air.

He drifted through the day, listening to family arguments, playing jazz records and admiring the cherry blossoms. Later that evening he began to come down from the twelve-hour trip. He wrote, 'Glad I sailed through this peyote test without any of the mental imaginables – the horror of accidents, I didn't cut my thumb or bite anyone or tip my mit . . .' But the peyote did cause a shift in consciousness, which he sought; though not as extreme as his Blake experience, it indicated that he was on the right path.

In the summer of 1951, Joan Kerouac had found that she was pregnant. Despite his Catholic upbringing, Jack tried to get her to have an abortion. She refused, and he pretended that the child was not his. Their marriage now broke down completely, and Joan went to stay with her mother in Albany. Jack refused to pay for prenatal care, and Joan had to get a court order. He eventually coughed up four payments of five dollars. That fall, after swearing his friends to secrecy, he left New York to stay with Neal and Carolyn in California. Neither Allen or Lucien Carr approved of his behaviour, and by the time he left he was on bad terms with both of them.

Neal, meanwhile, was now taking his responsibilities seriously. Working seven days a week to earn money for a family vacation, he did a daytime shift as a brakeman on the Southern Pacific Railroad, and in the evenings he recapped tires. Jack couldn't understand this commitment to family and complained about Neal's 'materialistic attitude'. This inevitably led to problems. Neal grew increasingly irritated by Jack's failure to contribute enough toward his upkeep, and for the household pot, which he smoked continuously. Jack's parsimony was legendary; he never even shared his cigarettes with his wife.

On 16 February 1952, Janet Michelle Kerouac was born, and the Brooklyn Uniform Support of Dependants and Abandonment Bureau began searching for Jack. Meanwhile, he was worried, not about his wife and their newborn child, but that he might not be able to live safely with his mother again without being sued for maintenance. Burroughs's grim 1945 prediction that Jack would eventually be strangled by his mother's apron strings was already coming true.

John Clellon Holmes's *Go* was published at the beginning of 1952, and Allen was shocked to read Holmes's vision of him and thought the treatment of his Harlem vision of Blake was crude and vulgar. 'You haven't really caught the way it felt,' he told Holmes, referring to the Blake experience, 'but you've caught something else. You've caught the solemn funny little kid I guess I must have been in those days.' When in 1976 he was asked, in his role of elder statesman, to write a preface for a new edition of the book, Ginsberg had to refuse. He had not looked at it in twenty-four years, but on re-reading it he was angered by it all over again. 'I was too ashamed of the prose to write a preface,' he said, 'so Holmes, whom I love, got mad at me.'

Kerouac also disliked the book but his problem was mostly one of frustration and jealousy at seeing Holmes get an astonishing twenty-thousand dollar advance, when Allen, who was acting as Jack's unofficial agent, trying to place *On the Road*, had only been able to secure an offer of one thousand from Carl Solomon, who was working as an editor for his uncle at Ace Books, publishers of cheap pulp paperbacks. Allen was also working on Bill's behalf, toting the manuscript of *Junkie* from publisher to publisher. Though he didn't think of it in those terms, this was the beginning of Ginsberg's self-appointed Ezra Pound role, which resulted in so many of the Beats getting published.

In May, Jack took a bus to Mexico City to stay with Bill Burroughs who had often invited him. Jack finished his revision of *On the Road* in Mexico City and mailed it to Carl Solomon. The manuscript was mostly material that finished up as *Visions of Cody*. Carl read it and passed it on to Allen, who read it and passed it on to John Clellon Holmes. On 12 June 1952, Allen wrote to Jack, 'I don't see how it will ever be published, it's so personal, it's so full of sex language, so full of our local mythological references, I don't know if it would make sense to any publisher – by make sense I mean, if he could follow what happened to what characters where. The language is great, the blowing is mostly great, the inventions have fullblown ecstatic style . . . Where you are writing steadily and well, the sketched, the exposition, it's the best that is written in America.'

Allen told Jack he was concerned: 'Ace I'm positive won't take it now. I don't know who will . . . Will you be revising it at all? What are you trying to put down, man? You know what you done?' In his opinion, it had to be pulled together; otherwise it would never be published. Allen's assessment of the book's reception with publishers was accurate, and *Visions of Cody* was not published until Kerouac had died, and even then only after considerable pressure from Ginsberg.

Allen had better luck with Burroughs. Bill had been sending him sections of prose ever since Allen got out of the P.I. *Junkie* was a controversial autobiographical account of his life as a heroin addict in New York and Texas, beginning in 1944 when he met Phil The Sailor and Huncke. There were two related texts, called *Junk* and *Queer*. *Junk* was the more complete of the two, and it was this that Allen took on his rounds. Carl Solomon decided to publish it, paying a thousand-dollar advance. Bill wrote to Allen, 'You really are a sweetheart. I could kiss you on both cheeks. We should get used to calling each other sweetheart, I understand it is the standard form of address between agent and author but this time I mean it.'

In 1952, Allen made an abrupt change in his writing style. For some time he had been trying to find a way to speak naturally in his poems. The two major influences upon him at the time were William Carlos Williams and Jack Kerouac. Two years earlier, shortly after the publication of Kerouac's *The Town and the City*, he had written Jack, 'I have to learn how to talk naturally in verse again; find out how to say great things or beautiful things naturally.' One of Kerouac's influences was his technique of sketching. Kerouac's architect friend Ed White had suggested, 'Why don't you just sketch the streets like a painter, but with words?' Jack gave it a try and was amazed by the results. The idea was, of course, not a new one, but to Kerouac it was a great innovation and his enthusiasm rubbed off on Allen.

Allen went back through his old journals, where he had many passages just like that: straightforward prose sketches of what he saw before him, written in a clear, detailed style, with no attempt to be poetic or 'break everybody's mind open'. He took a couple of paragraphs containing word-pictures out of the journals and arranged them on the page in lines like Williams's. Sometimes he arranged them by counting the syllables, sometimes by the breath lengths, and sometimes he just balanced the lines visually on the page. Years later he told a class of literature students, 'These were just the ordinary, unselfconscious notebooks, prose, and I took the nuts out of it, the intensest moments of prose, pushing everything else aside, isolating it, framing it on the page.' He was quite pleased by the results, which looked like Williams's work, but, unaccountably, he didn't realise the importance of what he had.

In January 1952, he dug out the poems and sent a group of them to Williams, because 'I had nothing else to send and felt washed up as a writer.' He told Williams that they were 'Fragmentary notes I picked out of a journal and put in lines just as experiment about a year ago. I gave up then, thinking they were nothing, thinking also that I was aimlessly trying to make poetry out of prose scraps.' He could not have anticipated Williams's reaction.

Writing from the Hotel Weston in New York City, where he was taking a few days vacation, Williams wrote, 'Wonderful! . . . How many of such poems as these do you own? You *must* have a book, I shall see that you get it. Don't throw anything away. These are *it*.' Allen, deliriously happy, wrote immediately to Jack and Neal in San Francisco. He enclosed copies of ten poems and said, 'Now you realise you old bonepoles, the two of you, whuzzat means? I can get a book out if I want! New Directions (I guess). Whew! An you realise further, Williams is also nutty as a fruitcake. It also means we can *all* get books out (just you and me and Neal) . . . I have a new method of Poetry. All you got to do is look over your notebooks (that's where I got those poems) or lay down on a couch, and think of anything that comes into your head, especially the miseries, the mis'ries, or night thoughts when you can't sleep an hour before sleeping, only get up and write it down. Then arrange it lines of 2, 3 or 4 words each, don't bother about sentences, in sections of 2, 3 or 4 lines each. We'll have a huge collected anthology of American Kicks and Mental Muse-eries. The American Spiritual Museum, A gorgeous gallery of Hip American Devices.' It is entirely typical that Ginsberg's first thought was to find a way for his friends to share in his good fortune.

The earliest poem composed by this method was 'The Brick-layer's Lunch Hour', which Allen wrote as a prose sketch in his journal while looking out of Carolyn's hotel window just before he and Neal left Denver for Texas in 1947. In it, a young bricklayer sits on a ladder on top of a wall, eating a packed lunch, and plays with a cat. Allen typed it out as lines of poetry without changing a word and had a poem. 'This is probably the earliest text I published which makes real sense,' Ginsberg later told a class of literature students, and quoted the three final lines, 'It is darkening as if to rain/ and the wind on top of the trees in the/ street comes through almost harshly.' He discussed the lines with his students, 'Without even intending it, there is that little shiver of a moment in time preserved in the crystal cabinet of the mind. A little shiver of eternal space. That's what I was looking for.'

Inspired by Williams's letter, he began reading furiously through all his old journals, searching for the poems hiding there. Two weeks later, he was able to tell Jack, 'I have been working steadily at typewriter, piecing together mad poems – I have already 100 of them. I'm jumping.' These he winnowed down to eighty or so and sent off to Williams.

This was to be the beginning of an association that lasted for the rest of Williams's life. Allen had finally found a poetry teacher able to show him the craft. That March, Williams took Allen to a small cocktail party and afterwards they sat in the car in his garage. 'Get locale, local speech, accents and rhythm,' he told Allen. 'Write in that idiom.' Williams took up the offer in Allen's letter that they explore the River Street section of Paterson. They went to the old swimming hole of Allen's youth, behind the silk factory; picking up a handful of trash at the riverbank, they made up a poem on the spot about what they had found. Allen wanted to take Williams on to the bars of River Street but he said he was too old and wanted to go home. Allen later recorded their conversation. They sat in the car in the darkness. Williams said, 'What's it all for?'

'Why?' said Allen.

'I'm getting old,' Williams said. 'Two years more and I'll be seventy.'

'Are you afraid of death?' asked Allen.

They sat in the car looking at the asphalt suburban street, and he said, 'Yes, I think that's it.'

Allen's friends were astonished by his new poetry. John Hollander thought that he had burst forth like Rilke. He stared at Allen in amazement and suggested he give them Greek titles so they would look like poems. Lucien liked the 'amusing ones' best, whereas John Kingsland preferred the 'recherché ones about Marlene Dietrich'. Allen told Jack, 'Dusty liked (eek!) the metaphysical ones best.'

On 4 April, Allen delivered a copy of the manuscript of his book, now called *Empty Mirror*, to Williams, who had agreed to help him make the final selection of poems. Williams wrote an introduction in which he stressed how Allen used the language of the crowd to reach the crowd; 'what can he do, in the end, but speak to them in their own language, that of the daily press?' Allen dedicated the book to Huncke.

Allen sent copies of his manuscript to *Partisan Review*, *Hudson Review*, *Commentary* and *Poetry Chicago* with no luck, and in May he showed it to Van Doren and Random House, and sent a copy to Kenneth Rexroth, who was a reader for New Directions, but all to no avail. *Empty Mirror* was not published until 1961, by which time Ginsberg was well known.

His grand plan to publish Burroughs, Kerouac, Alan Ansen, Jean Genet and various others through Ace Books was also upset. In June, he reported to Bill that Carl had broken up with Olive; stopped traffic on Eighth Avenue by throwing his shoes and briefcase at passing cars, smeared paint on the walls of his apartment and flooded it; attacked his books with a knife; run screaming in the streets; and been in and out of Bellevue. 'This has been going on for two weeks and I can't get anything done at Ace till he calms down. Gad.'

Dusty Moreland was living with Allen in his attic room, so he had little time to himself, particularly when Dusty's cat died and she went on a six-day binge. Everyone Allen dealt with seemed to be behaving strangely. Carl was going through an emotional crisis, Jack was paranoid that his wife might find him and angry that his book was not being hailed as a masterpiece; and Bill was planning a strange jungle expedition, in search of the hallucinogenic drug yage. 'Everybody seems off their heads, blowing tops around me,' Allen wrote Bill. 'I don't have a moment's peace from these people with their cats and yages and wives and voids and anger at the universe, why can't everybody calm down, I always say, like the nice people in the boobyhatch.'

Allen had been collecting unemployment compensation; when it ran out in October, he took a job with George Fine Market Research, on 42nd Street, as a market analyst on cosmetics, deodorants and other commercial accounts. With a regular income coming in again, he moved to a better apartment: 206 East 7th Street, on the Lower East Side of Manhattan, an area that he would live in for the rest of his life.

He and Dusty had decided to separate. He told Neal: 'With Dusty I seldom lay and it's no good really though I like her alright.' When the time came to move to the new apartment, Dusty had nowhere to go, so she moved with him. Allen tried to get her to go to work and help out financially; he wrote Jack what happened. 'She got totally annoyed, went around drunk for weeks, had a phase of insisting she was hot for me. We finally had one great sweet screw full of innocence and hotness on both sides, then she disappeared up Third Avenue.' Dusty didn't contact Allen for months, though all her clothes and furniture were in the apartment. 'She's mad at me,' Allen told Jack. 'Thinks I betrayed her – and I did because I came on real stern and annoyed after a while . . . I didn't want chaos, it was unsettling my mind.'

Jack, meanwhile, was brooding in San Jose, where Neal and Carolyn now lived. No publisher was interested in *On the Road*, and Jack looked for the villains of the piece and saw them all in New York. In a three-page temper tantrum, fuelled by his wounded pride, he directed his resentment and anger at all those who had dared criticise his book. The letter, dated 8 October 1952, was addressed to Allen, but it was John Clellon Holmes who bore the brunt of the attack: 'The smell of his work is the smell of death. Everybody knows he has no talent . . . His book stinks, and your book [*Empty Mirror*] is only mediocre, and you all know it, and my book is great and will never be published. Beware of meeting me on the street in New York . . .'

To Allen, he raged, 'And you, who I thought was my friend – you sit there and look me in the eye and tell me that "On The Road" I wrote at Neal's is "imperfect" as though anything you ever did or anybody was perfect? And don't lift a finger or say a word for it . . .' Jack declared dramatically: 'I shall certainly never find peace until I wash my hands completely of the dirty brush and stain of New York and everything you and the city stand for.' And so he continued, reviling everyone who had tried to help him get his book published; Allen, Lucien, Carl Solomon and John Holmes.

Allen had had a great deal of experience with paranoia. He gave Jack time to cool off, and less than two weeks later, he received the manuscript of *Doctor Sax* which Jack wanted him to place. They were reconciled, but Allen retained the uncomfortable knowledge of Jack's true feelings about his friends. When Jack returned to live with his mother that winter, the old intimacy between them was tarnished.

In January 1953, Allen went to visit Naomi at Pilgrim State for the first time in many months. He took the elevator to the women's ward, and two buxom nurses in white uniforms led her out. Allen gasped, horrified at how much his mother had changed. She had had a stroke. The flesh on her face was wasted and lined with age. She had lost a lot of weight and no longer had the robust, healthy look of past years:

> Too thin, shrunk on her bones – age come to Naomi – now broken into white hair – loose dress on her skeleton – face sunk, old! withered – cheek of crone –
> One hand stiff – heaviness of forties & menopause reduced by one heart stroke, lame now – wrinkles – a scar on her head, the lobotomy – ruin, the hand dipping downwards to death –

There was another change. Even when she was raving, she had always had self-confidence; now Allen saw 'pitiful batbrained hysterical fright and lack of sureness'. She was out of her mind. 'Are you a spy?' she asked, 'Who are you? Did Louis send you?' Allen's eyes filled with tears as he sat at the small table. Naomi weaved back and forth to the door of the visiting room, asking why he was crying, then ordering him to get out before he was struck down. 'You're not Allen,' she said. After a few minutes a nurse came and led her away. Allen staggered into the men's room, 'sobbing, saying "Horror, the horror of it," and groaning with grief and the reality of her death's hand . . .'

In the spring of 1953, Allen met a girl called Elise Cowen. She had attended Barnard with Joyce Johnson, then Joyce Glassman, who wrote movingly about Elise and Allen in her autobiographical volume *Minor Characters*. She pointed out the strong resemblance between them: 'They could have been born into the same family, brother and sister, they looked so much alike. Their broad foreheads and somewhat heart-shaped faces, the vulnerability at the corners of their mouths, their same darkness. They even wore nearly identical black-rimmed glasses, through which their large brown eyes absorbed the world nearsightedly.'

Allen saw a lot of Elise and she told Joyce Johnson, 'He seems to think I'm very deep.' But Allen did not invite her to move in with him. She became a part of Allen's circle of friends. Lucien Carr always called her Elipse; 'She was a sweet girl. I was very fond of her. She was very shy and like a wounded bird. You couldn't help feeling sort of protective about Elipse.' Joyce Johnson succinctly summed up Ginsberg's relationship with Elise when she said, 'Elise was a moment in Allen's life. In Elise's life, Allen was an eternity.'

Allen planned to publish *Junkie* (as they then spelled it) in the spring of 1953. Bill had decided to use the *nom de plume* William Lee, in case his parents saw it. They had been very critical after reading his thinly disguised exploits in Kerouac's *The Town and the City*, and since they were bringing up his son and still providing him with an allowance, he did not want a repeat performance. It was curious, therefore, that he chose Lee – his mother's maiden name – as his new surname. To publicise the book, Allen had provided material for David Dempsey's 'Literary Notes' column in the *New York Times*, but Jack refused to allow his name to be used there, since Bill was publishing under a pseudonym. In a letter dated 21 February 1953, addressed to Allen, Jack, referring to the Dempsey article, also said that he did not want *The Town and the City* mentioned in connection with *Go*, and denied permission to place his name next to Clellon Holmes's as an expert on the Beat Generation. Had Kerouac not been so jealous, this would have been the first article on the inchoate literary movement. Curiously, Jack still regarded Holmes as a friend; he continued to stay at his apartment and go drinking with him.

Ace aimed *Junkie* strictly at the news-stand market and printed up 100,000 copies at thirty-five cents with a lurid cover that showed a man and a woman struggling to get possession of a hypodermic syringe. To cover themselves against any suggestion that they might be advocating the use of drugs, Ace added a publisher's statement disassociating themselves from Burroughs's views on drugs and published the book as a double volume with *Narcotic Agent* by Maurice Helbrant – 'a gripping true adventure of a T-man's war against the dope menace'. Thinking that some of the slang used in *Junkie* would be incomprehensible to their readers, they added a glossary, partly compiled by Allen, which included such esoteric terms as 'yen pox', 'flop' and 'mud'.

Despite his refusal to help publicise Bill's book, Jack wrote to Allen on 7 May to ask if he would act as his agent again and try to place *Doctor Sax* and his bildungsroman *Maggie Cassady*, because his agents, MCA, had found no takers. *Doctor Sax* was one of Allen's favourite books, but it was still incomplete. When Jack returned to the city, he and Allen walked around Greenwich Village in the spring sunshine trying to find an appropriate end. As the text then stood, a great black snake, hundreds of miles long, was just emerging from the deep. Allen suggested a Shakespearian-style ending: 'Ah! 'twas a husk of doves'; meaning that the snake, representing all the evil in the world, was just a dead outer skin, within which would be a flock of doves. Jack went home and finished the book, saying that Satan was enamoured of doves and that 'his Snake would not destroy the world but merely be a great skin of doves on coming-out day.'

At the end of April, Allen discovered Chinese painting and spent days in the Fine Arts room of the New York Public Library poring over books of reproductions. He wrote Neal, 'You begin to see the vastitude and intelligence of the yellow men, and you understand a lot of new mind and eyeball kicks.' He also said that he had 'begun to familiarise myself with Zen Buddhism through a book by D.T. Suzuki, "Introduction to Zen Buddhism".' This was typical Ginsberg understatement. He had embarked on an ambitious study plan and took out more than seventy books on the subject from the Columbia University library alone. In one of the art books, he found a scroll painting by Liang Kai called 'Sakyamuni Coming Out From The Mountain', which showed Buddha exhausted after his enlightenment. Allen sat with the book open before him, entranced, and wrote a poem with the same title, using a long line and W.C. Williams's triadic form, breaking each line into three:

> He drags his bare feet
>> out of a cave
>>> under a tree.

It was the beginning of a new form of writing for him. Pleased with the results, he immediately set out to write something more ambitious: to set his feelings about Neal Cassady down on paper once and for all. He called the poem 'The Green Automobile', a private homosexual reference to the green robes of the *galabanti*, the male whores of Imperial Rome, to whom Oscar Wilde paid homage with his green carnation. It was also a reference to Neal's 1932 Pontiac clunker, known as the Green Hornet. Allen later described the poem as his 'first breakthrough as a poet. First time I let my imagination and desire dominate over what, in the mental hospital, I had been taught to accept as an adjustment to reality, to limit my demands of the external world to what could be workable so as to avoid excess suffering.'

It was a joyful poem, celebrating his love and friendship for Neal. It was written in very long lines, each one broken into quatrains:

> He'd come running out
>> to my car full of heroic beer
> and jump screaming at the wheel
>> for he is the greater driver.

Allen wrote Neal, 'In new poem I am beginning to explore some of the uncharted verbal rhetorical invented seas that Jack (&

yrself) sail in ... After my "Empty Mirror", which for me strips yakking down to modern bones, I would like to build up a modern contemporary metaphysical yak-poem, using the kind of weaving original rhythms that Jack does in his prose, and the lush imagery. I been dry too long. The Green Automobile ... does this, at least begins this.' He let his imagination run wild:

> This time we'll buy up the city!
>> I cashed a great check in my skull bank
>> to found a miraculous college of the body
>>> up on the bus terminal roof

It was a long poem, of thirty-four such stanzas, and he was still working on it in September. He told Neal, 'The point of this poem is to rewrite history, so to speak, make up a legend of my poor sad summer with you, and try to create some recognisable human-angelic ideal story, too.' The whole poem was a 'legend of love', idealised, as only then, six years after that painful summer, he was able to do.

In the summer of 1953, Ginsberg began work as a copyboy at the New York *World-Telegram*, where he had short, sociable hours for a change. Gregory Corso was more or less living with Allen, supported by Allen's forty-five-dollar-a-week salary, an echo of the Ginsberg-Huncke situation. Early photographs show Corso looking a lot like the young Frank Sinatra, with classic Italian features, and Allen enjoyed having an attractive 'soulful' poet around. All this would change when Burroughs came to stay.

A year had passed since Joan's death, but sentence had still not been pronounced. Then in November 1952, Bill's lawyer was involved in a car crash. A seventeen-year-old driver sideswiped Jurado's Cadillac, damaging one of its fins. During the ensuing argument, Jurado shot the boy in the leg. Tetanus developed, and the boy died in hospital. Jurado left immediately for Brazil, after first advising Bill to do the same.

Jurado's partners began demanding money to keep Bill out on bail, so although it meant forfeiting his bail bond, Bill took Jurado's advice and skipped the country. He visited his family, then spent most of the spring and summer travelling in Ecuador, Columbia and Peru in search of the legendary hallucinogenic drug yage.

Bill arrived in New York in the middle of August, intending to stay for one month en route to Tangier. He and Allen had not seen each other for six years, not since Allen and Neal visited him in New Waverly, Texas; but they had been in continuous correspondence, particularly over the publication of *Junkie*. Allen found Bill changed. He told Neal, 'He is really exciting to talk to, more so for me than ever. His new loquaciousness is something I never had the advantage of. I'm older now and the emotional relationship and conflict of will and mutual digging are very intense, continuous, exhausting and fertile . . . One of the deepest people I ever saw.' Bill decided that he was in love with Allen, and would give Gregory blood-curdling looks as he slowly and methodically used his machete to chop up the two suitcases of dried yage he had brought back from Peru. Gregory prudently decided to spend his time elsewhere.

Bill and Allen worked hard on the manuscript of *The Yage Letters*, which was typed for them by Alene Lee, a friend of Allen's who went on to have an intense relationship with Kerouac, the subject of his book *The Subterraneans*, where she is called Mardou. Allen got home from work at 4.45 p.m., and he and Bill would talk and work continuously from then until 1 a.m. or later. Allen was not getting enough sleep and couldn't concentrate on his job. 'I'm all hung on a great psychic marriage with him,' Allen told Neal. Thirty years later, Ginsberg recalled the time: 'Burroughs fell in love with me and we slept together and I saw a soft center where he felt isolated, alone in the world and he needed . . . a feeling of affection, and since I did love him and did have that respect and affection, he responded. I kinda felt privileged.'

Many of the ideas that appeared later in Burroughs's *Naked Lunch* had their genesis in this period. The futuristic vibrating city of Interzone, with its levels connected by a web of catwalks, was inspired by the fire-escapes and washing-lines in Allen's backyard. Another, more sinister, idea to emerge that fall was 'schlupping', Burroughs's proposition that he and Allen should become soul-mates and somehow merge into one entity. Bill kept making up weird routines about parasitic symbiosis, like Bradley the Buyer in *Naked Lunch* who 'schlupps up' the District Supervisor in some unspeakable manner. Bill was hoping to amuse and please Allen, but in fact he was sending chills down Allen's spine.

It seemed that Bill was serious. He wanted an ultimate telepathic union of souls. Ginsberg explained, 'Schlupp for him, was originally a very tender emotional direction, a desire to merge with a lover, and as such, pretty vulnerable, tenderhearted and open on Burroughs' part.' Allen's uneasiness grew. Part of the reason was sexual. They slept together a lot, and Allen did everything he could to please Bill, even though he preferred younger men. 'But I thought he was my teacher, so I'd do what I could to amuse him,' Ginsberg said. 'In bed, Bill is like an English governess, whinnying and giggling, almost hysteric . . . He liked best to come while being screwed.'

Allen tried hard not to reject Bill or withdraw from him emotionally, but the intensity of the affair frightened him. At one point they were discussing future plans, and Bill told Allen that he wanted him to come to Tangier with him. The idea of the situation continuing indefinitely so shocked Allen that he blurted out, 'But I don't want your ugly old cock.' Years later Ginsberg recalled, 'It wounded him terribly because it was like complete physical rejection in a way I didn't mean. Like a heart blow that severed the trust, because I'd freaked out for that moment, and regretted it ever since.'

In December 1953, Bill left New York by boat for Europe and Tangier. Allen prepared to go in the opposite direction. In November, when things had been at their most intense with Bill, Allen had arranged to visit Neal and Carolyn in California. His plan was to send a trunk of books and papers on ahead and hitch-hike there via Mexico. Allen began to close down the apartment. He borrowed money from Eugene and various friends, and the *World-Telegram* owed him back wages. There was a security deposit on the apartment and he was able to sell the refrigerator for thirty-five dollars. The biggest problem was trying to get rid of the ungainly home-made Reichian orgone accumulator that Bill had built in the bedroom.

Allen decided to go first to the Yucatán and see the ancient Mayan ruins, before travelling on to Los Angeles by bus. He told Neal, 'This is a rare and marvellous trip I need to feed (and free) my soul from ten years of NYC which I can afford to make – and as you must agree, should make, so when I see you I'll be able to talk for hours, not only about NYC intellectual beauties, but also manly savage solitude of jungles we've never seen – will add to our store of souls.'

Allen hitch-hiked to Florida and spent Christmas with Bill's family who had moved to Palm Beach, then flew from Key West

to Havana, his first plane ride. Havana was a big disappointment.
Instead of the wild sex orgies he had heard about, he found only a
shabby city run by gangsters. He reached Mexico in time for the New
Year celebrations. Before he left New York, Allen had been to the
Museum of Natural History, where he was given the name of Alberto
Ruz, the head of archaeology at Villa Hermoa Museum. As a result, he
was given a pass to stay, free of charge, in the archaeological camps in
that part of Mexico. At Chichén Itzá, he slept in a large square concrete
room with a dusty floor, right next to the late-eleventh-century pyramid
known as El Castillo. On his first night there, high on paracodene, he
climbed the ninety-one steps to the top of the great pyramid, spread out
his hammock in front of the main entrance to the summit chamber and
lay for an hour in the tropical night. Bats flew around the ruin, and the
forest seemed to close in on him. A creak in the stone rooms below,
which encased an earlier Toltec-Maya castillo, startled him. After an
hour, he saw Naomi, young and dark-haired, seated at the piano at a
party, close up, facing him, svelte and enjoying life.

So spent a night
   with drug and hammock
at Chichén Itzá on the Castle . . .

Before supper he would go to the tourist hotel, the Mayaland,
for a drink, but at night he was the only living person in the dead
city. A single clap of his hands in the Court of the Thousand
Columns would echo back from a half-dozen structures before the
sound was absorbed into the forest, filled with night birds and
chirruping insects. He would light his old Coleman lantern and
wander through the great stone portals of the Temple of the
Warriors, and examine the wall of the skull-rack platform in the
moonlight. He sat before a deathshead and wondered about the
unknown artisan who carved it, seven centuries before.

On 12 January 1954, he set off for the ruined city of Uxmal.
Uxmal was the crowning achievement of the Mayan builders, a
huge complex of large quadrangles with a palace on each side.
There were a number of pyramids and ancillary buildings, all
covered with low reliefs and sculptures, the enormous structures
connected by vast plazas; and when Ginsberg was there, just after
the excavations and restorations of Alberto Ruz of 1951–52, the
cleared area extended for more than a mile.

The main ruins were surrounded by unexcavated mounds in the jungle, which could be reached by winding mule paths. Dressed in army pants, walking shoes and a sunhat, Allen strolled along the criss-crossing paths, watching the ants on the cracked dried-mud surface, inspecting the huge orange fungi and the fan-shaped banana plants. He was surrounded by the constant twitter of birds in the tall trees, and the paths would pass overgrown, unexcavated houses and walls of the ancient city. The paths were littered with potsherds, and periodically he would come upon a pile of carved stone pediments, stellae and serpent heads gathered from the jungle.

When the light faded and the chorus of chattering insects and bat-squeaks began, he would go to the Bar and Restaurant to eat his evening meal and listen to the manager complain about his life. At night, alone in the moonlit ruins in his archaeologists' hut, he often felt lonely. 'Worrying about my fate again,' he wrote. 'That a small breeze of nostalgia fluttered in my heart, thinking a moment past I had someone in the room I loved with me – no ghosts – a man of flesh to talk to and hug.'

Allen arrived in the state of Chiapas in a bad temper. He had had a persistent head cold for several weeks and a touch of dysentery, and had run out of water on an expedition through thorn bushes and mud trying to get to a particular jungle view. He was already low on money and his faulty command of the language meant that he often lost his temper with the bewildered Indians when he tried to buy something.

At the Palenque ruins, Allen stayed as usual in the archaeologists' hut. Palenque lay on a small tributary of the Usumacita called the Otolum. The ceremonial buildings were all built on high ground at the foot of the hills that rose to become the Sierre Madre. It is a very old site. Palenque was at its height between the sixth and eighth centuries AD, before being abandoned to the macaws and monkeys.

The small area which had been cleared when Ginsberg visited was dominated by the palace, with its three-story astronomical observation tower, and by the Temple of Inscriptions where only two years before, in June 1952, Alberto Ruz discovered an underground crypt containing a giant carved sarcophagus and the remains of a priest-king wearing a jade death mask. In his thirteen-hundred-year-old tomb were the Mayan inscriptions that led eventually to the decipherment of Mayan glyphs. Most of the buildings and pyramids were still overgrown with thick jungle cover, and the forest was loud with the buzz of *chicharras grandes*, locusts and crickets; the distant roar of jaguars could be heard in the deep forest. Allen's visit to Chiapas was transformed by a chance meeting in the Palenque ruins with the 'White Goddess'.

Her name was Karena Shields. She was about fifty years old, and had been brought up in Palenque. She learned about the Maya from the Karivis Indians, their direct descendants, and had studied their metaphysics, symbolism and history. The ruins of Palenque stood on her land, but she had discovered lost cities and explored sites all over Chiapas and neighboring Guatemala. She had written various scholarly papers and a popular book, *Three in the Jungle*. Shields had been educated in the United States and had played Jane in early Tarzan movies. She lived on a cocoa *finca* (plantation), which she ran, single-handed, deep in the forest. She was just the sort of person Allen needed to meet in order to see the real Mexico and when she invited him to visit her cocoa *finca*, he readily accepted.

In Palenque, Allen had a series of vivid and melancholy dreams in which he embarked for the 'ancient parapets of Europe'. He dreamed of closing down his apartment and making arrangements with his family. He heard the fog horns sounding in the mist of NY harbour and dreamed of ships' captains, bunks and cabin lights. After a particularly powerful dream of being with Burroughs in an Italian train, Allen decided that he must, as soon as possible, go and live for a time in Europe. The Mayan ruins had evoked a desire to see the antiquities of his own culture.

> Yet these ruins so much
>   woke me to nostalgia
> for the classic stations
>   of the Earth,
> the ancient continent
>   I have not seen . . .

On 19 January 1954, Allen, Shields and three others set out on the seven-hour journey to the *finca*. They took a Jeep as far as the jungle track, then continued on horseback. This was a new experience for Allen, but he acquitted himself satisfactorily.

Karena Shields had lived at the Finca Tacalapan de San Leandro since she was three years old, when her parents moved from Ohio to manage a rubber plantation in Chiapas. There was a large, open-sided shelter with a thatched roof, and a fire burned constantly at one end for coffee and the tortillas and frijoles they ate at every meal. They slept in hammocks slung across the room. Behind the house were six native huts for the families who worked the plantation. In front was Mount Don Juan, densely covered by trees that obscured Mayan ruins. Legend had it that craftsmen came back to a large tree on the summit, to complete work left unfinished at their death. The area was called Xibalba (pronounced Chivalva), and the Mayans believed it to be a region of limbo or purgatory.

Allen went fishing by flashlight at night with the Indians, carrying a long pronged stick to spear crawfish as big as lobsters. He rode horses and took long walks through the jungle, often wading up the rocky riverbed of the San Leandro River in the midday sun, wearing just his shoes and surrounded by giant mahogany trees filled with monkeys. He could choose to wade ankle deep or, if he got hot, walk neck deep on the sandy bottom. There were clear rockpools surrounded by great ferns, ideal for swimming, and further upstream, he discovered a deep canyon with rapids and waterfalls. He washed away ten years of New York soot in a tropical paradise.

From logs, Allen built himself a set of drums ranging in size from three to seventeen feet, suspending them by vines from a wooden stand. He tapped a rubber tree to get the proper hard black tops for his foot-long drum sticks. He played several times a day, especially at dawn and in the evening in front of the fire. Usually he played with a very soft beat but sometimes, when a file of Indians rode through, he would break into wild rhythms that could be heard for miles. He wrote Lucien Carr, 'People come from miles around to listen to me play my drums. It really goes over big: this because I can actually bong out a variety of interesting African-type rhythms, and because their own native drumming is so awkward and inept . . . that my smooth easy-to-dance-to style is a great wonder.'

Weeks passed. Allen grew a goatee and mustache, which made him look like a German professor. He tried his hand in the banana groves, and worked at most stages of cocoa production. He particularly liked standing in the river with the Indians, each with a woven basket of the beans, swishing them around in the water. On 5 February, there was a meteor so bright that it illuminated the whole sky in brilliant red and blue, and on the same day they felt an earth tremor strong enough to shake the house and make the hammocks swing. A few days later, a rumour reached them that the earthquake was the result of a volcanic eruption at Acavalna, which had killed eight people in the town of Yajalon and toppled its four-hundred-year-old church. The population was said to be fleeing en masse.

After weeks of rumours but no hard facts, Allen decided to investigate. From Salta de Agua, the settlement nearest the *finca*, he hitched a ride to Yajalon with a reckless American pilot who flew a 1914 biplane over the jungle. A two-day trek by mule through the mountains, it was only minutes by plane. In Yajalon the old church still stood. Allen started the journey to the volcano on foot. Halfway there, he met a rancher, who loaned him his mule. Two men from Yajalon caught up with him, wanting to join the expedition, and at each village Allen passed through, his party grew larger. The first night was spent at Zapata, a small coffee-producing village.

At dusk, Allen heard what sounded like a colossal subway train passing beneath him. The ground shuddered. The village dogs began to bark. He was told by the villagers that they felt twenty such tremors a day; sometimes they were stronger. A hollow drum summoned everyone to the little thatched church at seven-thirty. The women sat in a circle on the floor and the men on logs against the walls. Each women held a long wax taper, the only illumination in the room. The prayers were in Tzeltal, the native language, and the responses in Latin. After a silence, the boy next to Allen produced a bamboo flute from inside his shirt, another produced a small drum, and they began to play. A half-hour later, they were joined by two guitarists. Suddenly, the mountain roar began again, this time much louder. As the room began to shake, the women shrieked and ran for the door. Lumps of adobe began to crack from the walls, plaster fell from the beams, the roof creaked ominously. The whole mountain seemed to shake, and the roar became deafening. Pieces of adobe the size of tortillas were falling all around, grazing Allen's shoulders. Just as it seemed as if the church must surely topple, it was suddenly quiet. Allen stood trembling, regretting the stupid arrogance that had brought him to this dreadful mountain. He began to have second thoughts about the expedition he was to lead the next day.

When they set off the next morning, Allen's expedition numbered fifty-four. They climbed steadily. Everywhere was evidence of the tremors, and the path was strewn with rocks and rubble. At the summit, they found no sign of volcanic activity. The whole mountain, in fact, looked like a gigantic pile of ancient volcanic rocks rather than a dormant volcano. They looked out over the surrounding mountain ranges. A thin layer of smoke haze hung in the valleys, as all over the countryside Indians were burning the *milpa*. The Indians pointed out the various villages below, and they watched a coffee company's plane enter the other end of the huge valley. Suddenly Allen heard the crackle and roar of flames. The Indians had set fire to a large dead tree and were jumping about in front of it, warming their hands in the cold mountain air. The fire caused clouds of smoke to billow from the top of Acavalna. The Indians were much amused. They knew that as soon as the people in the village below saw the smoke, they would abandon their village. Satisfied that Acavalna was still extinct, the expedition set off for Zapata.

They got back in the late afternoon, and Allen prepared a report to be sent to all the nearby towns and villages to calm people's fears. They made a copy for the Instituto Geologica and for the government. Allen spent the night at a *finca* half-way down the mountain. The next morning, he rose early and went to the gate to look at the view of the Hunacmec valley. There at the gate he found about forty Indians from the town of La Ventana. They had trekked to the *finca* at dawn and waited patiently for him to finish breakfast. The Indians wanted him to come with them to the east side of the mountain, where there was a huge cave. Two of the men had been there many years before, and they wanted to know if the earthquake had destroyed it.

The new expedition set off at eight-thirty, with twenty men going on ahead of Allen to open up an old path through the *milpa* with their machetes. Eventually the men at the front began yelling that they had found something. When Allen reached the head of the column, he found all the men lined up on rocks in front of a drop. Above them towered the huge arched entrance to an immense cavern.

Allen reported to Neal, 'When I came out in the clearing, I saw a hole in the side of the mountain as big as St Patrick's Cathedral, entrance to the great legendary cave – first stranger other than Indians ever there – solving riddle of the name of the mountain – House of Night – dark cave. Indians have great poetic imagination for names – a mountain anciently named house of night & forgotten why except for one or two who nobody believes centuries later.'

The morning sunlight illuminated the great cathedral space. The floor near the entrance was carpeted with moss. Part of the roof edge had collapsed in the earthquake, bringing with it boulders and trees which now littered the floor, their leaves still green. They all stood in awe for a while, then Allen, feeling obliged to take the lead, climbed down ten feet or so of rock and went in first. 'I had to do something brave to justify the honour,' he told Neal. Most of the Indians followed him. To their left was a great hole, its upper levels hung with stalactites. They could hear the steady drip of calcareous water.

Some of the stalactites were connected to stalagmites to form columns. There was rubble everywhere, caused by the tremors. They heard a distant rumble and felt a movement deep in the mountain, but nothing fell from the ceiling. Afraid to venture too far within, they spent an hour climbing among the stalagmites nearest the entrance. Allen collected some fragments and they left. As they filed into the intense green light of the jungle, they heard the rumble of rocks falling deep in the cavern, though they neither heard nor felt a tremor.

On his return to Yajalon, he wrote Kerouac, 'It was a real great *Life* magazine intrepid American adventurer situation, I really was a great hero and nobody knew except in Yajalon where I lived in the Presidente's house and strode the streets in my beard and all the Indians saluted me respectfully and asked me for volcano advice (they were all terrified) and all the merchants invited me in back of their shops for coffee and the priest and I had many long afternoons over beer and theology and geology and I ate in the restaurant every evening and dined with the pilots of the crazy air service, heroes of these mountains, (my friend who piloted me around was killed two weeks later with four passengers in the mist) and my restaurant bills went to City Hall, and everybody in town loaned me mules and guides for further exploration, other caves came to me, I went to Petalcingo, Chillon, all the little villages and towns in central Chiapas.' He sent to Salta de Agua for his camera, and together with some officials from Yajalon, he returned to the cave to take photographs and explore some more.

Down to his last ten pesos, Allen decided not to wait until his welcome grew thin, and returned to Karena Shields's *finca*. In response to the information provided by Allen, a team arrived from the Instituto Geologica with generators and equipment to measure the cave, which turned out to be one of the largest in the western hemisphere. Allen and the Indians who had accompanied him became local heroes, and their picture went on sale all over central Chiapas.

Allen had been writing regularly to his family and friends, but unknown to him, the Mexican postal service had lost all but a few of his letters. Bill Burroughs in Tangier wrote to Jack: 'Allen's neglect will drive me to some extravagance of behaviour. I don't know what I will do, but it will be the terror of the earth. You must remonstrate with him. I didn't expect him to act like this (not a line in four months) and I didn't expect I would feel so deeply hurt if he did.' He asked Jack to write to Allen and tell him of the pain he was causing.

In the last letter to reach Bill from Mexico, Allen had told him to write him care of American Express in Mexico City. This Bill had done, but his letter was returned unclaimed. 'I don't mind he doesn't write if he wants to feel completely free for a while,' Bill told Jack, 'but he could have spared me all this hurt – (which I am not playing up, which is worse than I describe in my letters to him) – by simply dropping me a line (as he apparently did to you) saying he would be out of touch for a while . . . P.S. No matter what Allen says I want to hear it understand? If he says something that you know would hurt me, please don't keep it from me. I want to know. Nothing is worse than waiting like this day after day for a letter that doesn't come . . . THIS IS SERIOUS JACK, DON'T let me down.'

Unaware of the great drama unfolding in Burroughs's mind, Allen remained at Karen Shields's *finca*. He spent most of April and the beginning of May, working on an eight-page poem, 'Siesta In Xbalba' (misspelling 'Xibalba'). He told Neal, 'I seem to be back on ball, art *developing* and real serious. All old forms of "Empty Mirror" poems now falled together and synthesised in such a manner that the casual fragments of thought utilised for short poems before are now linked together in a natural train of thought or images, very much paralleling the development of an intense meditation lying in a hammock just thinking along . . .' He told Neal that he wanted to make something sublime out of his visit to Chiapas, and described the central passage of the poem as a 'meditation on a carving of a skull I saw in Chichén Itzá months ago.'

> In front of me a deathshead
> half a thousand years old . . .

Allen could not continue his journey until money arrived; Karena Shields was also broke, waiting for her book royalties. Storms washed out the track from the *finca* to Salto de Agua and made the rivers impassable. When they were finally able to make the trip, Karena found the Mexican postal authorities had returned her royalty check to Harcourt, Brace the day before she and Allen reached the town. They spent most of the time lying in their hotel rooms with nothing to do but wait. Eventually twenty dollars arrived from Eugene, and Allen was able to repay Karena and pay his hotel bill, but this left him almost completely broke again. He had to wait for Karena's royalty check so that he could borrow enough to get to Mexico City, where money from Neal and, he hoped, his back wages from the *World-Telegram* were waiting.

Bill Burroughs, meanwhile, had become sick with worry. Allen had written Neal on 6 April, urgently requesting money, which Neal had sent at once. The reply came from Salto de Agua that the funds were 'unclaimed'. Burroughs asked his parents to cable Allen thirty dollars from his next month's allowance, which they did, but the money disappeared en route. Bill deluged Jack with letters to forward to Allen. He wrote to Louis Ginsberg, suggesting that he should make inquiries at the US embassy in Mexico City, and asked Lucien to contact the Mexican branch of U.P.I. Bill told Jack, 'I am afraid he may be in serious trouble, perhaps held incommunicado in jail. To stupid people he *looks* like a communist . . .' He concluded, 'I don't know what I would do if anything happened to Allen. I guess you have seen the letters I wrote to him and have some idea of how much he means to me.'

Neal was also getting concerned; three letters in a row had been returned. Allen, of course, was happily writing letters to his family,

Bill, Neal, Lucien and Jack, but they were all lost. Then a letter from Yajalon, telling Bill about the volcano expedition, finally got through to Tangiers and calmed him down.

The intensity of Bill's feelings began to worry Allen, and he wrote Neal, 'He sure is lonely or imagines himself such and I guess it drives him off the road at times ... This kind of need, with which I cannot but sympathise and try to do something real about ... will be a real problem. But of our friendship, so complicated now and in some ways difficult ... I hardly know what to do to straighten out and think probably the loco elements too deep to resolve and so must be put up with – too ingrained with the genius. My confidence to Bill always – though was relieved leaving New York to have his intensity off my back for a period. However a creative intensity which catalysed me to where I am now – much better off.'

Karena Shields' check finally arrived, and Allen was able to set out for California, having built up high hopes of renewing his love affair with Neal.

He found Neal, Carolyn and the children living in San Jose in a nine-room wood-frame house with a large porch, its yard filled with every variety of fruit tree. In the front was a gigantic palm. Roses thrived in the constant sunshine, as did the pot plants in the adjacent vacant lot. The mountains of the Diablo Range loomed to the east. Allen's room had French windows and an oversize desk. Neal provided him with a typewriter, a clock radio and even put his Ekotape tape recorder at his disposal. Allen unpacked the box of books and papers he had shipped from New York and made himself comfortable.

The balmy climate of that part of California had over the years attracted a considerable number of eccentrics, followers of fringe religions and cranks, and the ground was thick with phrenologists, Theosophists, Rosicrucians, Reichians, flying-saucer spotters, flat earthers, Kirlian photographers, Vedantists, vegetarians, vegans and nudists. It had also been a centre for the late psychic theurgist Edgar Cayce. Both Neal and Carolyn had become followers of his philosophy. Cayce would go into a trance state and prescribe medications and treatments for the sick. He knew nothing about medicine and his cures were usually herbal or homeopathic. A believer in the lost kingdom of Atlantis, Cayce was also a traveller on the astral plane. He made predictions and gave 'life readings', going into a trance and revealing his followers' previous incarnations.

Neal, now working as a brakeman on the Southern Pacific Railroad, took all this very seriously. Since Allen had last seen him he had grown cold and emotionless. His passion for life had soured and become a series of obsessions: for driving, sex, marijuana, chess and the philosophy of Edgar Cayce. His driving was faster and more frantic. Whereas he used to take pleasure at being at the wheel, now he was filled with hatred for everyone else on the road. He and Carolyn were having personal problems and were no longer having sex. Carolyn later said, 'Neal never enjoyed it unless there was violence. He couldn't manage it any other way. The only times he was ever not able to do it was when I was offering or willing. It had to be rape. Until finally I only submitted because I was afraid of him. At last, then, I said, "I can't stand it anymore, kill me or whatever," and much to my surprise he was very nice about it, he seemed to understand.'

Kerouac had stayed with Neal and Carolyn earlier in the year, expecting to meet up with Allen, but when Allen was delayed at the *finca* Jack had returned home to his mother. Jack had also found Neal to be very cold and had been irritated by his blind allegiance to Cayce. Unable to understand how Neal, his All-American hero, could fall for something so anodyne, Jack began to look up the original Oriental texts that the Cayce people drew on, in order to undermine Neal's credulity. In particular, Jack studied Dwight Goddard's *Buddhist Bible*, an anthology of most of the standard Buddhist texts, including the *Diamond Sutra*. He and Neal argued furiously, Cayce versus the Buddha, and in the process, Jack became a Buddhist. He submerged himself in the Buddhist texts and wrote a dreamy letter to Allen in Mexico professing his love and asking to hear about his Mayan discoveries and poems, but he warned Allen not to expect him 'to get excited by anything anymore'.

When Allen arrived, he was soon given the word on Cayce, and though skeptical, he read Cayce's *Extracts from Readings* and Gina Cerminara's *Cayce System Book*. He concluded that Cayce was a 'crackpot', which didn't help his relationship with Neal. No matter what subject they discussed, Neal seemed to have memorised Cayce's views, and once those were announced, no further discussion was possible. Allen reluctantly concluded in a letter to Jack that Neal 'really is suffering some incipient insanity'. The emotional closeness Allen had been hoping for, the main reason for his trip, was lacking. Allen put this to Neal and he agreed. 'I have no feelings, never had,' he said. It was a far cry from Allen's idealised dream fantasy of the situation, set down in his, 'Love Poem On A Theme By Whitman', which opened with Whitman's line, 'I'll go into the bedroom silently and lie down between the bridegroom and the bride,/ those bodies fallen from heaven stretched out waiting naked and restless . . .'

Allen's occasional sex with Neal was aggressive, harsh and frantic, and his enormous desire for Neal was frustrated night after night by Neal's indifference. His journal records the unhappy catalogue of his frustration: how he arranged the shades, turned down the lights and waited for Neal to finish seven games of chess with his neighbour. But then, instead of joining him, Neal suddenly retired to his own bed without a word. 'Once again, I've manoeuvred myself into a frustrating idealistic situation where I'm reduced to pathetic beggary,' he recorded.

The Cayce people had told Neal to stop writing; 'I was writing about sex, you dig, it's sinful, I know . . .' he told Allen, and Carolyn agreed: 'What good is that sort of thing? You call that art? It's just dirt!' Allen lamented the pages and pages of Neal's manuscripts that had been thrown in the trash. Neal hardly talked to Allen, except in a disassociated way. Allen thought that Neal probably hated Carolyn, but felt trapped by the children and, in any case, had nowhere else to go. Earlier in the year, Kerouac had been horrified when Neal had knocked his daughter Cathy clear across the room. When Allen tried to talk to him about it, Neal just said that there was 'No way out for me', and he drove even faster, played chess with even more maniacal intensity or just went blank. Allen wrote Kerouac, 'Everything seems impossible as far as any real contact – he really gets no kicks from me.'

Carolyn, meanwhile, had withdrawn protectively into herself and was grimly devoting herself to her three children and trying to save her marriage. She had asked the Cayce people for advice on how to live with Neal, and Hugh Lynn Cayce told her, 'All you have to do is keep your mouth shut.' Allen completely misunderstood her plight, and complained to Jack, 'She doesn't dig new things (statues or paintings when pointed out) – I mean she has no active curiosity or aesthetic or kicks interests and lives by this ruinous single-track idea of running the family according to her ideas strictly, ideas which are mad copies of House Beautiful and are really nowhere.'

Allen thought that Neal had been unfair to invite him to come out and then reject him, 'making things unclear, leaving me hung up when he knows my habit so well.' The situation brought out the masochistic side of Allen's character, and he began to record sex fantasies in his journals, 'I want to be your slave, suck your ass, suck your cock, you fuck me, you master me, you humiliate me – humiliate me, I want to be tied and whipped, spanked on the behind over knees, want to be made to cry and beg and weep for love.'

But Neal simply said, 'Do what you want.' The situation was frustrating and painful. Unfortunately, Allen was trapped by poverty. Neal was paying for his upkeep. Allen wrote, 'I feel like a strange idiot, standing there among wife and children all to whom he gives needs of affection and attention, aching for some special side extra sacrifice of attention to me – as if like some nowhere evil beast intruding I were competing for his care with his children and wife and job.'

Early one morning in August, Allen was in his room reading as Neal prepared to go to work. Somehow Allen enticed him into his room. Carolyn burst in and caught Allen giving him a blow-job. She screamed in horror and revulsion, then recovered herself enough to order Allen from the house. Neal went blank and ran off to work, leaving Allen and Carolyn to work it out.

'You've always been in my way since Denver,' Carolyn accused him. 'You're trying to come between us.' Allen went cold with horror and felt 'steeped in evil'. The same tired despair and hopeless futility he had felt when, as a teenager, he had taken Naomi to Lakewood returned now as Carolyn raged at him. Allen did not sympathise with her plight, nor did he see himself as in any way responsible for, or contributing to, the shaky state of their marriage. He was focussed on Neal, and on his own desire.

Allen said nothing in reply to her accusations, just 'went blank with a kind of hopeless feeling she was mad . . . I didn't come to screw her up.' But Carolyn was adamant. She forbade Allen to ever see Neal again. She drove him to Berkeley and lent him twenty dollars. The ride was tense, but she asked Allen to try to understand and forgive her. He wrote Jack, 'I know what I was doing with Neal sounds on the surface like a monstrous thing, as Carolyn, with some justice, suddenly exploded out with, but that is not the cause of their woes.'

Bill Burroughs, for one, was not surprised at this turn of events. He wrote to Kerouac, '[Allen] wrote me about he had been throwed out of the Cassady house. Hardly surprising. You know how women are. Come on broadminded and understanding . . . Well I guess Caroline [sic] has what she wants now. What every U.S. bitch of them wants. A man all to herself with no pernicious friends hanging about.'

After Allen's departure, Carolyn and Neal finally had some serious talks and decided that they both should take the Rorschach inkblot test, a personality and intelligence test, very popular at that time, used in determining levels of clinical insanity. Neal's test showed that he was sexually sadistic; that he was pre-psychotic; that he had a 'delusive thought system'; and that he was intensely anxiety-prone. Allen, who had previously not believed in the idea of 'clinical insanity' now began to think there might be something in it, certainly as far as Neal was concerned.

In San Francisco, Allen looked up Al Sublette, who had received him with great civility when Allen visited a few months earlier. Sublette, a friend of Kerouac's, was a black seaman with an ear for good jazz and an eye for women; he lived at the Hotel Marconi on Broadway. Allen checked in, and that night he met a girl in Vesuvio's bar and fell in love.

Her name was Sheila Williams Boucher, and he described her excitedly to Kerouac: 'A *great* new girl who digs me, I dig – 22, young, *hip* (ex-singer, big buddy of Brubeck, knows all the colored cats, ex-hipster girl) *pretty* in a real chic classy way, . . . she has a wild mind, finer than *any* girl I met – really, a real treasure – and such a lovely face – so *fine* a pretty face – young life in her – and real sharp . . .' He continued to extol her virtues, particularly the fact that she wasn't crazy, 'What a doll. *And* she's not a flip thank God. Not a stupid square in any way but *not* a flip, . . . instant digging each other – how wild and great.'

Sheila was small, with short blonde hair, and when Allen met her she was not yet divorced from her husband. She had a job writing advertising copy for the May Company on Market Street, and tried to get Allen a job there. For the first week they did nothing but talk and neck, spending most of their time wandering around the streets of San Francisco in the warm evening air or sitting drinking coffee in her apartment on Nob Hill. She liked Al Sublette and was quite familiar with marijuana from her days as a singer in roadhouses. Allen was especially pleased at her appreciation of particular lines in his poetry, rather than just expressing approval of the poems in general. The only drawback was that she had been married at eighteen and had a four-year-old son, Michael, living with her. Allen was now prepared to be paternal.

Neal, meanwhile, either out of guilt or sheer perversity, suddenly wanted sex with Allen. Whenever his railroad job brought him to San Francisco he would stay with Allen. 'I had a torrid romance then with Neal while I was at the Marconi, some really wild sex scenes,' Ginsberg remembered later. On one occasion Allen and Neal went to bed with Sheila. They both made love to her, and while she slept, Allen and Neal crept out of the room, 'went into the bathroom and started screwing. That was probably the dirtiest we ever got.'

Allen found himself a job with the market research firm of Towne-Oller. His hair was close-cropped, he was clean shaven and wore a good tweed suit. He seemed to enjoy his transformation, as described in an unpublished poem, 'In Vesuvio's Waiting For Sheila', which opens: 'Here at last a moment/ in foreign Frisco./ Where I am thoroughly/ beautiful/ Dark suit – dark eyes/ no glasses,/ Money in my wallet –/ Checkbook abreast –/ Toward an evening/ of fucking and jazz . . .'

Shortly after Allen's arrival in California, Neal had driven him into San Francisco, where he visited Kenneth Rexroth, who, at forty-eight, was already the doyen of the Bay Area literary scene. He held weekly seminars at his house, in which political, religious and literary subjects were discussed. Rexroth was an old-time anarcho-pacifist, with an interest in Oriental mysticism. He translated from the Greek and Latin, Chinese and Japanese in addition to writing his own open form poetry. Allen came armed with a letter of introduction from William Carlos Williams and had with him the manuscript of _Empty Mirror_. He had also corresponded with Rexroth in 1952, at Williams' suggestion, so Rexroth knew who he was. Rexroth had a reputation for being prickly, but Allen found him very easy to get along with. Now that he was living in San Francisco, Allen naturally renewed the acquaintance and began attending Rexroth's literary salon.

He got to know Robert Duncan, seven years Allen's senior, who, together with poet Jack Spicer, had his own literary circle. Though Allen liked Duncan as a person, he found his poetry too aesthetic and precious. There was always a slight distance between them. Allen began to meet the local North Beach characters. Peter DuPeru, a sensitive, curious and intelligent soul, reminded Allen of Carl Solomon because he had received shock treatment. DuPeru wandered the streets without socks, looking at San Francisco's baroque architecture, which was his great love. 'He has the best mystic mind I've met here,' Allen reported to Kerouac, 'Digs me too.' In the first draft of 'Howl', several lines were devoted to the Peter DuPeru story; 'Who limped over the city hills with half a mustache growing on the sinister side of his lip, looking for an example of baroque architecture carrying *Butler's Analogy*.' He met Hube the Cube, and also Hubert Leslie, who discovered Mort Sahl and scribbled proto-Beat poetry. Allen also met Kenneth Patchen, the author of *The Journal of Albion Moonlight*, who lived a few blocks away on Telegraph Hill. Patchen lent him a rare Black Sun edition of the Dos Passos translation of Blaise Cendrars' *Transsiberian Voyage*, a long poem which later served as one of the models for Ginsberg's travelogue-style works, *The Fall of America* and *Iron Horse*.

It was only a matter of weeks before Allen moved into Sheila's Nob Hill apartment at 759 Pine. Three decades later, Ginsberg recalled that it was a 'deep affair, really fell in love and wanted to fuck and could get hardons. It was the first time I'd had a balanced heterosexual life, to the point where I really wanted to get married and have kids and settle down to a life in advertising.'

Burroughs was horrified: he had been planning to move to San Francisco and live with Allen. He wrote to Kerouac, 'Now Allen is talking about making it with a chick, and I am really upset and worried. If I get out to Frisco and he is making it with a chick I might as well turn round and start back. You know how U.S. chicks are. They want it all. It would be the end of my relationship with Allen. At this point I couldn't stand to be around him all the time with no sex. It would be too much strain on me.'

Burroughs left for the States in September 1954, and Allen grew increasingly worried. 'God knows what will happen,' he wrote Jack. 'The impossibilities of his demands are ultimately inescapable unless I let him carry me off forever to Asia or something to satisfy his conception of his despair and need . . . I do like him and would love to share a place with him here, if it could be done, which it will be – but he is going to be frantic and possessive you know . . . The situation with Sheila will be a madhouse. I don't know how to manage it . . . It's a real bitch, man.'

Allen's visit to Neal was in some ways a flirtation with danger; though he had had high hopes for a renewed emotional relationship, Neal's rejection hurt him most in terms of sexual frustration, and he was able to retain his composure. Dealing with Burroughs's infatuation was an altogether more difficult task. It meant finally rejecting his teacher. It was also a big test of his hard-won independence. His choice was to either surrender himself to Bill, thereby losing his own identity, or reject Bill and continue to build his independent new life. Although it worried him enormously, he knew it was only a matter of time before he had to make the break.

Allen had settled into an approximation of a comfortable middle-class American life. He was earning $250 a month, and lived in an elegant large apartment on Nob Hill with a beautiful woman, a child and a friendly cat. He worked all day at the advertising agency, where he had two secretaries, and in the evenings he and Sheila entertained.

Neal, no longer feeling any emotional pressure from Allen, began to drop by once or twice a week to deliver or borrow pot, sometimes bringing his pusher with him. Often Neal would sit on the floor of the living room with his pot spread out on a newspaper in front of him, chopping and cleaning it, blowing the seeds to one side, while Allen busied himself around the apartment, picking up the child's toys, tidying up and taking out the garbage. One evening Neal settled himself down on the white shag rug, smoked a joint, and began to read aloud from Marcel Proust, just as he used to in New York City back in 1947. 'A quiet sweet nite,' Allen called it in a letter to Kerouac.

But Allen soon began to feel the strain of his middle-class lifestyle. He hadn't written anything since he was in San Jose, because he never had any time alone, and he was very worried by Burroughs's impending arrival. He began to find fault with Sheila, complaining to Kerouac that she was 'younger and more prey to girlish psychological semi-dramatisations (I'm an old man, tired sort of, I can't make the flux of love illusions) and undoubtedly the seeds of dissolution of this affair have already set in, now that we are established.' But later in the same letter, he confided, 'Sheila hates me because I am a stuffy old nag – saying [I'm an] abstractionist and not a Dostoyevskian lover. I screw for the first time regular these days, by the way, what a relief to come home to.' By the middle of October he found time to continue work on 'The Green Automobile' and began to thumb through his full notebooks for other passages that showed promise as raw material for poems.

Truly dreading Bill's arrival on the coast now, fearing an inexorable involvement, Allen told Jack: 'There would be a bust with the cops ultimately, and I'd be coming late to work, and I'd have to sit and listen to him and routines mercilessly applauding and so on . . . I lack solitude here and Bill is a power of solitude – got to give him all attention.' Allen tried to let Bill down gently and kindly, pointing out all the many problems, but Bill simply interpreted this as Allen being coy. Unfortunately, the situation was exacerbated by Kerouac, who, feeling sorry for Bill in his misery, told him a white lie, that Allen secretly wanted to be with him, 'otherwise he wouldn't have talked about it so much.' Eventually Allen screwed up his courage and wrote a severe, stiff letter of rejection which finally brought home the truth of the situation to Bill. Burroughs was absolutely shattered. 'I think I'm responsible for single-handed destroying Bill's belief in love,' Ginsberg said later.

Bill gave up the idea of moving to the Coast, and it was to be another twenty years before he saw California. He went instead to see his parents in Florida, where he received more bad news. The garden centre they operated was not as profitable as before, and they had to halve his allowance to one hundred dollars a month. Since he was broke and owed Jack money, he wasn't even sure that he could make it back to Tangier.

Allen was annoyed with Jack for giving Bill encouragement, and it took several letters to straighten out matters between them. When Allen was staying in San Jose, he and Jack began to exchange letters about Buddhism, and Allen asked Jack to be his teacher. Jack had made a thorough study of the material available in the San Jose public library when he was there but had not made contact with any Buddhist teachers or groups. Nevertheless he was prepared to go along with Allen's request. He sent him a 'correct bibliography' and rather pompously instructed Allen to listen to him, for his beginning studies in Buddhism, 'as tho I was Einstein teaching you relativity or Eliot teaching the formulas of Objective Correlation on a blackboard in Princeton.' Allen did not tell him that he had already read a massive amount of material on Zen Buddhism when he was studying Oriental art in New York City.

Jack's understanding of Buddhism, however, seemed to be basically theistic, since he never gave up his Catholic faith. As Lucien Carr mentioned in a letter to Allen later that year, 'The old kannuck bean peddler; eye think he thinks Buddha is the pope.' In fact Allen apparently was the only one of Jack's friends who took his Buddhism seriously.

Meanwhile, life on Nob Hill continued. Neal spent more time in San Francisco and taught Al Sublette and half of North Beach how to play chess. To Allen's constant irritation, Neal was even more deeply involved with Edgar Cayce and brought him up at every possible moment. His work on the railroad was deteriorating because he was high on pot all the time. The other railroad workers were complaining about him, and he had come up before three separate company investigations. To bring them nearer to San Francisco, Carolyn sold the house in San Jose and moved the family to Los Gatos.

Allen's relationship with Sheila hit serious trouble when he finally revealed to her his long sexual history with Neal. He had decided to begin analysis again, and a factor in his decision to reveal his homosexuality to Sheila may have been so that he could talk to her about everything that came up, just as he had done with his father. Looking back, Ginsberg said, 'We had developed a tremendous trust and I felt that she accepted me for myself and I no longer had to hide anything from her.' But homosexuality was not something spoken about casually in 1954, and for Sheila it seems to have been an unknown, terrifying and revolting thing. 'She threw a big fit and apparently it destroyed our relationship at least for the time being,' Ginsberg said, recalling the situation, years later. 'She didn't want to sleep with me any more, so I went through all sorts of masochistic tortures, with a girl this time for a change, which was a relief, a break in my pattern.'

Ever since Allen arrived from Mexico he had been under stress, first from Neal, then from Carolyn and Bill. On 10 November, he went for his initial one-dollar-an-hour therapeutic session at the Langley Porter Clinic, a division of the University of California at

Berkeley Medical School. Allen's doctor was Philip Hicks, but he was pleased to find another psychiatrist there who was an old friend from Columbia, Steven Schoen. They had long talks, and Allen felt reassured by Schoen's sensitive approach to his problems.

Allen continued to live with Sheila, and though she wanted him to move out, life in many ways continued normally. Allen entered into a very productive correspondence with Bill, who returned to Tangier in December. Bill sent long 'routines', flights of imaginative writing, three or four pages long, with virtually every letter he wrote. These routines were destined to become part of *Naked Lunch*. Allen resumed his role as Bill's agent and took some of the pieces to Kenneth Rexroth, who was a reader for New Directions.

Allen showed him the 'Roosevelt After Inauguration' routine, written the previous May in Lima, in which (among other things) Roosevelt replaces members of the Supreme Court with purple assed baboons. Rexroth grimaced and said, 'I don't think that's funny.' Bill was incredulous at Rexroth's response, 'It's not supposed to be *accurate*. Does he think it has anything to do with Roosevelt?' A series of incidents such as this gradually brought Bill and Allen back together again as old friends doing battle against the philistines.

At the end of November, Al Sublette shipped out to Chile. Allen helped him carry his precious collection of jazz records on board and as they stowed his things, Allen suddenly got a tremendous desire to ship out again himself and make enough money to fulfill his dream of going to Europe.

He continued his extensive correspondence with Kerouac which was for the most part concerned with spiritual matters, though, by the end of the year, Jack had reconsidered his 'Einstein' role in acting as Allen's teacher of Buddhism. He decided that he was too ignorant to be a master and told Allen that they were 'fellow disciples before the Awesome Law'. Their other discussions were usually political. Kerouac had become a great supporter of Senator Joseph McCarthy's crusade against communism and began to rail against old friends like Al Hinkle, whom he labelled a 'commie', criticising Allen for defending him. It has been suggested that Kerouac shifted to the political right sometime in the 1960s, but in fact he had always retained the reactionary political values of his parents.

Allen and Sheila argued constantly about their affair and the reasons why Allen didn't really love her deeply. Perhaps he loved men too much, though he wasn't sure if that was still the case. He did still have an idealised fantasy of a boy lover, but, 'What would I do with a pilgrim soul if I did find a real one here in San Francisco?' he asked her in the middle of one argument.

At the beginning of December Allen was walking alone through the night-time streets after yet another row with Sheila. He wandered aimlessly, a little drunk, and came to Polk Gulch, which was then an artistic bohemian neighborhood. Entering Foster's Cafeteria, he looked for Peter DuPeru who lived nearby, but no one he knew was there.

There was a table of young artist types and Allen went up to the one who had a beard and looked the most interesting. He was a twenty-six-year-old painter named Robert LaVigne. Allen introduced himself, and they talked about art. Allen soon impressed him with stories about Franz Kline, Willem de Kooning and Larry Rivers, whom he knew from New York. LaVigne invited Allen to come back with him and see his paintings. He only lived a few blocks away, in a large apartment on the first floor of a wooden Victorian house on Gough Street.

Allen was at once enthralled by a large oil painting of a naked boy with yellow hair and a frank youthful expression, who looked right out of the canvas at him. He felt his heart leap and asked who the boy was. 'Oh, that's Peter,' said LaVigne. 'He's here. He's home.' And into the room walked Peter Orlovsky, with the same youthful innocent expression on his face, only a little shyer. He was twenty-one years old, a tall, silent, gentle Russian youth.

They invited Allen to return, which he did, about a week later, bringing Neal Cassady with him. Another of LaVigne's paintings was a nude study of an attractive red-haired girl. Neal reacted in the same way that Allen had to the painting of Peter; he fell in love with her. The woman also lived in the apartment, having moved in about three months before. Her name was Natalie Jackson.

LaVigne had an exhibition opening in San Diego, and told Allen that once the show was over, he was intending to leave town to paint. He requested Allen to see as much of Peter as possible because Peter 'needed a sweet companion'. Allen shuddered. He felt doomed. He could already feel his heart melting towards Peter. 'Oh God, not again!' he exclaimed. 'Lord, what are you asking me for?' LaVigne was being very mysterious. He clearly felt that his own season with Peter was terminating, and he wanted Peter to be looked after. It seemed to Allen that LaVigne was behaving like a *shadchen*, an arranger of marriages.

Allen spent a night at Gough Street with Peter. He wrote Jack, 'Real sweetness in my breast, too much, I'd almost cry, but it's such a poor pitiful fleeting human life, what do I want anyway? Nature boy – to be loved in return. So followed a night of embraces, not sex.'

Allen had to leave the city for a few days. His brother Eugene was getting married to Connie Herbert, a minister's daughter. On 14 December 1954, Allen flew to New York, still a major trip in the early 1950s, involving stopovers in Los Angeles and Chicago. The wedding was a big happy family occasion, marred only by Buba's annoyance that Eugene had chosen a girl who wasn't Jewish. She took Eugene aside and pinched him viciously on the arm. Before the wedding, Allen went out to visit Naomi. She was quiet, tearful and she looked very old. She complained about the wires in her head and asked to be taken home. It was the last time Allen saw her.

Back in San Francisco, Allen found that there had been a number of changes during the five days he was away. Neal was living with Natalie in LaVigne's apartment, and had introduced the household to pot. Neal's friend Al Hinkle and Sheila had started sleeping together. This pleased Allen, because when he returned, LaVigne and Peter asked him to come live with them. 'Good, that's what you deserve,' was Sheila's response. 'Get out of here.'

Ginsberg has described his first sexual experience with Peter in some detail: 'I went to Peter's room. We were to sleep together that night on a huge mattress he had on the floor. I took off my clothes and got into bed. I hadn't slept with too many people. Never openly, completely giving and taking. With Jack or Neal, with people who were primarily heterosexual and who didn't fully accept the sexualisation of our tenderness, I felt I was forcing it on them; so I was always timid about them making love back to me, and they very rarely did very much. When they did it was like blessings from heaven. If you get into it there's a funny kind of pleasure/ pain, absolute loss/ hope. When you blow someone like that and they come, it's great! And if they touch you once, it's enough to melt the entire life structure, as well as the heart, the genitals and the earth. And it'll make you cry.

'So ... Peter turned around (he was in his big Japanese robe), opened up the bathrobe – he was naked – and put it around me and pulled me to him; and we got close, belly to belly, face to face. That was so frank, so free and so open that I think it was one of the first times that I felt open with a boy. Then, emboldened, I screwed Peter. He wept afterwards, and I got frightened, not knowing what I'd done to make him cry, but completely moved by the fact that he was so involved as to weep. At the same time, the domineering, sadism part of me was flattered and erotically aroused.

'The reason he wept was that he realised how much he was giving me, and how much I was demanding, asking and taking. I think he wept looking at himself in that position, not knowing how he gotten there; not feeling it was wrong, but wondering at the strangeness of it. The most raw meat of reasons, for weeping. Then Robert hearing, seeing the situation, came in to comfort Peter a little bit. I was very possessive and I pushed Robert away. That got me and Robert into a funny kind of distrust that lasted for a year or two ... Peter was primarily heterosexual, and always was. I guess that was another reason he was shocked – the heaviness of my sadistic possessiveness in screwing him. For the first time in my life I really had the opportunity to screw somebody else!'

Allen wrote the poem 'Malest Cornifici Tuo Catullo' and addressed it to Jack:

I'm happy, Kerouac, your madman Allen's
finally made it: discovered a new young cat,
and my imagination of an eternal boy
walks on the streets of San Francisco,
handsome, and meets me in cafeterias
and loves me ...

Allen liked the Gough Street apartment, with the smell of oil paint from Robert's front room studio. The big messy rooms and the kitchen where everyone met and talked reminded him of 115th Street, New York. Peter's room was in the middle and Natalie's was in the back. Neal was constantly rushing in and out like Oliver Hardy, happy, pulling off his pants as he ran down the corridor to make it with Natalie, giggling. He and Natalie played games together, and sometimes wore each other's clothes while they sat and smoked pot in her room. One day Allen and Neal met at the door and nodded to each other in agreement; they had both 'gained so much tender youth kicks in the last two weeks entering the apartment,' as Allen wrote Jack. 'So sweet and promising . . . tender joy entering the house again for me and Neal feels the same.'

Despite these enormous changes in his personal life, Allen continued his market research with Towne-Oller and his analysis with Doctor Philip Hicks at Langley Porter. He confided all his fears to Hicks: 'You know, I'm very hesitant to get into a deep thing with Peter because where can it ever lead? Maybe I'll grow old and then Peter proabably won't love me – just a transient relationship. Besides, shouldn't I be heterosexual?'

'Why don't you do what you want?' asked Hicks, 'What would you like to do?'

'Well,' said Allen. 'I really would just love to get an apartment on Montgomery Street, stop working and live with Peter and write poems!'

'So why don't you do that?' asked Hicks.

'What happens if I get old or something?'

Hicks laughed, 'Oh, you're a nice person. There're always people who will like you.' Allen was amazed. At last, an authority figure had given him permission to be completely free.

Robert LaVigne had second thoughts about giving up Peter. After a few weeks of emotionally stormy weather, during which Allen and Peter lived in separate hotels, Allen took an apartment at 1010 Montgomery Street. A week later, in mid-February, Peter moved in. Allen proposed that he and Peter take a marriage vow, similar to the one he had persuaded Neal to take at the rainy crossroads in Oklahoma. Sitting in Foster's Cafeteria one morning at 3 a.m., 'We made a vow to each other that he could own me, my mind and everything I knew, and my body, and I could own him, and all he knew, and his body; and that we would give each other ourselves, so that we possessed each other as property, to do everything we wanted to, sexually or intellectually, and in a sense explore each other until we reached the mystical "X" together, emerging two merged souls. We had the understanding that when our (my particularly) erotic desire was ultimately satisfied by being satiated (rather than denied), there would be a lessening of desire, grasp, holding on, craving and attachment; and that ultimately we would both be delivered free in heaven together. And so the vow was that neither of us would go into heaven unless we could get the other one in.'

As with with Cassady, the vow was very much an attempt by Ginsberg to formalise and make permanent their erotic relationship. It was also similar to Burroughs's 'schlupp' proposal. In a long soliloquy in his journal addressed to Peter, Allen wrote, 'So I don't care who else you screw, make it with girls, only to be sure to keep compassion for me, answer call when I break down to need of love moment – initiate my liberation and sexual revelation of self. Far as I know I want to be tied to bed and screwed, whipped, want to wrestle and blow and come in unison, sexual ecstacy . . . In return . . . my role as teacher already well defined but also promise to deliver with two special talents – creative sense & literary craft kicks . . . Which amounts to exchange of souls and bodies . . . So in this, you be master in bed, and I be master in book . . . Peter, I feel as if I'm in heaven. If this works out, I could end notebooks here and go on to impersonal existence. I'm on the verge of a great discovery. And the poems to write . . .'

Peter later said: 'I fell in love with him because he would recite a lot of poetry from memory and I had never heard anything like that before – so I was dazzled.' Though Allen and Peter's relationship was to last a lifetime, it had within it the fatal flaw of Peter's heterosexuality. Over the years, he had a number of long-term relationships with women, creating more than one *ménage à trois* of unusual complexity, which caused a great deal of tension and strain.

Peter's family would add another complexity to the relationship. His father, Oleg, was a cadet in the csar's army in St Petersburg. During the Revolution, he narrowly escaped death while guarding the Winter Palace. He was captured, escaped and eventually made his way to the United States, arriving in New York City in 1921. There he met Katherine Schwarten, a New Yorker, born in Yonkers in 1909, who left home at seventeen and moved to the Lower East Side to become a writer. They were married in 1926, and Peter, born 8 July 1933, was the third of their five children – Nicholas, Julius, Peter, and the twins Lafcadio and Marie – born between 1927 and 1941.

Katherine and Oleg were dogged by ill-fortune. In 1927, a mastoid operation performed by an incompetent doctor left Katherine deaf and with a partially paralysed face. Oleg's business did badly; he ran a silk-screen shop in what is now SoHo, in Manhattan, where his sons were pressed into working long, exhausting hours, but he was put out of business at the end of the war by cheap imports from the Far East. Oleg began drinking and released his disappointment and frustration through violence towards his family. Eventually he and Katherine separated. Katherine took the children and moved to Queens, where Peter went to school. His mother made him drop out when he was seventeen because she said she was too poor to continue feeding him. By this time Peter's elder brother, Julius, had been sent to Central Islip Mental Institute, suffering from catatonic schizophrenia.

Peter took a menial job at a hospital in Queens, washing dishes for seventy-five cents an hour. He worked twelve hours a day, six days a week, then got a better job at a state mental hospital, where he worked a forty-hour week tending senile patients. He changed their sheets, mopped the floors and fed them. He attended night school and finished the requirements for his High School Diploma. The job depressed him and sometimes, while he was on ward duty, he cried at the bleak, hopeless lives of the patients.

In 1953, during the Korean War, he was drafted into the army. Peter had always been quiet and dreamy, and one day at boot camp in West Virginia a lieutenant found him reading a book by Erich Fromm, and demanded to know if he was a communist. 'An army is an army against love,' Peter told him. They sent him to work as a medic in the army hospital in San Francisco for the duration of his military service. He was very lonely and took long, solitary walks around the city on his weekends off. It was during this vulnerable time that he met Robert LaVigne.

LaVigne was very friendly. Peter was still a virgin, though he felt attracted to girls. However, he desperately needed friendship and human contact and allowed himself to be seduced by LaVigne. 'I was very scared. I was trembling all over. He was showing me these big thick art books. I knew something was going on. I don't remember too much after that,' Peter said. 'I was young. I've always liked girls, but I couldn't make it with them yet. I didn't know how to do it. I was a dope, a creep, a hermit, a moron. I was going to spend the rest of my life by myself unless I had a brainstorm. But Bob LaVigne came along and there was a whole new friendship, exciting sexual knowledge facts.'

On Montgomery Street, Allen and Peter each had their own room, separated by a hallway, so they both had privacy. Turkish rugs covered the living-room floor, there was a large fireplace and a soft armchair to read in. Allen bought a three-speed Webcor phonograph from a pawn shop. Peter spent a lot of time brooding. He would go into dark Russian moods, lock himself in his room and weep for days on end, then emerge cheerful and friendly as if nothing had happened. Allen soon learned that it was best not to interfere. Allen happily unpacked all his books, records and papers and arranged them on his big work desk. In addition to his own journals and poetry, he had manuscripts by Kerouac, Burroughs and Cassady with him that he was still trying to place with publishers. He gave Jack's *Visions of Cody* to Kenneth Rexroth, who showed it to Robert Duncan. Allen respected Duncan's high literary standards, so he was delighted when Duncan said it was obviously a work of genius: 'Any man who can write fifty pages of description of reflections within a car bumper is a great genius in the tradition of Gertrude Stein consciousness prose,' Duncan told Allen. Rexroth, on the other hand, was not impressed.

Allen was surprised by the amount of literary activity in the Bay Area. Duncan ran his poetry workshop at San Francisco State College, and at the end of 1954, Ruth Witt-Diamant founded the San Francisco Poetry Center. The inaugural reading was by W.H. Auden; Allen ran into the poet Michael McClure at the reception afterward; they first met at Duncan's class. Neither of them was impressed by the reading, and as they talked, they discovered a mutual interest in William Blake. McClure remembered, 'One of my first memories of Allen was how different his idea of Blake was from mine. How profoundly both of us resonated with the work of Blake, yet how extremely different our views were. It was almost as if there were two Blakes.' For McClure, Blake was the liberator, whereas for Allen, he was a prophet.

Poet Lawrence Ferlinghetti's City Lights Bookstore on Columbus Avenue was an extraordinary mecca for poets. 'One of the original ideas of the store was for it not to be an uptight place, but a centre for the intellectual community,' said Ferlinghetti, 'to be non-affiliated, not tied up with, not belonging to any official organisation.' The store was an immediate success, and they literally had a hard time closing their doors. The manager, Shigeyoshi Mureo, kept the store open until midnight during the week and 2 a.m. on weekends. 'We seemed to be responding to a deeply felt need,' Ferlinghetti said. Ferlinghetti began a paperback series called 'The Pocket Poets', beginning with his own *Pictures of the Gone World* which he published in August 1955. Ginsberg became friendly with Ferlinghetti. Their student days at Columbia had overlapped (both studied under Lionel Trilling and Mark Van Doren), though they had never met there. Ferlinghetti got his M.A. in 1947 and went to France; he attended the Sorbonne on the GI Bill until 1951, getting his doctorate. Writing poems and a novel, he lived on the Left Bank, where he met Seldon Kirby Smith. They returned to the States in 1953, married, then moved to San Francisco, becoming part of its artistic community. Ferlinghetti worked as an art critic for *Art Digest* and was the poetry reviewer for the *San Francisco Chronicle*.

Born in March 1919 in Yonkers, New York, in World War II Ferlinghetti served as the commander of a sub-chaser in the North Atlantic. After VE day, he was transferred to the Pacific theatre and arrived in Nagasaki six weeks after the bomb had been dropped. Seeing the ruins reinforced Ferlinghetti's deep-seated hatred of war. 'You'd see hands sticking up out of the mud . . . all kinds of broken teacups . . . hair sticking out of the road – a quagmire – people don't realise how total the destruction was.' His experiences led him to develop his life-long commitment to left-leaning, libertarian, anarchistic political philosophy.

Spring came. Allen and Peter bought a used car and went on weekend excursions to Monterey, Point Lobos, and over the Golden Gate to Mount Tamalpais, Muir Woods and Stinson Beach. There were lots of visitors at Montgomery Street: Neal and Al Hinkle would spend afternoons playing chess by the sunny front room window, and Neal and Natalie sometimes spent whole weekends camped out in Allen's bed. Later that spring, Neal and Carolyn decided to split up. Neal arrived in San Francisco with his typewriter and clothes and took a room in North Beach. He had a telephone installed so that the railroad could contact him if they needed a brakeman, and leaving his typewriter with Peter, told him that he was going to 'do nothing but fuck and play chess'.

Allen still saw a lot of Sheila though their friendship had been severely strained by his declaration of homosexuality. Once she appeared drunk at Montgomery Street and caused a scene, demanding to know why Allen left her. 'You can fuck *me* in the ass if *that's* what you want!' she yelled, 'If that's what it's all about!' and tore down his flimsy fireplace.

Although leading a settled life with Peter and making good money, Allen was persistently reminded of his past insecurities and worries by the letters he received from Naomi. 'The wire is still on my head, and the sunshine is trying to help me. It has a wire department, but the wire that's outside of my head the sun doesn't touch, it is connected with the inside of me,' she wrote from Pilgrim State. She told him she was taking Thorazine and added, 'If I were home I could be out in the sunshine. It doesn't cost anything. When are you getting a regular sweetheart?'

On 1 May, Towne-Oller closed down their San Francisco office. Allen wrote Jack: 'I'm being replaced by a mechanical brain.' In fact, it had been Allen's idea that an IBM computer could do his job more efficiently, and he spent two months correlating the information for transfer to the machine. Allen was delighted and looked forward to six months of thirty-dollar-a-week unemployment money. He could now relax and spend his time writing. He celebrated by spending thirty-five dollars on Bach recordings.

On his twenty-ninth birthday his love life was in one of its pendulum swings, and he was gloomy because Peter was refusing to sleep with him. He wrote Jack, 'I am passing, like all others, out of youth, into the world . . . faced with financial problems that must be solved. How the hell are we going to get the $s to get to Europe, and when that $s gone, what are we going to do? How can we live with no future abuilding? That's what's bothering me.' That night he made love with the girl downstairs and felt a little better.

He was still recording his dreams, and his 'Record Of A Dream-Vision Night 6 June 1955', which was later reworked and published as 'Dream Record', was an early appearance of the famous Ginsberg long line: '– I revisited Mexico City and saw Joan Burroughs sitting at ease in a garden, clear eyes and ironic smile as eternalised in my imagination, her face restored to a beauty tequila and salt had made strange before the bullet in her brow.' He worked hard on the poem, perfecting every line, then sent it to Burroughs who was startled by it. 'About your poem on Joan,' he wrote, 'I think it is completely successful. I experienced a distinct shock at the end, I could see the picture of her talking and smiling so clear and precise like a telepathic image. I knew that I was seeing exactly what you saw.'

Allen also sent a copy to Rexroth who said, 'You went to Columbia University too long. You're too old to be going on with all this formal stuff like that. What's the matter with you?' Allen accepted Rexroth's criticism, but at the same time he knew he was on the right track. The year before, in San Jose, he had written 'In Back Of The Real', which was composed in a mode of variable measure following the later Williams. Williams himself had praised the poem, and Allen thought it was his best so far. In 'Dream Record', Allen used a system of relatively even syllable count, with a squarer line. Working out of William Carlos Williams, he evolved a style in which he would write 'Howl'; a variable system of measures adaptable to long free-verse lines by dividing them into three.

For some time, Peter had been concerned about his younger brother Lafcadio, who was now fifteen. Peter thought that he would be better off with him in San Francisco and decided to take on the responsibility of looking after him. At the end of June, Peter set out, hitch-hiking, for New York to retrieve him. Allen accompanied him as far as Reno, and they spent a few days sight-seeing in the Sierras before Peter continued on to New York.

On 28 July, Allen enrolled at University of California at Berkeley to complete his English M.A., a decision which cheered his father. He knew that he would have to get a job to support himself at college, but the unemployment money was still coming, so he settled down to assemble a collection of his work from the past four years and continue with his reading: the Latin translations he had been studying since 1954 – he was deeply immersed in Catullus – and modern Spanish and French poetry, particularly Lorca and Apollinaire.

One afternoon early in August, he sat at the typewriter in his large front room on Montgomery Street, with the intention of writing whatever came up. He had taken Rexroth's criticism to heart and decided that his poetry was too formal and too tight, so instead of sitting down to write a poem, he tried for something looser, more like prose, which would give him more freedom. 'I thought I wouldn't write a *poem* but just write what I wanted to without fear, let my imagination go, open secrecy, and scribble magic lines from my real mind – sum up my life – something I wouldn't be able to show anybody, writ for my own soul's ear and a few other golden ears.' He began to write about his life, again using William Carlos Williams's triadic verse form, only with the lines extended out to his own long breath length – each line a single breath, like blowing an extended cadenza on a saxophone:

> I saw the best minds of my generation
>   destroyed by madness
>   starving, mystical, naked,
> who dragged themselves thru the angry streets at
>   dawn looking for a negro fix . . .

6 Howl and the San Francisco Renaissance

I began typing, not with the idea of writing a formal poem, but stating my imaginative sympathies, whatever they were worth. As my loves were impractical and my thoughts relatively unworldly, I had nothing to gain, only the pleasure of enjoying on paper those sympathies most intimate to myself and most awkward in the great world of family, formal education, business and current literature.

Allen sat at his desk in the corner of the room by the first floor window overlooking the steep street, a few houses up from where Montgomery meets Broadway. Afternoon sunlight filled the room as he fed more paper into his big black second-hand office typewriter. He wrote using the rhythms of speech from the American street – black speech, phrasings overheard on street corners and in bars – and the rhythms of bebop and jazz, of sports commentators and the cool DJs on the all-night jazz programmes. It had a new rhythm and used new language. It was 'a tragic custard-pie comedy of wild phrasing, meaningless images for the beauty of abstract poetry of mind, running along making awkward combinations [of images] like Charlie Chaplin's walk, long saxophone-line chorus lines I knew Kerouac would hear *sound* of – taking off from his own inspired prose line, really a new poetry.'

He depended on the anaphoric 'who', which opened each line, to keep the beat. It was the base to which he would continually return before taking off on each long flight of the imagination: 'who sat in rooms naked and unshaved listening to the Terror through the wall,/ who burned their money in wastebaskets amid the rubbish of unread Bronx manifestos.' As he piled line upon line, he grew ecstatic: 'continuing to prophesy what I really knew, despite the drear consciousness of the world,' as he later described it. He was writing the tale of the tribe, 'Ten years' animal screams and suicides!', and the characters in his life appeared to take up their positions on the page:

He described Herbert Huncke's first appearance at York Avenue in 1947: 'who wandered all night with their shoes full of blood on the snowbanks of East River looking for the door in the river to open on a roomfull of steamheat and opium, picking his scabs saying who is my friend?' and remembered the story of his friend from the San Remo bar, Tuli Kupferberg, 'who jumped off the Brookyn Bridge and walked away unknown and forgotten into the ghostly daze of Chinatown soup, alleyways & firetrucks.' Overcoat thief Bill Garver, 'who pondered his cherries in Longchamps waiting to kidnap an overcoat on a coathanger, apparition of a week's rent,' appeared alongside Russell Durgin, in whose apartment Allen had his vision of William Blake: 'Who coughed up celluloid balls in Harlem with their lungs full of sixth floors of tubercular sky and orange crates of theology.'

He wrote of Ruth Goldenberg, one of the 'Three Graces' from the San Remo: 'who talked continuously seventy hours from park to pad to bar to Bellevue to Long Island to the Brooklyn Bridge ...', of Peter duPeru; and of course Neal Cassady, who was very much on his mind: 'N.C., secret hero of these poems, cocksman and adonis of Denver ...' But he only made oblique references to his oldest friends, Jack and Bill. They didn't really fit in the poem; they had not been destroyed by madness, and their stories lacked the raw power of Carl's shock treatment, Huncke's despair or even the saga of Louis Simpson, 'who threw their watches out of the window in the ballot of eternity.' To have described his relationship with Jack or Bill would have required a very different poem.

Recalling the stories of the 'best minds' of his generation, he paraphrased incidents from his own life: 'who were expelled from colleges for printing obscene odes in the dust of the sexless windows of men's dormitories and burned alive in bloody flannel suits of innocence amid the cannon blasts bestsellers and shrapnels of leaden verse and nitroglycerine shrieks of fairies and mustard gas of sinister intelligent editors.' He referred to his wait for a ship in Houston after the failure of his season with Neal in Denver: 'who lounged hungry and lonesome thru Houston seeking jazz or soup; & ate candy for six days and followed the brilliant Spaniard to converse about America & Eternity a hopeless task,' and of the part-time cleaning job he had taken to supplement his unemployment money: 'who mopped all night in desolate Bickfords listening to the crack of doom on the hydrogen jukebox.'

He wrote solidly, with copious crossing out, till he had filled seven pages. He quickly found that the theme he kept returning to was the story of Carl Solomon: 'who threw potato salad at Dadaist lecturers at CCNY & subsequently presented themselves on the granite steps of madhouse with shaven heads and harlequin speech of suicide demanding instantaneous lobotomies and who were given instead the concrete void of insulin metrosol electricity hydrotherapy psychotherapy occupational therapy pingpong & amnesia and who in protest only overturned one symbolic pingpong table.'

Recognising that the poem was about Carl, he began a second section, specifically addressed to him:

Carl Solomon! I'm with you in Rockland
    where you're madder than I am
I'm with you in Rockland
    where you must feel very strange . . .

Ginsberg later wrote, 'The rhythmic paradigm for Part III [which this section later became] was conceived and half-written same day as the beginning of 'Howl'. I went back later and filled it out.'

Allen went through the manuscript of the first section, labelling all those lines that belonged together A, B, C or D. Those about Neal were 'A', those about Carl were 'C' and so on. He made a few vital changes to the text, such as 'mystical' to 'hysterical' in the first line, then retyped the lines in their new order, so that the poem now led up to the long climactic passage of Carl in the madhouse. He ended the first section on a positive note by heralding the 'madman bum and angel', as these were most likely to have visionary awareness, and listing practical methods of attaining the widened field of consciousness that he had experienced through the use of art: 'the use of the ellipse the catalog the meter and the vibrating plane', a reference to Céline's use of staccato ellipsis, to Walt Whitman's extended catalogues, to William Carlos Williams's metre and the hot advancing colours and cold receding colours that create Cézanne's 'shimmering space'.

With a pink editing pencil he wrote across the top of the page, 'Howl For Carl Solomon'; not a poem dedicated to Carl, but an empathic howl of grief and rage for Carl's plight and the plight of all the others like him he had known. As Ginsberg later described it, 'A lament for the Lamb in America, with instances of remarkable lamb-like youths.' He bundled together the first six pages of the manuscript and sent them off to Jack Kerouac in Mexico City. (The seventh page of the manuscript had so much crossing out on it and was so messy that he did not think Kerouac could make any sense of it.)

Jack, instead of recognising the great breakthrough that the poem represented for Allen, responded on 19 August, to say: 'Your HOWL FOR CARL SOLOMON is very powerful,' but that he wanted 'spontaneity or nothing'. Kerouac did not like the crossing out in the poem and wanted Allen to stick to his first thoughts, not make corrections as he worked, which was Jack's method of working.

Allen misunderstood him and replied, 'The pages I sent you of Howl (right title) are the first pages put down, as is. I recopied them and sent you the 100% original draft. There is no pre-existent version. I typed it up as I went along, that's why it's so messy.' Allen also misunderstood Jack's use of the title of the poem; Jack was not suggesting a title for it, he was quoting the title that Allen had already given it. But Allen had clearly forgotten that he had titled the poem before sending it to Jack because from then on, he always believed that Kerouac had suggested the title 'Howl' to him and even thanked him for it on the poem's dedication page.

Peter returned from the East Coast. He had hitch-hiked with Lafcadio, a copy of Rimbaud's *Illuminations* in his pocket. He walked into 1010 Montgomery at 3 a.m. and threw his arms around Allen. It had been a traumatic trip for Peter. His two older brothers, Nicholas and Julius, sat mute in the Central Islip madhouse, and he had seen that Lafcadio was heading in the same direction. But now that he had Lafcadio with him, he sat scratching his head over his new responsibility. Lafcadio spent six hours a day in the bathroom, and talked incessantly about striking it rich and making twenty million dollars. Allen found living with Lafcadio very difficult and wrote to Jack, 'I am trying to shepherd fifteen year old Orlovsky around thru life, like being married and having overgrown problem child crazy kicks pathos of real life.'

One of the biggest problems was that Lafcadio ate everything in the ice-box. Allen would shop for groceries, but by mealtime he would find that Lafcadio had eaten all three steaks intended for supper. Allen complained to Burroughs, who suggested an obvious solution: 'In your place I would take a firm stand with Peter's brother and his appetite,' he wrote. 'Sounds to me like he needs a boot in the ass figuratively and literally. I mean, why kowtow to an obnoxious young punk?' Clearly the problem did not improve because two months later Bill wrote again, 'Why do you take all this crap from Peter's brother? People are better off if they don't get all they want to eat. It's been proved with rats.'

A few days after Peter returned, he and Allen took peyote. It was Allen's third time; a very disturbing experience. They stood on the corner of Broadway and Columbus Avenue, in front of City Lights: 'I looked into Peter's eyes, and I couldn't find anyone there,' Ginsberg said. 'He looked into mine and couldn't find anyone there. There was a total absence, a vacancy and emptiness. It was a shock when we looked at each other and perceived two phantom ghosts with empty eyes, laughing fiendishly. I got scared, thinking "Oh, oh, it's all empty."'

They went out in the night-time streets. 'We wandered on Peyote all downtown, P&I, met Betty Keck & saw Molock Moloch smoking building in red glare downtown St. Francis Hotel, with robot upstairs eyes & skullface, in smoke, again,' Allen wrote Jack. The word 'Moloch' came to Allen on the clanging Powell Street cable car, and he sat muttering it till, seated in the cafeteria at the foot of the hotel, he wrote the opening stanzas of 'Howl', Part II: 'Moloch! Moloch! Whose hand ripped out their brains and scattered their minds on the wheels of subways?/ Moloch! Filth! Ugliness Ashcans and unobtainable dollars! Beauties dying in lofts! Harpsichords unbuilt! . . .'

He was continuing in the same vein as 'Howl' Part I, opening with a reference to Bill Cannastra's death and following it with a reference to his friend Bill Keck's passion for harpsichords (he had just met Betty Keck on the street), but then he changed and became less specific in his metaphors: 'Children! Children! The very children breaking their backs under the subways. Breaking their backs trying to lift the Whole City on their backs – Pavements! Buildings! Trees Rockefeller Center Tons . . .' It would go through nineteen separate drafts before he was done with adding to it and shaping it, but he now had the beginning and end of 'Howl' Part II.

Allen had for some time been negotiating with City Lights to publish *Empty Mirror*, his book of Whitman-inspired poems, but Ferlinghetti had rejected it. However, when Allen showed Ferlinghetti 'Howl', his response was much more positive, and Allen wrote Jack, 'City Lights Bookstore here ... will put out "Howl" (under that title) next year, one booklet for that poem, nothing else, it will fill a booklet.'

Due to start college in September, Allen found a one room rose-covered garden cottage six blocks from the university – at 1624 Milvia Street, Berkeley. He moved in on 1 September; Peter and Lafcadio stayed on at Montgomery Street. Allen spent his first night there alone: 'home at night to pancakes high and Jupiter symphony and garden and moonlight and loneliness – the huge horror of Berkeley ahead – it could be nice, but ugly forebodings all day, job worry and study fears and the million books of scholars unreadable.' His first poems written there were 'A Strange New Cottage In Berkeley' and 'Supermarket In California', written on the same day. This time he used the long line to write short, quiet, lyrical poems.

Allen began his studies. To support himself, he washed dishes and read examination papers for the American Literature course. The twenty or thirty dollars a week he made were sufficient for his modest needs. His studies, homework and part-time jobs meant that he had time to see Peter only on weekends.

One day early in September, Allen ran into Michael McClure, who had been asked to organise a poetry reading at the Six Gallery but didn't think he would have time. Allen had been contemplating putting on a reading featuring Jack, Neal and himself, so he immediately volunteered. He consulted Rexroth, who recommended Gary Snyder, a young Berkeley poet. Allen went over to see him at once.

Snyder had been intending to go to the State Fair in Sacramento that day to see the long-haired angora goats, but in the end he stayed home to work on his bicycle. He had it propped up in his backyard when Allen arrived. Thin and wiry, with blond hair and a little goatee, Snyder had slanting, almost Oriental-looking green eyes, and his face was creased with laugh lines. He was twenty-five, a graduate student of Chinese and Japanese at Berkeley, who planned to go to Japan to study on a grant from the First Zen Institute of America the next spring.

He had been studying Buddhism since the late 1940s, when he was at Reed College, and did Buddhist meditation practice with the Berkeley Young Buddhist Association, who had published a number of his poems in their magazine *Berkeley Bussei*. He was muscular and tanned from spending the summer working with a trail crew in the Sierra Nevada. His cottage was tiny, and had a monastic feel. Ice axes and climbing ropes hung from the walls, and orange-crate bookcases housed a valuable collection of books on the Orient, many of them in Japanese and Chinese, as well as a good collection of modern poetry. His table was also made from orange crates. There were no chairs, just straw mats. In the yard was an almond tree, and Gary had arranged a few rocks and boulders to make his own Zen garden.

There was an immediate rapport betwen the two men. Allen later said: 'Gary kept his poems in spring board binders, like I did, and I opened one up, and it looked like a page of William Carlos Williams!' Allen liked the poems very much. Gary had been very impressed by Williams when the poet spent a week at Reed College in 1950 and had been influenced by him ever since. Gary also told Allen about a poet friend of his, Philip Whalen, also from Reed College, who was arriving the next day from the mountains. Allen, in turn, told Gary about his friend Jack Kerouac, a great poet, who was arriving any day from Mexico City. They discussed the upcoming reading, and it was dark by the time Allen walked home through the warm night air.

As Allen and Gary talked, Kerouac came hitch-hiking into town. He found Allen's cottage and, high on Benzedrine, sat and played the *Saint Matthew Passion* at full volume until Allen returned. Next day, Allen and Jack had dinner with Gary and his friend Philip Whalen.

Philip Whalen had spent the summer fire-watching from a lookout tower on Sourdough Mountain in Washington's High Cascades. Before arriving in Berkeley, he had stopped off with friends in Seattle and taken his first peyote, a subject of great interest to Allen. He and Allen quickly became friends. Whalen, a big, gentle man with a wide easy smile, was studying Zen Buddhism (eventually he became a Buddhist monk, after studying in Japan). He was born three years before Allen, in 1923, in Portland, Oregon. A wartime job in a B-17 aircraft factory delayed his entry to Reed College, but once there he became close friends with two other young poets, Gary Snyder and Lew Welch. The three of them shared a house at college, and then all moved down to the Bay Area. Kerouac described Whalen in *The Dharma Bums* as 'Booboo big old goodhearted Warren Coughlin a hundred and eighty pounds of poet meat.' Allen quickly put Whalen's name down for the reading.

Philip Whalen and Gary Snyder now joined Peter, Neal and Jack in the inner circle of Allen's friends. The San Francisco chapter of the Beat Generation was getting underway. Allen busied himself organising the reading. The poets decided that the readers would be Allen Ginsberg, Michael McClure, Gary Snyder, Philip Whalen and Philip Lamantia. Carl Solomon had introduced Allen to Lamantia in the San Remo in 1949. He was a year younger than Allen and had gone to New York when he was sixteen to present himself at the offices of the Surrealist journal *View*, in whose pages Andre Breton subsequently hailed him as an authentic Surrealist. Kerouac refused to read, claiming he was too shy.

Snyder suggested that Rexroth be the master of ceremonies. Rexroth, delighted, went to a thrift shop and bought a pinstripe cutaway for the occasion. Allen disseminated a postcard to advertise the reading. He listed the poets, and the date, 7 October 1955, and continued: 'Six poets at the Six Gallery. Kenneth Rexroth, M.C. Remarkable collection of angels all gathered at once in the same spot. Wine, music, dancing girls, serious poetry, free satori. Small collection for wine and postcards. Charming event.'

The Six Gallery was a converted auto-repair shop at Union and Fillmore. At one end was a small stage, on which they arranged six large chairs in a semicircle. Jack and Allen arrived with Lawrence Ferlinghetti and his wife, Kirby, to find over a hundred people squeezed into the small space. The whole bohemian poetry intelligentsia of the Bay Area appeared to be gathered together in one room for the first time, and there was an atmosphere of great gaiety and excitement. For most of the poets, including Allen, it was their first public reading.

Rexroth made a short speech and introduced Philip Lamantia, who chose to read the posthumous poems of his friend John

Hoffman. Hoffman was also a friend of Carl Solomon's and an acquaintance of Ginsberg's; he was rumoured to have died in Mexico City of a peyote overdose.

Lamantia was followed by Michael McClure who, at twenty-three, was the youngest poet there. McClure's life-long involvement with the ecology movement and its new emphasis as a motif in American poetry was prefigured by his reading of 'Point Lobos: Animism' and 'For The Death of 100 Whales', the latter being his response to the news that bored GIs at a NATO base in the Antarctic had destroyed a pack of killer whales. This was McClure's first meeting with both Gary Snyder and Philip Whalen. Whalen read next and took the reading up to the ten-thirty break with his 'Plus Ça Change . . .' lines of American speech, as suggested to him by Williams.

Although Jack had refused to read, he still wanted to be in the limelight and to share the excitement. He collected money for wine, then rushed out and bought gallon jugs of Californian Burgundy, which the audience passed around. He sat, with his own bottle, on the edge of the stage and sometimes appeared to have blacked out. Ruth Witt-Diamant, who was to play an important role in promoting the new San Francisco poetry, was shocked by the wine and the irreverent tone of the meeting but enjoyed herself.

Then, at about eleven, with the wine circulating freely, Allen made his way to the front of the room, nodding to his many acquaintances, and, as the house lights dimmed for the second half, he began the first public reading of 'Howl': 'I saw the best minds of my generation destroyed by madness, starving hysterical naked, dragging themselves thru the negro streets at dawn looking for an angry fix, angelheaded hipsters burning for the ancient heavenly connection to the starry dynamo in the machinery of night . . .'

He was nervous and had drunk a great deal of wine. He read with a small, intense voice, but the alcohol and the emotional intensity of the poem quickly took over, and he was soon swaying to its powerful rhythm, chanting like a Jewish cantor, sustaining his long breath length, savouring the outrageous language. Kerouac began cheering him on, yelling 'Go!' at the end of each line, and soon the audience joined in. Allen was completely transported. At each line he took a deep breath, glanced at the manuscript, then delivered it, arms outstretched, eyes gleaming, swaying from one foot to the other with the rhythm of the words. Rexroth sat with

tears in his eyes and ignored Ruth Witt-Diamant's gestures to him
to tone it down. Allen continued to the last sob, the audience
cheering him wildly at every line.

Afterwards Jack said, 'Ginsberg, this poem will make you famous
in San Francisco.' Rexroth corrected him: 'No, this poem will make
you famous from bridge to bridge.' Michael McClure, in *Scratching
the Beat Surface*, wrote, 'Ginsberg read on to the end of the poem,
which left us standing in wonder, or cheering and wondering, but
knowing at the deepest level that a barrier had been broken, that a
human voice and body had been hurled against the harsh wall of
America and its supporting armies and navies and academies and
institutions and ownership systems and power-support bases.'
McClure later told Ginsberg that he thought 'Howl' was 'Allen's
metamorphosis from a quiet brilliant burning bohemian scholar,
trapped by his flames and repressions, to epic vocal bard.'

Gary Snyder was left to follow Allen, and sensibly let the
clamour fade before reading 'A Berry Feast', his poetic invocation
of the first fruits festival of the Indians of Oregon. He read well,
in a deep resonant voice, and was able to capture the attention of
the excited audience. Afterwards the poets and their girlfriends and
boyfriends all went to Snyder's favourite Chinese restaurant to
discuss the remarkable evening, and thence to the Place, a favourite
poets' bar on Grant Avenue. And after that there was an orgy.

When Lawrence Ferlinghetti got home, he sat at his desk and,
paraphrasing the message sent by Ralph Waldo Emerson to Walt
Whitman on receiving *Leaves of Grass* a century before, sent Allen
a telegram: 'I greet you at the beginning of a great career. When
do I get the manuscript?'

The Six Gallery reading catalysed the Bay Area literary commu-
nity, and all who took part in it became local celebrities. With the
success of the first part of 'Howl' at the Six Gallery, Allen set to
work to complete the other sections of the poem. One afternoon,
he sat at his typewriter, looking out at the garden bushes, and filled
page after page with suggestions for the middle section of Part II,
the naming of 'the monster of mental consciousness that preys on
the lamb'. Gary Snyder was sitting cross-legged, Japanese-style,
before a writing frame on the rug, translating Han Shan from the
Chinese. Allen was muttering and sometimes laughing out loud in
his trance-like self-absorption as he thought of more and more

outrageous verbal associations to go with 'Moloch', and Gary called out, 'Moloch who reaches up thru the toilet bowl and grabs my pecker everytime I try to crap.' It was not long before the middle section of the poem was more or less complete, but the fine-tuning of the lines and phrases went on for months.

Allen began working on Part III, some of which he already had. It had a fixed base in the phrase, 'I'm with you in Rockland,' which was then followed by a graduated longer response, just made for reading aloud:

I'm with you in Rockland,
  where we are great writers on the same dreadful
    typewriter.
I'm with you in Rockland,
  where your condition has become serious and is
    reported on the radio.

Ginsberg took the form of this section of the poem from Christopher Smart, the eighteenth-century English poet whose 'Jubilate Agno' ('Rejoice The Lamb') he had been familiar with since the forties. Each line of 'Rejoice The Lamb' is a statement, opening with the word 'Let', followed by a counterstatement, opening with 'For':

Let Nahshon rejoice with the Seabreeze, the Lord give the
sailors of his Spirit. For he that walked upon the sea, hath
prepared the floods with the Gospel of peace.
Let Helon rejoice with the Woodpecker – the Lord
encourage the propagation of trees! For the merciful man is
merciful to his beast, and to the trees that give them shelter.
Let Amos rejoice with the Coote – prepare to meet thy God,
O Israel. For he hath turned the shadow of death into the
morning, the Lord is his name.

Allen used 'I'm with you in Rockland' as the statement and opened his counterstatement with 'where':

I'm with you in Rockland, where there are
twentyfive-thousand mad comrades all together singing the
final stanzas of the Internationale.

I'm with you in Rockland, where we hug and kiss the
United States under our bedsheets, the United States that
coughs all night and won't let us sleep.

The final section of the poem (called 'Footnote To Howl' rather
than 'Howl Part IV' because it was a variation on 'Howl Part II'
with 'Moloch!' replaced by 'Holy!') was written as Allen sat
weeping on the Kearny Street bus in San Francisco. The manu-
script was hastily scribbled in ballpoint on a page from a notebook
and needed very little work.

Holy the groaning saxophones! Holy the bop apocalypse!
Holy the jazzbands marihuana hipsters peace & junk &
drums!
Holy the solitudes of skyscrapers and pavements! Holy the
cafeterias filled with the millions! Holy the mysterious river of
tears under the streets!

After a few weeks, Allen gave up his attempt to get an M.A. at
Berkeley and settled down to enjoy his new fame. His friendships
with Gary and Phil grew deeper. With Gary he spent pleasant
afternoons gardening, carving poems into tree trunks, or watching
Gary prepare his esteemed horse-meat sukiyaki with sweet and
sour sauce. He learned an enormous amount about Zen Buddhism.
There were also Zen discussions with Philip Whalen, as well as
long talks about Williams and Gertrude Stein, whom Whalen had
been studying since he was in the army. On Thursdays, Gary
would appear at Allen's cottage with a slim grey-eyed girl, and he
and Allen would practice 'yabyum' with her. It was an Oriental
form of sex based on the mystical formula: 'Om, the thunderbolt
in the void'. They were the 'thunderbolt' and she, of course, was
the 'void.' Jack was initially upset by this. He had been brought up
to think that nakedness was a sin and had also been celibate for a
year, in keeping with his attempt to become a Hinayana Buddhist.
Gary sometimes tried to get Kerouac to meditate, but Jack had
wrecked his knees when he was a football player and couldn't sit
still very long. 'He was too jumpy,' Whalen said.
A year before, Peter had been a virgin, too shy to approach a
woman. Now Allen wrote to LaVigne: 'Peter and I wandering
around finding, finally, various pretty girls to make it with

menage-a-trois.' He told LaVigne about one girl they had been seeing together, 'finally, I screw dog her and she kneeling blows Peter, then we change around. She shy at first but after a while we all began goofing happily with our cocks and cunts and everybody woke up pleased.' Allen and Peter took their clothes off every chance they got. Peter particularly liked orgies. Philip Whalen remembered the parties, 'Allen got a kick out of seeing who was there, and sometimes deciding to upset them and get them going by disrobing. I remember a number of parties at Berkeley, as far as I was concerned at the homes of complete strangers, many of them academics, and Allen thought he could loosen them up by saying, "Let's all get naked!" He would remove his clothes and everyone would say, "How interesting," or "My goodness," and some would leave. Very funny reactions. It happened a lot.'

Allen was interested in seeing people's reactions: 'In Frisco when Peter and I and Gary and Jack, and everybody would go to parties, if we got drunk enough, because we were all feeling very happy at the time, feeling that it was a real renaissance of naked poetry, and feeling the beauty of the world and the beauty of men, almost, so we would take our clothes off. And everybody liked it really, nothing wrong with it.'

One afternoon, Allen, Jack and Philip Whalen were strolling around the Southern Pacific railroad yards at China Basin, near the Third Street flophouses Jack was so fond of (in the days before this area was transformed by the freeway) when Allen made a strange discovery and asked Philip what it was.

'It's a sunflower,' said Whalen. Allen had never seen one before. It had gone completely to seed and was all black and sooty from the locomotives. 'He was completely enthralled and really went into it,' Whalen remembered. That evening at the cottage, just as they were preparing to go out to a party, Allen had an idea for a poem. 'Just give me a minute,' he said, 'I'll write this down,' and as Jack waited by the door, Allen quickly scribbled down a poem using Jack's sketching style and his own long lines. In twenty minutes he was done and they left for the party. The poem was 'Sunflower Sutra' with its famous long final line:

> 'We're not our skin of grime, we're not our dread bleak dusty imageless locomotive, we're all beautiful golden sunflowers inside, we're blessed by our own seed & golden hairy naked

accomplishment-bodies growing into mad black formal
sunflowers in the sunset, spied on by our eyes under the
shadow of the mad locomotive riverbank sunset Frisco hilly
tincan evening sitdown vision.'

At the end of November Natalie began acting crazy. Neal had
persuaded Natalie to forge Carolyn's signature on bonds worth ten
thousand dollars, her life savings, so that he could pursue his
'system' at the track. He lost all of the money. Natalie's guilt at
stealing from Carolyn precipitated a nervous breakdown. She took
enormous amounts of amphetamine and within days became
skeleton-thin, with huge, terrified eyes. She was convinced that the
police were coming to arrest them and tried, unsuccessfully, to cut
her wrists. Neal's friends began seriously to recommend that she
be hospitalised.

On 30 November 1955, just before dawn, after Jack had gone
back to Allen's cottage and while Neal slept, Natalie went up to
the roof in her bathrobe and broke the skylight, to cut her wrists
with the jagged glass. A neighbour saw her sitting on the roof
bleeding and called the police. Thinking they had come to arrest
her, she ran away terrified. Despite the efforts of one of the
policemen to tackle her, she fell six floors to her death.

Allen had been worried by her paranoia, but hadn't realised how
serious it was. In an unpublished poem he wrote:

Your truthful eyes troubling me too late.
In the car coming over for Thanksgiving
You gave me look so tearful I knew it was death,
or thought so . . .

Natalie's death threw a pall over the entire community. Long-
suffering, all-forgiving Carolyn took Neal back, and Allen joined
them for a quiet Christmas in Los Gatos. Jack decided to spend
Christmas with his mother and hitch-hiked to Rocky Mount,
North Carolina, where she was living with his sister.

That December, Allen concentrated on making final revisions to
'Howl' and sending copies of it to family and friends. On 9
December, he mailed it to William Carlos Williams, along with 'A
Strange New Cottage In Berkeley', 'A Supermarket In California'

and 'Sunflower Sutra'. 'Look what I have done with the long line,' he wrote. 'In some of these poems it seems to answer your demand for a relatively absolute line with a fixed base, whatever it is . . . all held together within the elastic of the breath, though of varying lengths. The key is in the jazz choruses to some extent; also to reliance on spontaneity & expressiveness which long line encourages; also to attention to interior unchecked logical mental stream. With a long line comes a return, (caused by) expressive human feeling, it's generally lacking in poetry now, which is inhuman. The release of emotion is one with the rhythmical buildup of long line.'

He sent copies of the poems to his father; 'Howl' he thought too revealing. Louis responded enthusiastically: 'Read with interest your "Sunflower Sutra." I did not like the dirty words dragged in, nor the long long lines. However it had feeling and fervour and good concrete details. The ending builds up well . . . Bet you're making a literary reputation! Keep it up! You'll land somewhere in time!'

Louis was not so positive about all Allen's activities. In their correspondence, Allen continued to test his ideas. He engaged in a spirited defence of the values of the 'Beat Generation' – complete openness, free love, marijuana, etc. – which Louis looked upon with distaste. 'All your vehement, vaporous, vituperations of rebellion move me not one jot,' he told Allen. 'Your attitude is irresponsible – and it stinks!'

Allen was taking some concrete steps towards getting to Europe. The recently passed Taft-Hartley Act had opened up the shipping unions, and he thought that a three- or four-month stretch at sea would give him enough money for seven or eight months in Europe. In December, he began applying for ships. One finally came up in May.

Jack was intending to return to the coast to work as a fire-watcher that summer, and when he heard that Gary Snyder had moved to a new cabin where there would be room enough for him, he immediately hitch-hiked west. Shortly after Jack arrived, a huge poetry reading was presented at a theatre in Berkeley. Robert LaVigne, back in town, had made a seven-foot-high Lautrec-like poster for the reading and decorated the hall with pen drawings of Allen and Peter making love. On stage there was a row of throne-like wooden chairs left over from a stage set, one for each poet. It was the same line-up as the Six Gallery reading, a repeat by popular demand for Berkeley, and the audience knew by now what to expect. Kerouac passed the hat for wine and kept the bottle moving. Allen, wearing an unravelling, crumpled sweater, stood beneath the brilliant white spotlight and delivered his lines like a saxophone solo, putting everything he could into it. This was the first public reading of 'Howl' Part II and the audience booed and hissed at each mention of 'Moloch!' The excitement was tremendous. As Allen finished there was a triumphant burst of light as the coloured stage lights were turned on. All the other poets jumped to their feet to hug and congratulate him.

Everyone was aware that something special was happening. Rexroth told Allen that his presence was the catalyst for a major poetry renaissance on the West Coast, and Rexroth's wife later informed Allen that Rexroth had been waiting all his life for a situation like this to develop. Photographers had come from as far away as Vancouver, and the entire reading was professionally recorded. Rexroth wanted to form a poetry-jazz combo with Allen and a group of local musicians, and another group of jazz musicians proposed writing a musical setting for 'Howl' and touring the West Coast with him, performing 'Howl' as a 'Jazz-Mass'. Fantasy Records, the Berkeley jazz-label, also wanted to record him with a jazz backing. Literary magazines were eager to publish Allen's work, and three separate organisations had sprung up to organise poetry readings, so that there was now at least one a week. Robert Duncan was leaving town for Europe, and Ruth Witt-Diamant arranged for Allen to take over his poetry workshop one evening a week at San Francisco State. Allen told Louis, 'You have no idea what a storm of lunatic-fringe activity I have stirred up.'

The influential literary critic and poet Richard Eberhart arrived in San Francisco and was the guest of honour at a party at Ruth Witt-Diamant's house, where Allen gave him a private reading of 'Howl'. They got along well, and Eberhart took Allen with him to visit the poet Karl Shapiro, who was teaching at Davis College. This visit further confirmed Ginsberg's dim view of the establishment. He described Shapiro to Louis as, 'blank eyed, dull, acts like advt. executive and about as sympathetic.' They talked about Shapiro's trip to India.

'India was nasty,' said Shapiro.

'Karl didn't like it at all,' said his wife.

Shapiro said that the only way to deal with the suffering there was to ignore it. 'There was no light in his spirit at all, just money,' Allen told Louis. 'The theme of his poems is moderation and the virtues of middleclass existence, which is for him a refuge from experience. And HE teaches a creative writing course, and is admired by a flock of dull-eyed professors.'

Allen set himself a deadline of the end of April 1956, to finish revising 'Howl' and selecting poems for the book. When he handed in the final version of the manuscript, Ferlinghetti was so pleased that he decided to give him royalties. Robert Creeley made Ditto copies of the poem for use in Duncan's poetry-workshop, and Allen sent copies to Eliot, Pound, Van Doren, Trilling, Eberhart, Meyer Schapiro, William Faulkner and other literary celebrities, each with a long letter requesting the reader's reaction. He also sent copies to Louis, Eugene, Naomi, Lucien and other friends. Louis' reaction to the complete poem was positive: 'My first impression at first blush, is that it is a wild, volcanic, troubled, extravagant, turbulent, boisterous, unbridled outpouring, inter-mingling gems and flashes of picturesque insight with slag and debris of scoraic matter. It has violence, it has life, it has *vitality*. In my opinion it is a one-sided neurotic view of life, it has not enough glad, Whitmanic affirmations.' But Louis also conceded, 'The poem should attract attention and perhaps be a sensation. You will hear defenders and detractors. But it should give you a name.' His immigrant aspirations for his son to be a success were being fulfilled in an unexpected way.

Allen had sent William Carlos Williams the completed manu-script in March, and a month later received a strange Introduction from him. It read almost as if he were confusing Allen with someone else, except that he recalled Allen's father and back-ground. He described Allen as 'physically slight of build and mentally much disturbed by the life which he had encountered about him after the first world war as it was exhibited to him in and about New York City . . . Now he turns up fifteen or twenty years later with an arresting poem.' Williams had had a stroke, which may have made him forgetful. But he understood the poem well and sympathised, despite his private reservations. He thought 'Howl' should be cut by half, and didn't like Allen's long lines: 'He went back. His longer lines don't seem to fit in with the modern tendency at all. Retrograde. I didn't like them at all in "Howl". If he had paid attention to what Olson was doing it would have been more successful.' However, he clearly enjoyed the power of it and ended his Introduction: 'Hold back the edges of your gowns, Ladies, we are going through hell.'

Allen was determined to wrest a response from Ezra Pound, and wrote to him a second time, enclosing poems. 'Please READ at least one page of the enclosed ms. Or 1 line for that matter so long as you can judge the rhythm,' he demanded, but Pound wasn't having any of it. Allen mentioned in his letter that William Carlos Williams had written the Introduction to the book, so Pound mailed the letter and the poems to Williams with a note: 'You got more room in yr/ house than I hv/ in my cubicle. If he's yours why don't yu teach him the value of time to those who want to read something that will tell 'em wot they don't know.' Pound had been judged insane and sent to Saint Elizabeth's mental hospital in Washington, DC, in order that he not be put on trial for treason, a charge stemming from his wartime broadcasts on Radio Rome. Living in a madhouse himself, he was already quite familiar with 'best minds . . . destroyed by madness.'

On 19 May 1956, Eugene's wife Connie gave birth to Alan Eugene Brooks (Eugene had used his middle name when he became a lawyer; now he used the English spelling of Alan). Allen was very touched, and wrote, 'Thanks for naming the baby after me. It'll be an illustrious name (but perhaps temporarily in disrepute when my poems are published.) I almost cried thinking you cared that much to name it Allen.' In addition to celebrating the new birth, there was much discussion in the family about Naomi. Allen thought that if she was well enough to leave the hospital, she could be boarded with Peter's mother in Northport, Long Island, but when Eugene visited the hospital to make enquiries, he was told that Naomi was in no condition to leave. A letter from Naomi to Eugene, written that spring, showed how sick she was. Eugene passed the letter on to Allen, who later used the phrases in 'Kaddish'. Naomi wrote, 'God's informers came to my bed, and God, himself, I saw it in the sky – it was after Jan 1, 1956. The sunshine showed it too, a key on the side of the window for me to get out. The yellow of the sunshine, also showed the key on the side of the window for me to get out. I'm begging you to take me out of here.'

In May, Allen joined the USNS *Pvt. Joseph F. Merrell* as a yeoman-storekeeper at $5,040 a year. He walked around San

Francisco with a military haircut, wearing a leather jacket and khaki shirt and pants, and carrying a leather suitcase filled with poems. Moving his things to Peter's apartment, he left Philip Whalen in sole charge of the Milvia Street cottage.

On Saturday night, 9 June, a telegram arrived. Allen was in Berkeley, but Peter was home and accepted it. It read:

> Allen Ginsberg, care Orlovsky, 5 Turner Terrace, San Fran. Naomi Ginsberg died suddenly Saturday afternoon. Would appreciate your communicating this to Allen Ginsberg. He may call me at Hotel Regent.
> Eugene Brooks.

Knowing that Allen would stay over at Milvia Street, Peter set off for Berkeley. Allen was not home when he arrived, so Peter scribbled on the envelope, 'I got this at 7:30 p.m., and here at 10:45 p.m. Out to find you. Be back soon. She's in the sunshine now. Love Peter.' In 'Kaddish', Ginsberg wrote:

> Returning from San Francisco one night, Orlovsky in my room – Whalen in his peaceful chair – a telegram from Gene, Naomi dead –
> Outside I bent my head to the ground under the bushes near the garage – knew she was better –

Allen did not go to the funeral; there were only seven mourners. At a funeral parlour in Hempstead, Long Island, a sexton muttered a few prayers in Hebrew. He had to stop and ask her name in the middle of the short service and still did not get it right. The cortège went to the Beth Moses Cemetery in Farmingdale. As the casket was lowered the sexton prayed again but would not say the Kaddish because a quorum of ten males (a *minyan*) was not present as required by Jewish law. Louis stood, blinded by tears, recalling his happy early days with her, the pathos and tragedy of her well-meaning life, and the constant struggles she had within her. 'As I saw her coffin lowered into the hospitable earth, I thought that now she would at last have peace and rest, something I had struggled all my life to give her,' he wrote to Allen.

A few days after Naomi's death, Allen sat on the dockside in San Francisco and wrote, 'Everything changes toward death. My mother. Myself . . . My childhood is gone with my mother. My memory becomes less clear. My body will go. There is no me left. Naomi is a memory. Naomi is a memory. My 30 years is a memory to me.' Eugene was also moved to write about his mother's death and his poem 'To My Mother' appeared on 25 July in the *New York Times*.

Knowing that Naomi had been denied the Kaddish at her graveside, Allen attempted to get one said for her. He, Peter and Jack were taking one of their long walks around San Francisco, when they found themselves in the old Jewish neighbourhood between Fillmore and Buchanan. Seeing a synagogue, Allen suggested that they go in and say a Kaddish for Naomi. 'I showed the letter saying that there was no Kaddish said, and talked with some of the fellows there,' Ginsberg remembered. 'They asked Peter, "Are you Jewish?" "No." Kerouac, "Are you Jewish?" "No." They were friendly, I was a nice little Jewish boy whose mother had died so they tried to get a *minyan* together, but they couldn't come up with enough Jewish men. I remember Kerouac was very sweet about it, very accomodating.' Finally, Allen decided to write a Kaddish for her himself and asked Louis to get him a copy of the prayer. Louis complied with his request, and commented: 'Those chants therein have a rhythm and sonorousness of immemorial years marching with reverberations through the corridors of history . . . laden with the tears of things.' Several years would pass, however, before Allen completed his task.

Allen joined a new ship, the USNS *Sgt. Jack J. Pendleton*, taking with him the proofs of 'Howl' from City Lights which Villiers Press in London had begun typesetting at the beginning of June. The long verse line breaks of the poems were very poorly set. 'This being my first book I want it right if I can,' Allen wrote Ferlinghetti on 3 July. 'It looks as if the whole book will have to be reset practically,' and he offered to pay up to two hundred dollars for the cost of resetting. In his anxiety to extend his good fortune to his friends, Allen devised a dedication that managed not only to proclaim Neal Cassady's unpublished *First Third* and Burroughs's *Naked Lunch* but to name all eleven of Kerouac's unpublished manuscripts. Lucien he congratulated on being appointed Night Bureau Manager of United Press; a compliment Lucien could have done without. Allen was still thinking of the book as a slim volume of obscure verse published in the provinces.

Allen's ship was on its way to the Arctic Circle to deliver matériel to refurbish the Distant Early Warning line radar system, and weeks were spent assembling the cargo from military depots in Portland, Seattle and Tacoma. Philip Whalen forwarded mail to Tacoma. One of the letters came as a shock. It was from Naomi. It had been mailed by the hospital two days after her death, but unlike her recent letters, it was quite lucid. She congratulated Allen on his birthday and talked about the mimeographed copy of 'Howl' that he had sent her. 'It seems to me your wording was a little too hard. Do tell me what father thinks of it,' she said. She worried about Allen's prospects and continued:

'You know you have to have a good job to get married. I wish you did have a good job. What did you specialise in when you went to college? This going to the North Pole, who supplies the wearing material? They say when you visit the Eskimos you need a double coat of fur. Are you fit for that flying job? Don't take chances with your life! I wish you get married. Do you like farming? It's as good a job as any. I hope you behave well. Don't go in for too much drink or other things that are not good for you . . . As for myself. I still have the wire on my head. The doctors know about it. They are cutting the flesh and bone. They are giving me teethache. I do wish you were back east so I could see you . . . I am glad you are having your poetry published. I wish I were out of here and at home at the time you were young! Then I would be young. I'm in the prime of life now – Did you read about the two men who died at 139 and 149 yrs of age? I wonder how they lived. I'm looking for a good time. I hope you are not taking drugs as suggested by your poetry. That would hurt me. Don't go in for ridiculous things. With love and good news. (mother) Naomi.'

Allen was comforted by the thought that she seemed to be in calm spirits before her death, and he forwarded the letter to Eugene, asking him to show it to Louis.

Seven days out of Puget Sound, they sailed through the Bering Strait into the Chukchee Sea, but it was foggy and Allen couldn't see anything except white-breasted birds flying across from Alaska to Russia. He wrote a haiku: 'One fingernail dirty and the Bering Sea', and threw it in the water along with seven cents as a tribute to Naomi, being so near to her Russia. The ship continued up the Alaska coast to Icy Cape where, along with forty other ships, they had to wait for the ice to break up further north before they could continue. The sky was filled with clouds, and sometimes the ship was buffeted by rainy wind. They could see ice floes in every direction but no icebergs, nor was land in sight, though a radio antenna rose from an invisible beach just over the horizon.

Allen had access to the ship's mimeograph machine, and on the weekend of 26–27 July, he made copies of his poem 'Siesta In Xbalba', which he stapled into a twenty-two page booklet, dedicated to Karena Shields. He sent copies to Ferlinghetti and one to Louis, who responded encouragingly: 'It's very interesting with cinematic flashbacks of scenes and people. There is entangled in your lines a nostalgia for the past and for ruins that make a pulpit for mortality. Congratulations!'

The ship moved slowly up the coast and, by 4 August, was anchored off the Eskimo trading-post town of Wainwright; but the crew were not allowed ashore lest they infected the Eskimos with measles. A few days later, they completed their journey and arrived at Point Barrow, 340 miles north of the Arctic Circle, and the northernmost point of the United States.

In early August, the mail brought Allen a package from City Lights Books, and he saw for the first time the stark black and white cover of *Howl And Other Poems*. He was pleased by the way the type had been reset and also happy that it cost him only twenty dollars to have it done. He wrote to Ferlinghetti, 'Received the copy of the book you sent me promptly and was excited to see it ... I shuddered when I read the poetry tho, it all looks so jerry-built sloppy and egocentric most of it. "Greyhound" looks fine, I'm glad you told me to put it in. Reading it all through I'm not sure it deserves all the care and work you've put into it and the encouragement you've given me, in fact, to tell you the truth, I'm already embarrassed by half of it but what the hell . . .' He thanked Lawrence for publishing it and asked, 'I wonder if we will actually sell the thousand copies.'

Allen was in the land of the Midnight Sun. He described the scene to Kerouac: 'Dread ghastly pallor all night through clouds, and this week fantastic burning iron sun going down at edge of horizon for a few hours, clear weather. The water always moving, clouds always moving, birds same, clouds and me same, like a transparent shifting layer everywhere changing.' The *Pendleton* spent a month in the Arctic and delivered goods to various camps and bases during the week of midsummer when the sun never fully reached the horizon.

Coming directly after the death of his mother, the trip to the Arctic was mostly a period of solitude and contemplation. Ginsberg was unable to relate to his Jewish heritage but was moved by an as yet undefined spiritual quest. He had long talks about Muhammad with two black shipmates from the mess hall and gave them his copy of *The Diamond Sutra* (The Bible was not the only holy book he had with him). He told Kerouac, 'I spend a lot of time on the prow at night, often on my knees praying, but don't know to who or what.' He was still searching.

Back in San Francisco at the beginning of September, Allen immediately set to work sending out his book. Copies went to Carl Solomon, still in Pilgrim State, to Charlie Chaplin, Henry Miller, Robinson Jeffers, Louis Zukofsky, W.H. Auden, T.S. Eliot, Louise Bogan, Marianne Moore, Ezra Pound, Kenneth Patchen, e.e.cummings and the celebrated lesbian Natalie Barney, as well as to Burroughs, Kerouac, Holmes, Carr and all his friends. Lucien wrote Allen, 'I was touched at being included in your dedication. But I value a certain anonymity in life and it always jars me when my friends, of all people, find it desirable to include mention of me in their works – dedication page as well as text.' He asked Allen to remove it from subsequent editions of the book, which he did.

Allen mailed out over one hundred review copies of *Howl*, but the review that mattered the most had already been written. Richard Eberhart's long, serious article, 'West Coast Rhythms' appeared in the *New York Times* on 2 September 1956 and, though he mentioned Snyder, McClure, Whalen and the benevolent influences of Patchen, Jeffers and Rexroth, the article was centered on Allen, whom Eberhart identified as a major young poet. 'The most remarkable poem of the young group, written during the past year, is "Howl" by Allen Ginsberg,' wrote Eberhart. After describing Ginsberg's background, Eberhart went on to say: 'After years of apprenticeship to usual forms, he developed his brave new medium. This poem has created a furor of praise or abuse whenever read or heard. It is a powerful work, cutting through to dynamic meaning. Ginsberg thinks he is going forward by going back to the methods of Whitman. My first impression was that it is based on destructive violence. It is profoundly Jewish in temper. It is Biblical in its repetitive grammatical build-up. It is a howl against everything in our mechanistic civilisation which kills the spirit, assuming that the louder you shout the more likely you are to be heard. It lays bare the nerves of suffering and spiritual struggle. Its positive force and energy come from a redemptive quality of love, although it destructively catalogues evils of our time from physical deprivation to madness.'

Eberhart went on to point out the humour in Ginsberg's work, citing the line in 'America': 'Asia is rising against me/ I haven't got a Chinaman's chance,' and also mentioned 'Sunflower Sutra' as 'a lyric poem marked by pathos'. Ginsberg could not have asked for more.

Louis was overjoyed by the article: 'I was happy to see it. Edith keeps a copy in her purse and shows it to all and sundry. I have passed it around the Newark folks. I rejoice that your book is coming out. I predict it will make a name for you. You may wake up one morning and find yourself famous. I hope so.'

Allen was now famous enough for him to write to Kerouac, 'Agh! I'm sick of the whole thing, that's all I think about, famous authorhood, like a happy empty dream ... How beautiful tho,' Allen continued. 'I guess I really feel good about it. It's assuming proportions of an "it" in my life.'

Allen and Peter saw a lot of Gregory Corso, who had moved to San Francisco and was living in North Beach with a French woman. Gregory, with his spiky New York humour and paranoia, antagonised both Michael McClure and Neal Cassady, causing difficulties within the group which Allen took it upon himself to smooth over – a role in which he would frequently find himself with Gregory over the decades. Allen's tremendous loyalty to his friends meant that he would do anything to keep peace among them and maintain a working poetic relationship.

Allen single-handedly *willed* the Beat Generation into being by his unshakable belief that his friends were all geniuses. Without Ginsberg, Burroughs would almost certainly never have published *Junkie* and would not have continued his writing career. Without Allen, it is unlikely that Kerouac would have published anything other than his first book, and even that was done with Allen's aid. Over the years, he devoted an enormous amount of his time to promoting Kerouac, Burroughs, Corso, Snyder, Whalen, Orlovsky and the other writers loosely known as the Beats, as well as promoting post-Williams poets he was less close to, or didn't know personally at all, such as Levertov, Oppenheimer, Marshall, Zukofsky and Niedecker.

In *Jack's Book*, Robert Duncan was quoted as saying, 'Ginsberg always lived in the romance that he was going to know overwhelming writers. Allen came to San Francisco because of Rexroth and Patchen. Even meeting me, and I was nothing, was to him overwhelming, as Kerouac had been and Burroughs was. He invented the sky with new stars in it, and his invention of it was a poet's.'

Allen had his reasons. He viewed the literary establishment of Trilling, *Partisan Review, Kenyon Review* and the Southern School as ultimately reactionary: 'They were liberal but in the long run they would go along with a police state if it happened – they wouldn't go to jail.' They seemed preoccupied with fighting communism and Stalinism. To Allen, theirs was a 'cultural resistence to communism . . . so I was reacting to that conservative group with a hip shot. The reason I was so eager to ally with Rexroth and Duncan and the old San Francisco renaissance was because we basically had the same politics – which was like philosophical anarchism. I thought it was urgent for the poets to make an united phalanx: Black Mountain, North West, San Francisco, Renaissance, Beat, and New York School, to try and correlate our efforts and publishing. Because to me, Williams's "open form" meant "open mind" . . . I wasn't just plugging and promoting my friends. I had a much larger agenda.'

McClure said, 'The group that Allen was trying to get together smacked of New York, of homosexuality, and on the other hand, something I admire very much, a social commitment that I did not have within myself. As a matter of fact the thing that I've learned from Allen is social commitment.' At the time, however, Allen denied that he was consciously trying to form a group. 'We're all friends,' he told Lawrence Lipton later that year, 'but not organised as a literary movement.'

Not all the poets liked the idea of the 'San Francisco School', as Eberhart had called them, and preferred to jealously guard their own individualism. Robert Duncan in particular felt that his work was being overlooked, and McClure wanted to keep his identity very much separate. Squabbles were inevitable. 'The lines were drawn, the battles were horrific,' said McClure. 'We were pretty macho, but we really didn't want to do any damage to each other.

I mean, there were only about a dozen of us. No matter how territorial we were or how ferocious our internecine wars might be, we had a lot more in common with each other than with anybody else out there. So there was probably some yelling and name calling, but only once or twice.' One thing which highlighted the factionalism of the poetry scene was an article in *Mademoiselle* magazine on the San Francisco scene. Allen, Jack, Gregory, Peter and the others wanted a group photograph to accompany the article, but Duncan and McClure insisted on having their photographs taken separately. Allen could simply not understand competitiveness between poets and rather naïvely, but genuinely, wanted everyone to be friends and unite against the philistines.

That September, Allen decided his season was coming to an end. The inner group was beginning to split up and it was time to move on. Gary Snyder had already left to live in Japan. Allen was ready for his European trip.

He had achieved a lot in San Francisco. He arrived unknown and unpublished, and in three short years he found himself at the centre of a dynamic new literary movement, the famous author of a powerful and critically aclaimed work. He was now able to view himself as a poet and see a future for himself in literature. It would have been easy to remain in San Francisco and be a big fish in a small pond, but he knew that if he stayed he would become more and more embroiled in the social scene and never get any work done. Success and local fame had given Allen confidence and stability, and he now wanted, more than anything, to help Bill with his writing. 'The Beat Generation was just beginning to burgeon, and I was very conscious of leaving the scene to do something more serious and steady,' he said. 'I already thought Bill a genius writer teacher, so I thought that was important and it was dramatically interesting to be involved with something onward going rather than the past.'

Between himself and Peter, he thought, all of Bill's needs could be met. He felt protected by his relationship with Peter, which was working out well, and would have perhaps been less eager to go to Tangier alone. Allen had promoted a great growth in Peter. His sympathy and encouragement had enabled Peter to become much more self-confident, and by setting up orgies and threesomes Allen had enabled Peter to conquer his shyness as well as stave off any problems arising from Peter's preference for women. However, it was Allen who dominated the relationship. Allen always needed to be in charge, even if his role was sometimes a masochistic one; this Neal had only occasionally acquiesced to and Jack hardly ever allowed. In Peter he seemed to have found his ideal lover.

The European trip was something he had been planning ever since Mexico. His original idea had been to continue on to Russia, but it was to be another eight years before he achieved this. He intended not just to see the sights of Europe as a tourist but to settle down, living and working in one place.

It had been three years since he last saw Burroughs, and in his letters Bill sounded a little miserable. Peter had never met him but, as Ginsberg said, 'Peter and I decided that since he was so lacklove, the two of us would take him on and do anything he wanted. Satisfy him. So we went to Tangier to fuck him – to exhaust his desires.' Bill, delighted, replied that he expected Allen and his entourage in January 1957. He went on to extol the beauty of Tangier: 'This place relaxes me so I am subject to dissolve. I can spend three hours looking at the bay with my mouth open like a Kentucky Mountain Boy.' Allen had been a bit worried that Bill would want him all to himself, but Bill said: 'By all means bring Jack and Peter. I assure you I will not be jealous, in fact, jealousy is one of the emotions of which I am no longer capable. Self-pity is also impossible for me.'

Jack then revealed his worries about going to Morocco. Writing from Mexico City, he told Allen he wanted to go to Europe, but was afraid the Arabs would kill them if they went to Tangier. Bill scoffed at Jack's fears, and told Allen, 'Jack must not be afraid of Arabs, I am in a position to officially abolish fear.' He also mentioned that he had recently acquired a large machete.

Plans were made. Allen, Peter, Lafcadio and Gregory would go first to Mexico City and stay there for a few weeks with Jack, who had gone on ahead, then proceed to New York to make preparations for a long sojourn in Europe. Allen had not seen his father or brother since Naomi's death and wanted to spend time with them before leaving again for a long spell. They expected to arrive in Mexico City by 7 November, and asked Jack to look around for somewhere that they could all live for a few weeks.

Allen and Gregory set out to hitch-hike to Los Angeles, on the first leg of the journey, leaving Peter and Lafcadio to close down the apartment. Allen had sent advance warning of their arrival in Los Angeles. A consummate publicist for the group, he wrote to Anaîs Nin, whom he did not know, asking her if she could organise a reading for them and invite Christopher Isherwood, Aldous Huxley, James Dean and Marlon Brando. 'I don't know what you can do with us,' he wrote, 'but if you can figure anything you're welcome; and the occasion, whatever it is, will not, please understand, be just a big nowhere bore. I mean our poetry swings and is literate & OK . . .'

Allen and Gregory arrived in Los Angeles on 30 October, intending to stay only a week. Lawrence Lipton had arranged a reading for them on Saturday night. Allen and Gregory arrived drunk, Allen carrying an open bottle of wine. Anaîs Nin came with a group of friends, though not the ones that Allen had requested. He gave an inspired, drunken reading of 'Howl', addressing his delivery exclusively to her, and in his enthusiam he knocked over his bottle of wine, spilling it on himself. As it happened, someone in the audience had also been drinking, and began to heckle. Allen politely asked him to hear out the reading and said that he would be pleased to hear his opinions afterwards. This stopped the heckler for a bit, but when Gregory stood up to read, the drunk interrupted, wanting to go outside and fight. 'What are you guys trying to prove?' he demanded. Allen immediately yelled out, 'Nakedness!'

'What do you mean nakedness?' asked the drunk.

'I meant spiritual nakedness,' Ginsberg explained later, 'poetic nakedness – candor. Then I suddenly realised what I had said. Inspired, I just started taking off my clothes.' 'All right,' Allen challenged the drunk. 'You want to do something big, don't you? Something brave? Well go on, do something *really* brave. Take off your clothes!' The man was speechless. Allen advanced on him, tearing off his shirt. 'Come and stand here, stand naked before the people. I dare you! The poet always stands naked before the world.' Allen threw his shirt and undershirt at the man's feet, and he began to back away. 'You're scared, aren't you?' asked Allen, 'You're afraid.' Allen kicked off his shoes and socks and pulled down his pants. Doing a little hopping dance, he kicked them off and followed them with his shorts. He was now completely naked. The drunk had by now retreated to the back of the room. The audience sat in stunned silence.

Suddenly the room exploded in cheers, jeers, applause and angry argument. The drunk was booed and hissed until he left. Anaïs Nin was impressed and wrote in her journal, 'The way he did it was so violent and direct, it had so much meaning in terms of all our fears of unveiling ourselves . . .' Gregory wanted to leave at once and take Anaïs Nin with them, but Lipton restored order and Gregory was persuaded to finish his reading. Allen took his time in putting his clothes back on, smiling quietly to himself through half-closed lids. He finished the reading with 'Sunflower Sutra' and 'A Supermarket In California'. He wrote to Ferlinghetti, 'Reading we gave in L.A. was the most wild ever. I disrobed finally. Been wanting to onstage for years.' Burroughs got to hear of it in Tangier and wrote, 'What's with you? You wig already and remove your dry goods inna public hall?'

Peter and Lafcadio joined Allen and Gregory, and they headed south to Tijuana. In Guadalajara, they stopped to visit the young British poet Denise Levertov. Allen told Ferlinghetti, 'She was nice to us, we liked her a lot. I was surprised how much a good Joe she was . . . Levertov is a good poetess, certainly. I read a lot of her work there.' Allen added a folio of her poems to the collection of manuscripts he carried with him to show editors and publishers.

During their two-week stay in Mexico City, some Mexican boys took Allen, Peter and Jack home with them to play Spin the Bottle. They all took off their clothes and had a gay orgy. Jack took Allen to meet Esperanza, the young prostitute who inspired him to write *Tristessa*. She was thin and weak from morphine addiction, and it was clear to Allen that Jack had a hopelessly sentimental view of her. Gregory saw nothing romantic in the grinding poverty and filth of Mexico City and wanted to leave as soon as possible. He moved to an expensive tourist hotel to wait for his girlfriend to cable him the air fare back to the States. Allen, Jack, Peter and Lafcadio took an expense-share car ride to New York City through a newspaper ad. It was a very uncomfortable trip.

The news that Allen and Jack were back in town travelled fast. No one was more thrilled to see Allen again than Elise Cowen, who was living with her girlfriend Sheila in Yorkville. Allen and Peter found Lafcadio a place in a rooming house, then moved in with Elise and Sheila in their sixth-floor walk-up. They dragged another mattress into the bedroom, and all four of them slept together.

Sometimes Allen slept with Lafcadio, and Elise also took a liking to him and promised she would always look after him. Allen had a lot of catching up to do, visiting his father and stepmother in Paterson, and Eugene who had moved to Hicksville, Long Island. Eugene drove him out to the snow-covered cemetery where Naomi was buried. Crows circled the graves.

Allen met Peter's family in Northport. Peter could still not decide whether to accompany Allen to Europe. Allen and Peter had hired a lawyer to organise the release of Peter's brother Nicholas from the mental hospital, and Peter knew he was the only one in his family capable of handling matters if anything went wrong. He felt torn between nursing his brothers and living his own life.

Allen meanwhile ran around town, visiting. He had arrived in New York with manuscripts and books by Gary Snyder, Philip Whalen, Robert Duncan, Ed Dorn, Robert Creeley, Philip Lamantia, Denise Levertov, Michael McClure and Charles Olson, determined to extend the San Francisco Poetry Renaissance to New York. He threw himself into the task with enormous energy. He presented himself at the *New York Times* and asked them to review *Howl*. He was interviewed by Harvey Breit, whom he inundated with material. Breit wrote an informative, though unenthusiastic, piece as a follow-up to Eberhart's earlier *Times* article. *Mademoiselle* printed Denise Levertov's poems and also some Burroughs material. Allen was interviewed, at his insistence, by a cynical feature writer from the *New York World Telegram*, where he once worked as a copyboy; and Allen, Gregory and Jack were interviewed by the *Village Voice*.

Allen approached *Time*, *Life*, *Esquire* and the *Hudson Review*. The *Partisan Review* and *Kenyon Review* agreed to review some of the books he left with them. He persuaded James Laughlin, at New Directions, to include some San Francisco material in the upcoming *New Directions Annual*, and gave John Clellon Holmes's editor at Scribners a big pile of books and manuscripts to look through. At *The New Yorker*, Louise Bogan agreed to review *Howl* and other San Francisco publications. Allen gave Louis Simpson an enormous selection of material to consider for the anthology he was editing with Donald Hall, *New Poets of England and America*. The fact that Simpson rejected them all is a measure of how conservative the New York establishment was. Allen's best reception came from editor Don Allen at newly founded Grove Press, where *Evergreen Review* was in the works. It was decided that the entire second issue of the magazine be devoted to the San Francisco scene.

One of the poets that Allen visited was Diane di Prima. Ginsberg remembered his first meeting with her: 'She sent a bunch of funny poems, and then, when we went back to the East Coast, Jack Kerouac and Peter and I all got into bed with her and a couple of dancer friends she had, and we all had a big all-night orgy – she and Jack and me sucking the cock of this really pretty looking dancer boy fellow.' Ginsberg joked about orgies in the narration for a film sound track in 1979: 'Yes, we did quite a few. Peter would always get the girls and I would always get the guys, or we'd get a guy and a girl and take them home with us. I would make it with the guy if I could, and Peter would make it with the girl. Sometimes they were fifteen-year-old boys and sometimes they were sixteen-year-old girls. Good times. Fun.'

When Allen was away in Paterson or out in the literary jungle, Elise washed and ironed, made soup, took endless telephone messages for him. The fact that Allen was with Peter didn't seem to bother her unduly.

Allen encountered Salvador Dali at a gallery opening and introduced himself as a poet. 'Do you know the poet Lorca?' Dali asked.

Allen took two steps back and began reciting. 'Not for one moment beautiful aged Walt Whitman/ have I failed to see your beard full of butterflies . . .'

'But do you know his "Ode To Salvador Dali"?' he asked, but Allen had never heard of it. 'It is a beautiful poem, one of his best,' said Dali. 'What is your address? Do you have a group? I am interested in meeting the young poets.' They had a short, intense talk about Surrealism, then Dali, returning to the subject of his old friend Lorca said, 'Ah, "The Poet In New York", that is not the great Lorca. It is too Surrealist. The early gypsy ballads are more solid.' They arranged to continue their conversation another day at Dali's hotel.

Allen, Peter, Jack and Gregory arrived at the St Regis dressed so badly that Dali's wife, Gala, took one look at them and postponed the meeting for a week. Allen reported their initial enounter to Robert LaVigne, 'It was all very weird to have contact with dreamlike Dali . . . He seems intelligent and more serious than I'd have imagined.' Gala arranged Sunday lunch for them at the

Russian Tea Room, and Allen, Peter and Jack dressed as well as they could for the occasion. Jack wore a huge vicuña coat that reached the ground, and had a ski cap pulled over his ears to protect him from the vicious cold. Dali and Gala were waiting, Dali leaning forward on his cane. He ordered 'One grapefruit . . . peenk.' Allen explained his vow of poverty; he had decided never to read for money. Dali disagreed completely, 'The measure of genius is gold!' he told them. Allen said that they wanted to meet Marlon Brando, who they knew ate in the Russian Tea Room. Dali pointed at Jack and said, 'He is more beautiful than Marlon Brando.' They asked about his politics, and Dali said, 'As a politician I am a Royalist. I would like to see the Throne of Spain return, Franco and the others out.' He told them, 'Last night I finished my latest painting, using a pubic hair for the last final touch.' Peter explained rock 'n' roll to them and offered to take them to one of the big concerts at the Paramount. The Dalis went on their own and later marketed a 'Rock and Roll' perfume.

Allen, Peter, Jack and Gregory visited William Carlos Williams in New Jersey. He was then seventy-three, but youthful and alert. They all read their poems, while he stared out the white-curtained windows at the traffic ploughing through the slush and snow. Sometimes he seemed a little bored. They stayed all afternoon and into the evening, drinking the cheap wine they brought with them, until Flossie, Williams' wife, went to the cellar and brought up something better. Williams liked Peter's poems (he had written two), but most of the time it was Ginsberg and Williams talking. As they left, Kerouac asked, 'Before we go, Doctor Williams, do you have any wise words for us?'

Williams stared out the window, 'There's a lot of bastards out there.'

'They were dressed as bums, they were bums,' Williams said later, and remembered that they had smoked some funny-smelling stuff while they were there, but he was enthusiastic about the younger poets, and after their visit, he wrote Theodore Roethke, 'I think you've heard of Allen Ginsberg and his gang, Karouak and Corso. What does it mean? At least we live in an age where anything goes and I for one welcome it.' Williams, like Richard Eberhart, considered this group to be Ginsberg's creation.

Jack was the first to go. Allen lent him $225 and on 15 February he sailed for Tangier. Ten days later, Gregory left for Paris, to meet up with his girlfriend Hope Savage. Peter finally made up his mind. He and Allen each paid $185 for a one-way passage, and on 8 March they kissed Elise and Sheila goodbye and set sail on the *Hrvatska*, a Yugoslavian freighter headed for Casablanca.

7 The Classic Stations of the Earth

It was a magical interlude, and like all such interludes, all too brief: 'The things we have never had remain: it is the things we have that go . . .'

William S. Burroughs. 1983.
[Introduction to *Beat Hotel* by Harold Norse.]

Bill Burroughs had been in Tangier since December 1953 and had lived in a number of places including a celebrated male brothel. After a spot of trouble with his most recent landlady, who objected to the constant flow of visiting Spanish boys, Bill found 'the original anything-goes joint', the Villa Muniria (or Villa Delirium, as it came to be known) in the old French quarter. It was owned by an ageing Frenchwoman who had an 'in' with the authorities and had previously run a whorehouse in Saigon. The ex-madam poked Burroughs in the ribs and said, 'You can be *free* here, you understand.' Bill's room was small and damp, but he liked it because the door opened out on to a garden, where he was able to grow some roses and play with the housekeeper's two cats.

Bill's room was painted white and he had covered one wall entirely with snapshots, mostly from his 1953 expedition to the South American jungle in search of Yage. Another wall was his shooting gallery, pockmarked with bullet holes. As usual, Bill was heavily armed. He had an assortment of razor-sharp knives, including a meat cleaver and a machete. When Kerouac was in Tangier, Bill scared him by producing a rifle and waving it drunkenly over Jack's head.

In the corner of the room stood a home-made orgone accumulator, in which Bill used to sit, doubled-up, smoking kif. He had his own little stove, on which he made hashish candy, or majoun, of which he was very proud; finely chopped kif was mixed with caraway seeds, ground nutmeg, cinnamon and honey (mostly kif), then heated until it became the 'consistency of sticky shit' as Ginsberg described it. One tablespoon of Bill's majoun would see you through the night.

The floor was littered with bottles that once contained Eukodol – a morphine-based painkiller – and with pages and pages of typewriting, which lay thickly around the legs of his desk and which the sea breezes would blow out of the open door and into the garden. Bill would sit hunched over his portable, sometimes chuckling to himself, mopping his brow, hair awry. He would tear a page of manuscript from the machine and scribble all over it in his spidery calligraphy, before throwing it over his shoulder to join the pile. Sometimes he found his routines so funny that he would roll on the floor, doubled up with laughter. The manuscript had the working title of 'Word Horde'. It was later published, much revised, as *Naked Lunch*.

When Kerouac arrived in Tangier in late February 1957, Bill got him a roof-top room in the Villa Muniria. A tiled patio looked out over the topsy-turvy roof-tops and palms to the tower of the Catholic church and the bright green water of the bay. In the distance could be seen the coast of Spain and the mountains further inland, and sometimes Gibraltar was visible in the bright Mediterranean haze, a small bump of coastland to the north east.

One evening, Bill treated Jack to a fine meal, complete with fine wine and liqueurs. Back at the hotel, they collected Bill's binoculars and went to Jack's rooftop patio to look at the breathtaking night-time view. Bill stared out to sea. 'When will Allen get here?' he asked. Bill began to cry. He was still obsessed by Allen, after three-and-a-half years, he missed him dreadfully. He leaned on Jack's shoulder sobbing.

Within a month of arriving Jack was homesick for America and missed his mother. He began complaining about the high cost of whores (three dollars). He had a bad experience with opium, and became violently ill after smoking hashish that had been cut with arsenic. Jack couldn't understand Bill's obsession with Allen, nor could he relate to Bill's ordered European ways. He described his feelings in *Desolation Angels*: 'On the opium overdose I had snarling dreary thoughts about all Africa, all Europe, the world –

all I wanted somehow was Wheaties by a pine breeze kitchen in America . . . So by the time Allen and Peter finally arrived for their big triumphant reunion with us in Africa it was too late.' Jack had already made plans to move on. As Allen said, 'Jack was no good out of America.'

On 19 March 1957, Allen and Peter docked in Casablanca, where they spent three exciting days. Disregarding Burroughs's grim warning never to enter a Muhammadan establishment, they headed straight for the Medina to explore. After investigating in the capital, they continued their voyage round the coast, and as their boat pulled into dock, they saw Bill and Jack waving to them from the sunny harbour wall.

The excitement of seeing Allen was too much for Bill, who got very quickly drunk. He waved his machete about until Allen told him to stop frightening everyone. Allen wanted to do everything: hike to the countryside, go swimming in the harbour, explore the Medina and the Casbah, visit the circus, go inland to Fez by train, sit in outdoor cafés sipping mint tea and smoking kif. Bill's orderly life was thrown into chaos.

They rolled Bill's majoun into balls and chewed on it for hours, washing it down with hot plain tea. After an hour or so it produced a slow, strong marijuana high that was like peyote. Allen and Bill would stay up half the night talking, Bill stumbling around the room, endlessly stirring his drink with his index and middle fingers, visiting the two or three kif joints that he had burning in various ashtrays around the room, his voice sometimes raised high in protest as Allen gleefully proposed one contentious idea about art or literature after another for the sheer pleasure of watching Bill attempt to shoot it down.

Jack left for France in April, and Allen and Peter immediately moved into his wonderful roof-top room. Kerouac later regretted leaving; he accused Allen and Peter of putting pressure on him to go, so that they could have his room. With a room of their own, Allen and Peter settled into more of a routine. Allen got up at dawn and wrote on the patio, watching the sun rise, then spent five or six hours working on Bill's manuscript.

Each day, the Chinese maid brought a delicious lunch to Allen and Peter's room as they lay reading or writing. Cigarettes cost twelve cents a pack, Egyptian hashish was plentiful and opium was fifty cents a gram, enough to keep one awake for twenty-four hours. They spent a lot of time out on their patio, looking out at the harbour and the boats, or leaning over the concrete parapet to watch Bill putter about in the garden with the cats. The warm Moroccan nights were spent in conversation with friends. Paul Bowles often visited them there and recalled Allen's conservatory: 'I have an acoustical memory of the clicking of Allen's typewriter accompanied by the ceaseless rattling of the windowpanes as the *levant* roared outside.'

Alan Ansen arrived and joined the typing pool. By late May, there were over two hundred pages of finished manuscript. They were approaching the harder task of going through Bill's letters to Allen from 1953–56, pulling out biographical material, routines and narrative fragments to add to the main text. As the work progressed, Bill had liver trouble and had to stop drinking. He also cut out majoun. The manuscript gradually took shape, and Allen wrote Lucien: 'It's quite a piece of writing – all Bill's energy & prose, plus our organisation & cleanup & structure, so it's continuous and readable, decipherable.' According to Bill, Allen had considerable reservations about the book, despite his later efforts to champion it: 'Allen did a lot of typing, retyping parts of the manuscript, which he didn't like at all. He said, "I don't like it."'

They got to know Bill's friend, the English painter Francis Bacon, who said that he would paint a big pornographic picture of Allen and Peter. Allen gave Bacon some photographs taken of him and Peter in bed together in Tangier, but the painting was not done. Bacon later commented: 'Those photos were terribly useful. The lovers weren't very interesting, but there was something about the mattress spilled over the metal spindles of the bed that was so despairing that I decided to keep them and use them.' Bacon scholar Michael Peppiatt says that the ticking on which Bacon's nudes of the early sixties are displayed derives from these shots. It was through Bacon that Ginsberg met Paul Bowles. He had been in Ceylon when they first arrived but had just returned. Bowles had close-cropped blond hair and was wearing a suit. Allen found him very courteous and lively, but also a little remote. They spent the day smoking Tanganikan marijuana. That evening Bacon and Bowles went to eat at L'Escargot, an expensive French restaurant, and Bowles insisted that Allen join them, knowing that he would not be able to pay his share. Allen and Bowles talked about Gertrude Stein throughout the meal and Bacon picked up the check.

Bowles lived with the Arab naîf painter Ahmed Yacoubi, whom Francis Bacon had first enouraged to paint. Allen found Yacoubi very straightforward and sincere. Jane Bowles reminded Ginsberg of Joan Vollmer, 'cool and shy and intelligent like Joan,' he wrote, though his first introduction to her was not a success and she never liked him. When he first arrived Allen had introduced himself to her on the telephone as 'the bop poet'.

'The what poet?' she asked, and Allen had to repeat himself a number of times before she understood and said, 'I see.'

Then Allen asked, 'Do you believe in God, Jane?'

Jane snapped back, 'I'm certainly not going to discuss it on the telephone.' She wrote to Paul Bowles in Ceylon, 'I suppose I must see him, but he is much more up your alley than mine.' Jane had suffered a stroke a few weeks before Allen and Peter arrived, which left her disabled; she could not read and was afraid she was losing her sight. She worried she was going mad and was in continual dithering panic. Allen told her that William Carlos Williams had some of her symptoms and he ended up half blind and deaf, and joked that maybe she'd better get a good seeing eye dog. This was the wrongest possible approach with Jane; she was furious, she never wanted to talk to him or see him again and she never forgave him. Peter, however, she regarded as a saint.

Peter was unhappy in Tangier and wanted to go to Europe so he could meet some western girls. He was getting on badly with Bill who, despite regarding himself as incapable of jealousy, constantly teased Peter and put him down. Bill's condescending attitude towards Peter also offended Allen, who had hoped, perhaps naîvely, that Bill would like Peter and accept the situation. One evening, when they were all high on majoun, Allen could not take Bill's mocking attitude any longer. He leapt up and ripped open Bill's khaki shirt with a hunting knife. Peter, for his part, was glad when Allen began reading guide books to Spain.

They left Tangier in June 1957, bound for Granada, then took the train to Seville and stayed for two days. They zigzagged back to the ancient university city of Cordoba, arriving late at night, and the next day, they investigated the Great Mosque, with its hundreds of Arab pillars and coloured arches. They arrived in Madrid on the overnight train, took their travel-stained clothes to be cleaned, and rested up. They ate mostly as the Madrilenians did, standing at bars and stalls, dining on delicious small portions of lobster, crab and prawns, yoghurt or fresh fruits; a small but tasty steak was only eight cents. They strolled in the crowded evening streets and drank in the overcrowded student bars.

Allen, naturally, headed straight for the Prado, where he was astonished by the vibrant colour and intricacy of detail in the paintings of Breughel and Bosch, El Greco, Goya, Velasquez and Rubens. He spent an hour examining the details of Hieronymus Bosch's *Garden of Earthly Delights* before leaving it. *The Annunciation* by Fra Angelico was, he thought, simply the greatest painting he had ever seen.

Allen wrote to Kerouac: 'At that instant I got Europe hungry and museum hungry and realised all the treasures of Europe all over, in Italy & Spain & Moscow & Paris, all the vast collections of infinite pictures.' Allen's hunger for museums and cathedrals and works of art remained with him and over the decades he managed to visit virtually every collection of significance throughout the world.

Allen and Peter liked Madrid and made an effort to find work in order to stay the summer, but no job materialised. They made arrangements to spend the summer with Alan Ansen in Venice instead, and meanwhile concentrated on seeing as much of Spain as they could.

For Allen, the greatest thing in Barcelona was Gaudí's magnificent Segrada Familia. He and Peter climbed its unfinished towers and also visited Gaudí's Guell Park. They walked on the Ramblas and explored the dim alleys and high dark fortress-like stone tenements of the Barrio Góthico. They visited Jean Genet's Barrio Chino – a cheap slum, half medieval, half rebuilt after Franco's bombing during the Spanish Civil War – filled with whorehouses, artists' bistros and workingmen's cafes. They took a large garret room, high in the rooftops with a small window through which the setting sun turned their bedsheets first orange, then pink. They wandered the streets, looking for the life Genet had described, but it was long gone.

They arrived in Venice on 1 July 1957, having taken a train along the French Mediterranean coast in a heatwave, and spent a day and a night in Milan. Allen and Peter stayed up all night talking with Alan Ansen and at dawn watched the sun rise over the lagoon. They settled into Ansen's apartment on the Calle della Carrozze. Allen could put his head out of the window and see the blue water of the Grand Canal, half a block away, with the gondolas bobbing past and the water taxis leaving wakes which slopped against the striped mooring poles, as in a Canaletto painting.

Each day, like most tourists, Allen was drawn inexorably to the Piazza San Marco, the vast colonnaded plaza fronting the cathedral, where the orchestras of the outdoor cafes battled with each other, playing Italian light opera, Strauss and gypsy dances as great flocks of pigeons whirled and swooped among the tourists. Allen never grew tired of visiting the basilica, its five Byzantine onion domes fronted by a group of giant bronze horses looted from Imperial Rome. He found the edifice even more impressive inside where the warped mosaic floor tiles rose and fell in waves and curves, the ancient wooden piles beneath having settled unevenly into the mud of the Lagoon. The walls and ceiling were covered by thousands of square feet of delicate mosaic, the famous 'golden gloom' of ninth- and tenth-century Byzantium. This was the Old World of Europe that Ginsberg dreamed of in Chiapas and California, and he was utterly enthralled.

On 21 May 1957, acting on orders from Captain William Hanrahan of the San Francisco Police, Juvenile Division, two police officers went to City Lights Bookshop and bought a copy of *Howl*. The officers then obtained a warrant for the arrest of Lawrence Ferlinghetti as the publisher and as owner of the bookstore, and a John Doe for Shigeyoshi Murao for selling the book. Shig was taken the three blocks to the Hall of Justice, where he was fingerprinted and photographed, then locked in the drunk tank, which smelled of piss. Two hours later, an ACLU lawyer bailed him out. Ferlinghetti arrived not long after with his lawyers and was also fingerprinted and photographed but was not detained. The *Howl* trial was under way.

Two months earlier, US Customs had confiscated 520 copies of *Howl* arriving in the USA from the English printer. Ferlinghetti had immediately referred the matter to the American Civil Liberties Union, whose lawyers said that in their opinion the book was not obscene and they were prepared to fight the seizure. At this, the US Attorney in San Francisco backed down, and the books were returned. Now that the police had decided to prosecute, the ACLU again stepped in.

They planned a defence based on the first amendment rights of freedom of speech and press, and assigned one of their best lawyers to the case, J.W.K. ('Never Plead Guilty') Ehrlich. Opposing him was Ralph McIntosh, who had a long history of prosecuting nudist magazines and 'pornographic' films. The trial was a great *cause célèbre* for the Bay Area literary community. Kenneth Rexroth rose up in arms; Robert Duncan, Ruth Witt-Diamant and dozens of others offered assistance, and it was to be the main topic of literary discussion that summer. The trial date was set for 22 August.

With all the heavyweight literary intellectual support on his side, Allen didn't foresee any trouble winning the case. There was Richard Eberhart's article in the *New York Times*; William Carlos Williams's introduction to the book; the moral support of Louise Bogan, Randall Jarrell, James Laughlin and Grove Press. 'The literary backup was impeccable,' Ginsberg later said. 'You couldn't possibly lose the case, so I didn't take it seriously as a threat, and Ferlinghetti in his letters didn't sound too threatened.' The trial, of course, gave enormous publicity to the book, and Kerouac wrote Allen to complain that everywhere he went he was introduced as the guy *Howl* was dedicated to, and now he couldn't be famous on his own.

After a month in Venice, Allen and Peter made their first big sightseeing trip to the Italian mainland, first to Florence and then on to Rome, where, in the Protestant Cemetery, Allen plucked a clover from Shelley's grave to send to Corso in Paris, and took another to send to his father. He was overcome by emotion at seeing Keats' grave and wept. The rest of the day they spent on the beach at Ostia (where twenty years later they would read poetry to audiences of thousands at open-air festivals).

A visit to the Vatican Museum confirmed Allen's anti-Catholic sentiment. He found that drapery had been painted all over the naked bodies of Michelangelo's *Last Judgement* and fig leaves fixed to all the torsos in the Vatican's great collection of classical statuary. Allen expressed his indignation to his father, 'I never saw the Church in such vulgar and ugly relief. After Florence and its classical openness and after seeing statuary in the Forum and various State museums, to go to the Vatican and see them desecrating the very significance and point of ancient sculpture – idealised human beings, but real ones ... It stands out like the piece of dirtymindedness that it is.'

They took a train to Assisi, the beautiful mountain town overlooking the Umbrian valley. He and Peter arrived in the town dirty and unshaven, footworn, with Allen wearing a broken straw hat, much as Saint Francis himself must have appeared in his tattered cloak, begging and singing in the streets. They presented themselves at the Franciscian monastery, but the monks first refused them refuge, then solicited donations. They toured the churches, saw the tomb of Saint Francis and his relics and robes. They climbed the mountainside to visit the secret hermitage where Saint Francis spent his winters, and Allen tried out his bed. Some of the monks spoke English, which gave Allen a chance to vent his anger about the fig leaves in the Vatican.

Since the monks would not provide shelter, Allen and Peter unrolled their sleeping bags and slept on the monastery's front lawn. The monks were much put out. It was a beautiful warm night and the experience moved Allen so much that when he wrote his 'History of Visions – A List' in Peru three years later, he included that night among them: 'With Peter in Assisi, the clouds afright over the Umbrian plains in moonlite; cocksucking in the darkness on the grass in front of the cathedral doors.' They awoke early the next day to see the rising sun illuminate Giotto's frescoes in the church. Allen was in fine form and ready to continue his arguments with the monks. He read them his poetry and disturbed their whole routine. They showed him the bed of roses into which Saint Francis had thrown himself, which thereafter had grown no thorns. Allen could see the thorns as clear as day and took pains to point them out. The monks regarded him with even greater suspicion as a hell-bent atheist. Allen concluded that the Catholic Church was nothing more than a 'vast nasty thought control organisation'. He thought that the monks walked, talked and prayed like zombies, and that their arguments were crude, flat and pseudo-logical. 'I never was struck by what a bunch of namby pamby amateurs they were before,' he wrote his father. And to his brother he wrote, 'Close up, in Rome and in the great Franciscan center of Assisi they're nothing but a bunch of hard up, fig-leaving, psychotic politicians.' He had been hoping to find a deep under-standing of mystical experience and possibly a model beatific lifestyle among the Franciscans but was sadly disappointed. They spent a second night on the monastery lawn, then hitch-hiked back to Venice. He had not found the answer to his spiritual quest but had had one of the best and funniest times since their arrival in Europe.

Time magazine telephoned from Rome, wanting to interview Allen about the upcoming trial. Short-staffed because of the summer vacation, the editors readily agreed to Allen's proposal that they pay his way down there and give him two days' living expenses. They sent him a round-trip air ticket and thirty-five dollars. The interview itself was a depressing experience – the *Time* interviewer accused him of being insincere – but Allen was able to stretch the money to last two weeks, enough for him to make a trip to Naples and Ischia, where he hoped to find W.H. Auden.

After making the rounds of the Rome bars, Allen rose the next day at noon and took a train down the coast to Naples, where he did the usual tour of museums and saw the collection of art from Pompeii, including the famous room of Roman pornography. On the second day, he climbed Mount Vesuvius and spent an hour sitting and watching the steam oozing from the walls of the great crater. He walked around the rim, looking out over the Gulf of Naples to Capri and beyond. Then he slid and ran, arms outstretched to the sun, scattering powdered black lava sand, all the way down the side, running and walking through the lava fields until finally he came to beautiful vineyards, where he picked delicious blue grapes as he walked to the ruins of Pompeii. There he spent the afternoon in the strange deserted streets. A lot of statuary and painting remained, including a number of naked Venuses, satyrs and drunken Bacchuses, which pleased him. He also discovered the Priapic illustrations on the walls of the ancient ruined bordello, before returning, exhausted, to his youth hostel in Naples.

Allen found a fisherman to take him to the Isle of Ischia, where Auden had spent his summers for the last decade. Auden disliked sunshine and only came out in the evenings. Allen located him at Marie's bar, where he was sitting with a group of friends, 'a tableful of dull chatty literary old fairies,' as Ginsberg later described them. They were probably not at all pleased to have Allen intrude upon them, since he spent the evening drinking copious amounts of wine and arguing furiously and angrily with them on the merits of Walt Whitman. Allen found Auden's approach to the argument long-winded and rationalistic. Writing to his father the next day, he described the conversation:

'I doubt if Auden respects his own feelings anymore. I think his long sexual history has been relatively unfortunate and made him very orthodox and conservative and merciless in an offhand way. He sounds like an intelligent *Time* magazine talking, approaching such questions as capital punishment and literary censorship as if they were complicated bureaucratic problems as if they have no right to have private feelings but only a series of pseudo-factual logical considerations – a sort of fetish of objectivity – which strikes me as no objectivity at all, but a sort of abject distrust of people and their loves . . .

'I quoted the first line of Whitman, "I celebrate myself," etc., and Auden said, "Oh but my dear, that's so wrong, and so shameless, it's an utterly bad line. When I hear that I feel I must say, 'Please *don't* include me' " (Re: 'What I shall assume, you shall assume'). Said he was an orthodox Englishman, not a democrat (in this context). It all boils down to some sort of reactionary mystique of original sin.

'Auden is a great poet but he seems old in vain if he's learned no wildness from life. Said he "intensely disliked" Shelley. He thought my own book was "full of the author feeling sorry for himself" and saw no vitality or beauty beyond that as far as I could see. All this strengthens the conviction I have had, that the republic of poetry needs a full-scale revolution and upsetting of "values" (and a return to a kind of imagination for life – in Whitman's "Democratic Vistas" that I have been reading in Venice).'

By the end of the evening, Allen was drunk, and as he left he called them all 'a bunch of shits'. Actually Auden liked Ginsberg's work and often defended him in private, so the incident was probably more an example of Auden's having fun with an uninvited guest than a record of his real opinions.

Summer was coming to an end, and Allen and Peter began preparing to move on to Paris, where they intended to spend the winter. In order to see as much of Europe as possible, they travelled via Austria and Germany, stopping off in Vienna to see the museums, and then in Munich, where they visited the Dachau crematorium.

*   *   *

Allen's expectations of Paris had been high, but still it amazed him. He wrote Louis, 'Paris is beautiful. The only city I've seen so far that would tempt me to expatriate and settle down . . . Paris has universal interest and permanent charm as a living place. I'll try to stay here half a year and then come home.' It was to be almost a year before he left. Allen headed straight for the Louvre to see the Mona Lisa and spent several afternoons there. He and Peter took the creaking old elevator to the top of the Eiffel Tower, which was much bigger than he had expected. 'Very vast, like dream machinery in the sky,' he wrote Louis.

Most of all, Allen and Peter enjoyed ambling through the ancient twisting streets and alleys, and sitting in outdoor cafés on Haussman's grand boulevards. 'Everything as charming and arty and free and grotesque as advertised,' Allen wrote Louis. 'The very faces on the streets look like they've stepped out of paintings by Lautrec and Van Gogh. The streets look like impressionist streets . . . and all the millions of Hemingway and legendary cafe and boulevard and movie recollections of Paris I've stored up since I got to college.'

Kerouac's *On the Road* had been published that summer by Viking, and in Paris, Allen read Gilbert Millstein's laudatory review in the *New York Times*. 'So fine and true,' he wrote Jack. 'Well, now you don't have to worry about existing only in my dedication & I will have to weep in your great shadow.'

Allen heard in October that Judge W.J. Clayton Horn had pronounced *Howl* to be not obscene. Judge Horn's handling of the case was exemplary. He read all the relevant case histories, including the trial of *Ulysses*, and identified the constitutional aspects of the case: that to be considered obscene, a book had to be shown to have no redeeming social importance. He announced: 'I do not believe that "Howl" is without redeeming social importance. The first part of "Howl" presents a picture of a nightmare world; the second part is an indictment of those elements in modern society destructive of the best qualities of human nature; such elements are predominantly identified as materialism, conformity, and mechanisation leading toward war. The third part presents a picture of an individual who is a specific representation of what the author conceives as a general condition. "Footnote to Howl" seems to be a declamation that everything in the world is holy, including parts of the body by name. It ends with a plea for holy living ... The theme of "Howl" presents "unorthodox and controversial ideas". Coarse and vulgar language is used in treatment and sex acts are mentioned but unless the book is entirely lacking in "social importance" it cannot be held obscene.' The judge concluded that 'In considering material claimed to be obscene it is well to remember the motto: *Honi soit qui mal y pense*,' and found the defendant not guilty.

The trial had generated tremendous excitement in San Francisco, with letters to the *Chronicle*, mimeographed public statements circulated to the press, round table discussions on the radio and statements of support streaming in from editors and publishers. Barney Rosset and Donald Allen gave the most dramatic support by publishing the full text of 'Howl' in their special San Francisco issue of *Evergreen Review*. All the press attention resulted in terrific sales of the book; by the end of the trial, more than ten thousand copies were in print.

When they were in Venice, Alan Ansen had introduced Allen and Peter to Guy Harloff, a Dutch artist who lived in a cheap residential hotel at 9 rue Git le Coeur, a tiny medieval lane in the Quartier Latin. There were forty-two rooms, but the hotel was always full. Residents' guests slept on the floors and sometimes out in the hallways. Harloff introduced them to the landlady, Madame Rachou, who said a room would be available on 15 October. The building was over three hundred years old, and the floors sloped crazily. The plumbing was subject to backups, fierce loud vibrations, clankings and leaks. One had to give advance notice of the desire to take a bath, so that the water could be heated. Naturally there was a surcharge for this service. There were no carpets or telephones in the rooms, and the toilets consisted of a French-style hole in the floor on each stair landing. It was a big event if the sheets got changed. The electrical system was extremely sensitive and periodically plunged everyone into darkness if someone overloaded the circuit by plugging in a tape recorder or other device. Small and blue haired, Madame Rachou, who bought the hotel in 1933, could tell by consulting her electrical switchboard if anyone had smuggled in an illicit hotplate or even a radio.

Hookers, shopping bag ladies, artists' models and a giant black man from French Guyana lived side by side with jazz musicians and poets. Artists painted over their ceilings and walls, there was a photographer in the attic who spoke to no one for two years and one artist filled his room with straw. Rooms were 120 francs a month (thirty dollars) but Madame Rachou sometimes allowed her guests to pay with paintings or manuscripts, none of which she kept, not for a moment realising that they would ever be valuable. Madame treated her tenants as she would her own children and so, as Burroughs noted, she 'was very mysterious and arbitrary about who she would let into the hotel'.

Madame Rachou presided over a small bar, which served coffee, beer and wine and closed at ten-thirty. Next to the bar was a dining area where she would cook huge cheap lunches of cassoulet or rabbit stew, and would sit talking endlessly to her tenants over cups of watery espresso. Madame gave lunches for the local police inspectors, with whom she endeavoured to maintain a very good relationship.

There was a separate entrance to the hotel for residents and this door was never locked or controlled, but Madame had an uncanny clairvoyant knowledge of everything that went on in the hotel and in the street and was able to materialise at the door to protect her residents from con-men, occasional police visits, creditors and sometimes from themselves.

Allen and Peter were given a small furnished room with paper thin walls, a roof that leaked when it rained, walls of discoloured plaster and a small round table covered with oilcloth. Madam Rachou promised that a cheaper room, in which they could make as much noise as they wanted, would come free in a week or so, which it did. They moved to Chambre 25, third floor front. Their new room was much better. It had whitewashed walls and French windows with long drapes. There was radiator heat all week and hot water on Thursday, Friday and Saturday. They had a two-burner gas stove, on which Allen cooked lentil soup, beef stew and mussels which he bought at the magnificent open-air market on the nearby rue de Buci.

Before moving into the hotel, they visited with Gregory Corso in Amsterdam for a few weeks, and he returned with them to Paris. Allen, Peter and Gregory all slept together in a big sagging bed. Allen unpacked his red portable Royal typewriter from its carrying case and set his papers out on the worktable. For the next ten months this was to be his home.

* * *

Back in the States, *Life* magazine ran a big article on *Howl* and the trial. Soon the book was a best-seller. The subsequent publication of *On the Road* led to enormous interest in the 'Beats', and Allen began to consider that he might actually be able to live off his literary activities. Royalty checks were arriving with regularity. *Howl* was in its fourth printing, and sales showed no signs of abating. Grove Press had issued an album of modern poets, including Allen, reading their work, and Fantasy Records in Berkeley proposed that he should record a whole album of his work in a Paris studio. *Evergreen Review* and *Partisan Review* bought some poems, and Citadel Press wrote asking to include 'Howl' in an anthology of 'Beat' writing that they were assembling.

As Peter had feared, things had not gone well for his family without him, and he decided that he should return to Northport to protect his family and get his other brother Julius out of Central Islip hospital, where he had been for years.

Peter applied to the US Embassy to get a Veterans Administration loan, since neither he nor Allen had enough money for his fare. Allen was hoping that Kerouac would repay the $225 he owed him, since Jack knew about Peter's situation and was making a lot of money from *On the Road*. Although Jack kept promising, he never sent it, much to Allen's frustration. It wasn't until the next year that the V.A. finally loaned Peter the passage money.

Allen found that the heroin in Paris was much cheaper and better than anything he had ever taken with Bill Burroughs or Garver. Sniffed, it had an effect that was longer lasting and stronger than when shot in the vein, and the initial hit was almost as strong. Marijuana was also cheap and easy to get, and he liked to smoke it before visiting the Louvre: 'stared back at the Mona Lisa high on T.'

Now that he was settled, Allen began to write poetry again. The six months of running around Europe had been too frantic for him to do much more than write letters. He had, in the meantime, concluded that he needed to change his writing style. He found himself addressing his mother's death.

In November 1957, he wrote to Jack Kerouac: 'I sat weeping in Cafe Select, once haunted by Gide and Picasso and the well dressed Jacob, last week writing first lines of great formal elegy for my mother –

Farewell
with long black shoe
Farewell
smoking corsets & ribs of steel
Farewell
communist party & broken stocking . . .
with your eyes of shock
with your eyes of lobotomy
with your eyes of stroke
with your eyes of divorce
with your eyes alone
with your eyes
with your eyes
with your death full of flowers
with your death of the golden windows of sunlight . . .

'I write best when I weep, I wrote a lot of that weeping anyway and got idea for huge expandable form of such a poem, will finish later and make a big elegy, perhaps less repetitious in parts, but I gotta get a rhythm up to cry.' The poem was to be 'Kaddish'.

A young French artist, Jean-Jacques Lebel, had introduced him to the poetry of André Breton, and Ginsberg used the structure of Breton's 'Free Union' in this section of 'Kaddish':

My wife with the back of a bird fleeing vertically
With a back of quicksilver
With a back of light
With a nape of rolled stone
. . .
My wife with a sex of mirror
My wife with eyes full of tears

Winter came but no snow. Athough a vicious wind cut down the Seine, the narrow alleys were sheltered. Allen would get up around noon and spend the afternoon walking the grey streets alone. He took long strolls by the river beneath the grey branches of the plane trees and bought the unexpurgated Olympia Press editions of Henry Miller, Jean Genet and Apollinaire's pornographic novels from the bookstalls there.

The evenings were spent cooking supper then reading or writing; there were visits to movies, to the Chinese Ballet. The first local French people they got to know were a pair of shopgirls, one of whom, Françoise, was very attracted to Allen. 'She was really hung up on me. I didn't realise the consequences. I didn't take it seriously. I didn't realise it was real,' Ginsberg recalled, and said that his reactions were always the same whenever that situation arose. 'I keep thinking it's my mother whenever a woman gets emotional over me. It's apparently a big neurotic problem of mine, not recognising genuine affection. I thought anybody in love with me must be crazy! Since I'm gay anyway, and I've been living with Peter, that if anybody gets fixated on me there must be some misjudgement of some sort. I didn't see it, as I might now, as an indication for an open situation, more as a fixed obsession on her part. So I probably hurt her a great deal, being so closed off. She was very young. I was thirty by then.' Allen and Peter both made love to her, and when she was not around, Peter would go down to visit the whores in the truck warehouses near the Gare de Lyon. Later a girl named Joy Ungerer became a good friend of theirs. She was half-French, half-Malaysian, very cheerful and friendly. She grew quite attached to Peter but was happy to sleep with both of them.

People stopped by Allen's room all the time for supper, marijuana, heroin or whatever was on the menu. Strange beat characters wandered in and out, and Gregory Corso came up with a name for Madame Rachou's establishment; he called it the Beat Hotel (a sobriquet Allen never liked).

They continued to explore Paris. They visited the catacombs, and walked a mile underground in the eerie haunting dampness and sickly sweet odour of millions of human skulls and bones, stacked like fire logs along the sides of the tunnel. Gregory stole a legbone, which they displayed on their hotel wall alongside the portrait of Rimbaud.

Letters arrived from Bill, sometimes several a week. He appeared to have resolved his feelings for Allen and no longer thought they would ultimately be together. Allen wrote to Lucien, saying that Bill 'seems unhungup on me now, which is a relief, relations turning to normal again. It always made me nervous.' Allen was being deluged with fan mail, in addition to the copious correspondence he received from family and friends. He wrote Louis, 'Spend, or waste, a lot of time answering strange letters, everything from Jesuit appeals to Christ to young poets who write in on toilet paper.'

The letter on toilet paper came from a young poet named LeRoi Jones, who had just moved to Greenwich Village. He had read 'Howl' and was very moved by it. In his autobiography, Jones later said, 'Wanting to be as weird to him as I thought he was to me, I wrote him a letter on toilet paper, sent to the 9 rue Git le Coeur address, asking was he for real. He sent me back a letter, also written on toilet paper, but the coarser European grade that makes better writing paper. He told me he was sincere but he was tired of being Allen Ginsberg. (The notoriety was just starting.) He signed the letter and had a drawing under his signature of a lineup, a parade of different beasts and animals, all with halos over their heads in some weird but jolly procession.' Allen sent Jones poems, some of them Gregory's, for the magazine he was just starting, *Yugen*, and suggested that he contact Philip Whalen, Burroughs and Kerouac. He particularly tried to get LeRoi to publish Kerouac's poems because Lawrence Ferlinghetti had just rejected Jack's *Blues* poetry collection.

Allen was too broke to celebrate New Year's Eve,1958. Peter was out with friends and Allen wandered around the Place Pigalle in Montmartre all evening 'under the noisy stars', walking back at midnight through the Les Halles red light district where the drunken celebrants staggered in the street. His lack of money was serious. He didn't even have enough to pay his grocer's small bill for milk and eggs. He wrote again to Jack, pointing out his dire straits and asking him to pay his debt.

Allen had been encouraging Burroughs to visit Paris for some time. In January, a flurry of letters announced his imminent arrival. Allen rented Bill a room in the hotel. Bill flew in from Tangier on 16 January 1958, the day before Peter left for New York. Both Allen and Peter were apprehensive. As they parted, they kissed and waved goodbye awkwardly, filled with doubts and worries both about the future of their own relationship and, especially, Bill's intentions. Bill behaved at first as he had in Tangier – poker-faced and impassive, mocking and distant – but this didn't last. Something had happened to Bill, as Allen was to find out a few days later.

The evening after Peter left, Allen fell into a deep depression. He sat sobbing on his bed, then took some heroin. He had sex with

Bill for the sake of their old friendship, then they started arguing and misunderstanding each other according to their old pattern. Allen smoked some pot, but that only made matters worse, giving him an anxiety attack. Françoise came in and tried to climb all over him. Feeling paranoid and at his wits' end, he fell silent and terrified on the bed. There was a knock on the door, and it was Gregory, back from Germany where he had been trying, unsuccessfully, to sell encyclopedias to GIs. Allen was enormously pleased to see him. He was so familiar and reassuring, a solid connection to the happy days that he and Peter had spent living in the room together. 'I also thought he would save me from sordid sorrows with Satanic Bill,' Allen wrote Peter.

The next night, Bill and Allen sat facing each other, eye to eye, across Allen's kitchen table and had a serious talk. Allen confessed his doubts and misery, and Bill revealed what had been happening to him in Tangier. As Bill spoke, he was transformed in Allen's eyes. In the last months of 1957, Bill had stopped drinking and stopped writing. Every afternoon he sat on his bed, thinking and meditating, working things through slowly, until he finally became conscious of what he called 'a benevolent sentient center to the whole Creation'. He had apparently had, in his own way, a vision of what Ginsberg called a 'big peaceful Lovebrain'. It had given him the courage to look at his whole life, and his relationship with Allen, more dispassionately, he said; his trip to Paris was not to claim Allen, but just to visit; he wanted to see a psychoanalyst to clear up the unconscious blocks that remained.

He and Allen talked late into the night, finally establishing a rapport so exquisite and delicate that Allen trembled. It was a closeness similar to the one he shared with Peter, only it was not sexual. Bill even began to recognise that, while Allen was willing to have sex with him, he didn't really want to, so he stopped putting pressure on Allen. Allen wrote Peter: 'He no longer needs me like he used to, doesn't think of me as a permanent future intimate sex schlupp lover, thinks even he'll wind up maybe after difficulties with women.' Allen's dread of Burroughs cleared up overnight, and he awoke the next morning with 'a great bliss of freedom and joy in my heart.' He wrote Peter, 'Bill's saved, I'm saved, you're saved, we're all saved, everything has been all rapturous ever since . . . I cried the other night realising you'd gone, thinking that love would go away with you and I'd be alone without connection – but now I see Bill is really on same connection and I begin to feel connected with everything and everyone, the universe seems so happy.'

The new rapport was real. Bill and Allen began to discuss the means of extending 'Love bliss' to others and spreading the connection between them without sacrificing intimacy, which was what Allen and Peter had been trying to do in San Francisco, New York and Tangier by bringing other people into their relationship, and bed, but with little success. Allen now felt confident. 'We'll solve that problem too before we're done,' he wrote Peter. It took them a few years, but by the mid-sixties, their ideas of love and peace, open sexuality, and the use of consciousness-expanding drugs, had reached hundreds of thousands of people world-wide. The hippie movement, in this respect, had its roots directly in the Beat Generation.

Thomas Parkinson, Allen's English professor from Berkeley, invited him to visit London. Parkinson was making a series of programmes for the BBC and hoped Allen would record his poetry. Ginsberg crossed the Channel on 2 February 1958. On the ferry, he cried at the thought that he would soon see the 'sad fogs of the land of Blake' and wrote a small poem. His first view of Britain was of the White Cliffs of Dover, stretching away in the mist. In London, with his pack still on his back, he spent several hours mingling with the Saturday night crowds in the West End. He saw Piccadilly Circus and the winter moon over Big Ben before finally taking the tube to Parkinson's house in Hampstead.

He spent the next day in the National Gallery, where he delighted in the Rembrandts and Vermeers, but he told Peter, 'The greatest here is *Turner*. The only British painter and great genius like Van Gogh.' He saw many Blake watercolours amd drawings and spent hours examining the Elgin Marbles, writing Peter: 'Elgin Marbles Naked Love in British Museum. Greatest thing in Europe.'

Ginsberg recorded his five-minute contribution to Parkinson's series on American poetry. As soon as he began to read, the programme director, Donald Carne-Ross, stopped the recording and rushed in excitedly to ask Allen if he would record both 'Howl' and 'A Supermarket In California' complete. Feeling confident, Allen began again and gave a slow sorrowful reading, gradually building up the tempo. He almost broke down in tears, dreaming that he was talking through the huge BBC microphone to the 'Soul in the Fog'; that he was reading to Blake himself. Parkinson agreed that it was a great reading and afterwards Allen went out drinking with Carne-Ross, who drunkenly promised to record Jack and Gregory and everyone. Allen spent a night in Oxford where he gave a small informal reading. He read Creeley, Whalen, Levertov and 'Howl'. The students responded with great enthusiasm. Allen wrote Peter, 'I feel great again, communicating and crying in public – in front of the mild withdrawn English.' Thomas Parkinson drove him to Salisbury Plain to see Stonehenge and to visit Salisbury Cathedral, 'a big sweet cathedral looks so calm on the huge green lawn, big as daytime.' He sat up all night talking to Kerouac's schoolfriend Seymour Wyse and met a few English poets. He climbed to the Whispering Gallery in the high dome of St Pauls to look out over London. London was then the largest city on earth, a sprawling dirty metropolis. Signs of post-war reconstruction were everywhere, men clearing bomb sites and the skeletons of new buildings going up. Allen wrote a long prose sketch of the scene from his high perch in the pale winter sunlight.

He arrived back in Paris, to find Bill gloomy and with a light paregoric habit. Paregoric, an elixir of opium, legal in France, could be bought cheaply in any drugstore. Bill claimed that he was making experimental use of it in his analysis, but Allen took him to a doctor and got him some apomorphine, and he began withdrawing. 'He was glooming about the state of the world, all them armies and armories,' Allen told Peter.

Spring came and Madame Rachou celebrated by changing the curtains in the rooms and washing the bedspreads. The painter Larry Rivers arrived in the city, and Allen spent a wonderful week drinking with him in the spring afternoons, sitting in outdoor cafes, watching the passing show. Allen and Gregory were walking down Boulevard St Germain one day when someone hailed Allen. It was Dom Moraes, a young Indian poet from Bombay, whom Allen had met in London. They joined him and his girlfriend at the table and immediately got into a deep discussion about God. Allen and Gregory saw a lot of them, taking them sightseeing, driving around Paris in a convertible, and making spontaneous poetry tapes. They introduced Moraes to Larry Rivers, who had a young

American woman with him. In his autobiography, Moraes said, 'They leapt at her, suggesting that we all strip and make love on the pavement, "Like William Blake and the angels, man," cried Corso. The girl became very upset and burst into tears and the poets were much concerned, petting her with repentant hands, and offering her poems and candy which Corso pulled from his pocket.'

Moraes liked them, and offered to arrange readings for them in Oxford if they visited England that summer. Gregory did not want to wait, and the next week they were in London, looking at the sights. One evening, after a round of Soho pubs, they wound up broke and hungry at midnight on the pavement in Piccadilly. The bookdealer David Archer came and rescued them after an emergency phonecall from Allen; he fed them and gave them a little money, 'for poetry's sake'. Archer had a legendary bookshop in Holborn in the 1930s, and had published the first books by Dylan Thomas, George Barker and David Gascoyne at his Parton Press. Through him, they met Barker and caught a glimpse of the remnants of the Dylan Thomas era of literary London, mostly in the pubs of Soho and Fitzrovia.

Dom Moraes, who came down to London to get them, was surprised to find that they had already met up with his friend David Archer. Archer was delighted with Allen and Gregory, 'Charming chaps, what? And really talented,' he told Moraes. Their first reading in Oxford was at Jesus; Ginsberg did a fiery rendition of 'Howl'. At University College they demanded to know where Shelley's rooms were. Dom Moraes, not having the slightest idea, vaguely indicated the nearest door. Gregory flung it open and fell to the ground, crawling over the carpet, kissing it reverently, while the occupant of the room, who had been making himself a pot of tea, stared at him in horrified silence.

W.H. Auden had forbidden Moraes to bring any Beat poets near him, but Allen and Gregory had already found out where Auden's rooms were. Auden, taken by surprise, was noncommittal about their remarks on poetry, but later he warmed to them and took them to tea. Gregory asked him, 'Are birds spies?'

Startled, Auden said, 'No, I don't think so. Who would they report to?'

'The trees,' said Allen. Allen had heard that Auden regretted his aloof behaviour in Italy, so he brought him a volume of Artaud as a gift. It was unclear what Auden really thought of Ginsberg's poetry at the time, but Charles H. Miller, in his account of Auden, recalled a heated discussion of 'Howl' in which Auden defended the poem against Chester Kallman's negative appraisal. Auden also announced, in Miller's hearing, sometime in the late 1960s, 'Of course Allen *has* contributed to literature. "Howl" *does* have much to say, and Allen may well grow to even larger achievements. Give him time.'

Auden showed them around Christ Church Cathedral. They described this as the high spot of their visit, despite having been around it with a guidebook the previous day. To Auden's acute embarrassment, they attempted to kiss the hem of his garments, but he swiftly moved his trouser cuffs out of range and said goodbye. Moraes commented, 'This curious mixture of true innocence combined with a sharp eye for the main chance was very attractive.'

Dame Edith Sitwell arrived in Oxford for a performance of her 'Façade', at the Town Hall. Allen and Gregory were taken to the afternoon rehearsal and introduced to her. Allen told Dame Edith that he was editing an anthology of poetry, to be illustrated with photographs of the poets in the nude, and invited her to contribute. The seventy-year-old Dame declined gracefully.

Allen and Gregory's reading at New College was invaded by a large number of home-grown Beats and the cause of some controversy. New College was the main Campaign for Nuclear Disarmament stronghold in Oxford. Gregory's lighthearted approach to the subject of the H-Bomb in his new poem 'Bomb' was regarded as outrageous: 'O Bomb I love you/ I want to kiss your clank, eat your boom . . .' Gregory read. The members of the New College Poetry Society threw shoes, accusing the poet of being a fascist. Allen wrote to Peter, 'The students got mad and attacked him for being, they thought, anti-social.'

Edith Sitwell invited Allen and Gregory to luncheon at the Sesame Club in London and made a reservation in the inner dining room, 'So that the old ducks would not have so much to quack about.' Dame Edith, wearing a tall wimple-like conical hat, a long satin dress and a fur coat, led the way past the expensively dressed diners, leaning upon her ebony stick. Her escort was Quentin Stevenson from Oxford. Her secretary, Elizabeth Salter, followed with Allen and Gregory who were wearing turtle neck sweaters, jeans and sandals. Sitwell later described Ginsberg as having the 'look of a starved wolf'. Allen sat to her left and Gregory to her right, and they slowly ate their way through a specially ordered meal of smoked salmon, Lobster Thermidor and, possibly as a reference to Gregory's Oxford reading, the club's specialty, an ice cream 'bombe à l'Americain'.

Dame Edith opened the conversation by praising American poetry for its vitality, saying she particularly liked the work of Jose Garcia Villa, e.e. cummings and Marianne Moore. A discussion of Aldous Huxley's experiments with mescaline led to the subject of drugs, the use of which the Americans defended on the grounds of 'heightened sensibility'. Dame Edith's position was that 'no poet should need a drug to produce extreme sensibility, which must be, if he is any good, a part of his equipment'. A report in *Life* magazine suggested that at this point, Allen offered Dame Edith some heroin, which she refused on the grounds that it brought her out in pimples. When she read the account afterwards she was most offended, not only by the suggestion that she had used heroin, but that she might have spots. 'I'm hardly the spot queen,' she said. They talked for hours, and she told them that she liked their work and that they were the hope of English poetry.

The Algerian War had polarised the French population, and the arguments and accusations, political moves and repercussions changed constantly. Back in Paris, Allen followed events with interest, and the war was the subject of a long correspondence with his father. There was a huge anti-de Gaulle march and demonstration at the Place de la Republique. Silver-helmeted riot police waited down the block but there was no violence. It was the first large political demonstration that Allen had seen since his childhood days handing out leaflets against Mayor Hague in Journal Square, Paterson. These were the same types of people, arms upraised in comradely salutes, shouting 'Vive La République', and 'Front Populaire'. Allen almost cried, imagining that he saw Naomi and Aunt Eleanor among the marchers.

The news coming in from the States looked bad. Neal had been busted and was put in the San Bruno County jail to await trial for selling pot to a narcotics agent. In the course of their investigation, the police had found that Neal was Dean Moriarty of *On the Road* and were, as Ginsberg wrote Eugene, 'apparently doing all they can to be evil about it'. Allen was very worried and wrote asking Kerouac what was to be done. Allen proposed getting people such as Kenneth Rexroth and Ruth Witt-Diamant to write letters as character witnesses saying that Neal was a writer, but Jack wasn't prepared to do anything at all to help the hero of his books.

One of their friends in Paris was the painter Jean-Jacques Lebel, son of the art historian Robert Lebel. Early in June, Jean-Jacques's parents gave a party for Marcel Duchamp at their elegant apartment on Avenue President Wilson, and Jean-Jacques invited Allen, Bill and Gregory. Gregory disgraced himself by throwing up on the staircase before they even reached the party. Jean-Jacques introduced them to Marcel Duchamp, Man Ray and Benjamin Peret. Jean-Jaques had mixed memories of the evening: 'At the end, when people started to leave, I see them going up to Duchamp, Gregory holding hands with Allen. Duchamp was sitting in a chair, speaking to people. The first thing Allen does, he gets down on his knees and starts kissing Duchamp's knees – thinking he was doing something Surrealistic. And Duchamp was so embarrassed. So embarrassed! Allen being totally drunk – he made a mix of whiskey and red wine. And then the most embarrasing thing was to come. Gregory had found, in the kitchen, a pair of scissors, and he cuts Duchamp's tie. It's such a corny childish thing. Knowing Gregory and Allen it's lovely, it's trying to be humble, it's trying to say "We're children, we're fools, we admire you."' Jean-Jacques's father was less than enamoured of his son's new friends. Two days later Allen told Jean-Jacques, 'You know, I think we fucked up a little bit.'

The day before the party they had run into Tristan Tzara, the dadaist poet, at the Deux Magots restaurant. Ginsberg thought that his 'Dada Manifestos' were very good poetry, and had always liked the line, 'Dada is a virgin microbe.' Allen began reading Motherwell's *The Dada Painters and Poets* and went to see a few Surrealist movies including the famous *Un Chien Andalou*, made by Luis Bunuel and Salvador Dali in 1929. The shock scene of a girl's eye being sliced by a razor, which had been censored in the United States, was not as horrifying as Allen had been expecting.

Allen and Bill visited Louis Ferdinand Céline, the author of *Death on the Instalment Plan* and *Journey to the End of the Night*. Céline and his wife, Lucette, lived in a large house with a mansard roof on a cliff in Meudon, a southwest suburb with a view overlooking the Seine and the spires of Paris. Céline was dressed almost as a clochard in three moth-eaten sweaters. He had long hair and there was brown mould under his fingernails. There were ferocious dogs barking when they arrived but Céline assured them that the animals were just noisy and not dangerous. Bill, who hated dogs, was not so sure.

'I keep them for the noise,' said Céline. 'I take my dogs to the village because of the Jews. The postmaster destroys my letters. The pharmacist won't fill my prescription . . .' The dogs continued to bark and howl in their compound.

Rusty bedsprings stuck up from the overgrown lawn near the gate, and they sat outside at a rusty garden table. Madame Céline brought them tea and wine. Céline was friendly and the visit lasted for several hours. Allen got the impression that Céline did not get many visitors, though his work was enjoying a critical revival at that time. They spoke in broken French and English, but his English was no longer very good. Céline and Bill discussed the various prisons they had been in, and Céline said that one could only know a country by seeing its prisons. Bill told him about his days as a morphine addict, which prompted Céline to recall the time when he was a ship's doctor and had calmed panic on a sinking ship by injecting all the passengers with morphine. He still practiced as a doctor but said, 'All the young women want a young doctor to look at them, and all the old women want to stand naked in front of a young doctor,' so what could he do. 'It's too filthy here to practice.' He showed them where he wrote, in a huge messy downstairs room, cluttered with books. Allen and Bill were very respectful and Céline appreciated it. They left him copies of *Howl*, *Junkie* and Gregory's book *Gasoline*. As they left, Allen said, 'We salute you as the greatest writer in France!' to which Lucette playfully added, 'In the universe!'

Allen had been abroad eighteen months and was feeling homesick. He began to consider ways of raising the funds to buy passage back to New York. Louis offered to loan him the money, but Allen first tried to get hired on a New York-bound ship, to no avail. He made a few calculations to see if he could sell enough poems to pay his way but found that he could not. That spring, Kerouac had finally repaid the $225 he owed Allen, but the money had very quickly been used up. Allen hinted heavily in a letter to Kerouac that he was in need of ticket money, but Jack, despite his earnings from *On the Road*, was as tight-fisted as ever; anyway, his mother would never have allowed it. In the end, Allen accepted Louis' offer.

Allen tried to persuade Bill and Gregory to return with him. Gregory had no one in New York to return to, could live more cheaply in Paris and was scared of the police in the United States. Bill was not interested. He told Allen simply, 'I have told no one to wait.'

Allen met one final literary celebrity before he left. Jean-Jacques Lebel and his friend Henri Michaux bumped into Allen in the street. Allen expressed his admiration for the poet's work and said how interested he was in Michaux's experiments with mescaline. Michaux gave him his address and Allen fired off a drunken postcard inviting him to visit. A few days later, Allen was sitting in his room, naked and without his eyeglasses, washing his feet, when someone knocked on the door. As usual, he sang out 'Come in,' and there was Henri Michaux waving Allen's postcard. He told Allen that he hardly ever came out, but was having a day off and wanted to make the most of it. He promised to return and later that evening, Allen, Gregory, Bill and Michaux got into a long conversation about mescaline. It seemed that they had had similar experiences, and agreed about everything they discussed. They became immediate friends, and Michaux arranged to come back the next night, which was Allen's last in Paris, and bring a chicken for dinner. They had a wonderful evening. Allen explained the structure of 'Howl' Part II to him, and translated Gregory's poem 'Lost Watches' which Michaux laughed over. A few months later, when Allen was in New York, Gregory wrote to complain: 'Did you pee in the sink when Michaux came to visit? One of us did and what's wrong with that? But rumour has it that Michaux told people about it and thought that we were trying to impress him, really, so fucking European to even detect such an action.'

Allen sailed for New York on the *Liberté* the next morning, 17 July 1958. Bill was in tears when he left, and Allen wondered if he would ever see him again.

8 Kaddish

> *O Naomi, the photographs I have of 1920, you sitting on the grass, with long black hair, a mandoline upon your knees O beautiful Garbo of my karma, then, lovely young woman, Communist beauty . . .*
>
> 'Kaddish' (early draft)

The winking neon and floodlit towers of the Manhattan skyline loomed through the mist as the *Liberté* pulled into dock. 'Like all the spires and architecture and cathedrals of Europe all put together on one shelf and more massive height,' Allen wrote Gregory. 'You get a sense of eternity looking at Manhattan from a boat arriving – the buildings look as if they were manufacturing cosmic jazz.'

For the last two years, Allen had managed to live entirely on his poetry and literary skills. He had emerged from the *Howl* trial a famous literary figure, and upon his return to the States, the press seized upon him as the leader and spokesman of the scene. Despite the tag 'King of the Beats', Jack Kerouac was now little more than a right-wing alcoholic, hiding at home with his mother in Northport, and in no condition to give interviews. With Bill and Gregory still in Paris, the mantle of leadership fell on Allen. He organised poetry readings, pressured editors to publish the new work, and lobbied the press on a variety of issues, from legalised marijuana to free love. He took pains to show the difference between the Beat Generation and its philosophy of love and tenderness, and the Beatniks, who were mostly weekend bohemians out for a good time, but the press generally blurred the distinction, and public perception was that Allen was the progenitor of all the bearded young men who wandered around Greenwich Village in hand-made leather sandals, carrying bongoes and a bottle of chianti. Certainly they all had a copy of *Howl* in their jeans pocket.

When Peter had arrived back in New York six months earlier, he had an unexpected reunion with his father, Oleg, whom he had not seen in five years. They rented a large room together, and Peter took a job as a nurse on the night shift at the Psychiatric Institute, where Ginsberg was a patient in 1949. Peter checked out armfuls of books from the library and was usually able to read for five hours each night, when the patients were asleep. He spent a lot of time with his brothers; Lafcadio was at home in Northport with his mother, and Julius was still in the mental hospital, where Peter visited him every week. Julius now recognised him. Peter wrote Robert LaVigne, 'It's gotten to now where he imitates me, like flicks his ash from cigarette when I do, he puts his hand on his hip when I do. At least he notices me. Kind of a social thinking in his mind. Seems he wants to be close to me . . . There are few people in whose eyes have I seen such constant fear, as if Julius were continually looking over a battle field like in Bosch's Hell painting.' Peter wrote sadly, 'Seems I am married to my sick brothers.'

When, on his return, Allen arrived at Lucien's with his brother Eugene, Kerouac was there, already a little drunk, and he insisted on picking Eugene up, saying, 'I want to lift the Ginsbergs.' He was bloated from alcohol and had grown heavier since Tangier. Jack told them he was a Republican – no surprise, since he had always been a supporter of Senator McCarthy and his anti-Communist witch-hunts. Jack may have been feeling guilty about certain letters mailed to Allen in Paris, which Allen had not yet seen. Jack did not mention them.

Jack's mother had read a long letter that Allen wrote Jack when he was high on cocaine, and her immediate reaction had been to fire off a hate letter to Allen in Paris, warning him not to write to Jack or try to contact him through other people. Not realising that extra postage was required to send letters abroad, she put a six-cent stamp on; it went sea-mail and didn't reach Paris until after Allen had left. It was a masterpiece of the genre, calling Allen an immoral lout not fit to associate with Christians like Jack and herself. She told Allen that her husband, on his death bed, had made her promise to keep Allen away from Jack, and she swore that she would honour that promise. She had given Allen and Bill's names to the FBI. 'You miserable bums all you have in your filthy minds is dirty sex and *dope*.' She warned them, 'Don't ever mention Jack's name or write any more about Jack in your "dirty" "books" I'll sue you and have you in "jail" . . . We don't want sex fiens or dope fiens around us.'

Allen had asked Bill to open any mail that came after his departure, and Bill's initial reaction was to dismiss her; 'A stupid, small-minded vindictive peasant incapable of a generous thought or feeling,' Bill wrote, upon forwarding the letter. 'I mean, she really is evil in her small way. In your place I would show Jack the letter. If he is content to be treated like a child and let his mother open his mail and tell him who to see and correspond with, he is a lost cause.'

Jack *was* a lost cause. When his mother told him what she had done, he quickly wrote to defend her actions. Bill's reaction to Jack's letter was more extreme: 'I herewith forward Jack's weak and cowardly letter, like some cat explaining to a former friend how he can't have him to the house anymore because of the little woman don't like Jews and after all I am out of "all that now. Not that we can't meet now and then (not too often) for a glass of beer someplace maybe," etc. Weak and cowardly, "and of course you understand I can't help out with Neal or Julius. After all why should I involve myself. Must consider Mother first. She is easily upset you know, and I *did warn* him after all." And a *Catholic-Buddhist* yet, My god! She really has him sewn up like an incision.'

Bill asked Allen to tell Jack from him that no one could achieve the fence-straddle he was attempting. 'No one can simultaneously stand behind those filthy letters of Mrs Kerouac and be in any meaningful sense a friend of the person to whom those letters were addressed. Jack has reaped fame and money telling Neal's story, recording his conversation, representing himself as Neal's lifelong friend. Maybe the fuzz got onto Neal through Jack's book. In any case he sold Neal's blood and made money. Now he will not lift a dollar to help. I don't see it, Allen.'

Bill brooded over the matter. The next day he added a postscript to the letter, feeling that Allen was being very badly treated by Jack. 'He seems to forget all your hours of work getting his manuscripts before publishers, agents, etc. I don't like the way he shrugs off the horrible injustice of Neal's imprisonment. All he wants is *security for himself*. A weakling and a coward who cannot be trusted under any pressure. He doesn't want *his name* mentioned. What about *your* name and Neal's and mine in his books??' Meanwhile Mrs Kerouac continued to bombard Bill and Allen with letters in Paris; Jack had not told her that Allen was back in New York. The last letter Bill received he burned in his bidet, and then wrote to her saying he would not forward any more of her insane letters to Allen but would destroy them unopened.

Allen went to visit Peter's family in Northport. The Kerouacs lived only two blocks from the Orlovsky household. While Allen and Lafcadio hid from Jack's mother in the bushes, Peter asked him to come out for a visit, but Jack refused. He told Peter he was afraid his mother would know if he saw his forbidden friends, and anyway, 'What good would it do?' As they waited in the bushes, Lafcadio was confiding to Allen that a rocket from Mars had flown low over Northport and signalled to him as he ran naked out of the house to hide in the woods. They were coming back for him because he was the one perfect man, and they were going to save him from the coming apocalypse. Allen, realising that Lafcadio was crazy, and that Kerouac and his anti-Semitic mother were both crazy, wondered what strange chain of events had led to him hiding in the bushes like a ten-year-old, waiting for the King of the Beats to sneak out to play.

However, Allen had no intention of abandoning his friendship with Kerouac, and eventually his perseverance paid off. Within a few months, he had managed to drag Jack a little way from his mother's apron-strings, and that fall and winter they saw quite a bit of each other.

Towards the end of August 1958, Allen and Peter found an apartment at 170 East 2nd Street, overlooking an all-night Jewish bakery. Noisy trucks came and went all night, and the bakery had a big clock in its front window, which was useful since Allen didn't own one. The apartment had four medium-sized rooms; there was steam heat, hot water, a kitchen tub, an icebox and a new stove, all of which seemed quite luxurious after Paris. The rent was sixty dollars a month which Peter paid until Allen had money. Allen's room in the Beat Hotel had become like a railroad station, with a constant stream of people sleeping on the floor and visiting, making it very hard for him to get any work done. With his new East Village apartment, he was determined to stick to a policy of no visitors. 'It's a silent castle for sleeping, balling, cooking and writing,' he told Kerouac, whom he invited to come and stay anytime. He and Peter bought a pallet for the spare room.

They quickly developed a routine. Allen saw Peter off to work at eleven every night, then toured the bars. He would go down to the Five Spot where a waiter he knew let him in free. Thelonious Monk was the resident musician, so Allen heard hours of magnificent jazz. He was intrigued by a gnome-like figure, sitting at table near the door using a stop-watch to discover the principles behind Monk's timing and noting the variations in a tune from one night to next, or as Allen put it, 'notating Thelonious Monk's hesitancies and after thoughts clonks on piano, syncopations in and out of time.' He had heard of Harry Smith, a 'strange alchemist hermit mysterioso character' who, in 1948, had made film experiments using light directly on to film. He was best known for a six-record anthology of American folk song, issued by Folkways with his copious scholarly notes. They went to Harry's hotel room and he screened some of his films. Harry was to become a constant, nagging presence in Allen's life for the next four decades.

He gave a copy of *Howl* to Thelonious Monk, and a week later ran into him standing outside the Five Spot. He asked him if he'd read it.

'Yeah, I'm almost through,' said Monk.

'Well?' asked Allen.

'It makes sense,' replied Monk.

After the Five Spot, Allen would often go to Lucien's and watch the Late Show with him and talk politics. Then he would go on to the San Remo or the Cedar Street Tavern, to see if any of his old friends were there. Allen wrote Jack, 'I visit them all, sneak up like a ghost and spend all evening talking about what happened to them. Then I go home.' There was eighteen months' worth of gossip to catch up on. 'I am slowly going round digging every one of the multitude of people that I know, or knew, sneaking silent thru the streets and surprising them in their lives. No big mad scenes.'

He finally got to meet LeRoi Jones, to whom he had been writing from Paris, and went to big parties at his apartment, where the painters Willem de Kooning and Franz Kline and the Cedar Street Tavern art crowd mingled with black jazz musicians. 'An acme of good feeling,' Ginsberg later called it. 'A lot of mixing, black white hip classic.' Jones was publishing *Yugen* magazine and in 1960 began editing a series of books for Totem Corinth, by

Snyder, Whalen, Kerouac, Joel Oppenheimer and Ginsberg (his early poems, *Empty Mirror*), many of which Ginsberg had originally tried to get City Lights to publish. Jones also edited the anthology *The Moderns* which did for contemporary prose what Don Allen's *New American Poetry, 1945–60* did for poetry.

Sheila Boucher, Allen's old girlfriend from 1955, showed up. Running away from her husband and children, she crossed the country in true Beat style, spending four days in jail for vagrancy somewhere in the Midwest. She met up with a young painter on the road, and they arrived in New York together. She got an advertising job in the Empire State Building, but since they had nowhere else to go, she and the painter took over the spare room in Allen and Peter's apartment. Allen felt guilty for resenting it. He really wanted to be alone to work, but there seemed to be no way that he could ever manage it.

One night Allen went on an FM talk show, where he drunkenly and enthusiastically explained why marijuana should be legalised. The producers were horrified, thinking that they must surely be breaking the law. Afterwards, still elated, he showed up at the Five Spot at 3 a.m. and read Gregory's 'Bomb' to the musicians and a handful of remaining customers.

Allen spent a lot of time in New Jersey, visiting his relatives and having heart-to-heart talks with his cousins, who all seemed to have grown up, married and had children since he went to Europe. Sheila Boucher and her boyfriend stayed on at Allen's apartment. Her job hadn't lasted, and now they spent all day sleeping, then got up and vanished into the night-time streets. Sheila Plant, a San Francisco girlfriend of both Peter's and Lafcadio's, came to stay at the apartment while she prepared to return to the Coast. She had been in and out of mental institutions since Peter last saw her.

The apartment threatened to grow even more crowded. Carl Solomon was getting out of Pilgrim State soon, and his mother wanted him to live near Allen. Robert LaVigne wrote from San Francisco to say he wanted to visit New York and asked if he could stay. Allen could not bring himself to refuse, but told him, 'Now I want, weep for, need, prolonged solitude. I've come to the wrong place for it but I'm hung up with Peter and his brother's problems, which is so much to handle. I dread what's to come.'

Allen had a meeting with James Laughlin, owner of New Directions, and collected a copy of William Carlos Williams's

Paterson in which Williams had reprinted portions of Allen's letters. He talked at length to Laughlin about unpublished works by Philip Whalen and Gary Snyder and discussed 'Ferlinghetti's blindness' at not seeing how good all these new authors were. Allen believed so strongly that Ferlinghetti should publish Jack's book of poems, *Mexico City Blues*, that he offered to pay the costs out of his own future royalties, but City Lights finally turned it down, as well as rejecting an anthology of Buddhist poems by Kerouac, Snyder and Whalen. Ferlinghetti was also uninterested in Burroughs, though Allen still had hopes of persuading him to publish a short ten-to-twenty-thousand-word Burroughs pamphlet. 'You make a big mistake to pass him up,' Ginsberg wrote Ferlinghetti. 'DIG BURROUGHS HE'S A BIG GENIUS.' Allen was also trying to get Ferlinghetti to publish a second book by Gregory Corso, who was now penniless in Greece, but to no avail. New Directions eventually became publishers of both Gregory Corso and Gary Snyder, and their books sold in large numbers throughout the 1960s. Allen put too much pressure on City Lights, forgetting that Ferlinghetti wanted an editorial voice of his own.

By now, Allen was well aware of the problems of being published by a small press. He kept reporting to Ferlinghetti that New York bookstores were out of stock of *Howl*, or had written repeatedly for copies, which had not been supplied. Nevertheless he remained loyal, and continued to press Ferlinghetti to publish his friends. In the end he took the manuscript of *Mexico City Blues* to Don Allen, and Grove published it in October 1959.

Kerouac's *The Dharma Bums* was published by Viking Press in October 1958. Allen sat down with an advance copy and read it through. He wrote Jack: 'The whole thing's a great piece of religion testament book, strange thing to be published ... You settling down in simpler prose, or just tired like you said? Montgomery is great in there, and Gary is fine too. I don't dig myself (too inconsistent mentally) (in the arguments). It is a big teaching book which is rare and spooky.' Although he didn't regard the book as up to Kerouac's usual standard, this didn't stop him from promoting it for all he was worth.

Allen was concerned that Kerouac's publishing career was going astray and did his best to intervene. Kerouac had a number of good unpublished manuscripts, among them *Mexico City Blues*, *Doctor Sax* and *Visions of Cody*. However his agent, Sterling Lord, had

persuaded him to write a follow-up to *On the Road*, continuing
the adventures of his characters – *The Dharma Bums*. Now Lord
wanted him to write a travel book about Paris for Viking.
Meanwhile, Grove Press was clamouring to be allowed to publish
Doctor Sax. They had been promised it long before, and had
signed their side of the contract, but Lord had still not sent them
the signed contract. Grove editor Don Allen met with Allen to see
if he could influence Jack, pointing out that Grove had done well
for him with *The Subterraneans*, which was true. Allen wrote to
Jack: 'I say, perhaps Viking and Lord are neglecting your good
books and trying to get you to write "potboilers" according to
their idea of what your writing career should develop like.' It made
no sense to Allen for them to put off the publication of *Doctor Sax*,
which in his view was one of Kerouac's best books. In another
letter he spelt it out: 'My opinion – don't let Madison Avenue try
water you down and make you palatable to reviewers Mentality
by waiting on Wildbooks and putting out commercial travelogues
(however good) – *Sax* is logical next book and you're in a position
to do what you want now.' Allen's pressure made Jack act, and
Grove published *Doctor Sax* the next April.

Allen began a long-delayed course of dental treatment. The
dentist, Allen's cousin, suspected that the nitrous oxide he admin-
istered as a painkiller would have a profound effect on his patient.
As the office muzak receded into the distance, Allen had a glimpse
of another area of consciousness. 'Kerouac, Snyder and Whalen are
all correct as far as I can see,' he reported to Ferlinghetti. 'The
whole fabric of existence is illusion. If you can get the kind of
explicit Nirvana thru meditation as you can thru Nitrous Oxide,
Contemplation here I come. I never saw anything like *that* before
– whole friggin cosmos slipped into the void like lizard's tail into
crack in black wall. Sort of immense obvious cosmic joke.' He
began work immediately on the poem 'Laughing Gas.'

Delighted, he wrote Kerouac: 'Dammit it's all a big cheat – great
universal razz like ridiculous woody woodpecker disappearing
laughing into the receding eyehole of cosmic cartoon, all the
universes disappearing all at once. I'm sorry I was so deaf, I was
hung on Harlem God – I still don't understand how both absolute
impressions can exist without contradictions in same universe.'

For the past year, Allen had been reading Keats, Shakespeare,
Crane, Thomas, Mayakovsky, Essenin, Artaud, Christopher

Smart's 'Rejoice The Lamb', Lorca's 'Poet In New York' and, after finally succumbing to eight years of pressure from Gregory, was now reading through Shelley for the first time since his childhood. He found a similar rise to rhythmic and poetic ecstasy in Shelley's 'West Wind', 'Adonais', 'Epiphany' and 'Hymn To Intellectual Beauty' and in Crane's 'Atlantis'. Both poets rose to wild heights of prophesy that interested him greatly, 'Like the earth opening up and you see all creatures moving around at once in eternity.' It was a poetic form that he was trying to attain in his own time. He wanted to write something that he would himself regard as 'awesome'. Weeping as he read Shelley's 'West Wind', he knew that he wrote best himself when he cried; he hadn't wept over his typewriter in a year.

One night, Allen sat up until dawn with his friend Zev Putterman, at his Greenwich Village apartment, playing Ray Charles records. At about 3 a.m. he injected morphine and metamphetamine, and together they chanted passages from Shelley's 'Adonais'. The drugs made him talkative, and Allen began to tell the tragic story of Naomi, and how, at her funeral, a *minyan* of ten Jewish men could not be assembled, so she was denied the Kaddish, the prayer for the dead. Putterman found his old bar-mitzvah book of Jewish ritual, and they read aloud the central passages of the Kaddish. Still thinking about Naomi, and with the powerful rhythms of the Kaddish ringing in his head, Allen left his friend's apartment at the corner of West 4th and 12th, turned and headed east through the deserted Saturday morning streets of the West Village. A whiff of wood smoke hung in the crisp subzero air, as he hurried along the shadowless street, ghostly in the predawn light, burning with a tremendous desire to write.

His route took him through the very heart of Greenwich Village – Sheridan Square and Washington Square – past all the familar bookstores and corner groceries, closed and shuttered. This was the neighbourhood where, in the early 1920s, Naomi and Louis had moved on the fringes of New York's avant-garde intellectual and bohemian circles. Allen crossed Second Avenue, which in Naomi's day was the Jewish Rialto. He passed the one surviving Yiddish theatre on First Avenue and reached the East Side, where fifty years earlier Naomi, a frightened ten-year-old girl, fresh off the boat from Russia, had lived with her parents on Orchard Street.

Finally arriving at his apartment on East 2nd Street, he sat down at his desk, snatched up a blue ballpoint pen, and began writing. He was filled with 'a kind of visionary urge that's catalyzed by all the strange chemicals of the City – but had no idea what Prophecy was at hand – poetry I figured.' He was writing what was to become his most celebrated poem: a Kaddish for his mother Naomi.

He scribbled in blue ballpoint and when that ran out continued in red. From 6 a.m. that Saturday morning until 10 p.m. Sunday, he filled page after page with his unintelligible scrawl, writing non-stop except for trips to the bathroom, often moved to tears, sustained by the combination of morphine and liquid methadrine injected in the vein. 'I began quite literally assembling recollection data taken from the last hours – "Strange now to think of you, gone without corsets and eyes while I walk . . ." etc . . . I wrote on several pages till I'd reached a climax, covering fragmentary recollections of key scenes with my mother ending with a death-prayer imitating the rhythms of the Hebrew Kaddish – "Magnificent, Mourned no more . . ." etc.

'But then I realised that I hadn't gone back and told the whole secret family-self tale – my own one-and-only eternal child-youth memories which no one else could know – in all its eccentric detail. I realised that it would seem odd to others, but *family* odd, that is to say familiar – everybody has crazy cousins and aunts and brothers.

'So I started over again into narrative – "this is release of particulars" – and went back chronologically, sketching in broken paragraphs all the first recollections that rose in my heart – details I'd thought of once, twice often before – embarrassing scenes I'd half amnesiaised – hackle-raising scenes of the long black beard around the vagina – Images that were central to my own existence such as the mass of scars on my mother's plump belly – all archetypes.'

Peter brought him boiled eggs and cups of coffee. As the day wore on, Allen took a few Dexadrine tablets to keep the creative energy flowing. After the twentieth hour, his attention began to wander and the writing became more diffuse. He found it harder to hold together the associations but he persevered until he had completed the whole chronology of Naomi's sad life ending in a prayer, 'Blessed be death in us all!' He had written fifty-eight pages.

Ginsberg used a new measure in the poem. Whereas he had previously followed Williams and looked for his measure in everyday American speech, he now observed the fixed rhythms of deeply emotional expression: wailing, crying, the moaning at a deathbed or states of extreme stress, on which he thought he could build huge poetic structures, as he had tried and succeeded in 'Howl' Part III.

The only way that he knew to build a mighty rhythm was through repetition and syntactical parallelisms, repeats and litanies, because these were all present in natural speech. The hysterical screaming of a twenty-year-old boy from the Bronx stuck in his memory of the Psychiatric Institute. The boy had had an attack of hysteria in the shower and was dragged off to the padded cell in a straightjacket, yelling: 'All you patients on the eighth floor, all you patients on the seventh floor, all you patients on the sixth floor, everybody on the fifth floor, doctors, nurses, all you attendants, YOU'RE ALL GONNA DIE!'

The boy had drawn his breath out like the howl of an agonised dog at the end of each line till he was winded with the force of it, then he inhaled an enormous breath before the next. He screamed the last line at the top of his voice. Here was everyday language under great emotional stress. Allen used the same repetition in 'Kaddish':

With your sagging belly
with your fear of Hitler
with your mouth of bad short stories
with your fingers of rotten mandolins
with your arms of fat Paterson porches . . .

He repeated it twenty-eight times over, each line change like a sob.

The final section of 'Kaddish' came to him when he was standing on a street corner at dusk. He realised that the alternation of 'Lord, Lord' with the 'caw, caw' of the crows that circled over his mother's grave would make a powerful rhythm. At home he began typing rapidly:

Caw caw caw shriek the crows in the white sun over the
    grave stones in Long Island
Lord Lord Lord time breaks me down to this my
    mother's tomb & piece of grass . . .

He built on this litany, until he reached the final lines:

Caw caw all years my birth a dream caw caw New York
    the bus the broken shoe the vast high school caw
    caw all visions of the Lord
Lord Lord Lord Caw caw caw Lord Lord Lord caw caw
    caw Lord.

It was mid-November, 1958. The poem was complete. The bulk of it, the first two sections to the end of 'Hymmnn', had been written in the one mammoth forty-hour session, the fourth part he had done in Paris, and the short third part was provided as a link to the main text. It was not until January that he began the massive job of revising the text.

Film-maker Robert Frank and painter Alfred Leslie were making a low-budget fifteen-thousand dollar movie, based loosely on the third act of Kerouac's play *The Beat Generation*. In it, Neal Cassady came home from the railroad bringing with him a group of friends, the Bishop stopped by to visit, and eventually Carolyn threw them all out. Neal was played by painter Larry Rivers; Jack Kerouac was played by Gregory Corso, who had returned to New York; Richard Bellamy, who ran the Green Gallery, was the Bishop; composer David Amram played a cowboy and also wrote the music. Carolyn was played by actress Delphine Seyrig, the only professional in the film, who was later to star in *Last Year at Marienbad*. Allen and Peter played themselves. At one point, Kerouac tried to bring in a bum to drink with him; the man was so filthy that Al Leslie banned Jack from the set for the remainder of the shooting.

Allen, Peter and Gregory thought it was wonderful to be paid eighteen dollars a day to clown around. They just sat drinking wine, pouring water on each other, taking off their clothes, juggling and performing circus tricks. Allen refused to put his clothes back on during one of the scenes, and Larry Rivers shouted that Allen was stealing the scene from him. '*Anyone* can draw attention to themselves by being nude in a movie!' he yelled, but Allen still refused to co-operate. Rivers began to march around the studio playing his saxophone. Alfred Leslie stood in the middle of the room, shouting at the top of his voice to no avail.

The shooting started in January 1959, and lasted six weeks. Then it was found that MGM had cunningly copyrighted the title *The Beat Generation*, so they used *Pull My Daisy* instead, after the ditty that Allen and Jack wrote in the 1940s. The film became a classic of the new American cinema and the forerunner of the underground film movement of Andy Warhol and Jonas Mekas in the early 1960s.

On the literary front, Allen made a last attempt to get Ferlinghetti to publish Whalen and Snyder, using both flattery and financial inducement. He offered to pay the cost of printing both books and said, 'They are so historically important for S.F. Muse and you are the historically important S.F. pioneer so it would work out madly great if you'd relent.' But there was no relenting. Ferlinghetti turned them both down.

Allen had also been trying to help the Living Theater raise money to put on William Carlos Williams's play *Many Loves*, and gave a benefit reading. The play opened in January. Allen's next mission was to go to Chicago.

Irving Rosenthal and Paul Carroll had been printing much of the new Beat writing in *Chicago Review*. They published numerous pieces by Kerouac, Ginsberg and Burroughs. Then the *Review* was attacked by Jack Mabley, a gossip columnist for the Chicago *Daily News* who, under the headline of 'Filthy Writing on the Midway', ended his column: 'But the University of Chicago publishes the magazine. The trustees should take a long hard look at what is being circulated under their sponsorship.' The trustees did take a long hard look and decided that the chapters from *Naked Lunch*, Kerouac's 'Old Angel Midnight' and a prose piece by Edward Dahlberg would all have to be dropped from the forthcoming winter issue. Dean Wilt told Rosenthal that the winter issue had to be 'completely innocuous', and wouldn't even allow him to run an article on German Expressionism. Rosenthal resigned as editor, and so did Carroll, the poetry editor. They formed a non-profit trust to publish the suppressed winter issue in a new magazine to be called *Big Table*. Allen and his gang flew into town like the Lone Ranger, to help fight the forces of reaction and to do benefit readings that would raise money towards the print bill.

With the suppression of the winter issue of the *Chicago Review*, Allen, Gregory and Peter became big news. The Chicago *Sun–Times* devoted half its front page to their arrival. They met

Rosenthal and Carroll and were taken to a welcoming party given by society couple Mr and Mrs Albert A. Newman in their Lake Shore apartment. There, photographers from the local press and reporters from *Time–Life* interviewed them in front of works by Picasso, Monet and Jackson Pollock. Each day, the gossip columns detailed their every move. It was the Beats' first big-time news coverage. *Time* devoted almost a whole page to them, including a photograph.

On 29 January, despite a winter rainstorm, nearly eight hundred people made their way to the Sherman Hotel, where, in the Bal Tabarin Hall, Allen read from 'Kaddish' and did a powerful reading of 'Howl'. It was the recording made that night that Fantasy Records finally released as an album.

On 5 February, Allen, accompanied by Gregory and Peter, made a triumphal return to Columbia to read at McMillin Theatre. The moderator was F.W. Dupee, a founder of the *Partisan Review*, who placed the event in historical perspective by pointing out that the last poetry reading he had seen in McMillin was by T.S. Eliot. But even Eliot had not been able to pull the crowds Allen commanded. Fourteen hundred people managed, after some scuffling, to get into the hall, while a further five hundred were turned away at the door by the police. Allen was in his element, and even dedicated 'The Lion For Real' to Lionel Trilling. Trilling was not there, but his wife Diana was, which caused some embarrassment later, when she wrote a long, patronising account of the evening for *Partisan Review* and misinterpreted 'The Lion For Real' as a love poem to her husband. In fact Ginsberg's ironic dedication to Trilling referred to the line 'a lion myself, starved by Professor Kandinsky, dying in a lion's flophouse circus.'

Allen described the reading to Ferlinghetti, who had also gone to Columbia: 'It's my old school I was kicked out of so I suppose I'm hung up on making it there and breaking its reactionary back. In fact I almost went mad on the stage weeping over a poem ("Kaddish", and my Pop in the audience) and denouncing the English faculty as a pack of ignorant amateurs. Gave long lecture on Prosody etc and we answered questions, even Peter read two poems. Strange night . . . God, reporters all over, all asking the same questions and no end in sight, it's getting stranger and stranger, life. Beginning to get invites from TV programs but have been holding out for scene where I can read poetry rather than discuss Beatnikism. The world is really mad.'

They began to take their poetry out on the road. Allen and Gregory read at Harvard, and Allen, Gregory, Peter, Ray Bremser and LeRoi Jones read at Howard and at George Washington University in Washington DC. Allen read at Brooklyn College and gave impromptu readings at the Gaslight Café on MacDougal Street, which was the first of the coffee shops springing up all over Greenwich Village that had poetry readings.

Allen made plans to spend the summer in San Francisco. Thomas Parkinson offered to fly him out and pay him one hundred dollars to read at UC Berkeley, and Ruth Witt-Diamant offered him the same amount to read at San Francisco State. Philip Whalen wrote to say that he would have a place to stay, 'enormous bathtub, huge orgy bed, Mike Nathan painting. Kirby Doyle's old apartment,' so he was all set. Allen and Peter flew out in April.

The Mental Research Institute in Palo Alto was conducting a research experiment on the effects of LSD 25, or Lysergic acid, and Allen was invited to participate. He jumped at the chance; he had been trying to track down some LSD since hearing of its existence in 1957.

Allen described his first trip to his father: 'It was astounding. I lay back, listening to music and went into a sort of trance state (somewhat similar to the high state of Laughing Gas) and in a fantasy much like Coleridge world of Kubla Khan, saw a vision of that part of my consciousness which seemed to be permanent and transcendent and identical with the origin of the universe – a sort of identity common to everything – but a clear and coherent sight of it. Rather beautiful visual images also, of Hindu-type Gods dancing on themselves. This drug seems to automatically produce a mystical experience. Science is getting very hip.'

Allen read the later parts of 'Kaddish' in Berkeley, with one surprising result. Stephen Spender was in the audience and afterwards objected to the intrusion of personal material in the poem. A few days later Spender stopped by Thomas Parkinson's office and said that he had not been able to forget the reading and had begun writing poems again after several dry years, this time using personal material. A few days after that, he visited again and asked if Parkinson could get Allen to send 'Kaddish' to *Encounter*, which he edited, but Allen had already promised it to *Yugen* and *Big Table*.

Allen was still wrestling with the first long part of 'Kaddish', but he sent the rest of it to his father. Louis wrote back immediately,

'I like it very much; it is nostalgic and poignant; some lines are heart-wrenching, what with not only you but me being at that time in the middle of the anguish. Some of the lines are poetically magnificent and imaginatively vivid. I do object to one line: about the "beard about the vagina". It's bad taste and offends my sensibilities. Alas, to a lesser degree, I have reservations about all those "caw caw"'s though you might have something there.'

Allen replied: 'The line about the "beard around the vagina" is probably a sort of very common experience and image that children have who see their parents naked and it is an archtypical experience and nothing to be ashamed of – it looks from the outside, objectively, probably much less shocking than it appears to you I think – it's a universal experience which almost everyone has had tho not many poets have referred to it but it can do no harm to be brought to consciousness.

'Caw Caw I still rather like since it's the climax of a sort of musical form – two themes (Caw Caw and Lord Lord – representing realistic bleakness-pain-materialism, versus Lord Lord which is mystical aspiration) that alternate and in the last line merge into one Cry. I've read it aloud here and it sounds alright.'

Louis changed his mind about the 'caw caw's, but not about the vagina. 'I think on reconsideration, that the lines "Caw Caw and Lord Lord" are good; the unity of the assonance and the contrasting implications of the two names do hover over the grave. However, I still have reservations about "the beard . . ." It still offends my taste, and I object to it. But the decision is yours . . . In words begin responsibilities.'

Allen received a flood of letters from Gregory in New York, begging for money, and Barney Rosset and Lawrence Ferlinghetti reported the same. In the end, Allen wrote to say he was tired of trying to hustle money for Gregory and refused to ask Jack for any more on his behalf, 'It's too much, trying to pull loot out of Jack's teeth.' Earlier, when Gregory was still in Paris, Allen had started a Gregory Corso fund which he wrote about in the *Village Voice* and actually received some contributions. On 15 May, Gregory revealed in a letter that he had just lost four hundred dollars at the Belmont racetrack. Allen took more of the little LSD pills at Palo Alto and wrote to his father exhorting him to try the drug, 'You would enjoy it and it's not exhausting. Good as a trip abroad.'

Back in New York, meanwhile, Gregory realised that his return to the States had been a mistake and sold enough things from Allen's apartment to enable him to take off for Greece. Gregory wrote to Allen asking him to set up another Corso fund and, in August: 'Sorry about the cats, the bed, the chair, the TV but I had to get away from the USA.' Gregory's check to the shipping line somehow bounced, and apparently he was put off the ship before his intended destination.

Summer came, and Allen and Peter prepared to travel, to 'swing into the west and wander hand in hand in small towns by deserts and forget the world a while,' as Allen wrote Kerouac.

It was the middle of the August heat when they finally reached New York. The Lower East Side's hydrants were all on, flooding the pot-holed streets, making pools among the rubble and the overflowing garbage cans. Allen slept through the day and lived mostly at night, when it was cooler.

The publicity surrounding the beatniks continued unabated. Greenwich Village was filled with tourists, and weekend beatniks in beards and berets packed the newly opened coffee houses.

On Avenue C, near Allen's apartment, the Scottish writer Alexander Trocchi had his 'Methedrine University', where the lights burned all night and every meth head in the Lower East Side assembled to take drugs and do garbage art. They would find interesting pieces of wood in the street and spend hours cleaning them, as only a speed freak can, then they would paint them with shiny enamel in savage, totemic, clashing colours. At night, when the whole street was dead and quiet, Trocchi's place stood out like a beacon, with the bare high-intensity lightbulbs shining into the street.

One evening after midnight, Allen took Norman Mailer, Carl Solomon and a few others over to visit. It was like entering a blazing white universe. About thirty people sat around mumbling to themselves, scrubbing little bits of wood and painting in intricate detail. Sometimes one of them would go over to the table and help themselves to another shot of speed to give them the concentration needed for the task. Alex beamed all over his bony face as they came in, and tried to find something for them to sit on. The University couldn't last; it was eventually closed down by the police after one of the regular students, a thin girl called Tessa, discovered that Trocchi had all along been listening to her brain and called the cops.

Meanwhile, there were exciting new developments in Paris. Maurice Girodias read the ten chapters from *Naked Lunch* in the first issue of *Big Table* and told Bill that he wanted to publish the book immediately. Bill signed a contract with Olympia Press. *Naked Lunch* was published in late August. Allen read it straight through and was astonished. 'Burroughs gave me a gasp,' he wrote in his journal. 'I shivered in my room on East 2nd Street, seeing suddenly a flash out of nine years work with Burroughs on "Naked Lunch". He delivered. I grasped what was beyond (us) in the living grave.' His previous doubts about the book were immediately dispelled.

Herbert Huncke was out of jail, broke and homeless as usual, and he turned again to his old friends. Jack sent a small check care of Allen, to whom he wrote to say he wasn't Frank Sinatra and wanted to be repaid, making the transaction somehow Allen's responsibility. (Jack had just spent $2,500 fixing up the attic in the house he bought in Northport.) Three days later, Allen received one of Gabrielle Kerouac's letters: 'I want this to be the last time I have to tell you to leave Jack alone and don't you ever again ask him for money for Bums.'

Lawrence Ferlinghetti wrote to say that he and Allen were invited to a literary conference in Chile in January 1960. Allen began to plan a big South American trip which would include Bolivia and Peru.

He continued his heavy schedule of readings, including an East Coast tour with Michael McClure and Philip Whalen that was organised by Elsa Dorfman from Grove Press – one of the first big poetry tours. Allen was also handling Burroughs's affairs in New York, arranging the Grove edition of *Naked Lunch*. He was advising *Big Table*, *Evergreen* and *Yugen* and circulating manuscripts to many other magazines. Allen spent a good deal of time helping editors and anthologists with collections of 'Beat' writings. Kerouac, on the other hand, was constantly making their lives difficult and undermining Ginsberg's work by demanding exorbitant fees. He justified his position to Allen in a letter: 'Sterling [Lord, his agent] only claims that in every beat anthology I should get "premium" payment because they cant make it without my name. That's all.'

Allen saw Jack one last time before leaving for South America, and it was not a pleasant encounter. Peter's younger sister Marie, who was training to be a nurse, was staying with them. Jack arrived wildly drunk in the middle of the night and stormed into her room, giving her a bad fright. Allen described it as 'Some great traumatic boogie-man shot, which he thought was funny, being drunk, which scared her back to the bug house.' As he pointed out later, Kerouac would have been terribly annoyed if anyone had visited his home and behaved badly – or if any of them had visited his house at all – yet he felt free to cut loose in other people's households. 'What are you doing in my house, at this hour, at four o'clock in the morning?' Allen demanded.

Kerouac collapsed on the kitchen floor laughing, and with a disdainful look on his face said, 'Ginsberg, you're a hairy loss.' At the time, Allen resented Kerouac's arrogance and was hurt by it. However, on reflection, he transformed his remark into something profound and significant, which he cited in lectures as an example of Kerouac's Buddhist insight.

9 Ayahuasca in Peru

I will have to accept women
if I want to continue the race, . . .
Between me and oblivion an unknown
woman stands;

'This Form Of Life Needs Sex'

In January 1960, Allen made the exhausting twenty-four-hour flight from the sleet and snow of Newark Airport to Los Carrillos Airport, in Santiago, Chile. It was the beginning of six months of solitary exploration of volcanic peaks, Inca ruins and Amazonian jungle. The most unexpected and astonishing experience he was to have, however, was an overwhelming desire to love women and have children; an insight which came to him on the drug ayahuasca.

It was not until their arrival in Chile that Allen and Lawrence discovered that the literary conference was sponsored by the Communist Party, though as Ferlinghetti said, 'It didn't make any difference because at that time, being Communist down there was the only thing to be if you were humanitarian at all. It wasn't like Stalinism. Most of the intellectuals and poets in Peru and Chile were Communists.'

Twenty-seven writers from fifteen American countries attended the conference, at the University of Concepción. There was a lot of debate and argument, particularly over the recent events in Cuba, where Fidel Castro had led a socialist, but at that time non-Communist Party revolution into power.

Allen gave his speech in a mixture of Spanish, French and English. He read from John Wieners's *Hotel Wentley Poems*, Philip Lamantia's *Narcotica* and Gregory's *Bomb* as part of a long lecture on prosody, jazz, drugs and the soul. 'It was a big mad speech and they dug it,' he wrote Peter. 'I think it was probably the best of the speeches.' The San Francisco *Chronicle* reported: 'Ginsberg was liked both as an artist and as a melancholy, black-bearded Boy Scout in exile. He talked in Spanish, made numerous speeches, danced and asked questions.'

The extreme contrast between rich and poor in South America, the excitement generated there by the Cuban revolution and the ongoing Marxist debate between the intellectuals, writers and poets from the South American countries, made it inevitable that Allen should try to figure out just where he stood on the political spectrum, and for the next six months his journals were to contain his ruminations on the subject. It is the only time that overtly political material appears in his journals on a regular basis. He wrote: 'I live as if indifferent to the suffering of animals and men who die and groan to feed me and make my houses warm and bright – as if shielded from their sufferings, from knowledge and share of theirs by my tricky beard and wit. So that my poetry is all a half-celestial con, worth nothing to the bloodshot eyes of Physical sufferers in the mines and factories and fields. My original vow to help mankind in its sorry world-fate, on the boat to Columbia, is now being tested. Can I, as the Marxists claim [I do], remain aloof from the "final conflict" to bring bread and love to the masses?'

Allen's next destination was Bolivia, where he planned to take cocaine with the Indians. He spent three weeks in La Paz. The market was the most fantastic he had ever seen. It was an enormous web of streets, and he explored them all. The old Indian ladies in their brightly coloured scarfs wore coloured bands over their noses and brown bowler hats. Allen sat and chewed coca leaf with them, but he found it only mildly stimulating. After a few days of chewing, the corners of his mouth were stained green, and he was nauseated by the smell of coca on his breath. He strolled through the market in a black hat and dungarees, buying little silver flies, spiders and butterflies, and green and purple women's shawls. The poverty was so extreme that he felt out of place.

He continued on to Peru; Allen and fifty Indians were crammed together in the back of the truck with nowhere to rest their feet as they bounced along the dirt road for twelve hours in the rain. At Puno, Ginsberg took a train to Cuzco and the old Inca ruins of Machu Picchu. His health was beginning to suffer from the privations of his travels. He had not been able to take a bath for two months, and the prolonged lack of toilet facilities had aggravated an anal fissure, which caused him discomfort.

A week later, Allen was living in the caretaker's hut above Machu Picchu proper, following the Inca trails and staying in rough *pensiones*, living on *asado*, eggs and rice, and writing in his journal by kerosene lamp or candlelight. He had arranged to spend the night in the ruins. The mountainside was loud with the chirruping of crickets, and butterflies danced over the eroded brown soil as he climbed the treacherous rocky path to the fourteenth-century Inca city. He watched the sunset from the Intiwatna Stone. The mossy green stones blackened as dusk fell, and when darkness descended, the last tourist bus was halfway down the mountain. The Temple of the Sun, the Royal Tomb and more than three thousand stone steps were all his to explore in the moonlight, just as he had done in the Aztec cities in the Mexican jungle.

The writer Peter Matthiessen had arranged for Allen to receive a half gallon of ayahuasca, or yage, the powerful hallucinogenic used by the Amazonian Indians, which supposedly enabled them to see wonderful cities and tell the future. Allen took it for the first time, lying in his hotel room in Lima. After drinking the strange tasting liquid, he noted the results in his journal: 'Slowly drifting away but still thinking in my body, till my body turned to passive wood and my soul rocked back and forth, preparing to slide out on eternal journey backwards from my head in the dark. An hour, realising the possible change in consciousness, that the Soul is independent of the body and its death, and that the Soul is not Me, it is the wholly other "whisper of consciousness" from Above, Beyond.'

On ayahuasca he wrote: 'I have come home, I am the God, and I demand admittance thru the door.' But he knew that the drug he was able to get in Lima was nothing to that used by the *curanderos* in the jungle, and that he would have to follow in Burroughs's footprints to track it down.

Three days later, on 31 May, he left Lima at dawn, by train, heading to Pucallpa in quest of yage. By the end of the day he had reached Cerro de Pasco, a dirty little town, 14,350 feet up in the Andes, full of Indians and with a good market, which sold the traditional white-and-orange-striped mantas blankets. His journey took him through Huánuco and Tingo María, on towards

Pucallpa. He made the final stretch lying in the back of a creaky old truck covered with spiderwebs, on top of sacks of sugar. They bumped through the jungle at seven miles per hour, giving Allen time to look at every tree they passed, all of them hung with orange orchids. As night fell, he watched the stars and moon, feeling very solitary as he passed the unrelenting jungle, mysterious in the darkness. He felt, 'as if I had really left all behind and were now a permanent traveller in a world with no return to Peter or home – that pure solitude which makes the stars sharper and life seem more new strange dream, all universe an old familiar phantom.' He had been travelling alone for six months.

In Pucallpa, he was introduced to a *curandero*, called Maestro, a mild, unassuming man of about thirty-eight, who lived with a wife and children on the outskirts of town, at the edge of the jungle. An apprentice *curandero* is trained by a witch doctor, who takes him into the jungle and gives him ayahuasca day after day, until he has explored every facet of it and been to every place that the people in his future care could possibly go to. Only then is he ready to be a *curandero*.

On a moonlit night in June, Allen took his first Pucallpa Ayahuasca, which was drunk like beer. Maestro had prepared it from fresh young *Banisteriopsis Caape* plants that grew in his backyard; they were mixed half and half with a catalyst, the *mescla*, which was another leaf called *chacruna*. The two leaves were cooked all day and the liquid strained off. The resulting brew was served with full ceremony.

Allen lay on the ground in a robe and 'entered the great being again'. It was much stronger than the drug he had taken in Lima. At first, he saw a spectrum of different-coloured designs, similar to the pottery and blankets he had seen all day at the local market, then the bands of colour took on an organic form: flies, bees, golden bugs and serpents appeared and eventually became a seething fabric before his eyes. In the centre was a small black hole, and it was through this that Allen went. His concentration had been disturbed at first by the mosquitos that buzzed around and bit him, but finally, accepting their high pitched whine as part of the jungle music of locusts, frogs and distant dog barks, he lay still and allowed them to buzz and bite, all part of the same universe.

Allen lay there for several hours. Later, he went into the house where four other people had taken the yage. He experienced 'a great feeling of communal fraternity and a sharing of a realisation of Infinite Intimacy.'

Allen became obsessed by ayahuasca. He lay in bed all afternoon to escape the sun, waiting to go again to the *ayahuancero* at night and writing the long poem 'Magic Psalm' about his experience of the previous night, which would appear, much abbreviated, in *Kaddish and Other Poems*. Allen approached his next session with fear and anticipation but soon found himself experiencing 'the great squid of Eternity opening and closing its mouth in vast slow motion in the inner phantasmal recesses of imagination during hallucinated state – with undersea fringed labia.'

His third session took place the following night. There was a bright light at the *curandero*'s door, and thirty or so men and women sat around on the wooden porch or squatted under nearby trees, slapping mosquitoes. Maestro was distracted; his wife was in the final stages of labour in the next room. After the baby was born, the *curandero* came out carrying a flashlight and stood staring into the darkness. He lit a cigarette and announced that the ceremony would begin soon. Allen saw a meteor, with a red and blue glowing centre, arc through the black sky near the full moon.

Maestro dipped an enamel cup into the green-brown liquid and held it in front of his mouth. He inhaled on his cigarette and blew the smoke over the lip of the cup, whistling a sad little tune through the smoke. Then, after more puffs, he hummed the same tune straight down into the cup. He passed the cup to Allen, who had to light a cigarette, blow smoke on the surface of the brew, and drink it straight down. He wrote Burroughs what happened.

'Lay down expecting God knows what other pleasant vision and then I began to get high – and then the whole fucking Cosmos broke loose around me, I think the strongest and worst I've ever had it nearly – (I still reserve the Harlem experiences, being Natural, in abeyance. The LSD was perfection but didn't get me so deep in, nor so horribly in).'

He felt that he was confronting death itself. He became nauseous and staggered out on the porch and into the garden to vomit. He was all covered with snakes. Brightly coloured serpents wrapped themselves around his body. He felt he was a snake, vomiting out the universe. In the trees around him he could hear the other drinkers vomiting in the night, 'all around the noise of vomit, of the universe vomiting up parts of itself – the snake that eats itself, vomiting back forth into Being – I was a vomiting snake, that is, I vomited with eyes closed and sensed myself a serpent of Being, or Serpent of Isolation, the Serpent of Allen, covered with Aureole of spikey snakeheads miniatured radiant and many coloured around my hands and throat – my throat bulging like the Beast of Creation, like the Beast of Death – to vomit forth my physical misery to Be – I heaved it out four or five times and remained standing in a trance, horrified at my Serpent Self.'

As he walked home in the moonlight, one of his new friends told him that the more you saturate yourself with ayahuasca, the deeper in you go, till you 'visit the moon, see the dead, see God, see the Tree Spirits.' Allen was worried, wondering if he had the nerve to go back, let alone go up river six hours to drink with an Indian tribe, as he had planned. He was afraid of real madness, of entering a permanently changed universe from which there was no way back.

Knowing that Bill had been there before him and would be able to advise him, he wrote telling Burroughs his worries about going mad and of the drug permanently changing his consciousness. He said that he was now worried about bringing the drug back to New York as he had originally planned, in case it drove Peter crazy. Bill would reply mysteriously, 'There is nothing to fear ... Your Ayahuasca consciousness is more valid than Normal consciousness ... Why are you surprised to see me? You are following in my steps. I know the way. And yes, know the area better than you think.'

The next day, Allen examined his situation. He found that the right lens of his eyeglasses was cracked, probably broken while he was vomiting in the jungle. He began to record his experiences in his journal. Terrifying as the ayahuasca experience was, he felt that he was now reaching into a forbidden area of such fundamental importance that it was worth the fear and risk involved. In his quest to enlarge his field of consciousness, he had finally come upon a drug which enabled him to encounter at first hand the great cycle of birth and death; to understand his mother's death and the future deaths of Louis and Eugene. He felt his own acute fear of death and had a realisation that the escape from the inevitable is to reproduce. This insight made him confront his homosexuality.

'Naomi dead, in madhouse,' he wrote. 'My mother who I am afraid to (be) return to in sex – all Mother the same – Birth – yet what was she, and what am I that I am her product and continue to live in the world of her madness? Is that my curse, which forbids me to live or die, to give birth, but be neither man nor woman, fucked in the ass, or fucking poor Peter – I resolved to bear babe, to bear Women, learn women – again.'

He recalled all the women he had rejected – Natalie, Elise, Aileen, Dusty, Françoise: 'Horror! They maybe are sent to save me, and I, not knowing in my pride, act Prophet over them and withdraw from their embrace and copulation and vomit of new birth.'

He realised that for all those years he had clung to Peter, Jack, Lucien and Bill as family, because he was afraid to be alone with the knowledge of death, with no one to love him, 'no soul to *sign* to me what is the way of life, no seraph to be my father and protect me – afraid to be born the lone seraph of Existence – which each man is? The lone and Final seraph of Being. *The seraph that is alone, and dies into the void, not knowing the next transfiguration if any, to come* – leaving a part of Babe Angel behind in human children to guard the garden of Existence?'

It rained all day, and the streets of Pucallpa turned into brown mud. Colourful parrots stretched their wings and screeched over his door. He slept till four in the afternoon, feeling lazy, defeated by the rain and the tropical heat. He began to weep, afraid of what might happen that evening, feeling the death of his family and the 'vast Wheel of Time turning invisibly'.

And so Allen went back. About ten people were already gathered there when he arrived. He again took the brew and lay down on the porch, afraid to close his eyes as he felt the intoxication stealing over his senses. He vomited and found himself back in the familiar ayahuasca universe, 'with snakescales gleaming all over, hat of feathers and savage grass, and a look of skull-trance on my visage, a Devil worshipper. A snarling, savage cat, at bay.' Again he found himself, 'a self condemned to worry about its extinction.' He realised that God is death itself, and as the *curandero* hummed a strange tune, and the toads croaked in the mud, and distant tom-toms echoed from the huts on stilts down the track, and a thousand locusts whistled in the vegetation, he had a long conversation with God.

'What should I do about women?' Allen asked God.

'Make love to them,' came the answer.

He returned to Lima by air from Iquitos, flying over the Amazon jungle. He had gathered samples of the various elements of yage – the leaves and the different catalysts – to take home. In Lima he spent long hours meeting with government officials, getting proper authorisation to carry the bottles of the drug to the States.

During the flight home, Allen assessed his months of solitary travel and learning. 'I'm a poet,' he wrote, 'I've striven to record Beauty, and now my memory is going to be grabbed from me – all gone – yes, let this life pass. I hope I give up my memory without screaming.'

Allen devoted much of the next six months to further drug experiments, ranging from the ayahuasca he brought back from Peru, to the magic mushroom drug, psilocybin, which he took at Harvard. Drugs seemed to be a method of achieving an approximation of the expanded consciousness he had glimpsed with his Blake vision. His experiences convinced him that drugs were a possible means of altering public consciousness, a way of introducing ideas of a lifestyle closer to the Beat ideals of spontaneity, sexual openness, candour, literary honesty and spiritual liberation. He lobbied extensively for the legalisation of marijuana and gave much thought to methods of introducing psychedelics to the general population.

Meanwhile, in his own apartment, he was surrounded by speed freaks and heroin addicts and was engaged in a constant battle to keep the hard drug pushers away from his door. The spiritual questions thrown up by his drug experiments caused him to begin planning another long quest, this time with Peter, to India.

Allen had brought back a gallon of ayahuasca, for him and Peter to experiment with. Even in New York, Allen had the horrifying black hallucinations. He read all he could find that related to the experience, including Robert De Ropp's *Drugs and the Mind*, W.Y. Evans-Wentz's translation of *The Tibetan Book of the Dead* and Alexandra David-Neel's various books on Tibet. He found the section on 'Centering' in Paul Reps's *Zen Flesh, Zen Bones* to be useful.

Allen continued his work on 'Kaddish' but the August heat filled him with depression and lethargy. In September, fuelled by

Benzedrine, he finished 'Kaddish' in a characteristic thirty-one-hour marathon session. He wrote various hymns in a sob-wracked trance state and completed the final draft of the long first section. This he sent to Ferlinghetti and, still unsure about the poem, said in his covering letter: 'I don't know what it'll look like to you, poetry or not – huge white elephant maybe – you figure out what to do with it . . . Let me know what it looks like to you – I have lots of doubts.' But Allen need not have worried. Ferlinghetti was enormously impressed. On 11 October, Allen sent him the final version. Without breaking stride, he immediately began assembling poems for a subsidiary volume, since *Kaddish* only covered poems 1958–60. He thought he would call it 'Hiccup, Poems 1955–58' but fortunately he changed it to *Reality Sandwiches*, a quote from one of the poems.

When Fidel Castro visited New York in September 1960 to appear before the United Nations, his party stayed at the Hotel Teresa in Harlem. The Fair Play For Cuba Committee arranged a reception for them in the hotel and Allen, Peter, LeRoi Jones and other friends were among the invited guests. Allen and Peter pushed their way through the assembled FBI men to shake Castro's hand.

There was a press conference, and Allen astonished the gathering by saying, 'Marijuana is revolutionary, but the imperialists have invented all kinds of stories about it just so no one will smoke it and rebel. What does the Cuban Revolution think about marijuana?' The Cubans were surprised by the question, since it was not something that the Revolution had any position on. There had been clandestine farmers in the Sierra Maestra for whom marijuana was second only to coffee as a cash crop; at first, Castro turned a blind eye to them, but then he began to crack down. At the time of the press conference, marijuana was illegal in Cuba, just as it had been before the Revolution. With so much work to be done, the Cubans said they didn't relish the thought of people sitting around stoned.

Allen wrote Gregory about Castro's visit, 'N.Y. horrible with U.N. hysteria and Americans acting like a bunch of jerks, I am losing my sense of humour and having stomach trouble I get so mad. Went to reception for Fidel who's an honest rat, now my name in the paper as pro-Fidel. Which I am.'

Allen's political uneasiness was not helped by watching the first of the four Nixon–Kennedy television debates at Lucien's house.

That night, still angry, he amused himself by rattling off a letter designed to irritate Kerouac: 'This country is Evil and Whitman and I now spit on it and tell it to be nice or die, because that's what coming. I HATE AMERICA! Ugh. And Nixon and Kennedy combine all that's most obnoxious, but Nixon does take the cake.'

Kerouac left his mother and came to town in mid-October for a drinking binge. Allen noted in his journal, 'Jack in for three days, finally ending in bed w/ me & Peter like Silenus nekkid – his big thighs and belly.'

At a 'Beat Generation' symposium organised by the Group for the Advancement of Psychiatry, Allen learned that Harvard University was conducting experiments with psilocybin, the magic mushroom drug. When asked to participate, Allen needed little convincing, and a few days later, he, Peter and Lafcadio were on a plane to Boston, where they would stay with Dr Timothy Leary at Harvard. The atmosphere seemed very academic, with a small drinks party for them when they arrived at Leary's house on Beacon Street in Boston, but Leary's infectious grin and Irish gift of the blarney soon relaxed everyone.

Leary at forty was six years older than Allen and at the height of his career. He had spent a decade as the director of the Kaiser Foundation for Psychology Research in Oakland, then in January 1960 joined the Department of Social Relations at Harvard, where he taught a graduate seminar entitled 'Existential Transactional Behaviour Change.' Each year, Leary had taken his son and daughter to a villa near Cuernavaca and it was there, in 1960, that he had his first experience of the hallucinogen extracted from the fungus *Psilocybe mexicana*. When he returned to Harvard that fall, he received permission to begin a research project on the behavioural effects of the drug.

Though the drug experiments had Harvard's written seal of approval, it was completely against Leary's contract to take his research home with him. But Leary had little regard for Harvard's scientific traditions; that evening, he gave Allen a large thirty-six milligram dose; eighteen pills of psilocybin. Allen bustled round his room, preparing for the trip. Leary had given him his daughter Susan's record player, and Allen had selected Wagner and Beethoven from the record library in the study. Once he was ready, he took off his clothes, turned off all the lights and lay on the bed listening to the music. Peter lay down naked next to him. Leary said that he would check on them every fifteen minutes.

The drug took effect, and Allen saw himself lying on the bed with two choices: he could either withdraw into mystical introspection and vomit, or he could swallow back the vomit and live in the present universe. 'I felt intimidated by the knowledge that I had not reached yet a perfect understanding with my creator, whoever he be, God, Christ, or Buddha, or the figure of octopus as before [in Pucallpa]. Suddenly, however, realised they were all imaginary beings I was inventing to substitute for the fear of being myself – that one which I had dreamed of.'

When Leary checked on Allen, he was lying on top of the blanket with his glasses off and his pupils completely dilated, feeling scared, unhappy and nauseous. Peter lay next to him with his eyes closed, sleeping or listening to the music. Allen asked Leary what he thought of him. Leary later wrote, 'I leaned over and looked down into the black liquid eyes, faun's eyes, man's eyes, and told him he was a great man and that it was good to know him. He reached up his hand.'

Ginsberg would write, 'Professor Leary came into my room, looked into my eyes, and said I was a great man. That determined me to make an effort to live here and now.' He swallowed back the vomit.

Suddenly, out of the window, Allen saw a flash of light, which reminded him of the Star of Bethlehem and, as the music of Wagner's *Gotterdammerung* thundered in the room, 'like the horns of judgement calling from the ends of the cosmos – calling on all human consciousness to declare itself into the consciousness,' it seemed to Allen as if all the worlds of human consciousness were waiting for a Messiah, 'Someone to take on the responsibility of being the creative God and seize power over the universe ... I decided I might as well be the one to do so – Pronounced by nakedness as the first act of revolution against the destroyers of the human image. The naked body being the hidden sign.'

Allen thought of Milton's Lucifer and wondered why Milton sided with the rebel in Heaven. He got up from the bed, put on his eyeglasses and walked downstairs naked, closely followed by Peter. They headed for the study where Frank Barron, Leary's co-worker, who shared the house, was sitting at his desk. They stopped in front of him. As Leary came into the room, having ushered his young daughter up to the safety of the third floor, Allen raised his finger in the air and waved it. 'I'm the Messiah,' he said. 'I've come down to preach love to the world. We're going to walk through the streets and teach people to stop hating.'

'Well Allen that seems like a pretty good idea,' said Barron.

'Listen,' said Allen to Leary. 'Do you believe I'm the Messiah? Look, I can prove it. I'm going to cure your hearing. Take off your hearing machine. Your ears are cured. Come on, take it off. You don't need it.'

Barron sat smiling, and Peter looked on earnestly as Leary took off his hearing aid and placed it on the desk.

'That's right,' said Allen. 'And now your glasses. I'll heal your vision too.'

Leary took off his glasses, and Allen beamed round for approval at his healing abilities. Then Leary made a good point. 'But Allen, one thing . . .'

'What?'

'Your glasses. You're still wearing them. Why don't you cure your own vision?'

Allen was surprised at his oversight. 'Yes, you're right,' he said and took them off and put them on the desk next to Leary's. 'Come on,' he said, 'We're going down to the city streets to tell the people about peace and love. And we'll get lots of important people on a big telephone network and settle all this about the Bomb once and for all.'

'Fine,' said Barron. 'But why not do the telephone bit first?'

'Who we gonna call?' asked Peter.

'Well, we'll call Kerouac on Long Island, and Kennedy and Khrushchev and Bill Burroughs in Paris and Norman Mailer in Bellevue . . .'

'Who we gonna call first?' asked Peter.

'Let's start with Khrushchev,' suggested Allen.

'Why don't you start with Kerouac?' suggested Barron. 'In the meantime, let's pull these curtains. There's enough going on in here so I don't care about looking outside.'

After some squinting, Allen found the white telephone and dialled the operator. 'Hello operator, this is God. G-O-D. I want to talk to Kerouac. Try Capitol 7-0563, Northport, Long Island.' There was a pause, then the operator could be heard telling Allen something. 'No such number? Oh, right. That's the house in New Jersey where I was born. Look operator. I'll have to go upstairs to get the number, then I'll call back.' Allen, looking a little sheepish, explained what had happened, then skipped upstairs to get his huge address book. He reappeared moments later and this time was able to get through. He began to shout at Kerouac to come to Boston.

'Take a plane up here immediately. The revolution is beginning. Gather all the dark angels of light at once. It's time to seize power over the universe and become the next consciousness!'

Kerouac laughed and said, 'Whazzamatter, are you high?'

'I am high and naked and I am King of the Universe. Get on a plane. It is time!'

'But I got my mother . . .' Kerouac protested.

'Bring your mother!' Allen commanded, serious.

'Aw, I'm tired,' Jack complained, but he remained interested. It was the first time that Allen had ever dared to challenge Mrs Kerouac's control of his life.

'What do you want to do?' Allen asked.

'Lay down and die,' he said.

'What's the matter with you?' Allen shouted. 'Are you AFRAID?' Allen told him that he was afraid of God, that he didn't realise that he already *was* God! Jack was surprised to hear such authority and conviction in Allen's voice. It was the first time that Allen had spoken to him like that in years. 'Who else but us is *it*, the life-force, is God?' thundered Allen, and Jack had to agree. Allen was rapturous and made Jack promise not to die. Allen began to think that he could save everyone, take over the universe and freeze it into a permanent eternal present. He decided that William Carlos Williams should not be allowed to die and began to look up his number. Wagner's horns surged from the loud-speakers, inspiring him, 'Da dam, da dam, da da Dee!' 'Revolt in Paradise, the Messiah had broken loose!' Allen could see all the population of Earth linked by radio, television, telephone, computer, into one simultaneous transmission of consciousness which would turn on the universe!

Finally, Leary and Barron prevailed upon Allen to lie down on the couch and stop running up their phone bill. They put on a recording of James Joyce reading from *Finnegan's Wake* and, as he listened, Allen realised that the drug consciousness would sooner or later wear off. '[I] saw control of the universe slipping out of my hands,' he wrote. Eventually, in a dressing gown and over a cup of hot milk, Allen began to describe what he had seen. The psylocybin had reinforced the revelations of the ayahuasca and had finally opened the door for him to women and heterosexuality. He could see a womanly body and family life ahead, a view confirmed a few days later when he wrote to Neal Cassady and Carolyn and told them the news: 'I will have babies instead of jacking off into limbo ... All's well ... we're starting a plot to get everyone in power in America high ... Hurrah!' The latter proved easier to accomplish than the former.

Allen and Tim Leary began plotting the psychedelic revolution. To Allen, it was simple and egalitarian, an example of his deep belief in American democracy. Everybody should be allowed to have the mushroom drug and explore his or her own mind; it should not be reserved for an elite of professors and experimenters. But Allen knew that there would be a problem if it were introduced suddenly. It would get outlawed, and there would be horror stories in the newspapers. The correct way to introduce it was to get a series of respectable people to endorse it, and talk about the experience, so that by the time the authorities found out what was happening, there would already be a solid body of respectable opinion in favour of the drug. He felt that he should not campaign too much himself, but was prepared to do a lot of the legwork. 'Big serious scientist professors from Harvard' should do it, he said. 'I can't do it. I'm too easy to put down.'

He produced his big address book and began to compile a list of people to be turned on: Robert Lowell, Jack Kerouac, LeRoi Jones ... he listed painters, editors and publishers. The plan was that Allen would make the initial approach, and if the people were interested, Leary would write to them and send them research papers to sign. Allen would then make the arrangements, and Leary would come down to New York on weekends and run magic mushroom sessions with them. The programme aimed to discover various reactions, to test the drug's limits, and to find out from serious, thoughtful people what could be done with the drug. 'These people will have more confidence in you than in me,' Allen said. Within seven years, over four million Americans would have taken LSD. 'Allen Ginsberg came to Harvard and shook us loose from our academic fears and strengthened our courage and faith in the process,' Leary later wrote in *High Priest*.

In January 1961, Allen wrote to Leary with the addresses of the first four people he had selected to give psilocybin pills to as part of the Harvard Behavior Study project. They were Willem de Kooning, Franz Kline, Dizzy Gillespie and Thelonious Monk – two painters and two jazz musicians. Allen would convey the pills and the report to be returned to Harvard. Monk was given fifteen pills to swallow in the security of his home. Allen called him after five hours, and he said he felt fine. A few weeks later, Allen went round to Monk's apartment in West 63rd Street to find out what happened and to write up the report. Monk said, 'Well, I took 'em, but ain't you got nothin' stronger?'

Leary came to town one weekend for a series of sessions that Allen had set up. The first was with Jack Kerouac. Jack was already drunk when Tim got to Allen's apartment. 'So what are you up to Dr Leary, running around with this communist faggot Ginsberg and your bag of pills?' he demanded. 'Can your drugs absolve the mortal and venial sins which our beloved saviour Jesus Christ, the only Son of God, came down and sacrificed his life upon the cross to wash away?'

'Why don't we find out?' suggested Allen, getting out the pills.

Kerouac continued to behave like a small-town drunk, stamping around the room and standing on chairs. He climbed on Allen's couch and declared, 'I'm the King of the Beatniks.' All took the pills, and Leary, who had experienced mushroom sessions with over a hundred people, found himself propelled by Kerouac's behaviour into his first ever bad trip. He curled up in a fetal ball in the dark bedroom. Allen found him and played the role of the soothing *curandero*. Kerouac was in the other room, still yelling, red-faced, drinking red wine, smoking cigarettes and telling stories. Allen and Tim attempted to explain the philosophical implications of altered mind states, but Kerouac, unconvinced that enlightenment could be attained that easily, replied, 'Walking on water wasn't made in a day.'

Leary later analysed the session with Kerouac in *Flashbacks*: 'Throughout the night Kerouac remained unmovably the Catholic carouser, an old-style Bohemian without a hippie bone in his body. Jack Kerouac opened the neural doors to the future, looked ahead, and didn't see his place in it. Not for him the utopian pluralist optimism of the sixties.'

Allen, Tim and Peter went uptown to visit Robert Lowell and Elizabeth Hardwick at their Riverside Drive apartment. On the way there Allen told Leary, 'We're not dealing here with a Dionysian fun lover. He's a good guy with a psycho streak. We should be cautious about the dose.'

'Why are we giving psilocybin to Lowell?' asked Peter.

'We hope to loosen him up, make him happier,' said Allen. 'And on the political front, if Pulitzer Prize-winner Robert Lowell has a great session, his product endorsement will influence lots of intellectuals.'

While Allen guided Lowell through the experience, Peter and Tim talked with Hardwick in the kitchen. Three hours later, Lowell was beaming. According to Leary, he shook his hand and said, 'Now I know what Blake and St John of the Cross were talking about. This experience is what I was seeking when I became a Catholic.' Allen, however, remembered a less enthusiastic reaction. At the door, leaving, he said, '*Amor vincit omnes*,' to which Lowell replied, 'I'm not sure.'

Once they were out of the apartment, Leary said he wasn't sure that the dose was anywhere near large enough to have produced such a transcendental result. 'Maybe we should have given him the option to have a heavy-dose experience and go all the way.'

'That could have been risky for us,' Allen said. 'I wouldn't want to be known as the guy who put America's leading poet round the bend.'

But psilocybin was not the only new drug around. Methadrine was everywhere in the Lower East Side, and particularly in Allen's apartment. Huncke, Elise, Peter and his girlfriend Janine were all taking it. At that time, before he saw what terrible damage it caused, Allen's attitude to it was benign. 'All the young kids are shooting (needle) a drug called methadrine,' he wrote Leary in February. 'An amphetamine semi-hallucinogen – havn't tried it yet. It's all the vogue.' Allen took it for the first time later that month, mixing it with heroin and some psilocybin pills as a writing cocktail. From 8 p.m. until noon the next day he wrote a ten-page, single-space, clearly Methadrine-influenced poem, which was eventually published in a shorter version as 'Television Was A Baby Crawling Toward That Deathchamber.'

For some time Allen had been planning a trip to join Gregory in Athens and get a little peace. The situation in the apartment had become so crazy that he found it very hard to get any work done. Peter was on junk. He, Janine, Lafcadio, Huncke and Allen were all crammed together in the small tenement, and Elise was next door and visiting all the time. Allen often found complete strangers taking a bath or making themselves tea in his kitchen. He couldn't wait to get out. The plan developed that Peter and Allen would visit Bill in Paris, where Gregory would join them, then would continue on to India.

Jack was around a lot, very frequently drunk. He was obsessed with the idea that the New York Jewish intelligentsia were out to get him, and Allen, typically, tried to use reason against his irrationality, pointing out that many of the people who had helped him were Jewish: Allen himself, Seymour Wyse, Gilbert Millstein at the *New York Times*, whose rave review launched *On the Road*. 'The lineups are too mixed to categorise your "enemies" as Jewish,' Allen wrote Jack. 'You could make similar lineup of Catholics, Protestants. You are talking Jewish to annoy me, and it does because you think I am a *Jewish* Truth Cloud. Are you a *Catholic* Truth Cloud? You may be too drunk to remember you were screaming how Hitler was right – and your mother was too.'

Had Ginsberg not persevered, there is no doubt that his friendship with Jack would have terminated long before this. Lucien Carr, speaking about the friendship, said, 'On Allen's part, it was one of real devotion. On Jack's part, it was sort of a love-hate thing. One moment Allen was his oldest truest friend and the next moment Allen was nothing but a Jewish schemer. But Jack was funny that way. He never turned on me, but then, providentially I wasn't Jewish.'

Allen and Peter were to leave New York on 23 March 1961, and Peter managed to kick his heroin habit just in time. Allen made complex arrangements for Lafcadio, Huncke and Janine. He paid the rent on the apartment until the end of March and gave Janine and Huncke letters of authorisation to get back the deposits on the utilities. He left money for the outstanding bills, but, as was to be expected, without Allen there to take charge, everything fell apart the moment he left. Huncke and Janine were both injecting Methadrine into the vein and Allen's money simply disappeared. Marie Orlovsky came from Northport and rescued Lafcadio. Janine and Huncke got themselves a place with Elise in a renovated tenement building. Bill Heine moved in with them, and his speed-freak friends began to hang out there. Alexander Trocchi and his wife Lynn, who had both been shooting speed for years, moved in, and the apartment became a shooting gallery. Janine's weight dropped to ninety-five pounds. One day she came home to find Huncke and Heine gone. They had both been arrested. Elise was carried away to Hillside mental hospital, diagnosed as acutely schizophrenic. The terrors of the Methadrine plague were beginning to be seen.

10 Cut-Ups

*The basic Nova technique is very simple: Always create as
many insoluble conflicts as possible and always aggravate
existing conflicts.*

William Burroughs: *The Soft Machine*

A small group gathered at the dock to see Allen and Peter leave
on the S.S. *America*. The Empire State Building was wrap-
ped in mist and, though it was the end of March, snow lay
on the ground. Eugene and Louis, Carl Solomon and LeRoi Jones
were among those who came to see them off, knowing it would
probably be years before they returned. Elise stood on the dock,
peering over her eyeglasses. Janine, white-faced and blonde-haired,
wearing a black jacket, waved her scarf. Lafcadio gestured with a
straw hat, a half smile on his face, as the huge ship pulled away.
Peter stood at the rail waving in a Russian hat, his hand over his
heart. Allen was at the bow, 'And when I called their names I saw
them, drifting away with their skulls,' he wrote. He got his feet wet
in the sleet.

'I hope America will still be there when we get back,' said Peter.

They had been expecting a grand reunion with Bill in Paris at the
Beat Hotel, but a few days before they left, Bill wrote to say that
he would not be in Paris: 'I am leaving for Southern Spain or
Tangier so will see you there? Or what are your plans? . . . Right
now I want to get out of Paris as quick as possible. Don't like it.
Never did.' Bill's three month residency period in France was up
and he had to either re-enter the country or apply for a *carte de
sejour*. For some months his letters had mentioned that he was
thinking of making a trip south so Allen was not surprised.

They checked into the Beat Hotel, and immediately encountered
Bill's friend, the painter Brion Gysin. Gysin was a large man with

sandy hair and the mottled skin of a mountain man. He was born in England of a Swiss father and a Canadian mother, and held an American passport, having been in the US Army during the war. He was mysterious and aloof, as if privy to great secrets. He told Allen that Bill had left to avoid seeing him, and indicated that dark forces were at work. Allen thought he was being very paranoid and the two men never liked each other.

The root of the problem lay in cut-ups, a literary technique that Bill had first written to him about late in 1959. Cut-ups were invented that September, when Gysin was cutting a mount for a drawing and sliced through a pile of old newspapers and back issues of *Time* and *Life* with his Stanley blade. He noticed that the sliced-up strips of newspaper made new texts when a piece of one article overlapped another and was read across. He was delighted with his new discovery. He was literally reading between the lines: 'Cut through the word lines to hear a new voice off the page.' When Burroughs returned from England a few weeks later, he immediately recognised the potential of the method. He looked serious and prophesied, 'A project for disastrous success.' Cut-ups were to preoccupy Burroughs for most of the next decade.

They showed their discovery to Gregory Corso and Sinclair Beiles, who were living in the hotel, and soon everyone was doing it. The first cut-ups were juxtapositions of random newspaper and magazine articles, but soon printed books were used, and new poems made from the cut-up words of Rimbaud and Shakespeare. These initial cut-ups by Burroughs, Gysin, Corso and Beiles were published as *Minutes To Go*.

Soon Burroughs began to cut-up his own texts, and it was here that he parted company with Corso and Beiles, who believed that inspiration and imagination were essential ingredients in all forms of literary or artistic activity, no matter how depersonalised the work. To Burroughs and Gysin, fighting subjectivity, cut-ups meant that anyone who owned a pair of scissors could write poetry. Corso and Beiles were not going to let the poetic muse die that easily. The ensuing arguments got so bad that Beiles had a nervous breakdown. Then Burroughs cut up some of Corso's poems. Corso was furious and disassociated himself totally from cut-ups, and when *Minutes To Go* was published, he refused to sign copies of it. Throughout 1960, Burroughs produced literally thousands of pages of cut-ups.

Burroughs came to believe that the only way to find out what people was really saying, was to cut up their words and get at the meanings hidden inside. He extended his method. With the aid of his English friend Ian Sommerville, he began work on a series of tape recorder experiments and photographic collages. Finally, Burroughs applied this technique to people, metaphorically dissecting his friends and aquaintances to 'see who was inside', who they really were. His training as an anthropologist at Harvard enabled him to be quite unsentimental about this, regarding old friendships as simply mere encumbrances that had to be cut through in order to reach the reality of the person inside. This was the stage he had reached by the beginning of 1961, when Allen told him they were coming to Paris. He had developed his cut-up theories with Gysin, and wanted Gysin to explain the importance of cut-ups to Allen before their reunion.

He wrote, inviting Allen to join him in Tangier. Allen, Peter and Gregory Corso arrived in Tangier early in June, expecting to find Bill waiting at the dock with his binoculars, as before, since they had wired their arrival time and written several letters telling him their plans, but he was nowhere to be seen. He was in fact at home, ignoring their arrival. When finally they met, Allen was delighted; Bill, however, had changed. He was strangely distant and very suspicious, asking Allen who had sent him.

His cut-up experiments had led him to conclude that everyone had been conditioned by language and that all apparent sensory impressions were in fact illusory. He was now attempting to trace back along the word lines, to find out when and where the programming had taken place, and who was responsible. He suspected that the entire fabric of reality was completely conditioned and that someone was running the universe like a sound stage, with banks of tape recorders and films. He was determined to find where the control words and images were coined, and to locate the image bank. He thought that *Time* magazine's newspaper clipping morgue controlled the lives of millions of Americans, telling them what to think, believe, eat and behave. The image banks of the FBI and the CIA were also prime suspects. However, with the aid of a great deal of majoun, Bill had finally determined that everybody was in fact an agent for a giant trust of insects from another galaxy.

In Allen, Bill could detect certain parts of Louis Ginsberg and traces of ancient Jewish culture; in the intonation of Allen's voice and in his choice of words he identified aspects of Columbia University's English department: 'If we cut you up, who would we find inside? Lionel Trilling!'

Bill was encouraged by two young Englishmen, Ian Sommerville and Michael Portman, with whom he was living at the Villa Muniria; Sommerville was his lover and Portman had the room next door. 'My feeling was that they had replaced us in Bill's affections and intimacy,' Allen said later.

'Mikey' Portman was the scion to the Portman family, who owned a chunk of London's West End. He was young and angelic-looking, arrogant in an English public school way, and obsessed with Bill. Allen found it increasingly hard to relate to Bill because Mikey was always there, interrupting and making facetious remarks. Allen wrote Lucien: 'Bill's all hung up with eighteen-year-old spoiled brat English Lord who looks like a palefaced Rimbaud but is a smart creep – Apparently Lady Portman his mother gave him into Bill's hands to look after here – platonic anyhoo – But Bill got some kinda awful relation with him and the kid bugs everyone so intimacy with Bill is limited and Bill absentminded all the time – however very busy with his cut-up experiments and applying it to pictorial collages and taking brownie photographs and very busy and creative – also did new book in cut-up method, very pure experiments and strangely good reading tho oft toneless, "The Soft Machine."'

The Villa Muniria had become too expensive for their budget, so Allen, Peter and Gregory took two rooms around the corner at the Hotel Armor. Allen and Peter had a whitewashed, tiled room on the roof, with a harbour view from a small porch. Their old habits were reinstated, and Allen, along with Bill's neighbour Paul Lund, was soon cooking baby tuna and fresh perch from the harbour on Bill's little portable kerosene stove.

From the moment they arrived, Peter was given a particularly difficult time by Bill and his boys. This was a time when Burroughs seriously considered women as perhaps not human at all, having been sent from outer space as agents for the insect trust that was manipulating the planet. Burroughs proposed that all women should be exterminated just as soon as males had found some form of parthenogenesis. Peter, instead of accepting these discourses as Swiftian routines, always argued back in favour of love and sex and women, which of course only encouraged Burroughs and his entourage to come up with even greater outrages to upset him. Peter would get hoarse from the arguments, and Allen would get upset to see Peter so pained by it all. The boys felt threatened by Peter's ebullience and energy, and his openness and vulnerability made them deeply paranoid. Their reaction was either to ignore Peter or put him down. 'What if we cut up Peter? Peter likes girls so we'd probably find a Venusian inside,' cackled Burroughs, and Mikey Portman chimed in, 'That's right! Peter's a Venusian!'

Bill was now so inhuman that Allen was worried and frightened. He tried to get Peter to ignore the put-downs, but Peter preferred to confront them, so Allen and Peter wound up quarrelling as well. The argument went right to the heart of Allen and Peter's relationship. Although the fundamentally heterosexual Peter had become inextricably involved in a homosexual relationship with Allen, he was not prepared to sit back and let Burroughs and a couple of neurotic kids attack the things he held most dear, and argued forcefully on behalf of women and normal sex. But he was no match for their combined cynicism and sophistication, and each argument left him more frustrated.

Allen felt trapped by the situation, because he was unable to display the same indifference toward Bill that Bill felt towards him. Bill criticised Allen's attachment to Peter and to himself, and was scornful of Allen for depending so much on the brotherhood of old friends, which Bill dismissed as sentimental.

The conflict between Peter and Bill was exemplified in a series of mutual interviews conducted for a magazine Ferlinghetti was starting. Allen and Gregory interviewed Bill who said such things as: 'I feel like I'm on a sinking ship and I want off,' and Gregory interviewed Allen. Peter chose to emphasise his commitment to love in the face of Bill and his gang by transcribing a love-making session between Allen and himself. The results were awkward but strangely powerful, particularly in Peter's own unique spelling:

AG: 'Kiss me?'
PO: 'I do for a short wile & then get back to'
AG: 'Why dont you put the typewriter on my back then I can blow you directly?'
PO: 'He now is in my ear – & has his hand on my head'
AG: 'Does that feel good or am I just bugging you? . . .'

Allen didn't think that the transcripts were suitable for Ferlinghetti's magazine. 'At the time I was ashamed of it. We were supposed to be interviewing each other on world politics for City Lights' *Journal for the Protection of All Beings*, and I thought Orlovsky was being irrelevant,' Allen said later. 'However, now I see he had the right heart: bringing everything mental right back down into the body and disclosure of the secrets of the body's feelings ... Orlovsky's humanity was waked while I was in the power of my spectre – thinking I could make great angry pronouncements about the universe. All I wanted was love. All anybody wants.'

Another of Peter's transcripts conveys the tensions between Allen, Peter and Bill:

AG: 'After all the tender lovings we've given to each other.'

PO: Well, thank God I didn't charge you anything. That is, I wasn't. I wasn't a whore boy!'

AG: 'Yeah, well I guess it's all lost now. I'm getting older and creepy middleage looking. I guess you get disgusted when you realise what male potbellied being you wound up with for wife. But that's inevitable. I guess it's time we started out toward female, or me started, and see how that feels again. I still have that nightmare emptiness from someday when I'm dying and I've left no me behind, or child. Whole sisters and full sons to futurity, perpetuate this being. Awful if we didn't have a chance to settle down and get married and issue new Allens and Orlovskys before, Wham, the Bomb falls and ends that whole ecstatic story. That's the last moment fantasy I was telling Gregory about. I had it in Peru when I was high on Ayahuasca. It was so real it made me vow to get married and die papa, not even thinking of Bomb! ... But that's what I mean, a specific example of widening area of consciousness. The drug trance opened my soul and made me aware of the whole void side of my life and tenderised me to all the girls I'd ever had romance with and denied. So I'm talking about something real now that general men and women can dig ...'

PO: 'I didn't want to do it. You made me queer. It had to be you. Big cocky you. But you pulled me so and then I knew. I tried hard to fight it.'

AG: 'That's right you did. You always did keep telling me at the beginning you just wanted to be friends and you were afraid I was just acting nice so I could get in your ass. And now look at us.'

PO: 'But now I'm a bonefide queer on the witness stand.'

AG: 'Did I make that come true?'

PO: 'Make it? You hypnotised it true.'

AG: 'And now the dehypnotisation is begun. I'm getting old and you're realising you're no longer in my power . . .'

William Burroughs: 'Yeah, man. It's best for you to be away from him now. I mean now.' [Bill staggers drunkenly to his feet and knocks over his chair.]

AG: 'Oh really Bill! Don't wimper like that to me. I mean, I'm feeling something right now. Don't you realise I have to sooner or later find a girl and get married so I got a junior?'

WSB: 'Take a tip from me, kid, and steer clear of 'em. They got poison juices dripping all over 'em. Fishy smell too. Downright pornographic. Up a stretched asshole, that's where they make ya look. Wise up Allen and picture yourself right for once in a while can't you?'

PO: 'I know there's a lot of love to go around. And a lot of people are missing the ball. For me? I want to stop smoking and breathe some starry air.'

AG: 'Well, let's go in the room and make love again. Is that the answer to the World Question?'

PO: 'Yup. No, because I can't give you a baby.'

AG: 'I didn't want to stop coming with you just on account of that.'

Peter had mild jaundice, dysentery and a cold, and spent much of his time in bed brooding. After a week in Tangier, he finally had enough of the pressure and the put-downs and announced his decision to leave for Istanbul alone, breaking up their seven-year marriage. He refused to be moved by any of Allen's tearful arguments. Depressed, Allen recorded in his journal: 'July 9. Yesterday in the Socco, sitting at the Cafe Fuentes table overlooking the street filled with passing Arabs and ill-dressed youths, while Peter was visiting the whorehouse for half an hour, I wept, thinking of all the happy and past years we had lived together – how with his departure the sense of assurance and unity I enjoyed would be gone – and the sense of purpose to seek love – for what to seek now? As I am 35 and half my life now past, I have no sure road ahead, but many to choose from, and none seem inevitable.'

Timothy Leary arrived in Tangier at the end of July. At Allen's suggestion, he had corresponded with Burroughs and had invited him to Harvard to take part in a symposium on psychedelic drugs that he was organising for the September 1961 meeting of the American Psychological Association. Burroughs had agreed, and Leary flew down from Madrid to discuss the arrangements with him, as well as to visit with Allen. He was surprised to run into Peter, passing through customs in the other direction. Leary brought psilocybin pills with him, provoking what Burroughs referred to as 'the psychedelic summer'. Burroughs didn't like psilocybin, and he was unable to get Leary to try majoun, which in Bill's opinion was a stronger, better high.

Allen wrote to Peter in Greece, which was his first stop. 'Beautiful to see you ride off and I felt good that you were off into World alone, just tearful that we had been quarreling with each other and separating in soul, but that will be ok I hope next time we meet – I felt lost when you said "years" but if years alas, then years alas. I'll still cry to see yr old eyes.' He wrote to Ferlinghetti about Peter's leaving, 'We had big arguments about future of universe in Tangier. He wanted it to be sex-love, Burroughs wanted it to be unknown Artaud mutation out of bodies. I was undecided, confused. I still am except Burroughs seems to have killed "Hope" in any known form. The Exterminator is serious. Peter wanted innocence and sex apocalypse. It got very serious. I was vomiting.'

Bill's attack on word and image, supported by Leary, had confused Allen completely. Allen's opinions were always taken from people he respected. When something went so against his gut feeling, he was placed in a quandary. He thought that maybe poetry was redundant and found that he could only write journals and letters. In a letter to Gary Snyder, he said: 'Harvard opinion is that "arbitrary conceptualisation" is located in a specific brain area – cortex – and that drugs knock out cortex activity and leave open brain. Thus the present world psychic struggle is a war over Control of the nervous system. I see no way of writing at the moment since my original interest was something like mind transmission and present scientific research techniques have made great leap forward and perhaps now obviated words. At least that's Burroughs/Leary's opinion. That is, any aesthetic thrill or awareness a poem can bring can be catalyzed by wires and drugs, much more precisely.' Although there was, and is, no evidence that science is yet able to achieve this, Allen was so shaken by this idea and so trusted the opinions of his friends, that he developed a block against writing poetry that lasted for several years.

A few days after Peter left, Allen wrote him a long letter, covering most of the areas of their arguments and discussions: 'Leary told me he agreed with Bill that poetry was finished. Because he felt the world was really moving on to a new super consciousness that might eliminate words and ideas. It's just this point that had bugged me with Bill and hurt my pride – so I realised that at any rate part of my pride was hurt – or better dependence for security on my identity as a poet and my life work as a poet.

'I told Bill I wanted to see him alone and he said yes, and then we began a rapport again – I think aside from my own vanity pride (which his basic ideas were attacking and so it hurt me temporarily) – and aside from his carelessness and vanity and sloppiness because he is so busy – that Michael has been in the way. He kept hovering around the door when we were talking inside, and when Bill and I went out for lunch he said, "I guess I'll come along," and intruded on us. Bill said while he was gone for a second, "He is *too* dependent on me, that's his problem" – so Bill sees that – I see it *less* as a conspiracy of Bill and Michael now – Bill does want everybody included – or thinks he does – probably truly does – but the basis of *inclusion* must be that we drop our minds. i.e. my mind says I am poet and Orlovsky's lover, so when I got high I vomited with anxiety when I realised I was not that separate self but the same as everybody else.

'I guess your leaving must have robbed me of last prop, and it was courageous of you to do the same thing for yourself and take off and be a cloud and no more part of the idea we had together which was partly beautiful idea, but an idea doomed to fail after Zen-cut-up-loss of role-identity. The beautiful shiver tho always remains.

'As to sex, talked with Bill about that – his objection is to the use of sex as part of idea of identity, as part of re-affirmation and support of me-ness and ego – he admitted that sex might be a way of merger of souls on ego-less basis like we have had it, – and so he doesn't put it down, finally, in itself, but only where it is corrupted especially in civilised countries where it is part of power ego-grab. There is no real argument between you . . .

'I think one trouble here was you were isolated, I was confused and since I was clinging to my identity with you I could not see thru your identity to your heart, and I think you wound up over-affirming your identity and pressing down harder on it while it was under attack, instead of just giving it up and coming out free . . .

'All in all I think our idea of sex was right and beautiful and led us (or me) forward and I thank you Peter . . . Anyway it's worked out magically for the best and you and I are both free now so forgive me and take me in thought hello and I'll see you soon whenever we both can on free basis, I hope sooner than ten years because that would mean it would take ten long years for both of us to be really free . . .'

The scene began to break up. Leary went to Copenhagen, and Alan Ansen, who had been visiting, returned to his house in Venice, leaving only Gregory and Allen in their hotel and Bill with the boys in the Villa Delirium, with a strange sort of cold war between them. Bill, Ian and Mikey prepared to go to London, and Gregory decided to go with them. So Allen was left alone in Tangier to mop things up. He was almost broke; ever since Paris, he had foolishly lent Gregory money, all of which Gregory lost at the Casino. They arranged that Gregory would repay the money as soon as he reached London, sending it to the American Express in Athens so that Allen could collect it on his arrival.

Allen left Tangier on an August afternoon in 1961. Standing on the ship's deck, 'alone, solitary, hopeless, tranquil, still with knapsack,' he watched the familiar church spire, the hillside cluttered with Arab houses, and the white apartment blocks disappear into the blue sea haze. His only plan was to meet Gary Snyder in India on New Year's day.

Allen arrived in Athens in the evening and immediately went out exploring. He stayed up all night talking to people he met in all-night cafes and in the morning went to American Express to collect the money Gregory was to have sent. As he left his hotel, he caught a glimpse of the Parthenon and was all prepared to spend a pleasant day sightseeing, but at American Express he was brought down with a jolt. Despite all his promises, Gregory had let him down. Allen wrote angrily to him: 'So now I have about three bucks left and am totally bugged . . . Will you please send me what you said you'd send me which is $120 borrowed plus the $70 earlier . . . It's all a big fat stupid fucked up drag.' Gregory wrote back to say that he felt guilty and enclosed five pounds, about fourteen dollars.

Allen was also owed money by *Show Business Illustrated* for an article that he wrote on the Cannes Film Festival, and fortunately this check arrived the next day. The magazine however objected to his use of the word 'shit', which he had mentioned because it was used so frequently in the film *The Connection*. Despite his desperate need, Allen wrote back and said that he would repay the money if necessary, but they could not censor his text. The article was never run, nor was the $450 reclaimed.

Allen liked Athens and wrote Gregory, 'It's like a small town and very cute and toylike.' Thirty-five years later, he still retained the photograph of one of the boys there, and remembered: 'The boy I hired in Athens, strong and solid muscled, like Ally Oop, blond – Alan Ansen suggested the meeting with several friends.' His travels around Greece produced many beautiful pieces of descriptive prose, which would be published in *Journals: Early Fifties, Early Sixties*. With two new friends, he visited Delphi where they spent four days with the Greek poet Sikilianos, drank from the Castalian Spring and explored the Cave of the Muses. Allen climbed Mount Parnassus and walked its crags naked to salute Apollo.

He spent three days in Hydra, then visited Epidauros and Mycenae.

Back in Athens, he spent an evening with Leslie Fiedler, the literary critic, who later recounted how 'surprised and shocked' he had been at Allen's melancholy. Allen was walking round Greece in a daze, still not entirely sure what had happened to him in Tangier. From Athens, he wrote to his friend Howard Shulman and told him the story: 'We looked into Bill in Tangier and I met *someone I didn't know*; who rejected me, as far as Allen and Bill were concerned and all previous relationships they built up. And if I don't know Bill I sure don't know myself because he was my rock of Tolerance and Friendship and true Art.' He told Shulman about the cut-ups, then said: 'He was cutting up his own consciousness and escaping as far as I can tell outside of anything I could recognise as his previous identity. And that somewhat changed my identity since that had been something built, I had thought, and permanently shared with him. And Peter and I suddenly broke thru the automaton Love-Faith habit we were junked-up and comfortable in, and looked in each other's eyes – and nobody was there but a couple robots talking words and fucking. So he left for Istanbul and I stayed in Tangier and vomited off the roof.

'Now the serious technical point that Burroughs was making by his cut-ups, which I resisted and resented, since it threatened everything I depend on – I could stand the loss of Peter but not the loss of Hope and Love: and could maybe even stand the loss of them, whatever they are, if Poesy was left, for me to go on being something I wanted, sacred poet however desolate; but Poesy itself became a block to further awareness. For further awareness lay in dropping every fixed concept of self, identity, role, ideal, habit and pleasure. It meant dropping language itself, *words*, as medium of consciousness. It meant literally altering consciousness outside of what was already the fixed habit of language-inner-thought-monologue-abstraction-mental-image-symbol-mathematical abstraction. It meant exercising unknown and unused areas of the physical brain. Electronics, science fiction, drugs, stroboscopes, breathing exercises, exercises in thinking in music, colour, no thinks, entering and believing hallucination, altering the neurologically fixated habit pattern Reality. But that's what I thought Poetry was doing all along! *But* the Poetry I'd been practicing depended on living inside the structure of language, depended on words as the medium of consciousness and therefore the medium of conscious being.'

All of these methods, of course, achieved widespread use as the 1960s continued, being applied in a variety of art forms, from underground rock music to the theatre. In 1961, however, this was a forbidding and unknown area, and it was Burroughs, Ginsberg and a few other pioneers who first mapped it out, albeit at some personal cost to themselves, as Allen went on to tell Shulman:

'Since then I've been wandering in doldrums . . . I can't write, except journals and dreams down. As the next step if any for Poetry I can't imagine . . . I also stopped reading newspapers two months ago. Also the paranoid fear that I'm a degenerate robot under the mind-control of the mad spectre of Burroughs. Except that it finally seems (after dreams of killing him) that he has only taken the steps, or begun to take, steps toward actual practice of expanded consciousness that were on the cards for me anyhoo, since the first days of mind break up with Blake, and of which direction I was repeatedly reminded in drug trances.'

Feeling desolate, Allen decided to try and meet up with Peter in Haifa, where, by Allen's calculations, Peter's mother would be forwarding his next V.A. check. Allen arrived in Haifa in October but found no sign of Peter. Allen was not overly impressed by the place. He wrote to Kerouac: 'Haifa is like a ratty looking Bronx, amazingly full of Jewish people who all think they're Jewish, under a Jewish sky with Jewish streetcars and Jewish airplanes and armies and Jewish speeches and dances and theaters and Jewish newspapers, so after a while I felt like an Arab. Except like being surrounded by millions of relatives from Newark, so I felt lost and lonely.'

Ten days later Allen and Peter had a joyful reunion on a streetcorner in Tel Aviv. Peter had grown long hair and was very tanned. After Greece, he had gone all through Turkey to Alleppo in Syria, then to Damascus and Beirut, where he took a boat down the coast to Port Said and Cairo. He was so broke at one point that he had to sell his blood in order to eat. In Egypt he climbed the Great Pyramid and looked the Sphinx in the eye. He took a boat back to Beirut, and went from there to Jordan to explore Jerusalem, and finally to Tel Aviv to find Allen.

Allen and Peter visited Jerusalem for a week and met Martin Buber there. Looking like the classical image of a wise man, with his mouth hidden in his long white beard, he gave them a very friendly reception. Peter asked him what kind of visions he had had, and he told them that he had seen ghosts coming in his bedroom window when he was younger, but was not interested in visions like that. Allen tried out Burroughs's theories on him, saying that he thought that loss of identity and confrontation with the non-human universe was the main problem – that man had to evolve and change, and maybe become non-human in order to 'melt' into the universe. Buber disagreed vigorously. He was interested in human-to-human relationships, for it was a human universe that we were destined to inhabit. 'Mark my words young man,' he said. 'In years to come you will realise that I was right!'

11 India

> *Allen Ginsberg to Kushwant Singh, 'Do you know any nice young poets?'*
> *Peter Orlovsky to Kushwant Singh, 'Can ya introduce me to some drug addicts?'*

Allen and Peter landed in Bombay in mid-February 1962, with exactly one dollar. Fortunately, Lawrence Ferlinghetti had forwarded Allen's royalties. They changed their money on the black market, getting seven rupees to the dollar. At this rate, a meal cost them about fifteen cents. In Tangier Paul Bowles had issued dire warnings about staying only in good hotels and eating only in the best restaurants, but Allen and Peter were delighted to find that neither the water nor the one-rupee vegetarian meals upset their stomachs. Since they were hoping to live on twenty rupees a day between them, this meant that they could stretch their money a long way.

Their original arrangement had been to meet Gary Snyder in Bombay on 1 January. They were almost two months late, but there was no message waiting from him at American Express. They spent two days looking round the city, taking fifteen-cent rides in the horse-drawn carriages through the incredibly crowded streets. Then, since there was still no message from Gary, they took an all-day, all-night, third-class train to Delhi. They had air mattresses, so they spent the journey lying comfortably, watching India flow past their window, a panorama of huge plains and distant brown mountains, of palm trees and cows and people in loincloths tending water buffalo in muddy rivers.

In Delhi they stayed at a Jain dharmasala on Lady Hardinge Road. Dharmasalas are big hostels, near the temples, established in all towns and cities to provide free lodging and cheap or free food for anyone on a pilgrimage or visiting on business. They were introduced to the dharmashala by a Jain businessman from Jaipur whom they met on the train.

Despite his having read so much about India, the enormous part played by religion in India still came as something of a shock to Allen. He told Kerouac: 'Everybody in India is religious, it's weird, everybody ON to some Saddhana (method) and had family guru or Brahmin priest who knows all about how the universe is a big illusion; it's totally unlike the West – it really is another Dimension of time-history here ... It's assumed that all Gods are unreal so one should respect all Gods as purely subjective forms of medita-tion to fix the mind on one image and still it down and be peaceful – the Gods are all interchangeably friendly – Saraswati for people hung on music and learning; Lakshmi for people hung on moviestars beauties and loot; (Rhada for young lover devotees); Krishna for cocksmen-coyote types; Ganesha the elephant head god of prosperity and slyness for the Jerry Newmans and Peter Orlovskys of the universe (Peter has become a Ganesha devotee), Buddhas for the Jacks, Kalis and Durgas for Bill and ilk, anything you want – a huge cartoon religion with Disney Gods with three heads and six arms killing buffalo demons – everybody so gentle about it all it's unbelievable – except the Moslems swept down in the 12th century with their One Allah like a bunch of hysterical Jews and smashed all the pretty Walt Disney statues before they calmed down and got happy like the Hindus. Weird thing is we met hundreds of retired householders (sunyassis) all over, they really do retire from the world – Imagine my father wandering around New Jersey in orange robes with big serious expression – it's like that.'

Gary Snyder finally arrived in Delhi, with Joanne Kyger. Allen had not seen Gary in six years; he and Joanne had been living in Japan. Allen noted that he had aged. After a joyful reunion, they spent a week sightseeing in Delhi, visiting the Red Fort, the mosques and temples, and the old walls and gateways.

Now that the team was together, they set off on the road, heading first for the foothills of the Himalayas, where they were to visit the Ashram of Swami Shivananda. It was a jumble of half-finished brick buildings surrounded by groves of mango trees in a gorge on the banks of the Ganges, at the edge of the Siwalik Mountain Range. They were given a dusty room in a building on a hill overlooking the main complex. They ate in the dining hall, where they received unusually small portions of vegetarian food.

At the evening meeting, a series of swamis got up and read or recited inspirational works, until Shivananda got tired of them and cut them off with an 'Om.' Joanne had to sit with the women on one side of the room, while the men sat on the other. There were about five western women, dressed in saris. Shivananda asked Allen, 'How many of you are there?'

'Four,' he replied.

'That's an auspicious number,' and Shivananda winked at Allen as he passed along, supported by his two assistants. He gave the four of them each an envelope containing five rupees, and sitting on his padded chair, he directed his assistants to place a wreath of flowers around Joanne's neck. To Allen he gave a small book called *Raja Yoga For Americans*.

It was at Shivananda's ashram that Allen learned the Hare Krishna mantra, in which the various names of Vishnu are repeated: 'Hare Krishna, Hare Krishna; Krishna Krishna, Hare Hare; Hare Rama, Hare Rama; Rama Rama, Hare Hare.' Ginsberg was one of the first to popularise this to the United States and chanted it at readings and public meetings throughout the 1960s. Now it can be heard on the streets of most big cities in the United States and Europe, chanted by the devotees of the late Sri Bhaktivedanta. Bhaktivedanta arrived in the Lower East Side of New York from India in 1965 at the age of seventy and received enormous help and encouragement from Ginsberg in getting his first centre started.

Allen had an audience with Shivananda, which he described to Kerouac. '[He's a] charlatan of mass-production international nirvana racket – but actually quite a calm holy old man . . . I rather liked him. I asked, "Where can I get a guru?" and he smiles and touches his heart and says, "The only guru is your own heart, dearie" or words to that effect, and adds, "You'll know your guru when you see him because you'll love him, otherwise don't bother." Well, not quite that funny but that was the message. Which made me feel quite good after all that Tangier austerity and loveless gurus.'

Ginsberg found this message very reassuring, as he told Tom Clark in a 1965 *Paris Review* interview: 'That is the sweetness of it I felt – in my heart. And suddenly realised it was the heart that

I was seeking. In other words, it wasn't consciousness, it wasn't petites sensations, sensations defined as expansion of mental consciousness to include more data – as I was pursuing that line of thought, pursuing Burroughs' cut-up thing – the area that I was seeking was heart rather than mind.' The meeting with Shivananda set him on a new direction.

They had to move from the ashram the next day because a large crowd was expected for Shivaratri, the Night of Shiva, but they were directed to another ashram, just across the Ganges. A free row-boat service connected the ashrams. They walked along the glittering white sand on the banks of the Ganges and did their washing and bathing in the cool, clear water. They spread their clothes on the rocks to dry and dozed in the sun. The woods around were filled with little white huts of hermits, and further up river they came across a group of Shiva-worshipping sadhus, sitting motionless under trees, deep in meditation. They had bloodshot eyes and long matted hair, and their naked bodies were smeared with ashes. They sat on deerskins, and had small tridents stuck in the ground around them. One had a pet cow. Allen could not understand how they sat so still and was surprised when Gary said he could sit like that. Gary had learned Zen sitting in Japan, and during the course of their travels in India he taught Allen how to do it.

The next day, they took a walk on the hill behind the ashram to see the hermits' huts and the cow pastures. A teenage youth with long hair, wearing orange brahmacharia robes, was sitting on a big swing that hung from a flowering tree with a mass of fresh banana leaves beneath it. He spoke English. He told them he was on his way down from the Himalayas for spring and invited them to an 'astral lunch'. Allen asked him about the red-eyed sadhus in the valley below, and he dismissed them with a laugh. 'Ah, they're just the advertisement posters for the real yogis whom you can't see way back in the mountains.' India was proving to be everything that Allen had hoped for.

They continued their sightseeing with trips to Almora, where they enjoyed spectacular views of the Himalayas, and to the maharajas' palaces in Jaipur, which Allen found terribly dull. The long overnight train rides, the nights on the floor, sometimes four to a room, began to take their toll. Gary and Joanne argued frequently, and Joanne became irritated by Allen and Peter. In a letter quoted in her journals, she said: 'Peter Orlovsky locks himself in the bathroom all night and smokes opium and then vomits all the next morning so we travel slowly.' In the same letter she described Allen and Peter's appearance: 'Allen Ginsberg is running around in an unwashed white Indian (grey) pajama outfit with flapping arms and legs, or else very short shorts from Israel, and a Greek shirt and red nylon socks. He is balding on top, his curling hair down his neck. But if you think his hair is long, you should see Peter Orlovsky whose hair actually falls over his face to his nose in front (but that's all right because he can take drugs behind it easier) and down to his shoulders in back and a tee shirt that doesn't quite cover seven inches of his stomach in front and some tennis shoes full of holes without any shoelaces. The Indians for their own perverse reasons seem to adore him.'

They made arrangements to stay in the Triund Forest Bungalow in Dharmsala, and set out the next day to hike the seven miles up the hill to the ten-thousand-foot level with their rucksacks. They passed the Dalai Lama's headquarters and stopped to make an appointment to meet with him the next day at noon. His compound was guarded by armed Indian troops, as it had been since he fled Tibet in 1959, aided by the CIA.

Next day, the four Americans were quickly cleared through security and taken to a waiting room in a group of low wooden buildings. Tibetan prayer flags were strung like washing on lines between deodar trees and fluttered constantly in the breeze.

Eventually they were shown into the chamber where, dressed in red and black robes, the Dalai Lama reclined on a velvet couch surrounded by colourful Tibetan tankas, or painted scrolls. Gary prostrated himself, and the others greeted him more conventionally. He was then twenty-seven years old and looked to Joanne like a 'gawky adolescent'. His interpreter remained with him, though he spoke English well.

Allen described his many experiences with drugs and asked about their relationship to the spiritual states reached in meditation. Gary recorded the conversation in his journal: 'The Dalai Lama gave the same answer everyone else did: drug states are real psychic states, but they aren't ultimately useful to you because you didn't get them on your own will and effort. For a few glimpses into the unconscious mind and other realms, they may be of use in loosening you up. After that, you can too easily rely on them, rather than undertaking such a discipline as will actually alter the structure of the personality in line with these insights. It isn't much help to just glimpse them with no ultimate basic alteration of the ego that is the source of lots of the psychic-spiritual ignorance that troubles one.'

Allen asked him if he would like to take LSD, and the Dalai Lama said: 'If you take LSD, can you see what's in that briefcase?' He said he would be interested in taking psilocybin to see what Westerners were always talking about, and Allen said that he would arrange for Timothy Leary to send him some from Harvard. Allen was hogging the conversation, and eventually Gary said, 'Really Allen, the inside of your mind is just as boring and just the same as everyone else's. Is it necessary to go on?' Gary proceeded to discuss Zen meditation techniques. The Dalai Lama asked how he sat, where he put his hands, how he arranged his tongue and what sort of breathing he did.

Asked by Allen how many hours a day he meditated, the Dalai Lama replied, 'Me? Why I never meditate, I don't have to!' which prompted Joanne to write in her journal: 'Then Ginsberg is very happy because he wants to get instantly enlightened and can't stand sitting down or discipline of the body. He always gobbles down his food before anyone else has started. He came to India to find a spiritual teacher. But I think he actually believes he knows it all, but just wishes he *felt* better about it.' She asked the Dalai Lama if it was necessary for Westerners to sit in the full lotus position in order to meditate, since it was so uncomfortable for them. He replied, 'It's not a matter of national custom.'

Next they took the famous Pathankat Express to see the stupas at Sanchi. The huge stone domes with elaborately carved walls and gateways dated from the second century BC and were among the oldest Buddhist monuments in India. The smaller stupa had beautiful bas reliefs on its posts and rails; Joanne spent a whole day making rubbings of the carvings.

From there they continued to Faridpur, where the Ajunta caves were cut deep into the cliffside where a river makes a great bend in a steep gorge. There were five temple caves and twenty-four monastery caves, the oldest dating from the first century BC and the most recent from the eighth century. Some were as much as seventy feet deep, and a few still had painted walls and ceilings, though the colours had faded and were eroded and stained. Gary discovered that the caves had wonderful acoustics and chanted the Prajnaparameta Sutra in one, his voice echoing through the caverns and little side rooms of the complex. Allen was impressed and wrote Kerouac: 'He knows how to chant sutras in Japanese Sanskrit with big Tibetan Noh play sepulchral voice reechoing in caves and syncopating jijimuje syllables.' Allen learned the words from him and later added the sutra to his repertoire of chants for public readings.

The Ellora caves at Aurangabad came next: more than thirty caves, all painted, about half Buddhist, half Hindu and some Jain. They were astonishing. Cave number 16, Kailasa, was not a cave at all but a full size Hindi temple carved from the living rock. Allen described it to Kerouac: 'The great rock cut cave temples of Ellora where the great GLORY of Indian art really is, makes Michelangelo's renaissance look Western little. I mean, they got great dancing shivas balanced with ten arms doing cosmic dances of creation 20 feet tall, and fantastic skully Kalis invoking nightmare murders in another yuga, thousands of statues dancing all over huge temple built like Mt. Kailash the Himalayan abode of Shiva – And Ganesha with fat belly and elephant head and snakehead belt and trunk in a bowlful of sweets riding on his vehicle a mouse – How can DaVinci beat an elephant on a mouse?'

Their travels led eventually to Bombay, where Radhika Jayakar, an elegant young Indian woman Allen knew from New York, invited them to stay in her large comfortable house on Malabar Hill. The luxuries there contrasted vividly with their recent travelling experience. Each morning, Bhima, the barefoot servant, brought them tea and eggs as they lay in beds with fresh white sheets and pillows or beneath huge shade trees in the garden.

They collected their mail. Allen was shattered by news of Elise Cowen's suicide. Released from the Hillside Mental Hospital into her parents' care after her amphetamine breakdown, she was taken to their apartment in Morningside Heights, where she sat and brooded. One cold February day she leapt from the living room window into oblivion. Allen wrote Gregory: 'That really gave me a turn. I had felt a little responsible for her welfare and hadn't been much help to her when I was around, always felt revulsion for the deathsmell in her hair and so always held myself distant from her, and then she lived upstairs in East 2nd Street ... Everyone that took amphetamines regularly wound up a thinfaced paranoiac nervous wreck like Elise ...' The news depressed Allen for a long time.

Gregory reported from New York that Kerouac was in bad shape: 'He is not so fine, drunk, and can't talk straight with him, wanted to, he just cares about his self and demands I respect that self, but I can't if he just sits there bubbling drunkenly how great he is and how bad who else is, so unreal, unrelated, that he truly bored me.'

Peter also received grim news. Lafcadio was causing trouble at Central Islip Hospital, and his mother, hospitalised after her attempt to stab him, blamed it all on Allen. She wrote to Peter that it was Lafcadio's 'getting fucked up the ass and choked and beaten up' by Allen that had driven him crazy. Peter replied that he didn't think Allen desecrated that much; whatever happened occurred when Lafcadio had a 'general love' for Allen. Allen had worried and asked him if he should have sex with Lafcadio; Peter said it was all right where friendship and love existed, and it didn't seem to upset Lafcadio. 'But it's not that sex cock play with Allen that sent Lafcadio back to Bughouse,' Peter wrote. 'It was me and my stupidness making bad arrangements for him when I left NYC and also my leaving him.' Peter told his mother that he was considering coming home to get Lafcadio out of the hospital and take an apartment with him. It was fortunate for Allen that Lafcadio's mother did not press charges; and unfortunate for Lafcadio that Allen could not control his predatory instincts towards the mentally defective adolescent.

Allen spent much of his time sitting around reading *Hymns to Kali*, the classic poetry of Kabir, Ganeshwar, Ghalib and other Indian texts. He gave a reading with Peter and Gary, and over a hundred people came to sit in the warm evening air and hear their controversial poetry. The American Consul was in the audience. Peter read first, loud and brash, warming up the audience for the others. Allen used the occasion to give one of his rare readings of 'Kaddish'. A few days later, Gary and Joanne took the boat back to Japan.

Now that he was settled in one place for a few weeks, Allen gradually began to connect with Indian intellectuals. He was interviewed by the *Illustrated Weekly of India* which treated him and Peter like visiting saints, and they met a group of five young poets who were very interested in the Beats and were translating Beat texts into Marathi, the language of Bombay. Allen took them to literary tea parties where Indian critics sat around discussing Robert Graves in Oxford accents, and they, in turn, took Allen and Peter to the Bombay opium dens. They spent six hours walking through the red light district where Peter spent two rupees for a girl. There were houses full of hermaphrodites, transvestites; on one block, eunuchs lived on part of the sidewalk, their charpoy cots arranged neatly with their cooking stoves and other goods. The eunuchs were mostly middle-aged, with brightly rouged faces and bald spots; they sat combing long black hair that fell to their waists, as they camped it up for passers by. A policeman sat on the corner in his hut, peacefully surveying the scene and keeping everyone from harm.

The enormous tolerance in India for every possible form of eccentric behaviour and religious excess made Allen feel that most of his friends in North Beach and the Lower East Side would be better off here. The pressures that drove Elise Cowen out of her window just did not exist in India. He felt that even his mother would have been able to live happily in a tolerant society where everyone was accepted as a sadhu, following their own path, and there was an elaborate support system of ashrams and free lodgings and food. Allen wrote to Paul Bowles: 'Indians really sophisticated as far as letting everybody be as crazy as they want and taking it as formal personal method of relating to Gods, all very proper and dignified. The Moslems and Jews and Christians seem really mean and stinky in this respect, the more I think of it.' Allen had not read of the horrors of partition; the torture and murder that accompanied the expulsion of Muslims to Pakistan, or the destruction of Mughal culture in Delhi. He saw tolerance and acceptance, and in a way it was.

One small example was in the way that the Indians took to Peter. Friendly and open, they clearly related to him as some kind of American sadhu, with the result that Peter became expansive and talkative, in direct contrast to his misery in the uptight atmosphere of the Burroughs circle in Tangier, or in middle-class America. Peter strode through the streets in a flowing silk shirt, humming Bach, on his way to visit the opium den, or sometimes he just ambled after the white cows in the street, talking to the cow-girls – *gopi* girls, whom he called goopy girls. No one gave a second thought to his long hair and clothes. As Allen wrote to Kerouac: 'Everybody, workers, walk around in the streets in underwear, regular striped Hollywood nightmare shorts with open flies like Americans have nightmares being caught in the streets in.'

India was slowly working its magic on them, changing and relaxing them both. After eleven weeks in India, Allen was able to tell Kerouac: 'The subjective result on me of India has thus been to start dropping all spiritual activity initiated since Blake voice days and all mental activities I can discard, and stop straining at heaven's door and all that mysticism and drugs and cut-ups and gurus and fears of hells and desire for God and as such, as result, in sum, I feel better and more relaxed and don't give a shit and sometimes sit in cafe downtown Bombay and my brain does get empty and filled with big thrilling cosmic Indic Persian Gulf sunset XX Century.'

Allen now attempted to dissolve his writer's block by embarking on an ambitious 'Hymn To Kali', based on a classical formal hymn that he read in translation. The result was 'Stotras To Kali Destroyer of Illusions', which appeared in *Planet News*.

Allen and Peter began to feel they were overstaying their welcome on Malabar Hill, so on 11 May 1962, they said goodbye to Radhika and boarded the train for the long journey across the sub-continent to Calcutta.

In Calcutta at the end of May, Peter had to take his Veterans Administration examination to make sure he was still crazy enough to merit his pension. He passed easily and had guaranteed funds for the next two years. Allen meanwhile went on an expedition to the Himalayan foothills in the north. In Kalimpong, he visited many monasteries, and the head of one lamasery offered to get him a boy; Allen didn't take him up on it because he was too busy trying to find a tantric lama who would give him initiation. An old English lama with blackened teeth gave him the name of Dudjom Rinpoche, the head of the oldest school of Tibetan Buddhism, the Nyingma sect. Allen saw Dudjom on his thirty-sixth birthday, 3 June 1962.

Dudjom was suffering from asthma. He looked strangely like a woman with his hair done up in a bun, his smooth round face like an American Indian's and his Tibetan skirt. Allen talked with him about his fear of the hallucinations caused by LSD and Ayahuasca. Dudjom sucked the air in between his teeth and advised: 'Watch the wheels within wheels but don't get attached to anything you see. Let it pass into you but be inactive and not grasping nor rejecting. If you see anything horrible, don't cling to it. If you see anything beautiful, don't cling to it.' Allen did not immediately grasp what Dudjom had told him. Only later did he achieve the realisation that he was hopelessly attached to his Blake vision and the idea of a widened consciousness. When he finally severed this attachment, it transformed his life. Then he took Dudjom's advice to heart, and he quoted it often in interviews, lectures and readings.

Next, Allen took a jeep to Gangtok, the capital of the tiny Himalayan state of Sikkim, to visit the Karmapa, the head of the Kagyu sect of Tibetan Buddhism. Gyalwa Karmapa was recognised by his followers as an incarnation of a line of lamas that stretched back to the yogi poet Milarepa, who founded the sect in the eleventh century AD. A jolly, fat man with a baby face, Karmapa was very interested in what Allen had to say about drugs and said that he would like to try mescaline. He called Allen a manjusri, a bodhisattva of wisdom and learning, and told Allen that there was something definite that he could teach him if he could spend a week there. But Allen had been given only a three-day pass to Sikkim and had to leave the country the next day. He felt extremely frustrated.

Back in Calcutta, Peter had found them a place to live on the top floor of a third-rate Muslim hotel called the Amjadia, in the downtown bazaar district. They had a small whitewashed cell-like room with a ceiling fan, two beds, and creaking green shutters. Everywhere there were people sleeping on the sidewalks and in doorways, and the streets were filled with lepers, beggars and holy men with ashes in their hair.

Calcutta is the centre of Kali worship in India, and 8–10 October were the Durga Puja holidays. In all the Hindu quarters of the city, huge papier-maché statues were set up in big tents, and the streets were filled with people drinking bhang – a legal infusion of marijuana and almond milk – banging on drums and cymbals, smoking ganja – high-grade marijuana – singing and swaying in their rags in honour of the Goddess of destruction. Ginsberg described her as 'The official traditional dignified image of the nature of the universe here, representing what IS, like, power, electricity, force, being – all that is created, preserved and then destroyed.' Allen mingled with the crowds, smoking ganja and sitting in the tents with the half-naked, ash-smeared sadhus under the giant iron Howrah Bridge that spanned the Hooghly River (as the Ganges is called when it reaches Calcutta). The sadhus passed the pipes around and sang mystical songs to Shiva and Krishna. Allen soon learned the rituals: a devotional heap of flowers was placed in the middle of the circle and special incense lit. The devotees would raise the clay-bowled ganja pipe to the sky and shout, 'BOOM BOOM MAHADEVA', before blasting on it. Allen was soon behaving like a professional and became very good at yelling the invocation.

He went to the Nimtallah Ghats where, on the steps leading down to the river, the bodies were burned according to traditional Hindu funeral rites. To Allen, it was like entering a strange Bosch-like visionary world. Fakirs and sadhus sat in circles of five to twenty men, passing the ganja pipe. The mourners, groups of respectable white-robed men of all ages, smoked ganja and sang hymns. Sadhus with long, matted hair and beards danced with rolling hip movements to the drumbeats of blind beggars. The smoke from the funeral pyres rolled through the trees and swirled around Allen's head as he watched the show.

One of the pyres was for a three-year-old boy, and Allen looked on as his body was oiled to make it combustible. On the next pyre was a lawyer; his abdomen was already consumed, but attendants were still poking sticks at his chest and half-burned head. Allen stared at the puffed and blackened eyes, with the skull showing where the skin had burned away, and thought: 'There's nobody inside his head anymore. They're burning an old pillow. It's all okay.' Tantric ascetics in red robes and white beards sat around in alcoves facing the six corpse fires. One white-robed ascetic sat right in the ashes of the dead.

Allen decided to spend a night there alone with the sleeping sadhus. He bought two packages of ganja from the pipe shop on the main street and sat on a bench by the first ash pit to smoke and watch a body burn: 'Pile of wood and the head slowly bubbling up around mouth and nose – Cheeks blackened with sheets of flame clasping the volume of the face – splitting, and pink underskin sizzling open . . .' After five minutes he moved on to the Mandir, where he bought food for one of the dancing sadhus and drank tea. He wandered around the pyres as the sadhus were quieting down for the night, though a few still sat chanting. Back in the Mandir, he settled himself next to a handsome sadhu, and one of the attendants gave them a pipe. 'I blasted enough till my throat dry and panicky – then walked up and down, my body trembling, my neck constricted, till I peed, and still the trembling wait, as if I vomit or Ramakrishna appear in the river – or Krishna in every animal eye all around, each of the beggars – lay down to sleep finally on a marble bench in inner waiting room with rows of Baul singers and rags sadhu buttocks sheeted on the floor.' He took off his rubber sandals and put them under the bench; in the morning they were gone, and he had to walk barefoot for tea, puris and potatoes before hopping on the number 19 tram to go home to the hotel and Peter.

Allen began spending nights regularly at the burning ghats, usually Tuesdays and Saturdays, the nights of the biggest ganja-smoking rituals. One day while he was there, the attendants placed a young woman on the pyre, but she was not dead and fortunately awoke before the wood ignited. Allen spent long nights walking the Calcutta streets, looking at the thousands of homeless people murmuring in their sleep on the roadsides and sidewalks, scattered everywhere like bodies on a battlefield. In his journal he wrote, 'It isn't enough for your heart to break because everybody's heart is broken now.'

Calcutta became Allen's home. The painting of dancing skeletons on the wall of their room, Peter's cracked brown guitar, their knapsacks stacked neatly against the wall, the crude green shutters, the red paper kites fluttering outside in the hot air, the constant rickshaw bells, the bearded grocery seller wailing to Allah, the transvestite singing on the corner – all became familiar. The cool marble tables of the Hotel Amjadia's restaurant, the Baul Saints in their strange waistcoats and skirts, the lepers and beggars, became everyday sights. He got to know the tram system and the lamplit stalls at Burrabazaar where he drank bhang. He sat regularly beneath the mile-long black iron Howrah Bridge, listening to the roar of traffic and watching the tidal bore surge by.

On 10 December 1962, they took the Doon Express third-class sleeper to Benares. The Hindu equivalent of Mecca or Rome,

Benares is an ancient city built on the banks of the River Ganges at the time of Thebes, Babylon and Nineveh. At the water's edge is a cliff-face of ancient maharajas' palaces, temples, dharmasalas and worn cracked steps leading down to the water: a jumble of masonry and turrets and narrow crooked alleys, all teeming with people. It was on one of the narrow streets that Allen and Peter found a room, 'a few steps from Ganges near main mangy dog leper sadhu bathing ghat', where they would live for the next five months.

The room, on the third floor of a house on Dasaswamedh Ghat, overlooked a market square on one side and the steps of the ghat on the other. French windows opened on to a balcony, which encircled the room as on a Parisien *ronde point* and from which they could see the Ganges flowing and the pointed turrets of the temple across the street. Chicken-wire grills over the windows stopped monkeys from coming in and stealing bananas from the table.

There was a desk and plenty of shelves for Allen's books and manuscripts. They bought a hundred-watt bulb to prevent eye-strain when they worked at night; straw mats for the floor; clay pots to store water; and a big pail for cleaning. They arranged their blankets on the charpoy, a rope bed on a wooden frame, and bought a kerosene stove for a dollar. It looked and felt like home. Allen would tune his portable radio to Radio Peking, take a shot of morphine-atrophine, and lie back on the charpoy, relaxed and happy.

The street below Allen's house was constantly noisy with women vegetable-sellers calling their wares and lepers and beggars catching the bathers on their way to the river and back. Sacred cows and monkeys roamed at will, and all the marriage or first haircut or special funeral processions came past the house, often two or three of them each day, a gang of drummers preceding them, sometimes with eunuchs dancing ahead or with camels and elephants leading, 'a great surf of noise from dawn to midnight, statues of Gods passing on litters and holymen and attendants coming to take a bath'.

Allen spent a lot of time at the Manikarnika burning ghat, the holiest in all India, which he regarded as the 'best show here'. Geese and swans pecked among the leaf boats and marigold petals at the ash-blackened water's edge, boats with rectangular sails floated past downstream.

Two weeks after settling in Benares, Allen and Peter took a trip to Agra, about 350 miles away, towards Delhi, to spend Christmas at the Taj Mahal. Christmas was the anniversary of the death of Shah Jehan's wife, for whom the tomb was built, and the hereditary Muslim guards held a two-day festival of Urdu singing and poetry. The monument was open forty-eight hours for the celebration, and Allen and Peter bedded down in a marble alcove screened from the light as the amplified Urdu voices echoed and re-echoed around the vast dome, 'Great waves of sound frothing out of the arch.' Allen wrote Paul Bowles they had 'lots of ganja to make the symmetries more awesome'. He was deeply impressed by the building and enthused over it to Lucien Carr: 'Taj Mahal an awesome surprise – the picture postcards don't tell the Vibrational story – it really is a sublime joint – like being inside a perfectly symmetrical 3-D DeChirico canvas – you get that particular infinity sensation around it – like a time machine – Fortunately we *lived* in it for three days so we got quite an exposure ... Friendly atmosphere – most stupendous motel in Universe I'm sure – Worth a trip to India just for that.'

They spent the next week in Brindiban, Lord Krishna's home and the centre of bhakti yoga, whose cultists offer their gurus devotion, faith and love. There, in his quest for gurus, Allen met Srimata Krishnaji, and Bankey Behari, who told him to 'Take Blake as your guru,' to practice bhakti to Blake, since he was obviously Allen's guru, and stop looking for a living one. When Allen returned to Benares, he tacked a postcard of Blake's death mask, from the National Portrait Gallery in London, on the wall between the windows.

Allen gave a free reading at the Benares Hindu University. At the end, the head of the English department, a professor O'Brien, stood up and said that Allen's poetry was obscene and vulgar. Allen looked him coldly in the eye and said, 'Not half as vulgar as the speech you're making now.'

O'Brien, who was clearly used to everyone deferring to his opinion, got angry. 'You have the nerve to make us sit here and listen to that obscene "poetry" and won't even listen to our criticisms?'

To which Allen replied sarcastically, 'Must you make a *speech*?'

The professor exploded, 'You'll never be invited to Benares Hindu University again!'

'Oh come now!' said Allen, bored. He later realised that instead of insulting O'Brien and undermining his authority, he should have neutralised his hostility and given him a way out. But the damage was done, and the professor's acolytes, members of the Indian Communist Party, turned on Allen: 'You wouldn't have talked to him that way if his skin was white. You Americans with your airplanes and your rotten wheat. Now you come here with your filthy fucks to corrupt our pure Hindi poetry!' They sent a copy of *Howl* with all the dirty words underlined to the Criminal Investigation Department of the local police, requesting that Allen be run out of town.

The CID were already investigating Allen and Peter: why would Americans want to stay in India so long and mix with such low-class people? India was in a State of Emergency: there was a border dispute with China. Allen and Peter might be spies, possibly from the CIA. What had really focussed CID attention on them was the arrival, in February 1962, of Peter Turner, a photographer from *Esquire* magazine, whom the Indian Tourist Bureau had commissioned to do a photo essay on Allen and Peter in Benares for an *Esquire* special issue on tourism in India. Allen and Peter took Turner out on a boat at dawn to photograph sunrise on the Ganges and showed him the city.

Then began a period of harassment. The next day, an arrogant young CID man walked unannounced into their rooms. He refused to identify himself and demanded to see their passports. He asked what Allen did, and Allen said he was a poet. To Allen's surprise, he asked to see Allen's writing, so Allen showed him a copy of *Howl*. The man left, and later that day Turner flew off to his next assignment.

The CID man hung around all the next day, talking to the neighbours and spreading lies. He told Pandit, their landlord, that Allen and Peter were immoral foreigners and that he would get into trouble for renting them a room. This upset Pandit, who knew them well and thought that they were some sort of new type of American sadhus. The CID man shocked the dentist downstairs by saying that they had been buying whisky from the liquor store across the street. In fact, the bottles he had seen contained apple juice, bought for Turner who could not drink the water.

All of this was guaranteed to cause suspicion, generate more rumours and sour their previously good relations with their pious neighbours, but before Allen could do anything about it, he was visited by Mr Singh from the Foreigners' Registration Office. Allen complained to him of the harassment, and Singh said he knew nothing about it. No one but his office had the right to ask for papers, and the CID man was possibly a fake; if he came round again, they should seize him and send for the police. He said that they were living quite within their rights and departed, leaving Allen and Peter puzzled and confused.

The next morning, the CID man was sitting in the shop across the street, questioning the local tea sellers about them. Allen went down and asked to see his identification papers. When he refused, Allen insisted on taking him to the police station. There, Singh took the man into a side room and returned saying that the man was from the CID but was working under secret orders, so his identity could not be given. However, said Singh, the man apologised for spreading rumours. Allen, angry, said the damage was already done in the neighbourhood.

He took the matter to Singh's superior, who didn't see what all the fuss was about, so Allen demanded to see *his* superior. In the end, Allen went to the Special Police, and eventually the CID man, and his boss, came to reassure the landlord that everything was all right and that it had all been a mistake.

Singh was the next to harass them. A few days later, he walked into their room without even knocking, and when Allen asked him why he was there and if it was an official or an unofficial visit, he said that he was just passing and that he was their friend, 'or take it any way you wish'. Singh continued to come around late at night on 'social' visits, which clearly disturbed and worried the landlord.

An *Esquire* reporter was arriving on 26 February, so Allen went to the tourist board and asked them if they could make discreet enquiries into the reason for the harassment, which, he pointed out, hardly made for good tourist publicity. The reporter, Alice Glaser, arrived and stayed in Benares for a week, taking a lot of notes. Allen and Peter liked her even though her high heels prevented her going with them to the burning ghats or walking by the river. The day after she arrived, a clerk from the Foreigners' Registration Office delivered a visa denial and an expulsion order, which said that Allen and Peter had to leave India at the 'earliest possible time'. In a typical Indian bureaucratic slip-up, the denial was for the August 1962–February 1963 visa, which had already expired. The clerk said they should come to the office the next morning to make another application, but he took the landlord and the dentist aside and told them that the application would be denied.

That evening only Peter was in when Singh made his usual nine-o'clock harassment call. He told Peter that he and Allen had two to three days to leave India, otherwise they would be arrested and given a five-month jail term and fined five thousand rupees. Peter said they couldn't leave because they were waiting for money and that if they put them in jail, 'Thousands of journalists will come to visit us in Benares in our jail cell. There'll be stories in the paper about what's happening.'

'Let them come,' Singh replied. 'India's in a State of Emergency. In these times there are more important things.'

There was nothing for it but to go to Delhi and try to find someone who understood the situation. They left immediately. Allen began at the top with a telegram to Pandit Nehru, asking him to invite them to tea so they could explain the situation. He didn't get the interview. Allen reported to the Home Ministry bureaucracy, until at last they found an official who understood their reasons for wanting to stay. 'Oh, you're here on an intellectual level,' he said, and stamped their visa applications good for another six months.

Back in Benares, the Communist Party had learned about its members who had sent the marked copy of *Howl* to the CID; they were ordered to apologise. Singh stopped his visits, and the landlord was again a happy man. It was later revealed that the Benares CID had been acting on orders from Delhi and that a fifteen-page report had been filed, detailing everyone Allen and Peter knew and everywhere they went. The report had been requested because certain respectable people had made complaints about them and their 'immoral' poetry.

All this led Allen to the conclusion, as he wrote Kerouac, 'that I really should treat people gentler and not insult and drive them into a corner so they claw out in self defence. I have a tendency to flip into heroic outrages, Jeremiah-like, but aside from letting off my steam that generally complicates the situation rather than resolves it in understanding . . . So my Peace Program is to pacify myself to begin with.'

Allen continued his search for gurus. He visited Kali Pada Guha Roy, and Allen told him his doubts about poetry as a discipline fit for the void. The reply: 'Poetry is also a Sadhana, and Yoga also drops before the void.' Ninety-year-old Citaram Onkar Das Thakur told Allen that if he really wanted to find a guru he should not eat meat, fish, eggs or onions. He should stop smoking and masturbating and say, 'Guru, guru, guru, guru . . .' under his breath for a week, and then come back and see him. Allen kept it up for two days on the principle anything was worth trying.

Allen did seem to give some credence to the notion that he take Blake as his guru. From that time on, there are frequent references to Blake in his journals:

> Blake on the wall last week
>   eyes closed frowning on my
>   insults to the Professor
> I skipped in the room ashamed & fluttered
>   my face with my fingers—

The weather grew warmer and it was soon hot enough for Allen to bathe in the Ganges again. Whenever he felt too hot and sweaty, he would grab his red towel and, wearing just his pyjama bottoms, walk the few feet from his house to the steps of the river. A collection of holy men in orange robes were always gathered there, sitting on platforms under their umbrellas, gossiping with each other, and smoking ganja. One had no arms, just tiny little flippers, and wrote with a pen held in the toes of his left foot. Lepers sat under the trees in a little park, surrounded by dogs and cows. Row-boats and flowers crowded the water's edge where Allen washed his underwear on the wet steps with hard red soap.

Allen spent a lot of his time at the ghats, watching the corpses burn. He told Gregory that it, 'ended a lot of my anxiety about dying, especially always getting high with naked holymen in burning ghats, watching the roast.' He gave Gregory a graphic description: 'Yesterday I sat all afternoon writing random free little notebook pages. They were burning a woman and after an hour her thighs and arms were burnt and half her head. They pushed the armless legless face and chest upright over the fire and flopped it face down in the orange coloured flames – I got up close and saw blood dripping through the nose hole burnt away – one time I saw brains afire – anyway, nobody left inside to feel it.'

Allen was walking across the campus of Benares University on the night of 20 March, talking to a professor of German, when the man turned and told him that William Carlos Williams had died. Allen stopped under the trees and, wide-eyed asked, 'Williams is dead?' The instructor had *Time* magazine with him, and together they stood on the porch of the International House Annex bungalow, so that Allen could read the obituary under the electric light. As insects buzzed around the bulb, the news sank in. He looked up at the night sky. 'I saw the Big Dipper in the sky, that's all,' he wrote to Gregory the next day. He went home, smoked a little ganja, and wrote the lines in his journal which were later published, unaltered, as the poem, 'Death News':

> Williams is in the Big Dipper. He isn't dead
> as the many pages of words arranged thrill
> with his intonations the mouths of meek kids
> becoming subtle even in Bengal.

Many beggars lined his street, but Allen couldn't help noticing one who, particularly hideous, crouched in a foetal position, naked, against a urinal, looking like one of the skeletal survivors of Buchenwald. He was covered with loose brown faeces, and huge festering yellow sores on his hips and elbows crawled with flies. He was obviously dying. Somewhat fearfully, Allen gave him some milk, but he was too weak to take the rupee that Allen put in his hand. The pathetic creature was a deaf mute. There was yellow pus in his eye, and old curry stains dribbled down his chin. One hand was withered to a paw, and his swollen, shiny-skinned feet looked over-large at the end of his thin stick legs. One toe seemed to be leprous, and there were maggots coming out of his ear. Flies covered his eyes and his ass. That night Allen heard him screaming a piercing high pitched wail. The next day the beggar gurgled heavily as he breathed.

Allen and Peter knew an orphan boy who lived in the small leper park where the ghat met the river. The boy's parents had died, and he grew up there serving the beggars. Allen, Peter and the boy carried the man-corpse and his few rags to the Ganges to bathe, and Allen went for a doctor. The diagnosis was that nothing was wrong except starvation and its complications, so Allen and Peter began to feed him milk and fruit and bought him a mattress to lay on. Peter put hydrogen peroxide in his ears to kill the maggots and sterilise any infection. He put penicillin powder and afterwards talcum powder on the open wounds, demonstrating for the boy, whom they hired for fifty cents a day to feed him and wash him in the river every day at noon. They bought him white pyjamas and a sheet, and propped him in the shade of the Bo tree in leper park, where he sat stupefied.

He was incontinent, and every day they took his mattress to the river to wash the shit off and dry it in the hot sun. Slowly, he began to stir, and one day wrote in the dust, 'dood', the word for milk. Allen brought him a notebook and a pencil and he began to write in broken English, 'Sir I want to die because Hearing anybody magi saying to me he is thief Hardwar.' This was followed by some scrawls in Urdu and Hindi and a couple of Sanskrit letters. Then he wrote, 'I want to go to my house where my family is I want to go to Hardwar I want my bed and clothes.'

Allen had planned a visit to the ruins of the Buddhist university of Nalanda, which took him out of Benares for a few weeks. When he returned he found that the sick beggar was a little stronger. Peter had been looking after him, administering the medicine and paying the boy. One day, the beggar spoke to them in a high squeaky piercing voice. His tongue had been cut out by Muslims during the Partition of India, and he had been repeatedly stabbed, which had crippled him. Another day, as they were crouched, attending to him, a Hindu postal clerk came over and took down the man's name and address, offering to write to his family. Shortly afterwards the clerk came with the family's reply. He had disappeared six months before, and his mother had been crying every day since, thinking him dead. His brother was travelling to Benares from the Punjab, a thousand miles away, to get him. In the meantime, Allen had managed to get the man admitted to a hospital, where his health improved immediately.

Allen found that the hospital was free, but patients weren't admitted unless someone important or a foreigner brought them in. It was an attitude Allen found hard to believe. When he had first gone to the Municipal Health Bureau, which was only a few hundred feet from where the man lay dying, he was told to return the next day, because the official there would have to consult with his superior. Allen made a fuss but it was still some time before he was able to get the beggar admitted. Having once achieved success, he returned to the hospital the next day on behalf of a dying woman and eventually got her admitted as well.

Now that he was involved, Allen went to the top, the mayor of Benares, to complain about the situation, but the mayor just gave him a polite runaround. It took Allen a week to corner the bureaucrat in charge at the hospital. The facilities to treat the sick and dying beggars were there, but the bureaucrats were so self-centered and lazy that they would rather allow people to die in the street than stir themselves. Allen described his experience in a letter to Paul Bowles: 'We got another into hospital and tended a few others, so got inside the beggar starvation decor ... Everybody afraid to bother for fear of getting inextricably involved in insoluble problem ... I've seen four people die on the street downstairs in last month.' With the thousands of people on the streets, he could not do much, but instead of trying to ignore the starvation and squalor, he confronted it, and in doing what little he could, he understood it and experienced a side of India that most people preferred to pretend did not exist.

Allen accepted an invitation extended by Robert Creeley to come and teach poetry for three weeks at Vancouver University in July and August 1963, which offered a round-the-world ticket as payment. Peter had been opposed to the idea, but Allen wanted to go. Peter became surly and incommunicative. They had developed separate sets of Indian friends and had not done much together in Benares. Peter had been taking a lot of drugs: in Calcutta he had smoked opium and in Benares he shot up morphine. Now they lived together in silence, broken only by Peter's curt answers to Allen's questions. Neither of them raised his voice with the other, Allen containing his sadness and Peter his irritation. One night, on morphine, Peter revealed that he thought Allen was washed up; by going to teach at Vancouver University he had broken his vow never to read poetry in public for money. Peter obviously felt that Allen was abandoning him and perhaps truly realised then that with Allen's ever-increasing fame, they could never be equals in the relationship. Allen had no reply for him. He felt desolate and empty. He later told Allen it was just 'opium blues'.

Allen left Benares by train for Calcutta. Peter saw him off. 'That was a nice look you gave me at the RR station,' Allen wrote him from Calcutta. 'I always feel bad to part from you if we're cold to each other, and I feel happy to be alone when I know there's still a little tender look between us left in eternity. For no matter what happens, I always *want* to love you – I don't feel good with the barren-ness of kissless silent hopeless goodbye.' Years later, Ginsberg confessed that he had never really noticed Peter's excessive use of drugs; he was so used to being surrounded by crazy and eccentric behaviour that it seemed quite normal. He was prepared to let their relationship drift, confident that they would reconcile back in the States. Allen's plan was to visit Gary and Joanne in Japan on his way to Vancouver and to stop off in Thailand, Cambodia and Vietnam en route. On 26 May, he flew from Calcutta out across the Bay of Bengal and the Andaman Sea to Bangkok.

12 The Change

I believe sexuality is the basis of all friendship.

Jean Cocteau

n Bangkok, Allen enjoyed the cheap Chinese food and the
delicious iced sodas. He visited the museums, guidebook in
hand, and saw the sights, the Dawn Temple and the huge golden
reclining Buddha, 'big as a ship'.

In the park at night, rock 'n' roll boys in blue pants and neat
lightweight shirts lounged on the grass or on the steps of the statue
to King Rama VI, while music was piped through loudspeakers. In
his one week there he twice took boys back to his hotel, but as he
wrote Peter, 'Only trouble is they stick to me like adhesive tape
afterwards.' One of them was able to supply him with some
morphine. On 1 June, he left for Saigon.

Buddhist protests against premier Ngo Dinh Diem, the Catholic
puppet installed by the Americans when it became apparent that
democratic elections would result in a win for Ho Chi Minh, were
continuing when Allen arrived in Saigon. He was in Saigon for four
nights and spent most of his time hanging out at Neal Sheehan's
office at the United Press where all the US newsmen socialised.
There he met reporters from *Time*, *Newsweek*, the *New York
Times* and the agencies. He wrote Peter that he 'got the whole story
of Vietnam war gossip from them – EEEEK – it's like walking
around in a mescaline nightmare – I can arrange to fly inland and
see "model hamlets" – battles, but decided no and am scairt . . .
The war is a fabulous anxiety bringdown. It's *awful*.'

Allen allowed himself a week to visit the ruins of Ankor Wat in
central Cambodia. The ruins were huge, much larger than anything
he had seen in India. 'Very extensive like secluded vast park full of
old stone Cony Island ruins,' he wrote Peter. Ankor Wat was
surrounded by and often encroached upon by thick forest and

jungle. Great roots curled over the carved stone heads, slowly dislodging the nine-hundred-year old masonry. Bas reliefs were just visible behind barriers of vine and creepers. Snakes and insects lived in the rooms and cavities beneath the statues. Allen took photographs and wrote extensive journal notes about the ruins, which were published as *Ankor Wat* by Fulcrum Press in 1966: 'The huge snake roots, the vaster/ serpent arms fallen over/ the octopus roof . . .'

It rained much of the time he was there, silencing the parrots and filling the jungle with the sound of millions of raindrops dripping through the leaves and pouring over the statues, deepening their colours; nevertheless, he wandered among the buildings for hours.

It was night when he arrived in Tokyo. Hotels were all five or ten dollars a night, so he slept on a sheet of cardboard in the station, waking at dawn to catch the early train for the seven-hour journey to Kyoto, where he was to stay with Gary and Joanne. The top of Mount Fuji was cloud-covered as the train sped by, but Allen still wept at the sight, so familiar from Hiroshiga prints.

The Snyders' little Japanese house reminded him of Mill Valley, California. A rock garden with moss and leafy trees was visible through the open screen walls and glass door of the main mat room, where Allen sat at the floor desk to write. He liked the Japanese food Joanne prepared – fish and beancurd soup – and the neat clean feel of the country, which was the height of civilisation after the countries he had been in for the past two years. In Japan, girls were free to travel by themselves without a chaperone, teenage couples walked together on the streets and sat together in buses, and there were no starving beggars – all in stark contrast to India, where kissing in public was illegal and the image of death lined the streets.

Gary was in the middle of a Zen meditation week, so Allen signed up for four nights and sat cross-legged next to him for several hours each night. His ankles hurt after the first session, but he realised that the position kept him naturally balanced, his back straight. He found the Japanese style of sitting much simpler than the complicated Hindu style and the method much easier: breathing deeply into the stomach naturally and exhaling slowly and easily, keeping mind and thoughts on the feeling in the stomach. Whenever his mind wandered, he just went back to the rising and falling of the abdomen.

The monks wore black robes, and everything was very formal and silent, like a ballet. It was so still that Allen could hear the fish plashing in the pond outside. He learned more about 'sitting' in those four days than in the previous year and a half. It was all in great contrast to the noisy religions of India.

He began to get into the swing of things and did a tour of the queer bars and latrines of Kyoto. Impressed by how neat and sexy all the Japanese boys and girls looked in their tight-fitting drip-dry pants, he bought a pair of permanent-press pants and a drip-dry shirt for five dollars. He wrote Peter: 'Japan first place I seen where modern radios clothes cameras are all nice toys everybody got.'

He began to feel different, lighter, less death-haunted. He told Peter: 'Maybe it's the change from gaunt ascetic India sorrows.' He realised that India had depressed him. 'The depressed humanity brings down the atmosphere, it's real, but it's the Indian universe. Japanese universe much *funnier* and more cheerful.' The poverty in India had been 'man-made in a way – you can see it here in Japan – It's also overcrowded but everybody's neat and clean.' Allen was happy. With the weight of India off his back, he could begin to understand what he had learned there, 'the sweetness of all those gurus sinking into me'.

He was sorry to leave, but on 17 July he boarded the Kyoto–Tokyo Express, to spend a few days in Tokyo before flying on to Vancouver. As the train pulled away from Kyoto, he looked back over the events of the past two years. A great deal had happened since he and Peter boarded the S.S. *America* and stood in the snow flurries, waving at the little group of family and friends standing on the dock. At that time, Allen had painted himself into a corner with drugs. After his Blake vision, he had vowed to widen his area of consciousness and had systematically explored his mind, using stronger and stronger drugs: heroin, mescaline, peyote, LSD, psilocybin, ayahuasca. But with the more powerful hallucinogens he encountered an inhuman serpent monster, a vision of death, and it got so that if he took drugs he would start vomiting with anxiety. Yet he still felt a duty to take them, for the sake of an expanded consciousness. He felt compelled by his Blake vision to break down his identity and seek a 'more direct contact with primate sensation, nature'.

All through India he asked the holymen and gurus for their advice on how to deal with this problem, and they all, in one way or another, pointed him straight back to his own body: from Swami Shivananda's 'The only guru is your own heart,' to Dudjom Rinpoche, whose advice was for Allen not to cling to visions, be they horrible or beautiful. Allen realised he was clinging to his Blake vision. He was hung up on the memory of an experience and trying to reproduce it.

The gurus all told him to get into his body, to live in and inhabit the human form and not try to escape it with drugs or other methods. Allen had thought he had to break out of his body if he wanted to attain complete consciousness; that if he wanted to attain God, he had to die. Now he felt that he had been wrong, that maybe he had even misunderstood Blake and that Blake's 'Human form divine' was to live completely in the human form.

All through India he had questioned the validity of his search for a means to higher consciousness, and by the time he reached Japan he had already changed his position a good deal. Joanne Kyger, in her journals, noted that Allen no longer spoke about the significance of his drug visions when he stayed with them in Kyoto. Removing himself from the weight of the Indian experience permitted what he had learned there to come through, and as the train sped towards Tokyo, Allen realised that he did not want to be dominated by the inhuman serpent drug experience anymore, or even dominated by the moral obligation to enlarge his consciousness, or do anything, except be in the present, accepting himself for what he was.

'I had a very strange ecstatic experience then and there, once I had sort of gotten that burden off my back, because I was suddenly free to love myself again, and therefore love the people around me, in the form that they already were. And love myself in my own form as I am. And look around at the other people and so it was again the same thing like in the bookstore [in 1948], except this time I was completely in my body and had no more mysterious obligations. And nothing more to fulfill, except to be willing to die when I am dying, whenever that be. And be willing to live as a human being in this form now. So I started weeping, it was such a happy moment.'

Between the tears, he scribbled in his notebook the long poem later published as 'The Change': 'In my train seat I renounce/ my power, so that I do/ live I will die.' Abandoning the quest for immortality and cosmic consciousness that would live forever, he returned home to his own body. In renouncing visions, he had of course renounced Blake as well. He was amazed to find himself free at last. He now knew that in order to attain the depth of consciousness that he had experienced back in 1948, he had to cut himself off from the Blake vision, otherwise he would be perpetually hung up on its memory. He said later, 'The remarkable thing is that I stupefied myself from 1948 to 1963. A long time – that's fifteen years preoccupied with one single thought.'

Allen arrived at the University of British Columbia jubilant in the knowledge of his new realisation and clearly in a delicate emotional state, crying all the time and fondling people, demanding to be loved for what he was, and loving everyone in return. He was treated with the utmost tenderness, particularly by Creeley, who recognised the change in him. Allen was to teach poetry with Robert Creeley, Charles Olson, Robert Duncan and Denise Levertov, and it seemed that they were all talking about the same thing and must have had the same realisation as he, Olson saying, 'I am one with my skin,' and Creeley talking about 'The place we are.' Allen and Duncan were even able to get over their mutual paranoia and make up their differences. One of the first things Allen did was persuade Creeley that Philip Whalen should also be there. Creeley agreed, and he and Allen sent Whalen money to fly up to Vancouver.

Allen in fact caught, or created, the mood of the entire conference. The students all appeared to be lovelorn, and it was a period of change for many of the poets. It turned into what Allen described to Lucien Carr as 'three weeks teaching poesy, free love and belly sighs to lots of unhappy students who want heaven.' The poets all lived together, and many of the students spent nights with them. Allen was in ecstasy and wrote Peter, 'I'm telling you, the Cold War's over. Hurrah, all we gotta do is really love each other.' Allen had written a similar letter to Peter from Paris in 1958 when he and Bill had first proposed the idea of a 'love generation' but such an idea was premature in the Eisenhower era. Now, as the 1960s got underway with Kennedy in the White House, it was an idea whose time had come.

It was not until the third week of the conference that Allen began to come down from his elated state, but as he wrote Peter, 'Can open up at will and cry for love anywhere – even to police –

everybody gotta be included, you were always right. Burroughs trouble is he cutting up his feelings as well as mind. Mind needs cut ups to release feelings.' Allen had brought Peter's Indian harmonium back with him from Benares and used it to accompany himself in singing the Hare Krishna mantra. 'He drove us all mad with that,' Whalen remembers. 'It meant a lot to him. He actually was singing, which he loved to do anyway, but he was singing this thing and getting into, for all practical purposes, a bhakti yoga, a devotional yoga . . . He was just beginning to get into the idea of using music and chanting for part of his poetry reading.'

Allen practiced what he preached, as usual, in the extreme, whether it was the chanting Hindu mantras or his new-found acceptance of his own body as a love centre. He could be very persuasive. On 16 August, the Poetry Conference ended with a huge party, during which Allen sat on the floor and chanted 'Hare Krishna', weeping and ecstatic, kissing everyone and feeling everybody's stomach.

Allen arrived in San Francisco in August 1963, and stayed in the roomy attic of Lawrence and Kirby Ferlinghetti's rambling Victorian house. He ran around town visiting all his old friends. Allen thought Michael McClure looked older and even more handsome, and was pleased when for the first time McClure gave him a kiss, their old differences settled. McClure thought Allen had changed for the better. Whalen found him more mellow, with less 'hopping around' than usual. However, not everyone was pleased with Ginsberg's new message. Jack Spicer's poetry circle was very suspicious, both of his new interest in Oriental religion and his attitude to sex. Poet Larry Fagin, who first met Allen in Paris in 1958, and who was living in San Francisco in 1963, remembered, 'He was put down by Spicer's circle . . . Zen was okay, but this smearing your eastern goo on everyone was unheard of.' And as for Allen's new message of free love to save the world, Fagin said, 'Spicer found the orgy scenes utterly repulsive.' Just as in 1956, 'Allen wanted everyone to be one big happy family.'

A surprise visitor to San Francisco that August was Lucien Carr, bringing some of the original 1940s Beat Generation spirit to the West Coast. His wife was away in the country, and he had got drunk one night with a girl named Lois and just taken off on the spur of the moment. 'I said, "Let's go to San Francisco!"' They arrived drunk and practically penniless. Lucien remembered Allen saying that North Beach was the place to be, so they went there and checked into a cheap Chinese hotel. They sat in their room with a box of Saltines, a couple of cans of sardines, two quarts of gin, and no money. Lucien called City Lights and spoke with Ferlinghetti. Identifying himself, he asked, 'Is there anyone in town I know? And if there isn't, can you lend me fifty dollars?'

'As a matter of fact,' Ferlinghetti said, 'Ginsberg's just come to town.'

'Ginsberg came and somehow found us in this rabbit warren,' Lucien remembered. 'And we'd been locked in there for two days with nothing but all this gin and saltines. Anyway, he rescued us and took us to Ferlinghetti's attic ... Allen was conducting all sorts of poetry business at one end of this attic and we were at the other end, but the stairs that you got up to the attic were in such a place that you had to step over the mattress that Lois and I had, to get down to have your poetry discussions with Allen. And there we were constantly drunk, constantly fucking, people stepping over us, until Ferlinghetti finally told Allen, "You've got to get your fucking friends out of here!"'

Allen made arrangements for them all to move down the hill to a house owned by an eccentric doctor. 'It was the same situation,' Lucien remembered, 'one great big room with Allen conducting his business at one end, and Lois and me at the other. But this crazy man had two big apes, in a cage that was half outside the wall and half in the livingroom, and the apes would go into an absolute frenzy when they watched all this screwing going on.' After about a week Lucien decided that it was time he returned to face his wife. Allen had just received royalties from Scandinavia and gave them to Lucien to get himself and Lois back to New York.

One night some friends of Michael McClure's gave a big party. Allen went along and was surprised to find that it was at 1403 Gough Street, Robert LaVigne's old apartment, where Allen had first met Peter, eight years before. There was a spare room there, so he moved in. To complete his sense of déjà vu, Neal Cassady also moved in with Anne Murphy, his girlfriend of the past eighteen months, just as he had joined Allen to live with Natalie in Gough Street all those years before.

Neal's arrest in 1958 for offering a couple of joints to undercover agents in trade for a ride to work had resulted in two terms of five years to life. In actuality, he spent two years in jail –

three months in Vacaville and the remainder locked in San Quentin. There he became a devout Christian, memorising the names of all 262 popes and devising prayers to be said at different times of day. He was released on 4 July 1960, and took a job changing tyres – his good railroad job was gone forever. He began to violate his parole by hanging out in North Beach and down in Palo Alto, where a new friend lived, the writer Ken Kesey, who had a place in the woods where a permanent party seemed to be going on, celebrating the joys of LSD. He had a string of girlfriends, many of them coeds from Stanford, then settled down with Anne Murphy. For the sake of their three children, Carolyn had waited for him when he was in jail, but since it was clear that nothing had changed, she filed for divorce in the summer of 1963. When Allen met up with Neal again, he had given up work and was living on unemployment, most of which he lost at the racetrack, trying to prove his 'system'.

The Gough Street apartment belonged to Charley Plymell, a poet from Wichita, who was editing a literary magazine called *Now*, and his girlfriend Ann Buchanan. Allen, naturally, was sleeping with everyone in the apartment and this soon began to cause problems as he noted in his journal: 'All week in and out of bed with red bearded Charley and little girl Ann ... Charley slowly jealous of my role flesh over to Ann and Ann jealous of my role flesh to Neal. So I alone in bed tonight as last night.' His arrangement with Charley and Ann culminated with Charley marching stark naked into Allen's back room and threatening to kill him for trying to steal his girlfriend. 'He was absolutely mad,' Allen said, 'Which was totally uncalled for, because it was his ass I was obsessed with, not hers ... And I got scared, I said "What have I got myself into with this guy?" ' The arrangement wasn't working, and the tensions that it caused began to make Allen close up, despite his determination to love everyone. He wrote, 'Seems no hope for me caught between Men and Women, I can't love or don't open up to – retreating further and further into an old subjectivity and now lethargy after months of euphoria and good feelings and kisses and ass holdings and tenderness to everyone.'

It was Plymell that introduced Allen to the music of Bob Dylan. *The Freewheelin' Bob Dylan* had been released that February, and on a visit to Bolinas, Plymell played it for him. Allen listened to 'A Hard Rain's A Gonna Fall' and wept. He remembers, 'I thought,

"Oh, we got a second generation of prophets, it's gonna be great!" '

On 28 October, Madame Nhu arrived in San Francisco to address a gathering of businessmen and civic leaders at the Sheraton Palace Hotel. After Buddhist monks in Vietnam had died and been injured in clashes with Diem's police and soldiers, a number of monks immolated themselves in an effort to draw world attention to the religious policies of Diem, and his fiercely Catholic sister-in-law, the beautiful and sinister 'Dragon Lady', Madame Nhu. To try and counter this, Diem sent Madame Nhu on a coast-to-coast tour of the United States to present his claim that 'There is absolute religious freedom in Vietnam'. Married to Diem's brother, Ngo Dinh Nhu, the chief of the secret police, Madame Nhu did not help her cause by telling reporters that she enjoyed the monks' 'barbecues'. Everywhere she went, she was met by student demonstrations, and it was only at the Roman Catholic Fordham University in New York that she spoke without interruption and received enthusiastic applause.

Over five hundred people held a protest rally and formed a picket line outside San Francisco's Sheraton Palace Hotel, Allen among them. It was his first political demonstration, and he approached it with characteristic individualism. He made a placard. On the left side, he carefully painted his three-fish 'Buddha's Footprint' symbol, using patriotic red white and blue fish tails with gold and silver scales. On the right he carefully printed a poem:

War is black magic
Belly flowers to North and South Vietnam
include everybody.
End the human war.
Name hypnosis and fear is the
Enemy – Satan go home!
I accept America and Red China
To the human race.
Madame Nhu and Mao Tse-Tung
Are in the same boat of meat.

He held the placard aloft for fourteen hours, singing various Hindu mantras. He told a local journalist, 'I'm here today on the picket line trying to be tender to Madame Nhu and Mao Tse-Tung. Or better, asking them to be tender.' He explained his political philosphy: 'Anger and fury of left wing will only drive the humanoid bureaucrats and cops into deeper humanoidism. Be kind to cops; they're not cops, they're people in disguise who've been deceived by their own disguise.' It was pure hippie rhetoric, enunciated for the first time; the direct result of his experience on the train in Japan.

Allen now looked the way that most people remember him from the sixties: black curls to his collar, thinning hair on top, wise rabbinical beard, and large sad brown eyes magnified by thick-framed glasses. He was already a public figure, as he found out one day while strolling through North Beach. He came upon a fight between groups of black and white youths and watched as the police arrived with sirens blaring and red lights flashing. It seemed to Allen that the police were being unduly rough on the black youths, so he walked up to one of the police officers and began to stroke the back of his neck. 'You should be more understanding,' Allen told him. 'You must learn to love, not hate.'

The officer pulled back, aghast, flung open the back door of the police car and yelled, 'Get in, you're under arrest.' Allen climbed in and they drove off.

As they drove along, the officer said, 'Say, you're Allen Ginsberg, aren't you?'

Allen nodded modestly.

'The poet?'

Allen nodded again.

The cop got furious all over again. 'Now why would a famous man like you, a man who knows so much about life, want to get mixed up in a street fight?' he asked. 'Now get out and be a good boy.' He stopped the car and Allen climbed out.

On 22 November 1963, Ginsberg was sitting at the kitchen table eating some eggs, when Neal rushed in and yelled, 'Kennedy's been shot!'

They turned on the television and watched as Lee Harvey Oswald was described as a pro-Castro leftist. The assassination was called a communist plot, and even the liberal Fair Play for Cuba Committee was dubbed a violent organisation. There was an orgy of anti-left feeling propagated by television and the media, which went on for weeks, most of it having no bearing on the killing at all. The outpouring of hate, represented by the assassination itself and the media reaction to it, strengthened Allen's desire to get his message of love and peace across before the country was consumed by a wave of neo-McCarthyism. Many people found his views shocking.

His vision of universal love applied to every area of politics, including his views on Israel and the Jews. When Israel invaded Egypt in June of that year, many of Allen's left-wing and pacifist Jewish friends found themselves in a quandary but not so Allen. He saw no reason to abandon his anti-war views simply because he was of Jewish ancestry. Although normally reluctant to appear in anthologies of Jewish poetry or to be interviewed by Jewish magazines, he spoke four days after the assassination of Kennedy to Leland Meyerzove, the editor of the Jewish magazine *The Burning Bush*. With Kennedy's death and the burgeoning Civil Rights movement very much in mind, Meyerzove asked two questions: What should be the Jew's relationship to the Negro, and what was Allen's opinion about American and Israeli Jews?

'I think Jews should start making it with Negroes,' Allen said. 'My Jewish family in New Jersey doesn't have any Negro friends – and they think they are big liberals – and they really would get upset if one of their daughters married a Negro ... When my brother brought home this Southern Baptist minister's daughter as a bride, then my grandmother, God rest her soul, took him aside into the bathroom and started pinching his arm in anger. In other words, Jewish race consciousness is built upon the same stuff that killed President Kennedy, to the extent that it excludes other human images as clan to its family consciousness ...

'And the trouble with the Israelis is that they are *Jewish*, they were hypnotised by the Nazis and all the other racist magic hypnotists of previous eras. Astonishing mirror image resemblance between Nazi theory of racial superiority and Jewish hang-up as chosen race. They didn't desire it – any of them. Any fixed categorised image of the Self is a big goof. Open wide the doors of the future! Hurrah! Messiah has come!'

Needless to say his position did not endear him to his family or to some of his friends, particularly during the various Arab-Israeli wars, but he always stuck to it, refusing to make racial distinctions or to take sides just because of his Jewish ancestry.

*   *   *

Allen returned to New York in December of 1963. He was met by Eugene at La Guardia Airport and driven out on Long Island to stay awhile with his brother's family. It had been almost three years. Eugene and Connie now had five children, including their new baby, Anne. Allen also spent a few weeks in Paterson, telling Louis and Edith his traveller's tales and catching up on their news. While Allen was in San Francisco, Peter had hitch-hiked at remarkable speed through the Middle East and Europe to London. He reached New York in November, a month before Allen got there.

Allen made an attempt to see Kerouac during a visit with Peter to see the Orlovsky clan in Northport. Allen hid in the bushes, as before, while Peter knocked on the door, but Jack's mother turned him away. Allen telephoned Jack four times in one week, but no one answered. He decided that Jack must have a signal system, so he phoned, let it ring three times, then hung up and dialed again. Kerouac's mother answered and said that Jack was not home. Allen asked her to give Jack his number, but she refused and hung up. Exasperated, Allen wrote to Jack, 'I think she's carrying things too far. Goddamit what's the matter at your house?' Kerouac methodically labelled and filed the letter.

Allen and Peter stayed with Ted Wilentz and his wife. Wilentz had handled many of Allen's affairs while he was away in Europe and India and had published *Empty Mirror* under his Corinth Press imprint in 1960. He also published Kerouac's *Scripture of the Golden Eternity* and books by LeRoi Jones, Gary Snyder, Philip Whalen and Diane di Prima, as well as *The Beat Scene*, a heavily illustrated poetry anthology which spread not only the new poetry but images of the life-style around the world. Ted's daughter was away at college, so Allen and Peter had a room to themselves. One of their first visitors was journalist Al Aronowitz, who showed up one day with his friend Bob Dylan.

Dylan was familiar with Allen's work and that of the other Beat writers, and Allen, in his turn, was interested to meet the author of 'A Hard Rain's A-Gonna Fall' and 'Masters Of War'. They talked about poetry and got along very well. Dylan was about to play a concert in Chicago and invited Allen to fly out with him, but Allen was too busy looking for an apartment and getting back into New York, and also too proud. 'I thought he was just a folksinger, and I was also afraid I might become his slave or something, his mascot.'

The meeting with Bob Dylan had a curious outcome. Dylan owned the manuscript of a group of Allen's rhymed poems from 1948 to 1952 which Allen had assumed were lost forever; he had neglected to make copies of many of the poems before he let the folder out of his hands. He had been unable to get the book published in New York, so when a friend left for London, Allen gave her the manuscript on the off chance that she might meet someone who would be interested in publishing it there. The manuscript passed from hand to hand, and when Dylan was in London, someone gave it to him, knowing his interest in Ginsberg and the Beat Generation. He returned it when Allen went to visit him in Woodstock. *Gates of Wrath* was published by Don Allen at his Grey Fox Press in 1972.

Shortly after they met, Allen went with Dylan to a concert in Princeton. Photographs taken backstage appeared on the sleeve of Dylan's album *Bringing It All Back Home*. Allen was shown clean-shaven and wearing a smart top hat. Film-maker Barbara Rubin was in one of the pictures, ruffling Dylan's hair. Allen had been introduced to Barbara in the back room of Max's Kansas City by Jonas Mekas. Barbara had short dark hair and big eyes that always seemed to be darting around the room, checking who was there. The way she held her jaw suggested that she was impatient for you to finish speaking. Much of her time was spent trying to figure out how she could fit people into her various schemes. Barbara took enormous quantities of acid. When they met, Barbara at once took Allen to the Mekases' Film-makers' Co-operative nearby, to see her experimental film *Christmas on Earth*. Allen was very impressed by it. 'It was a lot of porn, beauty, in which she made an art object out of her vagina. I thought that was in the right spirit. We got into a very funny rapport, we were just there alone, and we actually ended up screwing on the floor that very night. She was really young and pretty and I liked her.' Her method of film-making consisted largely of swinging the camera around her head. She superimposed the film strips on top of each other to make flowing, abstract images so it didn't really matter much what the raw material was.

In the first week of 1964, Allen and Peter moved into an apartment at 704 East 5th Street. Their apartment was very light, and they could see the towers of Wall Street over the rooftops from the back windows. They bought a rug and found furniture in the streets; Allen made himself a sawhorse desk. Their Chinese scrolls and Tibetan tankas were hung on the freshly painted white walls.

In San Francisco, Allen had begun work on a movie script of 'Kaddish' with Robert Frank, but the writing had not gone well. Now he spent most of his time with Frank, blocking out the script and elaborating on all the details about Naomi. Allen became part of the new underground film scene. He wrote Ferlinghetti: 'The Lower East Side movie world here is really thrilling, like a poetry renaissance, excitement, parties, tragedies, masterpieces in lofts, etc. Best thing in NY.'

Films were being made everywhere, but Andy Warhol's silver-lined Factory was the most prolific studio of them all. Warhol made his first films in 1963: *Kiss*, *Haircut*, *Eat* and the six-hour *Sleep*. Warhol filmed every day. Whoever dropped in was the star of that afternoon's film. He made one of Allen, Peter, Jack Kerouac and Gregory Corso, in his 'Couch' series, three-minute silents of people sitting on the Factory couch, but perversely he shot it from the side, so that it was difficult to see what was happening or who was who (probably because Kerouac tried to tell him how to do it).

Allen usually went to the Factory with Barbara, who was very involved with Warhol through her film work. Allen renewed his friendship with Warhol's assistant, the poet Gerard Malanga; in 1958 Malanga had organised a poetry festival at Wagner College in which Allen took part. It was Malanga's job to silk-screen the paintings of Marilyn and Elvis, the car crashes, and the flowers that became Warhol's most famous images. Allen could see certain parallels between Warhol's factory and his own place. Despite the drugs and sex and madness, there was always work going on. Describing the Factory years later, Ginsberg said, 'There were people taken in to work with them, to work with their neurosis and work with their colourfulness and maybe turn it to artistic advantage and value, and maybe get therapy that way. I always thought it seemed like a good project.'

Allen did not get too involved in the Warhol scene, in part because of the pervasive amphetamine use; Allen had already seen its destructive effect on his friends. Half the people hanging around Allen's apartment were taking Methadrine and it would have been foolish to expose Peter to even more at the Factory. 'I was interested in the films, the civil liberties and the beautiful boys he had,' said Ginsberg. 'But they were unobtainable or in another realm of some sort. I didn't find any serious Angels there to talk to who wanted to know about poetry.' Over the next several years, Warhol invited Allen to screenings and his parties, but Allen mostly saw him in the back room at Max's Kansas City, which was virtually the private club room of Warhol and his so-called superstars.

Two big legal campaigns preoccupied Ginsberg in the spring of 1964. The city was insisting that in order for coffee shops to hold poetry readings, they should meet cabaret standards, with sprinklers, fire exits and kitchen flues; since most of their customers bought only one coffee a night, this was clearly uneconomic. It meant the end of the free readings at Le Metro and other popular haunts. In a model lobbying campaign, Allen and ACLU lawyers petitioned the various politicians involved and won the case.

Simultaneously he was testifying, along with Susan Sontag, in defence of Jonas Mekas who was charged with obscenity for screening Jack Smith's *Flaming Creatures* and Jean Genet's *Chant d'Amour*. He spent hours on the phone with lawyers and journalists, concerned poets, film-makers and coffee shop owners. His telephone rang continuously.

He also engaged in a frenzy of literary activity, publishing Burroughs's *Roosevelt Routine* – which had been censored from *The Yage Letters* – through Ed Sanders's mimeograph Fuck You Press, editing Huncke's stories, writing introductions and pestering editors. He went on TV shows and revised foreign language proofs of his books. He got no poetry written but enjoyed himself enormously.

Allen still saw Jack from time to time and continued to behave as if there was a real friendship between them. He listened to Jack's late-night drunken anti-Semitic phonecalls, trying to reason with him. Sometimes, however, he just hung up on him: A journal note of 12 May 1964, read, 'I had cut him off the phone yesterday dawn when he began repeating same accusations against Jews – "All the bureaucrats of Soviet Hungary are Jewish" – called drunk, I was sleepy.'

Ginsberg described their relationship in a lecture: 'So, from 1963 on, the relationship was – contentious, sometimes close, odd, occasionally he'd come by, really drunk, and want me to blow him, and get very insistent. "Nobody loves me, c'mon, give me a blow job! You're a fairy, give me a blow job! Nobody loves me, I'm too fat and old and redfaced. I'm lonesome!" Careless. He didn't give a shit anymore, what I thought or what anybody thought.'

Spring came, and Gregory Corso arrived from Cleveland with his wife, Sally, and their baby girl. They moved in with Allen. Robert LaVigne was also staying. The days grew warmer, then turned hot and muggy. There were riots in Harlem. Cassius Clay took the World Championship from Sonny Liston. *Dr Strangelove* was released, and Rudy Gernreich marketed topless bathing suits. The 1960s were getting into their stride. Allen moved into high gear, answering letters and writing poetry, mostly at night when the other people in the house were asleep and there were fewer telephone calls. He would often finish up watching the dawn break over the city. He wrote, 'How I love the poetry of the lovely roofs, the city purring muffled in the cars.'

He and Peter took Peter's brother Julius out of Central Islip Hospital, where he had been living for the previous twelve years, and brought him back to live at East 5th Street. After a few weeks of silence, Julius began to talk non-stop. 'Do you want to live or die?' Allen asked him.

'I don't know,' said Julius.

Allen began to visit the Kerista collective, a Lower East Side commune of about eighteen people living in a store-front on Ludlow Street, described as 'a sort of benign Manson family' by Rosebud Felieu, who lived there. She described Allen's first visit: 'He was always hot for whatever was new on the scene and this was one of the first weird drug sex communities around at that time. Everyone there was very odd, like very skinny or fat or nervous. They all thought Allen was bad news because he had an ego or something but I thought he was amazingly funny and kind.' She didn't know who he was when he arrived, but he looked very sweet, so she sat on his lap, tickled him and asked him his name. 'Allen was pretty surprised I think that some school girl liked him just for being a fine guy.' He told her if she ever needed a place to stay, to come over to his place; which she did.

Allen and Peter had big orgies with Rosebud and Ann who lived next door, the English poet Harry Fainlight, a local poet named

Szabo, and many others. Ann would drag her mattress across the hall to help cover Allen and Peter's floor. Allen wrote Charles Olson, 'Been making it with some nice young girls and boys – what a pleasure to be a clean old man – More I see it I think there is a big sex upsurge revolution which will alter and enlarge family unit – long house – with everybody making it like on the bed in Vancouver. Huge pot-love circle here in Lower East Side busted this week.'

It was also in 1964 that Allen met Maretta Greer, a painfully thin, blonde mendicant who had just returned from India. She presented herself at his door and said that she had heard of his interest in Eastern philosphy and wanted to meet him. 'She needed a place to stay,' said Ginsberg, 'and she was mystical and pretty and we immediately got on.' She was to be his girlfriend on and off for a number of years, whenever she was not in India. There was always room for another young person in the apartment.

Sally Corso returned to Cleveland with the baby, leaving Gregory in New York. In September, he cracked up and had to be taken to the hospital, 'raving on goofballs, screaming about the baby,' Allen noted. Gregory calmed down, visited his family in Cleveland, then went to stay with friends in Buffalo.

Haydée Santamaría, the Cuban minister of culture, invited Allen to attend a writers' conference in January 1965 at the Casa de las Americas in Havana. The Cuban government would pay all expenses. He could fly there from Mexico City, but because of pressure from the United States, Mexico would not give re-entry permits to travellers from Cuba, so he would have to return via Prague. Allen accepted the invitation with alacrity, and was even pleased by the cumbersome travel arrangements, because he thought that he stood a very good chance of finally reaching Moscow if he got as far as Prague. The State Department initially refused to issue him with the required travel permit, but a lawyer friend of Allen's threatened an injunction, and the State Department gave in.

Ken Kesey and his Merry Pranksters arrived in New York in November, with Neal Cassady at the wheel of their famous bus. They immediately telephoned Allen, and he and Peter went to see them at the luxurious Park Avenue apartment in the eighties where they were staying. Allen and Peter got there at about 1 a.m. The psychedelic bus, with its 'Further' destination sign, and its ad, 'A

Vote For Goldwater Is A Vote For Fun' was parked across the street. In the elegant apartment, the Pranksters were jumping all over the furniture, filming each other to the rhythm of the Grateful Dead. They were smoking a lot of pot and several were high on acid. Although Neal was completely exhausted from his driving, he continued out to Northport to collect Jack. Kerouac was unwilling to come, but Neal cajoled him and he finally relented.

It was a tradition with the Merry Pranksters to celebrate the American flag; they wore stars and stripes on their shoes, on their teeth and on their faces, so in honour of Kerouac's arrival they draped a huge flag over the couch for him to sit on. Jack picked it up and carefully folded it. Allen took note: 'He very carefully folded up the flag as an object lesson, how to treat the flag and respect it, which I thought was a bit reactionary. After all, he didn't have to go to that length.' Jack was withdrawn and silent. He occasionally slugged from a wine bottle, but turned down all offers of pot or acid.

It was Neal's big moment, introducing his new hero, Ken Kesey, to his old hero, Jack Kerouac. It was almost impossible for them to talk in that atmosphere. The situation must have been particularly confusing to Kerouac, who, apart from a few drinking buddies at the local bar, was isolated and had no idea what was going on with young people in the 1960s. He didn't know who the Merry Pranksters were or their orientation or philosophy. Kerouac didn't say much. Ginsberg thought later, 'To Jack, when he came in, it must have looked like a bunch of weirdo apes jumping up and down in a cage.'

On 11 November, Allen and Peter flew to Boston as guests of Harvard where Allen was scheduled to give four readings. These were the first public readings where he sang as part of his performance. He and Peter chanted mantras, using Peter's harmonium as accompaniment. At Brandeis University, Allen gave a seventy-minute ecstatic, tearful reading of the whole of 'Kaddish', which astonished the audience and moved many of them to tears. Fortunately, it was recorded and in January 1965, Allen signed a contract with Jerry Wexler at Atlantic Records to release it as an album. Allen and Peter spent long evenings visiting old friends and drinking at the Harvard Tavern, and having sex with dozens of people, male and female. They were quickly banished from

Harvard's Lowell Hall by their hosts, and had to stay with friends for the remainder of their visit; Peter read his 'Sex Experiment' transcription at Lowell Hall, which proved controversial. After three weeks of poetry and orgies, they returned to New York to find that Methadrine freaks, let into the apartment by Barbara Rubin, had stolen all of the Tibetan tankas and scrolls they had collected on their travels. Many books were missing and also Allen's typewriter.

For years, Allen had been speaking out in favour of the legalisation of marijuana; now he got together with the poet Ed Sanders and others and founded LeMar, whose aim was to legalise marijuana. On 27 December 1964, they staged their initial demonstration, probably the first of its kind. The nearest piece of Federal property they could find was the Department of Welfare building on Avenue B at Tompkins Square. Here, nineteen men and women gathered to demonstrate in favour of legalisation. Allen carried a sign that read 'Smoke Pot, It's Cheaper'. Two bored policemen and a handful of puzzled local people looked on, but it was too cold for a big crowd to gather. Interviewed by the *New York Herald Tribune*, Allen said that he thought marijuana would be legalised in the US within five years.

On 11 January, he flew to Boston again, this time to testify along with Norman Mailer and John Ciardi at the obscenity trial of *Naked Lunch*. Elequently, he praised Burroughs's ear for common speech, quoted lines of pure poetry from the text and pointed out the high moral tone of the book. He expressed admiration for Burroughs's courage to make such a total confession and said that the book had influenced him greatly, 'particularly because it was such an enormous breakthrough into truthful expression of exactly really what was going on in his head, with no holds barred. He really confessed completely, put everything down so that anybody could see it.' They lost the case, but Grove Press appealed and on 7 July 1966, the Massachusetts Supreme Court finally declared *Naked Lunch* not obscene, reversing the earlier decision by the Superior Court of Boston and removing the threat of a nationwide ban on the book.

13 The King of May

It's another universe here, rather a shock in fact – not much place for a dribbling subconscious to sit down.
Allen Ginsberg to Ed Sanders, Moscow, March 1965

G insberg was unprepared for Cuba. He had not studied the history of the country or the Revolution and could not adjust to the radically different lifestyle that the people there were forging for themselves. He appeared to not appreciate the seriousness of the pressure being put on Cuba by the United States. The US had already tried to invade the country and had set up an economic blockade, which was very damaging to the Cuban economy, making it more reliant on the Socialist countries than Castro would have liked. Cuba was still struggling to build enough schools and hospitals to educate and provide medical care for its people, while developing its industry to self-sufficiency in the face of the American embargo.

The delegates to the writers' conference were put up at the Havana Riviera, a luxury hotel originally built by Meyer Lansky and the mob during the corrupt regime of Fulgencio Battista. Now it was one of the few hotels where foreign visitors could stay. Allen was given a room overlooking the Caribbean.

During his first foray to explore Havana's night life, he was approached by three youths, who asked whether he was Allen Ginsberg. They had been trying to reach him all day at his hotel. The youths published a literary magazine called *El Puente* (*The Bridge*) but said that the people responsible for funding were conservative and kept them under-financed.

They all went to a nightclub where the youths got tipsy and complained about the crackdown on homosexuals by the special police division *Lacra Social*, and about arrests in the street of 'Sick' types, a term derived from the 'sick' jokes and cynical Beat

Generation humour associated with the comedian Mort Sahl. However, they told Allen, they supported the Revolution. They spoke quite freely and openly about the situation in Cuba. When Allen said that he thought that Cuba should put an end to capital punishment, they told him to tell Fidel his views. Allen had not realised that he might actually meet Castro, but they said, 'Sure you will.'

On his second day in Havana, Allen met the assistant editor of *Cuba* magazine. Although he had been in Cuba less than forty-eight hours, he began complaining about Lacra Social, saying that its policies toward homosexuals, marijuana and the 'Sick' youths of La Rampa Street had led to the arrest of a number of people, many of them teenage poets from the Writers' Union, wrongly suspected of being homosexuals just because they wore tight blue jeans and beards. This was the beginning of Allen's troubles.

Naturally the man from *Cuba* was very interested to hear Allen's views and told them to his colleagues. Allen had not realised that in a country with a population about as big as that of New York City, gossip, personal contacts and meetings often constituted the social debate. In fact, two of Cuba's leading poets had already visited the minister of the interior, and complained to him about persecution of homosexuals on La Rampa. Not only was the persecution stopped; Lacra Social was dissolved. That was how things were done.

After dinner that second day, Allen was interviewed by a well-dressed, bearded reporter from *Hoy*. They were interrupted by a telephone call from the lobby. Two youths from *El Puente* had brought their translation of 'Kaddish' but had been prevented from going up to his room. Allen rushed downstairs in anger, dragging the reporter with him as a 'witness'. The hotel staff directed Allen to the official government guide, who explained that the hotel rules forbade visitors to the rooms because of the large number of whores hanging around and also because visiting farmers had a habit of bringing chickens and even cows with them, which they tried to put into the elevator. However, in this case, the boys would be allowed up 'as long as they can identify themselves'.

The guide was clearly embarrassed by Allen's anger, quite unjustified since many European hotels have the same rules. One of the youths, José Mario, had his Writers' Union identification with him, but Manuel Ballagas had nothing but his manuscript of

'Kaddish' which Ginsberg clumsily seized and thrust in front of the guide's nose, saying, 'That's *his* identification. He translates some texts of mine.' Then Allen realised that he had over-reacted and that the boys had already been given permission to go up, added, 'Besides, the doctor told me to stay inside and not go out [he had 'flu] ... so obviously I have to receive people upstairs, journalists, poets, et cetera.' The situation was saved.

They sat talking in Allen's room until midnight. Allen corrected the seventeen-year-old Ballagas's translation of 'Kaddish' and quizzed him about persecution of homosexuals. He dictated a page-long appreciation of the Revolution to the *Hoy* reporter, which was mostly sympathetic but complained about the persecution of homosexuals by Lacra Social, and ended by quoting Voznesensky: 'Communist comes from the heart.' What would Allen ask Fidel Castro if he met him? He would ask about the persecution of 'Sicks' and homosexuals, ask why marijuana was not legalised and suggest that Cuba end capital punishment. Rather than execute bomb-throwing terrorists, Allen said, they should give them magic mushrooms and jobs as elevator men at the Havana Riviera Hotel.

Since these remarks seemed unlikely to get into print, Allen tried to put crude pressure on the reporter by saying that if Blas Rosa, the editor of *Hoy*, wouldn't publish the interview, Allen would write about it in *Evergreen Review*, and his article would be translated into French and seen by Jean Paul Sartre and other supporters of the Cuban Revolution.

His influenza was better next day. He had been invited to dinner by Maria Rosa Almendres, the head of Casa de las Americas. In conversation, her husband agreed with Allen that there was no free press in the American sense: 'But so what? Everybody knows everybody! You can always complain to Fidel, or take up a grievance with someone in power.'

That night, Allen watched Fidel on television: 'A real hairy creature for president,' he wrote in his journal. 'Ten times more natural than Johnson, in fact human ... One finger up – talks rapidly like Cassady.' Allen completed the night's journal entry with the line, 'Communism/ Socialism/ Revolution, constantly under discussion. I'm obsessed with Lacra Social.'

The next day, a nineteen-year-old youth, Reglo Guerrero, brought a handwritten poem for his opinion. They were interrupted by Nate Gonzalez Frere from *Revolucion*, come to interview him. Both had been prevented from going up in the elevator without permission, but the Cultural Friendship Office gave it immediately. Allen got angry when the journalist said the policy made sense because of the whores, farmers with their cows, thieves and especially the counter-revolutionaries, who might seek publicity by attacking a foreign visitor. This was one of the few hotels where visiting government officials and foreign guests stayed, making it a terrorist target. But it was no use, the elevator, along with the disbanded Lacra Social, became something of an idée fixe for Allen during his stay in Cuba.

In his interview with Frere, he discussed the changes in American poetry caused by William Carlos Williams and described the Lower East Side scene. He explained Indian mantras to her and then spent an hour complaining to her about Lacra Social. She told him that she couldn't report his views on that because she was interested in literary matters, and in any case, Lacra Social, which she agreed had been terrible, had been dissolved. 'Oh no!' said Allen, relying on the street gossip of his teenage informant. 'They arrested a boy on La Rampa last week.'

The conference got under way with a big meeting at the Casa de las Americas. Haydée Santamaría explained the rules of the poetry competition they were to judge: 'Give the prize to the best work outside of politics and go talk to anyone you want.'

Allen's complaint that *Hoy* wouldn't publish his interview on the 'Socialist acceptance of homosexuals' had repercussions. *Hoy* sent another reporter, who wanted to know why Allen had proposed such a strange subject. Was he serious? Was he saying it to shock? The Cubans genuinely could not understand what he was talking about. Even in the United States his views were controversial, but at least his fellow Americans could understand them. To the Cubans, whose primary concerns were building hospitals and schools, and teaching the mostly illiterate population to read and write, Ginsberg's preoccupation with homosexuals, Lacra Social and the legalisation of marijuana was incomprehensible.

He noted in his journal: 'Having had this interview already over and over, it's become an obsessional subject of explanation, like I'm sick of it and my own opinions, except the whole lack of communication on the subject indicates either I'm neurotic special case out of step with the universe, or they're just plain insensitive – So I have to go into long painful explainations of why I lust for boys and men and that gets sticky. Wound up trying explaining my early image of women was affected by my mother died in a bughouse. The journalist was very sympathetic but altogether the point was lost.'

He got down to the serious work of reading the submissions for the competition. He was faced with ninety-one manuscripts, all carbon copies and all in Spanish. He was pleased when the young poet Manuel Ballagas came by to help him out.

The next morning, Ballagas telephoned Allen with the news that when Allen's limousine dropped him off the previous night, he had been taken to the police station and questioned. Ever since the Bay of Pigs, the police were paying particular attention to anyone consorting with foreigners, particularly with Americans. Ballagas was taken home, and his mother had to sign a paper saying that she would bring him to the station if they ever wanted to see him. It was not a serious matter. The Havana waterfront was patrolled by teenage girls with sub-machine guns; the Cubans were expecting to be invaded by the United States at any moment. Government paranoia was justified, as it was later revealed that the CIA were at that very moment devising methods to assassinate Castro.

Two more reporters from *Hoy* interviewed Allen that day. Allen gave them a long literary interview about exploring consciousness by association rather than by metaphor. He told them that he was gay but he liked girls and that he smoked pot, then asked them about the persecution of gays in Cuba. They responded, 'You must understand the Revolution is more concerned with basic issues like raising production, feeding and educating the people, cutting sugar and defending ourselves from US pressure. Later on these aesthetic issues can be discussed.'

That evening a large group of delegates went to hear the new 'Feeling' music. Allen sneaked Ballagas and a few others into the delegates' free box. Afterwards, as he sat writing in his hotel room, he received a call: Ballagas and another poet had been arrested as they left the theatre.

Maria Rosa Almendres tried to explain the situation to Allen. 'Perhaps you don't understand how hard we have to struggle to keep the Revolution clean. You have to understand that the stupid ones, the squares here, think it's bad for us to have the young ones washing our dirty linen in public, discussing problems with foreigners. After all, *we* have to struggle with the conflicts, and worse, with threats from outside, not you!' She was obviously irritated by Allen's lack of understanding.

Allen had an appointment to see Haydée Santamaría, the minister of culture, the next morning. He described her in his journal: 'Looks about 45, Russian, blonde buxom, talks like a woman making a speech to high school girls, too rapidly and with too much authority, as if her words were some kind of governmental policy, which it is, which is dangerous, since she doesn't know much more about psychic life than my Aunt Clare.'

Allen's harsh assessment was not shared by the Cubans, who held her in high regard. Haydée Santamaría was a great hero of the Revolution. She took part in the famous raid on Moncada barracks with Fidel in 1953, where she was captured, jailed, and forced to watch as her brother and his fiancée were tortured to death by Batista's troops. When she was released in 1955, she joined Fidel and the rebels in the hills and was later made a member of the Revolutionary Council. She could have had virtually any high position in the government, but her passion for the arts led her to the Ministry of Culture.

Explaining to Allen the need for society to deal with homosexuals who made a spectacle in public and seduced unformed young people, she told him that the *El Puente* youths were filling his head with gossipy complaints. Allen interrupted her to ask about the problem of the boys in jail. (They were only held three hours, but he didn't know that at the time.) They talked at cross purposes for a while, but Santamaría promised to investigate how such a mistake could have been made and told him the boys would be released.

As she left the room, Allen reached over and gave her a slap on the backside. Within an hour, ten people had come up to ask Allen what he had done to insult her so. It was almost as if he *wanted* to be deported.

Allen began to feel nostalgic for his New York City scene and wrote, 'All these people, even old Paris fairies here, all going around saying that they don't think it's right elders seduce the young. They have absolutely no idea what goes on – Oh for my New York bed full of teenage boys and lost wandering Tibetan/Amphetamine girls of twenty.' Rather than meet Castro and the others who made the Revolution, to find out about it first-hand, Allen preferred to hang out with the *El Puente* teenagers. Certainly much of his time was spent trying to seduce one of the *El Puente* youths, with eventual success.

The next evening, at dinner, he overheard criticism of the *El Puente* boys for complaining to Allen. Apparently, gossip about them was everywhere. Allen now became paranoid, fearful of the situation he had created. His own gossip was coming back to him, fifth-hand, transformed amost beyond recognition, undoubtedly partly as a result of his faulty Spanish. In his journal for 7 February he wrote: 'Total collapse today – woke totally isolated, didn't know who to talk to to confide in ... Entering Orwellian dreamworld – Total supression of conscious and unconscious fantasy everywhere ... Can't trust anyone. Like having a nervous breakdown, "I got the fear." '

Another of the boys who had shown Allen his poems was taken in for routine questioning, detained for several hours, then released. A group that had invited Allen to read his poems at the university had the reading cancelled by the Rector, and the students were advised not to have private meetings with Ginsberg. Allen was asked not to go with the rest of the delegates to a meeting with Prime Minister Dorticos. Maria Rosa Almendres had a long meeting with Haydée Santamaría and reported that Haydée was very angry with him. Had he said that Raoul Castro was a fairy and that he wanted to sleep with him? Allen had said it, but he couldn't remember to whom. There was also a lot of gossip around the Casa because Allen had told a reporter that he'd had a sex fantasy about Che Guevara. In a country that was 85 per cent Catholic, such statements were bound to be controversial and found offensive, particularly by people who had fought alongside Raoul or Che, and most particularly coming from an American.

At the conference, Allen gave a slow, deliberate explanation of poetry as an exploration and expansion of consciousness. Speaking in Spanish, he explained the technical means that he had adopted for this purpose: dreams, waking fantasies, marijuana, mushrooms, peyote, spontaneous composition. He explained meditation, yoga and mantra singing by comparing them to the trance state induced by the dancing and chanting in Santeria ceremonies of the African Elequa cult, which in 1965 had a million adherents in Cuba. He amplified his explanation with a lengthy catalogue of anti-brainwashing techniques that could be used for combatting universal sloganism, dogmatism and mass-media hypnosis, concentrating on an explanation of the cut-up technique of William Burroughs. This part of his lecture was probably not understood by most of his audience, and he was hampered by not having the appropriate texts. Out of concern for the Casa, he did not speak about any controversial subject.

On 3 February, Allen was wakened by a phone call from a professor at the University School of Letters, cancelling his Walt Whitman lecture. That day the delegates were all taken in cars to a luncheon at the Old Country Club. Waiters circulated with ice-cold rum drinks. When Haydée Santamaría arrived, she went up to Allen, shook hands, and immediately launched into a long conversation that he was unable to follow because her Spanish was so rapid. He calmed himself by inwardly repeating a mantra a couple of times. She was telling Allen the facts of the Revolution: 'We have established 20,000 schools, and we need more cement. Work and cement is our need. Afterwards will come other matters.' After a while Allen shifted the conversation.

'There's one thing I want to clear up,' he said. 'Perhaps you misunderstood. You see when I left you last time, I was quite happy and relieved at the rapport we had and felt so good I slapped you. Sort of exuberant and affectionate. I hope you didn't misunderstand. In my country . . .' He had trouble pronouncing the words because he had already consumed three of the delicious iced rum drinks and they seemed to be affecting his command of Spanish.

She tried to explain to him that he had formed his bohemian ideas in another country and that they didn't apply in Cuba. She mentioned his use of marijuana, which was illegal in Cuba. 'It has always been a crime and it's definitely a crime and that's how it must be for the time being. That's the policy we've adopted.' Allen tried to explain that he was aware that it was illegal, and was only trying to introduce some legitimate information into the discussion of marijuana as a social problem. He reported the conversation in his journal:

'She replied, leaning now against the piano and apparently willing to talk to me for a while – which surprised and excited me and I began to relax – getting into it – huge room full of artists and functionaries all dressed up and she the chief personage there, and here I was all involved alone talking to her – a kind of egotistical amazement at the position I found myself in, being such a serious/embarrassing problem for her to handle – "Yes, but we have work to do and cannot afford these extra luxuries which impede the senses ... We have to raise the young children here with revolutionary ideals ... the Revolution is for them, the life, the reason for being ... Though you may discuss such matters (as marijuana) with people on a high level or mature officials, you understand we cannot have you spreading such ideas which are against the laws of our country and our policy among the young people. They are too young, too impressionable. You came as a foreigner and invited here by us as a great poet of fame, and we cannot support that you spread ideas to the young against our own policies that we have arrived at ...""

Tom Maschler, the chief editor of Jonathan Cape in London, strolled by and Allen introduced him. Maschler, who had just published John Lennon's *A Spaniard in the Works*, suggested that the Cuban government invite the Beatles to Cuba as a gesture of world harmony, and as a propaganda gesture. Allen excitedly seconded the idea, saying how well loved the Beatles were by the youth in the US.

Santamaría said that very few people in Cuba knew who the Beatles were, and besides, they had no ideology. 'Yes,' said Tom. 'But they're like Frank Sinatra, the young girls swoon over them and weep. If you want to attract the young, invite the Beatles.'

Santamaría patiently explained that they wanted to build something permanent: a life and a hope for the future; the Revolution wasn't a marketing exercise. 'Without a true ideology, a true understanding of life, there can be no future for the young ... The Beatles will come and it will be like our Fiesta. Everybody will be excited for a few days and then that will be the end of it. We want to give our people something *more*. Some truth and work and food.'

Allen and Tom explained that it would change US State Department policy and end the cold war if Cuba and the Beatles accepted each other joyfully and that it would cause the brainwashed children of the US to see Cuba in another, friendly light. The idea that a Beatles concert in Havana would improve US–Cuba relations illustrated the lack of comprehension between Allen and Haydée Santamaría. To the Cubans and their supporters, one of the most important points of the Cuban Revolution was that a Latin American country had removed itself from the American sphere of influence.

Despite his misgivings, Ginsberg still felt able to enter in his journal for 4 February: 'They obviously do have a tough struggle to survive, that their defiance and resentment of US obnoxious intrusion and blockade is understandable completely, and even their blank dumb miscomprehension of my own queer rare literary extravaganza, and they do suffer too much to take it easy.' He began teaching US poetry informally at the Writers' Union, reading from Creeley's *For Love* and Williams' *Collected Poems*. He felt that things had lightened up and that people were getting used to him.

Allen had arranged to visit Yves Espin, an architect who knew and liked his poetry. He had been educated at MIT and was Raoul Castro's brother-in-law. Picking Allen up at the hotel, Espin drove him to his fine apartment on the Vedado, where a group of his elegantly dressed friends had gathered and were drinking rum and ice-water. Allen was the centre of attention, and they asked him many questions, including, inevitably, what did he think of the Revolution? Allen liked the look of them, so he answered honestly:

'Too much suppression of communication of unconscious content, dreams, fantasies, intuitions and jokes here. Actually too much fear. Everybody in Cuba secretly thinks they're anti-revolutionary in one part of their soul, so everybody's afraid. Actually the words "revolutionary" and "counter-revolutionary" have lost their meaning and are just a fear stereotype now. How could an artist sit down and write blind poesy and know in advance if it would be catagorised as pro or anti? If he thought about it he'd be paralyzed. If a big Dostoyevsky, with no sense of guilt, and a huge brown humour, wrote a novel here about Lacra Social and terrible in-group club and art-school, and everybody's sex lives and Marxist dogma and gossip, could it be published here? Nobody here wants that kind of genius art!'

Espin laughed and agreed with him, 'They'd never publish it here.' Allen, relaxed, sat on the floor and talked about magic mushrooms, Tim Leary and Hitler's sex life with Eva Braun. He drank and sang the Shiva mantra with his finger cymbals. Espin and his wife were charming, friendly and relaxed, and the party went on into the night. It was 2 a.m. when Espin drove Allen back to his hotel. Just as he was going to bed, Caballo, a Mexican dramatist, telephoned and said, 'Ginsberg! We're all here having a party. Come and join us!' He immediately pulled on his white Indian pyjamas, put on both sets of his Chango beads, put finger cymbals and cigarettes in his pyjama pockets and walked barefoot to the room.

For the first time, all the *invitados* were gathered in one small room, happy, drinking. They all shouted greetings and applauded Allen's late arrival in costume. They sang songs, and the party eventually disintegrated into a drunken political argument. Allen got back to his room at 5 a.m. and fell into a deep sleep.

Three hours later he awoke to a sudden knock on his door. It was someone from ICAP, the cultural organisation. The man was accompanied by three soldiers in neatly pressed olive-green uniforms. Allen was told to dress immediately and accompany them. He should bring all of his belongings. They were going to the immigration department, where the chief wanted to see him.

'I realised the jig was up,' Allen wrote later that day, 'and got a cold chill thru my back – adrenalin panic – more like a cold fear thrill – everything sharp and clear as in a dream.' The soldiers began looking around the room. Allen stumbled about sleepily, trying to wake up, looking for his underwear. He suddenly remembered that the black notebook on his bedside table contained a detailed description of making love with one of the *El Puente* boys. He had used only initials, but it would have been easy enough for them to discover his identity.

'Have you called the Casa de las Americas?' he asked. They told him that it was not usual to call them. 'I think you should call Haydée Santamaría,' Allen said, 'and check out if this procedure is regular.' He dressed awkwardly and went to the bathroom to brush his teeth. One of the soldiers remarked on his electric toothbrush. Allen began emptying his drawers. 'I want to call the Casa,' he said, but they told him he was not allowed to make any calls.

He packed his knapsack, sliding the incriminating notebook under his jeans at the bottom. He stuffed the masses of papers he had accumulated into some large envelopes and put them in the knapsack. It was now full, and he still had a big pile of Cuban books and newspapers. One of the soliders loaded them on to a handcart.

They took him to the old Immigration building and put him in a room to wait. He found his finger cymbals and began chanting very slowly and quietly, so as not to disturb anyone. After a while he was taken to a small room with a large barred window, a chair and a bed. One of the soldiers brought him cigarettes and a copy of *Hoy*. Allen flicked nervously through the paper.

Another uniformed man appeared and said, 'We have arranged your departure this morning on the plane to Prague, London and New York.'

'Fine, but if I may ask, what is this all about? Have you not made a mistake? Have you consulted the Casa de las Americas?' Allen asked the man's identity. He was the head of Cuban Immigration, Carlos Varona.

They got back in the car with the soldiers and drove off along Malecón, passing the ships in the harbour. One cargo boat had the name *Mantric*, prompting Allen to pull out his finger cymbals and begin a low chant, 'Ooom Oom Oom Sarawa Buda Dakini . . .' which he followed with the Hare Krishna mantra. 'It cleared my senses a bit,' he wrote, 'very useful and good steadying influence.' Varona reached for the car radio, and Allen put his cymbals away. He asked yet again why he was being kicked out.

'Respect for our laws, compliance with our laws . . . You'll have to ask yourself that.'

Allen wanted to know which ones, but Varona was not specific. 'Just general immigration policy . . . also a question of your private life, your personal attitudes.'

'What private life?' laughed Allen. 'I haven't had much of that since I've been here.' Varona laughed with him. 'Are you sure you're not making a mistaken judgement on the basis of gossip?' continued Allen. 'I mean, Havana is a small town and full of exaggerated gossip.'

'Havana has more work to do than gossip,' said Varona. 'Havana is a serious place. Do you understand?'

'Yes certainly, but are you sure you're not mistaking rumour for real acts and kicking me out for nothing serious?'

'We may be making a mistake.'

'Then why not take your time and discuss it with Haydée Santamaría?'

'I have called her,' said Varona. 'I am sure she will accept our decision. I have an appointment with her at noon.'

'What time does the plane leave?'

'Ten-thirty.'

Outside on the strip stood a huge silver jet with CESKO-SLOVENSKE painted on it. Allen shook hands with Varona and the soldiers and walked out to the waiting plane. Before boarding, he turned and waved goodbye. The soldiers waved back.

Allen had very few contacts in Czechoslovakia. One of them was the writer Josef Skvorecky, who had written to Allen asking him to explain some of the references in 'Howl' in order to help his friend Jan Zabrana, who was translating it into Czech. Allen found Skvorecky's number and phoned him. Skvorecky, astounded when Allen said he was calling from a phone booth in the Prague airport, immediately drove out to collect him. That evening, they went to Jan Zabrana's apartment; they talked late into the night. The next day Zabrana took Allen to the Writers' Union.

It turned out that Allen had royalties due him for a book of poems, and back money for publication of his work in *Literarni noviny*, the foreign-literature magazine. He also had two years' back royalties for performances of his poetry at the Viola poetry café. In addition, he was invited to stay in Prague as a state guest of the Writers' Union, given seventy-five dollars spending money in crowns, and a free hotel suite at the beautiful nineteenth-century Hotel Ambassador, in the centre of town. There he had a large sitting-room to work in and a bedroom with a huge bathroom. His windows looked out on to the tramcars and black cobblestones of the main street of the old city. Outside, snow was falling.

Allen loved Prague, with its blue-grey stone buildings and the ancient stone bridges over the Moldau, or Vltava, its royal statues and red tramcars. 'Over the river again today in Breughel's wintery city/ the snow is white on all the rooftops of Prague' he wrote in 'Message II'. He told Ferlinghetti: 'Prague is lovelier in miniature than Paris almost.'

Allen worked with Jan Zabrana on translations of his poems for a forthcoming book and gave him 'Message II' to translate for the Writers' Union literary weekly. When Zabrana saw the lines 'I lie/ with teenage boys afraid of the red police,' Zabrana said, 'Allen, you know you can't publish this, "afraid of red police", because it wouldn't pass the censor.' Allen thought for a while, then crossed out 'red' and inscribed 'pink.' Zabrana told him, 'This doesn't really help.'

With all his Czech money, Allen found that he had enough crowns to live well in Prague for a month and also take a train to Moscow, to return via Warsaw. He wrote to Peter apologetically, 'Forgive me for setting foot in Russia without you, but I am so near, so eager! And the money's got to be spent here too!'

Allen was very well received in Prague, particularly at the Violacaff, the poetry and jazz nightclub in the centre of town where jazz musicians would gather after gigs for jam sessions. The cellar was decorated with huge blow-ups of Fred MacDarrah's photographs from the anthology *The Beat Scene*, featuring Allen and Peter. The idea of combining poetry and jazz was suggested by the records they had heard of Kenneth Patchen, Rexroth and Kerouac performing to jazz.

When Allen was taken there, on his second day in Prague, the beautiful young poet Vladimira Cerepkova was sitting at the bar, talking with a friend. She exclaimed, 'My God, every bum nowadays looks like Ginsberg!' and Allen, recognising his name, said, 'That's me!' No one had known he was in Prague, and to the regulars of the Viola it was if the pictures on the wall had come to life. Even to Allen it seemed a little incongruous when, a few days later, he sat in the audience watching his poem 'Message' performed on stage with a musical accompaniment. One of the young students Allen hung out with on his visits to the Viola was Vaclav Havel, who reminded him of it when Allen was entertained by Havel as head of state after the overthrow of the old regime. Allen hadn't recognised him: 'He was prettier in the sixties.'

The Czechs were amazed not only at Allen's being there, but at his life-style. It was February, and yet all he wore on his feet in the snow were a pair of thin Cuban tennis shoes. On the other hand, he had with him an electric toothbrush, something that no one in Prague had even heard of in 1965, and was to them the height of bourgeois luxury. Sadly, it broke down before he was able to demonstrate its abilities.

Within a few weeks, Allen was the best known member of the Prague underground scene and the hero of the student dormitories. One night, a gang of young kids took Allen back to their place to drink, and at the end of the evening one nineteen-year-old boy crawled into bed with him. Homosexuality was quite legal in Czechoslovakia, and by 12 March, Allen was able to write to Peter, 'I'm having a ball here, as long as I don't open my dirty mouth like in Cuba – in public . . . I'm making it with teenage kids in orgies and going to wild Turkish baths and screw boys by the Moldau River and blowing in dark alleys.'

He gave a big poetry reading at Charles University, the oldest in Europe, before an audience of five hundred students, who overflowed the hall. He read the whole of 'Howl' and his new Prague poems, including 'Message II' with its line about the 'red police'. He wrote, 'They let me loose, I talked freely, the walls of the State didn't fall.'

He also spent time with Skvorecky and with Igor Hajek, the editor of *Literarni noviny*, who was preparing a major article on Allen and his poetry – which he had no intention of publishing, however, until Allen was safely out of the country. Having seen Allen in action the year before in New York, he feared that the visit to Prague might end abruptly and with a scandal. He waited until Allen left for Moscow, not realising that he planned to return to Prague before going on to London.

Warm March sun was melting the heaps of snow on the black cobbled streets of Prague as Allen began the two-day train journey to Moscow: 'Trembling at the Railway Station, amazed at the great red train Moscoka – Prague,' he wrote. He had paid Intourist in advance for four days in Russia and was also invited for one week as the official guest of the Writers' Union. He was equipped with a small English–Russian dictionary and some strong new shoes for Red Square.

As the train approached the Carpathian Mountains, Allen scribbled excitedly in his notebook:

My Slavic Soul, we are coming home again –
    once more on Red Square by Kremlin wall
    in the snow to sit and write Prophesy –
Prince-Comrades of Russia, I have
    come from America to lay my beard
    at your beautiful feet!

At dawn they arrived at Chop, just over the Russian border. The train rolled on, past villages of thatched houses surrounded by pink mist, through snow patches and black fields, horses in the distance drawing sleighs through mud. They passed isolated dwellings, where figures in black clothes trudged up snowy lanes, and came to Lvov, with its onion-domed cathedral and police in long nineteenth-century coats with epaulets. It was in Lvov that Allen's grandfather Pinkus was born a century before. All of Allen's paternal ancestors came from the towns and villages of this part of the Ukraine.

Ylena Romanova, the head of the Western Literature department of Moscow University, met him at the station. He was taken to the modern glass-and-brick Minsk Hotel and given a small room, then they went to the Writers' Union to meet Frieda Laurie, who was to look after him. The Writers' Union was an enormous building from another age. They took a table in the restaurant beneath carved mahogany balconies and great chandeliers and were served a classic Russian meal of borscht, smoked salmon, caviar, steak and vodka. Allen explained at once what had happened in Cuba and told them he had no intention of voicing such opinions to reporters in Moscow.

'You will stay here a while,' said Frieda Lurie, 'but let me advise you that we have an experience, the war, and a different life to you, so that certain things are best not spoken about, especially to journalists. People don't and won't understand. We hope you'll come to see our point of view.' The subject of homosexuality was raised. 'We all have a normal love life here,' explained Frieda Lurie. 'Russians may not appreciate your interests, though possibly you may have some truth or some valuable opinion, still, your proposal to be silent and watch is best.'

Allen went straight to the Kremlin. He wrote his first impressions: 'Then walking in thru Kremlin estate – the surprise of the 16th century vastness – the medieval fortress still in postatomic operation, offices and central bureaus there with the formal front of the old Feudal shield and wall and turret and clock and gold onion dome and peaked gate keep solid as Bronx Park Zoo right in the middle of Moscow – and the spaciousness – as if all the steppes of a Siberia and "Asiatic vague immensities" were on display in the Central Powerhouse Castle – Capital of the Future Spacy Universe Nation – huge walks in thru gates, fields with palaces and old cathedrals, a 16th century iron-embroidered cannon – I felt like a provincial from Pinsk or Magnitogorsk, seeing the Worlds Fair Ancient Center.'

The next day Allen arranged to meet his relatives. Joe Levy, seventy-two years old, came into the hotel, hesitated a little, then walked up to him. Allen said, 'Joe?' They last met when Allen was five years old, before Joe and his wife decided to return to Russia to live. They sat and talked, and Allen finally got straight the story of his mother's family's emigration from Russia to the United States. Then Joe took him home, where his wife, Annie, was preparing supper.

Joe was Naomi's cousin; his father, Isser, and Naomi's father, Mendel, were brothers. In 1931, a group of thirty friends and relatives from Newark went back to visit Russia. Joe and Annie were so impressed that they decided to stay. Annie returned to Newark alone to pack up the furniture and ship it all to Moscow. It was still there, including a 1922 Victrola with Caruso records and a big American bed.

Anne produced the photograph album: Allen's Aunt Eleanor with husband Max smiling on the beach, Naomi and her girl-friends staring at Allen through time. Allen found a photograph of himself as a cute four-year-old in shorts, with a thin belly. It was all too sad: Eugene staring painfully at the sky through spectacles; Louis and Naomi in the 1920s: Louis with his teacher's moustache; Naomi in the 1930s wearing tennis clothes; Allen and Eugene, Newark 1933; Edie and Aunt Rose; and pictures of other cousins, still alive in Russia, some who never left. Then came the 1960s photographs in colour: pictures of weddings and grandchildren in a land almost forgotten. 'The expression, the sad tragic aloneness never changes in half a century, surviving them the unknown decendants,' Allen wrote. 'Anne and I were sad and tears rolled down our cheeks as we came to the end, the last pictures of the unknown newly grown children in America.' Joe and Anne had no children.

When he had arrived in Moscow in 1931, Joe had taken a job as an electrician on the Moscow subway; after the anti-Jewish campaign under Stalin, he was transferred to a job stuffing horsehair into sofas. He had a nervous breakdown. 'It wasn't Stalin,' he said. 'Beria misled him! Beria was working for Scotland Yard. It was all Beria's fault.'

Anne sighed, 'Oh Joe, you still believe that?' But Joe had to; he had staked his life on it. 'The collective heart is the most important thing about Communism,' he affirmed to Allen, but Anne seemed dubious. Allen sang them the Hare Krishna mantra and Hare Om Namo Shiva, but when Joe took Allen back to his hotel on the subway he said tentatively, 'That kind of singing doesn't seem to have effect here.' Allen wondered what he meant.

Allen was drunk when he met Yevgeny Yevtushenko, Russia's most famous living poet and literary activist. Accompanied by the interpreter provided by Frieda Lurie, Allen had been to dinner with two members of the Writers' Union. On the restaurant stairs, he encountered a tall, thin, handsome, bright-eyed man, dressed in a striped suit, who said, 'Yo soy Yevtushenko.' Allen drunkenly knelt to touch his knees, but Yevtushenko stopped him. This was Yevtushenko's first day out of bed after a bout of pneumonia, and he was still suffering from vertigo. He wore his thin blond hair brushed forward over his brow. 'I love you,' said Allen, impressed by the Russian poet's good looks. Allen kept touching and saluting him, and in Cuban Spanish tried to get him to understand that he admired his nose and hair and mouth. Yevtushenko arranged a meeting for the next night.

Yevtushenko lived in an old apartment building in an area of unfinished streets where a few old wooden buildings remained. He took Allen's coat, gave him a bowl of soup to warm him, and told him, 'You were very drunk last night.' In fact Allen remembered very little about their conversation of the previous evening. Yevtushenko continued, 'I saw you were a good man. Here, we hear many bad things about you, that you are a pederast, scandals, but I know it is not true.'

'It's all true,' Allen said. Through his interpreter, he explained to Yevtushenko, in some detail, his Blake vision and said, 'As for homosexuality, that's my experience and that's the situation I'm in. So the scandal comes from talking openly about it.'

'I know nothing of such matters,' said Yevtushenko. 'It is a private affair of yours.' Next, Allen began a long explanation of the use and qualities of different drugs. Yevtushenko seemed restless and asked, 'But why are you interested in such matters?'

Allen tried to explain, citing religious use of ganja in Shivaite sects in India, and LSD in the US. Allen was in the middle of trying to explain *what* the unconscious felt like, when he finally lost Yevtushenko, who said, 'Please Allen, I like you. I like you as a poet, but these are your personal problems. Please don't speak to me about them. They are not interesting to me. I respect you as a great man, a great poet, but these two subjects, homosexuality and narcotics, are not known to me, and I feel they are juvenile preoccupations. They have no importance here in Russia to us. It only disturbs my impression of you. Please don't talk about these two matters.'

'I feel rejected,' said Allen.

'I have problems more important than these,' said Yevtushenko.

'Okay,' said Allen. 'Tell me all your problems, and tell me the problems of Russia.'

Yevtushenko told him of the twenty million people who had been arrested during the era of Stalin. He said that as many as fifteen million may have been killed or died in prison. Yevtushenko's own grandparents both disappeared. 'But after all, we believe in Russia and in our system,' he said, and tried to explain. 'What would it mean to be anti-Communist? To go back to monarchy or capitalism? Nobody, very few people, want that in this country, so we have to work our problems out. It's slow. It's terribly slow, but I think we'll win.'

He told Allen of his difficulties with the censors. His last major long poem had been ready in proof for a year, but not published. He had to make 450 changes to it to get it passed, but he thought it was worth it because the magazine had a circulation of more than a million. He said that he once read to fourteen thousand people, in Moscow. He played Allen a recording of himself reading in Paris. Talking about his work had cheered him. He stood up, hugged Allen and kissed him on the mouth. Allen was embarrassed, unused to Russian customs.

They went to a Georgian restaurant to meet Yevtushenko's wife, Genia. Allen tried to explain Kerouac's spontaneous prose style, but Yevtushenko couldn't accept it as a valid theory. Allen felt the cutural gap between them was immense, and the next day he woke up depressed, convinced that they had achieved no real communication. He wrote Peter, 'Saw Yevtushenko. He nice but square – couldn't talk deep soul – *another* kind of poetical soul. I'm lonely.' Allen may not have realised, possibly because of faulty translations of their conversation, that he had already made an impact on the Russian poets. In a conversation in 1986, Yevtushenko said that in the 1950s, issues of *Evergreen Review* were eagerly passed around and Ginsberg's work was given very careful study. 'You know, in the late fifties, you were my idol,' he told Ginsberg, 'my idol!'

After a trip to Leningrad, devoted almost entirely to museum visits, Allen returned to Moscow where he finally met Andrei

Voznesensky, the other Russian poet whose work bore some resemblance to that of the Beats. They spoke in English, and Voznesensky invited him to his home. There, Voznesensky sat relaxed, in an armchair, and both he and his wife were very friendly. They discussed poetry, Allen saying, 'Yes, sometimes I think in rhythm,' and Andrei replying, 'Yes, I think in rhythm!'

Allen was excited; it seemed that they were making real contact.

Andrei asked him, 'Does rhythm come to you, and do you carry it around for several days?'

'No,' Allen told him, 'the first draft is the last, ideally. That is the ideal, not to touch the composition. So the rhythm comes as an impulse to writing. Or comes during the composition. Sometimes, maybe two or three times in my life, I've had the full rhythm, a complete rhythm from my whole body, when the whole physiology moved in one strong rhythm, a sort of cosmic rhythm. I never know when that will happen. I sometimes get minor rhythms, but those are beautiful too.'

'Cosmic rhythm,' Andrei translated it to his wife. 'That's good. Here's a toast first to cosmic rhythm!'

Allen gave a long discourse on different drugs, but Andrei, like anyone else in Moscow, could not understand his interest in them. Andrei asked if Allen's strongest rhythm came with or without drugs, and Allen said both. Once with, once without, and once half and half. Then Andrei asked him to read from his work, and he read, softly, parts II and III of 'Howl', for him to hear the rhythm. Voznesensky said afterward, 'I don't fully understand the words but I was with you in the sound.'

Later Allen chanted mantras, then it was time for Voznesensky to attend a performance of his poems set to music. Allen accompanied him, and in the car he began to weep. Andrei told him, 'You look beautiful now.' Allen, a little drunk, said, 'This may be the only time we see each other. You have no idea the trouble I went through to get here. It was very difficult and I am unhappy that I can't stay more than a few days.' His visa was due to expire shortly.

Andrei told him, 'I am glad to see you. We are both poets above all else. We are together, that's supreme.'

The train journey to Warsaw passed less than fifty miles south of Naomi's hometown, Vitebsk. Allen arrived in Warsaw just as the sun was setting behind the peaked roofs of the old town. He checked into the Europeski Hotel and went to walk the wide streets. Allen went to the Writers' Union, which welcomed him as a guest of the Ministry of Culture, arranged to pay one week of his hotel bill, and gave him a hundred zlotys spending money. He ran into Dan Halberstam, whom he had last met in Saigon. 'It's a goddam police state,' Halberstam told Allen, 'Never saw a country like this where there's a total split between populace and government.'

Halberstam gave Allen a tour of the city, which ended at the site of the Warsaw Ghetto, now a vast stretch of greensward surrounded by new apartment projects. Children were playing on the stone steps of a large bronze commemorative monument. Allen recorded his impressions: 'I started crying – whatever happened was completely invisible – a whole new universe had emerged in the same place in space – nothing left of all that ruin and suffering except the monument and a few visitors.'

In a café he wrote: 'Old buildings rubbled down, gaiety of all night parties under the air bombs,/ first screams of the vanishing ghetto – workmen step thru prewar pink-blue bedroom walls demolishing sunny ruins,' lines that would become part of the poem 'Café In Warsaw'.

Voznesensky arrived in Warsaw and demanded to know what 'Wow' meant. Allen had left him a note at his hotel: 'I'll wait for you. Wow.' So he shouted, 'Wow!' and Voznesensky laughed. He had to leave the next day, but Allen was able to dine with him and exchange a little gossip. Voznesesnky's most amusing story was that Krushchev, now in retirement, had revealed to a Western journalist that he had become a poet. 'In his spare time he writes poetry for his family and friends,' said Voznesensky, laughing. 'He reads it aloud to them. It is Surrealist.'

Allen returned to Prague and checked into the Merkur, a cheap hotel. The next day was May Day; traditionally the day of Majalis, a medieval festival, when the students elected a May King and held a beauty contest to find him a May Queen. They paraded them through the streets and held a mock wedding ceremony. The festival had been suspended for twenty years, since the Communists came to power. Instead, the students traditionally rioted against the police in a small wooded park on a hill near the river.

Allen had made sure that he returned to Prague in time for May Day.

That year, 1965, with the growing liberal climate, the authorities had decided to let the students revive their Majalis festival and have their own parade in the afternoon. Each school of the university had nominated its candidates for May King and Queen, who would be paraded through the streets from their school to the Park of Culture and Rest where, in the exhibition hall, the winners would be chosen.

Josef Skvorecky had been nominated as May King by the Engineering School of the Polytechnic, but he had come down with influenza. Told by Jan Zabrana that Allen was back in town, Skvorecky called him at his hotel and asked, 'Allen, would you like to be the King of Majalis?'

Concerned that he would attract too much attention, Allen asked, 'Is it political?' Skvorecky assured him that it was just a student affair of no significance, so Allen agreed. The afternoon of the parade, Allen was met at his hotel by a large delegation of students dressed in 1890s costumes: men in top hats and waistcoats carrying canes, women in hoop skirts with parasols, surrounded by jesters who burst into the room blowing trumpets. 'Mister Ginsberg, we have the honour to beg your presence in procession to the crowning of the King of May, and to accept our support for your candidacy of Kral Majalis, and we humbly offer you crown and throne.' They placed a little gilded cardboard crown on his head and a sceptre in his hand and sat him in a chair covered with red drapes. He wrapped himself in an old Chamois coat, got out his finger cymbals and a statue of Ganesh, the Elephant God, that he happened to have with him, and was borne unsteadily down in the elevator to a waiting flatbed truck.

The streets were filled with students drinking wine and beer as the parade commenced. They reached the courtyard of the polytechnic, where a huge crowd of students had gathered to greet their candidate for king. There, a bigger truck was awaiting him, garlanded with roses, with a Dixieland band playing on the back and five pretty girl attendants. It was piled high with crates of beer, and a sign on the front read, in Latin, 'Ginsbergum Krale Majalis'.

Allen drank a beer and made his first speech: 'I'll be the first kind King and bow down before my subjects. I'll be the first naked King.' They lurched off into the streets of Prague, Allen drinking beer and wine. Every time someone put a bullhorn or microphone to his lips for a speech, he sang a mantra, 'Hare Om Namo Shiva' or 'Om Sri Maitreya.' No one was expecting the huge crowds that lined the streets. Following the truck were several thousand students singing and chanting, 'Long Live Majalis!'

The parade wound its way through the old town. They reached Staremeskaya Nameska Square, and Allen made another speech: 'I dedicate the glory of my crown to the beautiful bureaucrat Franz Kafka who was born in the building around the corner here.' Then the procession, fifteen thousand strong, moved on past the House of the Golden Carp where Kafka wrote *The Trial*. Allen excitedly pointed it out to the crowd, 'On your left comrades is the actual house where saintly Kafka lived and cleaned his teeth, and wrote his huge novels which your comrades have not even published!'

Allen drank more beer and wine and sang louder and louder. Finally, the procession passed over the old stone bridge across the Vltava. Townspeople sat on the river banks, leaned from windows, and waved from the rooftops. A crowd of 100,000 excited and happy people, filled the Park of Culture and Rest; a half dozen rock bands were playing. The organisers were amazed, and just a little worried, because they had expected only ten or fifteen thousand people that afternoon.

They gathered in the huge exhibition hall, and the election of the King of May began. There were four or five other candidates besides Allen, dressed as kings or clowns. The medical school candidate, wrapped entirely in bandages, made an eloquent speech in Latin. The law school candidate, in kingly robes, spoke entirely about fornication. The engineering school candidate, in dirty Levis and a work shirt, sang 'Om Sri Maitreya' for five minutes and then sat down. He had a landslide victory: 100,000 people elected Allen Kral Majalis, the King of May!

All that afternoon he ran around with his gang from the polytechnic, exercising his kingly powers by fondling everyone within reach, listening to the bands and drinking. At midnight, the people would choose a Queen for him. It grew late, and the students finally reassembled in the hall and began the beauty contest. Allen sat on his throne, looking out at the drunken crowd, the footlights dazzling him a little. As the selection went on, he spent a quiet fifteen minutes writing a poem in his notebook.

Jirí Hendrych, the Party Secretary for Cultural Affairs, was not pleased to find 100,000 drunken citizens in the Park of Culture and

Rest at midnight. He had been expecting to see the harmless drunken revels of a few thousand students. When he entered the hall and found that they had elected an American as King of May he was horrified. He turned white with rage, 'This is impossible! You have to get rid of him immediately!'

The student organisers had little choice but to obey. The students had a security force, dressed as American military police, in uniforms left over from a film that had recently been shot in Prague. As Allen sat musing on his regality, a line of ten American MPs appeared in front of his throne. The Master of Ceremonies spoke a few words into the microphone, saying that Allen had been deposed and made Prime Minister instead and that a Czech student was to be King in his place.

The 'MPs' lifted Allen from his throne and sat him on the side with the May Queen judges, while a drunken Czech student, who had no idea what was happening to him, was put on the throne in Allen's place where he sat, blinking, looking confused and embarrassed.

Allen, cheated out of the two hundred dollars he was supposed to receive as May King, grumbled in a letter to the poet Nicanor Parra: 'The May Queen was elected but I didn't get a chance to marry and sleep with her as was tradition for the night. In fact, I was supposed to have the run of Prague and do anything I wanted and fuck anybody and get drunk everywhere as King.'

Allen spent all night singing and talking with a group of students in the dormitory, undeterred by the presence of two middle-aged business-suited men with a tape-recorder and a supply of Scotch. They welcomed the men, knowing full well that they were secret agents. The Prague newspapers played down the extraordinary events as much as they could, but the authorities had been alerted. They took a dim view of Allen's disruptive presence and decided to get rid of him.

For the next two days Allen wandered around Prague making a movie with some film-makers, singing 'Hare Krishna' and tape-recording interviews with student magazines on the evolution of consciousness, sex logic and space-age feeling. He went to rock concerts, wrote poems, slept with boys and kept his journals. Then, on 3 May, he found that his notebook was missing. It contained the usual things: six poems, including the one that he wrote under the spotlights while on his throne; politics and gossip:

'All the capitalist lies about communism are true and vice versa.' It included descriptions of a few orgy scenes with students and gave a detailed account of masturbating in his room at the Hotel Ambassador, kneeling on the bathroom floor with a broomstick up his ass.

He went to the Viola café and saw the two men in business-suits who gave him vodka till he was drunk and reeled out into the street at midnight, singing 'Hare Om Namo Shiva'. A police car stopped and asked him for his identification, which he did not have as his passport was being held at his hotel. They took him to the station where he explained that he was the May King, and a tourist poet, and not really drunk, just happy. They let him go. From this time on, he was openly followed by plainclothes police. He decided to keep sober. His plans were to continue to travel in Europe, and he didn't want to leave Prague until his travel arrangements were complete.

On 5 May, he left the Viola at midnight with a young couple, Eva Metopel and Jendrick Measl, heading for the all-night post office at Pansher Corner. As they turned on to a lonely street, a man appeared, saw Allen, hestitated momentarily then suddenly rushed towards him, yelling 'Bouzerant! Bouzerant!' (Homosexual). He punched Allen in the mouth, knocking him down and sending his glasses flying. Allen scrambled to his feet, grabbed his glasses and began running. Allen's friends tried to hold his assailant back, but he pulled free and gave chase. He caught up with Allen outside the post office and knocked him to the ground.

A police car arrived instantly, and Allen looked up from the sidewalk to see four rubber clubs held menacingly over his head. 'Om!' he chanted, then stayed quiet. Allen, the couple, and Allen's assailant were all bundled into the police car and taken to the station. The stranger maintained that they'd been exposing themselves on the street when he passed by and that they had attacked him. Allen demanded a lawyer and to be allowed to speak to the American Embassy. At this, the police decided to let him go. Eva and Jendrick were held separately, interrogated until 5 a.m. then released, with no repercussions. They had both refused to sign a statement handed to them: she that Allen had tried to seduce her boyfriend, and she'd called cops; he that Allen had tried to seduce Eva.

Allen concluded that it was definitely time to leave Prague. He consulted with his friends at the Writers' Union and at *Literarni noviny*, and they agreed with him. He had only one remaining appointment, a radio interview on 6 May. Afterwards, he went with friends to a café in the heart of Prague, where he was approached by plainclothesmen. The police had found Allen's missing notebook. 'If you'll come with us and identify it, we'll return it to you and you'll be back here in half an hour.'

Allen apprehensively went with them to the station and identified his notebook. As soon as he signed for it, one of the detective said frostily, 'On sketchy examination we suspect that this book contains illegal writings, so we are holding it for the public prosecutor.' Allen was free to go.

The next morning, 7 May, the same plainclothesmen appeared and took him back to the station. In an upstairs room, Allen was seated before five pudgy-faced bureaucrats at a polished table. 'Mister Ginsberg,' they said. 'We immigration chiefs have received many complaints from parents, scientists and educators about your sexual theories having a bad effect on our youth and corrupting the young, so we are terminating your visa.' They told him that his notebook would be returned to him (it never was). Allen explained that he had a plane ticket to London and would leave on his own, with no fuss, the next day. He pointed out that letting him leave voluntarily would be more diplomatic and would spare them the embarrassment of exiling the May King.

His views seemed to have no impact, and he was taken to his hotel to pack his things. He ate lunch in his room with a detective. He was not allowed to telephone the US embassy, the Writers' Union, or any of his friends. They escorted him to the airport. Allen sank into his seat on the BEA jet and sighed, kicked out of a Socialist country for the second time in four months.

In the opinion of Igor Hajek, of *Literarni noviny*, Allen brought a lot of the trouble on himself by his provocative behaviour. He mixed with people in Prague that most individuals in literary circles would have avoided. As a foreigner unfamiliar with the norms of the country, he stirred things up more than could be tolerated, even in those comparatively liberal times.

Ginsberg's deportation served as a pretext for the Stalinist element to attack the Writers' Union and its rather liberal weekly newspaper. Since Hajek had written the original 'Introduction to Ginsberg' article, he also came under fire. *Mlada fronta*, the Communist Youth Organisation daily, ran a full-page article, written by its editor on the orders of the Ideological Department, attacking the Writers' Union, *Literarni noviny* and Hajek. The CIA-front Radio Free Europe issued a summary of the Prague press coverage on 17 May:

> Czechoslovakian Communist Party daily *Rude pravo* had accused American beatnik poet Allen Ginsberg of having abused Czechoslovakian hospitality and grossly violated the norms of decent world behaviour. The accusations were made one day after *Czedeka* [the Czechoslovak Press Association] reported that Ginsberg had been expelled from the country because of his negative influence on young people. Last Sunday Czedeka also had quoted Communist Youth Organisation daily *Mlada fronta*, which printed excerpts from his personal diary. *Ruse pravo* claimed that the documents printed by *Mlada fronta* testified to the fact that Ginsberg is a person with a sexual deviation and to narcotics addiction. They alleged that in his notebook Ginsberg described *in detail* sexual orgies he staged in various places with young men. Ginsberg's character is completed by the notes in which he speaks with disdain of our Republic and of the citizens whom he met and with whom he talked.

Czechoslovakian President Anton Novotny himself went on the air and attacked Ginsberg, explaining the official reasons for expelling him. A 2 June news dispatch from a Vienna newspaper was headlined, 'Deliberate Corruption of Czechoslovakia's Youth Is The Latest Charge Made Against The West By Czech President Anton Novotny'.

Much was made of Allen's deportation from both Cuba and Czechoslovakia, and he himself described his eviction from Cuba as 'one of the best things I've done'. His attempts to explain his behaviour in these countries were usually dismissed as 'unbelievable political naïveté'; certainly, as a result, a number – possibly dozens – of people were interviewed by secret police. In Cuba, Allen genuinely thought that his views – that homosexuality should not be persecuted and that marijuana should be legalised – were 'revolutionary' (as he had stated at the Cuban press conference in New York three years before). That was his yardstick, and when Cuba did not manifest his particular vision, he began to proselytise. The Cubans, for their part, expected him to be interested in the progress they had made since the revolution – thousands of schools and hospitals built, the fight against illiteracy, the rise in the percentage of live births – but Allen's interest was in individual freedom, not in collective advance. Allen and the Cubans had two very different definitions of 'revolution', forged from two very different viewpoints and virtually irreconcilable.

In Czechoslovakia, Allen could not have known that the Majalis parade would attract so many people, but since it was the first in twenty years, its student organisers should have anticipated its popularity. Unwisely, after his fears about his Cuban notebooks, he nonetheless continued to record compromising details in Czechoslovakia, which ultimately led to his expulsion. He behaved as he would have in San Francisco or New York, but in Prague, as Hajek said, his behaviour was seen as provocative and therefore insulting. In this, Allen played straight into the hands of the Stalinists, who were using any excuse to stem the tide of liberalism. Although Allen was acclaimed for his chutzpah – no one else would have *dared* to behave as he did – for his friends and acquaintances in those countries, his visits were not a conspicuous success.

On the plane to London, Allen wrote his version of events in Prague. The words flowed easily on to the pages of his notebook, and by the time he landed at Heathrow he had a complete poem, requiring no tightening or changes, a perfect distillation of his feelings and experiences. He called it 'Kral Majalis': 'And I am the King of May, tho' paranoid, for the Kingdom of May is too beautiful to last for more than a month.'

14 Into the Vortex

I lift my voice aloud
make Mantra of American language now,
I here declare the end of the War!

'Wichita Vortex Sutra'

Although it would be another year before the cover of *Time* magazine would proclaim 'Swinging London', the city was already the centre of a vibrant fashion and pop music scene. Allen arrived on 8 May, and the next night he found himself sitting in Bob Dylan's opulent suite at the Savoy, along with Joan Baez, Albert Grossman and Don Pennebaker, whose three-man crew were filming every aspect of Dylan's tour. Dylan himself was looking sharp in Beatle boots, narrow black pants, and trendy London shirt with high rolled collar. His hair was fashionably tousled. Joan's hair was still long and centre parted, but she wore the latest short skirt and puffy sleeved top. Though Dylan had not yet 'gone electric' in public, the folk-singing Bob Dylan of the early 1960s was now years behind him.

That night Dylan played the first of two nights at the Royal Albert Hall. Allen was detailed by Dylan to escort Marianne Faithfull, and they travelled in their own black limousine. Afterwards a large party gathered in Grossman's suite at the hotel. Dylan was in his own suite, entertaining the Beatles and everyone else was forbidden to go in. Then Allen received a summons to the presence. The Beatles and their wives were there, with their two personal roadies, Mal Evans and Neil Aspinall. The room was completely silent. 'Just totally frozen, not knowing what to talk about.' Allen sat down on the arm of Dylan's chair, even though there was not really enough room. 'Why don't you sit a little closer,' mocked Lennon. Allen responded by falling forward into Lennon's lap. Looking up into his face, laughing, a little drunk, Allen asked, 'Have you ever read William Blake?'

'No, never heard of him,' snapped Lennon.

'Oh John, stop lying,' said Cynthia, his wife, and everyone laughed. Allen asked if they were aware of the relationship between the 'Beatles' and the 'Beats' and if they knew what the Beat Generation was. He told them about Kerouac, Cassady and the others. Dylan had had a friendly meeting with the Beatles the previous year in America, when he had turned them on to pot for the first time. But now he was on their territory. Ginsberg remembered the evening well: 'Dylan wasn't giving anything and they weren't giving anything. Dylan was laconic with them too, they were all uptight.' Dylan must have realised that Allen was the only person capable of breaking the ice.

The next day Allen went to the American embassy to begin negotiations to retrieve his notebook from the Prague police. Afterwards he took a bus to the Savoy to visit with Dylan. Pennebaker was filming the credits for their film *Don't Look Back* in the lane next to the hotel, and as Dylan stood flipping lyric cards, Allen puttered about in the background. The streets were filled with fashionably dressed long-haired young people as London emerged in colour for the first time since the war. He spent the afternoon in the National Gallery, revisiting his favourite pictures, then returned to the Savoy to join Dylan's party going to the Royal Albert Hall for their second concert. After the performance, they all ate together at a trattoria in Soho, seated at a large round table. 'How lovely to be back again in England,' he wrote in his journal.

It was the first time Allen had been in Britain during the summer, and he took advantage of the good weather to explore the country, visiting poets and giving small readings in Worcester, Bristol and Cambridge. In Newcastle he met the Imagist poet Basil Bunting, a friend of William Carlos Williams and Ezra Pound. Bunting had recently been 'discovered' working at a local newspaper by the Newcastle poet Tom Pickard. From Liverpool, Allen wrote Peter: 'I spent all week in Liverpool home of the Beatles and heard all the new rock bands and gave a little reading and had a ball with longhair boys – it's like San Francisco in Liverpool except the weather is greyer – lovely city, *mad* music, electronic hits your guts centers.' He was so moved by the new dancing and music that he proclaimed, 'Liverpool is at the present time the center of the consciousness of the human universe,' a line still used by the city fathers.

Back in London, Allen found that he knew an enormous number of people. John Ashbery gave a reading at the American embassy, which was followed by a literary cocktail party at which Tom Maschler of Jonathan Cape introduced Allen to the London literati. The poet Pablo Fernandez, cultural attaché at the Cuban embassy, was there, and was intrigued to hear about Allen's experiences in Havana. Allen saw the gallery owner Robert Fraser, Andy Warhol's London dealer. With Allen was the Finnish poet and translator Anselm Hollo, finally met after years of correspondence, at whose flat Allen spent his first night in town. London was the place to be, and Americans were flocking across the Atlantic to join in the action. Among them were Lawrence Ferlinghetti and Allen's sometime girlfriend Barbara Rubin.

Allen used Better Books, London's main literary bookshop, as his headquarters and went to stay with the shop's manager in nearby Fitzrovia. He celebrated his thirty-ninth birthday on 3 June with a classic 1960s party, with Beatles and Stones records, Tamla Motown and Stax playing full volume, and girls in see-through lace and mini-skirts dancing with long-haired youths. John and Cynthia Lennon arrived with George Harrison and Patti Boyd. Allen rushed to embrace them but by the time they arrived he was completely drunk and had removed all of his clothing except his Jockey shorts, which were balanced on his head. A 'Please do not disturb' hotel sign hung around his penis. John and George shrank back, making sure that no photographers were present. They talked a little, and John told Allen that he had once produced a magazine at Liverpool College of Art called the *Daily Howl*, but the Beatles, nervous at Allen's nakedness, soon left for another party. Asked why they were going so soon, Lennon hissed, 'You don't do that in front of the birds!' Allen's arms had to be wrapped around a lamppost for support while a cab was found to take him home. Once in the cab, he lay on the floor, and was only able to make it up to the third floor apartment by crawling up the stairs on his hands and knees.

With Allen and Lawrence Ferlinghetti in town, Gregory Corso just over in Paris, and Andrei Voznesensky due to arrive any day, there was naturally talk of a reading. Barbara Rubin, never one to think small, hired the largest venue in London – the Royal Albert Hall. Though the reading itself was something of a flop, the event served as a model for the big international poetry festivals that were to become commonplace in Europe, occurring every summer from Amsterdam to Rome. The reading was also a catalyst for the burgeoning London arts community, and such diverse organisations as Europe's first underground newspaper, *International Times* and the Arts Lab, a multi-media arts centre for experimental films, avant-garde theatre, and performance work; both traced their origins back to the Albert Hall reading. This was one of the reasons Ginsberg is held in such high esteem by that generation of young English people; his presence in London during the summer of 1965 primed the pump of the London 'underground' and galvanised everyone into action. For Allen himself, his European trip was complete, and on 29 June, after half a year away, he flew back to America on his still valid Cuban air ticket.

Throughout the 1960s, Allen's fame continued to grow, until by 1967 he was a national figure; featured on talk shows, interviewed by *Playboy*, the subject of personality posters, a celebrity, famous for being famous. He had been abroad when the media had first shown interest in the Beats over the trial of 'Howl' and Kerouac's best selling *On the Road*. The press had quickly developed their own stereotype Beatnik, using the classic French Bohemian, with beard, beret and sandals, as their model. Allen's notion of the Beat Generation was more concerned with sensitivity, sensuality and lack of hypocrisy than with the fashionable coolness, lack of visible emotion and studied existential pose of the Beatnik; the press, however, lumped them all together. With the Kennedy era, things had loosened up and the 1960s really began: rock 'n' roll blossomed, birth control became truly feasible, a hundred different threads came together in the youth movement. Allen found himself one of its spokesmen.

He was obviously flattered by the media attention, but his primary motive was to get his various messages across, by all and every means. The years of market research training gave him a canny eye on how to present his ideas to the general population in the best possible light. He became expert at manipulating talk-show hosts, twisting questions in order to speak out against the war or in favour of legalising pot, and he used his massive contact book to connect up scholars and researchers, activists and journalists. Ten years before, he had spent his time putting together editors and poets; now his address books became the central switchboard of what became known as 'the underground'.

As Allen's legend grew, so did Peter's dependence on drugs. He had taken a great deal of methadrine in the Lower East Side in 1959, and heroin in France in 1961. In India he was addicted to morphine, which was one of the reasons that he didn't want to return to the United States with Allen. Faced with Allen's new role as guru to the burgeoning youth movement, Peter retreated into the false self-confidence of amphetamine, presenting a speedy, funny, distracted face to the world. His relationship with Allen grew more complex. Peter now had regular girlfriends, but his life was nevertheless dominated by Allen. He acted as Allen's chauffeur. He was Allen's secretary, answering the endlessly ringing telephone, fielding visitors and looking after the apartment during Allen's frequent absences. And he was also still Allen's lover. They were both living life very quickly, storing up problems for the future.

Peter was sometimes deeply depressed about his brothers or about his own life, but Allen was often too busy visiting, being Bob Dylan's confidant, or acting as guru of the youth movement to notice Peter's troubles and drug-taking. 'I didn't realise that it was a chronic problem that had distorted our relationship and distorted my whole behaviour towards him and his toward me,' Ginsberg later said. 'I just wasn't facing it. It went on for twenty years.'

When Allen arrived at US customs after his flight from London, he was taken into a side room and stripped down to his underwear. Agents examined the lint in his pockets with a magnifying glass but found only tobacco crumbs. He managed to get a look at their documents which had negligently been left face upward on the desk, and read: 'Allen Ginsberg (reactivated) and Peter Orlovsky (continued) – These persons are reported to be engaged in smuggling narcotics.'

In Allen's absence, his East 5th Street building had deteriorated. The water and heat had been shut off and the city had given each tenant one hundred dollars to relocate. Peter had found a third-floor walk-up at 408 East 10th Street, in a dangerous run-down block between avenues C and D. Allen arrived home to find that addicts had already broken in and stolen his typewriter and Peter's Indian sarod. He didn't have much time to settle into his new quarters, because no sooner had he visited his family and recovered from jet-lag than he and Peter headed out to California, where the Berkeley Poetry Conference would begin on 12 July.

The conference went down in history as a showcase of the most important younger poets working in America at that time: Gary Snyder, Robert Creeley, Robert Duncan, LeRoi Jones, John Weiners, Jack Spicer and Ginsberg. Charles Olson made one of his rare public appearances. Allen wrote, 'He got drunk and high on pot and bennies, and instead of reading, talked his head off for four hours to 700 people in the audience, concluding leading over the podium with his huge bulk and growling out like a lion, 'I love POWER!' Duncan got so scared that he fled in the middle. But it was a great night. I read drunk, but well, thank God.'

To the delight of his family, Allen received a Guggenheim Foundation grant. He used the money to buy a Volkswagen camper equipped with a refrigerator, a bed and a desk. In mid-August, Peter stayed behind in San Francisco with his girlfriend, Stella, while Allen, Gary Snyder and Gary's girlfriend Martine took off up the Pacific Highway to Oregon, camping on beaches and at riversides in forests. Once they reached the Oregon border, they turned inland to the Cascades and Crater Lake National Park, where they camped at the foot of Mount Scott. They spent two days back-packing on the Wonderland Trail in Mount Ranier National Park, looking down into foggy chasms, eating wild berries, tramping through the snow around the 14,400 foot peak and developing tremendous appetites. Every morning they read aloud from the Tibetan classic *100,000 Songs of Milerepa*, and one morning, Allen and Gary climbed the ten-thousand-foot Glacier Peak, using crampons and ice-axes on the snowfields. 'I've finally found a climbing companion,' said Gary, which made Allen very happy.

They were away a month and Allen was delighted to see Peter again. He wrote in his journal: 'Slept last night between Peter and Stella, naked, and turned this and that way, one to another on sofa bed, content.' On 1 October, with Peter at the wheel, his long hair tucked up under a woolly hat like a Rastafarian, Allen, his young friend Steven Bornstein, Julius, Neal Cassady and his girlfriend Anne Murphy left San Francisco in the Volkswagen for a week of camping and driving around to visit friends. They saw Ken Kesey in La Honda and Carolyn Cassady in Los Gatos and drove all around the Salinas and Monterey area before finishing up in Big Sur, where they spent a few days at Lawrence Ferlinghetti's cabin in Bixby Canyon.

The cabin stood next to a small stream at the foot of the steep canyon walls, where the mist rarely burned off before midday. A path led down through the trees and mossy cliffs to a small white beach, spanned by the Bixby Canyon Bridge, one thousand feet above. One day, Allen took an acid trip, sitting on the warm sand at the foot of the cliffs where the little Bixby Creek trickled into the sea. Afterwards he wrote Charles Olson, 'I took some LSD at Big Sur . . . and felt great – finally – no horrors or worries – just titanic ocean and terrific cliffs and Blakean planet – sunshine and beautiful Wordsworthian kelp.'

LSD had been giving Allen the same terrifying visions he experienced on ayahuasca in Peru, so he was very relieved. 'No monster vibrations, no snake universe hallucinations. Many tiny jeweled violet flowers along the path of a living brook that looked like Blake's illustration for a canal in grassy Eden: huge Pacific watery shore. Orlovsky dancing naked like Shiva, long-haired before giant green waves, titanic cliffs that Wordsworth mentioned in his own horizon. No harm.'

It seemed a long way from the 'real' world, where the cracker-barrel Texan President Johnson dominated the political scene and had become the prime target for anti-war protesters. That day, President Johnson underwent a gall bladder operation, and despite Johnson's escalation of the Vietnam War, Allen felt compassion. He wrote, 'Realising that more vile words from me would send out physical vibrations into the atmosphere that might curse poor Johnson's flesh and further unbalance his soul, I knelt on the sand, surrounded by masses of green bulb-headed kelp vegetable-snake undersea beings washed up by last night's tempest, and prayed for the President's tranquil health.'

Back in San Francisco, Allen, Peter, Julius and Steven Bornstein all stayed with their old friend Shig Murao from City Lights, in his two room North Beach apartment. Steven had a bad habit of inviting everyone he met to come and stay, so Shig would sometimes find his living room filled with people no one knew. They would all go out to eat, and Allen would invariably pick up the tab.

Allen first met Steven on the street in New York; he was living in a juvenile home on St Marks Place. Steven began to visit Allen regularly at East 10th Street, so Allen invited him out to San Francisco with them. Steven made a hundred-foot-long scroll illustrating the *Tibetan Book of the Dead*, drawing the various Tibetan deities with intense attention to detail. Allen wrote Huncke, 'He doth take too much speed and *is* not in best (nor worst) of health.'

Peter was also taking speed, and spent a great deal of time scrubbing and dusting at Shig's apartment. Although Shig was happy to have his toilet bowl scrubbed, he was less pleased when Peter cleaned his wok; 'You have to season a wok, and the patina is what gives it the flavour. He spent a whole day cleaning that thing and scouring it. He didn't know. Peter one day took a toothbrush and he scrubbed the whole sidewalk. It was like a Happening. He knew that everyone was watching him, he was trying to be funny, toothbrush and cleanser.'

They moved to a bigger place where Neal and Anne often stayed with them, using Julius's bed. Allen described Neal in a letter to Huncke, who hadn't seen Neal in years: 'Neal had entered a new space age dimension – all his old energy still full steam but after 13 years railroad, 2½ years jail and now divorced and years of intensive pot ... several years of obsession with the racetrack where he lost $10,000 and now several years omnivorous absorption of amphets by mouth, ("jumpers" he says) and company with huge crowds of Zonk-minded admirers, lovers of his legend, like, devotees of his energy and speed – he's become a sort of fantastic continuously talking (on 7 or 8 levels of simultaneous association) teacher, plus the fact that for 2 or 3 years he's gone into LSD mind too, also omniverously, more even than Barbara Rubin and friends did.'

Neal's home base was Ken Kesey's psychedelic community in the Penninsula backwoods at La Honda, near Palo Alto, where a continuous LSD acid test was going on beneath the redwoods, with films and tapes and huge speakers cranked up to full volume and dozens of kids smoking pot and tripping, wandering among the trees. Neal, of course, drove the psychedelic bus, which now had a microphone slung above his head to broadcast his acid-crazed travelogue as he hallucinated that the gas pedal had turned to spaghetti or that he was being attacked by phantom cockroaches. On acid, he drove through a forest fire and all the way to Idaho and back with no brakes, clutch, or reverse gear, with seven or eight kids lying on a mattress on the roof, high on acid, with the huge roof-mounted speakers blasting rock 'n' roll at startled passers-by.

Allen found the chaos at Kesey's hard to handle, and dealt with it by just being quiet and looking around, speaking when spoken to and trying to say something sensible. He usually stuck with Neal but occasionally had 'manly conversations' with Kesey. Peter's way of dealing with the acid-madness was to chop wood.

In Berkeley, following the wake of the Free Speech Movement demonstrations, an anti-war march was organised by the Viet Nam Day Committee, to go from the Berkeley campus, through the black district of Oakland to the Oakland Army Terminal. It was the height of the Black Power movement and since many disadvantaged blacks were against the war, the march organisers thought that they would pick up more protesters that way. At the Oakland city line, they were stopped by police wearing full riot gear, with gas masks and guns. Everybody sat down in the street and there were some speeches from the sound truck. At this point, a Hell's Angel named Tiny, who had been behind the police lines, rushed out with seven other Angels and tore down the 'Peace In Vietnam' banner that had led the march. Then he ran to the sound truck and cut the wires. The Hell's Angels – motorcycle street gangs who modelled themselves on Marlon Brando in *The Wild One* – inspired fear whenever they rode into town on their Harley-Davidsons. They were right-wing and patriotic in a populist sense. The police stood by and watched them disrupt the march.

Many of the marchers had been involved with the Free Speech Movement and were determined to exercise their constitutional rights, so another march was planned for November. There was a mass meeting to decide policy, during which the Angels were compared to Hitler's Brown Shirts and a proposal made that all the men on the march should carry long sticks to defend themselves. Allen proposed just the opposite: the march should be led by grandmothers carrying flowers, young women with babies in arms and girls dressed in pretty costumes. He printed up a leaflet entitled 'How To Make A March/Spectacle', suggesting that the march should have old-fashioned floats with big papier-mâché caricatures to dramatise the issues: a Vietnamese girl attacked by American soldiers in robotic battle gear or Lyndon Johnson with his pants down, surrounded by garlands of flowers and clowns and people playing music.

The Hell's Angels, for their part, threatened to beat up anyone who marched. Clearly something had to be done to avert a confrontation, so Ken Kesey proposed a meeting between the two sides to be held at Ralph ('Sonny') Barger's house in Oakland. Barger was the president of the Oakland chapter of the Hell's Angels, the most powerful of the outlaw gangs operating on the coast. Ginsberg, Cassady, Kesey, some Merry Pranksters in costume and one or two people from the Viet Nam Day Committee arrived, to be met by about twenty Angels, also in costume. The first thing they all did was drop acid, with the exception of Allen, who was certain that he would have a horrific trip. At first, the conversation did not go well. Kesey tried to explain to Barger that it was not a Communist plot, whereas the Angels said 'We gotta fight 'em here or there.' The Angels thought a Communist victory in Vietnam would lead to a Communist police state in America. Kesey and Allen's argument was why fight them at all. America invaded Vietnam, Vietnam didn't invade America. The discussion began to get acrimonious.

Allen pulled out his harmonium and began to chant the Prajnaparamita Sutra, the 'Highest Perfect Wisdom' sutra, singing in a deep-voiced monotone. After a few minutes, Tiny, the Angel who had torn up the 'Peace In Vietnam' banner, joined in, singing 'Om, om, zoom, zoom, zoom, om!' Gradually the other Hell's Angels began to join in, followed by Cassady and Kesey, till in the end, the whole room was chanting. 'I was absolutely astounded,' Ginsberg later said. 'I knew it was history being made. It was the first time in a tense, tight, situation that I relied totally on pure mantric vocalisation, breath-chant, to alleviate my own paranoia and anxiety.' In the end Barger put Dylan's 'Gates of Eden' on the record player and confessed to Allen that he liked Joan Baez. By the time the meeting broke up the tension had all been dispelled. Kesey said he was on the side of the Angels and knew they were all blessed. Barger insisted that they had been inaccurately reported and had already made American flags for their own, peaceful, pro-American counter-demonstration. One of Barger's lieutenants, Terry the Tramp, later told Hunter S. Thompson: 'That goddam Ginsberg is gonna fuck us *all* up. For a guy that ain't straight at all, he's about the straightest son of a bitch I've ever seen. Man, you shoulda been there when he told Sonny he loved him . . . Sonny didn't know what the hell to say.'

Several days later the Angels issued their Newspaper Edict, printed in the *San Francisco Examiner*, saying that it would demean them to attack the filthy Communist marchers and that they had sent a telegram to President Johnson offering to fight the Communists in South Vietman as Gorilla (sic) soldiers. The Angels had found a way to save face, and the march was safe from attack.

Shortly after the march, there was a party at Ken Kesey's huge house in the woods to which the Hell's Angels were invited. Allen, Peter, Julius and Steven drove down to La Honda in the camper and it was there, in early December 1965, that Ginsberg wrote the poem, 'First Party At Ken Kesey's With Hells Angels' at 3 a.m. while the huge loudspeakers blasted out Ray Charles, the Beatles and the Rolling Stones, and four police cars waited outside, their red lights revolving in the leafy night.

Bob Dylan arrived to play some concerts in the Bay Area and Allen saw him every day. They talked about poetry and fame, and again discussed the idea of doing something together; Dylan producing a record of Allen's mantras or appearing in a movie or TV show. They had been discussing the idea for some time. Ten months earlier, in February 1965, Dylan had referred to it on the Les Crane TV talk show:

Les Crane: 'Have you ever given any thought to acting; think you might enjoy acting?'
Bob Dylan: 'Well, I'm gonna try to make a movie this summer. Which Allen Ginsberg is writing. I'm rewriting.'
LC: 'Allen Ginsberg the poet?'
BD: 'Yeah. Yeah.'
LC: 'He was on this programme you know.'
BD: 'Yeah?'
LC: 'Extolling the virtues of marijuana one night.'
BD: 'Really? Allen?' (surprised) (audience laughs) 'Sounds like a lie to me.' (audience laughter)
LC: 'That's really – you think I'm lying?'
BD: 'No, I didn't mean that.'
LC: 'Allen Ginsberg was sitting in that chair where Caterina Valente is sitting right now, and he said that he thought we ought to legalise pot.'
BD: 'He said that?'
LC: 'Right on the televsion!'
BD: 'Phhewwwww!'
LC: 'Can you imagine that?'

BD: 'Nah. Allen is a little funny sometimes.' (audience roars with laughter)
LC: 'Allen's a little funny sometimes, huh? Yes. What's this movie going to be about?'
BD: 'Oh it's a, sort of a horror cowboy movie.' (audience laughs) 'Takes place on the New York Thruway. I play my mother.'

Dylan gave Allen thirty tickets for his concert at the Berkeley Community Center and asked him to spread them around. Allen invited McClure, Duncan, Snyder, LaVigne, Shig, Kesey and other friends, and gave half the tickets to the Hell's Angels. At the concert Sonny Barger, Terry the Tramp, and the other Angels sat quietly in the front row along with Joan Baez, who sang along with Dylan from her seat. When Dylan reached the line in 'Gates of Eden' about the motorcycle black madonna two-wheel gypsy queen, Allen screamed it out in unison. Afterwards Allen took Sonny Barger backstage and Barger produced a huge bag of pot, making Dylan very paranoid.

There was a big party afterwards at Robert LaVigne's studio in the Mission district, and Dylan, Joan Baez, the members of The Hawks (Dylan's musicians, who later changed their name to The Band), Ken Kesey, Michael McClure, people from the Viet Nam Day Committee, Sonny Barger, Freewheelin' Frank, Terry the Tramp, Tiny and the other Hell's Angels all danced to an all-woman rock band, their differences forgotten.

Feeling generous, Dylan gave Allen six hundred dollars to buy himself a top-of -the-line portable reel-to-reel Uher 1000R Reporter tape recorder, which would run for ten hours on batteries and could be plugged into a socket to recharge. Dylan also bought an amplifier for Peter and an autoharp for Michael McClure.

On 15 December, Allen, Peter, Julius and Steven left San Francisco to drive slowly across the USA. They began by spending a week with Lawrence Ferlinghetti at his cabin in Big Sur. Allen had got a prescription for morphine to relieve kidney stones, and he spent a lot of time sitting, high, on the beach, mumbling into his new tape recorder, getting to know it as a writing tool. 'A new ax for composition,' as he described it to Gregory. There was a big rock in the middle of the white sand beach, and he sat there and made a number of recordings of mantras, accompanying himself on his finger cymbals, while the sea sighed in the background. He practiced deep 'Om's, which blended in with the waves, and began to use the machine to record his impressions. When they were transcribed, they gave his journals a conversational tone. He described the walk from the cabin, following the creek down to the beach:

> The mossy rockface ... many colors of green and yellow, tendrils of vines ... reddish brown. Velvet moss. The brightness of the sun ... all the little twinkling branches at the end of the path trembling in the wind, and the gurgling of the stream ... weeds in the surface brown ground like animal hair – Camel hair weeds – tender little green creepers crawling up a tree. All the trees looking like St Francis in Ecstacy – Snaky Reptilian Dinosaur tracks in the mud ... Blue snout tip of ocean thru the rock path ... God it's beautiful here now – a few birds flutter down the path – a robin?
>
> – Here you are little birdy, ... Oh, there's Steven perching and looking in his solitude and smiling – Hello Steven!

In the evenings they sat around the big stone hearth, putting logs on the fire and talking quietly. Allen reread Kerouac's *Big Sur*, written four years before in the same cabin, when Jack was having D.T.s and thought that the canyon walls were going to close in and crush him. Kerouac's graffitti were still on the wall of the outhouse: 'Read three pages of Poe's The Gold Bug' and 'Useless, useless,/ the heavy rain/ Driving into the sea.' At night, they could hear the shifting of the ashes in the fireplace and the tinkling of the stream by the side of the house.

On Christmas Eve, they cleaned the cabin, put fresh kindling and small logs under the porch, piled chopped wood by the fireplace, and set off south down the Coast Highway, intending to spend a month in Los Angeles. Christmas Day, they camped in the Santa Lucia Range. Allen wrote Gregory: 'I'm heading down to L.A. .... Hang around Wally Berman's Canyon home there and drive around to parties in the camper and play my tape recorder by my pillow and fuck Peter and Steven and tell Julius to wash the dishes.'

Wally Berman, a friend of Allen's from North Beach, was an artist and editor of *Semina* magazine. He was living with his wife Shirley and their son, high in the Santa Monica Mountains. There,

Allen and the others quickly settled into the strangely beautiful world of canyon living, with coyotes howling at night and the glittering web of lights spread out below. Allen did a couple of television debates about narcotics laws, met Laura Huxley and had a brief visit with Christopher Isherwood. On 10 January 1966, he did a reading at Riverside University and sent the check to Ed Sanders, copies of whose *Fuck You/A Magazine of the Arts* had just been seized by the police in New York. Allen advised Sanders to contact the ACLU and organised a benefit reading in Los Angeles, which brought in another three hundred dollars for the defense fund.

It was impossible not to get involved with the music scene in L.A. Through Dylan's manager, Albert Grossman, Allen met The Byrds, the rock group who took Dylan's acoustic 'Mister Tambourine Man' and recorded a sweetly harmonised rock 'n' roll version of it with a jangly twelve-string electric guitar. It was released in May, and inspired Dylan to 'go electric' himself. Allen mentioned in a letter to Ed Sanders that he was also seeing a lot of a 'Teenage Rock King kid named Phil Spector'. Spector was the creator of the famous 'Wall of Sound', the genius behind the Ronettes, the Crystals, the Righteous Brothers and many other acts. When Spector heard Allen's mantra-chanting, he offered to produce him singing 'Prajnaparamita Sutra' as a jukebox record. Regrettably, this was one of the 'little symphonies for the kids' – Spector's term – that he never got round to making.

On 26 January, the Volkswagen bus set off to discover America. Peter drove, Julius and Steven sat in the back, while Allen, in the front, held his microphone and recorded impressions as they travelled. They headed east for San Bernardino, with Nelson Eddy singing 'Oh What A Beautiful Morning' on the tinny car radio, followed by news of the war. The poetry notations taped on the trip became 'Hiway Poesy LA-Albuquerque-Texas-Wichita', published in *The Fall of America*. Their first destination was Albuquerque, to visit Robert Creeley. They spent the night camped in snow in the vast empty Arizona desert. Peter drove steadily: through the Painted Desert, past the Meteor Crater to the Petrified Forest, through the lands of the Navajo and the Hopi, past gas flares and oil refineries emitting smoke and steam – 'High aluminum tubes winking red lights over space ship runways' – till they finally crested a hill and saw night-time Albuquerque sparkling below in the black desert.

They had an enjoyable but short visit, and the Volkswagen was soon rolling along Route 66 again, this time toward Kansas, 'Center of the Birchite Vortex' as Allen described it in a letter to Lucien Carr. They dropped off a pair of hitch-hikers at Tucumcari and drove on into Texas. They were in the Bible Belt:

On radio entering Texas/ Please For Jesus!/ Grunts & Screams
& Shouts/ Shouts for the Poison Redeemer,/ Shouts for the
Venomous Jesus of Kansas./ Onward to Wichita!/ Onward to
the Vortex!/ To the Birchite Hate Riddles,/ cock-detesting,
pussy-smearing/ dry ladies and evil Police/ of Central Planes
State . . .

They entered Kansas at Liberal, past radio towers with red blinking beacons transmitting the *Hebrew-Christian Hour* and *Lifeline*. They passed a small herd of buffalo, their backs shining in the sun, slowly cropping the frosty grass at the edge of the Ninnescah River. The radio picked up nothing but religious broadcasting or news of the war. After the annual Tet truce, the United States launched Operation Rolling Thunder, bombing to within four miles of the centre of Hanoi in a still undeclared war. American casualties were running at one hundred dead, six hundred wounded each week. 1966 was to be the year when Johnson more than doubled US troop numbers, from 181,000 in January to 400,000 by December. The United States dropped as many bombs on Vietnam as had been dropped in the whole Pacific theatre during World War II, and by the end of the year another 4,800 Americans were dead and 335 American planes shot down.

'Martial music filling the airwaves –/ only the last few weeks/ waves of military music/ drum taps drum beats trumpets/ pulsing thru radiostations/ not even sad . . ./ What Patriot wrote that shit?' The music was Sergeant Barry Sadler's 'The Ballad of the Green Berets', a patriotic novelty song which was climbing the charts. It reached number one on 5 March 1966, and stayed there for five weeks, such was the mood of the country.

They gave readings, which were sold out, and there were big parties with all the local poets, professors and young people. Allen was at the height of his fame. All the newspapers wanted interviews, and *Life* magazine reporter Barry Farrell followed him around as if reporting on a royal tour, writing a huge story entitled

'Guru Comes To Kansas'. Robert Frank flew out and filmed the Kansas City reading and also shot footage of Ginsberg and Orlovsky in a Kansas wheatfield. 'It was a very romantic time and a very creative time,' Ginsberg recalled. 'It really dazzled me because there was so much going on.'

In Wichita, Allen found the Chances R club, where the 'fairy boys of the Plains' danced to the Rolling Stones' '(I Can't Get No) Satisfaction' and Nancy Sinatra's 'These Boots Are Made For Walking'. His poem 'Chances R' later appeared in *Planet News*. They drove to Topeka to give a reading at the Menninger Clinic before an audience of psychologists and psychiatrists. Peter built up high hopes that the renowned clinic might be able to help Julius and might even take him on, but they didn't have anything new to suggest. Peter, on amphetamine, let his anger and frustration show. Ginsberg remembered his reaction: 'So Peter took off all his clothes at this gathering of psychiatrists and showed 'em his asshole standing on a table, angrily. And then, driving back to Lawrence with me and Julius, he was very drunk and was driving very fast and suicidally. I got really scared and that was the one and only time I have been totally frightened [by Peter].'

As their Volkswagen bus circled Wichita, driving through McPherson and Emporia, straying north to Lincoln, Nebraska, the radio crackling with news of the war dead and cattle prices, Allen filtered the images of the winter farms, the advertising signs, the newspaper headlines – 'Vietnam War Brings Prosperity' – the endless highways through the flatlands, the continual chatter of the car radio, into a series of spoken stanzas, two or three long lines at a time, murmered directly into the microphone of his Uher as they sped along.

The triangle-roofed Farmer's Grain Elevator/ sat quietly by the side of the road/ along the railroad track/ American Eagle beating its wings over Asia/ million dollar helecopters/ a billion dollars worth of Marines/ who loved Aunt Betty/ Drawn from the shores and farms shaking/ from the high schools to the landing barge/ blowing the air thru their cheeks with fear/ in Life on Television.

He was dictating the lines that became 'Wichita Vortex Sutra', possibly his best-known poem of the 1960s and regarded as one of his finest. He collected Midwestern images, glimpses of the snow-covered farms and silent afternoon small towns, and collaged them with the hysterical headlines, reactionary radio editorials, quotes from political speeches, books and articles, until the poem reached its climax when Ginsberg summoned all the powers of his imagination and, calling upon all the various gods and gurus at his command, from Krishna to Blake, to empower him, he proclaimed the End of the War.

> I lift my voice aloud
>   make Mantra of American language now,
>   I here declare the end of the War!

He wrote Gregory: 'I wrote huge 17 page "Wichita Vortex Sutra" big Shelleyan poem ending Vietnam War – wrote it on tape machine betwixt Lincoln and Wichita.' In print the poem came out at twenty-three pages, twice as long as 'Howl'. It was instantly recognised as the strongest, most heartfelt response to the horror of the Vietnam war and the wanton destruction in Southest Asia, as well as its effect on the United States.

The *Village Voice* published it on 28 April 1966. It was quickly picked up by the burgeoning underground press and appeared in the *L.A. Free Press*, the *Berkeley Barb*, the *Fifth Estate* and *Ramparts*, among others. In England *Peace News* ran it across their centerfold and issued it as a pamphlet. Coyote Books in the States also released it as a pamphlet, distributed by City Lights. *Life* magazine used a large section of it at the end of Barry Farrell's profile, and next to 'Howl' and 'Kaddish', 'Wichita Vortex Sutra' soon became one of Ginsberg's best-known works.

Despite the quotations and topical references, it was completely lacking in slogans and in the hectoring, self-righteous tone which flawed so many anti-war statements. Because it was not topical in that sense, the poem did not date, and it would come to be highly regarded for capturing, perhaps more than any other work, the precise atmosphere of the country at the height of the war.

They stayed in the midwest for a month, travelling in Kansas, Nebraska and Indiana. They were stopped by the vice squad in Wichita, visited by the police after a reading in Lincoln, and in Bloomington, where they had visited Dr Kinsey's Sex Institute, they were threatened with investigation by the Indiana state legislature because Peter had read one of his transcribed 'Sex

Experiments' from Tangier. But they escaped without being arrested and continued on east, heading to New York City.

The most pressing item on Ginsberg's desk when he returned was the case of Dr Timothy Leary, who on 11 March, was convicted of transporting and tax avoidance and given the maximum sentence on both counts, a total of thirty years in prison and a fine of thirty thousand dollars, and was commited to a hospital for psychiatric observation. This draconian sentence was immediately appealed to a higher court but the heat was on and for the next decade Leary was hounded by the authorities, unable to pursue his research and forced to devote most of his time to defending himself from legal harassment.

Allen immediately got involved in the Timothy Leary Defense Fund and began gathering signatures and money for an advertisement in the *New York Times* condemning the sentence and calling for changes in the law. The advertisement was signed by Leslie Fiedler, Richard Alpert, Charles Olson, Robert Lowell, Norman Mailer, Jules Feiffer, Susan Sontag, Jonas Mekas, Kenneth Koch, Albert Grossman, Laura Huxley, Peter Fonda and even Allen's *bête noire*, critic Norman Podhoretz.

Allen continued his flirtation with the world of rock 'n' roll. Phil Spector's idea of recording mantras stuck with him. He wanted to make records and be a star, but his recording career got off to a slow start, and it was not until 1969 that he cut his first album. Thereafter he managed to record more albums than the average rock band.

In April 1966, Andy Warhol and Paul Morrissey hired an old Polish dancehall, the Dom, on St Marks Place, and began a series of public performances. Allen went along and danced to exhaustion with Barbara Rubin and her girlfriends, to the music of the Stones and the Beatles. 'I Want To Hold Your Hand' was a great favourite at the club. Barbara arranged for Allen to sing with the Velvet Underground, and he climbed onstage and sang 'Hare Krishna' while Gerard Malanga danced around cracking his whip, and the group provided appropriate backing. 'I was trying to introduce a big serious note of spiritual materialism in the middle of all that!' joked Ginsberg. His role as the spiritual adviser to the underground scene was becoming more defined.

When Allen was in London in 1965, he had made arrangements to have his collected poems published there by Jonathan Cape;

Penguin would issue the paperback edition. This naturally brought up the possibility of a similar volume in the United States. The problem was that City Lights was still very much a small press, with correspondingly poor distribution. Allen enjoyed his relationship with City Lights because he was dealing with friends and was able to use them as an informal office to send out books to people and handle all the messy details of foreign editions and anthologies. They took a percentage for this service of course, but it did relieve Allen's desk load. The mid to late 1960s was a period of enormous success for Beat writers and writers influenced by the Beats. Richard Brautigan sold over two million copies of *Trout Fishing in America*, Lawrence Ferlinghetti's *Coney Island of the Mind* sold close to one million and his publisher, New Directions, constantly reprinted his other books and those of Gregory Corso and Gary Snyder. Though it must have been galling for Ginsberg to see rows of Ferlinghetti's books in the stores, and rarely any of his own, he stayed with City Lights. One of his reasons for doing so was that he was easily their best selling author, and without him the press might have had to close.

The idea of a hardcover version of his collected poems, therefore, posed something of a problem. He had just returned from the Midwest, where, despite his tremendous fame and sold-out readings, he was unable to find any of his books in the stores. He wrote to Ferlinghetti and suggested the idea of a joint imprint: Doubleday/ City Lights or Grove/ City Lights, with the New York publisher handling the distribution and City Lights taking a share of the profits. 'I wd give the book to City Lights to do hardcover,' he wrote, 'but having been in Lincoln, Nebraska and Wichita etc., I don't think its possible in next few years for City Lights alone to compete with Grove etc for distribution. I wanna big mass distribution if I can.'

Allen had been offered a ten-thousand-dollar advance on a hardcover edition, and he offered to forgo this if City Lights could be brought in as a profit-sharing co-publisher. 'Please say OK,' he begged Ferlinghetti, 'unless you have a groovier alternative.' City Lights were naturally unwilling to lose its cash cow, and in the end Ginsberg was persuaded to stay with them, largely because he could not face the unpleasantness of a break. He was at the peak of his fame, he could command enormous sums for poetry readings, and with proper distribution he would certainly have been America's best selling poet. With a good literary agent and a New York publisher he could have sold at least four times as many books. In 1970, he was offered a one-hundred-thousand-dollar advance by a New York publisher, but it would have meant leaving City Lights altogether, and he turned it down.

Most of the money he made from his readings he gave away to other poets, and to avoid paying tax on these funds, some of which would go towards the Vietnam war, Allen, with the legal assistance of his brother, set up a charitable foundation. On 12 April 1966, the paperwork was completed and the non-profit Committee On Poetry came into being, making Ginsberg probably the first poet in America, and possibly the world, with his own charitable foundation. Over the years, COP was to distribute tens of thousands of dollars to small presses, underground newspapers, impoverished poets and other projects, to further the cause of poetry.

Shortly after Allen had been strip-searched as a 'narcotic trafficer' on his return to New York from Paris in 1965, there was another attempt by the authorities to curtail his activities as a marijuana legalisation advocate. A jazz musician called Jack Martin was arrested for possession of pot, and four narcotics agents, including the supervisor of the New York Bureau of Narcotics, had a private meeting with him during which they told him that his bail would be raised from five to ten thousand dollars and that additional charges would be added to his indictment, unless he helped them out.

Agent Bruce Jensen acted as their spokesman. 'We want Ginsberg,' he said. 'How would you like to see your wife in jail? . . . We don't want you, we want the guy you get it from . . . Do you know Ginsberg? . . . Can you get him for us? . . . Can you set up Allen Ginsberg?' To the enforcers, it was inconceivable that Ginsberg would campaign for the legalisation of marijuana unless he was somehow involved with its sale and trafficking.

Jack Martin had been arrested with a friend of his, George Wilbourn, and on 11 August 1965, there had been a benefit to raise money for Wilbourn's bail. Though Martin had never met Ginsberg, he got up and gave a brief speech in which he described how Jensen had tried to get him to set Ginsberg up. At this point, three undercover agents in the audience came forward and, after a shouting match and a brief scuffle, Martin was arrested for a second time. Arrested with him were film-makers Jack Smith and Piero Heliczer, who were charged with assault and resisting arrest. The narcotics agents had shown no identification, nor did they have arrest warrants. Smith and Heliczer thought that Martin was being attacked by thugs which was why they intervened. They were all taken to the Fifth Precinct Station where Jack Smith was brutally beaten by Detective Imp, who seemed quite unconcerned that many people were witnesses to his actions. Allen Ginsberg, meanwhile, was still in California, quite unaware of what was going on.

Martin and Wilbourn pleaded guilty in the original marijuana case and received two-year suspended sentences. The cases of assault and resisting arrest didn't reach court until 11 April 1966, when the jury was selected. By this time, Ginsberg had been informed, and he turned up in court. He told the *New York Times*: 'I feel like the noose of the police state is closing in on me. I've had experience of police states in Prague and it's very similar here.' On 13 April, Narcotics Agent Bruce Jensen testified that he had asked Martin if he knew whether Ginsberg ever possessed or sold narcotics in New York and that he had once asked Martin 'if he would assist the Bureau of Narcotics as an informant'. On 15 April, Martin, Smith and Heliczer were all found guilty of assault and resisting arrest.

Meanwhile, Tim Leary's case was slowly winding its way through the appeal courts, taking up much of his time and costing a huge amount in legal fees. Among his supporters were Billy and Peggy Hitchcock, heirs to the Mellon fortune, who placed at his disposal a mansion set in a 2,500-acre estate in Millbrook, New York. On 17 April, the Dutchess County police raided it. Among the twenty-nine guests that night were four medical and psychological doctors, three physical scientists, five journalists on assignments and three photographers. There were twelve children. The police swept through the house, entering all the bedrooms without knocking and body-searching all the adults. They searched all sixty-four rooms in the mansion, and though they found no drugs on Leary, he was arrested along with three of his guests for drug possession. It was a straightforward case of police harassment. Allen wrote to Ferlinghetti, 'Shit's hit the fan on Leary and LSD in New York and phone's ringing in every direction.'

On 14 June, attired in a new Brooks Brothers suit, Ginsberg flew to Washington to testify at the Congressional Hearings on LSD before Senator Edward Kennedy, Senator Jacob Javits and others. Allen had prepared his presentation very carefully. It was one of his most persuasive appeals and also a superb piece of scholarship, basically proposing government funded research into the safety of the drug, but none of his suggestions were heeded and, predictably, LSD was made illegal.

The next day, still in his new suit, he flew to San Francisco. This was to become the pattern of Allen's life, logging more air-time than most businessmen as he flew around the country and the world attending readings, conferences, workshops and arts festivals, giving interviews and appearing on television talk shows.

In the early hours of 24 July 1966, the young poet Frank O'Hara was hit by a dune buggy on Fire Island in a freak accident; he died the next evening. Allen had first met O'Hara in the early 1950s, but it was when he returned to New York from San Francisco in 1956 that Allen got to know his poetry. Later, O'Hara and Ginsberg both lived on the Lower East Side, and they would often visit each other. The two men had a lot in common: they were the same age, both homosexual, both poets who moved in circles which were not strictly defined by their literary work. O'Hara was an Assistant Curator at the Museum of Modern Art, and Allen admired the way he dealt with that uptown world. 'Frank taught me to really see New York for the first time, by making of the giant style of Midtown his intimate cocktail environment. It's like having Catullus change your view of the Forum in Rome.'

They dedicated poems to each other: Ginsberg's 'My Sad Self' was to Frank O'Hara, and O'Hara wrote a poem called 'Fantasy/ dedicated to the health of Allen Ginsberg'. O'Hara's death was a shock and Allen went out to Springs, Long Island, with Larry Rivers for the funeral. Two days later, late at night, Allen took some heroin and as Peter stared out of the apartment window, distracted by amphetamine and the noisy night-time Lower East Side clamour, Allen sat and wrote a poem for Frank O'Hara, 'City Midnight Junk Strains'.

I stare into my head & look for your/ broken roman nose
    your wet mouth-smell of martinis
        & a big artistic tipsy kiss.

Allen awoke to the news that Bob Dylan had been thrown from
his motorcycle near his home in Woodstock and broken his neck.
After three weeks he was permitted to have a few visitors and on
19 August, Allen went to spend the afternoon with him, taking a
pile of poetry for him to read: Rimbaud, Blake, Shelley and Emily
Dickinson.

Dylan later telephoned from his bed in Woodstock and asked,
'What's *your* poetry like now?' As for himself, he told Allen, 'What
I'm trying to do now is not too many words. There's no line that
you can stick your finger through, there's no hole in any of the
stanzas. There's no blank filler. Each line has something.' Dylan
had stopped his amphetamine babble and now seemed mostly
interested in country music. He was writing *John Wesley Harding*.

On 23 October Allen gave a reading with his father at the Paterson
YMHA. It was Allen's first reading in his home town and
something of an occasion, with a heavy turn-out of family
members and press. Afterwards, while he was still on stage, there
was some casual conversation with reporters, and Allen revealed
that earlier that day he had gone to the falls on the Passaic River
and smoked some marijuana. The Mayor of Paterson, Mayor
Graves, promptly swore out a warrent for Allen's arrest. Allen
wrote Gregory: 'My first reading in Paterson! With my pappa! ye
Gods!' He was unable to return to New Jersey to see his family
until the matter was cleared up.

His itinerary for November involved a three-day trip to Kansas,
a trip to Toronto and five readings in five days in Boston, where
he made a speech in favour of LSD at the Arlington Church, which
was widely reprinted in the underground press. He gave TV and
press interviews and attended several peace marches and rallies. He
appeared on the *Mike Wallace Show* on CBS and was on NBC the
next night. There was, in addition, his paperwork. That month he
wrote an introduction to a book of poems by Charley Plymell and
transcribed most of his 'auto-poesy' tapes, filling hundreds of pages
of his notebooks with an almost unintelligible scrawl, which he
would later cut and edit, then type up. He wrote ten or more letters
a day and fired off Committee On Poetry checks to the needy; from
an underground newspaper in trouble with the police in London
to sending Gregory Corso $350 to get back to New York from
Athens. 'Just about keeping my head above water by furious

energy at desk,' he wrote Ferlinghetti. 'But it's not natural. Something got to give.'

The Arts Council of Great Britain, in a surprise move, invited Allen to attend an international poetry festival planned for the summer of 1967. He was also invited to London by the 'anti-psychiatrist' R.D. Laing who was organising a conference on the subject of 'The Dialectics of Liberation'. Allen decided to accept the Arts Council offer and stay on for the conference. Since he was now bringing in two to three hundred dollars for each reading, he could now afford to take Louis and Edith to Europe. He made plans for them to join him in London after the conference and to continue on from there to Paris, Venice and Rome. Louis was now seventy-two, and Allen wanted to show him the sights before he got too old to travel.

Allen himself was forty-one, and his life seemed to be falling into a pattern. His enormous appetite for work and travel was, if anything, growing, but as a celebrity, he was spending much of his time presenting his message to the world not only in words but in person.

At the beginning of 1967, Allen, Peter and Allen's mantra-chanting girlfriend Maretta Greer flew to San Francisco. Allen took part in a round-table discussion with Tim Leary, Gary Snyder and Alan Watts organised by the *San Francisco Oracle*, the local underground newspaper which was distinguished by its rainbow printing and psychedelic designs. The *Oracle* came from the Haight–Ashbury area, which was rapidly becoming the centre of the hippie universe. In 1966 there had been a dozen or so hippie communes and a few crash pads in the area; now there were hundreds.

The youth of America, in distancing themselves from the mainstream, had set up their own newspapers, their own music, cafés, bookshops; and in areas where there was a large hippie community they set up crash pads, centres that provided legal advice, free food and medical care, and even job-finding centres run by hippie capitalists. Large communes in the country grew organic produce to be sold by the burgeoning health-food shops. Allen, recognising the hippies as literal descendants of the Beats, saw them as the hope of America. He thought they would transform society, fulfilling the prophesy of Walt Whitman and bringing a new spirituality and a new sexuality to the nation. He identified with their free-wheeling sexuality, their use of psyche-delics and soft drugs, their mysticism and rejection of middle-class mores; it was precisely their ideas about sex, drugs and the Vietnam war that divided them from middle-class America.

The tentative experiments with psychedelic drugs conducted by Allen and Leary had mushroomed so that now over one million Americans had taken them. A large number of kids had gone further; following Tim Leary's dictum, 'Turn On, Tune In, Drop Out', they dropped out of college or jobs and headed for the Lower East Side, Haight-Ashbury or country communes. Acting as a central switchboard for the scene, Allen gave enormous assistance to the underground newspapers, doing benefits and interviews and providing contacts with like-minded people throughout America and the world. Everywhere he went, he spoke of legalising pot and the benefits of LSD. With his luxuriant black beard and huge calm eyes, his beads and finger cymbals, he became almost symbolic of the movement itself, even though he was of a different generation. He assumed the role of the elder statesman of the counter-culture, one of the few older people the hippies felt they could trust.

All the Beats were highly regarded. Snyder was pleased by the widespread interest in American Indians, ecology and tribalism. McClure delighted in his new role as anarchist prince, and both he and Snyder participated in be-ins and love-ins and wrote for the underground press. William Burroughs, living in London, followed the scene with great interest and wrote for the British underground paper *International Times*. Neal Cassady had found his niche as driver of the Merry Pranksters bus. Only Kerouac remained apart, trapped in a 1950s Cold War sensibility along with his mother. Kerouac was convinced that anyone who demonstrated against the Vietnam war was a Communist. Peter Orlovsky said, 'Over and over again he got drunk. He had a vision that he would go up in a tree top with a gun, ready to pop us off. He wanted to shoot the red Communists because we were demonstrating against our country. When it came time to come out and demonstrate; when it came time to write and talk in public; he wouldn't do it.'

On 19 January 1967, Allen, Maretta, Gary Snyder, Tim Leary and many others were all on stage to chant mantras at the Human Be-In held at Golden Gate Park, San Francisco, where an incredible thirty thousand people assembled for what was advertised as a 'Gathering of the Tribes'. The Grateful Dead, Jefferson Airplane and the Quicksilver Messenger Service all played, using a PA system guarded by the Hell's Angels. The Diggers distributed thousands of free turkey sandwiches laced with LSD; Leary told the audience to 'Turn On, Tune In, Drop Out', Jerry Rubin said things like, 'Our smiles are our political banners and our nakedness is our picket sign'; and the audience themselves took up the mantra of 'We Are One! We Are One!' Someone parachuted from a light aircraft and floated gently down to the middle of the meadow causing many people to think that they had just seen God. Gary Snyder ended the gathering by blowing a long note on a conch shell as everyone turned to watch the sun sink into the Pacific. Thousands of people walked to the beach to sit and watch the gathering dusk, and thousands more cleaned up. The memorable day was marred for Allen by an argument with Peter, who was high on amphetamine and refused to join them at the event.

It was the last innocent, idealistic hippie event. That night the police swept down Haight Street; all soft-drug dealers were driven off the scene or arrested, and within weeks the area was flooded with amphetamine and heroin. The communal nature of soft drugs – pot and acid – as demonstrated by the cleaning up of the park, was destroyed and replaced by the amphetamine culture, which would produce Charles Manson.

Poet Larry Fagin regarded Allen's appearance at the Be-In as the occasion which finally made him a household name. 'Allen really became the Allen that we know in 1967. He got out into the public and could never really withdraw completely again. The Be-In skyrocketed the whole Ginsberg cottage industry into outer space. It was the highest visibility that he had up to that point.' There had been jokes and cartoons in the press about Ginsberg as far back as 1959, but now his picture cropped up everywhere as a pictorial shorthand representing the counter-culture and hippie movement. Many of the kids who had a poster of him on their wall had probably never read his poetry.

Allen attended the 1967 Spoleto Festival, where he met Ezra Pound, who shook his hand but remained silent. Afterwards he flew to London for the Arts Council poetry festival. The night Allen arrived, a big party was held at James McNeill Whistler's old house on Cheyne Walk which had been used by Antonioni for the orgy scene in his film *Blow-Up*. Many of the same people were there for the party: young women in velvet and lace and diaphanous scarves and men like dandies from a Beardsley drawing, with long hair and ruffles at their neck and cuffs – the London style that year. The eighteenth century panelling was hung with medieval tapestries, softly illuminated by a huge Moroccan chandelier. *Sgt. Pepper* played quietly in the background, and the butler offered brownies on a silver tray. Unfortunately, there had been some confusion about just how much hashish Alice Toklas's celebrated recipe for brownies actually called for, and half the people at the party succumbed to cannabis poisoning. Allen was talking with Mick Jagger and Marianne Faithfull, when it dawned on Mick and Marianne that the drug had been too powerful. They ran vigorously up and down Cheyne Walk; on returning, Marianne pronounced herself 'high but cool'. People began to panic; some members of Parliament telephoned their physicians and were taken away to have their stomachs pumped. 'Groovy scene here,' Allen wrote Peter the next day.

His first reading was on 12 July. The evening began with W.H. Auden, who shuffled on stage in his carpet slippers and read familiar material. He was followed by Stephen Spender, and the first part concluded with Charles Olson, then living in London. Allen led the Italian poet Giuseppi Ungaretti on stage for the second half and remained at his side to read the English translations after Ungaretti read in Italian. Allen finished the evening with mantras and recent poems. He had more time to stretch out three days later, when he did a solo reading as part of the same festival. He attempted to dispel the formal atmosphere by laying out bananas and incense on the stage, and opened with his usual mantras, but though he read well, the reading was strained and not a great success. 'Horrible. So much like an opera singer's performance,' he said later. 'I worked at it instead of just letting it come.' After the reading, friends took him to Cavendish Avenue, in St John's Wood, to visit Paul McCartney.

All the other Beatles had bought country mansions, but McCartney lived in town, with actress Jane Asher, in a large but unostentatious Regency house. The living room had French windows leading out to a patio. Two paintings by René Magritte hung on the wall, next to one of the versions of the drum skins painted by Peter Blake for the *Sgt. Pepper* album sleeve. A sculpture by Takis stood blinking in a corner next to an Indian sarod. Mick Jagger and Marianne Faithfull were already there.

Mick sat in a rocking chair, his long white silk scarf trailing on the carpet. Paul and Allen sat on the carpet. There was a slight nervousness at first, but everyone worked hard to dispel it. Allen sang a few mantras with his finger cymbals, and tea was served.

They discussed acid, which Paul had taken, and William Burroughs, whose face appeared on the sleeve of *Sgt. Pepper* and who had made recordings in a small studio Paul had provided for poets and experimental musicians, but mostly Paul preferred to tell stories about the old days in Liverpool and about his family. He tried to explain to Allen the nature of British eccentricity and said that most of the exploits of the Beat Generation would have been regarded as perfectly normal in Liverpool. They talked at cross purposes some of the time but it was a friendly visit.

As they talked, Paul had been idly opening boxes of gifts from fans. In one he found a bright red satin shirt, and began to draw paisley patterns, eyes and psychedelic designs on the front of it, using coloured magic markers. When it was time to leave, Paul reached over and gave the shirt to Allen. 'A souvenir of swinging London,' he said.

The next day there was a rally in Hyde Park to demand the legalisation of marijuana. Brian Patten and Adrian Henri read their poems but no one heard them. Allen arrived late with friends wearing his McCartney satin shirt, which was much too tight for him, and carrying a flower. Walter Cronkite immediately appeared with a camera crew and got in a quick interview before Allen reached the podium. Allen began chanting, accompanying himself on the harmonium. A young policeman came forward and informed him that the playing of music was not permitted in a Royal Park. Allen obligingly stopped playing and gave the policeman the flower he had been carrying. The policeman blushed.

A few people smoked joints, and members of the Balls Pond Road commune danced and sang, their bodies and faces painted with psychedelic colours, but it was a small gathering and most people drifted away early, leaving Allen sitting on the grass surrounded by a group of friends and admirers, all chanting the Hare Krishna mantra. That evening, BBC Television's national news carried the music, and the announcer made a *namaste* hand gesture as he said goodnight, a degree of levity never before seen on the BBC.

The month before Allen arrived in London, Rolling Stone Keith Richards had been found guilty of permitting his house to be used for the smoking of marijuana and sentenced to one year in jail and a fine of five hundred pounds. Mick Jagger, found guilty of the illegal possession of amphetamine on the same occasion, was sentenced to three months in jail and a three-hundred-pound fine. Now free on bail, pending an appeal, both had spent one night in jail. They responded to the situation by writing a song. Allen was invited to the recording session.

Through the thick glass of the control room window, Allen saw not only the Stones, dressed in their flowing scarves and ruffled shirts, but John Lennon and Paul McCartney, who had come to sing in the chorus as a gesture of support. Allen was ecstatic. 'It was wonderful,' he told friends the next day. 'They all looked like little angels.' The song they recorded was 'We Love You', which opened with the sound of footsteps and a prison door slamming. Allen wrote Peter, 'Last night I spent at recording studio with Mick Jagger, Paul McCartney and John Lennon looking like Botticelli Graces singing together for the first time. I conducted through the window with Shiva Beads and Tibetan oracle ring.'

Allen was an invited speaker at the Dialectics of Liberation conference, organised by 'anti-psychiatrist' R.D. Laing at London's Roundhouse. The conference was quickly dominated by Stokely Carmichael, a leader of the American Black Power movement, whose plans for a separate black nation gave rise to many late-night arguments. The distinguished group of speakers included Paul Goodman, John Gerassi, Gregory Bateson, Mircea Eliade, Ernest Mandel and Paul Sweezy. Allen's theme was 'Consciousness and Practical Action', which he began by quoting at length from Burroughs's *Nova Express*, as an example of police state methods. He was responding to Gregory Bateson's exposition on the greenhouse effect, which he accurately predicted would manifest itself within ten to thirty years. The entire conference was tape-recorded and released as a set of albums. Subsequently, a woman at the pressing plant, listening to a test pressing of Allen's speech to check for faults, was so upset by the quotes from *Nova Express* that she became ill and had to be sent home. The plant refused to press the record, and other means had to be found, holding up the release of the entire series.

On 28 July Allen drove to Wales with publisher Tom Maschler to spend the weekend at his country cottage in the Llanthony Valley in the Black Mountains. They stopped en route at the magnificent ruins of Tintern Abbey, the inspiration for Words-worth's ode. That afternoon, feeling relaxed in the tranquil setting, Allen took an acid trip. While on LSD he wrote 'Wales Visitation', a nature poem:

> I lay down mixing my beard with the wet hair of the mountainside,
>   smelling the brown vagina-moist ground, harmless . . .

Allen's idyllic summer was interrupted by news of Peter, whose methadrine addiction caused him on one occasion to hallucinate that the house was on fire and, on another, that the window mouldings were bugged or electrified; he began to dismantle them. He was taken to Bellevue to detoxify. Allen was worried, not just for Peter's health, but for his own manuscripts and papers. He wrote to Peter: 'I wish you would quit playing with meth completely, you've seen it in others, it's always created sensory or ideal quirks that you didn't like from the outside. There's now so much chaos and craziness on all sides that I wish we two could be calm and not swept into violence. I say, fix up the house, fix windows fast, quit all needles and all meth, clean up and come over here to England . . . If you get in such state that you lose weight, are obsessed with spy-bugging, call fire-dept. for imaginary fires, wind up with police in house and yourself temporarily in Bellevue – things is gone too far.'

It was a pattern that was to continue for the rest of Allen's life, whenever he left Peter alone for any length of time. In their correspondence that summer, they had been analysing their relationship and clearing up some of the misunderstandings that had grown up between them. Peter felt that Allen needed lots of young boys like Steven Bornstein and was dissatisfied with him. Allen wrote:

'Well, I'm happy making it with you alone as long as we make it. I just chase after boys as a substitute when I get the idea that you don't want to be stuck with me and that I'm generally too old and repulsive to you now after so much familiarity. I mean, I really got the idea, the last year especially, that you basically don't dig making it with me, and so as not to lay my needs on you, I diverted sex lovemaking to others and accepted the situation cheerfully rather than getting hung up on it and laying guilt on you or me. I don't in any case want to monopolise all yr sex imagination and don't fantasise monogamy for you or me. If you've been at all avoiding lovemaking with me because you think I need or deserve younger various cats, well stop that thought and let's make it more again. I'd rather stick with you, if it were still pleasant to you. But basically – I think you've told me – that I'm getting physically too unappealing – which is no betrayal or fault of yours, that's nature – so I've not wanted to force myself on you lest I seem even more unappealing in the cold light of detached awareness. I have need for love touch and sex come but I'm not so nuts as to think that you or anybody has to find me sexy – so I've just been taking what comes to me, without my having to force the situation by willpower . . .

'The worse thing has been the meth – I never know who you are or where you are in the universe – and yet as long as there are practical attachments, as long as there are sex attachments of some kind also, there has to be some reliable meeting place. Otherwise I get scared my mss will disappear or you'll change your mind in the middle of a trip and denounce me for being an old stinking fink.'

Allen's parents arrived in London, and stayed with him at the enormous house that New York society hostess Panna Grady had rented in Regent's Park. Allen and his father gave a reading together at the ICA in Dover Street which was later released as an album, and Allen showed Louis and Edith the sights: from a day visiting Buckingham Palace and Trafalgar Square to a celebrity-packed party at Kenneth and Kathleen Tynan's wonderful house at Thurloe Square.

After touring Europe with his parents, Allen went to stay with his translator, Fernanda Pivano, and her husband, designer Ettore Sottsass, in their beautiful Milan apartment. They spent a weekend with Nanda's mother, who lived at the seaside near Genoa. Nanda knew Olga Rudge and Ezra Pound, and she arranged a drive down to have lunch with them on the Saturday, 23 September. Olga Rudge, an American violinist, had been Pound's companion since the 1920s. They had a small terraced apartment in a large red house in Sant' Ambrogio, near Rapallo. The house was high on the mountainside and had a magnificent view out over Torquello Bay to Portofino on the promontory below.

Eighty-one-year-old Pound, who had been virtually silent for many years, said little during the meal. Allen asked him if he ever met Céline. Olga Rudge said that he had not, so Allen described the visit that he and Burroughs made in 1958. Allen recounted that he had asked Céline which French prose writers he liked, and Céline had mentioned three: C.F. Ramuz, Henri Barbusse and Paul Morand. While Allen tried to remember which of Morand's books Céline liked, Olga Rudge asked Pound, who was still digging into his plate of pasta, 'Ezra, what was the name of that book by Morand you liked so much? You didn't like what he did later.'

Pound looked up, and said in crisp French, '*Ouvert à la Nuit.*'

Allen had brought along his harmonium, and before lunch he had sung Hare Krishna and the Prajnaparamita Sutra. Nanda said afterwards that Pound had looked startled and a little scared when Allen began singing vigorous, loud 'Om's, but Olga Rudge said that he enjoyed it or else he would not have stayed in the room.

They returned to Milan and the next day resumed their translation work. A few weeks later, Nanda left for London, after making arrangements for Allen to visit Pound in Venice, his winter quarters.

Allen checked into the Pensione Cici, not far from the Salute, where Pound frequently ate his midday meals. As he stood in the lobby consulting a wall map of Venice, Olga Rudge and Pound emerged from the dining room. They all had coffee together and Rudge told Allen that if he had any trouble finding the pensione, 'Oftentimes Venetians will walk half a mile to show you a tiny alley.'

Pound suddenly broke his silence. 'Forty years since I've seen anybody do that.'

'Do what Ezra?' she asked.

'Take the trouble to walk you along to show you the way.'

Arrangements were made for Allen to come to luncheon the next day. On 22 October, Allen stood before the lion-faced doorbell of the narrow three-floor house on Calle Querini that Olga Rudge had owned since 1928. Pound was silent throughout the visit. Allen had brought some records for Pound to hear, so they went to the top floor of the house where the record player was. Allen recorded in his journals: 'He had come upstairs swiftly when I asked him to listen, and folded self in chair, silent hands crossed on lap, picking at skin, absorbed.' Allen put on the Beatles' 'Eleanor Rigby' and 'Yellow Submarine'. Pound smiled lightly at the line 'no one was saved'. Allen played Dylan's 'Sad-Eyed Lady of the Lowlands,' and 'Gates of Eden', sometimes repeating words aloud for Pound to hear clearly. Allen had even brought along Donovan's 'Sunshine Superman'. 'Is this all too much electric noise?' he asked. Pound smiled and sat still. 'Sat there all along,' Allen wrote. 'I drunk, he impassive, earnest, attentive, asmile.' Allen continued the concert by chanting mantras to Krishna, Tara and Manjusri. Hearing the Manjusri mantra, Olga Rudge came to the top floor and joined them, saying, 'It sounded beautiful down there.' Pound said nothing. That evening, Ginsberg went to Harry's Bar and got very drunk.

On 28 October, Allen was seated in the dining room of the pensione with the English poet Peter Russell, the critic Michael Reck and Reck's six-year-old son, waiting for Pound to arrive. An Italian crew making a programme about Pound waited outside, cables trailing across the floor. Rudge and Pound eventually appeared, and Pound seated himself on Allen's right. Allen had spent the previous week reading the 'Cantos' and walking around Venice, trying to find the places mentioned there. He had heard that Pound would respond to specific textual enquiries. 'I found the "Place of Carpaccio's skulls",' said Allen, 'but where's the place where "in the font to the right as you enter/ are all the gold domes of San Marco"?'

Pound looked up from his fish, 'Yes, when the font was filled, now they've changed it, it used to be like that.'

'I walked half a mile yesterday, looking for the spot in Dei Greci, in San Giorgio. Finally looked in San Marco.'

'It used to be like that,' continued Pound. 'The centre was filled with water and the reflection had the domes.' Olga Rudge added that the font in San Giorgio Dei Greci had been fitted with a copper rim, which they now filled with water; the centre was no longer filled.

After getting replies to a number of specific questions, Allen now decided to try some of his own work on Pound. He looked through his notebook, looking for a phrase. 'I've been trying to find language equivalent for that light on water. Yesterday I arrived at this: Leaped on Vaporetto,/ sun yellow in white haze, Salute's/ silver light, crooked-mirrored on the glassy surface.'

Pound looked Allen in the eye as he repeated the line, 'light, crooked-mirrored on the glassy surface.' Allen smiled at him. 'You approve of that?'

'That's good,' said Pound, and returned Allen's smile.

'The phrasing of your poems has had a very concrete value for me as reference points for my own perception,' said Allen. 'Am I making sense?'

'Yes,' said Pound, but after a pause mumbled, 'But my own work does not make sense.' Both Allen and Michael Reck assured him that it made sense to them. 'A lot of double talk,' said Pound. He seemed to search for words, then said, 'Basil Bunting told me that there was too little presentation and too much reference.'

Allen replied that the year before, the poet Basil Bunting had told him to look at Pound because Allen had too many words. Bunting showed Pound as a model for economy in presentation of sensory phenomena via words.

Michael Reck told Pound that reading his poetry, one was struck by how real the descriptions were, even if one hadn't experienced the thing oneself. 'Reading your poetry, I often feel this myself,' he told Pound. 'Your poetry is often shockingly direct.'

Pound sat silent, rubbing his hands, then said, 'At seventy I realised that instead of being a lunatic, I was a moron.'

Both Allen and Reck protested, but Pound insisted. 'My writing. Stupid and ignorant all the way through. Stupid and ignorant.'

Reck said, 'In your poetry, you have an ear. That's the most important thing for writing poetry. So it's hard for you to write a bad line.'

'It's hard for me to write at all,' Pound answered with a faint smile.

The conversation continued, and Allen asked if he would like to give a reading in the United States; in Buffalo, maybe, or San Francisco.

'Too late,' said Pound.

'Too late for what?' Allen laughed. 'For us, or for your voice?' Allen told him that it was never too late; that he had shown the way and that the more of Pound's work he read, the more convinced he was that it was the best of its time.

'The intention was bad,' replied Pound, 'that's the trouble. Anything I've done has been an accident. Any good has been spoiled by my intentions. The preoccupation with irrelevant and stupid things.' Then, speaking slowly and with emphasis, he said, 'But the worst mistake I made was that stupid suburban prejudice of anti-Semitism. All along, that spoiled everything.'

'Ah, it's lovely to hear you say that,' Allen said. It was Pound's first public expression of regret for the anti-Semitism of his wartime broadcasts for Radio Roma. Just as Allen had appeased Kerouac's anti-Semitism, so he had accepted all sides of Pound's character. 'Anyone with any sense can see it as a humour,' said Allen, 'in that sense part of the drama. You manifest the process of thoughts, make a model of the consciousness, and anti-Semitism is your fuck-up, like not liking Buddhists, but it's part of the model as it proceeds. The great accomplishment was to make a working model of your mind. Nobody cares if it's Ezra Pound's mind, but it's a mind like everybody else's.'

Allen leaned over to Pound, who was staring straight ahead, and told him, 'But you must go on working, to record the last scenes of the drama. You still have a great deal to say. After all, now you have nothing to lose. You *are* working aren't you?' But now Pound remained silent. Allen continued, 'Ah, well. What I came here for, all this time, was to give you my blessing, then. Because, despite your disillusion, unless you *want* to be a Messiah, then you'll have to be a Buddhist.' Pound smiled.

'But I'm a Buddhist Jew,' Allen continued. 'Perceptions have been strengthened by the series of practical exact language models which are scattered throughout the "Cantos" like stepping stones. Ground for *me* to occupy, walk on. So that, despite your intentions, the practical effect has been to clarify my perceptions. And, anyway, do you now accept my blessing?'

Pound hesitated, opening his mouth for a moment before speaking. 'I do.'

They all walked Pound and Ezra Rudge to their doorway, where Allen took Pound by the shoulders and looked him straight in the eye for a long moment before saying, 'I have told you what I came here to tell you, and I also came here for your blessing. And now may I have it, Sir?'

'Yes,' he nodded, 'for whatever it's worth.'

Allen stood talking with Olga Rudge as the others said their goodbyes to Pound. 'But if you wait,' she told Allen, 'and have patience, he needs to talk. He thinks all his work so bad, whereas when he reads it into tape, you can tell he reads with enthusiasm, some parts. Other parts of course he dislikes, but that's natural, after years to be self-critical, anyone would.'

Then Allen turned to Pound and kissed him respectfully on his right cheek. Pound held Allen's hand and said, 'I should have been able to do better.'

'It was perfect,' said Allen. 'I haven't properly yet sung Hare Krishna to you either. I'll be around a few days more anyway, maybe ... See you.' Pound stood at his doorway, hesitating, waving everyone down the alley.

The next evening at nine, Allen was waiting for the vaporetto at the Salute boat station, a floating platform on the Grand Canal. Pound and Olga Rudge appeared, on their way to the Carmini Church, where a woman friend of theirs was singing in a Vivaldi concert. Allen asked if he could accompany them, and Olga Rudge said, 'Certainly.' They climbed aboard the vaporetto, and Allen sat behind them, leaning forward to speak between the backs of their heads so that they could both hear him. He told them the story of Julius Orlovsky as a Manichaean who would not speak for fourteen years because he believed that all the evil in the universe came from his body and mouth. Olga Rudge laughed and asked, 'Are you a Manichaean, Ezra?' but he would not answer.

Allen sat behind them in the ornate seventeenth-century candle-lit nave and wrote a small poem-sketch of the scene: 'Old man sat before me,/ brown canvas shoes, one heel raised alert,/ hat and cane in hand/ Smooth woodslab resting/ under a fold in his coatback –/ white cheek beard dyed red by/ velvet light,/ black not entirely faded from/ back of his skull,/ fringed with grey hair,/ candle gleam through white web.'

A delicate theme played on the violin began and Olga Rudge rose, closely followed by Pound, and walked along the north aisle of the church to stand closer to their friend. When the piece was over, they left without waiting to hear any further pieces and began walking home through the alleyways. Allen spoke to Pound about the 'Cantos' and Pound's apparent inability to finish them, saying that the work was not a static crystalline idealised structure but an open-ended one, 'that is, epic, "including history," of movement of your mind and record of focused perceptions existing in *time*, and changing in time. Anything you write now will refer back to the beginnings and alter all that went before, like turning a Venitian blind,' Allen said. 'So *anything* you do now is OK and will be proper, appropriate, as means of altering preceding thought-flow by hindsight. Am I making sense?'

'It's all tags and patches,' replied Pound.

Allen spoke more about the 'Cantos' and finally asked, 'Is your problem one of physical depression that keeps you from recording and registering these final perceptions – whatever you are *now*?'

'The depression's more mental than physical,' Pound answered. They reached the house, and Allen went in with them and sat down while Olga Rudge lit a fire. Allen talked more about the 'Cantos', but Pound remained silent. Then Allen asked, 'Do you know the enormous influence you've had?'

'I'd be surprised if there was any,' Pound replied dubiously, but looked interested.

Allen recited a few short poems by Robert Creeley, then spoke of Charles Olson and John Wieners. He asked Pound if he was at all familiar with Allen's own work, but Pound shook his head. 'Well, oddly, it might even please you,' Allen told him. He asked if Pound understood that his writing had been a model for a whole generation of younger poets in the United States, including himself, who at forty-one was exactly half his age.

'It would be ingenious to see any influence,' replied Pound.

Olga Rudge brought in cups of Ovaltine and a copy of *Canto CX*. 'Has Mister Ginsberg seen this?' she asked. Allen said that he would return it, but she asked Pound to inscribe it to him.

Pound hesitated a long time, then said, 'Oh, he doesn't *want* it.'

'Well, yes. Sure, I do,' said Allen. 'If you want to check your perceptions. I absolutely do.'

Pound took the small volume and signed, 'Alan Ginsberg – dall'autore – Oct 29, 1967. Ezra Pound.'

Olga Rudge invited Allen to come the next day and sing to Pound on the night of his eighty-second birthday. Allen arrived at 10 p.m., wearing the red satin shirt given to him by Paul McCartney, a large Buddhist trikaya emblem around his neck. He carried his harmonium. Pound was sitting in the downstairs room, warming himself before the fire. Allen ran through the Prajnaparamita Sutra in both English and Japanese, then followed it with a rousing version of the Hare Krishna mantra. There was a break for some birthday cake and champagne, then Allen chanted the Three Buddhist Vows. He recorded the events in his journal:

'Then in silence till, to illustrate effect of his composition on mine, read – with indifferent voice alas – few pages of "Middle Section of Long Poem On These States." Oops! Silence. Eek! Put that down fast after asking, do you see the relationship in method of composition? Silence. So picked up harmonium and chanted 50 verses of "Gopala Gopala Devaka Nandina Gopala" – high and sweet, and low solemn. Then explained "Gopala means Krishna cowboy," and said goodnight and "Happy Birthday Krishna." He smiled at that. Leaving from door I demanded, "Well, say *Goodnight*!" He nodded amiably, said "Goodnight." So I left.'

Allen saw Ezra Pound a few more times, and once they met at lunch at the Pensione Cici. The elderly waitress carefully boned Pound's grilled trout. He did not look well, and though he shook Allen's hand when Allen said goodbye, he did not speak throughout the meal or when he left.

The season was over. Many of the pensiones had closed up, and few tourists braved the wind and rain to walk on the Piazza San Marco. The outdoor cafes had taken in their chairs and potted palm trees. The orchestras had all gone home.

15 Paterfamilias

. . . if the wisest man would, at any time, utter his thoughts in the crude indigested manner as they come to him in his head, he would be looked upon as raving mad.

Jonathan Swift

Allen did not fully accept his middle age; he worried about approaching old age and ill health, about his deteriorating looks and childless future. On the plus side, at forty-one, he now had a sufficient body of solid work behind him, enough to guarantee his place in American Letters. He was easily the most famous poet in America. He was witnessing the widespread application of many of his ideas about free love and the use of consciousness-expanding drugs. Hundreds of underground newspapers mixed anti-Vietnam War news with esoteric discussions of the philosophies of eastern mystics previously unheard of in America; there was extensive interest in meditation, mantras, the occult, astrology and every possible kind of spiritual quest from Shamanism to Aleister Crowley. Allen had seen the initial tentative ideas of the 'New Vision', which he first discussed with Lucien Carr, Bill Burroughs and Jack Kerouac, back in 1944, blossom into a widespread youth movement which involved possibly millions of people worldwide.

Other movements and rebellions took root and blossomed in the 1960s: women's liberation and the struggle for black civil rights. Of the three, the youth movement was the most fragile, containing within it the seeds of potential tragedy. But the 1960s were not yet over. Woodstock was yet to come, in 1969, but so, too, were the assassinations of Martin Luther King and Robert Kennedy, and the brutal clashes between authority and the counter-culture at Kent State and in the streets of Chicago.

Allen came back to New York on 15 November 1967. Peter was in San Francisco, and Allen wrote telling him to stay out there as long as he wanted but warned him to stay off methadrine. He added: 'I want to live with you but I can't live with meth, things are so chaotic outside the house I need calm in the house. And I know that what I want to do is live quietly, stay at home a lot and work on Poetry. I did that in Europe and it makes me feel good. No meth and maybe even no phone.'

Peter arrived in town a week later, calm and off speed. Allen was relieved of the guilt he always felt when Peter was taking a lot of meth. 'In the late sixties, Peter started going crazy, partly because of his speed trips, perhaps. I felt I was to blame, that this was the result of my demands on him,' he said. But now the atmosphere in East 10th Street was relaxed, and Allen slowly eased his way back into the New York scene, dispensing advice, contacts and money. His poetry foundation continued to distribute thousands of dollars each year to needy poets, and Allen himself gave endless benefit readings for pacifist groups, war resisters, deserters, little magazines, underground newspapers, small presses and the inevitable legal defence campaigns.

Ever since the Beatles had begun to extol the virtues of the Maharishi Mahesh Yogi in August 1967, Allen had wanted to meet him. With the Beatles' endorsement, the Maharishi was attracting an enormous number of young followers, including other rock musicians such as the Beach Boys. The Beatles had even announced their intention of going to India to study at his ashram (they did in fact go, in April 1968). In January 1968, the Maharishi came to New York. Allen had telephoned for tickets, and on the return phonecall he was invited to meet the Maharishi in his suite at the Plaza Hotel.

The room was filled with flowers, and Allen sat on the floor along with dozens of devotees, who were listening to every word spoken in the Maharishi's high-pitched, squeaky voice. Ginsberg had heard reports that the Maharishi had said a number of outlandish things at recent press conferences, such as 'Poverty is laziness' and 'Communism equals weakism', so he had a number of questions to ask him. Hippies were particularly vulnerable to this type of teaching since, having rejected their own culture and changed their own perceptions of reality with acid, they were wide open to exploitation.

Allen had no arguments with the dictum that everyone should meditate for half an hour each morning and evening, and he remained open-minded about the Maharishi's claims that his special mantra form was more effective than any other, since Allen hadn't tried it. Allen even thought that the Maharishi's high-powered, highly organised method of advertising meditation, and the setting up of what were, in fact, pyramid clubs of people meditating, would certainly tend toward a more general peacefulness in the land if they caught on. It was his political statements that worried Allen as being 'definitely dim-witted and a bit out of place'. Ginsberg described the meeting:

'After I was introduced, I sat at his feet and literally started yelling at him – spent half an hour almost, challenging, arguing – all in good humour tho his business managers and devotees gasped with horror occasionally, but I never got impolite and he stayed calm and rather sweet, so no harm.' Allen said that the Vietnam War was a problem troubling everyone in his audience that day, certainly all the young people there and that though, as the Maharishi had said, the United States was 'Creative', its creations were massively negative ones, as in Vietnam, and that was why people were restless and looked to persons such as Mick Jagger or the Beatles for spiritual guidance. It was because young people were 'bugged by war!' He said that the Maharishi had not confronted the problem satisfactorily.

Maharishi replied, 'Johnson and his secret police have more information than you, so they know what they are doing.'

'Ah,' said Allen. 'They're a buncha dumbells. Don't you know that your implicit support of authoritarianism is making a lot of people wonder if you're not some kinda CIA agent?'

'CIA?' the Maharishi giggled. His devotees began muttering.

'It's a common question,' Allen explained, 'so it should be proposed. You shouldn't stand around silent and fearful to talk.' Allen asked him, 'What about the kids who have resisted the draft? Should they go to war and murder people?'

'Either way,' the Maharishi said, 'meditate.' Allen asked him about the Hare Krishna mantra and the Maharishi said that one mantra does not fit everybody. Since everyone is different, everybody needed a different mantra. Allen thought that made sense, so he went on to ask about drugs, since the Maharishi had condemned drug usage.

'There wouldn't be anyone to see you today if it hadn't been for LSD!' Allen told him. The devotees gasped.

'Well,' said the Maharishi, 'LSD has done its thing. Now forget it. Just let it drop.' He said that meditation was stronger.

'Excellent,' said Allen. 'If it works, why not? If it works.' He said that he would be glad to try it and that it couldn't do anything but good. But then the Maharishi said that acid damaged hippies' nervous systems.

'I had six hippies visit me in a room in Los Angeles and had to take them into the garden because they smelled so bad.'

'What?' yelled Allen. 'Don't you realise that acid hippies were the largest part of your audience today?'

But the Maharishi was adamant. He would not be moved from his conviction that hippies smelled. As for a final judgement on the war, he didn't want to get into that. He only wanted to emphasise, meditation, meditation, meditation.'

'That's fine,' said Allen. 'I'll meditate.'

It was early on a cold February morning at East 10th Street. Peter was lying on his bed with a girl who had spent the night. Allen was in his room with Louis Cartwright, a friend of about six months. The phone rang and a friendly voice with a Denver accent, someone Allen didn't know, asked, 'Have you heard the news from the West?'

Expecting to hear of yet another arrest, Allen replied, 'No, been away all week.'

'You haven't heard the news from the West? Neal Cassady is dead.'

Peter, on the other line, gasped, 'Oh!'

On 2 February 1968, Neal had taken a train down to Celaya, a town in the mountains just north of Mexico City, and from there had gone by taxi to San Miguel de Allende, where his girlfriend Janice Brown, known to everyone as JB, was waiting for him. At noon on 3 February, Neal left JB's house to return to Celaya to pick up his 'magic bag' which he had left there. He told JB that he would walk the two and a half miles from her place to the railroad station at San Miguel, and would then walk all the way down the railroad tracks to Celaya, about fifteen miles, counting the ties as he went. JB thought that he was kidding.

He got to San Miguel by mid-afternoon, but got caught up in a Mexican wedding party, where he washed down a handful of Seconals with a large quantity of pulque, the sacred Aztec drink made from the fermented sap of the maguey plant. The next morning, a group of Indians found him lying beside the railroad tracks a mile and a half outside San Miguel. He had apparently been trying to make good his word to walk to Celaya. He had passed out from the drink and drugs, wearing only a T-shirt and jeans as protection against the cold mountain rain, and had died of exposure; the death certificate said 'generalised congestion'.

Allen's first thought on hearing the news was, 'Sir Spirit's now home in Spirit,' an idea he was to use in 'Elegy for Neal Cassady', a tearful poem, written a few days later:

Tender Spirit, thank you for touching me with tender hands
When you were young, in a beautiful body,
    Such a pure touch it was Hope beyond maya-meat . . .

After friendship fades from flesh forms –
heavy happiness hangs in heart,
    I could talk to you forever,
    The pleasure is inexhaustable,
    discourse of spirit to spirit,
    O Spirit.

The poem ends, 'Sir Spirit, an' I drift alone:/ Oh deep sigh.'

As the 1960s drew to a close, there was a great movement within the youth counter-culture to leave the cities and establish communes. In the country, they could grow organic vegetables, build tepees or geodesic domes, live in whatever sexual combination they favoured, have children and be free from the pressure of police, drug addicts, rape and street crime, which had begun to plague the hippie enclaves in the cities. Ginsberg was not immune from the trend. Ever since Gary Snyder had set up house on land that he and Allen owned in the Sierra Nevadas, Allen had been thinking about getting a place outside New York where, away from the pressure of the Lower East Side, Peter could kick drugs – something like a health farm where poets could dry out.

He asked Barbara Rubin to look around for a place in upstate New York. She found one five miles outside the small town of Cherry Valley, a sleepy little village of clapboard houses, about eighty miles west of Albany. The farm consisted of a tumbledown farmhouse, a barn and outbuildings set in ninety acres of well-drained land with a creek running through it. The land was surrounded by state forest. It seemed ideally private.

The house had four bedrooms and a large attic. There was a big kitchen leading directly off the porch with a large range and sink with an old hand pump. The foundations were made from huge slabs of stone, crudely piled but very strong, built by the original settler of the land. Allen bought the farm and appointed as farm manager underground film-maker Gordon Ball, a friend of Barbara's who also wanted to escape the city.

Barbara had taken Allen's request that she scout for a farmhouse for them all to live in to mean that she and Allen were going to marry. Though she told a number of friends in New York, she knew better than to mention this to Allen, perhaps fearful that he would shatter her dreams or, more likely, waiting for the right moment to manoeuvre him into it. Allen and Barbara arrived in Cherry Valley in mid-March, 1968. 'Barbara Rubin that first night in Cherry Valley sleeping next to me played with my pecker trying to rouse me, but I was indifferent in fact afraid. Didn't want to be active, didn't want to be drawn in ... I said aloud, "I didn't wanna, I didn't wanna, I didn't wanna, I didn't wanna," – four times.' – Allen knew Barbara's agenda: 'She wanted children, very serious – after our first copulation on floor of Filmmakers Archive office, she expected much more sex of me, or love, or children ...'

Allen's main motivation in setting up the farm was to get Peter out of the city and away from methadrine. That spring, Peter was still seriously addicted and was repeating his street-cleaning act, crawling about in the gutter on East 10th Street with its overflowing garbage cans, scrubbing the filthy sidewalk as Puerto Rican street kids watched him suspiciously from their stoops. It was almost impossible for Allen to communicate with him. Allen also had in mind to get Kerouac to the farm to dry out, rather like Alan Tate taking Hart Crane to the country, but Jack would not leave his mother.

In the fall of 1966, Gabrielle Kerouac had suffered a stroke, which paralysed her, confining her to bed. Needing a nurse for Mémère, Jack married Stella Sampas in November 1966. The sister of an old schoolfriend from Lowell, Stella was older than Jack and had never married. She was a reliable, efficient woman who had known Jack all his life. He knew he could trust her to nurse his mother, which she did. Jack bought a house in Lowell for the three of them, and Gabrielle's health began to improve. Jack spent his time at the bar owned by his new brother-in-law, Nick. He had no wish to live on a farm.

Peter, clearly in a bad way, arrived at the farm with his brother Julius. It soon became apparent that it was going to be hard to get him off methadrine; he had hidden supplies all over the farm. In his 'leper voice', so-called by Allen for its gruffness and despair, Peter would sometimes go off on long Shakespearian monologues, which were quite poetic; but he could also be frightening. On one occasion, as Allen and Barbara pulled up at the farm in the VW bus, Peter ran out wrapped in heavy chains, brandishing a machete. While Gordon and the others froze in horror, Allen walked straight towards him and took him in the house.

Peter was not the only problem; Allen and Barbara argued constantly. Barbara was a terrible driver and would drive down the middle of the road and even on the wrong side, because she was always looking at the person she was talking to, and she was always talking. She and Allen never had much of a sexual relationship, but now her megalomania began seriously to impinge on Allen's life. Many of the arguments concerned religion. Barbara was becoming more and more involved with Judaism and thought Allen should follow suit. Gordon remembered one terrifying car ride on the way to Cooperstown: 'I was holding on for my life in the back seat and . . . Allen finally got fist-shaking angry and said, "I'm a Buddhist Jew!" and kept resisting her . . . She was beginning to realise obviously that he wasn't going to come around.'

People began to visit and in April, Gregory Corso and Belle moved into the front bedroom vacated by Allen, as the first official Committee On Poetry residents.

It turned out that the house was not as isolated as they thought. Living on a patch of land adjacent to a corner of Allen's land was Ed the Hermit. Ed Urich had escaped to the country from Greenwich Village many years before. He lived in a small shack and kept a few goats for milk. He wore bib overalls and an Agway peaked cap. For a hermit, he had an enormous amount to say and would visit the farm every day to make predictions about the weather and advise on what to plant and when. He was lonely and the poetry farm was a godsend to him, particularly in the summer when the girls walked about naked. Allen and Ed soon struck up a friendship, and Allen would usually find Ed pottering about in the yard when he came down in the morning and went out on to the frosty grass to urinate, wrapped in an old coat.

In February 1968, the anti-war activist Abbie Hoffman had been to see Ginsberg in his 10th Street apartment. It was the height of the Tet Offensive in Vietnam, which was to kill over two thousand American troops. Hoffman said he and Jerry Rubin wanted to hold a Festival of Life in Chicago in August, the same time as the Democratic Party Convention, as an example of a life-style alternative to the one being promoted by the assembled politicians. To this end they planned to launch a Youth International Party – called Yippies – and run their own candidate, a pig named Pigasus. The idea was to emulate the Human Be-In in San Francisco, with a similar line-up of teachers, yogis, poets, musicians and anti-war speakers. Like everyone who had an idea for a festival, Abbie wanted Allen to contact the Beatles and Bob Dylan.

Allen, interested in the general idea, called Jerry Rubin. Allen had known Abbie only a few months, whereas his acquaintance with Rubin dated from the 1965 anti-war marches in Berkeley and the organisation of the 1967 Be-In. Rubin had run for Mayor of Berkeley in 1967, and Allen had supported him. Jerry told him that they would go soon to Chicago to apply for a permit and to try to arrange for thousands of kids to camp out. Allen, inundated with work, could not take a central role, but he did subscribe his name to the project and on 7 March, took part in a nationally televised press conference with Abbie and Jerry and the folksingers Phil Ochs and Arlo Guthrie. Allen outlined the purpose of the gathering as a manifestation of 'a desire for the preservation of the planet', then sang the Hare Krishna mantra for ten minutes before the cameras.

The country was in great turmoil. A Gallup Poll published on 31 March, showed that only 36 per cent of Americans approved of LBJ and only 23 per cent approved of his handling of the war. On 4 April 1968, Martin Luther King Jr was assassinated, provoking widespread rioting. In Chicago, Mayor Richard Daley gave riot police his infamous instructions to 'Shoot to kill', an ominous warning of what was to come that summer. On 23 April, students at Columbia University barricaded the offices of the dean, sparking a wave of college protests against the Vietnam war which affected nearly every campus in the nation. On 3 June, Valerie Solanas attempted to murder Andy Warhol, and the next day, Sirhan Sirhan killed Robert Kennedy. Everywhere, people seemed to be turning to violence to redress their grievances.

Mayor Daley's office refused to give the Yippies a permit to hold their Festival of Life. Allen met with Abbie Hoffman in Chicago to discuss the situation. Even if they cancelled the festival, thousands of people would come. Allen felt obliged to attend, since he had associated himself with the event from the beginning and felt a responsibility to make sure it was as peaceful as possible.

President Johnson's decision to withdraw from the presidential race caused the anti-war groups to rethink their tactics. Many had been going to Chicago specifically to protest against LBJ. A large coalition of anti-war groups was formed, headed by David Dellinger, Rennie Davies and Tom Hayden, and a series of marches and demonstrations was planned. The Yippies coordinated their festival with the coalition.

Mayor Daley's response was to put his 11,500 police on twelve-hour shifts, mobilise 5,500 National Guardsmen and air-lift in 7,500 troops under LBJ's command from Fort Hood, Texas. The police were armed with heavy wooden clubs and tear gas canisters. It was becoming clear that a Festival of Life with dancing, poetry and music was very unlikely, so Rennie Davies and Tom Hayden began courses in Karate and other forms of self-defence for their people. About a week before the convention, Allen went to them to advocate that they teach meditation and chanting instead. In Allen's view, 'It was an invitation to violence rather than preparing for a real festival. My role was of chanting "Om" and I thought the chanting of "Pigs" was the wrong mantra.'

Allen returned to Chicago on Saturday, 24 August, and met the Yippie 'leaders', Abbie Hoffman, Jerry Rubin, Ed Sanders, Paul Krassner and others. Thousands of young people, invited by Hoffman and Rubin, were converging on the city and heading for Lincoln Park. The police said that the park was to close at 11 p.m. The Yippies had no permit and no contingency plans. Violent confrontation was inevitable, but as it later turned out, this was what Jerry Rubin had wanted all along.

One of the editors at *Esquire* magazine decided to get a different angle on the convention; instead of sending a regular reporter, he commissioned William Burroughs, Terry Southern and Jean Genet to write their impressions of it. It was the first time Burroughs had been in Chicago in twenty-six years, and he didn't like it. That evening Allen had the chance to test the power of mantra in calming a violent situation. At ten-thirty, he and Ed Sanders were walking through Lincoln Park. It was very dark, and people had lit bonfires in garbage cans. There was a sudden burst of lights, and a wave of police moved in fast to clear the park. Allen was surprised and said to Ed, 'They are not supposed to be here until eleven!' He began to chant 'Om!' He and Ed slowly walked out of the park, gathering a group of people, until fifteen or twenty of them were uttering a solid deep vibrational chant as they walked towards the Lincoln Park Hotel. It took about twenty minutes to reach the road dividing the park from the hotel, by which time he had attracted about a hundred people, all calm and unharmed by the police.

The next day, Sunday, Allen went to Lincoln Park, where a PA system had been set up and John Sinclair and the MC5 were playing. Allen asked if he could do a bit of chanting, and they gave him the microphone. He chanted Hare Krishna for about fifteen minutes, then sang William Blake's 'The Grey Monk' to try and calm the crowd, still excited by the MC5's 'Up Against The Wall' rhetoric. The rock music resumed and Allen walked away, surrounded by a group of young people.

Suddenly they saw a great mass of police sweep through the centre of the park towards the PA system. Allen felt an adrenalin flash and, following his own precepts, sat down and began chanting 'Om!' He had originally intended to chant for about twenty minutes to calm himself, but when a crowd gathered, he continued – for seven hours. Many people joined in, some staying for a short period, others for an hour or so. At dusk the crowd grew to several hundred. A core group of about fifty remained the whole time. At one point someone passed Allen a note from an Indian saying, 'Will you please stop playing with the mantra and do it seriously by pronouncing the 'M' in OM properly for at least five minutes? See how it develops.' Allen realised that he had been using the mantra as a song instead of as a means of concentration, so he started to do it the Indian's way. He explained what happened in a *Playboy* magazine interview:

'After about 15 minutes, my breathing became more regular, even, steady, as if I were breathing the air of heaven into myself and then circulating it back out into heaven. After a while the air inside and outside became the same – what the Indians call *prajna*, the vital silvery, evanescent air. Then I began to feel a funny tingling in my feet that spread until my whole body was one rigid electrical tingling – a solid mass of lights.' By this time it was 8 p.m. and Allen had been chanting for more than four hours. He sat facing the John Hancock building which was just beginning to light up. 'I felt like the building, except I realised it wasn't alive and I was. I felt a rigidity inside my body, almost like a muscle armor plating. With all this electric going up and down and this rigid muscle thing, I had to straighten my back to make a clear passage for whatever flow there was: my hands began vibrating. Five or six people were touching them. Suddenly I realised that I was going through some kind of weird trance thing like I read about in books. But it wasn't mystical. It was the product of six continuous hours of chanting "Om", regularised breathing and altering body chemistry.'

He put his legs up into the full lotus position, something he could rarely do, and it felt good. 'I realised that it was possible through chanting to make advances on the body and literally to alter states of consciousness. I'd got to euphorias, ecstasies of pleasure, years before; but this was the first time I'd gotten neurological body sensations, cellular extensions of some kind of cosmic consciousness within my body. I was able to look at the Hancock Building and see it as a tiny little tower of electrical lights – a very superficial toy compared with the power, grandeur and immensity of one human body.'

He had never chanted that long before and was amazed at the effect it was having upon him. 'It felt like grace. It felt harmoniously right that some psychophysical rarity should be happening on that political occasion as dusk fell on Lincoln Park and the Hancock Building lit up on the horizon. If there'd been panic and police clubs I don't think I would have minded the damage. Clubbing would have seemed a curiously impertinent intrusion from skeleton phantoms – unreal compared with the natural omnipresent electric universe I was in. This was the most interesting thing that happened, for me, in Chicago.'

The next night Allen was walking in Lincoln Park with Burroughs and Genet. They came upon a crude barricade made from picnic tables, trash cans and police crush barriers. The police could have easily encircled it and pinned down the demonstrators. There were a lot of young people there, yelling and banging on metal trash cans. It seemed to Allen that they were looking for a confrontation with the police, since it was 11 p.m. He began chanting 'Om!' and was joined by more and more people until almost everybody at the barricades was doing it. After about fifteen minutes, a police car came rolling down the hill behind them and crashed straight into the barricade, with a tremendous sound of breaking glass. People scattered. Allen retained his composure and, still chanting, removed himself from the scene. People shrieked and screamed as the police attacked them. On this occasion 'Om!' was no protection.

Leaving the park, Allen, Bill and Genet saw a mob of police burst out of the trees in pursuit, not of kids, but of news photographers. The police had taken off their badges and name plates, and some had even removed their unit patches. The club-swinging mob advanced on the crowd, and at the end of the incident, seventeen media reporters, pressmen from the *Washington Post*, the *Chicago American*, the *Chicago Sun–Times*, *Life*, *Newsweek* and cameramen from ABC, CBS and NBC had to be taken to Henrotin Hospital for emergency treatment.

The next evening, Allen, Bill, Genet, Terry Southern and Dick Seaver from Grove Press made their way to Lincoln Park. A large crowd lined the outskirts of the park, ready to make a quick getaway, and an even larger one was moving towards the centre of the park where a group of about four hundred clergy and local people, horrified by the police brutality of recent days, had set up a ten-foot-high cross under one of the park lights to support the members of Students for a Democratic Society, the National Mobilization Committee and the Yippies in their fight for the privilege of staying in the park at night. The congregation was exhorted to join in a non-violent vigil and sing 'We Shall Overcome', 'Onward Christian Soldiers' and various pacifist songs and hymns.

The police began to set up their lines, and the clergy lifted up their cross and carried it away from the crowd to erect it facing the spotlights that marked the police lines, interposing the cross between police and demonstrators. Allen and his companions sat on a small hill overlooking the scene. Suddenly huge tear gas canisters came raining down on the crowd, crashing through the branches of the trees. Gas filled the air, a great white plume in the police spotlights, enveloping the crowd. People ran in panic, screaming, their eyes streaming with tears. The police fired a second volley, this time into the crowd. The ministers took up their cross and retreated. Allen grasped Bill's hand and Genet's, and they walked slowly towards the edge of the park, away from the scene of carnage, as the police advanced into the crowd, clubbing stragglers to the ground. Huge street-cleaning trucks, specially adapted, advanced on the crowd, spraying tear-gas. Some of the crowd fought back vainly, ripping up the sidewalk to throw at the truck windows. A dozen patrolcars were engulfed and trashed as the kids broke up into mobs, roaming the streets, vandalising everything in sight. Hundreds of people were arrested and hundreds more badly beaten by the club-wielding police.

The thousands of kids thrown out of Lincoln Park moved on to Grant Park, where they continued to sing 'We Shall Not Be Moved', hymns and anti-war songs. The police tried to tear-gas them out, but the wind blew most of the gas into the air-conditioning ducts of the giant Hilton Hotel overlooking the park, where most of the delegates and press members were staying. The kids chanted all night, and many of the lights in the hotel stayed on as press and delegates watched the extraordinary spectacle below. In the middle of the night, the National Guard was brought in. Armed troops in battledress arrived all through the night in jeeps and military transport, as tear-gas swirled through the hotel lobby and the noise of the trucks and the kids' loudspeakers ensured that everyone in the Hilton knew what was going on. By this time, many of the press and delegates shared Genet's opinion of Chicago. He told Burroughs, 'I can't wait for this city to rot. I can't wait to see weeds growing through empty streets.'

The main battle of Chicago occured outside the Hilton Hotel on 28 August. The National Mobilization Committee had organised a pacifist rally and march, starting at the band shell in Grant Park. The police and troops had sealed off the park but Allen, Bill, Genet and Terry Southern found a way in by climbing over some trestles. They reached the stage area, and Dellinger invited them onstage to address the crowd. Allen was unable to speak and just managed to croak 'Om!' The others said their bit and moved to the back of the stage as the speeches continued.

The peace march began assembling, and Dellinger asked Allen and his companions to lead. Allen Ginsberg, William Burroughs, Jean Genet, Terry Southern, Richard Seaver and the British photographer Michael Cooper, their arms linked together, all holding flowers, were an obvious target for press photographers, who swarmed around, delighted by the line-up. The march progressed for a couple of blocks until it reached the edge of the park, where National Guardsmen blocked the way with machine guns and jeeps equipped with barbed-wire shields.

The march was not allowed on to the city streets. Dellinger asked Allen to calm the crowd and the troops by chanting. 'There was this long line behind us, there was this great mass of armed people in front of us. It was a tricky, scary moment,' Allen said later. He took the microphone, and with the tattered remains of his voice, he began chanting 'Om Sri Maitreya'. People sat down, expecting a long wait, and quite a few began to chant along with him. When Allen's voice finally gave out everybody just sat quietly.

In the end David Dellinger announced that the march was over; the government had forced them to abandon their citizen's right to have a peaceable assembly for redress of grievances. The march broke up but it was impossible for anyone to get out of the park because the troops were still blocking all the bridges, which were the only exits. The police, however, tried to clear the park by firing tear-gas at the marchers. Allen and Bill finally found an unmanned bridge and escaped. Meanwhile, a huge group had managed to force a lightly guarded bridge and get back to the city across Michigan Avenue, only to run straight into the Reverend Abernathy's Poor People's Campaign march, complete with mules and wagons, which was just then progressing up the avenue. The police had had no choice but to grant the Reverend a permit for his march, unless they wanted the press and cameras to focus on a full-scale riot in Chicago's black South Side as well. It was like an episode in a science fiction book, with the mules contrasted against the troops in battledress and gas masks, and the thousands of ragged long haired kids breaking through the armour to join in.

Just before the Hilton Hotel, the mules and wagons were allowed across the intersection, then as the Poor People's Campaign marched out of sight, the others found themselves surrounded on three sides by rows of angry cops. The police, moving in arcs of twenty or thirty men, sliced into the crowd with their clubs and with Mace, beating people indiscriminately. Tourists, newsmen, people on their way home from work, were all attacked and beaten. The *New York Times* reported, 'Even elderly by-standers were caught by the police onslaught. At one point the police turned on several dozen persons standing quietly behind police barriers in front of the Conrad Hilton Hotel watching the demonstrators across the street. For no reason that could be immediately determined, the blue-helmeted policemen charged the barriers, crushing the spectators against the windows of the Haymarket Inn, a restaurant in the hotel. Finally the window gave way, sending screaming middle-aged women and children back-ward through the broken shards of glass. The police then ran into the restaurant and beat some of the victims who had fallen through the windows and arrested them.'

So many people were injured that the Eugene McCarthy campaign headquarters on the fifteenth floor was turned into a makeshift hospital, but the police even burst into that and swept through clubbing people, leaving great pools of blood on the floor. Ginsberg, with some poetic licence, described the scene in his poem, 'Grant Park: August 28, 1968':

> The teargas drifted up to the Vice
>> President naked in the bathroom
> – naked on the toilet taking a shit weeping?
> Who wants to be President of the
>> Garden of Eden?

Even those taking part in the convention had to acknowledge the blood in the streets after the seige of the Hilton, and it was Connecticut Senator Abraham Ribicoff who did it, in his nomina-ting speech. He told the assembled delegates, 'With George McGovern as President of the United States we wouldn't have Gestapo tactics in the streets of Chicago.' Mayor Richard Daley rose up from his seat, shaking his fist at Ribicoff and mouthing anti-Semitic obscenities, but the grey-haired Ribicoff stood his ground and simply said, 'How hard it is to accept the truth.'

The convention went on to nominate Hubert Humphrey. He would lose the November election to Richard Nixon, and the war in Vietnam would drag on.

Allen was only confirmed in his view that the United States was becoming a police state. He said in *Playboy*: 'I think everybody who watched television during the convention experienced a widening of consciousness because ... outright police brutality was shown so clearly that even TV and radio commentators were saying, "This is a police state!" Before Chicago, that would have been considered an impropriety, even though many already felt it was true, secretly. To make it official like that turns things over in people's minds; suddenly they wake up in a different country from where they thought they were. But it was there all along!'

When Allen had first told Kerouac – in one of their recent telephone conversations – that he was going to Chicago, they quickly got into an argument. 'Kerouac thought that Dave Dellinger, the leader of the anti-war movement, was Jewish,' Ginsberg said. But when Kerouac attacked Hoffman and Rubin, 'Ginsberg, what are you hanging around with all those dirty Jew Communists for, anyway?' Allen realised what the key was. 'I said, "What the fuck, is that what your mother put in your mouth? Tell your mother she's got a dirty cunt! And I'm gonna shove a coke bottle in it and put some gasoline in it and explode it!" and he started laughing. All of a sudden got friendly and pleasant and began talking common sense instead of the usual contentious macho trading of ego pinpricking. So I found what he was actually doing was just seeing how much ego I got, and how much attached to it I was, and if I could be upset still, until I finally just laid it back on him, realising that he was just being playful with me rather than really mean.'

Clearly the idea that he and Kerouac still had some sort of friendship was so important to Allen that he would go to almost any length to maintain it, even if it meant explaining away years of anti-Semitic insults as playfulness. He recognised that Kerouac was sick and made the same allowances for him as he had for Naomi. 'How do you draw the line between complete honesty and disillusionment?' he asked a class of poetry students. 'I never solved the problem because when I read his books I realise he was enormously brooding vaster of mind and heart than myself, and that my irritation was jejeune and egoistic and self-defensive and contributed to his death and disillusionment, so I always feel guilty. On the other hand, occasionally I'd come up against him

when I would realise he was full of shit. And *vain*! Totally vain!
That whole thing wasn't wisdom at all, it was like some kind of
complete paranoic vanity! That's why it rubbed so badly.'

After a few days in New York with Burroughs, who was writing up
his Chicago article for *Esquire* before going home to London, Allen
returned to the farm, where Herbert Huncke had joined the others.
Encouraged by Allen and by a grant from a wealthy patron, Huncke
was assembling more of his occasional writings and essays for a
book. His first, *Huncke's Journal*, had been published by Diane di
Prima in 1965. The farm was in full swing with a menagerie that
included a horse and chickens. Barbara had bought some African
geese which shat all over the front porch and bit everybody. They
kept them for a while because they were as good as guard dogs.
Allen learned how to milk Bessie, the cow, and the goats, and helped
pick the young cucumbers for the pickle barrel. Two acres that Peter
and Gordon had planted out on strictly organic principles yielded an
enormous amount of fresh, tasty vegetables, and they began to think
about self-sufficiency. A row of old maples grew alongside the patch
of grass next to the house, and Allen liked to sit in their shade at a
small table, working on his proofs and notebooks.

Allen's success with chanting had furthered his interest in music.
He had already set Blake's 'The Grey Monk' to music and
performed it in Chicago. Now he began work on the whole of
Songs of Innocence and Experience, which Blake had originally
sung but for which no musical notation survives, if there ever was
any. 'Finding right melodies for a dozen or more songs and taping
them – lovely extention of my mantra practice,' Ginsberg wrote.

Allen bought a dusty old upright pump organ at a barn sale,
cleaned it up, and installed it in the living room. In the evenings,
with his Aladdin lamp burning, Allen sat and painfully picked out
the melodies of his Blake songs, working on them over and over
again, until he was able to get the melody in his head recorded on
tape. The old organ whistled and groaned, the lamplight flickered,
and moths flew around its bright globe like a scene from the
previous century. Lee Crabtree, a musician who had played with
the Fugs, came to stay on the farm and taught Allen basic music
notation.

Barbara was getting more involved in the Jewish religion and
began to spend a lot of time at a yeshiva in nearby Sharon Springs.

She now realised that her master plan of marrying Ginsberg and converting him to Judaism was not going to work. By this time she had distanced herself from the other people on the farm, and in September she left to go and live at the yeshiva.

The nights got chilly, and Peter began cutting and stacking wood ready for the winter. He was in good health, ruddy and tanned from spending his days outdoors. It seemed that the farm was working.

Winter comes early to that part of upper New York State, but they were prepared. By the time the last of the leaves had blazed scarlet and fallen, they had more or less finished work on the house. Though it was not yet completely winterised, the house now had insulation in the attic, and the walls of all the bedrooms were panelled in raw pine. The cellar was filled with Ball jars of home-grown tomatoes, beans, beets and squash. Apples stood in rows on the wooden shelves, alongside jars of cloudy home-pressed apple juice. They had picked all the cucumbers and harvested all the crops. The barn had been fixed up to provide shelter for the cow and the horse, and plenty of hay and fodder was laid in. The chicken coop and the goat house were both weather-proofed, and thick waterproof winter boots and warm woolly socks and hats had been bought. They achieved a remarkable amount during that first season and things seemed to be going well.

In November, Allen fractured his hip and cracked four ribs in a car crash after taking Lawrence Ferlinghetti to the airport. He spent several weeks in the hospital in Albany, then returned to the farm for an enforced period of rest. He hobbled around on crutches and spent his time reading, composing Blake songs and answering his mail. He wrote Ferlinghetti: 'It's been a sort of pleasure to go through, I never had a broken bone before in 42 years.'

In January 1969, Maretta Greer arrived on the farm unexpectedly, having been deported from India. Gordon remembered her arrival: 'It was an average, cool winter day, overcast, temperature about zero. And here was this woman with short hair, with a blanket wrapped around her getting out a car and walking barefoot through the snow towards the house. I thought, "Terrific! Wonderful!"'

Maretta was installed in the attic where she set up a little altar and spent a lot of time crying and complaining how uncivilised the

United States was. She expected to be treated as an honoured guest and made no effort to help with the cooking or cleaning. Since Allen was leaving on a four-month reading tour at the end of February, Gordon asked Allen if he would ask Maretta to do a little of the work.

Allen broached the subject with her just as he was coming down the stairs. He was three or four steps from the bottom and asked, 'Say Maretta, while I'm gone, can you pitch in and do a little work around the place?' Maretta was outraged, 'I'll never tell you the secrets of the seven mysteries!' she screamed, and knocked his crutches out from under his arms.

'Keep on!' said Allen, encouraging her to let it all out. Her voice grew shrill. She was insulted that he should be leaving so soon after her arrival. '[She thought] I was leaving her there like in a mental hospital or a retirement farm,' said Ginsberg, 'she was very demanding.'

On 18 February, back briefly in New York City, Allen gave the first public performance of his Blake songs, accompanied by Lee Crabtree on piano and Cyril Caster on guitar. This was the beginning of Ginsberg's practice of using musicians as an integral part of his act. That June he went into Apostolic recording studio in Greenwich Village.

Rather than have a small combo play all the tunes, the producer, Barry Miles, treated each song individually: 'The Garden of Love' was arranged as a country and western number, whereas 'The Blossom' came out like a minuet. This meant that specialist musicians were needed for some of the tracks to achieve special effects. At the suggestion of Charles Mingus, they used Herman Wright on bass and Julius Watkins, famous for his work with the Thelonious Monk Quintet, to play French horn.

To get the appropriate sonorous drum rolls on 'The Grey Monk', Blake's powerful cry against tyranny, Elvin Jones was brought in. He arrived looking very sharp, accompanied by his Japanese wife, Keiko, who carried his drum kit and then assembled it. Jones listened carefully to the song, played exactly what was needed, collected his five hundred dollars and disappeared. It would be fifteen years before Allen played with him again. Percussionist and trumpet player Don Cherry added the finishing touches to many of the tracks. The whole project was recorded and mixed for ten thousand dollars. Though originally intended for the Beatles' Apple Records, it was released on MGM in 1970.

Allen was able to spend most of the summer of 1969 on the farm. There was a new calf and kittens, and an expensive new water system was being installed, which used the force of gravity to pump water up to the house. With a fifty per cent state grant, they constructed a pond below the barn and stocked it with fish. It rapidly attracted frogs and all the wildlife associated with ponds, and soon looked as though it had been there forever. Allen actually had time to relax. He walked around the fields a lot, knee-deep in wildflowers and grasses, listening to the birds and insects. He communed with the goats, the horse and the cows, kept up his gigantic correspondence and helped bring in the harvest.

That summer, Jane Kramer's biography *Allen Ginsberg in America* was published by Random House to generally favourable reviews. Even *Time* recognised his fame and influence: 'Ginsberg has also come to be legitimised by a wide public (*Life*, *Playboy*, TV talk shows) and all but officially designated as a peculiar national treasure of sorts.' Of the book itself, which was based on a two-part *New Yorker* profile, Ginsberg told *Publisher's Weekly*, 'I wish Miss Kramer had been more realistic about homosexual situations.'

Recognition in another form came earlier in the year, when Ginsberg received a grant of five thousand dollars from the National Institute of Arts and Letters, 'In recognition of his creative work in literature.'

On the evening of 21 October there was a phonecall from journalist Al Aronowitz. Gregory took the call, turned to Allen, and cried, 'Al! Jack died.'

The next morning, they rose early and dressed warmly. Allen and Gregory took a walk through the snow to the row of trees at the top of the property and there, at the end furthest from Ed the Hermit's cabin, they carved Jack's name in a tree.

Kerouac died the classic drunkard's death, from cirrhosis of the liver. At the end of 1968, he had moved his wife and mother to St Petersburg, hoping that the Florida sun would speed Gabrielle's recovery. Although Jack sometimes typed all night, he spent most of his time watching television, alternating beers with sips of whisky. His mother lay bedridden in the back room, tended by

Stella. On 20 October, after a sleepless night, he was watching 'The Galloping Gourmet' on TV when his liver finally collapsed. He dragged himself to the bathroom, where Stella found him vomiting blood. He was given emergency surgery but never regained consciousness.

Allen had a reading at Yale that day. The students had stretched a twelve-foot paper banner across the stage which read, 'In Memorium: Jack Kerouac, 1922–1969' and on the line below, 'Neal Cassady, 1927–1968.' Peter and Allen climbed on stage. Allen arranged his papers, books and harmonium, then said, 'We'll begin with a prayer.' He and Peter chanted the Diamond Sutra, Jack's favourite. When it was over there was scattered applause, but Allen quietly told them, 'You don't applaud a prayer.' He began by reading a number of choruses from Jack's 'Mexico City Blues', repeating the final lines of the '211th Chorus' three times, to make sure the youthful audience got it:

> *Poor*! I wish I was free
> of that slaving meat wheel
> and safe in heaven dead.

He ended his reading of Kerouac with the '242nd Chorus', the last in the book, and stressed the final stanza:

> Stop the murder and the suicide!
> All's well!
> I am the Guard.

Allen read his own work, and then there was the usual question period. Someone asked why Kerouac was so important and why had he turned so right-wing in his last decade. Allen waited almost a minute before venturing a reply. Finally he said, 'Well, he was the first one to make a new crack in the consciousness.' He told them that pot, rock, 'doing your own thing', 'making a new Jerusalem', etc had all come out of that crack.

'He broke open the fantastic solidity in America, as solid as the Empire State Building, that turned out not to be solid at all. His vision was what the universe as we will experience it is – golden ash, blissful emptiness, a product of our own grasping speed.' Allen said that Kerouac had tried to follow the implications of his sad–comic view of things to the bottom of his own nature, transcribe it in its own onrushing spontaneous flow, and leave it there for others. 'So he drank himself to death,' Allen said bluntly. 'Which is only another way of living, of handling the pain and foolishness that it's all a dream, a great baffling silly emptiness, after all.' Allen ended it there.

The next day it was crisp and cold as Allen and Peter, Gregory and John Clellon Holmes drove to the funeral in Lowell, Jack's hometown. It was then an ugly mill town with empty factories sprawled along the banks of the Merrimack, its miraculous self-renewal still many years away. They found the bar owned by Nick Sampas, Jack's brother-in-law, and sat reading the funeral announcement in the *Lowell Sun*. The bartender said that Nick had gone to the airport to pick up Stella, and that Jack's body had arrived in Lowell on an earlier flight. The funeral was to be held the next morning at eleven in Saint John the Baptist church, where Jack had been an altar boy thirty-five years before.

Nick and Stella arrived, and tearful introductions were made. Jack had told countless stories about them all, but Allen was the only one Stella had ever met because when Kerouac went into town to see his friends he refused to allow her to accompany him. The Sampas family insisted on putting them all up and feeding them, and they suddenly found themselves in another world, that of a close-knit Greek-American family, sharing their food and wine and their bereavement. They were plied with lobster, shrimp and steaks. Bottles of Retsina were produced. Suddenly they remembered that they had made no arrangements for flowers.

Gregory sketched an elaborate design of a heart on a lotus, but at that time of night the florist could only manage a simple heart of red roses with their names on the ribbons: Allen, Peter, Gregory, John, Bill, Lucien and Robert (Creeley). Across the centre was a ribbon reading 'Guard the heart'.

At the funeral parlour, Jack lay surrounded by flowers, a rosary entwined around his fingers, wearing a yellow shirt, a houndstooth sports jacket and a red bow tie with white dots. Allen reached over and touched his forehead. 'Touch him,' he said. 'There's really nothing inside.' He quoted a few stanzas from 'Mexico City Blues' while Peter fought back the tears. Gregory knelt at the side of the coffin weeping openly. Allen described the scene in a letter to Carolyn Cassady:

'Jack in coffin looked large headed, grim lipped, tiny bald spot top of skull begun but hair still black and soft, cold skin makeup chill to finger touch on his brow, fingers wrinkled, hairy hands protruding from sports jacket holding rosary, flower masses around coffin and shaped wrinkle-furrow familiar at his brow, eyes closed, mid-aged heavy looked like his father had become from earlier dream decades – shock first seeing him there in theatric-lit coffin room as if a Buddha in Paranirvana pose, come here left his message of Illusion-wink and left the body behind.'

Jack was given a high requiem mass, complete with priest circling the coffin with a swinging censer. Allen, in beads and beard, was a pallbearer. There were many cameras and reporters, and Allen was interviewed next to the hearse. At the cemetery, after a priest said final prayers, they all took roses from a wreath and placed them on the coffin before it was lowered. Allen was asked to throw the first handful of dirt. He did, and the others followed suit. The TV people packed up their equipment, and the gravediggers began to shovel the October earth.

The next day, Allen gave a teach-in at Columbia University. 1969 was an angry year, a time when much of the idealism of the mid-1960s began to sour. In May, during the battle for People's Park in Berkeley, an unarmed student was shot from a rooftop by police as he watched a demonstration. At Altamont the Hell's Angels murdered a member of the audience and roughed up the performers at a Rolling Stones concert. Moratorium Day on 15 October brought tens of thousands of people to the streets to protest the war, and on 15 November, in Washington DC, a quarter of a million marched against the war. By the end of the year, 31,000 American troops had been killed in Vietnam. There seemed no end to the slaughter.

On the farm, the telephone rang continually, and Allen would hurry to answer it, sitting on the little child's chair by the front door, where he spent hours receiving horror stories from New York, Newark, San Francisco and Seattle. He sat, brow furrowed, his huge address book opened before him, fingers dialling lawyers, the Civil Liberties Union, his father or the *New York Times* to complain angrily about distortion in their news coverage of demonstrations or arrests.

Allen's fall tour took him all through New England and Canada. Then in Chicago on 7 December, he delivered his testimony for the

defence in the so-called Chicago Conspiracy Trial. David Dellin-
ger, Rennie Davis, Abbie Hoffman, Tom Hayden, Lee Weiner,
John Froines and Bobby Seale were all charged with conspiring to
incite a riot at the 1968 Democratic Party Convention. Bobby
Seale's trial was quickly separated off, much of it occurring with
him bound, gagged and shackled to his chair, in full view of the
jury, which found him guilty. On appeal, he was acquitted of all
charges. The lumping together of the anti-war organisers with
media-freaks Hoffman and Rubin was also unfair, but they
decided to fight it together, with William Kunstler and Leonard
Weinglass as their defence lawyers.

Judge Julius Hoffman presided, and his encounter with Allen
manifested a total lack of communication. The large court doors
swung open, and Allen strode rapidly down the carpeted aisle,
paused, and gave Judge Hoffman a Hindu *namaste* salute of
greeting, holding his hands in prayer before his beard. The tiny
seventy-four-year-old judge peered down at him from his high
perch, then sank even deeper into his leather chair, his eyes
half-closed.

Leonard Weinglass, for the defence, led Allen through a
description of his profession: teaching, lecturing, writing and
reciting poetry. Allen explained in some detail his studies in India
and Japan and carefully spelt out the names of all the swamis he
met there, so that the court reporter could list them accurately. He
pointed out that all his studies involved chanting and praying,
'praying out loud and in community'. The judge looked puzzled.

Allen described his role in the February 1968 news conference
when plans for the Yippie Festival of Life were announced, and he
told the judge the contents of his speech, trying to show that their
plan had been to hold a peaceful festival, like the San Francisco
Be-In, not a riot. He said that he had concluded his speech by
chanting the 'Hare Krishna Mantra' for ten minutes for the
television cameras. Then, to demonstrate, Allen launched into the
mantra: 'Hare Krishna, Hare Krishna, Krishna Krishna, Hare
Hare, Hara Rama, Hare Rama, Hare Hare, Rama Rama.'

Prosecutor Thomas Foran, among others in the court, laughed.
William Kunstler objected, saying that the chanting had been a
serious presentation of a religious concept. 'I don't understand it,'
said Judge Hoffman. 'The language of the United States District
Court is English.'

'I know,' said Kunstler, 'but you don't laugh at all languages.'

'I didn't laugh, I didn't laugh,' protested the judge. 'I didn't laugh at all. I wish I could tell you how I feel. Laugh – I didn't even smile.' Allen pointed out, helpfully, that the language was Sanskrit. 'That's why I didn't understand it,' Hoffman said, and told Kunstler, 'You may use an interpreter for the remainder of this witness's testimony.'

Hoffman could not see what the mantra had to do with the case, and the prosecution agreed, saying, 'He is talking about things that have no conceivable materiality to this case.'

'It adds spirituality to the case, sir,' Allen offered. But Judge Hoffman had had enough.

'Will you remain quiet, sir!' he yelled at Allen, who murmured an apology.

Next, Allen's harmonium was presented in court, and Allen was asked to identify it.

'It is an instrument known as the harmonium, which I used at the press conference at the Americana Hotel,' said Allen, happily playing several ascending chords.

'All you were asked was what it is, and instead you played a tune on it,' snapped Hoffman, but as Allen tried to explain, the judge cut him off and adjourned the case until the next morning.

Allen testified for the whole of the next day, during which time he was able to deliver a spirited reading of Blake's 'The Grey Monk' and his own poems 'Going To Chicago', 'The Night Apple', 'In Society' and 'Love Poem On A Theme By Whitman', which the prosecution asked him to read, hoping that their homosexual themes would discredit him as a witness. At the close of his third day on the stand, he was asked to read 'Howl'. He did not have a copy with him but read as much as he could remember, which was quite a lot. For the most part he was questioned on his recollections of the days in Chicago, and of specific meetings with the defendants, many of which he was able to recall in great detail. The defence was trying to show that the intent was peaceful and that mantra chanting, as a way of calming crowds, had been planned from the very beginning, but most of the attempts to prove this were rejected by the judge, who sustained constant prosecution objections to the testimony. Some of Allen's testimony did genuinely seem to surprise the court, particularly the fact that he chanted 'Om!' for seven hours straight.

The case had a predictable outcome. The academics, Lee Weiner and John Froines, were aquitted of all charges; all the defendants were absolved of conspiracy; Hoffman, Rubin, Dellinger, Hayden and Davis were individually convicted of crossing state lines to incite a riot. Judge Hoffman then spent two days giving 175 contempt-of-court citations, totalling nineteen years in prison, to the eight defendants and their attorneys, Weinglass and Kunstler. Bobby Seale and Kunstler both received more than four years for contempt.

It was to be two years before the US Court of Appeals overturned the verdict and most of the contempt citations, finding that 'The demeanor of the judge and the prosecutors would require reversal if other errors did not.' Once all the jail time had been voided and the citations reversed, Jerry Rubin revealed, 'We *wanted* disruption. We *planned* it. We *were not* innocent victims. Guilty as hell! Guilty as charged!' Allen, who had accepted all along that the Youth International Party were planning a non-violent festival of youth, was as annoyed as everyone else to find that the original good intentions had been undermined. 'Jerry Rubin covering our karma with shame, disgrace,' Allen wrote. 'I alibied for him in Chicago, now he says peace was a lie, we meant to start a war. Guilty 1968.'

By 1970 five people were living on the farm: Allen, Gordon, Julius, Peter and Denise Mercedes. Denise, a guitar player from New York, had moved to the farm at the end of 1969 to be with Peter. Peter bought a banjo, and they spent hours together in their room off the porch making music. In the spring of 1970, the poet Ray Bremser, his wife, Bonnie, and their three-year-old daughter, Georgia, moved into the attic.

June came, and Peter's behaviour remained erratic. He was still taking amphetamines from time to time, his gravelly voice giving him away. Naturally strong and energetic, he was almost super-human on speed. He and Gordon built a fox-proof fence to protect the chickens. Peter fenced several acres of garden land to keep out deer, then he and Denise planted out an acre of soybeans. He embarked on the ambitious task of posting the entire land, all ninety acres of it, and early each day he and Julius would disappear and only return at dusk, their bare chests burned a deep tan by the sun.

Since Julius did only what he was told, he sometimes spent all day standing in the hot sun in the middle of the soybean patch, because Peter had forgotten about him. If he was not told to go to bed, Julius would sit all night on the settee, his big boots arranged neatly at his side; he was always waiting in the upstairs corridor in the morning for someone to tell him to make himself some breakfast. Sometimes several people would tell him, so Julius had several breakfasts.

Peter went through a phase of speedy good humour when he was fun to be with, but it was impossible to talk seriously with him. Then, at the end of June, he and Allen finally sat down and talked. Allen noted in his journal, 'Sad conversation with Peter. He'd secretly spent all his bank money on great stores of amphetamine. Plastic packages later burned in guilt in trashcan. So no money more in hiding though his checkbook said full.' The thousands of dollars spent on speed had originally been obtained by Peter's selling his letters from Allen, Jack and other friends. Although he told Allen he had destroyed the speed, he had clearly not destroyed all of it. It was hidden all over the farm, and Allen and Gordon had already discovered some of it in the barn. It was a very difficult time for everyone.

The speed made Peter very paranoid. He was convinced that the young redneck farmers from Cherry Valley were going to come and kill everyone on the farm, and he watched the lane suspiciously for lights. He and Denise had a small black-and-white television, which Peter thought was watching him. He destroyed it with an iron bar and threw it out into the yard, following it with the remains of the two car batteries that had powered it. He gave careful consideration to Allen's views on sex and decided that Flash, the horse, was not safe from Allen. 'That Ginzy, he'd fuck anything,' he muttered, and slept in the barn to protect Flash.

His withdrawal, when it came, was anguished. He lay outside the house, banging his head on a rock until he bled, crying, moaning and cursing himself, 'Why do I do it? It's poison, it's fucking poison!' Allen hovered over him, helpless, offering advice, knowing all along that Peter had more speed hidden away.

'Let's chant together,' suggested Allen. 'Maybe that'll ease the pain.'

'That stuff doesn't work,' Peter retorted angrily, 'You don't really believe in all that chanting do you?'

Allen looked sorrowful. He sat next to Peter and wiped the sweat away as Peter writhed and burned up on the damp evening grass. The windy darkness was punctuated with the green neon flashes of fireflies. Peter pulled through.

One day Peter and Ray Bremser got drunk, and Allen yelled angrily at them. The purpose of the farm was for them to dry out, he told them; alcohol and drugs were banned. The problem was that the ban was very difficult to enforce, since he did not feel that he could extend it to his visitors, or even other members of the farm like Gordon or Bonnie. It was a constant problem for him. Allen himself used drugs rarely: the occasional joint at a party or LSD in special circumstances, such as Big Sur or the Welsh countryside. It was also only sensible to keep the farm as clean as possible from drugs in case the police raided.

Shortly after Memorial Day, 1970, Peter and Denise bought a pig. Allen's face dropped as the piglet exploded from the sack and ran in confused circles in the front yard. The farm already had a horse that no one rode or groomed, a billy goat that did nothing but smell and eat; there were dogs, cats, geese and even a gerbil in a cage in the kitchen, but none of them did anything but consume food. The piglet was named Don't Bite Me, and lived in Denise and Peter's room. It followed them everywhere, rooting in the garden, digging up the lawn, and would come running whenever they whistled. It grew rapidly, but they still kept it in their room even when it weighed more than Denise.

More people arrived, and in July, Gregory moved in again. Trouble began almost immediately. He deeply resented not being allowed to drink and followed Allen around, telling him that the only reason he had come there was to kill him. 'You, you're dead already. And Peter! He's just a parasite on you!' he yelled at Allen, who sat under the maples, trying to read the manuscript of the French translation of *Planet News* that his translators had brought up to the farm to work on with him. 'This is Gregory, Allen. Your oldest friend. I have to kill you to save you from all this!'

Allen gave up trying to work and went inside, while Gregory tagged along, stamping his feet and shouting abuse. Allen flopped exhausted in a chair and said, 'You know, though I've known you for so many years, I don't think I like you so much anymore. It's been a long time since there was any friendship. It's all been unpleasantness.' The implications of this remark kept Gregory quiet for the rest of the day.

A few days later, beer cans were found floating on the pond. Everyone trooped down to look at them, and a full-scale investigation began at once, with all eyes on Gregory and Ray as the culprits. Allen wrote, 'Beercans found in the pond, and their smiling faces turned snarling and screaming at each other at dusk – Peter drunk also screaming in garage. Second day, all calm and a wave of happiness passed through tranquil grassy yard – yesterday more vodkas, swearing and threats of death.'

Gregory made life as unpleasant for Peter as he could, calling him 'Allen's little bum boy', abusing his poetry and accusing him of being a leech on Allen. Peter kept out of his way as much as possible because sometimes, when Gregory really provoked him, Peter had to hit him, which he always regretted afterwards. Gregory could also be violent when drunk, and on one occasion attacked Gordon and gave him a black eye because he refused to buy beer for him in Cherry Valley.

Allen wrote Ferlinghetti, 'Gregory's here. Several wild screaming drunk explosions. Quiet today. We'll kick his ass if he starts again.' A few days later Gregory returned to Buffalo, where he immediately wrote to ask Allen for an allowance of a hundred dollars a week.

Allen replied, 'It's maybe not practical supporting 13 people, 1 horse, 2 cows, 10 ducks, 30 chickens, 1 pig, 3 dogs, 3 cats, 1 jerbil and now one big white rabbit here and promising to support you at $100 a week in Buffalo – take it easy on me.' He told Gregory that he had set up the farm as a refuge, suggesting that the farm was where Gregory should be if he wanted Allen to support him, 'but since you don't live peaceably with others, or relatively peaceably, it makes domestic situation too tough to live with when you take such perverse pride in putting down everyone and attacking people when drunk. It's too hard to live with. If you really want to stop off here, you'll have to come to some kind of peaceably sober understanding with the household outside of me. Which basically means no lushing and exacerbation from fire-engine mouth and fists. I'm tired and just wanna get my desk work done.'

There was a constant stream of visitors that summer, with sometimes as many as two dozen people on a weekend. Poets Robert Creeley and Allen DeLoach were both teaching at Buffalo, so the farm was a convenient half-way stop on the drive to and from New York City. Artist Wynn Chamberlain and poet John Giorno came, dressed in flowing Indian cotton and chiffon. Paul Blackburn arrived looking thin and wan. He joked about lung cancer as he chain-smoked the Gitanes that later killed him.

Carl Solomon spent a few days on the farm after Allen reassured his mother that he would be safe there and told her how good for his health the trip would be. He arrived on the Greyhound and immediately called his mother from the drug store. That evening, Carl and Allen lounged in the living room. 'We're not young and pretty anymore,' said Allen.

'No, but we can still be old and bestial,' replied Carl, and they both laughed. Carl was very relaxed, but when the conversation took a political turn, Carl stopped and said that he could not discuss such things because his uncle would not approve and it made him nervous.

Elsa Dorfman, Herbert Huncke and a friend came to stay. 'Man, we got such boss wheels outside,' said Huncke, entering the kitchen as if it was a Times Square bar. 'Dig the threads,' he told Allen, grabbing his hand to make him feel the quality of his clothes. 'We've brought pink gin,' he said happily. 'Where shall we put it?' Allen was flustered and tried to explain that they must not give any to Ray and Peter, because they were supposed to be drying out. Among other visitors that summer were translators Claude Pelieu and Mary Beach, come to work on the French edition of *Planet News*, and Ann Charters, who came to interview Allen for her ground-breaking biography of Kerouac, published in 1973, which she dedicated to Allen.

Allen spent the summer evenings tootling away at the pump organ beneath the kerosene lamp. He often slipped into Denise and Peter's room to watch the news of the war on the flickering blue screen (they had replaced the TV). Leaving their room, he would stand in the yard and look up at the thick band of the Milky Way, and imagine the destruction taking place half the world away. The news that September was grim: The United States was bombing Cambodia, Laos and Vietnam from bases in Thailand.

Allen felt impotent in the face of the US war machine, but using his skill at 'reading between the lines in the *New York Times*', he found an area where his special knowledge of drugs and his anti-war efforts could be combined: he began a massive project to investigate the role of the CIA in opium smuggling in South East

Asia. He already had extensive files, which he now added to by gaining access to the files of *Time-Life*. His spring 1971 reading tour opened with a week in Washington, DC, and he used this time to visit Les Whitten in the office of columnist Jack Anderson, in search of a vital letter that had mysteriously disappeared from the files of a Senate government operations committee. Both the *New York Times* and *Ramparts* were researching the story (at Ginsberg's instigation), but whereas they had only telephoned Anderson's office to see if he had a copy of the letter, Allen appeared in person.

'To our surprise, his detailed files and probing questions were thoroughly professional,' Anderson's 'Washington Merry-Go-Round' column reported. 'The poet's theory is that the CIA has been compelled to help the opium farmers in the mountains of northern Laos in order to keep them fighting the communists. The CIA has raised a 10,000 man army from the Meo tribesmen. Without their opium trade, they might require massive US economic aid.' The letter Allen was looking for was written by a former CIA employee, S.M. Mustard, and was addressed to former Senator Ernest Gruening of Alaska. It charged that South Vietnam Vice President Nguyen Cao Ky 'took advantage of [the] situation to fly opium from Laos to Saigon.' With a copy of the letter in his folder, Allen went off to interview Walter Pincus, former Senate Foreign Relations investigator with a lot of inside information on Indo-China.

Ginsberg established that eighty per cent of the heroin on the streets of America came from South East Asia, via Saigon (twenty per cent was the official line). In charge of the opium traffic was Nguyen Van Thieu – the head of the US puppet government in South Vietnam – Madam Nhu, Marshall Ky and other top politicians, all aided and abetted by the CIA which provided the air transport. Allen's point was that the misery and violence on the city streets was directly related to US policy in South East Asia.

On 4 March, Allen and Louis Ginsberg gave a joint reading at the Corcoran Gallery, in Washington. The audience was filled with society hostesses and government top brass. Richard Helms, the head of the CIA, sat in the front row, and Allen delivered an impassioned version of 'Pentagon Exorcism', looking straight at him. He had met Helms at a reception before the reading and immediately quizzed him about the CIA's role in smuggling opium.

Helms, of course, denied that CIA-owned airlines had anything to do with it, and the discussion finished with a wager. Allen bet his bronze vajra (Tibetan thunderbolt) that he would prove that the secret CIA-Meo airbase at Long Chen was used as a depot for trans-shipment of Golden Triangle opiates to Saigon. Helms accepted the wager and agreed to meditate for one hour each day if he was proved wrong. (Senate hearings later proved Ginsberg right. It is not known if Helms began to meditate.)

16 The Lion of Dharma

Allen is a rabbinic sadhu *who can at need transform himself into an astute and hardheaded lawyer, and only this combination of fearless holiness, blazing compassion, and clear intellect has prevented him from being jailed or shot long ago.*

Alan Watts, *In My Own Way*

In April 1971, there was an important exchange of letters in the *New York Times Book Review* between Ginsberg and Richard Howard. Along with Carolyn Kizer and W.D. Snodgrass, both had been judges on the National Book Award poetry panel. The panel had chosen in favour of Mona Van Duyn, but Allen had disagreed with the verdict and disassociated himself from it. In his closely argued 2,500-word letter, Allen spelt out why he thought that Gregory Corso should have been awarded. 'So what are you proposing,' he wrote, 'that Mona Van Duyn has a better EAR than Gregory Corso, a greater juxtapositional economy, a more fertile sense of invention, a greater grasp of history, a greater involvement of person with poetics, a superior shrewdness in phrasing, a loftier metaphysics, even a more practical hand? Are you all mad? Have you no sense of modesty or proportion to your dreadful ambition to reduce all poetic judgements to domesticated mediocrity? There is nothing wrong with Van Duyn's book except that it is not the work of Genius, and there is nothing right about Corso's book except that it is the work of Genius.'

Allen then went on to extol the 'poetic genius' of McClure, Lamantia, Whalen, Snyder and Kerouac, and as good as claimed that there was still a conspiracy against them all. He signed his letter, 'Your disobedient servant.' Richard Howard in his reply began by querying the 'persistent association by you of Kerouac–McClure–Lamantia–Whalen–Corso in a pentad of "experimentalism" to which no other name has been added, not Merwin, not Ashbery, since you began to haunt these States.'

Allen was very widely read – except in modern fiction, which he rarely saw – and had assembled an enormous poetry library, but though he recognised the high quality and degree of achievement of many other poets, he remained convinced that his poet friends from the mid-fifties – Howard's 'pentad', to which a dozen or so others working in the 'open-form' Williams tradition, such as Creeley and Snyder, could be added – were the only 'prophetic' poets in the United States of world stature. Such loyalty was perhaps to be expected from members of any literary movement, but it was his insistence that his friends were 'geniuses' that rankled those writers and critics outside of his circle.

In the years to come, this sometimes resulted in accusations of nepotism, as Ginsberg's influence in literary society grew stronger and universities looking for writers in residence or organisers of foreign poetry festivals assembling an American contingent turned to him for advice and suggestions.

In his *New York Times* correspondence with Howard, Ginsberg distinguished between 'open breath poetry' and the traditional academic style of the time. That the 'Open Breath School' was possessed of genius was disputed by Howard; 'I wish I could come to terms with this Genius business, Allen,' he wrote, 'but I cannot. It seems to me you use the word the way hardhats use the word "American": and it seems to me that if "Genius" does not include Shakespeare's Sonnets and Milton and Wallace Stevens, it means merely madness, and that is what you want it to mean.' By touching on Ginsberg's high regard for madness and eccentricity, Howard certainly scored a good point. He went on to complain that Allen drew a line between art and genius, 'between excellence and ecstasy – as if the one had to, or could, preclude the other. You make out that if it's bad enough, it's got to be good, and that indeed is the parting between us.' Over the years, Allen's continuing preference for the Whitman–Williams lineage of 'mad scribblers', as McClure called them, was often to place him in conflict with the literary establishment – though less so in succeeding decades as the academic tradition itself shifted to a more open form.

In the 1960s, Allen had been a long-time public advocate of LSD, marijuana, mantra chanting and spiritual exploration as a means of expanding consciousness. During the 1970s he concentrated more on mantra chanting and meditation, and was proclaimed by the Luce press as the guru of the youth movement. His readings became more like seminars, consisting of poetry, mantra chanting and often an exposition of his current political preoccupations: the CIA role in dope smuggling in Southeast Asia, FBI infiltration of the anti-war movement or support of a worthy local cause. His stage props included incense, a Tibetan bell and brass thunderbolt (dorje), his ever-present Indian harmonium and, on one occasion, a large brass statue of Vajrasattva. To the incomprehension of many in the audience, he began his readings by chanting mantras, often at great length and often accompanied with explications of the poetic symbolism of the syllables. It was as if T.S. Eliot, at a poetry reading, were to sing plainsong.

Ginsberg, playing the role of teacher, had a limited practitioner's knowledge of the mantras he sang with such devotion. He had never taken a teacher in Hinduism or Buddhism, and had only recently begun to meditate, though he had chanted mantras for half the previous decade, encouraged by Swami Muktananda and various other gurus. In 1970, Swami Muktananda Paramahansa invited him to Dallas, where, for a week, Allen sat alone in his hotel room, meditating Hindu-style, repeating the Guru Om mantra with each breath, as instructed. Each midday and evening, Muktananda would come to see how he was getting on and to correct his posture. Back on the farm, Allen continued to meditate for an hour each morning before beginning work.

Over the years, he had met a large number of Zen masters, swamis and lamas, many of whom gave him teachings, particularly in India. Allen learned a good many mantras from Maretta Greer, though her explanations of their meaning were not informed by religious practice under a single teacher. Some of Allen's friends were concerned by his new preoccupation with chanting, thinking it was distracting him from his poetry. Then he took Chögyam Trungpa as a teacher, and he dropped all but a few of the mantras from his performances, in favour of explaining basic Tibetan-style meditation practice to his audiences.

Allen first met Chögyam Trungpa on the street in New York in late summer 1970. Allen was with his father, who was feeling weak from the heat. Trungpa had just hailed a cab, and Allen asked, 'Can I steal your vehicle?' explaining that his father was sick. Trungpa's Scottish assistant, Kunga Dawa, recognised him and they exchanged addresses. Ginsberg saluted Trungpa Indian-style and recited the common Padma Sambhava mantra: 'Om Ah Hum Vajra Guru Padma Siddi Hum'. Trungpa later told Ginsberg that he wondered if the poet knew its full significance. Not long afterward, Trungpa invited him to critique his poetic Buddhist ritual text, the *Sadhana of Mahamudra*, which Dawa had translated into English.

In the spring of 1971, Ginsberg moved to Berkeley to supervise the final stages of the assembly of a sixteen-hour tape of his best recorded readings. That May Chögyam Trungpa arrived in Berkeley and visited him. Trungpa had already been to the bar across the street from his hotel and was drunk. Helped back to his room by two of his students, he had fallen on the stairs and torn his pants. When he bent over his son, his wife yelled at him for breathing vodka all over the baby. 'Aren't you drinking too much?' Allen asked.

Down in the hotel restaurant, Trungpa looked at Allen. 'Why do you wear a beard?' he challenged. 'You're attached to your beard, aren't you? I want to see your face!' Allen sped to the hotel pharmacy and then into the men's room with a new pair of scissors. He reappeared five minutes later at the cocktail table where Trungpa was sipping his third Bloody Mary. 'You didn't shave it! All you did was cut it off two inches!' Trungpa teased.

'It's eight o'clock and you've got a lecture to give at eight-thirty,' said Allen. 'I'll shave there.'

'They know me,' said Trungpa. 'They know I'll be late. Shave now. Order another drink.' But Allen insisted they go.

Backstage at the lecture hall, half-way through shaving, Allen realised that he was free of his familiar media image and could now walk anonymously down Telegraph Avenue. He appeared from the bathroom clean-shaven, and Trungpa exclaimed, 'He took off his mask!'

Trungpa asked him why he always wore black shirts – Allen usually wore dark green work shirts – and Allen told him that he travelled a lot and they were easier to wash when he was on the move. 'Why don't you try some white shirts,' suggested Trungpa, 'and see how they feel?'

Allen followed his suggestion and went to the Salvation Army and bought about twenty shirts at fifteen or thirty cents each. 'I noticed that people were actually less scared of me,' he observed later. 'Less anxiety. Then I got a whole bunch of suits, tuxedos and everything.' The change from bearded guru to middle-aged businessman in an ill-fitting suit was so startling that when he presented himself to his room-mates at the Woolsey Street commune where he was staying, for a moment no one recognised him.

He enjoyed his new invisibility. In an interview with Irving Rosenthal he said, 'Several nights later I closed the Capri invisible and went to the Basket dressed in my Salvation Army $3.50 Montgomery Street suit and porkpie hat, white shirt and tie and close-cropped hair. I stood around watching everybody dance all night, got beat for a buck by a halfdrunk speedfreak kid I picked up in front of Finocchio's, and wound up taxiing alone to Pam-Pam's at 6 a.m. Great gathering of beautiful varied lads and queens at table, so I walked up hat in hand and said, "Can I sit with you? I'm lonely." They said "NO! No room here, we're expecting more people." And suddenly I was on the outside of gay hippie culture looking in and realised I'd stumbled on a new karma yoga treasure: anonymity.'

During his talk with Trungpa at the hotel, Allen had complained that he was fatigued by his endless cross-country poetry readings, and the extended air travel. 'That's because you don't like your poetry,' said Trungpa.

'What do you know about poetry?' exclaimed Allen, struck but amused.

'Why do you need to depend on a piece of paper when you recite poetry?' continued Trungpa. 'Don't you trust your own mind? Why don't you do like the great poets, like Milarepa – improvise spontaneously on the spot.'

That evening at Trungpa's meeting, Allen improvised a silly ditty, rhyming 'moon' and 'June', 'beer' and 'dear'; it was surprisingly easy. His father's example and all Allen's youthful years of writing rhymed couplets came to fruition. The next night, at a benefit for Tarthang Tulku's Tibetan Buddhist meditation centre in Berkeley, Ginsberg tested Trungpa's suggestion; he took no books or texts on stage. He chanted Tarthang Tulku's melody for the Padma Sambhava mantra for more than an hour, then, using just two harmonium chords, he improvised a twenty-minute lament beginning, 'How sweet to be born here in America.'

'It was the first time I ever got on stage without a text,' he said, 'and had to improvise it out of the whole cloth of what I was thinking at the moment. And it was really awkward and unfinished, but it was so profound . . . and so liberating when I realised I didn't have to worry if I lost a poem anymore because I was the poet, I could just make it up.'

Allen was deeply impressed by Trungpa, who, by quiet suggestion, over the short time he had known him, had inspired changes in his approach to poetry and his appearance. He began to realise that in Trungpa he had found his teacher.

Chögyam Trungpa, the eleventh Trungpa Tulku, was from the northern Chinese province of Tsinghai, a rugged primitive area of mountains between the upper reaches of the Yangtse and Mekong rivers. The plateau was divided into the territories of twenty-five tribes, each with its own hereditary chief, and despite being situated in the Amdo region, the people were culturally more akin to the Khampas to the south, though the society of the plateau was more primitive. The area was at the outer rim of influence of the Tibetan religion.

When the Chinese began much-needed land reform after the revolution, many feudal landowners and top religious leaders, including the Dalai Lama, decided that it would be advisable to flee the country, and as part of the exodus from both Tibet and the neighbouring regions of China, nineteen-year-old Trungpa left for the West, walking from Kham to Arunachal Pradesh in India with a group of attendants and followers. In the years that followed, many tens of thousands of Tibetans fled the country, mostly from Tibet proper.

It was a prescient move, given the near-complete destruction of the traditional Tibetan religion and the apparatus of the theocratic state. During the violence of the Cultural Revolution between 1965 and 1968, the army and the Red Guards levelled many temples to the ground, humiliated and tortured monks and sent thousands to detention camps. A disastrous bureaucratic attempt to cultivate wheat instead of barley on the high plateau resulted in widespread famine. Years later, the Chinese apologised and rebuilt a few of the temples, mostly those on the tourist route.

Trungpa learned English, studied comparative religion, philosophy and fine art at Oxford University and became the first Tibetan to hold a British passport. He attracted a group of Western

followers and set up the Samye Ling monastery in Scotland, but as
he absorbed the influence of the West he developed a fondness for
wine, women and fast cars. In May 1969, he crashed his sports car
into a joke shop, paralysing his left side. He gave up his monastic
robes and in January 1970 married a young Scots woman, Diana
Pybus; they moved to the United States with several of his
followers. 'I'm sure he will be much happier there,' said the
secretary of the sedate Buddhist Society in London, breathing a
sigh of relief. 'His style of Buddhism is much more suited to the
Americans, I think.'

This proved to be the case. Stories quickly spread about this
amazing new teacher of 'Wild Wisdom', an alcoholic who drank
beer all through his lectures, who was occasionally so drunk that
he fell asleep during meditation sessions, who was always at least
an hour late and was known to creep up on students who were too
comfortable in meditation, blasting them with his water pistol. On
one famous occasion, he drunkenly insulted a redneck truck-driver
in a road-house, and when it came time for him to leave, he and
his attendant, Kunga Dawa, found the door barred by the trucker,
who was fuming with anger and levelling a double-barrelled
shotgun at Trungpa's head. Not to be outdone, Trungpa pulled out
his water pistol and squirted the man. The trucker left in a squeal
of wheels.

His religious lineage was that of the Kargyü sect, but he was also
empowered to teach the N'yingma, the oldest of the Tibetan
Buddhist schools. Since the time of the Buddha, all major schools
of Buddhism comprised three types of practitioners: the lay
community; strictly disciplined monastic communities devoted to
scholarship; and non-monastic 'wild wisdom' yogis, known as the
mahasiddhas, some of whom retreated to solitary caves or forests,
while others lived secular lives as butchers, courtesans or house-
holders. All placed great value on meditation under the tutelage of
a personal teacher. They drank a lot, often exhibited 'divine
madness' and were known as the 'mishap lineage'. They were
reputed to be great meditation instructors, and their teachings were
handed down through the centuries by written and oral tradition
from guru to disciple. It was the Kargyü and N'yingma sects of
Tibetan Buddhism that embodied the mahasiddas' lineage.
Trungpa's 'Wild Wisdom' was in a classic tradition of Tibetan
teachers going back to the yogi poet Milarepa. Allen found this

method very attractive, combining, as it did, many of the traits of the Beat Generation: the emphasis on the 'sacredness' of immediate experience, sexual candour and absence of censoriousness, as well as the veneration of madness. It also helped that he was physically attracted to Trungpa. Trungpa's alcoholism – he claimed he drank 'to understand the American psyche', though he drank in England as well – which paralleled that of Kerouac and many of Allen's other friends, did not put Allen off. Trungpa became a major influence on Allen throughout the 1970s and into the 1980s.

Allen involved himself in the gay liberation movement from the beginning. The day after the famous riot in 1969, he had visited the Stonewall Bar, hoping to calm any further violence and to give his seal of approval to the gays who had finally stood up against police harassment. When he arrived, he was applauded by the crowd and allowed through the police line into the club; one police officer even asked for his autograph.

In the summer of 1971, Allen gave a very frank interview to the *Berkeley Barb* in which he spoke at length about his homosexuality. 'I'm very shy,' he said. 'I've always found it difficult to proposition people on the street or in urinals or anything like that. It's not my scene exactly. Although I have all sorts of heartbeats and heart throbs and longing desires walking up and down the streets for practically half the young cats I see, but it's really hard to communicate it. I'm also so busy I hardly have time for romantic dalliance, even if I could break through my shyness. I'm at liberty in case anybody wants to know,' he said. (Peter had stayed behind in New York with Denise.) 'I'm almost at the level of putting an ad in the *Berkeley Barb* for something like that: "Wanted: one young man, secretary, companion, body servant, who can drive, take shorthand, competent in business matters and correspondence, can cook, camp, good carpenter, a forest hippy."' His announcement paid off, as he remembered twenty-five years later: 'There was Boy George in Berkeley who answered my personals ad and secretary lover with a waterbed 1971. No joke, beautiful body corpse.'

Back in New York after a brief visit to India, Allen received a flurry of telegrams and phone messages from Yoko Ono, inviting him to join her and John Lennon in Syracuse for the opening of a show of their sculpture. It was 9 October 1971, John Lennon's thirty-first birthday, and a number of people had gathered in his Syracuse hotel suite to celebrate. There was a giant birthday cake, and toys and telegrams littered the room.

John sat on the bed wearing his little round eyeglasses, his hair very long, parted in the middle. Record producer Phil Spector was there, completely drunk, and insisted on holding Allen's hand. Ringo reminisced about the old days with the Beatles, who had formally broken up the previous year, but had not toured since 1966. John talked at length, attacking the concept of 'God', as he had done on his *Imagine* album. Allen seated himself in a half-lotus on the carpet and, arranging his Tibetan bell and dorje, incense and harmonium around him, began to chant the Padma Sambhava mantra: 'Om, Ah, Hum . . .'

John jumped up and said, 'Wait a minute, I'll get my guitar.' Ringo borrowed Allen's finger cymbals and upturned a waste-basket to make a drum. Someone gave Spector a guitar, and he took it upon himself to sing harmony with Allen. In the first hour or so, Allen led with mantras – 'Om Ah Hum', 'Om Namah Shivaye' and 'Om Manni Padme Hum' – all taken very slowly. He also did Blake's 'Nurse's Song' but he couldn't get the timing right. It didn't matter, and they all began to improvise blues.

They strummed their way through 'Yellow Submarine' and 'Give Peace A Chance', both of which had good choruses to join in on. They jammed for about six hours. 'Lovely day,' wrote Allen.

Afterwards Allen found himself in a limousine with John Lennon and a drunk Phil Spector. The car was surrounded by screaming teenagers, and Allen got some sense of what it must have been like to be a Beatle. 'Just like in *Help*,' he said. 'I think probably relations with Lennon and others easier in future. This is first time we really got together on art vibration.'

Peter and Denise wanted to spend the winter in New York, so Allen closed down the farm for the season. The animals were all given away, with great care taken in selecting their new owners. They even found a farmer who would take their three-hundred pound pig, Don't Bite Me, as a pet. Julius was sent to the Binghamton Hospital, still not talking but in good physical shape after his work outdoors.

* * *

Trungpa asked Allen to come and stay at his house in Boulder for a week, to appear with Gary Snyder and Robert Bly at a poetry reading to raise money for Vajradhatu, Trungpa's religious organisation. Allen already regarded Trungpa as his teacher, but now he took the formal vows of Buddhism. On 6 May 1972, he underwent the traditional Buddhist Three Refuges ceremony at Dharmadhatu meditation centre, with Gary Snyder in the congregation. Allen committed himself: to take refuge in the Buddha (either the historical Buddha or simply a state of 'awakened mind'); to take refuge in the dharma (the teachings, the cumulative body of Buddhist knowledge); to take refuge in the sangha (the Buddhist community or congregation; all sentient beings). Allen repeated the vows three times and accepted as his refuge name Lion of Dharma. Trungpa had already given him a new mantra for meditation.

Although not required to, he also took the Bodhissatva Vows. 'I was doing Trungpa's instruction so it seemed natural,' he said, 'but the Bodhissatva was the one which was most interesting.' The four vows begin: 'Sentient beings are numberless, I vow to liberate them all,' which Allen interpreted as meaning: 'Enlighten all, help all or get on with, which is the same thing I took on the Columbia ferry boat. I felt I was already on my road and this was merely like a formulation, in classical terms, of what was already my intuitive desire.' The vows continue: 'Obstacles are inexhaustible, I vow to cut through them. The gates of the Dharma are countless, I vow to enter every gate,' which Allen described as 'The notion of relating to every situation and not boycotting any situations. Not avoiding, but trying to alchemise every situation, by skillful means to turn it to advantage . . . To turn it from shit to roses.' The final vow is 'The Buddha Path (of awakened mind) is endless, I vow to follow through.'

It is easy to see why Ginsberg should be attracted to the Bodhisatva ideal, since one of his great strengths was always his willingness to take a difficult or painful situation and try to salvage something from it, whether it was in dealing with his mother's madness, becoming involved with the lepers and dying beggars in India or talking amiably with street people and bag-ladies. He would intervene in street arguments, talk to belligerent drunks and spaced-out junkies. If someone had a bad skin condition or disfigurement, Ginsberg would immediately ask about it rather than pretend it was not there. His enormous inquisitiveness and almost complete lack of embarrassment sometimes led him to quiz complete strangers about their income or sex life and volunteer the same uncalled-for information about himself.

The benefit reading for Vajradhatu was chaired by Trungpa. First Robert Bly, Gary Snyder and Allen read from Trungpa's English translation of the *Heart Sutra*, followed by the poet Nanao Sakaki reading it in Japanese and finally Trungpa reading it in Tibetan. Trungpa read his own poems with Allen reading the English translations, which he had helped to polish. Then Allen spontaneously improvised some songs. The second half opened with Bly and Snyder reading as a team, and then separately, to enthusiastic audience response. This seemed to irritate Trungpa, who turned to Allen, sitting next to him at the left of the stage, and declared that Snyder was boring. He accused him of laying his trip on everyone so that all they got was Snyder's trip and none of their own. Trungpa had with him a small gong, about a foot in diameter, which he placed on his head and began to bang. Snyder valiantly continued his reading. Trungpa then put the gong on Allen's head and began to bang it. Snyder was not about to let a noisy drunk prevent him from finishing his reading, though as Allen said later, he 'was not too sure where to put his feet'.

'If you think I'm doing this because I'm drunk,' Trungpa told Allen, 'you're making a big mistake.'

Allen did not understand, 'Is this just you?' he asked, 'or is this traditional manner or what?'

'I come from a long line of eccentric Buddhists.' Trungpa then took the microphone and apologised to the audience, not for his behaviour, but for what he described as the poets' laying a trip on them. 'I'm sure they don't mean what they said,' said Trungpa. He carried on in an incoherent manner for a bit longer before closing the proceedings with the 'Gaté' mantra. The audience joined in. Trungpa banged the gong on his head, smashed several glasses and the evening was over.

Both Snyder and Bly, who had been Trungpa's student in Scotland, were offended by Trungpa's behaviour at the reading, particularly since they were raising money for him. What was significant, however, was that Allen had been seen to side with his teacher against his fellow poets. Allen was normally overly protective toward his fellow poets, as when he threw Gregory Corso out of St Mark's Church for interrupting Robert Lowell, so this represented unusual behaviour for him.

For two years Ginsberg had been devoting more and more of his time on stage to singing lengthy versions of 'Om Ah Hum' and 'Om Mani Padme Hum' mantras, often to the irritation of those members of the audience who had paid their money to hear him read poetry. Although most of the audience were prepared to go along with it, many were clearly bored, others were puzzled and some simply regarded the whole thing as a massive ego-trip. Trungpa suggested that he stop using the mantras at his readings. 'It was rousing an expectation in the audience, getting them high,' said Ginsberg, 'but I had no further instruction to give. So it was just a trip, a buzz, which it was, but what good would it do unless I was aiming to provide something further. I can't deliver a teaching.' Allen's friends were much relieved.

Throughout 1972, both Allen and Peter were deeply involved in the anti-war movement. Allen used press interviews and television talk shows as vehicles for his message, sometimes angering TV hosts by twisting their questions to his purposes. His position was that the United States had split Vietnam unnaturally in two, and he often quoted Eisenhower who had said that eighty per cent of the Vietnamese would have voted for Ho Chi Minh if the United States had allowed democratic elections at the end of the Indo-chinese war with France. The statistics of the war filled Allen with horror, and he used every possible opportunity to protest. 'The thing that struck me,' he said, 'was that though there were big mobilisations, and although the majority of the country was against the war, there was no dialogue between the government and the people organising the antiwar movement. They weren't communicating.'

In 1972, he spent ten days with Gary Snyder at Kitkitdizzi, his house in the Sierras. Gary had no telephone, but while visiting a friend nearby, Allen phoned the White House and got through to Henry Kissinger. 'This is Allen Ginsberg – the poet,' he introduced himself.

'I know,' said Kissinger.

Allen suggested that Kissinger should get together with David Dellinger and the leaders of the peace movement and try to open a dialogue. Kissinger said that he was agreeable to a meeting, in principle. Allen told Dellinger, who approved of the idea. Senator Eugene McCarthy offered his place for a meeting, but there was no reply from the White House when he left a message to this effect for Kissinger.

Shortly afterwards, at a huge demonstration outside the White House, Allen found himself on stage, singing Blake, as tear-gas swirled about him again. He was often arrested and tear-gassed at demonstrations. One such occasion occurred in Miami during the 1972 Democratic and Republican conventions. The peace movement planned huge demonstrations and took great care to ensure that Miami 1972 was not a repeat of Chicago 1968. Given the strength of the anti-war movement in the country, the administration did not relish the thought of the media coverage that massive peace demonstrations would get and used every means to disrupt them. Even before the Chicago riots, the FBI had infiltrated the Yippies with agents. When the Yippies went to Miami, both they and the breakaway Zippies had agents provocateurs in their midst, whose job was to disrupt peaceful demonstrations and cause violent scenes; the media was bound to concentrate on them and ignore the much larger number of people engaged in peaceful protest marches and rallies. The tactic worked well and, as predicted, the press ran a number of editorials denouncing the peace movement for violent behaviour.

The Vietnam Vets had also been infiltrated by the FBI, and Allen was particularly incensed when a peaceful march of about two hundred mantra-chanting people, which he had helped organise, was disrupted by large numbers of veterans. The march had begun very peacefully. 'Walking down Collins Avenue, everybody was very pleased, chanting "Ah!" which sounded great, good vibration, people were being friendly. And the old folks in Miami Beach were on our side. All of a sudden, a block behind us bursting into the street, are all these Vietnam Veterans coming to join us, digging what we were doing, I thought. They scattered in our ranks and began overturning garbage cans, stopping cars, pulling out the spark plugs, totally wrecking the scene and creating a traffic jam. So immediately the police arrived, apparently notified in advance that this was the tactic of the FBI, because these were Vietnam Vets who were FBI agents.'

At first Allen couldn't understand why the Vietnam Vets would behave like that, then it became obvious that they were trying to get everyone arrested. 'So we kept our group together and went back, cleaning up the garbage cans and putting them right and trying to create order, but by that time the police had gathered about five blocks down and formed a line to stop us.' When they got there, the police ordered them to disband the march or be arrested for disturbing the peace. 'So we all sat down in the middle of the street and the police surrounded us and slowly rounded us up and one by one threw us into meat trucks that they hired for the occasion to take us to jail.' It took him three days to get out. Peter had also been arrested but was in a different cell.

Allen described the event. 'It was a real bitter political experience because it was the total sabotage of every possible good natured attempt to do a peaceful festival of life. And it was overt ... The press said we had rioted. The wool was pulled over the public's eyes completely in that way. It was difficult enough to realise that we had been that much infiltrated but then to explain it, and on top of that, how could we prove it until years later when the Vietnam Veterans [The Gainsville Eight] won their case.' It took five years for the proof to slowly emerge through the Freedom of Information Act – 'By which time nobody remembers it. But I remember it!'

Allen's desk was still filled with appeals for help. That year, Timothy Leary and Abbie Hoffman both found themselves in deep trouble with the authorities in ways far beyond any aid that Allen could give. Leary had escaped from jail with the aid of the Weathermen and gone to live in exile. He had been serving twenty years for two pot convictions: ten years for possession of two roaches weighing only a few grams, imposed in Orange County, California; and ten years imposed in Houston for his original conviction in Texas for possession of a half ounce four years before. So desperate was the FBI to get him back that American agents snatched his passport from him at Kabul airport and bundled him on to a plane for the United States. Leary was placed in solitary confinement and his bail set at five million dollars, the highest in American history. In a remarkable display of erudition, Allen responded by setting out the complicated facts surrounding the case in the form of a sestina – a lyric fixed form consisting of six stanzas, each comprising six lines, in which the end words of the first stanza recur as end words of the following five stanzas, and as the middle and end words of the concluding tercet. The end words should rotate in order, but in Allen's case they didn't, so he called it 'Mock Sestina: The Conspiracy Against Dr. Tim Leary.' It was distributed as a flyer in May 1973.

Equally imaginative, perhaps, was Allen's attempt to defend Abbie Hoffman, who was arrested while trying to sell more than three pounds of cocaine to undercover narcotics agents. Unable to deny that Hoffman was involved in a large-scale drug deal, Allen wrote, 'In time of communal Apathy synchronous with Abbie Hoffman's recent disillusioned withdrawal to private life (after crises of his public affairs to confound Government poice bureaucracy and war led him to be attacked left and right), Mr Hoffman is now to be congratulated on an arrest which by its very surprise, its simultaneous whimsicality and seriousness, re-unites many of his fellow workers once again to resist the steamroller of police state power crushing another live citizen's body.' Allen concluded his open letter, 'I pray with body speech and mind OM AH HUM for courts and government and public to recognise the strange delicacy and historical charm of the situation in which they are placed together with peace poet Abbie Hoffman and, myself, sincerely yours, recommending Hare Krishna to one and all, Allen Ginsberg.'

That fall, Allen spent a few weeks on the farm, where Peter and Denise were bringing in the harvest, boiling beets ready for canning, gathering apples to store in the cellar and bottling giant zucchinis. He spent long hours in his room with its hissing gas mantle, answering letters and preparing to attend Trungpa's three-month Vajrayana seminary in Teton Village, a ski resort in Jackson Hole, Wyoming. Trungpa intended to take eighty advanced students through the three *yanas* of Buddhism, devoting a month to the study of each. Trungpa wanted very much to get Allen involved with his organisation and asked him if he would teach poetics at the seminary. Allen felt flattered to be invited to teach, but soon found that he was being treated like everybody else. 'I could either take the position of student or pursue my own universe, and it seemed I'd learn more by being a student and not making a scene over my deflated ambition to be a teacher, though I was teaching.'

Before this, in New York, Trungpa asked Allen to be his poetry guru, which puzzled Allen. 'I couldn't figure on what level he meant it. Somewhat mockingly but also very serious . . . So I said, "Sure, I'll be your poetry guru. Please be my meditation guru." So we made a little deal. "You teach me meditation, I'll teach you poetry." Obviously somewhat playful, and he was being very courteous to me.' The deal is an interesting reversal of the 'vows' Ginsberg had taken with Neal Cassady and Peter Orlovsky. With Neal and Peter, Allen offered to teach spiritual and intellectual skills in exchange for physical love and practical help. In this case, it was Trungpa offering the spiritual advice and Allen the practical skill.

In Jackson Hole, Allen found the experience of intensive sitting 'painful and changing and rapturous and boring, like some kind of flattened out acid trip extending through time. Lovely.' Bearded again, he sat nine hours a day, staring through a giant plate-glass window, watching the dawn break pink on the powdered snow of the mountain peaks and the shadows move imperceptibly throughout the day till dusk fell and the light faded. He repeated his 'A Ah Sha Sa Ma Ha' mantra silently in his head, using it to measure his breath. His mind raced with thoughts, chatter and anger, frustrations and erotic fantasies, till each one was played out and he was still sitting there in bib-overalls, with balding head and greying beard, feeling calm and strangely high.

After nine days, Trungpa told him to just watch his breath moving out, otherwise he would get 'entangled in a body trip too heavily'. Allen did this simple samatha meditation – no mantra, eyes open – for the next decade or so, and incorporated instructions on how to do it into his reading programme. He described it in detail:

'Specifically, samatha – as distinct from Zen style – is paying attention to the breath leaving the nostril and dissolving into the space in front of the face . . . I've heard it described as touch and let go, touch and let go – or attention to the breath going out, and then dropping it as the breath ceases, and then attention again to the breath when it goes out. So it's practice in *re*-directing your attention constantly to the space in front of your face, outside of your body. In that sense, almost by definition, it's practice of egolessness because you're meditating on the empty space into which your breath dissolves, rather than into any psychological or sensational phenomena going on inside the body. Then there is constant daydreaming and drifting away from that attention to the space. You're constantly waking up – mindfully waking up to the actual space around you, into which you're breathing. You use the breath as a handle to get back into that space.'

This type of meditation is referred to time and time again in his poetry and is the subject of the title poem of his City Lights book *Mind Breaths*. He continued the intensive sitting, 'eye fixed on glittering tremble of gold aspen leaves all day, glittering like buds.'

It was the time of the CIA-sponsored overthrow of Salvador Allende's democratic government in Chile, and Allen's thoughts were dominated by despair, anger and confusion over the role of the United States in toppling a legally elected government. He worried over the fate of Nicanor Parra and his other Chilean friends there and vowed that if they were harmed he would somehow find a way to throw Kissinger in jail. He read in the Denver *Post* that Pablo Neruda had died of cancer but the military regime would not allow him a public funeral. Allen wrote several small poems for Neruda during his breaks from meditation:

Your poetry long as Chile
    epics, verses, sonnets,
    line by line lie empty . . .

On 30 September, he learned of the death of W.H. Auden and that afternoon sat weeping, remembering how he first met Auden in 1946, at Earle Hall in Columbia, and how he had ridden the subway with Auden all the way down to Sheridan Square, just to talk to him. He remembered Auden's apartment on Cornelia Street which had seemed so glamorous at the time, and his loft on 21st Street where he had read the manuscript of Allen's *Empty Mirror* and recommended that he study David Jones as a model for open verse. He recalled their shouted argument on the Isle of Ischia in 1957 and later, in the 1960s, sitting on his couch in St Marks Place, New York, offering to sing Blake for him, and Auden's reply, 'Oh no! I get so embarrassed when people sing to me alone. That's for the concert hall.' It had only been two months since Allen had read with him in London, and he had explained Welsh verse forms to Allen, counting the syllables. As he wrote his journal, Allen turned his thoughts to Auden's lover, Chester Kallman, weeping in Bavaria, to Christopher Isherwood mourning his old friend in Hollywood, and the sadness at Oxford, Harvard and Columbia. He wrote, 'The aspen grove lost its yellow leaft roof, 'tis end of September, kind Auden's gone away forever.'

The second two-week session went better than the first. Allen was more relaxed, and the sexual fantasies began to lose some of their power, 'less intensely hot and horny lov'd – and less painful to repeat phantom mind fucks o'er – sexual spectres more transparent than before, almost invisible asses and cocks, couldn't maybe even get a hard-on over real ruddy ass meat – all in my mind!' he wrote. On his last day there, he talked with Trungpa about sex and asked if maybe they should sleep together.

'I think that would be interesting,' said Trungpa, 'if there's ever time – and space – to explore those feelings.'

Allen's intensive meditation was interrupted by the beginning of his fall reading tour, but he managed to rearrange his schedule so that he could spend a further two weeks at Teton Village, midway through the tour.

Most of January 1974 Allen spent on the farm, meditating in the attic. He began by sitting for five hours a day, then slowly increased this to eight, 'staring open eye at horizon hill woods dawn and dusk west over the State land, snow all over pond fields and red barn roof, flies born buzzing in the sunny window.'

Back in New York City, he got caught up in the excitement surrounding Burroughs's return to the States to teach at City College from February until May, two hours a week – a position Allen had engineered for him, thinking that he was stagnating in London. He did a number of readings and found, to his surprise, that he was a natural performer. Bill still dressed in the same conservative suit and tie, which made the subject matter of his readings seem even more outrageous. His return to live in New York was much like that of the prodigal son and was the cause of a great round of parties, drinks and dinners. Allen saw a lot of Bill and taught him Trungpa's meditation system which, to Allen's astonishment, Bill approved of completely. Allen had been seeing Yoko Ono, and on Valentine's Day he took her over to visit Burroughs at his loft at 452 Broadway. Yoko, wearing a big floppy hat, sat holding hands with Burroughs, who was so drunk that the next day he had no memory whatsoever of their visit.

* * *

Allen's 1974 spring tour finished in California, and Allen, Peter and Denise left for the Sierras, to start building a house on the land Allen owned with Gary Snyder. Allen's journal happily recorded: 'May 28. Kitkitdizze Poets' Hermitage, Ponderosa Circle Site – birds chirping and titting. 5 a.m. dawn bell from Hindu ashram uphill bonging the morn.' The Ashram was near Gary Snyder's house, where Allen, Peter and Denise were staying. Another journal entry read, 'I wake up, Snyder with flashlights at his porch shelf in the pre-dawn rain in the Sierra foothill summer dark'; the feeling is that caught by Kerouac in *The Dharma Bums*.

The land was not far from Nevada City, a small town in the foothills of the Sierra Nevadas near Donner Pass, on the Truckee wagon train route to California. The whole area, studded with abandoned mines from the Gold Rush days, was thick with oak and fast-growing Ponderosa Pine. Peter worked naked, huffing and sweating, helped by Denise and a number of young 'Buddhist striplings living out their forest manhood with Indian headbands and leather carpenter aprons,' as Allen described them. They poured concrete, dug up bedrock, sawed and shaped wood. Allen learned to saw wood and hammer nails. They were working from an architect's drawing designed to their specifications, which included a proper kitchen and a sun deck. Gradually the house began to take form.

Allen and the poet Anne Waldman both gave readings and poetry workshops at Chögyam Trungpa's newly formed Naropa Institute in Boulder that summer, and when the sessions came to an end, Trungpa asked them to start a poetry school there. Anne was an obvious choice to co-direct the school, as she had years of experience in running the St Mark's Church Poetry project. Trungpa had already planned a 'national poetry conference' to be held at Naropa the next year, and the poet Lewis MacAdams had prepared a list of some sixty poets for Trungpa to choose from. Allen felt himself becoming inexorably entangled in Trungpa's world. The lecture that Trungpa had given on the 'Samya Vow' threatened Vajra Hell to those who refuse the guru. As Allen frequently did, he expressed his worries in his journal as a 'worst-case scenario', writing: 'I am caught in whirlpool of Ego Desire Ambition Power, to run the school and be elder poet host to such a large company of bards fighting for recognition and fame.' Allen seems not to have considered the fact that dozens of established universities would have been pleased and honoured to offer him a similar position and would have even offered him money, something that was very scarce around Naropa. The attraction of Naropa was the association with Trungpa. Allen agreed.

He was sharing an apartment in Boulder with Anne Waldman, and they began to discuss names for the new school. Anne suggested the 'Gertrude Stein School', but Allen wanted to honour his old friend. The 'Jack Kerouac School' was kicked around for a while, and then Anne came up with the 'Jack Kerouac School of Disembodied Poetics'. A student later asked why 'disembodied' poetics, when the emphasis was on getting back into the body. 'That's a joke,' Allen replied, 'because he's dead, so he's disembodied, so to speak. Also because we were fools and didn't know what we were getting into. We didn't realise it would be such a serious body. Also because of beatnik poetic inspiration that made it sound funny. I objected to Anne, saying "Wait a minute, this is contrary to all the basic principles enunciated by Pound and Williams and the Imagists," but Trungpa said, "Ah, it's pretty funny. Why don't you use it? It's too late to change it. Too late!" '

By mid-August 1974, Allen was back at Ponderosa Pine Circle helping Peter build the cabin. The structure was not habitable yet, so they slept outside in sleeping-bags. By mid-September, the roof was on and the windows were being hung. It looked like a tiny wooden castle amid the blue oak and Ponderosa Pine. Allen filled a journal with images from the four months of living deep in the woods: Peter yodelling as he worked, the Milky Way through the pinetops, the mosquitos at sunset, the time he found a rattlesnake curled up under a stone, how the helpers sat around in the evenings playing guitars by the light of the kerosene lamp, swimming in the cold pool . . . By October the house was finished, and it was also time to leave.

Allen returned to San Francisco on his way to New York, where he had several upstate readings lined up. One evening, he and Anne Waldman attended a concert by jazz pianist Cecil Taylor at a San Francisco nightclub. Sitting there, he noted in his journal, 'I want to be known as the most brilliant man in America.' Allen said later,

'I was so ashamed of what I wrote down that I wouldn't let her see it. I hid my notebook from her with my hand. Within a month I realised that the poem was funny. It's obviously a great burlesque, a take-off on myself, shameful, shocking.' He added to it, and it became 'Ego Confession', which appeared in *Mind Breaths*.

Allen had reason to feel confidence in his position. The Vietnam war was finally over, ended when the last helicopter left the roof of the American Embassy as the victorious Vietcong swept through Saigon. At home, Allen's deep suspicions about the Nixon administration were all vindicated by the Watergate affair, in which Nixon was forced to resign and many of his top aides were jailed for lying to Congress.

No major pastoral poems came from Allen's period in the woods. Instead, he proved once again that he was the master of the urban landscape, managing to turn a mugging into a successful poem. On 2 November, he left his East 10th Street apartment and walked past the usual throngs of Puerto Rican youths lounging on the stoops and leaning on wrecked cars. One block from his house, two youths tripped him and immediately dragged him into the basement of a burned-out store, where they relieved him of his week's seventy dollars spending money. Allen kept up a continuous chant of 'Om Ah Hum', thinking that this would calm them, till they yelled, 'Shut up or we'll murder you!'

'Om Ah Hum,' replied Allen, 'Take it easy.'

They pulled down his socks, looking for hidden hundred-dollar bills, while a third youth roughly tore off his wristwatch. 'Shut up and we'll get out of here,' they said and left.

'. . . I rose from the cardboard mattress thinking Om Ah Hum didn't stop em enough,/ the tone of voice too loud,' he wrote. 'My shoulder bag with 10,000 dollars full of poetry left on the broken floor . . .'

He stood up and found his eyeglasses on the edge of the step where he had thoughtfully placed them as he was dragged to the basement. Emerging into the half-gutted street, he called the police from a nearby bodega. He and a policeman examined the basement to see if his wallet had been discarded there before the muggers left. The neighbourhood kids had seen nothing. Still a little shaken, Allen walked along East 10th Street and crossed Avenue C to his own block, realising that he had lived there for ten years and didn't know anyone more than half a block away. He sold the resulting poem, 'Mugging', to the *New York Times* for seven times the amount that the kids had stolen from him.

In March 1975, Allen and Peter moved into a much larger apartment at 437 East 12th Street between First Avenue and Avenue A. It had six rooms, two of which were very small, and had been created by knocking together two small apartments: an arrangement that led, somewhat incongruously, to Allen's having a sink right next to his desk in his office. There were three south-facing front rooms, and Allen and Peter took one each, with the third becoming Allen's office. When Allen woke in the morning all he could see from the window was the top of the church opposite which, in the grey winter light, reminded him of his days in Paris. Denise had a small room of her own off the kitchen, where she practised her guitar. They painted the walls white, tacked their picture of the young Rimbaud on the wall and were home.

Allen's reading on 17 April 1975 in New York was a historic occasion. Allen, Peter and Gregory returned to McMillin Theatre at Columbia University for a benefit for Naropa Institute, billed as 'Another Night At Columbia'. The first night had been the historic reading of 5 February 1959, the subject of Diana Trilling's infamous essay. This time they had William Burroughs with them on stage; it was the first time they had all appeared together since their informal reading at George Whitman's Paris bookshop in 1958. Allen announced that he would read the best poems he had written since he was last there, sixteen years before. His choice was 'Kral Majalis', a section from 'Wichita Vortex Sutra', 'Wales, A Visitation', 'Please Master' (during which a few people in the audience groaned at the painfully explicit sexual revelations), 'On Neal's Ashes' and 'Ego Confession'. At the line 'I want to be known as the most brilliant man in America', the audience erupted into a great wave of applause and laughter.

After the summer sessions at Naropa that year, Allen spent two weeks in solitary meditation at Trungpa's Rocky Mountain Dharma Center, in Livermore, Colorado, attending lectures and counting his prostrations in a little cabin in the mountains. It was standard Tibetan Buddhist practice that in order to qualify to receive the higher level of teachings from the guru, the disciple had first to complete 100,000 prostrations. With each prostration, the disciple committed himself to his guru, the Buddha, the dharma and the sangha. Trungpa had said, 'Surrender to prostrations as you surrender to toilet bowl. You're a poet, so have some humour.' It was not until October 1975 that Allen got back to New York.

That spring, Bob Dylan had returned to New York, leaving his wife and children in Malibu. Looking his old self from his early 1960s days as a folk singer, with a scruffy leather jacket, dark glasses, and several days' growth of beard. He began taking part in late-night jam sessions at the rock and folk clubs in the Village. After the summer break, he was ready to go out on the road in a tour bus with a few friends and play small halls. His original idea soon grew into an elaborate project calling for a large road crew, a lighting crew, an advance party and management team. Then he decided to make a movie of the tour, which added two film crews, with their own sound men and their equipment and lighting handlers.

So many celebrities were interested in doing guest spots or in joining the tour for a few days that Dylan thought it would be a pity to gather so much creative talent together and just make a concert movie, so he decided to intercut the live footage with improvised scenes using the musicians as actors. Dylan phoned Allen one morning at 4 a.m. asking him to join the tour to help set up suitable scenarios. It was the first time they had spoken in four years. 'What're you writing?' Dylan asked. 'Sing it to me on the phone.' Allen did. Dylan said, 'Okay, let's go out on the road.'

Allen was delighted, particularly when Dylan told him, at a party a few days later, that his improvised songs 'have everything. They are understandable at every level'. Dylan told Allen, 'You're the King, you're the King, but you haven't found your kingdom. But you've always been the King . . . People get off on your energy.'

Allen was not exactly sure what was expected of him, since Dylan had also roped in Sam Shepard to write spontaneous scripts. At the rehearsal studio Allen asked Dylan, 'Bob, what do you want of me? What's your fantasy? Your idea?'

'Well, it's up to you to decide,' said Dylan, characteristically. 'You're the King. Whatever you want to do, get it together. I'm presenting you. It's about time. This country has been asleep. It's time it woke up.'

Allen suggested Anne Waldman, Peter and Denise, and Dylan agreed. Peter came along as a luggage handler, and Denise's job was to provide fresh flowers and fruit for Dylan's hat before each show. The tour, named The Rolling Thunder Revue, was organised under conditions of extreme secrecy. In order to be able to play small halls, not even the musicians were told which town they would be playing until the day of the concert. Dylan had not forgotten the last time he announced a tour: there were six million applications for tickets.

They began shooting the film before they even got out on the road. In one scene, Allen was supposed to be filmed from an 8th Street balcony while he stood in the road and read his poems. Behind the balcony, everyone in the room was high on drugs, and the film crew was shooting close-ups of Dylan's twitching face while Phil Ochs tried incoherently to explain the plot of *Hard Times* to him. Allen, in the street, kept calling up that he was ready, but no one seemed to hear. This standard of professionalism persisted throughout the tour, leading eventually to Sam Shephard's premature departure.

The touring band now consisted of Rob Stoner; his friend, drummer Howie Wyeth, whom not even Dylan's bad timing could faze; Luther Rix on drums and percussion; and Scarlet Rivera on violin. David Mansfield, described by Ginsberg as 'the boy with the Botticelli face', doubled on violin as well as dobro, steel guitar and mandolin. There were now four guitarists, not counting Dylan and Joan Baez: Roger McGuinn, Steve Soles, Mick Ronson and Bobby Neuwirth. Ronee Blakley played piano and sang. So many performers could not play at once, so the show was organised like a revue, with everyone but the rhythm section doing a small set, sometimes joining each other, then all coming together for the grand finale. To see if it worked on location, they booked the Seacrest, a resort hotel in Falmouth, Massachusetts, then half-empty because it was out of season, and did a run-through of some of the numbers in the lounge.

The only other occupants of the hotel were a party of 165 elderly Jewish ladies gathered for a fund-raising mah-jong championship. To their great surprise, late one evening the hotel manager rose to announce, in best Las Vegas fashion, that there would be a poetry reading by 'one of America's foremost poets, Mister Allen Ginsberg!' Allen shuffled to the podium, wearing a brown suit, rabbinical curls and a beard. He sat on a stool, hunched over the microphone, and announced that he would read 'Kaddish'. The ladies smiled encouragingly. Dylan filmed the reading and included a large segment of it in the final film. The camera team captured the tension perfectly. Sam Shepard, in his book of the tour, *Rolling Thunder Logbook*, described how he saw it:

'The mothers go from patient acquiescence to giggled embarrassment to downright disgust as Allen keeps rolling away at them . . . Since I was raised a Protestant, there's something in the air here that I can't quite touch, but it feels close to being volcanic. Something of generations, of mothers, of being Jewish, of being raised Jewish, of Kaddish, of prayer, of America even, of poets and language . . . The ladies sit through it, captured in their own seaside resort. A place they've all come to escape to, and there they are, caught.' Shepard was surprised at the burst of applause Allen received; evidently no one could fail to be moved by the poem. It was as if Allen was finally reading it to Naomi herself. Dylan sat silently throughout, absorbing the whole performance.

Joan Baez followed next and charmed the ladies with 'Swing Low Sweet Chariot', Dave Mansfield played some fancy classical guitar, then Dylan set things jumping with 'Simple Twist of Fate', accompanying himself on the piano. He was soon joined by the rest of the band and the Seacrest Motel was transformed into a late-night Greenwich Village rock club. The mah-jong players appeared to enjoy every bit of it.

The first concert was on 30 October 1975, in Plymouth, just around Cape Cod Bay from the Seacrest. Anticipating the bicentennial year, they could not overlook a chance to film a few scenes at Plymouth Rock, and a great deal of time was devoted to trying to lower Allen down from the granite portico which protects it from vandals. Allen was to sit on the rock while Dylan, at the helm of a rubber dinghy that also contained Bobby Neuwirth, Ramblin' Jack Elliott and Peter Orlovsky, landed on the beach and set foot in America. As the dinghy crew, shivering with cold, dragged their craft up the beach to stop it being swept away by the winter tide, Allen busied himself chanting and ringing his finger cymbals, much to the amazement of tourists visiting the historic spot, who stood gaping at him through the railings.

That evening Allen asked Dylan, 'Well, how do you like your party?'

'It's *your* party, it's not mine.'

'Well, is it giving you pleasure?'

'Pleasure? Pleasure? No, not at all. I wouldn't want that, would you? That's too dangerous. I do what I do without thinking of pleasure.'

'And when did you come to that state?' asked Allen.

'Couple of years back,' said Dylan. 'I mean, at one time I went out for a lot of pleasure, all I could get, because, see, there was a lot of pain before that. But I found that the more pleasure I got, subtly there was as much pain. And I began to notice a correspondence, the same frame. I began to experiment and saw it was a balance. So now I do what I do without wanting pleasure. Or pain. Everything in moderation.'

Allen asked if he believed in God.

'God? You mean God? Yes I do. I mean, I know because where I am I get the contact with – it's a certain vibration – in the midst of – you know, I've been up the mountain, and, – yes, I've been up the mountain and I had a choice: Should I come down? So I came down. God said, "Okay, you've been up on the mountain, now you go down. You're on your own, free. Check in later, but now you're on your own. Other business to do so check back in some time. Later." '

'I *used* to belive in God,' said Allen.

'You don't now?' said Dylan, surprised.

'No, I *used* to believe in God.'

'Well, I used to believe in God too,' said Dylan. 'Yes I *used* to believe in God. If you believed in God now you'd write deeper poetry now. I mean, there's no question I didn't get any answers. He's too busy to answer. I understand that – making elephants. Anyone who can make camels go through needles' eyes is too busy to answer my questions. I'm on my own.'

'Did you study Kabala?'

'Well yeah, but it's complicated, and not satisfactory.'

'Any good teachers?'

'Yeah, lots of good teachers, but . . .'

'So you said the other day that you had your own practice. What is it?' asked Allen.

'Oh, I'm not going to give away any secrets! Be sure! I'll cover for God, I'll alibi for God anytime. I'll cover for him. Sure. Absolutely! You don't want me to give him away do you?'

Allen obviously did, but tried another approach, 'Well then, how do you get on the mountain? Or where does the road to the mountain begin?'

'Oh, I can't tell you that. But I can take you there. I promise I'll take you there! You wanna go?'

'I'll come following you,' Allen sang one of Dylan's own lines.

Despite the enormous cost of keeping an ever-changing touring party of forty or more people on the road, Dylan stuck to the idea of playing small halls, though in most places they did two houses to bring in more money. Dylan was quoted in *Time*: 'We were all very close. We had this fire going ten years ago and now we've got it burning again.' The concert schedule accommodated the needs of the film crew; in fact, the cost of the film soon became so high that Dylan had to introduce some larger venues into the itinerary to help break even. The caravan of two touring buses, several cars, equipment trucks and Dylan's personal luxury mobile home slowly wound its way across New England, travelling in great secrecy, always staying twenty or thirty miles from the concert venue, in small, out-of-the-way hotels.

Allen's first idea for the film was, perhaps predictably, that he and Dylan should sleep together, and their subsequent conversation, naked in bed, should be filmed. When he addressed himself seriously to the problem of the film, he came up with a scheme that was nothing if not ambitious. The film, he thought, should 'wrap up all questions' on ecology, capitalism, communism, God, poetry, meditation and America, 'as best we can'. He also thought it should present their thoughts on acid, grass and sexual liberation and have dramatic cameos on the atomic bomb and war, and Jerusalem and the Jews. His notebook brimmed with ideas: a meditation sequence with Burroughs and Trungpa; a dialogue on God between himself and Dylan; Dylan's wife Sara (who was on the tour) as a mother goddess; a dialogue between Dylan and LeRoi Jones on black and white working together; 'whole cast and crew, Mich to Andy, Chris to Sara, lined up family naked for portrait perhaps by swimming pool'; Dylan giving Allen guitar lessons; Allen reading from Sacco and Vanzetti's speech . . . They shot several scenes at the Hillcrest Hotel before the tour began, including one improvised dialogue in a diner on 1 November, with Allen playing the Emperor and Dylan the Alchemist:

Allen: 'I've heard through the grapevine that you have certain powers.'

Dylan: (Evasive as ever) 'Oh, that's not me. But I know who you mean.'

One of the most successful early scenes they shot, and one of the most poignant in the finished film, was a visit to Jack Kerouac's grave. Lowell was the third town on the itinerary, and as soon as they got to town, Allen and Sam Shepard drove to Nick's Lounge. Nick Sampas and his brother Tony were delighted to see Allen again, and Tony drove them out to the cemetery so that Sam could examine the location and make plans for the next day's filming there.

At noon on 3 November, Allen, Dylan, Sam and Peter, accompanied by the camera crew and the soundman holding his Nagra, drove through the black iron gates of the graveyard. Allen and Dylan approached the spot where Kerouac lay and read the inscription on the small marble plaque set in the earth, half-covered by grass and autumn leaves:

> 'TI JEAN' JOHN L. KEROUAC
> MAR. 12, 1922–OCT. 21, 1969
> – HE HONORED LIFE –

Allen quoted Jack's favourite lines from Shakespeare, 'How like a winter hath my absence been . . . what freezings have I felt, what dark days have seen! What old December's bareness everywhere!' Allen and Dylan settled themselves cross-legged on the grass before the plaque. Dylan tuned his Martin guitar, and Allen unpacked his harmonium and quoted a few lines from *Mexico City Blues*, then Dylan borrowed the harmonium and they began to improvise a slow blues, trading verses back and forth, to Jack Kerouac beneath them, under the grass. Allen described the scene in a letter to Gregory: 'Then Dylan took guitar and played slow blues while I composed celestial triplet-rhyme lines, Jack looking down from clouds over trees weeping a big tear – Dylan stopped playing to stuff an autumn leaf in his breast pocket, I continued acapella on the beat, when he picked up the guitar hit chord in time to end my line in proper measure – like old time blues licks – then we walked harmonium and guitar together down vista of gravestones and November bare trees – bright . . . leaves blowing in our path in Graveyard.'

As the Rolling Thunder Revue continued, Allen's on-stage role increased. He was allowed to play finger cymbals on one of Rick

Danko's solo numbers and sing in the chorus on another, but he spent most of his time working on film scenarios. He and Ramblin' Jack Elliott discussed the old days and reminisced about the time, twenty-five years before, when Elliott had gone off with Helen Parker, Allen's first girlfriend, leaving Allen frustrated and broken-hearted. Allen composed a song to her:

> Here's to Helen Parker
> wherever she may be
> Cape Cod or on 14th Street
> in New York City
>
> She took old Allen's cherry
> his first radiant lay
> She stole Jack's ramblin' heart
> practically the same day

Although he was delighted by the communalism and creative energy of the Rolling Thunder Revue, Allen told Dylan that he couldn't stay on for the whole tour because his father was dying and he had to spend time with him.

'Bring your father,' said Dylan.

'What about me, when I'm dying,' asked Allen.

'We'll take care of you, when you're dying,' replied Dylan.

But as Allen said later, 'The next morning he was glum and he didn't remember. And I went up thinking that he was going to take care of me for the rest of my life! I didn't realise that his munificense was engorged with snow.'

It was the first time Allen had been on a big rock tour, and the amount of cocaine being used disturbed him; he wrote a triplet about it for the daily tour newspaper:

> Nobody saves America by sniffing cocaine
> Jiggling yr knees blankeyed in the rain
> When it snows in yr nose you catch cold in yr brain.

Dylan had become convinced of the innocence of the black boxer Hurricane Carter, in jail for murder, and in order to raise money for his appeal fund, they took the Rolling Thunder Revue to Madison Square Garden. The 'Night of the Hurricane' was on

8 December 1975 and tickets sold out in five hours. Louis and Edith attended their first rock concert, to see Allen onstage, in suit and tie and sneakers, not only with Dylan, Joan Baez, Joni Mitchell and Roberta Flack, but with Muhammad Ali, who came to introduce the show. The concert raised $100,000 towards Carter's appeal, and after the Christmas break they did another at the Houston Astrodome. Many years later, Dylan's support for Carter was vindicated when his conviction was reversed.

Allen saw the poet W.S. Merwin in New York, and got a first-hand report of the incident at Trungpa's Vajrayana seminary the previous fall that had become an exciting source of gossip in Buddhist and poetry circles. The event occurred at the three-month intensive seminar that Trungpa organised each year. Allen had attended the first one in 1973 and subsequently went to several more with Peter. In 1975, the seminar was held at the Eldorado Ski Lodge in Snowmass, Colorado, which Vajradhatu had taken over completely from the beginning of September until Thanksgiving.

Merwin had given a reading and a lecture on Dante at Naropa, and was spending the summer there with his new girlfriend Dana Naone. He asked Trungpa if they could attend the seminar. At first Trungpa refused; only a quarter of those who applied had been accepted, and enrolment was complete. The usual requirement was that the applicant had previously sat a *darthun* (a thirty-day sitting period) and taken training courses with Trungpa. Merwin and Naone were not students of Trungpa's, and had no retreat experience, but Trungpa wanted to get Merwin involved, so he gave him preference over the long waiting list.

Merwin's background was intellectual, monastic, contemplative and peaceful and as a pacifist he simply refused to participate in the chants dedicated to the aggressive deities. Whenever lines such as 'You enjoy drinking the hot blood of the ego,' or 'As night falls, you cut the aorta of the perverter of the teachings,' he simply put down his chant sheet, which was in English translation, until the passage was over. The blood-thirsty nature of the chants made Merwin and Naone less and less keen to take vows with Trungpa, and they told him so in a private meeting. They were not prepared to surrender to the guru, which Trungpa required.

31 October occurred in the middle of a period of sitting, and Trungpa declared a Halloween party to celebrate the beginning of

the Vajrayana teaching. At the party, Merwin and Dana danced to records for an hour or so with the other students. Trungpa arrived drunk at about ten-thirty held up by his 'vajra guards', who had already caught him twice when he fell over. Earlier that evening he had told an elderly woman student that he intended to take off people's clothes. When Trungpa arrived, she was the first to be stripped by his guards, who paraded her around the room on their shoulders. Later she said she felt 'trashed out'. Trungpa now did a strip-tease himself and was carried around the room. Dressed again, Trungpa pointed from one person to another, ordering his guards to 'Chop 'em up' – tear off all their clothing.

Trungpa decided to lecture on Vajrayana, and asked if everyone was there. When it was discovered that Merwin and Naone had already left, he sent William McKeever, the executive director of the Naropa Institute, to get them. They returned, but at the door they sensed the excited, violent atmosphere and decided to drive into Aspen for the night. As they prepared to leave, McKeever returned with a command that they attend. They explained they had already been back once and were not going again.

A mob began to gather so Merwin locked the door. McKeever returned a third time with orders from Trungpa to escort them to the party. A threatening crowd had now gathered in the hall, the telephone line had been cut and the mob began kicking the door. Then someone announced, with great satisfaction, that Trungpa had sent an order to bring them down, 'at any cost'. Trungpa suggested smashing the window. His guards did as they were told and planned a simultaneous attack on both door and window. As the door gave way, Merwin struck out with a bottle in the darkness as his attackers came pushing through the splinters. Merwin described what happened next, 'At that point Dana shrieked and there was a loud crashing as the big glass balcony door was smashed by McKeever, among others, with another heavy object . . . I crossed the room and started to beat the remnants of the glass door outward onto the balcony, pushing with broken bottles, but meantime the crowd forced its way into the room behind us from the hall. Dana was shouting, "Police! Why doesn't somebody call the police?" but they laughed at her, women too, and Trungpa later mocked her, for that, in one of his lectures.'

As they were dragged back to Trungpa's party, Dana again pleaded, 'Why doesn't someone call the police?' One of the women insulted her and a man threw a glass of wine in her face. Trungpa was sitting in a chair, surrounded by his disciples, who sat in a ring on the floor. He ordered them to sit down. Merwin's account continued. 'He said we hadn't accepted his invitation. I said that if we *had* to accept it wasn't an invitation. An invitation, I said, allowed the other person the privilege of declining ... I reminded him that we never promised to obey him. He said, "Ah, but you asked to come." Then dramatically, "Into the lion's mouth."

'I said that they'd developed big corkscrews, now, for forcing coyotes out of their burrows, and that maybe he ought to get one, to do his job more easily.'

During one of their exchanges, Trungpa threw a glass of saki in Merwin's face. 'That's saki,' Trungpa told him, then turned to Dana Naone. 'You're Oriental,' he said. 'You're smarter than this. You might be playing slave to this white man but you and I know where it's at. We're both Oriental ... we know where it's at.' He began to ramble drunkenly about, 'My country being ripped out from under me, and it was the Chinese communists who did it ... If there's one thing I want to see in my lifetime, it's to see my country back. Only one Oriental to another can understand that.'

According to Jack Niland, one of Trungpa's students, 'He kept doing this super racist thing ... very cutting, and her only response was, "You're a Nazi, you're a Nazi," and "Someone call the police." She was completely freaking out.' Then Trungpa asked them to join in the dance and celebration and take their clothes off. They both refused.

'Why *not*?' asked Trungpa. 'What's your *secret*? Why don't you *want* to undress?' and to Dana he said, 'Are you afraid to show your pubic hair?' Trungpa said that if they wouldn't undress, they would be stripped. Merwin described the stripping, 'He ordered his guards to do the job. They dragged us apart, and it was then that Dana started screaming. Several of them on each of us, holding us down. Only two men, Dennis White and Bill King, both of whom were married with small children there at the seminary, said a word to try and stop it, on Dana's behalf. Trungpa stood up and punched Bill King in the face, called him a son-of-a-bitch, and told him not to interfere. The guards grabbed Bill King and got him out of there. One of the guards who'd stayed out of it went out and vomited, as we heard later. When I was let go I got up and lunged at Trungpa. But there were three guards in between, and all I could swing at him through the crowd, was a left, which was wrapped in the towel, and scarcely reached his mouth. It didn't amount to much and I was dragged off, of course.'

As the guards lunged for Dana, she tried to hang onto Merwin but they were pulled apart. She tried to get at Trungpa but he was too well protected. 'Guards dragged me off and pinned me to the floor,' she wrote in her account of the incident. 'I could see William struggling a few feet away from me. I fought and called to friends, men and women whose faces I saw in the crowd, to call the police. No one did . . . Richard Assaly was stripping me while others held me down. Trungpa was punching Assaly in the head, urging him to do it faster. The rest of my clothes were torn off.'

'See?' said Trungpa. 'It's not so bad, is it?' They stood holding each other, naked, with Dana sobbing.

After meeting with Trungpa the next day for tea, Merwin and Naone elected to stay on at the seminary to attend Trungpa's climactic Vajrayana lectures, which took place as scheduled for the next two weeks. They made no public statements about the humiliating assault, but rumour and gossip soon spread throughout the Buddhist and poetry communities. Many Buddhists felt misgivings about Trungpa's methods – including several high-ranking Tibetan teachers – while Merwin's friends, outraged at the treatment he had received, felt an apology, at least, was in order. None came, and the affair tarnished Trungpa's reputation, particularly among critics suspicious of or hostile to Tibetan Buddhism, with its insistence that the guru can do no wrong. To supporters of the Chinese Revolution, it was further proof that change in Tibet was long overdue.

Louis Ginsberg's health was slowly deteriorating. In his eighties, he was now too tired to go out for a walk or even to reach down and take off his shoes. He needed help to rise from his velvet armchair where he sat looking out over the rooftops. 'Don't get old,' he advised Peter. Louis was diagnosed as having a tumour of the pancreas and spots on his lungs. Against the wishes of the family, Allen asked the doctor to tell Louis what was wrong. 'Thank God,' said Louis, 'I thought it was cancer of the brain.'

One evening, Allen took a walk through the old downtown section of Paterson. Entire blocks had been torn down, and new buildings and malls stood near Fair Street, where he grew up. The site of their old house now lay beneath the newly built Hamilton

Plaza. 'Massive poured concrete building sites and walkways, all downtown changed,' he wrote, 'ghostly and empty streeted.'

Louis and Edith's apartment on Park Avenue was so quiet that Allen was able to complete his first ten thousand prostrations, but he was still way behind everyone else in his group. Although Louis was very sick, the doctor thought that he would live for some time yet, so at the end of March 1976, Allen left to teach at Naropa. 'Off to see that Trungpo-Mumpo?' Louis complained.

Allen wrote to Gregory: 'Louis is dying in Paterson, wasted thin arms, wrinkled breasts, big belly, skull nose speckled feet thin legs, can't stand up out of bathtub ... I may have to leave Naropa to help him out of bed to die.'

Allen had readings booked in New Jersey in May, and spent as much time as possible with Louis. In Part III of 'Don't Grow Old' Allen described him, 'wasted arms, feeble knees/ 80 years old, hair thin and white/ cheek bonier than I'd remembered.'

Allen read to him from Wordsworth's 'Intimations of Immortality': 'Trailing clouds of glory do we come from God, who is our home . . .'

'That's beautiful,' said Louis, 'but it's not true.' He told Allen a story from his youth: 'When I was a boy, we had a house on Boyd Street, Newark. The backyard was a big empty lot full of bushes and tall grass. I always wondered what was beyond those trees. When I grew older, I walked around the block, and found out what was back there – It was a glue factory.'

Returning to New York briefly in early May, Allen was walking down Central Park West, and found himself at the Dakota Apartments at 72nd Street. He telephoned upstairs and visited John Lennon and Yoko Ono for an hour. In a bizarre arrangement, Yoko Ono had set Lennon up with a Chinese–American woman, May Pang, and encouraged them to have an affair. Ono controlled the situation by telephone – sometimes as many as twenty calls a day. The liaison lasted for eighteen months and became much more serious than she had expected. Lennon and Pang moved to Los Angeles, where Lennon cut two albums and produced a third with Harry Nilsson. The cocaine and madness of the LA music scene brought out the worst in Lennon, and he eventually returned home to Ono, dumping May Pang in a rather callous manner en route. Now he and Yoko had a child, Sean, and Lennon was devoting his time to bringing him up. John told Allen that he and

Yoko had gone on a forty-day fast after Sean's birth and were practising a very clean and healthy diet. John baked all the bread.

He said that he had been lying sleepless one night, listening to WBAI on earphones, when he heard someone reading a long poem. He thought at first that it was Bob Dylan and was surprised when the announcer said that it was Allen Ginsberg reading 'Howl'. He admitted that he had never read it before. Although he had a copy, 'my eyes saw the page, but I can't read anything. I can't get anything from print.' Now, hearing 'Howl', he understood why Dylan had mentioned Allen so often, how much Allen had influenced Dylan, and how close to Dylan his style was.

Allen wrote his friend Miles, 'It sure was nice hearing Lennon close that gap, complete the circle and treat me like a fellow artist as he walked me to the door goodbye.'

In the middle of May, Allen flew to Wichita, to rejoin the Rolling Thunder Revue, which had been touring Florida and the southern states. The film had completed shooting in January, and Allen, who spent a week hanging out with Dylan, decided to ask him for fifteen thousand dollars for acting in it and setting up the scenes and dialogue. He wanted a car and a stereo set and to give some money to Ray Bremser. The mention of Bremser, whom Dylan had heard read when he first arrived in New York in 1961, did the trick, and the money came through. Dylan took 120 hours of film into the Sound Factory in Hollywood and emerged twenty months later with a four-hour film called *Renaldo and Clara* in which Allen played a major dramatic role.

Allen continued to spend as much time as he could with his father. On 4 June, Louis felt strong enough to talk to a reporter from the *Village Voice*. He said that he didn't believe in life after death. 'I'll tell you what my attitude is,' said Louis. 'It's full of awe and wonder, because when you think about a galaxy with billions of stars, and you think of billions of galaxies sweeping throught the universe, you wonder, why this prodigious display of energy?'

Allen returned to Boulder to teach his summer classes at Naropa. A telephone call early in the morning of 8 July 1976, informed him that Louis had died peacefully in his sleep. Allen was on the first plane out of Denver for New York. As he flew over Lake Michigan in the morning sun, the poem 'Father Death Blues' came to him in rhyming triplets, complete with a tune:

Hey Father Death, I'm flying home
Hey poor man, you're all alone
Hey old daddy, I know where I'm going

Father Death, Don't cry any more
Mama's there, underneath the floor
Brother Death, please mind the store

The next day the *New York Times* devoted sixteen column inches to an obituary headed, 'Louis Ginsberg, Traditional Poet'. The subtitle read, 'Gave Readings With His Son, Allen, In Last Years.' The obituary, by Thomas Lask, quoted a part of Louis' poem 'The Fly', which concluded: 'All material/ Things depart/ Now all the world/ Is hinged on the heart.'

Not long after his father's death, Allen joined Peter at an intensive meditation seminary in Land O'Lakes, Wisconsin. Allen and Peter sat, looking out over the snow-powdered flatland day after day. Allen needed the solitude to come to terms with his father's death and with the reflected significance of his own middle-age. He wrote Gregory: 'I'm finished as a poet, no more magic, nobody left out there to yell at, nobody left to curse out, to take revenge on or feel superior to! Not even Rockefeller! God knows where you are! My book "Mind Breaths" ends up in my father's grave. Take care.'

Ginsberg had three important books published in the fall of 1977: *As Ever: The Collected Correspondence of Allen Ginsberg and Neal Cassady*, published by Creative Arts in Berkeley, with a forward by Carolyn Cassady; *Mind Breaths*, his new City Lights collection, which appeared at the beginning of December; and his first hardback, *Journals Early Fifties Early Sixties*, edited by Gordon Ball and published by Grove Press. The journals drew a lot of press attention, including a long review from Allen's old Columbia class-mate Louis Simpson in the *New York Times Book Review*. Simpson regretted the 'acres' of dreams in the book but also said: 'There are some entertaining "political ravings" in these "Journals," including insults to some people at Columbia who did not pay sufficient attention to his poems when they first came out. As I was one of those people, I am happy to have this opportunity to say that I was wrong – not merely wrong, obtuse.'

A remarkable – and an honourable – volte-face from Allen's old opponent.

As winter began, Allen worried continuously about the Merwin–Trungpa conflict. A journal entry for 28 November, in his habitual 'worst-case' stylisation of transient anxieties, noted that he felt 'trapped "like smoke going down a bamboo tube" between poesy and Dharma, Merwin and Trungpa, in their ghost war. Hypocrite, I take rides with each. I haven't pursued my prostrations, I push and preach Dharma and poetry in public. I *can*'t face Merwin, I get angry at my boyfriends and students, I am a hairy loss.' His journals indicate that Allen still had doubts about the whole guru–disciple relationship, as practised by Tibetan Buddhism. The Merwin incident intensified his unease. He wrote, 'This submission to Trungpa guru, this surrender, is it correct? A transfer of God failure debasement to a Living Body so at least the Adoration Devotion is to a real Entity not an image – and Merwin's war, is it mine, 'gainst the vulgar drunken Guru Sangha? – Am I a fool?'

He spent much of January 1978 on the farm with Peter, then fitted in a short reading tour before returning to Naropa in March to teach his students Blake's *Urizen* – a project that became a four-term course, a line-by-line discussion of Blake's works from early poems through the prophetic books to the Seventh Night of 'Vala, or the Four Zoas'.

Among the administrative problems facing him as co-director of the Kerouac Poetry School was the rejection of two grant applications by the National Endowment of the Arts, which had learned of Merwin's treatment at the hands of the president of Naropa. Although the Poetics Department did have complete independence in its teaching, it was still criticised by some for being a department of the institute of which Trungpa was chief director. Naropa also had a $35,000 grant from the Rockefeller Foundation to protect.

Naropa grew chronically short of funds; in 1977, many of the teaching staff did not receive their salaries on time. Allen donated most of his salary to Naropa, as did many of the staff who could afford to, and raised money with many benefit readings.

Members of the poetry community began to align themselves for or against Trungpa, but it was not until the spring of 1977 that Allen was first involved in the controversy on a personal level.

Among the most vocal in his outrage at the treatment of Merwin and Naone was the poet Robert Bly, who was using the term 'Buddhist fascism' to describe Trungpa's behaviour. This was a serious criticism, because Bly had been a student of Trungpa's and had even helped him edit his first book, *Meditation in Action*.

As Bly interpreted the situation, Allen, despite being in charge of the poetry school that had presented Merwin's lecture and reading, had sided with his teacher against the poetry community that he was supposed to be encouraging and protecting, poets he had devoted his whole life to promoting and nurturing. 'So what is this community of poets I was talking to you about?' he asked Allen. 'What happened to that? ... You're sacrificing that, for what? That teacher? You can't sacrifice human beings and poets you've been associated with your whole life!' It was this basic charge that Allen had to consider seriously, particularly when the Merwin affair resurfaced at Naropa that summer.

Poet Ed Sanders had been invited to teach a course on 'Investigative Poetics' and had expected his students to choose something like the strike against compulsory lie detector tests at the nearby Coors Brewery or an investigation into the local Rocky Flats Plutonium factory, south of Boulder. To his surprise, his class voted overwhelmingly to investigate the circumstances of the infamous Halloween party at the Vajradhatu seminary. Twenty-four students worked on the project, sometimes until dawn, intending to interview everyone even remotely connected with the incident, intending to reconstruct the events leading up to the final stripping. The 179-page report was finished in less than a month; the only person who refused to grant them an interview was Trungpa. To the relief of the Poetics Department and the Naropa administration, the students voted not to publish their findings for the time being, considering the controversy a private matter. Allen ended his teaching with a meditation retreat, this time devoted more to prostrations than to sitting. He managed 5,000 prostrations during his nine-day stay at the Rocky Mountain Dharma Center, bringing his total up to 26,600.

Trungpa's style had gradually changed, prompted by the visit in 1974 of the Karmapa, the head of his lineage; he now advocated short hair and neat dress. Suits and ties soon surplanted the casual hippie outfits of his original followers, and alcohol became the drug of choice. Trungpa was chauffeured around in a blue

Mercedes-Benz, and his home was staffed by students dressed as English butlers and maids; they were required to call Trungpa and his wife 'Sir' and 'Lady Diana'. He was protected by bodyguards known as the Vajra Guard, who wore blue blazers and received specialised training that included haiku composition and flower arranging. On one occasion, to test a student guard's alertness, Trungpa hurled himself from a staircase, expecting to be caught. The guard was looking the other way and Trungpa landed on his head, requiring a hospital visit.

As well as his involvement with Naropa, Allen still had other interests and campaigns. Twelve miles from Boulder, in Rocky Flats, the Rockwell Corporation made nuclear triggers for hydrogen bombs. In 1975 Allen had gone on one of the public tours of the plant, with W.S. Merwin, among others, and had also been involved in various anti-nuclear demonstrations directed against the factory. On 12 June, he began work on a long poem, his own version of Corso's 'Bomb', and two days later, after one of his typical all-night marathon writing sessions, he had the completed manuscript of 'Plutonian Ode'. The poem began: 'What new element before us unborn in nature? Is there/ a new thing under the Sun?'

The next day, he and Peter were arrested along with other demonstrators as they sat meditating on the railroad tracks, blocking the passage of a trainload of nuclear waste labelled 'Fissile Materials', which was being transported out of Rocky Flats precincts.

'Plutonian Ode' became the title poem of his next City Lights book and appeared in numerous underground newspapers and magazines. The poem was a good example of Ginsberg's mature style – 'glittering thoughtful galaxies, whirlpools of starspume silver-thin as hairs of Einstein!' – and he delivered the polemic by addressing himself directly to the strange new substance and details of its manufacture, describing the apparatus that his bardic chant was meant to penetrate: 'My voice resounds through robot glove boxes & ingot cans and echoes in electric vaults inert of atmosphere . . .'

Throughout the summer, the main subject of conversation was the Merwin affair. Of particular concern was whether or not Trungpa could do no wrong, since as a lineage holder of the Dharma, his every action was a teaching vehicle and could be learned from. 'If you make a mistake, you learn from it, therefore there are no mistakes,' said Ginsberg, referring to Trungpa's position as a member of the 'mishap Lineage'. The opposing view was that Trungpa had been an alcoholic ever since the late 1960s and was certainly capable of making mistakes. He misused his power to pressure dozens of female students to have sex, and when one student, illegally in the country, refused, he telephoned the immigration police to have her deported. It appeared, particularly to outsiders, that Trungpa was intent on recreating the feudal theocracy he had in Chamdo. The apparent drift of his teachings was toward the 'mandala-concept' of the Kingdom of Shambala, a non-democratic kingdom in which he had supreme power, using terms drawn in part from the Tibetan secular epic *Gesar of Ling*, and his inner circle became more and more like a medieval court, complete with court intrigue and rivalry.

Though Ed Sanders' investigative poetics team had voted not to publish their report on the Merwin incident, photocopies were circulating in the poetry community. Sanders had given poet Ed Dorn permission to distribute copies as he saw fit, and Dorn had mailed out fifty of them, mostly to other poets. There was widespread interest in the report, and Ferlinghetti asked Allen for a copy so he could consider it for publication by City Lights; Allen refused. Poet Tom Clark, now the senior writer on the local *Boulder Monthly*, also asked Ed for permission to publish the report, since he thought that Boulder residents should be better informed of the activities of the large Buddhist community in their midst. Sanders told Clark that the poetry class had been canvassed earlier that year and that they still voted against publication.

On 13 September, Ed Sanders wrote to Dorn saying that a majority of the class were now in favour of publication. He added, 'Report came in yesterday that the Vajra Guards were recently training wearing Canadian Mountie uniforms and that the word "democracy" is now being used apparently at Naropa as a catch-all word for the ills of the world . . .' Still, Ed was hesitant to publish, because it would mean a 'sure or probable break' with many of his old poet colleagues.

All this changed when the news broke of the events of 18 November 1978, when the Reverend Jim Jones led a mass suicide of 911 members of his People's Temple in Guyana. Horrific photographs of bloated bodies heaped in the temple compound filled the press and television screens, and religious cults became a national topic of conversation. Ed Sanders' investigative poetics group immediately voted overwhelmingly to publish their report.

Inevitable comparisons were made. Jones, like Trungpa, had forced men and women to strip in public and had sex with many of his female followers. When he ordered the mass suicide, not all of his followers aquiesced, and it was his armed guards who forced many of them to drink the cyanide-laced Kool-Aid. Trungpa's students did not consider that a Jonestown was a possibility in Boulder or at a seminary, but people further removed from the centre were less sure. What if Trungpa had ordered the mob to rape Naone? They would have surely complied. Allen realised that the fear of Vajradhatu stemmed largely from the traditionally hermetic nature of such teachings, and he began to wonder if the inner workings of Vajradhatu ought not to be made public. But Allen still gave Trungpa his general support, considering the real heat of the controversy to be an aspect of cultural xenophobia.

The first articles about the Merwin affair began appearing in the press, with the publication in the February 1979 *Harpers* of 'Spiritual Obedience' by Peter Martin, a writer who had taught two courses in literature at Naropa in 1977. The local newspaper, the *Daily Camera*, asked at Vajradhatu for any comment on the *Harpers* article and ran a piece about Trungpa. In a follow-up, the *Camera* carried an editorial headlined 'To Avoid The Name, Shed The Disguise', which commented on the *Harpers* piece and briefly described the Merwin incident. Regarding the charge that Trungpa was operating a Jim Jones-type cult, the *Camera* mentioned the guards, the limousine and the drinking, and suggested, 'To avoid being called a cult, it might help not to act like one.'

Tom Clark asked if he could interview Allen about the affair for *Boulder Monthly*. Allen had reservations about the magazine, and about talking about the incident since he had not been there. Though he knew Clark regarded Oriental meditation practice as a cultural anachronism and disapproved of Trungpa, he was confident of Clark's good intentions because their *Paris Review* interview in 1965 had worked out so well. As co-director of the poetry school, Allen agreed, assuming he would have a chance to edit his interview as he had done for the *Paris Review*.

* * *

The interview took place on 12 January 1979, with Ed Dorn and a student present. The first question put by Clark regarded the effect on Allen and the Buddhist community of Peter Martin's article. 'Universal paranoia, I think,' said Allen. 'Also some clarification of complexities that everybody feels within the Buddhist community. It brings to the surface a lot of thoughts that people have had anyway and discussed among themselves, but just didn't discuss publicly: fear of Buddhist fascism, paranoia about submission to a guru, the apparent incomprehensibility of the Merwin thing ... It's like reading your marriage troubles in the newspaper.'

Tom Clark was a skilled interviewer, and he almost immediately steered Allen to the heart of the matter: the political implications of the submissive relationship between disciple and guru. Allen demurred, 'You know you're talking about my love life,' he said. 'My extremely delicate love life. My relations with my teacher.'

Clark pointed out that people were interested in the subject more for its implications than just regarding the rights or wrongs of the Merwin incident itself. 'If you turn this around and say it takes two to make a master,' said Clark, 'you're not necessarily saying that one or the other's culpable.'

'I feel culpable,' said Ginsberg. 'It's my paranoia that I'm expressing.'

'I don't think that you personally were ever accused by anybody of anything in this regard,' said Clark.

'I assume myself all the time, of seducing the entire poetry scene and Merwin into this impossible submission to some spiritual dictatorship which they'll never get out of again, and which will ruin American culture forever. Anything might happen. We might get taken over and eaten by the Tibetan monsters. All the monsters of the Tibetan Book of the Dead might come out and get everybody to take LSD! ... The Pandora's Box of the Bardo Thodol has been opened by the arrival in America of one of the masters of the secrets of the Tibetan Book of the Dead.'

Allen trusted and had faith in Trungpa's intelligence and thought there had been no sexual motive in Trungpa's approach to Dana Naone. Clark pointed out that it was only natural, in the light of Jonestown, to be concerned when a large group of people appeared to condone the assault on two others by not helping, even when one of them was pleading with them to call the police. At this Allen grew passionate: 'In the middle of that scene, to yell "Call the police" – do you realise how *vulgar* that was? The Wisdom of the East was being unveiled, and she's going "Call the police!" I mean, shit! Fuck that shit! Strip 'em naked, break down the door! Anything – symbolically. I mentioned privacy before – the entrance into Vajrayana is the abandonment of all privacy. And the entry onto the Bodhisattva path is totally – You're saying, "I no longer have any privacy ever again."'

Clark pointed out, 'You only make that sacrifice if you *want* to.'

'Only if you want to,' Allen agreed.

'What if they didn't want to?'

'Then what were they doing at this Vajrayana seminary?'

To Allen, much of this seemed hypocritical. He complained that all poets demanded poetic licence, the divine 'right to shit on anybody *they* want to ... Burroughs commits murder, Gregory Corso borrows money from everybody and shoots up drugs for twenty years but he's "divine Gregory" but poor old Trungpa, who's been suffering since he was two years old to teach the dharma, isn't allowed to wave his frankfurter! And if he does, the poets get real mad that their territory is being invaded!'

The interview with Tom Clark was ill-advised in every way. Until that point, as Clark said, no one had blamed Allen for the Merwin affair, or even for encouraging some members of the poetry community to get mixed up with an Oriental despot.

Allen asked to see a copy of the transcript to approve the editing and accuracy of it. Clark had a deadline to meet, and as Allen was about to fly to New York to receive a poetry prize, he asked Clark to show the edited transcript to Anne Waldman; he did not. When Allen returned from New York, in late February, Tom Clark dropped a transcript of his interview off at his house. When Allen went to *Boulder Monthly* with his revisions, he was horrified to find the office piled high with cartons of the March 1979 issue, waiting to be shipped out. It contained Allen's interview, a section of Sanders's report, and an unflattering picture of Trungpa on the cover. Allen was enraged. Clark had retained all of Allen's most critical references to Merwin.

Meanwhile, all over town, the magazine was selling out, as Buddhists bought four or five copies at a time. Sanders flew in from California and picked up a bundle of the magazine to distribute, and Ed Dorn sent copies out to poet friends around the country.

The article provoked some strong reactions, including one from Bob Callahan, the publisher of the Turtle Island Press, who was so concerned that he organised a petition requesting the members of the poetry community to suspend any participation in the activities of the Jack Kerouac School of Disembodied Poetics until the Vajra Guards had been disbanded and efforts made to guarantee that such a thing could not occur again. It demanded that the 'rights of individuals to dissent according to conscience be at all times respected'. Callahan received between forty and forty-five signatures, with the Bay Area poets split roughly down the middle. Those not already connected to Naropa were usually happy to sign. Native American poets such as Jim Pepper, Leslie Silko and Simon Ortiz all signed, as did Black or Third World poets such as Ishmael Reed, Victor Hernandez Cruz and Allen's friend David Henderson. Many of the poets with Buddhist connections agreed in private with Callahan, but were not prepared to put their name on anything in public. Michael McClure telephoned Callahan and told him, 'Those wimps at Naropa are no threat to you. I've told Allen for years, privately, to get out of that scene. Still, Allen believes in it. It's his family. You can't attack him for it. You're trying to ruin Allen Ginsberg. You can't do that!' McClure then began a telephone campaign to stop people signing the petition.

Gary Snyder telephoned Callahan and said, 'Your response isn't generous enough.' Two weeks previously Snyder had told Callahan that he had 'grave doubts' about Trungpa's behaviour but now he said, 'Take off my clothes? Sure, I'd do it. It's a big joke to me. Just don't criticise Allen in public.' One of the strongest attacks on Trungpa came from Kenneth Rexroth, a long time student of Buddhism and translator from the Chinese and Japanese, who said, 'Many believe Chogyam Trungpa has unquestionably done more harm to Buddhism in the United States than any man living.' Few defended Trungpa, but few would criticise Allen or the Jack Kerouac School of Disembodied Poetics, which had, after all, engendered the original Sanders' Class Report.

Jim Hartz, the man who originally introduced Merwin to Trungpa, was the first person to openly criticise Allen in print, 'Allen's become a sort of lapdog and apologist for a Tibetan monarchist who loathes anything that smacks of democracy – no wonder they push Thomas Hobbes in the "Vajra Politics" courses at the seminaries – particularly Hobbes' "Leviathan." Frankly, as

Trungpa gleefully did a couple of years ago at Naropa proclaiming the "death of hippiedom" (Trungpa encouraged his students to vote for Nixon v McGovern, Ford v Carter . . .) I think the Beat trip is dead. For the cover of the investigation as far as I'm concerned, they ought to have a picture of Allen, in his Uncle Sam hat, wrapped in the Shambala flag, pissing on Walt Whitman's grave – and Neruda's too!!! At least, Allen as a "Beat" is dead. Ironic twist, to say the least.'

Allen was, as usual, his own severest critic. In an apologetic letter he later wrote to Merwin, he described his reaction when he learned that the unauthorised version of his interview had been printed: 'I was freaked out and yelled at Tom, thinking he had betrayed my trust and purposely got me into hot water. My main worry was that indiscreet put downs of your poetry, hyperbolic fantasies of Buddhist fascism, low grade gossipy opinions about scenes where I wasn't present, distorted paraphrases of conversations with Trungpa . . . would not only reveal my own basic hypocracy, but also confuse the public issue (if there was one) with my un-edited, private, and hysteric or irritable conversation with friends. I'd thought I'd have a chance to correct the interview or Clark have the friendly common sense to edit and clean up my solecisms.

'I stopped yelling at Tom when I realised it was a fait-accomplis irreversable and he thought he was doing it (aside from pressure from the magazine) as the rare bold action of an honest reporter, and that my yelling was only making the situation worse by solidifying my own and Tom's self-righteousness. I also breathed a sigh of relief, that I had hit bottom and my own hypocracies were unmasked to fellow poets and fellow Buddhists, and that was almost a service rather than a stumbling block.'

17 Eminence Grise

Poet, but sick of writing about myself/ Homosexual role model, noted for stable relationship, but separating out from companion & now worried about lacklove who's going to take care of me in deathbed senility/ Buddhist agitator, but bad meditator with high blood pressure/ Scholar but hardly read books no patience anymore/ Peacenik Protestor but coward and bored with confrontation/ Left wing but suspicious of communism & revolutions including American revolution/ Anti-bourgeois, but want a house & garden & car/ Democrat but following guru leader/ Anarchist individualist but involved in sangha

Journal, 1 September 1984

By the end of the 1970s, Ginsberg, now in his fifties, had established what his friends often referred to as the 'Ginsberg Cottage Industry', a team of people engaged to further Allen's projects and campaigns: a secretary, a file clerk, a booking agent, a bibliographer, teams of students to transcribe his journals, translators in dozens of languages, teaching assistants, lawyers specialising in the Freedom of Information Act, lawyers good at civil rights, lawyers knowledgeable about drug laws, accountants specialising in non-profit foundations. In addition to this, an unlimited supply of editors of little literary magazines and small presses remained anxious to publish his texts. The amount of paperwork generated grew to staggering proportions and became itself a subject for poems. Thousands of pages of transcribed journals sat unread, great files on the CIA, drug busts, censorship, and dozens of other projects filled the file cabinets in the apartment at 12th Street, all kept in some semblance of order by Bob Rosenthal, who had been Allen's secretary since the end of 1977. Rosenthal was his facilitator: 'I really worked, especially in the later 1970s, just on social activism. Allen needed people to write letters for him to governors and heads of state, and if Allen wrote these letters, he got responses. He could write to more people through me. I just had to learn some Buddhist jargon to throw in those letters: "grounded," "mindful" . . . I was facilitating his good deeds in the world. Or we thought they were good deeds.' Rosenthal was Allen's representative: he brokered Allen's position between rival factions in gay politics, negotiated and mediated on his behalf in Buddhist politics, eco-politics and government politics. He decided which group Allen would march with in the gay parade, whom he would stay with and who would be his translator.

Allen had now reached an age where his fame and notoriety were such that the establishment was forced to recognise his achievements. His pioneering work in promoting open-form poetry and the work of his friends in the Beat Generation had created a whole new genre of American letters. Recognition had first come in April 1974, when he was given the National Book Award in Poetry for *The Fall of America*. Next came the National Arts Club gold medal, and acceptance into that establishment on 22 February 1979, at the club's Gramercy Park South headquarters. The principal speaker was the commissioner of cultural affairs for the City of New York, Henry Geldzahler, who, to everyone's astonishment, chose this august occasion to come out of the closet. He announced, 'It is easier and more palatable for me to be an American and to be a homosexual because Allen has stood and spoken out. His eloquence allows us to share his victory.' After speeches by Norman Mailer, the previous year's recipient, William Burroughs, John Ashbery and Ted Berrigan, Allen remarked how pleased he was to have 'the stamp of the City's approval on cocksucking by the commissioner of cultural affairs', which drew roars of laughter. Afterward Allen examined the medal and found the word 'distinction' misspelled on its obverse. 'And these were the people we were fighting against!' he commented.

Following hot on the heels of the National Arts Club came the American Academy of Arts and Letters, which also inducted him as a member. He even received the Medal of Honour from the Commune of Rimini, in Italy. Allen was now an officially decorated member of the establishment. None of these honours, however, loosened his writer's block or relieved his preoccupation with his role in the Merwin affair. In his journals, he mused: 'I've difficulty knowing whether I'm lying to myself to cover Trungpa's hierarchical secrecy, or lying to Clark in not openly and continuously confronting him in his journalistic spitefulness and intrigue ... This inhibits my writing altogether since I don't want to waste my poesy and readers' time on gossip and spite, or exhibit my own confusion.' Ranged against him in his defence of Trungpa were his old friends Clark, Dorn and Sanders, as well as Merwin himself. At a meeting of the American Academy of Arts and Letters, Allen had run into Merwin, who looked at him calmly and said, 'I don't trust you, Ginsberg!'

In December 1979, *The Great Naropa Poetry Wars* by Tom Clark was published, closely followed in March 1980 by Ed Sanders's Naropa class report, *The Party: A Chronological Perspective on a Confrontation at a Buddhist Seminary*. Allen campaigned to limit the damage caused by Clark's book, taking it upon himself to correct every minor factual error and innuendo, of which there were many. Talking about the Vajra Guards, Clark wrote: 'The rumour is, they're armed with M-16s. Others say it's submachine guns.' Naturally, the local press was interested in a private Buddhist army in training, and Allen spent weeks anxiously following up the story until he found its source: someone on the other side of the valley who saw the guards practising bowing and thought they were doing bayonet practice. He tape-recorded all his telephone calls and drove himself so hard that he almost lost his voice, but he was finally able to assure the local *Rocky Mountain News* that there were no guns.

The book caused more than a temporary rift between friends. On the last page, Clark ran an appendix entitled 'The Big Payoff', which listed the recipients of the National Endowment for the Arts awards for November 1979 who had been staff instructors or faculty members of the Jack Kerouac School and who, in Clark's words, 'therefore are at least implicit proponents of what Allen Ginsberg has called the "experiment in monarchy" of Chogyam Trungpa.' He pointed out that the Literature Advisory Panel included Ron Padgett, a former Naropa poetics instructor. Clark said that he had suggested to David Wilk, the Literature programme Director of the NEA, that awarding $150,000 in fellowships to one small, identifiable group of writers amounted to wholesale federal subsidy of an avowedly anti-democratic literary movement. 'Personally, I'm upset about it,' Wilk responded 'but publicly I can't say a word.'

Some, but not all, of the poets listed in the book were Buddhists, yet as Allen and many others pointed out, the same group was more closely identified with the St Mark's Poetry Project in New York, but that did not make them Christians. Many of the people who had read or taught at Naropa – William Burroughs and Gregory Corso, for instance – were not Buddhists and did not agree with Trungpa's philosophy or politics.

This was no longer an internecine dispute between poets. Clark had handed the ultra-conservative Heritage Foundation and those who styled themselves 'neo-conservatives' a weapon with which they could attack not just Naropa but the NEA itself. Ginsberg said, 'It seemed to me an enormous mistake to make a political issue out of an aesthetic issue ... Ron Padgett went through a horror scene after getting money for all those friends of his who were worthy like Ted Berrigan and Alice Notley. That led to a round of critiques in *Coda*, saying we were a clique. And it was just the opposite. This was the first time there was ever any money given to the bohemian group. It was like a nightmare; them announcing they were anti-fascist and then aligning themselves with the Heritage Foundation.'

A series of articles appeared in *West Coast Book Review* and elsewhere, all attacking Naropa, Allen, Peter and Anne Waldman for garnering NEA grants or for claiming that Naropa was the 'centre of American poetry' (a line, in fact, taken from *Time* magazine). The articles led to the Heritage Foundation's denouncing Allen and the grants, which in turn led to the diminishing of NEA grants to magazines, and a cut-off of funds for autonomous community organisations like the St Mark's Poetry Project, the Detroit Institute programme, Beyond Baroque in Los Angeles and other poetry projects. A trend began that was still visible in September 1985, in an attempt by a group of Republican congressmen to withdraw funding from work that was thought to be 'obscene, and contrary to the taste of the public', a reference to Peter Orlovsky's book *Clean Asshole Poems and Smiling Vegetable Songs*.

Allen's defence of Trungpa led inevitably to conflicts with his friends. On a visit to the Bedrock Mortar Hermitage, as his cabin next to Gary Snyder's house was now called, he and Snyder quickly got into a challenging argument about Trungpa's imperial style of teaching. Allen referred to it, rather grandly, as 'Dharma King Monarchical', but Gary insisted that it was simply 'Theocratic'. Allen countered by saying that there was no God in Buddhism, but he was on shaky ground. He noted afterwards, 'I was troubled by my defensiveness in explaining role of Vajra Guards and his rational disapproval. The subject had sat with him long time and when it rose he was urgent to show his thought as if he'd rehearsed or feared this argument. Same for myself.'

Allen's position was not helped when the Dalai Lama, the spiritual head of all Tibetan Buddhists, very pointedly left out Trungpa's centre when he began a six-week tour of Tibetan centres in the United States on 3 August, that year, or by the fact that at the 1979 seminary Trungpa insisted that his students dress formally with suits and ties for the men and dressed his guards in military uniform. Trungpa himself wore British military uniform and the atmosphere was very stiff and correct. Trungpa was reported to be drinking a tremendous amount and keeping his talks very short.

There was also a tension between Allen and Gary over Allen's house and land. Several times Gary came over to Allen's cabin with his briefcase to try to get Allen to sign papers deeding his property to Snyder's children when he died, something Allen resisted.

Throughout the 1970s, Allen's reading tours had taken him to many of the European summer arts festivals. He developed a very accomplished performance style, which combined poetry with music – usually provided by guitarist Steven Taylor, Allen's arranger and accompanist since 1976. The tours were as filled with incident as any big rock 'n' roll tour, with leading roles sometimes played by fellow poets. In 1979, after touring Britain, they flew to Amsterdam to join Gregory Corso for Ben Posset's One World Poetry Festival. As they approached passport control at Schiphol airport, they observed that the glass wall of a police office had been smashed; glass was everywhere. 'Look at that,' said Allen. 'They got some Arab who didn't understand what was going on and got scared and jumped out of the window.' As they entered the passport control hall, in the corner they saw Gregory and his friend George Scrivani, surrounded by police, and knew at once who had broken the glass.

'Hey guys! It's me!' yelled Gregory as they tried to make themselves inconspicuous.

'No, no, no,' they gestured, but it was too late. The police took their passports and made them wait outside the office. The incident almost cost them virtually all the money they had made performing in England because the immigration people insisted that Allen had to pay for tickets for Gregory and George to be flown to San Francisco; Allen protested it was none of his business. Gregory had flown in drunk and sang and danced with a towel wrapped round his head in the passport control line. When an official asked him where he thought he was, Gregory called him a 'Fucking Nazi'. The Dutch are very sensitive to this insult after their wartime occupation by the Germans and the man gave Gregory a shove. Gregory had landed in a office chair, rolled across the room through a Venetian blind and smashed through a plate glass window which shattered in all directions. Fortunately the festival organiser, Ben Posset, arrived and calmed the situation, explaining that they were all famous poets. In the poetry tour bus, Allen and Gregory had a fist fight, stopped by Peter who simply reached from behind and hugged Gregory until he stopped struggling.

Allen continued to spend much of his time in Boulder. With Trungpa sick, Allen delivered the 1980 graduation day speech at Naropa. Like the thousands of other graduation day ceremonies all over the country, Allen's speech contained the same sincere platitudes, eulogising the founder of the school and giving praise for the graduating class. Lionel Trilling would have been proud of him; he was now literally a member of the establishment. Allen watched as the Boulder Buddhist community celebrated the 21 June mid-summer solstice with a purification ceremony complete with flags and military uniforms and realised how foolish they looked to outsiders, and maybe even to himself.

That fall of 1980, Allen, Peter and Steven made their first visit to Eastern Europe, performing in Yugoslavia and Hungary before making a gruelling six-week tour of Austria and Germany. They flew home from Frankfurt on 15 December, to find that Peter's eighty-one-year-old father was mortally ill. Oleg was hospitalised in New York and Peter took over some of his nursing care. Allen also learned that Barbara Rubin had died from a post-natal infection in October. Having finally accepted that Allen would not marry her, she had become a Hasidic Jew, married and eventually moved to an Orthodox community in southern France.

The European tour had exhausted Allen and he spent a week in bed with 'flu, depressed about the political situation. 'Cold war fear in my head, rueful of red, capitalist and bohemian Buddhist military police hierarchies,' he wrote.

He set up a low altar next to the window in his bedroom and covered it with red cloth. On it he placed a smiling Thai statue of the Buddha and arranged his bell, dorje, mantra beads and prostration-counter, a Chinese ceramic incense holder and a red box of Japanese temple incense. A Catholic lectern held a Vajradhara tanka that Allen had bought in Benares. His room had been freshly painted white by Lucien Carr's son – the future novelist Caleb Carr – and was very bright. Through the slatted blinds Allen could see the cornice of the Catholic church opposite and a Tibetan banner, now little more than a sooty rag after five years in the New York air, flapped from his rusty fire-escape.

Above the bed was a large framed example of Trungpa's calligraphy: Allen's mantra 'Ah!' At the foot of the bed was Louis' desk, upon which stood Allen's battered typewriter, with its red dust cover. The desk was piled with mail and manuscripts, overflowing from his office. Below the window was a silver-painted radiator, on which Allen dried his socks and which whispered and clanked while he was meditating.

Above the altar hung a framed illustration of the Kargyu lineage tree, used in visualising during prostrations. These he did on a sheet of shiny composition board laid on the wood floor. Stacked against the wall was a brown zabutan meditation mat and a brightly coloured zafu cushion for sitting meditation. One wall was covered from floor to ceiling with books. Another small room was filled floor to ceiling with books, and twice a year, those no longer in use were shipped to join Allen's archives on deposit at Columbia University.

Soon after the new year began, Allen lay ill, preoccupied with the inflated accounts of the celebration of the return of the American hostages from captivity in Iran. In the *New York Times*, ex-Nixon speech-writer William Safire thundered that the barbarians must be punished. From his sick-bed, Allen improvised another of his East–West songs, including lines about the hostages:

CIA's Col Roosevelt overthrew Mossedegh
They wanted oil, now they got Ayatollah's dreck

They put in the Shah and trained the police, the Savak
All Iran was our hostage quarter century, that's right Jack.

The release of the hostages seemed suspiciously well timed to coincide with the inauguration of Ronald Reagan. 'Reagan inaugurated with Hollywood pomp and Mafia banquets,' Allen noted gloomily. 'The Right Wing strong jawed movie star on the path of Supreme Power.' In El Salvador right-wing death squads were murdering people with impunity while the regime received massive grants of American military aid, whereas Nicaragua's application for aid was summarily turned down, forcing the Sandinistas to look elsewhere for deveopment money. Ginsberg's journals from December 1980 until February 1981 were filled with long catalogue poems of atrocities committed by the United States and the USSR. He felt paralysed into inaction by the world situation, which he felt was heading to another Vietnam, this time in Central America.

When Allen complained to Burroughs about world problems, Bill told him, 'No problems can be solved. As soon as they're problems they're insoluble. No problems can be solved and all solutions lead to more problems.'

Intrigued Allen asked, 'Who wrote that?'

'I did,' said Bill's flat voice over the telephone.

When Allen returned to Boulder for the beginning of the 1981 Naropa term, he moved into 425 Varsity Manor, in the Swiss-chalet style Varsity Townhouses complex. His two-room apartment faced an inner courtyard, across the hall from where Bill Burroughs lived from 1977 to 1979, in order to be near his son as he recovered from a liver transplant that gave him a few extra years of life.

Allen remained in Boulder when Peter returned to Cherry Valley to fix the porch and tend the fruit trees. Allen's course that term was a second series of lectures of 'The Literary History of the Beat Generation'. Despite the 'Naropa Poetry Wars', Allen had managed to do an enormous amount of work during his decade in Boulder. He had taught five terms of William Blake, doing a line-by-line analysis from the earliest poems to the 'Four Zoas', and from tapes of these classes he had developed a number of lectures and texts on Blake, the first of which would be published in 1988. He taught the work of William Carlos Williams and two

488 Ginsberg

terms on English lyric poetry, and he had assembled a massive teaching anthology, *Twentieth Century International Heroic Verse*, from Rimbaud to the younger modern poets writing in Allen's style, such as Antler. At one point he had five teaching assistants, all typing up his voluminous journals and putting his manuscripts in order.

Istvan Eorsi, a Hungarian poet with whom Allen became friends on his 1980 trip to Budapest, spent four nights at Allen's apartment en route to Chicago. During a walk in Chautauqua Park, a wide meadow overlooking Boulder, Allen asked him what criticisms he had of his work.

Taking Allen seriously, Eorsi said he had three points to make: That Allen in his older age seemed to have substituted Buddhism for all the enthusiasm and energy he once had for creating an open-hearted society. That, like many great poets, he wrote too much and published too many 'dead' poems. ('Time will edit them out for me,' Allen rejoined.) That the repetition of certain homosexual details were sometimes compulsive or too self-conscious or programmatic. Other than that, Eorsi said, he thought that Allen was the greatest poet in the world.

His judgement saddened Allen, who said that he was neither here nor there, with either meditation or revolution. Eorsi pointed out that, unlike Mayakovsky, who had to live with the revolution that he prophesied and helped to create, Allen had to live with the fact that the revolution he helped to create did not win, but lost. By this he meant the Beat, hippie, anarchic, flower-power, LSD-using, pot-smoking, sexual freedom movement of the 1960s, which was being swamped by the neo-conservatism of the late 1970s and early 1980s. Eorsi thought that Allen had used Oriental meditation as a substitute for his failed revolution and that, important as it was to him, meditation did not serve as a total inspiration to him and did not have an all-inclusive poetic intensity. Allen felt that this was appropriate criticism from a Middle European standpoint, which did not take into account American concerns with self-awareness and ecology. It was, however, a view that many of his friends – fellow American poets – also shared.

In New York once again, Allen went to the rock club Bonds on 10 June 1981. The British punk band the Clash was in residence. Their lyrics, when they could be heard through the buzz-saw guitars, had a strong left-wing populist slant: anti-racist, anti-elitist and pro-working class. Allen went backstage to meet them, and as he walked into their dressing room, Joe Strummer, the lead singer, greeted him by saying, 'Well, Ginsberg, when you gonna run for President?'

'Never, or I'll wind up in Diamond Hell' – a Tibetan Buddhist allusion.

'You got any poems you can read to our audience?' Strummer asked. 'We had somebody get up to lecture about El Salvador and they were throwing tomatoes.'

Seeing his chance to play with the Clash, Allen said, 'Well, I got a poem that has chord changes. You want to try that?' So for the next ten minutes, with the audience screaming for the band to appear, Allen and the Clash rehearsed the changes of 'Capitol Air'. Then they went out onstage and performed it in front of the violent crowd of three thousand rowdy punks. Everybody liked it, including Strummer. 'I think they were surprised that I was able to get up and belt out a song,' Ginsberg said later. 'They're all good musicians, Mick Jones particularly, and they're very sensitive and very literate underneath all the album-cover roughneck appearance. I don't know of any other band that would, in the middle of a big heavy concert, be willing to go on with a big middle-age goose like me who might or might not be able to sing in tune for all they know.'

He found the hard rock crowd very different from his usual audience. 'The real challenge is to be so clear and definite and so courageous and so authoritative as to lay down a story in front of three thousand screaming new wave heads that they actually listen to it because it makes sense.'

Again Allen was able to transcend the generation gap. He wrote 'Howl' just after rock 'n' roll was invented, but a decade later was able to relate to Lennon, McCartney, Jagger, Dylan and the other 1960s musicians. Now there was a new wave of rock musicians, who saw the previous generation as boring, lifeless and irrelevant, yet they regarded Ginsberg as a source of inspiration and as someone who would understand exactly what they were doing – as he did.

Medals and memberships aside, there were still many areas where Allen's views contrasted sharply with those of the establishment, in particular his views regarding sex. That summer, Allen had a number of students to whom he was attracted, and to his delight, some of them reciprocated. Allen's belief that a sexual relationship between student and teacher was not only permissible but salutary shocked a number of people, particularly educators. The issue came up during an interview for the *Washington Post*, when Nancy Bunge asked him how he got his poetry students to locate their own perceptions rather than just imitate his. He gave her many examples, ending with: 'Check out the students' own writing. In personal conversation and contact, or by lovemaking with the students in bed where appropriate.'

'Are you serious?' she asked.

'I'm totally serious,' Allen said. 'I believe the best teaching is done in bed and I am informed that's the classical tradition. That the present prohibitive and unnatural separation between student and teacher may be some twentieth century Wowser, Moral Majority, un-American obsession. The great example of teaching was Socrates, and if you remember "*The Symposium*", the teaching method involved Eros. So Eros is the great condition for teaching. It's healthy and appropriate for the student and teacher to have a love relationship whenever possible. Obviously the teacher can't have a love relationship with everyone in the class and the student can't have a love relationship with every one of the teachers, because this is a strictly human business where some people are attracted to others, but where there is that possibility, I think it should be institutionally encouraged.'

He went on to discuss the danger of exploitation of the student by the teacher and vice versa, but suggested that problems arise in any love relationship and didn't see why they should arise any more in a student–teacher relationship than in any other. 'My own experience is that a certain kind of genius among students is best brought out in bed,' he told Bunge. 'Things having to do with tolerance, humour, grounding, humanisation, recognition of the body, recognition of ordinary mind, recognition of impulse, recognition of diversity. Given some basic honesty, some vulnerability on the part of teacher and student, then trust can arise.'

Although some people have claimed that this was a self-seeking argument to legitimise Ginsberg's desire for his young male students, it did follow quite naturally from his ideas of sexual freedom, which began in the 1940s and which he promoted most actively in the 1960s. It was, in fact, the attitude people expected from him, whether it was practised or not. For the purpose of the interview, Allen was indulging in hyperbole in citing Socrates and his active recommendation of teacher–student love, just to shock Bunge. However, during his years of teaching and travelling, he had many relationships with young men in his classes, some of whom may have derived some good from this special attention, many of whom resented his attentions. Allen did not lust after boys, in his words he was 'not interested in hairless youths'. The youngest boy his staff ever saw him with was, at most, a few months under-age.

On the obverse side, women had often complained that Allen was inclined to pay less attention to females in his classes, and some even requested their money back. Allen himself admitted that he found it very difficult to memorise the names of his female students. There were, of course, no women among Socrates' students.

When he edited an 'Obscure Genius' special issue of *Friction, the Annals of the Jack Kerouac School of Poetics*, Bob Rosenthal asked Allen if he noticed anything special about the twenty-three poets he included; Allen puzzled over the question until Rosenthal gave him the answer: they were all male. Bob Rosenthal: 'Allen didn't hate women, but he ignored them. He didn't see them, he was blind to them. In his photographs, when he wrote down the names, he never named the women. In teaching that happened, he doted on the boys and he ignored the girls. And to many women's credit, they ignored that and they got what they wanted out of Allen, but they had to ignore a lot. And of course he shamelessly promoted many poor writers who were cute boys. Once after working for Allen for five or six years, I complained to Anselm Hollo about all these writers that Allen foisted on people, and he said, "Aw you know, Allen, he fell off the clothesline a long time ago. Dear Allen, we don't expect to get the avant garde out of Allen." '

This indulgent view, from Anselm Hollo, a teacher at the University of Colorado, was echoed by many of Allen's colleagues who identified quite narrow limitations in Ginsberg's vision. His revolution was one of candour, and in the promotion of open-form poetics, and it stopped there. When he read new writers, he looked for people who were imitating him. Of the younger poets he liked, Antler's work reminded him of himself, therefore of Kerouac; Andy Clausen had the protean energy of Neal Cassady; and David

Cope was post-William Carlos Williams – they were the grand-children of his idols.

Allen had little or no interest in the avant garde. Concrete poetry, the Language Poets, new developments in Black and women's poetry, all passed him by. In the visual arts, his taste stopped with the development of abstract painting which he never understood or liked. In music, he enjoyed working with his friend Philip Glass, but still puzzled over his work: 'Isn't it kind of repetitive?'

Allen travelled extensively during his 1981 summer break from Naropa, going first to Mexico City, in August, where he attended a Writers Conference along with Günther Grass, Andrei Voznesensky, Octavio Paz, Jorge Luis Borges and others. After one of the day's proceedings, he helped Borges to his car. 'Ginsberg,' said Borges, trying to place the name. 'Ah yes, I read a book by a man of that name. The Cabala, 1911, edited by . . .' Allen protested that this could not possibly have been by him and again told Borges his name. Borges was sure he had read a text, long ago.

'Maybe by my father, Louis Ginsberg?' Allen suggested.

'Perhaps,' agreed Borges, 'on the Cabala!' It was a classic circular Borges conversation.

Another day, after Allen had read a number of poems, including 'Capital Air', he took Borges' arm to help to help him off stage. 'Did you understand the English stanzas?' asked Allen. 'Of course,' he replied. 'I am Borges.' Later, in the dressing room, he complained about a line in 'Capital Air': 'I don't like police assassinating Argentine Jews.' It wasn't true, he said. 'Nonetheless,' he continued still referring to the poem, 'in the main I agree with your opinions.' Though blind, he told Allen that he saw lights and shadows, mostly at night, and a luminous sunset. He said that he did not like the poetry of Ezra Pound, whereupon Allen quoted 'Canto XIV' to him. 'He didn't write that in verse properly,' Borges complained. Allen explained that it was the quantitative aspect of Pound's prosody that he admired, and Borges allowed that he perhaps liked some of the early work, but not the 'Cantos'.

'I'll consider your opinions,' said Allen.

'Because I'm eighty-two doesn't mean my opinions are to be respected,' Borges replied.

*   *   *

After Mexico City, Allen visited Toronto to see a stage version of
'Kaddish.' From New York he flew to Rome, initiating one of his
frequent Italian tours. On 7 October, after having made the
gruelling twenty-three-hour flight from Naples to San Francisco to
work on the proofs of *Plutonian Ode* at City Lights, he finally
found himself back in Boulder and spent his first night at 2141
Bluff Street, where he was to live for the next few years. It was a
large house, set on a bluff, with a fine view out over the Flatirons,
which he would describe in many poems during the coming years.
Since 1978, he had lived at the Boulderado Hotel, or taken one of
the Varsity Townhouse apartments, and were it not for the Poetry
Wars, he would not have moved full-time to Boulder at all, for
despite the attraction of Trungpa and the Buddhist teachings
available, he regarded the town as 'a honky paradise ... with all
the advantages and disadvantages that that implies. The lack of
racial mix makes it bland, lacking colour.' However, as co-
administrator of the Poetics Department, he felt a duty: 'I moved
to Boulder in response to Clark and Dorn's attacks. I felt Naropa
needed my help.' Ginsberg always considered his helping to
introduce Tibetan Buddhism to the United States as one of his
highest achievements, and he never regretted the move, which
would keep him away from his New York office for five years.

He still had a crowded schedule of readings, the most important of
which was the highly publicised twenty-fifth-anniversary reading of
'Howl' at Columbia McMillin Theater on 14 November 1981. The
event was a complete sell-out, with people clamouring to get in.
During the two hour programme he sang Blake, read 'Birdbrain' and
'Capitol Air', and finally gave a twenty-seven-minute rendition of
'Howl'. The poem used to take him twenty to twenty-two minutes to
read, but he no longer had the long breath of his youth. The slower
delivery enabled him to emphasise the irony and humour of the
poem, and the audience frequently roared with laughter. The reading
was a great triumph, and even Allen's old adversary *Time* magazine
gave him a full-page review, headed, 'Howl Becomes A Hoot'. They
still disliked 'Howl', but Ginsberg himself was acceptable now.

That winter, the Clash returned to New York to cut their next
album at Electric Ladyland, Jimi Hendrix's old studio on West 8th
Street. They called Allen in Boulder to invite him to join in the
sessions. A few days into January 1982, Allen was in New York

for a reading, and stopped by the studio to see them. Joe Strummer greeted him in his usual gruff yet friendly way: 'You're the greatest poet in America, can you improve on these lyrics?' Strummer handed him the lyrics to 'Ghetto Defendant', and Allen began tinkering with the words, much as he corrected his students' poems at Naropa.

For 'the admiral lies asleep' he wrote, 'the admiral snores command', and instead of saying 'lines cross oceans' Allen wrote, 'submarines boil oceans'. Strummer liked all the suggestions and used them. Then they needed something on the track which sounded like the voice of God, so Allen wrote something and sang in deep bass in the studio; when the recording was mixed, his voice appeared beneath Strummer's main vocal on the track.

He spent about seven nights with the Clash, sometimes working through until 9 a.m. Strummer would hand him a Xerox copy of lyrics written out in his notebook, Allen would change a phrase or two and make other suggestions, then Strummer would go out in the studio and sing it. Maybe an hour later, Allen would have another idea of how to change a phrase to make it more pronounceable. He would join Strummer in the studio and show him his suggestion. Strummer would try it on a separate vocal track, and if it worked, would select all or part of it for the final mix.

In this way, Allen worked on three or four of their numbers. And during the time it took to get microphone levels and headphone volume levels and to set up equipment, he just kept them company, helping them smoke a large amount of very strong pot. He began to take books in to show them, including Gregory's new book, *Herald of the Autochthonic Spirit*, and Peter's new City Lights title *Clean Asshole Poems and Smiling Vegetable Songs*. The album was released as *Combat Rock*, with all of Allen's contributions on it, including his duet with Strummer. Allen was pleased to see it rise in the charts but, characteristically, asked for no payment.

Allen's next major trip was to Managua, Nicaragua, where his old friend the poet Ernesto Cardenal was now the Minister of Culture. Cardenal had organised a poetry festival to bring together 'poets of national liberation' from all over Latin America to honour the centenary of Nicaragua's great national poet, Rubén Darío. The exiled Argentinian poet José Antonio Cedrón was there, as was

Roberto Sosa from Honduras, but most of the press attention was focussed on the poets of the two superpowers: Ginsberg and Yevgeny Yevtushenko.

Allen and Peter arrived on 21 January 1982, and checked into the Hotel Intercontinental, where they had a fine view of Lake Managua and the dramatic volcanoes ringing the city. It seemed as if the great earthquake of 1972 had occured only weeks before; large buildings with their insides reduced to rubble still stood all over the city, their shattered remains used by squatters. President Anastasio Somoza, the US-backed dictator, had done nothing to repair the ruins after the earthquake, and had caused even more damage himself when, during the final offensive against his regime, he ordered his airforce to bomb those areas of downtown Managua controlled by the Sandinistas. Many of the Chevrolet taxis were still riddled with bullet-holes from those final days. The victorious junta was composed of leading businessmen as well as leftists and Marxists, and they pledged themselves to a free society and a mixed economy, but the scale of the problem they faced meant that it would be years before Managua looked like anything other than a war zone, particularly with an American economic blockade in force.

Allen and Peter went straight to a reception, and after pleasantries, Allen approached Commandante Daniel Ortega and asked for a minute of his time. Allen said that he didn't want to be a problem to Nicaragua, but that some of his texts might be regarded as controversial; he went on to explain what had happened to him in Cuba and Czeckoslovakia in 1965. In reply, Ortega asked him to try to understand the situation from their point of view in the face of threats made against them by the United States government. He said that they were dependent on their friends. 'You are free to do what you want, but please remember that we are up against the wall. My main task in the next few weeks is to deal with the threat of an American invasion. Anything you say critical of the Nicaraguans and their allies, the Russians and the Chinese, will be used in America and *La Prensa* as propaganda.' Ortega explained that no matter how well intentioned Allen was, even if in a friendly critical spirit, statements would be taken out of context and exaggerated and abused.

Allen understood that, but he said that for 'propaganda', it would be to the Nicaraguans' advantage to have him speak freely.

He told Ortega that the majority of Americans in a recent Gallup Poll disapproved of US violence or war in Central America and that it would look good if he could read the same texts in Nicaragua that he usually read at home. They talked at length, with Yevtushenko listening in and taking photographs. Ernesto Cardenal explained to Ortega that Allen had done benefit readings in the States to raise money for the fight against Somoza and to help the Sandinista cause. Before the revolution, Cardenal had translated Allen's poetry into Spanish; now he was presenting it to the people.

At the dinner following the reception, Allen spoke with Yevtushenko, who complained that as long as his novel had remained unpublished in Russia, he'd had big money offers for it from American publishers, which he had refused because he wanted to publish it first in his homeland. Now that the book was out in the USSR, however, American publishers would not touch it. They had wanted it for propaganda.

The next day, Allen met with the American poet Margaret Randall, who had been living in Managua since the revolution. He and Peter spent the day sightseeing and preparing for their reading, which was held at the Teatro Nacional. Allen opened with the first page of 'Howl', followed by 'Howl' Part II, then 'America', 'Elegy Che Guevara', 'Don't Grow Old', 'Father Death Blues', 'Homework', 'Birdbrain' and 'Meditation Blues'. The poems were all simultaneously translated, except for the final blues. On the musical numbers Allen was accompanied by Trio Las Turbas. It was 'Birdbrain' that the American press picked up, and it was quoted in several reports.

Birdbrain runs the World!
Birdbrain is ultimate product of Capitalism
Birdbrain chief bureaucrat of Russia, yawning
Birdbrain ran FBI 30 years appointed by F.D. Roosevelt and never chased Cosa Nostra!
Birdbrain apportions wheat to be burned, keep prices up on the world market!
Birdbrain lends money to developing Nation police-states thru the International Monetary Fund!

Allen was pleased by his reception; a lot of people had laughed and only a few got up and left. Afterwards he went drinking with

Yevtushenko and various members of the American press, Russians and Nicaraguans. 'Some Russians came to your reading, but no Americans came to my reading,' complained Yevtushenko, 'which tells you something about the nature of our countries' relationship. But do you know, Allen, the translator, he made one very big mistake because he mixed up 'hippie' and 'beatnik' and the only one who caught the difference was one Russian technician. This is because when the beatnik era was born in your country, there was a parallel time in Russia, an echo across the oceans, the same moment with some awareness of cultural differences.'

'I didn't know that,' said one of the Americans.

'But now things between us are culturally fucked up,' Yevtushenko continued angrily. 'We are separated by an ocean of shit! Oceans of shit!' He raised his glass, 'A toast! May our two shit countries not go to war!' Yevtushenko was on good form, and many empty rum bottles already littered the table. The waiters refused to serve them any more, so the party moved to Yevtushenko's room where he could order rum through room service. There Allen told him how Ezra Pound and Williams were a big influence in Latin America, largely because of Cardenal. 'You know,' said Yevtushenko, 'Pound is not published in the Soviet Union because he is so much connected with fascism.'

'Then you should start with publishing his late poems,' Allen suggested, 'where he renounced fascism.'

'Yes, we should publish him,' Yevtushenko agreed, 'but you know, we lost 20 millions (to fascism). I was asked to read one of his poems, and I like some of his poems, but I could not do it. I could not read Pound.'

The next morning, all the poets assembled for an outing to León, fifty miles northwest of Managua. On arrival, Allen, Yevtushenko and various reporters gathered at a sidewalk café outside the cathedral, and by 11 a.m. the drinking had begun, except for Allen. One of the American reporters asked Yevtushenko if he thought Managua was heading toward a totalitarian state that would not tolerate intellectual freedom. 'Maybe not totally,' he said, ambiguously.

Allen was more sanguine: 'Intellectual freedom can flourish here if the US doesn't continue putting pressure on them,' he said. 'But the US is fast making a situation where someone who wants to be open and liberal is put in the position where the Sandinista hard-liners say, "Look, you're threatening the security of our revolution" . . . In a situation where the US puts them in a totally defensive military posture, they're going to put all the energies of the society toward militarisation of the society.'

In Managua, Allen, Yevgeny Yevtushenko and Ernesto Cardenal sat down and wrote an appeal for the liberty of Nicaragua, which they addressed to the world's writers and presented at a press conference. They called it 'The Declaration of Three', and it said in part:

> We call the world's writers to come to Nicaragua to see with their own eyes the reality of Nicaragua, and lift their voices in defense of this country, small but inspired. They'll be welcome and can acquaint themselves directly with the true character of this revolution, of the efforts of the people to create a just society exempt from violence, a revolution whose image is being consciously distorted by those who have an interest in destroying the alternative which it proposes.
>
> The Damocles' sword of aggression now hangs in the air above these people.
>
> We trust that if the writers of the world get together, their pens will be mightier than any sword of Damocles.

As a member of PEN, the international writers' organisation, Allen had voted to denounce the Sandinista government for the repeated closings of the anti-government newspaper *La Prensa*, but now he began to worry if the shut-downs might have been justified, given the strong likelihood that *La Prensa* had been infiltrated by the CIA. The strongest evidence for this was the parallels in form and style between *La Prensa* and *El Mercurio*, the Chilean newspaper that the Church Committee of the US Senate proved had been infiltrated by the CIA, and which had whipped up anti-Allende hysteria prior to the CIA overthrow of the government. In a very short time, *La Prensa* had gone from being what Allen called 'a respectable NY Times-type newspaper, to a National Enquirer scandal sheet,' filled with horror stories of murders, car accidents and food shortages. The change was so dramatic, that on his return to the States, Allen wrote to the State Department to ask whether the CIA had in fact infiltrated the newspaper. Assistant Secretary of State, Thomas Enders, replied, '. . . the aspirations of the Nicaraguan people are being progressively betrayed by an anti-democratic vanguard mortgaging their country and their revolution to Havana and Moscow.'

Allen was impressed by what he saw in Nicaragua, and by the great changes that had already been made in the short time since the revolution. The Sandinistas had abolished the death penalty. The child mortality rate had decreased dramatically. The literacy rate had risen from twenty per cent to more than fifty per cent, thanks partly to the Cubans. Many of the Cuban technicians in the country, whom President Reagan and his secretary of state, General Alexander Haig were fulminating against, were literacy workers, who had accomplished a similar improvement in their own country after the overthrow of the dictator Batista.

Ginsberg's visit to Nicaragua revealed an enormous change in his political attitude. During his visit to Cuba in 1965, when it was under the same economic pressure and threat of invasion from the United States, he was obsessed with the twin problems of persecution of homosexuals and the legalisation of pot, to the virtual exclusion of all else. He showed no interest in the revolution or its achievements and did not take advantage of the situation to meet any of the revolutionary leaders. In Nicaragua, his primary concern was the revolution. Questioned by reporters on his return home about his opposition to US political interference, he said: 'It's a self-fulfilling prophesy. We're forcing them into Soviet hands, to mortgage their revolution as we forced Castro. They want a pluralistic society. They're just as aware of the abuses of Socialism in the Soviet Union and Cuba as we are.' In another interview, Allen stated: 'Castro came to Nicaragua and said, "Don't make the mistake we did of being dependent on the Soviet Union," and Haig recently called the Nicaraguans pawns of Russia. American strategy, in sum, is to make it hard for them, make them look bad and starve them economically.'

Ginsberg's views were backed up by the announcement of a $17 million CIA destabilisation plan. 'The United States has run Central and South America for the last century,' Ginsberg said. 'We had our chance but we drove them into the ground with dictatorships so painful, so unbearable, the people had to rebel. The rebellions were popular and influenced by Marxist theory.' He told the *Colorado Daily* that the real problem, as he saw it, was that the US military was 'so completely interconnected' with the militaries in Latin America that 'we can't let anybody go'.

*　　*　　*

Allen spent less than a week at home before he was off on yet another tour of Italy with Peter and Steven Taylor, which was followed by a short tour of California before he returned to Boulder. Peter had been in Cherry Valley, and in May he arrived at the house in Bluff Street in a very strange state of mind. He unloaded the car in silence, then carried a beautiful dead pheasant into his room, which he knelt over, pursing his lips, making a high-pitched moaning sound. The bird stayed in the centre of his room for two days, carefully arranged on a cloth. One night, Allen came downstairs at 1 a.m. to find Peter crouched over three bags of garbage, separating out the paper from the cans. 'Whatcha doin'?' asked Allen, nonchalantly.

Peter did not reply, then a few minutes later whispered, 'Compost'. He would make coffee in the middle of the night and tiptoe about the house, replying to questions in a whisper. Then one morning Allen looked out of the window and saw him cleaning the blue Volvo with his bare hands. Allen tried to talk with him, but he replied, 'I have no time, gotta do my prostrations.' It was while he was in this disturbed state that he gave Trungpa the $9,700 remaining from his controversial $10,000 NEA grant. Vajradhatu accepted it. Bob Rosenthal observed that it was after the publication of *Clean Asshole Poems and Smiling Vegetable Songs* that Peter began to go to pieces, as if having to be a poet was an intolerable pressure. Allen constantly brought him on stage to sing songs and read his work, something Peter often felt very uncomfortable doing.

Allen meanwhile was suffering from a bad kidney stone attack. He lay in bed delirious with the pain and from the opiate painkillers his doctor had prescribed. He had not the energy to do anything except occasionally read a fragment from Kerouac's *Book of Dreams*. Thoughts, visions and poems passed before his eyes, and he talked to himself in his sleep. The stones showed clearly on x-rays taken at Boulder Hospital, and it was a week before he recovered. Peter also recovered after a week, and life on Bluff Street returned to normal.

That spring the Poetics Department at Naropa was in a frenzy of activity, planning a Jack Kerouac conference, an idea sparked by the success of the 1976 anniversary reading of 'Howl' at Columbia, which had raised enough money to keep the Poetics Department going for a year. Since the school was named after

Kerouac, it seemed appropriate to mark the twenty-fifth anniversary of the publication of *On the Road*. From the very beginning, it was seen as a fund-raising media event rather than a scholarly conference, more concerned with the cult of personality than with academic study of Kerouac's texts. The original list of 'VIPs', as Allen called them, at the preliminary planning meeting in July 1981 included Bob Dylan, Tom Waits, William Buckley, Jr., Abbie Hoffman and Ken Kesey, but made no mention of Kerouac's widow, his daughter or his two ex-wives, whose contributions to a serious study would have been of value. Basically Allen was presenting his Kerouac: the sensitive footballer, intimate friend and confidante from the 1940s, the great genius writer who had 'heart', not the anti-semitic Kerouac, who abandoned his daughter to become a drug addict and prostitute, and wanted to shoot all anti-war protesters. It was an idealised, sanitised Kerouac, the greatest writer in America, the Kerouac Allen always wanted him to be.

The conference was to be held during the second summer session of 1982, and Allen had sensibly decided to repeat his 'Literary History of the Beat Generation' lectures during the first summer session so that he could devote more time to the conference. Naropa did not have the facilities for large gatherings, so most of the events were held on the University of Colorado campus. The conferees stayed at the Columbine Lodge in Chautauqua Park, overlooking the city; Robert Creeley, Gregory Corso, Ann and Sam Charters, Ray Bremser, Carl Solomon, Diane di Prima, Herbert Huncke, Joyce Johnson, Michael and Joanna McClure, Jack Micheline, Lawrence Ferlinghetti and others flew into town. The front porch of the lodge became the unofficial meeting place for everyone and was the scene of many reunions and introductions. Huncke had not seen Edie Parker Kerouac since the 1940s; Carolyn Cassady had never before met John Clellon Holmes. Few of the conferees knew William Burroughs, who had spent so much of his time out of the States and played no part in the San Francisco scene of the mid-1950s. Rather than film the conference itself, Robert Frank chose to set up his camera outside the lodge and simply filmed people gossiping on the porch. Also at the conference were Ken Kesey and his friend Ken Babbs, Paul Krassner, Timothy Leary, Abbie Hoffman, and other 1960s people who regarded themselves as keepers of the flame, as well as Beat critics and translators such as Dennis McNally and Nanda Pivano.

The proceedings took place before a twenty-foot-high backdrop by Karel Appel of Kerouac as a gentle, suffering saint with a large cross at his neck. Allen had written across the painting 'O Jack of Light, here's Your Cross of Tenderness'. Between three and four hundred people enrolled, paying either $160 or $240, depending on whether they wished to attend the writing workshops being given by Burroughs, Ginsberg, Herbert Huncke and others.

The conferees were nearly outnumbered by the press. Allen's publicity machine was almost too good, and in the end there were more than one hundred and thirty accredited reporters from over one hundred organisations to witness the historic reunion. There were representatives from the *New York Times*, the Washington *Post*, the Miami *Herald*, *Newsweek*, Swedish radio and Swiss television. Two NET television crews and three documentary film crews were on hand, as well as reporters from the three networks, AP and UPI. The perspective and composition of the conference changed somewhat during the planning stages, and the list of people invited grew to include practically all of Kerouac's old friends.

There was a series of well-received readings by all the principal writers and poets present, but the workshops and panel discussions received a more critical reception from the press and public. As the Miami *Herald* reported: 'Amid the conference's obsession with celebrity, [Kerouac's writing] was exempt from much measured assessment.' For the speakers, however, the entire event consisted of what Allen called 'delicious orgies of nostalgia'.

The conference was a success, a memorable reunion for the generations of the 1940s, 1950s and 1960s. It provided the press with a ready-made story and numerous photo opportunities. It made money for Naropa (but they did not pay Allen back the few thousand dollars start-up costs that came from his own pocket), and it was great fun for all who attended. It had little to do with Kerouac's work and a lot to do with him as a personality. Allen summed it up in his journal, 'No great revelations re Jack K. None of us brought up any big scandals, last letters. etc., just praised his heart and prose.'

It was also a tribute to Ginsberg's genius for organisation and publicity. All through the conference, he ran around frantically, sleeping a bare five hours a night. When it was over, he collapsed with food poisoning and spent three days vomiting.

*   *   *

On a visit to New York in late August 1982, Allen went backstage at a Clash concert at Pier 84 to wait for them to finish their set. The band brought him on stage for 'Ghetto Defendant', their second encore, and in front of eight thousand ratty-looking New York punks, Joe Strummer, in a fierce Mohawk haircut, announced 'Mister Allen Ginsberg' and pointed his finger at Allen, and began to sing the verses. Feeling completely relaxed in the situation, Allen chanted his own verses in response, as he had done on their *Combat Rock* album.

On the evening of 12 November, Peter's father died of cancer. Peter had been with him until the end of hospital visiting hours. Oleg's death exacerbated Peter's feelings of responsibility for his family; he had worried about their welfare ever since the 1950s, when he returned home from Paris to care for them. He felt 'married to my crazy brothers', and with Oleg gone, he now faced the possibility of having to look after his mother, sister and three brothers.

Allen had a three-month European winter tour through France, Italy, Holland, Denmark, Sweden, Norway and even Finland. On 6 December, he and Steven Taylor left New York for Paris, to appear at War On War, the first of a series of readings organised by Jean-Jacques Lebel for UNESCO; it featured nineteen poets from five continents. This was followed by one of Ben Posset's One World Poetry tours of Holland, which extended into the New Year. Whenever practical, Allen and Steven stayed in Amsterdam at Simon Vinkenoog's book-lined house on the bank of the Amstel River, and Simon often accompanied them to readings, acting as interpreter if needed.

On 23 December, Allen and Steven did a long performance at a Rotterdam jazz club with Allen singing 'Jessore Road' and delivering an ecstatic rendition of 'Plutonian Ode' to the television cameras present. Then came the long ride home through the fog, arriving in Amsterdam at 4 a.m. Allen slept in a bunk bed in the attic and when he awoke the next afternoon, Barbara Vinkenoog and the children were preparing for the Christmas meal. On Christmas day there was the thickest fog yet and it was dark by five p.m. Simon lit the candles on the Christmas tree which stood on a platform in the corner, hung with silver tinsel, then came the Christmas meal of turkey, cranberry sauce and stuffing. Allen sipped a little grappa afterwards though he did not normally drink.

The Vinkenoogs welcomed Allen and Steven into their family and they felt relaxed and comfortable.

Peter flew in on the morning of 29 December, seeming calm and in good shape. He slept all day, but that evening, at an important reading with Andrei Voznesensky at the Paradiso, he began to act strangely again. Allen sang, Voznesensky read his first group of poems, then came Peter's turn. First he delayed, drinking vodka, chortling and laughing to himself. Then he read, 'You Have To Stop And Think This Thing Out, Peter', smacking himself hard on the head with his fist between each line.

Allen grew nervous, knowing that Voznesensky did not like to be associated with anything that might jeopardise his freedom to travel. Peter was stopping after each word to ask Simon Vinkenoog to translate and spell it in Dutch, beginning with the word 'shit' until Simon finally objected. He explained to the audience that Peter had arrived that morning and that his father had recently died. Peter gurgled and guffawed, drank, and yelled at Simon, 'You want 'em clean or dirty? Dirty? I'll give you dirty!' Allen was eventually able to coax him off stage, then he read an abbreviated programme very self-consciously, anxious about what Peter might do.

The next day Peter stood in the kitchen from midnight until 9 a.m. practising the same short Jimmie Rodgers riff on his banjo, bare-chested, eyes closed. 'Don't wreck your voice,' Allen cautioned him when he returned. Peter slept two hours then began to clean the house. He cleaned all day, until they left that evening for Vlissingen, a resort town on the southwest coast of Zeeland. Peter read there with deliberate care, but the next morning he was up early and standing barefoot in the fog at the ocean's edge, strumming the same short riff over and over on his banjo. When Allen approached him, he snapped, 'Fuck you. Don't talk to me. Leave me alone.'

He was the same later in the morning, when Allen couldn't get a sensible answer out of him about breakfast. 'At that moment I recognised that it seemed finally a thread of communication had snapped, and he was refusing simple information,' Allen wrote later. The ride back from Vlissingen was a nightmare. Peter laughed, wheezed, yukked and cursed Allen all the way, through a pea-soup fog. Vinkenoog told Allen when they got home, 'You're a saint!'

John Lennon had suggested that Allen perform 'Jessore Road' with a string quartet, as the Beatles had done with 'Eleanor Rigby'. In Vlissingen, Steven Taylor had completed the last violin part of an arrangement of the poem for two violins, viola and cello. The tour promoter, Ben Posset, arranged for them to use the recording equipment at the Milky Way concert Hall in Amsterdam and hired the Mondrian String Quartet. They worked until 1 a.m. and got two good recordings. Allen's vocals were steady, only slightly wanting on the melody line.

When they returned to the Vinkenoogs', enthusing over the recording, Peter was scrubbing the kitchen sink. Wearing only his bathing shorts, which sagged below his pot-belly, he was sweating, eyes closed as if in a trance, repeating, 'Fuck Reagan, Fuck Reagan,' over and over like a mantra.

'I don't think I could stand a week of this,' said Simon. 'I don't like cursing in my house, there's children here.'

Allen said softly, 'You're upsetting the house. Simon doesn't like cursing and the kids are asleep.'

'Shut up!' Peter yelled at him. 'Don't talk to me. Fuck! Fuck! Fuck Reagan! Fuck you!'

It was all horribily familiar to Allen, who recognised it as Naomi's behaviour with Louis. 'Albephrenia,' said Steven. 'Uncontrollable talking and swearing to yourself,' and said he wondered whether Peter should continue the tour.

Allen remembered that the previous February, Peter had driven from the Vajrayana seminary in Pennsylvania to Cherry Valley and had so frightened the poet Andy Clausen and his family, who were staying at the farm, that they telephoned Allen for advice. When Peter had returned to Boulder that summer, he had been in the same trance state, talking and moaning to himself for several days after he arrived. He told Allen later that he had been in terror, thinking that the police and CIA were following him, and that Richard Helms himself was at the wheel of the car behind. Several people from the seminary were riding back to Boulder with him, and Peter imagined that they were watching him. The only way he had been able to ward off an attack was to control them by singing in a high-pitched voice all the way to Colorado.

Peter's crisis came a few days later, in the office at the Milky Way. He raged and yelled, shrieked and yodelled. Screaming 'Kill Reagan! Shit!' He smashed his banjo to pieces and broke his glasses. Allen considered calling the police to prevent him from hurting himself. Allen recorded Steven and Vinkenoog's comments that Peter's anger and frustration might be related to Allen's over-dominating paternal role: 'always ordering him around, constantly commenting on his behaviour, his readings – on being far too long a time over-interfering with his every common social moves, behavior, gestures.'

Dominating Peter was almost second nature to Allen, and he found taking their advice extremely difficult, but he made some progress, and Peter calmed down. The Danish promoter had arranged readings in every major town in Denmark. The comic aspect of the trip appealed to Allen's sense of the ridiculous, as he and Peter appeared in towns they had never heard of, and preached Buddhist meditation to people whose lives they knew nothing about. He wrote, 'Peter meanwhile daily waves his copy of Naropa at audiences, preaches Buddhist guru information, imitates Mila-Repa's cotton clad nakedness, and carries around his gomden [square sitting pillow] everywhere, while I hypocritically sing, "Do The Meditation" as a rock song. What a mess, mentally.' Allen hadn't meditated for months.

In Stockholm they stayed with Ann Charters, Kerouac's biographer, and her husband, the record producer Sam Charters. Sam asked Allen why he was getting so involved with music. 'I love to sing,' said Allen, detecting a note of disapproval.

'Everybody is waiting for you to write the Final Poem,' said Sam.

' "Plutonian Ode" is quite strong,' Allen offered. 'Why, do you think it's draining energy away from my writing?'

Charters didn't answer him directly, and Allen felt depressed and wondered if it was true. Certainly a number of his friends in the States thought so.

The tour continued: to Helsinki, where they were only two hundred miles from Leningrad which, to Peter's frustration, they had no time to visit. Allen was relieved, imagining dreadful consequences if Peter went crazy in the Soviet Union. They returned to tour Norway and Germany where the final performance, on 16 February 1983, at Friedrich Engels Haus in Wuppertal, was filmed; it was released as a commercial video: *Allen Ginsberg on Tour*. It was one of the most strenuous tours Allen had ever undertaken. Steven told Allen that he would never tour Europe with Peter again.

* * *

While they were in Europe, record producer John Hammond had released *First Blues*, containing twenty-four Ginsberg performances. Allen had barely recovered from jet-lag in New York before he was on the road again, this time to promote his record. For the album notes, Hammond had written: 'Allen Ginsberg is not only one of the world's best poets but one of its finest citizens as well. Long impressed with his musicial abilities, I recorded Allen in 1976 but CBS refused to issue the results considering the songs obscene and disrespectful. I am thrilled to finally be able to present Allen on my own label; not only the 1976 sessions but those from 1971 and 1981 as well. I will present "disrespectful" music like this as often as possible.' Coming from the man who first discovered Billie Holiday, Bob Dylan and Bruce Springsteen, this was praise indeed.

The album gathered together the best of Ginsberg's various sessions, including three tracks improvised with Bob Dylan in 1971; Allen suggested that Hammond talk with 'a photographer friend' about the sleeve. He turned out to be Robert Frank, who produced a montage of photographs which made the album look a little like his jacket for the Rolling Stones' *Exile On Main Street*. As befitted a rock star, the launch party was held at Studio 54. Allen performed many of the songs from the album with a five-piece backing group, surrounded by hi-tech glitz.

He toured all through the spring of 1983, this time doing more television appearances than usual. Keeping one foot in the rock 'n' roll world, he did a benefit for Naropa at the Peppermint Lounge in New York. He hadn't spent time at his desk in New York for months and was dogged by a mountain of paperwork and letters, which fortunately he approached with a sense of humour. He wrote:

I'm a prisoner of Allen Ginsberg
Who is this slave master that makes me answer letters in his
  name
Write poetry year after year to keep up appearances
Pays a dumb secretary Jewish boy to answer phone pay bills
  shuffle papers
Who is this egoist whose file cabinets leave no more room for
  pictures of me?
I want to escape his clutches, his life, his bank accounts, his
  Master Charge debts.

Who is this politician who has my life hypnotised by his
  favors . . .

Allen arrived in Boulder in late spring 1983. He opened up the
house on Bluff Street after being away for six months and hired
someone to come and clean the house from top to bottom so that
when Peter arrived he would not go on a cleaning jag. Allen had
decided to leave Boulder, having co-administered the Poetics
Department for a decade. He wanted to leave with no bad feelings,
particularly any residual gripes from the 'Poetry Wars', and made
a point of contacting all his old adversaries. As usual, he had not
had time to prepare himself properly for the course he was
teaching. His classes were on Poe, Melville and Whitman, and he
rushed to read their biographies and writings.

Allen found himself divided between envy of those students who
had started with him and were now far along in their Buddhist
studies, and the pull of the 'poetry rock 'n' roll world TV
newspapers politics fame'. He also knew that he was growing older
and that as things stood, he did not make enough money from
poetry to live. His City Lights royalties were only seven thousand
dollars a year, not much for a lifetime's work. Though he made
considerably more than that at readings, seminars and workshops
and for television appearances, almost all his money went towards
supporting Peter, paying his musicians and running his office, or
else into the Committee On Poetry, which was still giving grants
to poets. 'Maybe I'm getting too old to go out fight the world with
new wave rock and roll and platform oratory poetry,' he mused,
wondering what his next move should be.

Peter arrived in Boulder and cleaned the whole house. There was
snow in May as Allen began a poetry workshop, instructing his
students to use meditation breathing techniques, pay attention to
the sound of one word at a time in their heads with each inhalation
of breath, and write it down with each exhalation. His goal was
to teach concentration and economy of breath. Like Burroughs,
Allen was always able to see the possibilities of new techniques.

He was concerned about the future of the Poetics Department.
Anne Waldman was away, so Allen was the sole director, but there
were precious few students and even fewer faculty. One of the
staff, Michael Brownstein, told him that there was little he could
about it and that he should leave as he planned. 'You shouldn't

feel guilty,' he said. 'Trungpa doesn't feel guilty.' In fact it had been Trungpa's suggestion: 'Take more space,' he told Allen. 'Go to New York and make some money.'

Not long afterwards, on 3 June, Allen celebrated his fifty-seventh birthday with his brother on Long Island. Eugene was sixty-two the same day. Allen blew out of the ring of candles, and they both composed haiku. Allen's read:

Two brothers at table on their birthday
  Each his own thoughts, writing –
  think of our mother in the grave

On 15 July, Allen went on a month's retreat to the Rocky Mountain Dharma Center. During the day he attended the seminary, where he rapidly became accustomed to making prostrations; falling to his knees, then forward on to his hands, then stretching out on the floor while visualising the Kargu lineage tree of gurus with its many details. He had the help of sliding boards, a gomden, a Zabuton (a rectangular padded mat) and a pair of scarlet jogging shorts.

His tent was set at the edge of a meadow thick with wild flowers beneath pines, where the scent of lilacs filled the air. He looked at the surrounding mountain peaks and remembered his travels through other mountains long ago, in Bolivia, Peru, India. 'Another life,' he thought, 'What did I see, will I ever go back? I'm glad I kept a record or else even the memory of everything be gone.' He remembered his first trip to Mexico and the bougainvillea in the square by the mayor's house in Yajalon, Chulapas. 'God, what naïveté, my behavior then,' he wrote in his journal. 'Wiring New York thinking I'd discovered a giant earthquake and cave. On that basis I inadvertently conned the folks of that village to put me up for a week, doing nothing but wandering around emptyheaded and lost.'

At 3 a.m. one morning, Allen woke and crawled outside to relieve himself, taking care to turn off his electric lamp before unzipping the tent flap and stepping out under the dark pines. There was moonlight behind the hill to the northeast and a few bright stars. To the north there were clouds and the distant rumble of thunder. 'Well, finally all's quiet,' he thought. 'I feel better, Trungpa and his army's asleep resting.' Then, from the hill to the east where Trungpa had his Prajna house and dome, Allen heard a military shout followed by silence, then massed voices raised, chanting in unison Trungpa's Shambala anthem: 'Garuda spans the threefold world . . .' came drifting to him across the darkness. 'They must be tired,' he thought.

Many of Allen's old friends came to teach the summer writing programme at Naropa that August, including Burroughs, Gary Snyder and Timothy Leary. This was the first time that Burroughs and Snyder had met (Snyder had diplomatically bowed out of the Kerouac conference). Snyder gave a major reading in Boulder, but as Gary spoke lovingly about making an axe handle, Bill got up to go in search of a drink. It was not Bill's scene at all.

That August, Allen's friend Miles persuaded him to get a literary agent to handle his affairs and recommended Andrew Wylie in New York. Though this was something that Allen had shied away from all of his life, he finally recognised that his business affairs were a mess, with books coming out from myriad publishers all over the world, which he couldn't keep track of, and within a few months a deal had been struck with Harper and Row to produce a uniform edition of his work, beginning with *Collected Poems* and continuing with an annotated edition of *Howl* based on the Faber facsimile of *The Waste Land*; a volume of new poems, 1980–85; and volumes of letters, essays and journals. The advance on this multi-book contract took care of his immediate financial worries.

In February 1984, the United States Information Agency 'blacklist' of speakers surfaced in Washington; it was published by the *New York Times* on 15 March. The people banned from government-sponsored overseas speaking engagements numbered eighty-four; Ginsberg was among them. The list included James Baldwin, David Brinkley, Representative Jack Brooks, McGeorge Bundy, Shirley Chisholm, Walter Cronkite, Representative Thomas Downey, Betty Friedan, John K. Galbraith, Senator Gary Hart, Coretta Scott King, Ralph Nader and Tom Wicker. A USIA offical said that most of them were liberals whose views were thought to be inconsistent with administration policy, a clear indication that in the Reagan administration, even the cultural agencies had a political bias. Allen felt proud to be in such company.

In 1984, after two short European tours, Allen began a three-week teaching course at the Atlantic Center for the Arts in

New Smyrna Beach, Florida. Allen's secretary was booking him into more and more workshops, seminars and courses, which paid well and enabled him to stay in one place for a few days and not be continually zigzagging across the States from reading to reading. On this occasion he was given a luxurious wooden cabin set among scrub palmetto and live oak filled with squawking tropical birds. The campus buildings were connected by elevated board-walks, which passed between the palm fronds and branches. Allen felt slightly guilty about his accommodation and wrote, 'Gold in the sky, cool as an icebox in my giant wooden cabin. How many poems have I written denouncing air conditioning? I thought I locked myself out in the moist heat on the porch and got scared among the palmetto bird chirps ... It's an anxiety attack, well deserved. Haven't finished the long delayed preface to "Collected Poems".'

Despite his idyllic surroundings, Allen felt depressed. He filled his journal with his usual doubts and fears, but there was still an edge of irony and humour in his entries: 'I haven't sat in a year. Taken vows I can't remember for a lifetime devotions and saddhanas. Took a vow of sainthood 40 years ago, now potbellied my life's slipped by ...' He questioned his role as a teacher: 'Students in front of me for three weeks. What are their names? What do they need?' A decade before, when he began to teach at Naropa, Lucien Carr had asked him, 'What have you to teach my children?' Allen did not reply. Now he remembered Lucien's question and wondered, 'Why must I teach anyone? Where'd I assume that guruship? That's not poetry.'

It was not his only worry. He was growing concerned about the effect his work might have, in particular his myth-making about his homosexual marriage to Peter. It had been years since they made love, and now Peter was drinking heavily and Allen was fearful of him, yet in his poems he paraded their image as a model of gay love. 'How many people will go their wrong way?' he asked himself, 'defy their parents and die in hovels alone, childless, because they read, "I will be home in two months & look you in the eye".' As usual in his journals, he played out his ideas to the full in order to explore them, but there was a kernel of truth in his fears.

That summer, the Atlantic Center for the Arts also featured courses by photographer Robert Frank and jazz drummer Elvin

Jones, who had worked on Allen's 1969 recording of Blake's songs. Allen was pleased to see Jones again, and they made another recording together. The first take of 'Big Fish, Little Fish' was almost perfect, except for the guitar part, played by one of Jones's students. By the third take, the musicians were finally together, but Allen spoiled it by hesitating at one line and getting the order of the lines wrong in the second stanza. He was too ashamed to tell them, so they moved on and wound up the session with a recording of Allen's explosive 'Hum Bomb!' in one flawless take. 'We all felt good,' he wrote, 'because the quality of the music cooked.' Jones told Allen that it was the sanctified church beat that made it cook. 'At the bottom it's got to be religious,' he explained. 'It's all religious or it doesn't count.' Afterwards Allen noted in his journal, 'Sanctified church beat! And I flubbed the lyric!'

Allen had given up his Bluff Street house and shipped his library and belongings back to New York, so he spent that summer in Boulder in the Varsity Townhouses. There he maintained a tight work schedule in order to complete his *Collected Poems*, working through the nights when there were fewer distractions. He finished the last batch of three hundred pages of manuscript on 19 July and sent them to his editor with a feeling of great relief. He had been thinking about a *Collected Poems* since 1965 and, as the culmination of his life's work, he wanted it to be right. The 837-page volume included eighty-eight pages of notes on the poems; photographs; an index of titles and first lines; an index of proper names; it reprinted the original cover blurbs, dedications and introductions, and opened with an 'Author's Preface, Readers' Manual', in which Allen listed his best poems for the reader's convenience, an audacious move which would cause comment by reviewers. He asked his old friend Harry Smith to design an emblem, to be used on all the titles in the series. Smith used Allen's Buddha's footprint symbol as the basis for a formal design.

In the fall of 1984, Allen returned to New York in good health. He had quit smoking, was practicing t'ai chi and had been swimming regularly in Boulder Creek. He was getting himself in shape for a visit to China. The trip was organised by Norman Cousins, the former editor of the *Saturday Review*, and Robert Rees, a poet, who were both on the faculty of UCLA, the venue of the first meeting between Chinese and American writers, which had taken place two years before. Both Allen and Gary Snyder had been very eager and active participants in the earlier meeting, presenting the Chinese delegation with a list of '100 Questions That American Poets Would Like To Ask Chinese Poets'. The leader of the Chinese delegation said that they could answer some of them, that they could write and send back the information on others, but that for some of them, they would just have to come to China and see the answers for themselves – which was, of course, the idea. It was therefore not too much of a surprise, when Cousins and Rees chose Allen and Snyder as members of the American delegation to China for a reciprocal visit. The delegation, which landed in Beijing on 18 October 1984, also included Leslie Marmon Silko, William Least Heat Moon, Toni Morrison, Maxine Hong Kingston, William Gass and Harrison Salisbury, most of them accompanied by their wives or husbands. Gary brought along his wife, Masa, who was born in Beijing.

The subject of the conference was 'The Source of Inspiration', a tricky title designed to dodge the doctrine of art as revolutionary propaganda and allow the Chinese writers, as well as the Americans, a chance to discuss their real motivation and reasons for writing. 'The Chinese are heartbreakingly in love with the Americans,' Allen would tell the Boulder *Daily Camera* when he returned. 'They look to America for technology and knowhow and those who learn English get a thorough background in American literature.' Allen had been surprised to find that extracts from *On the Road* and Mailer's *The Executioner's Song* were among the required reading for every technician who wanted to study in the United States. His own 'Howl' was also widely read among intellectuals, who could relate immediately to the opening line, 'I saw the best minds of my generation destroyed by madness . . .' The reference for them was the persecution of intellectuals during the Cultural Revolution.

China was in the throes of self-examination in the wake of the excesses of the Cultural Revolution and the Gang of Four, and the Americans were there, in part, as a sounding board for the Chinese writers. In a report written for UPI, Allen said: 'In conversation, the Chinese express different emotions about the decade of upheaval. They feel bewilderment that China, which was the greatest civilisation in the world, went through this period of self-degradation.'

The four-day conference was wide-ranging, but one of the questions asked repeatedly was how contemporary Chinese litera-ture could be introduced to American readers. The Chinese were publishing a lot of American books, from Richard Nixon's memoirs to *Jonathan Livingston Seagull*. When the poet Yuan Kejia was asked about his literary influences, he named Walt Whitman, the works of T.S. Eliot and Allen Ginsberg. He had also recently read, in translation, work by John Cheever, James Joyce, Bernard Malamud and Saul Bellow. This surprised the Americans, who were expecting to be told about Marx, Lenin and Mao Tse Tung; none of the Chinese writers mentioned them. Some did, however, refer to China's glorious past, particularly the T'ang Dynasty (AD 618–907), which had produced such poets as Li Po, Tu Fu and Han Yü, and several mentioned the classic novel *The Dream of the Red Chamber*, which interested Allen because homosexuality is mentioned in the novel and he had decided not to discuss the subject unless the occasion seemed suitable.

With the conference over, the delegates set off on a ten-day sightseeing tour, beginning at Xi'an where the amazing Han army of life-sized clay figures, cast in full military regalia, had been buried with the emperor. Most of the soldiers had been uncovered and restored, 'stepping forward silent motionless underground,' as Allen described them.

In Shanghai, they saw the Temple of the Jade Buddha, the Bund and the waterfront of the Huangpu River with its rows of British colonial hotels. They took an excursion to the beautiful old city of Suzhou and visited the Cold Mountain temple where the T'ang Dynasty poet Han Shan (whose name means Cold Mountain) once lived beside the Grand Canal. Gary Snyder had published translations of twenty-four of Han Shan's poems in 1958, and he presented them to the Buddhist monk who now looked after the temple, improvising a new poem as he did so, which he called 'At Maple Bridge'. Robert Rees, moved by the occasion, improvised a poem about Gary improvising a poem. The local people began to gather to watch this display of poetry.

The official tour ended in Guangzhon (Canton) on 5 November, and the delegates returned to the States. All except Allen, who always tried to take advantage of conferences as a departure point for his explorations, as he had done in Chile, Australia, England and other countries. Before leaving for China, he had arranged to extend his stay, teaching at Beijing and Hebei Universities.

Before returning to Beijing, he spent a week exploring the interior, notably on an unaccompanied river trip through the famous Yangtze River Gorges. At the Beijing School of Foreign Languages, he gave morning lectures on William Carlos Williams, Robert Creeley, Corso, Kerouac and Orlovsky. He found the people open, friendly and inquisitive. The Cultural Revolution had cut everyone off from the outside world for a decade, and now they wanted to know what Allen and the Beats had been doing during that time. 'People now hopeful and cheerful and disillusioned with dogma,' he wrote.

In his UPI report, Allen said, 'Everybody had a story about the Cultural Revolution, about how they were sent to the country as a Red Guard, or how their parents were fired from their jobs as translators or physicists, or their mothers sent off to the countryside or how they themselves were exiled to jobs cleaning latrines. Elderly physicians were forced to stand bowed over, wearing dunce caps, answering questions day and night.'

At Hepei University in Baoding, eighty miles southwest of Beijing, Allen had his own apartment, three concrete rooms in the Foreign Teachers apartment block. The electricity was not very reliable, and Allen sometimes found himself writing his journal by candlelight after the lights had flickered out. It was cold, and he had had bronchitis for three weeks. Finally he was able to get a hot plate, for heating water and humidifying the room, which received only a few hours' heat and hot water. The boiling water plus herbal medicine from the university infirmary eventually cured him.

At the university he taught Williams's short poems, also work by Reznikoff, Creeley, Gregory, Peter and Kerouac. He mimeographed a sheaf of work by Philip Whalen, Philip Lamantia and Bill Burroughs, and also taught the work of Walt Whitman. Leafing through *Leaves of Grass* he felt a surge of affection that inspired him to write the poem 'I Love Old Whitman So'.

Allen's chill kept him indoors most of the time, wrapped in blankets, sleeping or reading in bed. Now that he was settled in his own rooms, and the guided tours were over, he began to write. Previously, every moment was filled with talk and sightseeing. In Baoding, he had time to poke about in the markets and shopping streets, jotting down observations, eating food from street vendors and absorbing everyday life. Baoding was not an open city, so there were no facilities for tourists. Allen was seeing the 'real' China. In late November he wrote:

> One morning I took a walk in China
> students danced with wooden silver painted swords,
>   twirling on hard pathed muddy earth
> as I walked to Hebei University's concrete north gate,
> crossed the street, a blue capped man sold fried sweet
> dough-sticks, brown as new boiled donuts . . .

Allen taught Whitman to the older students in a special class of advanced semi-professionals who had been displaced by the Cultural Revolution or who were middle-school teachers coming in for continuing education. Allen explained the references in Whitman to prostitutes, orgies and revolution, and watched his class carefully. There were many smiling faces and nods, but the students asked very few questions except technical ones. A student told Allen that anyone who asked too much, or was too curious, would stand out as too individualistic and this might be noted in his dossier. They were also inhibited by cultural timidity and a traditional Chinese Confucian respect for authority.

After one class, Allen went downtown to buy some Chinese ink and calligraphy brushes, accompanied by a student. As they waited for a bus, Allen asked him what unmarried men did for love. 'They must live pure lives,' his student told him.

'Why?' asked Allen.

'If their behaviour was loose, they would be considered trouble-makers.'

'You're married and have a place to live and a job, so you can talk,' said Allen. 'But what right have you or anyone to tell those without wives or jobs or station, to live loveless the rest of their lives? What kind of communist community is that? What kind of equality? It's barbaric exploitation! You expect to have those people dig your trenches and plant your rice and live without love?'

The student smiled, 'I really agree,' he said. 'That's what I think too.'

This was the first time since he had arrived that Allen was able to make contact with a Chinese citizen. Knowing that this world of secret personal views must exist, he had not been able to penetrate it. The longer he stayed, the more often this occurred, and he was eventually able to get the viewpoint of the individual Chinese, or at least those attached to the foreign languages departments of the universities.

On 1 December, he finished his two-week course of lectures. The faculty held a farewell banquet for him and for another American who was also leaving. An old cadre member at the dinner, whom Allen had always been suspicious of, thinking he was a police spy, revealed that in the mid-1950s he had managed a Chinese opera company. He sang to the gathering and then sentimentally recited a famous heroic poem by Mao Tse-tung:

> The mountains are dancing silver serpents
> The hills on the plain are shining elephants
> I desire to compare our height with the skies.

The old man wanted to show the departing Americans his great depth of feeling for China. 'Our farewell was warm with tipsy embraces,' Allen wrote.

Two days later, he took the train back to Shanghai where he was to teach at Fudan University. There he stayed in the guest room of the old President's House, carpeted and furnished with a shining armoire and two comfortable sofas beside a tea-table. Above his bed hung a mosquito net, tied in a giant white knot when not in use. The heat came from a noisy ventilator grill set high in the wall above his desk. The north wall was composed entirely of French windows, which were curtained at night, and in the garden below his balcony were a stone table and chairs. Nurses and children gathered in the garden beneath the trees in the daytime. Each morning, he awoke to the sound of music playing over the campus loudspeakers as staff and students did their morning exercises.

He spent the first two days in Fudan resting, recovering from his virus, but he had many visitors and was soon conversant with the latest Shanghai gossip. Whenever it was appropriate, he asked about sex, and always received the same answer: pre-marital sex, except if the couple were intending to marry, was considered immoral, and love between men was unheard of. One day after class, a professor asked Allen if he had a family. Allen told him that he was homosexual, and the professor asked if he would explain that to him. He said that he had asked other American visitors, but they said it was something disgusting.

One of his students had translated a number of Allen's erotic poems. Allen was surprised and asked him who he would show it to. 'My girlfriend,' he replied.

'What's your pleasure in that?' Allen asked.

'I'm young and I enjoy love,' he replied. 'I'm interested in love.' But he said that he would not be able to show the translations to very many people, just one or two friends.

In his UPI report, Allen wrote, 'There's an ambiguousness among the Chinese. The people are trying to sort out how much of the sexual repression, how much of the travel limitations, how much of the hyper-organisation is really a support system for keeping the whole society together and how much is a control system to keep power at the top.'

He finished teaching on 20 December, and prepared to leave China. Christmas Day he spent in Yunnan province, just above the Vietnam border, where he lectured at the National Minorities School and was given a Christmas meal by the faculty. He arrived in San Francisco on 28 December 1984, just in time for the publication of his *Collected Poems*.

Collected Poems 1947–1980 was published on 2 February 1985, to considerable critical attention, beginning with *Time* magazine which ran a full-page interview, with a colour photograph. The article, written by R.Z. Sheppard, took the standard *Time* line; 'Howl', which the magazine had put down, was called 'once effective as a counter-culture manifesto . . . now an unconvincing historical oddity'. 'Kaddish' however, which *Time* had ignored when it was published, could now be safely described as 'a masterpiece of candour and emotional persuasion'. In its reference to 'Howl', the article quoted a line from the 'Moloch!' section, leaving out the last four words: 'granite cocks! monstrous bombs!' Allen, interviewed for the Detroit *Jewish News*, protested: 'By leaving out "monstrous bombs!" which is a contemporary problem, they can declare it obsolete and archaic. They amputated the line in order to try and prove their point. That really is unfair journalism as well as being unethical and anti-literate to doctor my verse to fit their view. The one line which they quoted, they bowdlerised politically.'

It was not the only objection Allen had to the piece, which he must have known would be a hatchet job when he agreed to do the interview. *Time* was more interested in how much money his new book contract was worth than in the poetry, and the very title of their piece, 'Mainstreaming Allen Ginsberg', suggested that Allen had somehow gone commercial. 'It requires vision and careful work to make a life, let alone leave a literary legacy. This follower in Whitman's footsteps has shown that he is capable of both. One can see it in his eyes: one wide and innocent, gazing at eternity; the other narrowed and scrutinising, looking for his market share.'

'That was rather cruel,' said Allen. 'Look at my face. I have Bell's Palsy, so one eye and one part of my mouth is a little distorted. Paralyzed. So "one eye narrowed and looking for his market share" is a little like kicking a cripple.'

Allen for his part was clearly delighted with the book. When asked by the Philadelphia *Inquirer* what he would like to leave as his legacy, he laughed and said, 'A great big book of poems, a big fat book of poems. I just hope somebody will sit down and read it, beginning to end, familiar with the whole thing. It will be like reading through Yeats. It will actually alter slightly perceptions of the world and open up space and tolerance and humour. For one thing, the realisation that you don't have to be right, all you have to do is be candid ... I don't think any poet will be able to get around it. It's like a big roadblock. They're gonna have to talk about something real, about their phenomenal world.'

Seeing the poems presented in true chronological order for the first time invited comparisons with Pound's *Cantos*, Whitman's *Leaves of Grass*, and Williams's *Paterson* (what the *Washington Post* called 'the garrulous side to American poetry'). Allen said that all along his intention had been to make 'a graph or a picture of my mind over the seasons, months, years, decade' – the quantitative verse of Pound. He accepted that he didn't always succeed, and told the *Washington Post*: 'My intention was to make a picture of my mind, mistakes and all. Of course, I learned I'm an idiot, a complete idiot who wasn't as prophetic as I thought I was. The crazy angry philippic sometimes got in the way of clear perception.'

His intentions were recognised by some of the critics. Stephen Salisbury wrote in the *Inquirer*: 'by turns funny, personal, public, boring and quirky, the poems offer a record of life in postwar America, a map of his slowly evolving spiritual awareness and a frame-by-frame picaresque documentary starring the gamboling self in modern society.'

Even his enemies on the right had to recognise the seriousness of his undertaking. Robert Richman devoted six pages to attacking him in *Commentary*, and Roger Rosenblatt, senior writer for *Time*, gave him a three-page review in the *New Republic*, saying: 'What these 800 pages prove is that Ginsberg has always been a minor poet; that is, a poet who has produced a few remarkable pieces, but the bulk of whose work shows no philosophical growth (despite its ostentatiously philosophical preoccupations) and rarely any depth. It is no small thing to be a minor poet; few make the list in any century.'

18 The Good Grey Poet

*Be radical, be radical, be radical – be not too damned
radical.*

Walt Whitman to Horace Traubel

Most poets, on reaching their 60s and having seen the
successful publication of a doorstop tome of their collected
poems, would think it time for a rest, to slow down and
reap the benefits of long service to literature. Not so Ginsberg.
After *Collected Poems* came more trips, books, records and
readings. If anything, his work load increased. Signed with Harper
and Row, he faced publisher's deadlines for the first time; his
all-night work marathons were now undertaken to get manuscripts
in on time, as well as to keep abreast of his massive correspon-
dence. In 1986, Brooklyn College appointed him distinguished
professor; teaching one day a week, he made money enough so that
he no longer had to tour unless he wanted to, which dramatically
reduced his work load.

Allen discovered a new art form – photography. Throughout the
years, he had always taken pictures of his friends: Neal buying a
car in San Francisco in 1955; Peter posing before Robert LaVigne's
huge portrait of him; Bill reclining on Allen's floor in New York
in 1953; Gary Snyder pissing off a mountainside; Kerouac on the
beach in Tangiers in 1961. Allen described his approach to
photography in terms of the original Beat sensibility: 'It's like
looking through a telescope back into time at people who were
really interesting, in the period of their greatest creativity,' he told
a *Miami Herald* reporter. 'I'm not a photographer, but I was aware
of the sacredness and the poignance of the pictures. It's kind of a
poignance of the moment, like an appreciation of the colour of the
sky, the blue of the blue and the face of the face and the Jack
Kerouac of the Jack Kerouac.'

His photographs were the most utilised section of his archives on deposit at Columbia University and had appeared in many books on Kerouac or the Beats. Ann Charters chose the best of them in her photo-essay book, *Scenes Along the Road*, but the archive was incomplete. Originally processed by labs that serviced corner drugstores, many of the prints had been given away to friends over the years.

Photographs were disappearing and negatives were being roughly handled at Columbia, so Allen asked art curator Raymond Foye to organise and catalogue the collection. Foye printed up thousands of negatives on contact sheets, and the wide range and extent of the collection became visible for the first time. Allen asked Brian Graham, Robert Frank's printer, to print a few professionally and was surprised by the results. It was obvious that there was enough good material for an exhibition.

'It was like a whole other career going on that I didn't know was there,' said Allen. 'I had always enjoyed taking pictures of my friends, but I hadn't thought about it. Without knowing, I had made a record over the years, a chronicle of the scene.' His first show, 'Hideous Human Angels', was presented at the Holly Solomon Gallery on 57th Street in January 1985. It received wide press coverage and put Allen on the cover of the *Daily News* magazine. The New York Public Library bought a number of his photographs and presented them in their 'New Acquisitions' group show the next month. Ginsberg's office swung into action; one of his assistants spent her entire time organising the developing, printing and cataloguing of his photographs. Brian Graham found his work load dramatically increased as Allen had shows at the Middendorf Gallery in Washington, DC, the Dallas Museum of Art, Galerie Watari in Tokyo, the Fogg Museum in Boston and many other museums and galleries around the world.

Allen took advice from photographers like Berenice Abbot – who told him to make sure to get the feet in – and Robert Frank – who helped him with composition – and he bought a new camera, which he began to carry everywhere and used it constantly. He was absolutely unabashed about taking photographs: Julian Beck of the Living Theater smiled weakly for Allen's camera from his deathbed; Allen's Uncle Abe also managed a wave from his, days before he died. As the police carried a struggling Peter Orlovsky away to Bellevue after he smashed up the janitor's apartment in a drunken rage, Allen clicked away, recording everything for posterity.

He was just as uninhibited about pictures of himself, as Richard Avedon's famous nude shots of Allen and Peter demonstrated. Now he proudly showed visitors a new picture of himself, taken by a boyfriend: Allen naked, a chubby Modigliani odalisque, smiling sweetly for the camera. His technique improved rapidly, and soon at least half of the photographs in his shows were recent work. He took great pride in seeing his work in the photography journal *Aperture* and popular magazines such as *Vanity Fair*.

As part of a project with John Cage, he took a series of views of the four seasons from his kitchen window, which were widely exhibited. When Sony gave him a video camera, he made a twenty-minute video film of scenes around the house: Julius Orlovsky talking guardedly over breakfast; Harry Smith – 'film-maker, sound archivist, occult bibliophile' – delivering a monologue; a Russian poet who spoke no English smiling at the camera; fleeting appearances by Bob Rosenthal and the stream of visitors who filled the apartment at all hours of the day.

Nineteen eighty-five ended with a visit to Moscow and a writers' conference in Vilnius, Lithuania, then still a part of the Soviet Union. Allen's contribution was criticised by William Gass in the *New York Times* Book Review: 'I don't know whether the Soviet people feel any tenderness toward stupidity, but everywhere Allen Ginsberg walked he seemed to elicit an "ouch" . . . What is the difference between public pronouncement and private speech, he asked; if private speech is eloquent and public speech is constricted, what is the remedy? It isn't necessary to be right all the time – infallibility is a tyrant's tune – but we must be open and frank and honest with one another. Homosexuality was sometimes on his mind, so he unashamedly spoke of it. The shame would have been not to.' Allen cut straight to the chase, as usual, using any and all available platforms.

As his 60th birthday approached, Allen began to ruminate over his life. It seemed to him that Neal Cassady and Lucien Carr were the great loves of his life, with Peter 'familiar as life and death'. He wondered why he had never revealed his feelings to Lucien, why he was so hesitant, when all he had to do was pick up the telephone and 'ask him everything I never dared forty years ago'.

He fretted over his inability to relate to women, and wrote: 'Woke thinking, what unresolved trauma with Naomi inhibits or blocks my relations with world, with love, or with myself and women? Why not settle down with a young girl and bask in Carib or Mediterranean sea honeymooning and beach under palm tree potbellied with a floppy hat like Eliot? Was my dread of abandoning her to the ambulance in the Bronx and later to the hospital the trauma that set me apart from all women and family life, children and their continuous breath of flesh?' He vowed to find a woman and marry.

Allen arrived back in New York on 8 June 1986, from Naropa, and had a late Japanese supper with Lucien. They visited Lucien's mother and, as they walked the familiar streets of Greenwich Village, Allen told him he was thinking of marrying. Lucien warned him, 'You don't want a teenage sex doll. It means trouble later. I should know.' Lucien was in the midst of a divorce. Allen was chagrined. He had thought Lucien would encourage him to marry. They sat on a park bench in Sheridan Square.

Allen: 'Well, here we are, two old men on a park bench.'

Lucien: 'You're damn right, and it's a good thing too!'

At times they fell silent, but Allen wanted to discuss his feelings for Lucien. 'You know, I was in love with you when we first met – for at least twenty years, it was the most intense and – well about the deepest!' Lucien did not reply.

'Did you hear?'

'No.'

'You didn't even know I was in love with you almost forty years ago?'

'Never occurred to me,' said Lucien, then added, 'And now we're old friends.'

Allen went home to masturbate. He told Bill Burroughs about the conversation on the phone. Burroughs advised Allen: 'If people don't want to remember something, don't insist.'

After five weeks at Naropa, Allen flew to Lawrence, Kansas, to visit Burroughs. Bill's closest collaborator, Brion Gysin, had died of a heart attack in Paris on 12 July, ten days before Allen arrived, and Bill wanted to reminisce about his old friend. 'Brion was the only man I ever respected,' he told Allen. 'He understood everything I'd done.'

Allen had always felt a little jealous of Bill's high regard for Brion and asked him, 'What is it in me you find lacking, what blind area?'

'Your lack of interest in magic, in telepathy, paranormal, out-of-body experience, is a failing,' Bill told him.

Allen's big summer tour of 1986 was through Middle Europe: Hungary, to compile a PEN Club report on censorship; Yugoslavia, where he received the Golden Wreath for Poetry (the previous recipient was W.H. Auden, and benefit readings for Solidarity in Krakow and Warsaw. Allen bought a 1940s Leica in Warsaw which Robert Frank told him was the same model he'd used to shoot *The Americans*.

Allen had been having recurring fainting spells; during a visit to Boston in November, his cardiologist identified an irregular heart beat which he attributed to overwork, exhaustion and anxiety. Allen had not read his students' homework, had blurbs to write, and found more and more that he couldn't remember names. Harry Smith was living homeless at the Hotel West flophouse, calling Allen, demanding money for a room, and Peter's continuing problem with alcohol was raising Allen's blood pressure.

When Allen was in China in 1984, Peter had gone through a crisis. He stayed up for two days, drinking saki, Trungpa's drink, then scared Allen's staff by appearing naked in the apartment with a machete, threatening to cut his own head off. Exhausted from lack of sleep and overcome by alcohol, he was impossible to reason with. He waved around a pair of sharp scissors, and offered Bob Rosenthal a haircut, then began hacking off hanks of his own long hair. After hours of this, he lunged at Bob Rosenthal's groin with the scissors, stopping short so that Bob felt the point, but was not cut. Peter hissed in Bob's ear: 'I am going to sodomise your children!' Bob's children were then six and two.

Bob: 'Well, talk about taboo! The love drained out of me, it was gone forever. I went to call the police, because he tried to stab me, not because he threatened my children. When the officers arrived, Peter was standing in the kitchen, naked, waving a machete over his head.'

Peter asked permission to go to his apartment next door to dress. Bob had already fetched his clothes, but as he informed the officers of this, Peter had already reached his door. He wrenched from their grip and locked himself in. There had recently been much adverse publicity for the police when Eleanor Bumpers, a homeless vagrant, had been killed while resisting arrest. This time the police took no chances. Within twenty minutes there were ten police cars outside and the original officers had been replaced by a special hostage negotiation team. Television news crews and a large crowd gathered in 12th Street. Only when Peter had nothing left to drink did he eventually open the door when a friend from Dharmadhatu offered him saki. Peter was carried from the building, tied to a chair, howling at the top of his voice for the benefit of the media and the neighbours.

Bob Rosenthal committed Peter several more times after that, an unusual role for a secretary: 'I figured Peter was relying on me, he was out of control, he needed to detox, and Allen would never have done this, and he couldn't do it himself, and he knew I was daddy, and daddy sets limits.'

When Allen returned from China, he began attending the family service programme at Bellevue with Peter, seeing an analyst once or twice a week at low cost. A year later the analyst went into private practice; her rates went up considerably, but Allen continued to see her. Peter was in Bellevue only a few weeks, but following his discharge he began to drink again, and increasingly difficult scenes ensued. After several violent episodes, he and Allen were advised by their psychiatrists not to see or contact each other for a year. This was particularly hard for Allen because, for the first few months, Peter's then girlfriend, Juanita Lieberman, worked as Bob Rosenthal's assistant and was a constant reminder of Peter.

Since Peter could hardly remain in his next-door apartment without constantly encountering Allen, he spent most of their enforced separation at Trungpa's centre in Vermont. Reports from Trungpa's followers said that Peter continued to drink and that his behaviour was 'strange' and 'peculiar'. One of the conditions of the separation was that Peter should become economically self-sufficient and break his thirty-year dependency on Allen, which was the root of much of the problem. This caused more arguments at the end of their year apart, in 1986, because Peter believed that Allen should sell his archives and use the money to relocate himself, Peter, and Peter's mother, sister and brothers, to Trungpa's new centre in Nova Scotia, as Trungpa had suggested that his followers do.

After more difficult episodes, Allen attempted to get Peter to attend the family service course at Hazelden Hospital in Minneapolis. Peter refused to go, so Allen went with Beverly Isis,

Peter's current girlfriend. The family service programme was based on the notion that alcoholism is a family disease: the family becomes codependent with the alcoholic, in the sense that it attempts to keep order while the alcoholic causes disorder. Ginsberg said, 'It was very similar to my situation with Naomi . . . The key neurosis that all the codependents have, and the alcoholics, is a feeling of worthlessness, of not being able to correct the situation and feeling that it's their fault, a feeling of guilt, that if I can't stop Peter from drinking I must have been treating him wrong all these years and it must be my fault.'

Allen was told to go about his own life and stop taking on the burden of guilt, which came from trying to control the situation and constantly failing. 'That was very much my own situation with Peter and my mother,' Allen said. 'Peter repeating my mother and the chaos she created.' Bob Rosenthal detected an ambivalence in Allen's attitude to Peter's madness: 'Allen delighted in Peter's behaviour. Whenever Peter was going crazy, Allen had a twinkling in his eye: this was home, this was home life for him and he loved it, and never divorced it.'

Allen's talks at Hazelden and with his psychiatrist were revelatory. Allen was told that he had to realise that Peter was the only one who could make up his mind to stop drinking; all Allen could do was try to offer a supportive situation. He had spent his adolescence trying to control and contain the chaos caused by Naomi's madness: 'My father rejected me if I didn't believe him, and if I didn't believe her stories, she would reject me. So in order to win her affection, I would have to believe her delusions. It's a double bind that leaves a permanent sense of guilt.'

Allen identified that as the cause of his assuming a massive workload. 'Certainly the reason for my workaholism is a low sense of self-esteem and a constant need to produce something to feel that I've done something that people will accept me for.' On leaving Hazelden, he was supposed to make a resolution. He tried, with some success, to stop working at eight each evening. 'That was my resolution – take it easy, meet friends or go to a movie or have some human contact, instead of working until five in the morning.' It was only then that he realised he didn't have a real living-room. Most visitors were destined for the office or the bedroom; a set of uncomfortable chairs in the kitchen did duty for everyone else. Allen bought a television set and a video recorder for the living room and began entertaining there. When he purchased a new dish rack and an electric clock for the kitchen, Bob Rosenthal jokingly accused him of becoming a yuppie.

It was not easy to give up habits of a lifetime, but he now felt he had a better understanding of his own motivations. His duties at Brooklyn College consisted of one three-hour writing seminar a week but, characteristically, he stayed on afterwards to give tutorials until about nine in the evening. 'I had to do extra work to prove to them it was worthwhile having me there,' Allen said. 'I could've rested on my laurels.'

Nineteen eighty-six ended with Peter in Bellevue, and with Allen, Beverly Isis and Juanita Lieberman all seeing psychiatrists. The year's great achievement was the publication in December of *White Shroud* – 'a mellow sampler of Ginsberg in his prime', as Ann Charters described it in the *Los Angeles Times*. One of the most considered reviews came in a syndicated column by Allen's old adversary Tom Clark, who generously allowed: 'If Ginsberg isn't the world's first truly international poet, he'll do until one comes along.' Although, like many reviewers, he had reservations about the political 'list' poems in the book, he thought the title poem, a dream apparition of Naomi, more than made up for them. 'This memorable poem has a way of bathing the rest of Ginsberg's new work in its calm light, to some extent relieving the black-and-white stencilled-in spareness of "political" vision in the surrounding pieces.'

When Elise Cowen finished typing a fair copy of the original manuscript of 'Kaddish', she had told Allen, 'You haven't finished with her yet.' 'White Shroud' is an epilogue to 'Kaddish'. In a dream, Allen returned to the Bronx, scene of his earliest memories, and saw Naomi in an alley, living like a bag-lady: 'I/ was looking for a house, I thought, she has one, in poor/ Bronx, needs someone to help her shop and cook, needs her children now.' He and Naomi were at last reconciled in his dream. 'My breast rejoiced, all my troubles over, she was/ content, too old to care or yell her grudge, only complaining her bad teeth. What long-sought peace!' He awoke before dawn and looked out over the rooftops of Boulder.

> . . . I returned
> from the Land of the Dead to living Poesy, and wrote
> this tale of long lost joy, to have seen my mother again!
> And when the ink ran out of my pen, and rosy violet

illumined city treetop skies above the Flatiron Front Range,
I went downstairs to the shady living room, where Peter
　Orlovsky
sat with long hair lit by television glow to watch
the sunrise weather news, I kissed him & filled my pen and
　wept.

Chögyam Trungpa died of a heart attack on 4 April 1987, in
Halifax, Nova Scotia, having spent the previous year and a half in
a semi-coma. Allen went to see him a few weeks before he died
and recorded his impressions in his notebook: 'Brown great mouth
open red lips & upper teeth white visible, eyes closed with slits
eyeballs moved back and forth spasmodically within – once he'd
yawned as if to cough but hadn't strength to bring up mucus. A
bit of wet foam at his huge-slitted right eye tearduct, he lay on his
left side eyes closed.'

According to Tibetan Buddhist custom, Trungpa's body was
embalmed in salt and arranged in the sitting meditation position
inside an upright closed wooden box. The cremation was held
early on 26 May at Karme-Chöling, the 540-acre estate in the
Green Mountains near Barnet, Vermont, that had been Trungpa's
first centre in the United States.

'Nobody here is crying, "Oh, dear Guru, don't go away," ' Allen
told a *New York Times* reporter. 'His teaching is part of our minds
now. In a sense we look through his eyes as some look through
Hemingway's or Dostoevsky's eyes.' Trungpa's death, he said
later, made him understand the notion of the guru's mind being
everywhere: 'Certain perceptions and understandings are perma-
nent and affect your perspective on things. In this case, the notion
of emptiness, interrupting the build-up of anxiety and conceptual
thought by some trick of emptying the mind, either by thinking of
his [Trungpa's] face, or by stopping and meditating a moment, one
breath, or looking out at the sky. Any number of mind tricks.
Cutting through the build up of superficial anxiety, or illusory
consciousness, so the final resting place really is just open empty
mind. That's his mind, but also my mind, so space itself. I began
appreciating how helpful he had been in establishing that.'

Allen was not lonely in the apartment. Harry Smith came for a
short stay, hurt his leg, and, as in *The Man Who Came to Dinner*,
stayed almost a year. It was a stormy interlude; Harry's health was

poor, and he was a difficult, stubborn guest unused to sharing a dwelling. He took a perverse enjoyment in antagonising Allen, who was once reduced to slapping him in frustration. On one occasion, Bob Dylan came to meet Harry; many of the songs Dylan performed in the early days of his career he had taken from the Folkways *Anthology of American Folk Music* which Harry had compiled. To Allen's annoyance, Harry refused to get up. In the end, Allen's psychiatrist stepped in and told him that Harry had to go; he was raising Allen's blood pressure.

On 16 April 1987, the Federal Communications Commission warned the Pacifica radio network specifically, and the rest of the broadcast industry generally, not to air broadcasts of 'language or material that depicts or describes, in terms patently offensive as measured by contemporary community standards for the broadcast medium, sexual or excretory activities or organs'. All broadcasters in the USA received a notice concerning the airing of possibly offensive material headed 'New Indecency Enforcement Standards To Be Applied To All Broadcast And Amateur Radio Licencees'. In a letter to Allen, the executive director of Pacifica said, 'Pacifica, in this climate, cannot risk losing its licence . . . We must therefore, with great sadness, notify you that we are no longer free to air "Howl" and many other standard classics of contemporary literature . . .' Pacifica's lawyers naturally challenged the policy, seeking to set aside the new definition of 'indecency' and calling for a legally defined 'cut-off time'. There could not have been a project more perfectly tailored to the campaigning zeal and skills of Allen Ginsberg. He sent documents to the American Civil Liberties Union, the PEN American Center Freedom-to-Read Committee, and retained his own lawyer to work on the case. He discussed official censorship in interviews and circulated a massive folder of clippings and copies of correspondence to all interested parties. He devoted an enormous amount of time, energy and money to the project and, in 1989, Pacifica won their appeal against the new FCC regulations.

In January 1988, Ginsberg went to Israel, where he read at the huge Peace Now demonstration in Tel Aviv, protesting at the treatment of Palestinians in the occupied territories. A crowd estimated at sixty thousand gave him the loudest applause of the day for his 1974 poem 'Jaweh And Allah Battle', an attack on the role of the two religions in the Arab–Israeli conflict. In an interview, Ginsberg said he had come because he wanted to be 'a calm voice among a lot of ranting voices, polarised voices'. On his return to New York, he began attending weekly PEN meetings with Arthur Miller, Norman Mailer, Erica Jong, Susan Sontag, Ron Lichtenstein and a hundred other Jewish artists and writers, to organise a stand against Israel's treatment of Palestinians. At the end of February, the group sent a telegram to express solidarity with an association of Israeli artists and writers protesting Israel's conduct on the occupied West Bank.

While in Israel, Allen had compiled a dossier of information on censorship in that country for the PEN Freedom-to-Write Committee. He met Hana Siniora, editor of the much-censored Arab newspaper *Al Fajir*, and Elias Zananeri, managing editor of Palestinian Press Services, *Al Awdah*, and looked at their files of censored items. In June, the committee sent a letter to the Israeli government, urging it 'to cease its practice of censorship' of Palestinian writers and journalists in the occupied West Bank and Gaza Strip. The letter, the result of much heated discussion that divided some of the leading writers in the United States, called on Israel 'to end its policy of arrests of Palestinian and Israeli journalists, to reopen censored Palestinian newspapers, to reopen the Palestinian Press Service, and to cease its practice of censorship of books, school reading materials, newspapers and literary texts circulated in the West Bank and the Gaza Territories.'

In addition to Ginsberg, its initiator, the letter was signed by: Susan Sontag, president of the PEN American Center; Faith Sale and Rose Styron, the co-chairwomen of the Freedom-to-Write Committee; William Styron and Grace Paley. Faith Sale said, 'The letter is not a political statement. It's a statement about censorship – and that is PEN's mandate.'

As expected, the letter was opposed by Israel's supporters at PEN. Novelist Cynthia Ozick said in an interview: 'Criticism of Israel must have credentials and I feel no-one on the Freedom-to-Write Committee has such credentials.' But Allen had done his research and the letter went into considerable detail, listing specific charges of censorship, including the detention of 35 Palestinian journalists without trial or charges and the forced closure of several Palestinian newspapers and magazines, as well as the Gaza Press Service and the Palestinian News Service.

Allen had been a member of the Freedom-to-Write Committee since 1966 and had long used it as the vehicle for his various campaigns, beginning with LeRoi Jones's trial in Newark, where his writing was used against him in an assault case, and continuing with cases involving Timothy Leary, John Lennon, and FBI and CIA sabotage of the underground press. Throughout 1988 he was very involved with the opposition to the new FCC regulations which forbade his poetry from being broadcast in the USA except in the dead of night. He was a very active committee member and was eventually asked to become a vice-president.

Ginsberg would have achieved very little in taking on the powerful Israeli lobby alone, but his new position in the establishment gave him the ability to campaign on a much higher level, dealing with international affairs. The views of the committee members made headlines in the *New York Times* and were given serious consideration.

Ginsberg and the Beats had been an inspiration for a number of younger artists, many of whom had now reached the peaks of their careers. The Italian painter Francesco Clemente had great success working in New York and collaborated with Allen on an illustrated edition of 'White Shroud'. At the New York Shubert Theater benefit for Vietnam Veterans in February 1988, Allen and Philip Glass performed 'Wichita Vortex', Allen's poem set to music by Glass. Allen had also been approached by Robert Wilson, Glass's longtime collaborator, who was working on a performance called Cosmopolitan Greetings (after a 1986 poem by Allen), based on the life of Bessie Smith. Allen was originally asked for a new text, but instead of overloading himself with yet more work, he offered old material, which they accepted. 'I would normally have been flattered at working with these famous names,' he said, pleased that his anti-workaholic resolution was bearing fruit.

On 28 June 1988, an event dear to Allen's heart occurred: the opening of the Jack Kerouac Commemorative in the new $3.5 million Eastern Canal Park in Lowell, Massachusetts. The Commemorative – the word is used as a noun – featured fifteen passages from Kerouac's books incised upon eight three-sided granite columns arranged in a rough mandala, rather like a war memorial.

When the news was first announced that Lowell's City Council had decided to approve a new park in Kerouac's memory, Kerouac's old enemy, Norman Podhoretz, used the occasion to attack the Beats yet again. In the *New York Post*, under a headline 'Strange Honor for a False Prophet', he once more fulminated against 'Howl': 'In its glorification of madness, drugs and homosexuality, and its contempt and hatred for anything and everything generally deemed healthy, normal or decent, Ginsberg's poem simultaneously foreshadowed and helped to propagate the values of the youth culture of the 1960s ... Kerouac and Ginsberg once played a part in ruining a great many young people who were influenced by their "distaste for normal life and common decency".'

But Allen no longer rose to the bait. In an interview in *New Letters*, he said: 'Good old Norman Podhoretz. If he weren't there like a wall I can butt my head against, I wouldn't have anybody to hate. And why hate him? He's part of my world, and he's sort of like the character the Blue Meanie ... did I ever really hate him or was I just sort of fascinated by him? I saw him as a sort of sacred personage in my life, in a way, someone whose vision is so opposite from mine that it's provocative and interesting – just as my vision is interesting and provocative enough for him to write columns against it in the newspaper. In fact, maybe he's more honest than I am because he attacks me openly. So I should really respect him as one of the sacred personae in the drama of my own transitory existence.'

Allen began an affair with a seventeen-year-old boy from Atlanta called Mark; he felt that it could not last, but it cheered him.

That summer Harry Smith moved back into the apartment. He had been living in a 'Bowery cubicle Franciscan retreat Anthony House flop ill with pneumonia and anaemia, so moved to small room again. Says he wants to die.'

Allen's journals reveal an amazingly full life: visits with Robert Wilson, a trip to Japan, continuing problems with Peter, Harry and Gregory:

Gregory volatile and fiery when visiting ... tried to embrace me, I withdrew, his face darkened, he began arguing ... he called midnight yelling at me, said, 'I'm cashing in chips' on friendship. Morning he woke me on phone wanting money a little ... he'd come back to Roger Richards'; found a note with phone number, called it. It was the city morgue. In morning Gregory wanted me to throw money down out of window ... came down 15 minutes later (dressed) he was seated on stoop. I repeated what I said before, 'I won't see you when you're drinking.'

He said, 'I lost my wife and son refusing to stop drinking. Poo – that's part of me – you can't reject me your old pal – you only love me for my poetry.' Scowling, 'If I didn't give up for my son why should I change for you?' ... He stopped to argue in the street, yelling, between squealing, crying and angry accusation in front of the coffee and doll storefront on 12th Street near 1st Avenue ... seemed deliberate to embarrass me in my neighborhood.

Allen was not normally involved in giving handouts to this group of friends, as that was handled by COP, Allen's poetry foundation. So it was Bob Rosenthal's unenviable job to give money to Gregory, Herbert Huncke and Harry. Bob: 'I had scheduling problems, they all came over for money so often. Herbert and Harry didn't like to be in the room at the same time, so I'd have to coordinate their visits. Sometimes I'd maliciously let them meet. Harry once told me he liked me because I never tried to kiss him. I kept things very businesslike.'

However, problems with Corso and company were slight compared with the latest scandal to break at Naropa. Trungpa had appointed one of his students, an American called Thomas Rich, from Passaic, New Jersey, to be his successor. Rich changed his name to Ozel Tendzin, and assumed the role of Vajra Regent of Vajradhatu. On 15 December 1988, at a meeting in Berkeley, forty-five-year-old Tendzin revealed that he already knew he had AIDS when he had sex with a number of his male students. One young man had tested positive for the AIDS virus, and had unknowingly passed the virus on to a young woman in the Buddhist community who also tested positive. There was concern that Tendzin, 'might have passed this on to many, many people'. Tendzin's young male companion also tested positive, and it was this man's mother and sister who first spread the news around the Buddhist community. Tendzin had known he was infected as far back as 1985 when he had talked about it with Trungpa. Tenzin said he came away from the conversation feeling he could 'change the karma. Thinking I had some extraordinary means of protection, I went ahead with my business as if something would take care of it for me.'

Trungpa had said nothing, even though he knew Tendzin was sexually active, perhaps genuinely believing in the magical powers of all the chants and visualisations, even though Buddhism had never been shown to have cured any other ailments, not even the common cold. Trungpa designated Tendzin to lead the church until a permanent successor was chosen, and at his death in 1987 Ösel Tendzin succeeded to the post of president of Vajradhatu and the Nalanda Foundation.

The Vajradhatu International Church's board of directors, in Halifax, Nova Scotia, felt that he had abused his position by having sex with students, and had demonstrated reprehensible moral behaviour which would damage the sangha. They asked Tendzin to step down, but he refused, saying he would give initiations and hold that year's seminary. Predictably, the sangha split down the middle with some members feeling that important secret teachings would be lost by his departure, and others feeling that he should be taken to court by those whom he had knowingly infected and sentenced to death.

Allen was naturally in the thick of it: 'much gossip about the Regent's AIDs contagion'. The board seemed powerless to unite the entire sangha to a course of action; the various centres took sides for or against the Regent, money stopped coming in, rich benefactors withdrew their support, chaos reigned. Barbara Dilley, the Chancellor, who taught dance at Naropa, asked Allen if he could raise money from his many contacts. He balked; he had done scores, possibly even hundreds of fund-raising benefits for the Buddhists over the years and brought in rich patrons from all over, but with a scandal like this no one was going to want to support Vajradhatu. He glumly recorded: 'Barbara Dilley . . . pale cheeked, doesn't dance any more age 51, wants me to help raise money thru artist friends – a bottomless hole? I once tried Dylan ten years ago, he made fun of me for asking, said he skipped that part of my letter.' In the event, the Regent's health declined rapidly. He moved to Ojai, California and, on the advice of Dingo Khyentse Rinpoche, he entered into retreat. Tendzin died on 25 August 1990.

* * *

Allen's home situation seemed impossible to resolve. Peter, en-
sconced in the next-door apartment, was once more on ampheta-
mines: his huge potbelly shrank, he became thin-faced and gaunt;
eyes blinking, he growled and screamed to himself as he went
about his daily chores: cooking, cleaning or soaking his clothes in
the bathtub because Allen would not let him into his apartment to
use the washing machine. Allen despaired; he had spent tens of
thousands of dollars on the Cherry Valley farm to isolate Peter
from his city drug sources to no avail. Peter's downstairs neigh-
bour, poet Michael Scholnich, a family man with a new baby,
complained of Peter's unnerving noises as he yelled at the television
set, groaned and stomped on the floor, cursing at all hours of day
and night. His neighbours across the hall and in the apartments
above all complained to Allen about Peter's loud television and
screams. Allen, as owner of the lease on Peter's apartment, felt
responsible to his neighbours for Peter living there. 'What can I do?
Call the police, change lock, force him on street? It's inhuman
abominable behaviour, – nor can I live with him, he's out of his
skull, and may be dangerous tho I doubt he'd attack me. So's not
to "enable" him, I've cut off money aid; so's not to fear him I've
had him in court for "order of protection" in case he screams on
balcony or tries to come in my hallway drunk ... Meanwhile my
head buzzes with rumination ... How can I continue my life, with
Peter confronting me with crises like Naomi, and the Buddhist
family fragmenting with Naropa undergoing throes of conscience.'

In May 1989, Bob Rosenthal moved the Ginsberg office out of
Allen's apartment to fourth-floor premises at Second Avenue and
14th Street, sublet from a daughter of Alene Lee, the woman who
had typed up *The Yage Letters* for Allen and Bill; 'Mardou' of
Kerouac's *Subterraneans*. Alene often dropped by the office, and so
renewed her friendship with Allen. The room was once used as a
music school and had an echoing concrete floor. All the battered
filing cabinets, with labels such as 'Dope', 'Dope', 'Mostly Dope',
'Death and Asshole' – his will and medical records – and the many
drawers marked 'FYPC' – Faded Yellow Paper Clippings – as well
as the sagging boards that served as desks, the Apple Macintosh,
the Xerox machine and the boxes of books, were all cleared out of
the crowded office where Rosenthal and his assistant, Vicki
Stanbury, had struggled for so many years with the chaos of
Allen's paperwork. The move completed, Allen went at midnight

to the new office and browsed through boxes of photographs uncovered by the move. He worried about the increased rent, a total of $900 a month, including his apartment, and worried about having an office at all. 'I need Bob to keep track of mail, taxes, monies & exterminators, also poetry readings. But I have to work to maintain this luxury. Is it just to keep me company, have an office I can call for help with lightbulb replacements?'

He thinned out the books in his library and rearranged the apartment. He had privacy for the first time in fifteen years and wrote: 'Now that office moved out of the apartment, rooms are quiet, telephone still long afternoons, relieved of stress – waking mornings late to pee, Rosenthal and Vicki Stanbury used to be there, or afternoons afraid to nap lazy in their eyes, guilty, wandering in and out disturbed attracted by constant telephone, visitors, Brian Graham printmaker, messengers visiting, Susie Timmons doing books at kitchen table while I cleared a space for oatmeal or lunch soup, magnetised at desk, phone busy when I wanted to dial stepmother.'

Allen's health problems increased: he took Allopurinol for gout, and his sight was getting fuzzy, the first phase of cataracts. The medicines he took for high blood pressure prevented him from getting an erection but a newly purchased rubber dildo vibrator seemed to help.

He had a cardiologist in Boston, and an endocrinologist for his kidney problems. His macrobiotic advisor prescribed a diet for his diabetes; he also worked with Dr Ho, the Chinese acupuncturist, and a Tibetan doctor. The missing component was a general practitioner to coordinate all these efforts. He had Bells Palsy and, whenever he was fatigued, his face would droop and freeze. He had had kidney stones since the 1950s, and had had his gallbladder removed. By the late 1980s, he always had Demorol with him which he used to control the pain. He did not listen to his body's protests; instead he would work through pain. He aneasthetised it to do readings – but was often irritable – and when he got home he would totally collapse. He liked the total collapse because he got a lot of attention from his concerned staff. In 1989 he was feeling so run-down that he went to Bassett Hospital, in Cooperstown, upstate New York, near Cherry Valley, where his cousin Joel was a doctor. They did a liver biopsy and found cirrhosis.

* * *

Peter Hale, Allen's friend from Boulder, came to visit, and Philip Whalen passed through town. Allen read at St Mark's Church and afterwards Whalen said that he thought Gregory's yelling at Allen was tiresome. Allen was surprised; he hadn't even noticed it, he was so used to Gregory's disruptions. However, at a reading in Vancouver with Gregory, he had to work hard not to show his irritation when Gregory continually interrupted him, and talked loudly in the back of the hall. But Allen continued to deal with his tormentors. At a major reading at Rutgers' University, he brought Peter on stage, seemingly oblivious to Peter's erratic behaviour. Only afterwards did he criticise himself 'for failing to notice mad jerking & bikini'd incoherence on Rutgers' stage doing push ups behind my back, while I orated to a thousand mystified kid youths –'

In October Bill Burroughs came to visit and was charmed by Mark, the young man from Atlanta. Bill commented, 'Allen's got himself a beauty.'

In San Francisco that fall to receive the National Poetry Award for Distinguished Service to Poetry, Allen as usual stayed with Shig Murao on Grant. The front room had not changed in two decades: a straw mat on the floor, the walls lined with bookshelves – though there were now fewer books than before – Shig's desk at the bay window overlooking Grant Street at Vallejo, the Chinese laundry across the street, but there were now expensive new bistros up and down the the narrow street. Shig had had several strokes in the last ten years and limped around the room with his cane. He could no longer play zen flute. He and Allen sat in his television room in the back and discussed their mutual diabetes.

Allen had only been in San Francisco a few hours and already felt an empty sense of loss, the excitement of the 1950s poetry renaissance was long gone. 'No ambition or possibility to re-enter youthtime aura, new souls to meet & conquer & convert & befriend & start a hopeful revolution of poetry – won't stay here long, like visiting phantom stage after the play's over, an empty theater years later . . . a community of souls already dead in Hades, empty ghosts still hungry for action, severed from the living land.'

He saw Lawrence Ferlinghetti, Michael McClure, Philip Lamantia, Philip Whalen at his Hartford Street Zendo and AIDS hospice, and Gregory, who was also in town, hanging out with the bums on Broadway. Allen revisited his old haunts: the Trieste coffeeshop, Dante's coffeeshop on Columbus, Vesuvio's on Adler Place, now renamed Kerouac Alley. He wrote a poem, naming the other streets of San Francisco after his friends.

Christmas came, and Allen had not heard from Mark for a month. He had not returned Allen's calls before leaving for a month's holiday in France. 'Strange disappearance of his attention, his love vanished,' Allen noted. He showed Robert Frank a photograph of Mark in bed, naked, asleep, that he had taken a year earlier.

'Is he really asleep?' asked Frank.

Allen told him he was.

'That's what makes it so good.'

In January 1990, Allen received a letter from Mark, severing their relationship, and giving Allen his reason, 'I gave you my body, you didn't want to listen.' Allen recognised his complaint as justifiable; he had not been interested in Mark's opinions, only in his body. But Allen was not overly concerned because January also brought him a new flatmate: a young teacher he had met in China, who had now moved to the United States. Jack did the laundry, cleaned the windows, vacuumed and mopped the floors and unblocked the three pilot lights on the stove that had been without flame for fourteen years. He also 'enjoyed lovemaking, came to bed each morning for an embrace & kiss from his room.' He had not heard of the Beatles, so Allen played him the *Sgt. Pepper* album, 'It leaves me breathless,' he said at the end of the first side. 'I tried to breathe out slowly at the music but the last chorus went on so long. I wish I had this text to teach my students in Chung Ching.'

Allen was so overworked in the spring of 1990 that he began to fear a stroke: he was the keynote speaker at the Gay and Lesbian Writers' Conference in San Francisco; as the vice-president of the American PEN Center he was the host at a gala dinner; he spoke at the Earth Day Rally in Philadelphia and lectured at Rutgers. 'How can I stem tide of actions, papers, letters, phonecalls, travels, emergencies, cash flow, requests for money?' In April he was able to escape by boarding a plane for Prague – the May King was returning to his kingdom, this time to be welcomed with honour by Mayor Koran and President Vaclav Havel.

President Havel had instigated a search for the notebook taken from Allen by the Czech secret police in 1965, but it was reported destroyed. Allen had several duties as part of the May Day celebrations, begining with a speech. He told the Prague audience:

'As May King twenty-nine years ago, I have authority to advise: meditation, calm, cut through hysteria, muscle power instead of machine power, clarity of mind, tranquil nature, sensitivity at the time of loss of the planet, as it seems, in the next generations. Gate Gate Paragate, Parasamgate Bodhi Svaha.' His new guru, Gelek Rinpoche, had casually commented that in three or four generations, human life on Earth would become more difficult; that the sparks of accident and chaos would become more rapid – Chernobyl, the war in Iraq, Three Mile Island, frequent oil spills would make life unsustainable. Allen immediately passed the message on as his own.

Before going on stage, Allen introduced Anne Waldman to President Havel at a café table. Allen told Havel: 'My advice: candour ends paranoia, if you're afraid of secret police.'

'I'm not afraid of secret police,' said the president. 'Everyone tells me be afraid of Mossad, of PLO. I am only afraid of the people of Czechoslovakia, there has to be a spiritual element, that's why the Dalai Lama's visit was so important to us.' He told them: 'The Dalai Lama gave me this mantra . . .' He took a sheet of paper from his wallet and read:

Om Ture Tu Tarey Turey Goihah
Om Ku Re Kule Hri Svahah

'With instructions to say "Om Ture" every day. The second line is only for emergencies. Nothing so far a crisis, not Bush, not Shamir, not Gorbachev, but in case of real crisis; the mantra has special power.' He arranged to see them the following night when they would have more time to talk.

That evening, in the old town square, the Lord Mayor of Prague, Jaroslav Koran, introduced Allen to the assembled crowd as the old May King. He read 'Return Of May King' in an exalted voice, his amplified voice booming out over thousands of heads in the square. A translation followed, then Allen was given his paper crown. He knelt and presented it to the young student in a cloak and top hat who was to succeed him, and made *namaste*. He advised the new May King that it was the privilege of the May King to sleep with anyone he wanted to in Prague.

'That is not my interest, you know,' the new king told him.

'Alas,' said Allen.

Allen did the rounds of television stations and newspapers. President Havel attended all the public events, including a writers' conference and a big reading. Allen gave him copies of all the FCC censorship material from the PEN American Center, the American Academy of Arts and Letters, and newspapers, and asked him to sign a petition. Havel told him: 'I will try to hand it on ... I'll be able to sign it as a playwright writer, not as president.' Allen agreed that that was more appropriate.

He complimented Allen on his stage presence, and said Allen's voice was beautiful. He had been moved by the poems, he didn't need translations. He thought the double view of the self as an ironic reflection in 'Kral Majalis' was 'beautiful, enjoyable, brilliant'. Allen and Anne Waldman both kissed him, and saw him to his car. He pointed out the heart decal on the front windshield.

Allen returned to New York for a few weeks, where he had to deal with the continuing problems of the Orlovsky family. Peter had removed the front windows of his apartment and was howling at the street. He had also been bullying his sister Marie. Lafcadio had attacked his mother and was in King's Park Hospital leaving Marie at home alone. On one occasion Peter dressed in her clothes and paraded around the local supermarket. He had taken Marie's two-thousand dollar inheritance from Oleg, and returned another time and stole three hundred dollars from a drawer. When confronted, he angrily threw a Frisbee at her which hit her on the lip. Allen went to see her with Doctor Joe Gross – Harry Smith's doctor, and an old friend of Allen's who had been with Allen in Prague. Marie signed the committal papers that Doctor Gross brought, stating: 'Peter Orlovsky acts crazy and dangerous taking money that's not rightfully his.' Peter was committed to Bellevue.

By mid-June, Allen was in London, promoting his new record, 'The Lion For Real', just released on Island Records. He gave a reading at the Royal Festival Hall and wished he had more time to visit. He wrote to Edith, his stepmother: 'London with double decker buses feels nostalgic – I'd love to live here a season and take it easy sight seeing.' His next stop was Istanbul where he stayed with the American Ambassador and drove around in a bulletproof limousine.

In addition to the 1990 Naropa Institute Summer Poetics Programme, Allen attended a number of summer arts festivals before departing for Seoul, South Korea, on 19 August, to participate in the Twelfth World Congress of Poets. PEN had given him a dossier on government censorship, compiled from reports by Asia Watch and Amnesty International, and a list of writers and journalists imprisoned for their writing. Allen had faxed ahead to say that he would be representing the PEN America Center and that he would be 'speaking out' on writers in prison. He was told that he was free to speak his mind, he would not be censored.

On Allen's arrival in Seoul, he immediately got into an argument with the congress organiser, the poet Moon Duk Su, about censorship. Allen mostly kept his temper. He was told that writers were jailed for three principal reasons: private or organised attempts to contact North Korea, for organising labour unions in support of higher wages and better conditions, and attacks on the president or military. Allen decided on the cases of four dissident writers and poets to present at his morning press conference. At the congress he performed 'Father Death Blues', discussed meditation, and improvised a blues on the Korean National Security Act used to jail writers.

He changed his return ticket in order to give himself a few more days to explore, see the museums and get the feel of the streets. He wrote Edith: 'Lots of sightseeing, lots of walking and looking at fish markets, lots of salty food and fresh fish (raw, sliced off flounder still gasping occasionally on the plate) at East Sea.'

After a particularly acrimonious argument with someone from UNESCO about writers in prison, Allen retired to bed disturbed: 'because I'd been disturbing my hosts all week over "prisoners of conscience" as per PEN Club reports. And many I met had made fun of "your Susan Sontag" for her intrusive eccentric behaviour at 1988 PEN Club Congress here, insisting on raising the issue of writers and journalists in prison. I was ashamed, perhaps Dei Dao and Voznesensky (also present) would see me as an adolescent troublemaker with kneejerk habitual pattern of looking for prisoners or injustice to complain about, an egotistical announcement maker "bawling" blind complaints.'

He taught Blake at the university, and a class on Whitman. At one lecture, he was asked to explain his Blake vision: 'I answered that I probably experienced latent mature timbre of my own voice.' Then he recited 'Ah! Sunflower' 'with heart tones'. The students were enthusiastic, anxious for information, and his classes usually lasted several hours.

Before leaving for Seoul, Allen had visited Peter in Bellevue, along with Gelek Rinpoche and Beverly Isis. 'He'd shaved his bullet head, smirked, snarled, took off Gelek's shoe and rubbed his little foot. When we left, Gelek said he was crazy, thoughts jumping around from one to another disconnected.' When Allen returned to Bellevue after his trip, he found Peter altogether calmer, with several weeks' growth of grey hair on his shaven head. Allen took him cheeseburgers and french fries. Allen told him that he couldn't return to the next-door apartment; it was too disruptive for the neighbours, and for Allen himself. He would put Peter's papers in order and into storage.

Allen asked what was going on in his mind when he broke the windows in the apartment building hallway and front door. 'Insanity,' Peter said, 'alcohol – too much cocaine, you know the combination, lock myself in, look at pictures, sex and play with my titties and get paranoid, that's why all the confusion in the house.' Peter said the doctors were remanding him to Veteran's Hospital for thirty days.

Allen told him that he needed six months to a year of the rehabilitation programme. He had to change. If he did then Allen would get him another apartment and help support him if he had difficulty working, but he wouldn't help him commit suicide. Peter walked Allen to the door and kissed him goodbye. They hugged each other.

While Allen was away, his Chinese roommate had decided that he no longer wanted a sexual relationship with him. He took no enjoyment from it and had only been trying to please Allen. He wondered if he should move out. Allen was saddened, but insisted that he stay. Jack began restoring Peter's old apartment, trying to get the smell out and doing his magic with the blocked pilot lights on the stove. Allen realised that agreeing to cut sexual ties had removed a lot of pressure from their relationship: 'I needn't appear young, could display age and weakness, be helped, needn't scheme and compete falsities or pull in my belly to seduce him – with the sex making off my back he was more my subject and house slave or "Chinese house boy" as he wanted to be, more under my influence he said . . . I felt twinge of longing, sad happiness, relief, liberty – all mixed – like a new life, no ball and chain of meat.'

One of Trungpa's students, Jacqueline Gens, came to work for Bob Rosenthal to keep track of Allen's photographic career. Allen liked her and she sometimes accompanied him to events. In his journals for that summer, Allen even wondered if she would be prepared to have a baby with him. That October, Allen introduced her to Bob Dylan in his candlelit dressing room backstage after a concert.

'If you have any Buddhist questions, here's a learned Buddhist lady,' said Allen.

'Oh I don't know anything about Buddha. But there was a nightclub in KC called the Laughing Buddha.'

Allen was nonplussed. 'Thank you for the audience, sire,' he said and patted Dylan's neck.

'I'm honoured, sir,' said Dylan.

On 6 November, Peter was let out of rehabilitation and went to stay with Beverly Isis. Peter's mother, Kate, died in hospital a day or two later. Peter remained sober and was able to visit the hospital in time to hold his mother's hand for half an hour. Beverly reported to Allen that Peter had trouble following conversation and had a short attention span. Allen wondered if it was brain damage caused by alcohol.

In December Gelek Rinpoche came to spend a weekend. Allen cleaned the apartment and changed the sheets. He introduced Gelek to Lucien, who later told Allen that he was a sweet man, he liked him, but his description of death and after-death was incomprehensible gibberish. He could not understand a word of it. Allen spent Christmas with Jacqueline, taking her with him by train to visit his brother, Eugene, and sister-in-law, Connie, at Connie's family's house in Port Washington. Allen gave out books and scarves as presents.

One by one Allen's friends began to drop away; there had been a slow attrition ever since the death of Frank O'Hara in 1966, when Allen wrote (in 'City Midnight Junk Strains'): '[I] hear of one funeral a year nowadays–/ from Billie Holiday's time.' They each left an emptiness, and made Allen concerned for his own post-humous reputation. Ted Berrigan died of liver disease in 1983.

Julian Beck, co-founder of the Living Theater died of cancer in September, 1985. John Clellon Holmes, author of *Go*, arguably the first Beat Generation book, died of cancer in 1988 after a series of terrible operations in which his tongue was cut out and part of his jaw removed. Now it was Alene Lee on her deathbed at Lennox Hill Hospital. Allen spoke with her for half an hour on the phone, calmly discussing the death process. Allen told her Gelek Rinpoche's advice on dying: cultivate concentration on whatever level of practice you're at, 'practice compassion and empty open mind,' and described his experience with laughing gas. Alene told him of her fear of death: when she was sixteen, training to be a nurse, she had seen an awful grimacing corpse in the hospital which had traumatised her, and as a child she was made to kiss her dead stepmother's corpse, embalmed, cold and hard in its coffin. They discussed Kerouac, 'Her anger at him was tribute to her closeness, it was "personal" she said.'

Allen visited her on New Year's Day, then, ten days later, Christine, Alene's daughter, called and left a message saying Alene didn't want to die alone. Could Allen be with her? He had a Freedom to Write meeting at five, and worried that Alene might die before he got to the hospital. He remembered sitting alone with his Aunt Eleanor in the 1940s as she lay blue-faced, dying of septicaemia, in an oxygen tent. She asked him, 'Am I going to die?'

He had not known what to say without panicking her, so replied non-committally, 'I don't know,' and left soon afterwards.

Alene was down to 86 pounds, her body deteriorated beyond recovery. She lay propped on a pillow gasping for breath, skeletally thin, eyelids half-closed, with a plastic oxygen mask over her nose and chin. Allen told her he was there, then sat and did samatha meditation. He chanted a few mantras, then sat quietly. Allen left when Christine arrived, advising her to let her mother die in peace without intensive machinery.

Alene had revived at midnight and spoken with her daughter. Christine asked Allen to leave it a day before visiting.

I went in and sat with Christine and Alene, who was propped up on pillows, a tube strapped to the right side of her jaw. Each time she breathed her head moved a slight jerk, impelled by the blue air machine at her bedside pumping air in her lungs, it looked like. Her eyes half closed, pupils half visible, grey eyeballs, a little sweat on her hollow brow, losing pulse slowly and blood pressure lowering – Christine kept her head close to Alene's so I couldn't see Alene's eyes, I sat at window in chair and meditated, pacing my way through prostration sadhana and Gelek Rinpoche's 4 Reminders poem ('especially human life is like a bubble . . . this body will be a corpse . . .') Around 5.29 no more pulse, breathing had stopped, the doctors shone light in eyes, no pupil reaction, so Alene was 'pronounced dead'. Christine stayed on to watch the body being washed and wrapped in plastic.

As Christine left for a few minutes, I took photos of Alene 'like Egyptian queen or princess' in shroud-like sheet wrapped up with classic head sticking out of the sheets, as if wrapped embalmed the face showing, staring up, eyes opened still, jaw askew and teeth visible, from the long period, a day or more with breathing tube taped to her jaw. Christine saw me, said, 'I'm not sure anyone should see those photos, she was a very private person.'

The next morning Christine called and asked for the negatives. Allen gave her the roll to develop and asked her to return the photos taken earlier.

Allen's psychiatrist, Doctor Fortner-Lewis, closed her practice in order to study paediatrics. Allen was fond of her; she had solved most of his 'perplexities' with Peter. She told him that he was in better shape, calmer. She said that the break with Peter had provoked confusing resonances and memories of breaks and early troubles with his mother, and told him he could always call her for advice. As Allen walked around apartment 24, surveying the sorted piles of Peter's books and papers, he knew how Louis must have felt when Naomi finally moved to Manhattan to live with Doctor Luria. Allen and Peter had not had sex in ten years; now Peter was moving out completely.

Allen threw himself into his work. The previous September they had moved the office to Union Square, fourteen storeys up, with big east windows looking down on the square. On 20 June 1991 Allen stayed at the office until 4 a.m. dealing with a foot-high pile of mail left over from January. He mailed twenty-seven letters on his way home, then wrote poetry until five-thirty. Among his projects were a volume of 1950s journals that Gordon Ball was editing, selected poems for Viking, and a volume of new poems

1984–1991. A new book of photographs and a series of collaborations: 'End of Fall of America' with Roy Lichtenstein, 'Cosmopolitan Greetings' with Francesco Clemente, and 'Plutonian Ode' with Philip Glass. His religious practice was even further behind than the contents of his in-tray, but in July, he was able to go on a five-day retreat with Gelek and take the Heruka Initiation and Bodhisattva Vows with him. Unlike Trungpa, who was always surrounded by courtiers, and usually too drunk for an intimate conversation, Gelek was someone whom Allen could relate to, not only as a teacher, but as a friend. Gelek began to stay at Allen's apartment whenever he came to New York. Gelek said: 'We became friends. I was a bit surprised, I was expecting an angry poet.'

Allen was unable to let go of Peter, and Peter soon found himself back in his old apartment, despite an agreement with the landlord that he not live there. Inevitably he started drinking again, and inevitably there was a crisis. Peter was agitated, sleepless, up all night watching television, eating nothing but salami. He smoked six packs of cigarettes a day, coughing and gagging, and ate dozens of throat lozenges every few hours, crunching them up. The climax came on 2 November 1991, after a week of cocaine and vodka. Allen was meditating in his bedroom when Peter entered the apartment and threatened Jack, Allen's Chinese roommate, still living there. He slapped him across the face with a cloth, then, getting no rise from that, held a knife against his throat. After a few minutes, Peter retired to his room. Jack waited until Allen had finished his meditating before telling him. Allen called the police. Ten of them came with an ambulance. Peter's hands were cuffed behind him, he was bound to a chair with plastic strips, and carried out yelling, 'Nazis, read me my Miranda rights! Call my lawyer.' He was taken back to ward nineteen north at Bellevue. As they brought him in, a nurse said, 'Why Peter, how nice to see you again!'

Harry Smith died on 28 November 1991 in his tiny room at the Hotel Chelsea. Allen's friend Raymond Foye telephoned the news from Saint Vincent's. Allen took a cab to the hospital, and arranged with a young Catholic priest to go down to the morgue to sit with Harry. Allen was led to the basement through battleship-grey corridors. The priest and an attendant went inside while Allen waited: 'There may be corpses lying around.' They prepared the room and Allen was ushered in. They pulled out shelf eight from a wall full of long, stainless-steel drawers. Harry's body was covered by a bright-white shroud beneath a disposable clear plastic cover. Allen asked if they would fold the shroud back to enable him to see Harry's face.

His face bound with a long strip of adhesive bandage under the nose to the ears, a plastic drainpipe in his mouth jerked aside, blood on his greywhite beard, as if he'd again vomited his food as so often in restaurants, hair on head fine and silvery, right eye swollen shut where he'd fell over off chair upsetting a pile of books ... I put my hand on his brow, still somewhat warm – had forgotten my camera and Raymond had said, 'Personally I think, not to take photo' – so sat with Harry's body an hour, rehearsed prostration litany, four reminders and dedications and refuge and Bodhisattva and lineage prayers – silent awhile – then sex session yoga I'd learned from Gelek Rinpoche – put my right hand on the crown of his head, a swath of paper shroud over his skull, my palm covering that and fingers touching the side of his forehead and his silver hair – sat and meditated for while on breath then on thoughts.

A series of reminiscences of Harry passed through his head; Allen had known him for more than thirty years. Allen sat on the stool, looking down at Harry's swollen eye. 'How strange I took Harry on Earth for granted, now he'll be gone forever, and myself later on, but for now no more Harry Smith living so unique, so painfully suffering, so self abrogating, so devious, saintly.' Raymond Foye said he found a great number of uncashed social security and royalty checks among his papers. Arrangements were made to archive Harry's room, all the tapes to go to the Smithsonian, which already had so many of Harry's collections. Harry had died of a peptic ulcer; he had been coughing blood for years.

Allen spent New Year's Day, 1992, staying with his doctor cousin Joel Gaidemak. Joel checked Allen's various symptoms and diagnosed a congestive heart condition – he must have had a minor heart attack in his sleep; a forecast which prompted Allen to write a catalogue poem called 'Heart Attack Blues', a 27-page, 24 lines to a page, list of all the boys he'd had sex with who sprang immediately to mind.

Allen devoted more time to his classes at Brooklyn College than was necessary. He often brought in guest speakers for his ongoing series of lectures called the Literary History of the Beat Generation, including Ray Bremser, Carl Solomon, Gregory Corso and, on one occasion, Peter Orlovsky, taken out of Bellevue specially for the afternoon. In April, using Kerouac's *Essentials of Spontaneous Prose* as a model, he instructed his Brooklyn students in the art of poesy:

(1) Keep your hand moving 10 minutes (to evade critical 'monkey mind').
(2) Free to write worst shit in America.
(3) Don't worry about punctuation grammar syntax spelling.
(4) First thought the first way your mind flashes on something.
(5) Be specific. Car-Cadillac vegetable-onion flower-geranium. Writing is a visual art.
(6) Lose control, say what you really want to say.
(7) Don't be logical, life isn't.
(8) Go for jugular (energy or scaryness).
(9) 'If you go all this way with writing it'll take you [to] very place that zen does.'
(10) Spend it all.

That summer found Allen back in Boulder, staying at the Varsity Townhouses in the same apartment he had had for the last five years. Aside from Naropa, his projects included a four-CD box-set of his greatest recordings for Rhino Records in Los Angeles. His health continued to slowly decline: he had gout, kidneystones, high blood pressure, diabetes, misty eyes and dysesthesia – a lack of feeling in the soles of his feet, inside ankles, small of back, anus and the head of his penis. He dreamed still of Naomi, Neal, Charles Plymell, Robert LaVigne and earlier boyfriends. He had a head full of lineages, visualisations, mandalas, chants and Vajrayana Downfalls. Among the Fourteen Root Tantra Downfalls, he was most concerned with number fourteen: 'Despising women. For enlightenment in this lifetime need male or female heter partner without which we cannot. It is the source of all bliss.' There were also the Secondary Mother Tantra Vows, of which number eight: 'Never release seminal fluids,' seemed unlikely to remain unbroken.

Just after Christmas, Allen left for Gelek Rinpoche's centre in Ann Arbor, Michigan, to go on retreat in preparation for Yamataka induction; a fifteen-minute, Gelugpa-style practice he was obliged to perform daily from now on. 'What a bewildering array of symbolic practices prayers mudras mantras visualisations – all to prepare for ongoing deathbed.' His Yamantaka Initiation occurred on 31 December, forty years after he first was intrigued by the Evans–Wentz translation of the *Tibetan Book of the Dead*.

Nineteen ninety-three was to be a very busy year, with an enormous amount of travel within the United States, and culminating in a four-month European tour. His professional commitments had moved up a notch, more money was coming in, but the administration costs had also increased with the new Union Square office. Bob Rosenthal's staff now consisted of Jacqueline Gens and Peter Hale, as well as lawyers, part-time bookkeepers and archivists. One of his financial burdens was removed by the wealthy Japanese artist Hiro Yamagata, who gave a substantial grant to COP to help Gregory Corso's $100-a-day heroin habit. Allen's photographic career just about broke even; it cost him a lot in printing costs and administration, but he had a number of shows and sales, even though his natural tendency was to give his work away. The photographer Bruce Weber visited to conduct an interview and wanted several of Allen's photos. He insisted on paying for them, so Allen charged him three hundred dollars each but gave him the ones he'd taken of him on an earlier occasion.

Allen's life was still overshadowed by the spectre of Peter's seemingly insolvable problems. Before Christmas he was committed to Saint Luke's Roosevelt Hospital psychiatric ward after another manic drunken spree finished up with the police carrying him away from the Stratford Arms Hotel where he was then living. This time Allen was told to stay away. In May 1993, Peter was back in Roosevelt hospital after drinking what his case worker, Brian Davis, called, 'a toxic amount of alcohol'. Peter was remanded by the judge for at least ten days. Once more Allen was advised to stay away.

Allen was also concerned for Carl Solomon, who was in hospital with cancer lesions all over his body. The doctors told him he had six months to live but Carl refused to hear them, and began talking of finally moving out of the Bronx to live in Manhattan as he'd always wanted. Carl had received radiation therapy in the Veteran's Administration Hospital; this had cured the pain in his back, but he decided against chemical therapy and so went home.

In mid-March, Allen, accompanied by Peter Hale and his friend David Greenberg, took the subway out to Pelham Bay. Carl lived in a cold basement on Sands Place, two blocks from his old family apartment. He answered the door using a walking frame, then returned to the adjustable electric bed provided by the hospital. He had asked Allen to bring him a milkshake so they arrived with a giant-size Häagen Dazs, bought beneath the Pelham Bay elevated station tracks.

'Well, Carl, all that destruction between sanity and insanity, how do you judge that, or view it in perspective?'

'Ah,' he said wryly, 'It doesn't make any difference.'

He volunteered, 'An account of my homosexual history: it was experimental years ago, but now I prefer women. In this life you have to confront women . . . I've recently realised, life is and has been constant struggle against death.'

He was beginning to feel pain, but did not want to hear Allen's advice on a healthy diet. He received 'Meals on Wheels' supply food: egg and tuna salad, factory chicken, and was content with that. The V.A. hospital had not sent the Tri-codeine he was supposed to receive, so Allen offered him Vicodin (Allen always carried powerful painkillers in case of a kidneystone attack). Carl was dubious at first. 'Nothing to do but wait for relief, endure it and sooner or later it stops, or else get medicine.'

Carl had a flatmate, Tony, a stocky seventy-three-year-old man who was ill himself. He shuffled in and out and informed them that he had lived there for twenty-four years. Allen produced his camera: 'Carl's hair unusually combed over to cover bald front of skull, now flagged out on pillow. I took some Leica snapshots.'

In March, a bad attack of bronchitis kept Allen in bed all week in Boise, Idaho, but he still managed a reading at the university. One thousand students packed the hall, standing at the back: 'In slightly weakened and emotionally vulnerable condition I nearly wept several times thinking of the rare opportunity to vocalise aesthetic erotic vajrayana dharma to so many spirits eager for spiritual news and grounded candor.' It was a fairly typical evening's performance for this period: Allen took the stage, and spent two minutes arranging his books, manuscripts, tea and songsticks on a coffee table without looking up. Then he bowed to the audience, said good evening quietly and explained the structure of the evening. He scheduled a break after an hour and said he would read poems from 1948 until the present. He began with light material, to get the audience engaged: 'USA', 'Just Say Yes Calypso', 'Don't Smoke Rag', and 'Do The Meditation Rock'. As it was his first poetry reading in Idaho – he had read in every other state – he read 'Pull My Daisy' and 'Howl'.

He followed with 'Don't Grow Old', prefacing it with an explanation of Louis' role as a poet, his as a poet now. He explained that Peter was his boyfriend, who had worked as a nurse. Louis (formally a little leery of homosexuality) had turned to him in extremis while Allen and Peter were bathing and dressing him, and said, 'Don't ever grow old.' Allen recorded in his journal: 'The tone of that prosaic announcement or preface brought odd gasp of emotional clarity to some in the crowd – could hear the sigh.' He sang 'Father Death Blues' a cappella, tapping his hand on his knee occasionally for rhythm.

After a twenty-minute break, he discussed the nuclear waste dump site in Idaho and read 'Plutonian Ode' before moving on to the poems from *White Shroud*. After two hours he still felt good and ended with Blake's 'Tiger', accompanying himself with songsticks.

Allen prepared for his long trip around Europe with a week at the Jewel Heart Retreat, near Grand Rapids, Michigan. Gelek Rinpoche asked Allen to sing 'Don't Smoke', 'Father Death Blues' and 'September On Jessore Road' before the sangha of about seventy people. The days were hot with some heavy rain. Allen returned to New York refreshed. Because he had diabetes as well as a heart problem, Allen maintained a strict macrobiotic diet of no salt, no alcohol, no dairy products – basically a rice and fish diet. He lost weight and looked much healthier than he had done in years.

On 6 September Allen flew overnight, business class, to Vienna, to begin a tour which would take him through Bratislava, Budapest, Beograd, Krakow, Lodz, Warsaw, London, Dublin, Belfast, Oslo, Bergen, Munich, Paris, Berlin, Prague, Barcelona, Madrid, Athens and Tangiers, with many side-trips on the way. It was like a big rock 'n' roll tour, except Allen was travelling alone.

The tour got off to a gentle start with ten days of teaching poetry with Anne Waldman. Allen walked the streets of Vienna in his old Gore-Tex shoes until he got blisters and bought some new ones. He visited the art museums, studied Rembrandt's self portraits and works by Rubens and Breughel. Then the interviews began. On the eighteenth, his friend Istvan Eorsi arrived to drive him to Bratislava and on to Budapest where he stayed in Eorsi's studio room overlooking Buda and the Danube, the Elizabeth Bridge and Buda Castle. He had read in many of these cities before, and many of the people he met were friends, such as Vaclav Havel; wherever possible he used the same interpreter as before.

In London, staying at Hanson Street, Allen visited his old haunts in Soho and Fitzrovia: the beatnik pubs on Goodge Street – Finch's One Tun and the Duke of York – from his 1965 visit; the Fitzroy Tavern and the French Pub, where Allen first met George Barker in 1958. In the late morning of 15 October, after a flurry of phone calls and faxes, Allen left for Dublin: 'First visit to Dublin, Belfast, Sligo and Galway – what pleasure. Saw Yeats's grave and tower and recorded poem for Bono of U2 who came to Dublin reading.' Bono liked a number of Allen's poems and asked him to recite them in synch with a couple of their tracks for a television blockbuster they were planning. Allen recorded 'Hum Bom!' and 'Don't Smoke'. While they were in the studio Bono showed Allen some of the footage they had already shot, telling him, 'This is total Burroughs cut-up method.' Allen told the *International Herald Tribune*: 'He's read my poetry. He's really open.'

Like a rock 'n' roll tour, faces and places began to blur into one. A week in Norway, a week in Munich, a week in Paris – where he received his medal – then off to Berlin. In Prague, he read 'Please Master' at the Viola cafe and, unusual for him, was slightly embarrassed at the intermission to find the United States Ambassador there with his wife.

While Allen was away, Peter was broke, living on the street or sometimes in shelters for the homeless. He showed up at the office and Bob Rosenthal faxed Allen, asking what to do. Allen despaired: 'How protect Bob, my family problems none of his business work and he won't deal with Peter.'

On 22 December, his official duties over, Allen flew from Athens to Tangier, via Rome and Madrid, arriving in Morocco early in the afternoon; a sixty-seven-year-old man on a sentimental journey, revisiting the scenes of youthful happiness. He checked into his hotel, then walked up Blvd Pasteur, past the Café de Paris, to the corner of Calle Cook and rue Magellan, to the Villa Muniria – now the Hotel el Muniria – several blocks further than he remembered. He wrote Peter: 'I went inside and on stairway up to our old 1957 veranda room I cried to think how innocently happy we were together that trip to Europe, how much I loved you and miss your presence now. What happened to our lives together and can't we ever return to each other if we can't return to our light hearted youthtime? The upstairs room seemed smaller, the veranda now cracked concrete but still can go out on it.'

He went and looked around the garden, where they had taken the famous set of photographs with Bill and Paul Bowles against a big palm tree in 1961. The garden was smaller and more cluttered than Allen remembered. A housekeeper and his family now lived in the two rooms once occupied by Burroughs and Mikey Portman. Allen remembered that the second visit was a less happy time, 'but we survived thru all India, thru years with Trungpa, and now? How do you choose? I'm still waiting, tears in my eyes, hoping you will wind up safe, happy, calm genius as you were, dear Peter.'

The hotel was mostly empty, being out of season, and the rooms were slightly chill. Allen was able to rent his old room for ten dollars a night. He told Peter: 'I rented this same for two nights this week, and extra hideaway, nostalgic secret apartment as in old dreams though I'm paying $60 a night at the 4-star Hotel Minza (I'd never afforded to be inside 57 and 61).' Room eight on the top floor still had its brown, mottled, tiled floor, the same white walls, black table, bureau and armoire, the same double bed with a black headrest and sideboard. A yellowing curtain hung over the French windows overlooking the familiar porch, with its salmon-coloured tiles, where Allen used to type at dawn as the city came to life below.

Allen bought a full-length, old-fashioned white-and-black vertical striped djellabah to wear around town. He visited Paul Bowles several days in a row. He recounted his 1948 Blake vision, which Bowles had not heard about, and sang him Blake's 'Tiger', 'The Sick Rose' and 'Ah! Sunflower', with harmonium accompaniment.

Bowles lamented rising prices, the spoilage of Tangier by new architecture, corrupt police, and hashish and cocaine lords. He talked about Jane Bowles, how she had once returned a purchase to Saks Fifth Avenue, dumping her plastic bag on the counter. It was the wrong bag; coffee grinds and orange peel spilled out over the glass. She began laughing hysterically and fled to Saint Patrick's cathedral, said Bowles. He told Allen what torture it was for him to visit her in the hospital in Malaga. She was convinced that he would never return to see her again.

Peter Hale and Jacqueline Gens met Allen at JFK on 27 December to collect his bags. Allen continued on to Michigan for a week-long retreat before resuming his poetic duties. On 11 January 1994, he read a strong-voiced 'Howl' at Carnegie Hall with the Chronos Quartet at a celebrity event. Allen was a star and had the Maestro's suite. He felt the reading was somewhat detached because he could not see anyone's eyes in the huge hall, the house lights were too dim.

There were more celebrity events that year including a benefit reading for Tibet House, with Philip Glass, Paul Simon, Ritchie Havens and Natalie Merchant, and a week in London in early November, promoting his new book *Cosmopolitan Greetings*. Allen took Peter Hale with him as an assistant. He read at Saint James's, Piccadilly, moved to be presenting his poems in the church where William Blake had worshipped. That Sunday, he went by train with Miles for lunch with Paul McCartney in the country. Paul showed Allen around the house, which he had designed himself, and discussed his art collection: a Vuillard still life, a Rembrandt landscape engraving, a Renoir still life, a Matisse drawing, and lots of Magrittes. A Magritte drawing of a candle with a new moon as the flame was hung above a primitive of a seashore, which Allen identified as Hawaiian, and wondered which – the Magritte or the primitive – was the more valuable in God's eye. He said later that he regarded Magritte as 'just popular culture'.

Linda cooked one of her vegetarian meals; the four children were all there, as well as three Old English sheepdogs. Allen ate three helpings of the roast vegetarian loaf, and rather guiltily took what was left after everyone was finished, 'If no-one else wants it'. Allen was shy, quiet, soft-voiced; he read Paul his Beatles poem 'Portland Coliseum', talked about mutual friends, art, the paintings of George Condo. They discussed the press and politics; Paul was very anti big-business and Thatcher policies. Paul showed him a sheaf of his poems and Allen reverted immediately to Professor Ginsberg of Brooklyn College. He produced his fountain pen and began correcting them, crossing out the articles and enquiring deeply for more information about each subject, demanding more visual images, quoting at length from Yeats, Kerouac, Williams. Paul initially looked shocked, then got involved in the process, asking Allen to sign the corrections afterwards. (Later he said, 'You know, I think I'll keep 'em as they are. Allen turned them into American poems.')

Paul gave Allen a signed copy of the *Beatles at the BBC* CD, which had just come out, and a copy of a privately produced book of reproductions of his paintings. Allen, in turn, had several booklets with him to give Paul. Linda was very taken with him; they discussed photography and Linda said she never figured out how to use a light metre, some pictures came out too dark to use, some too light, but most were OK.

He continued on to Paris, where he stayed at the Ritz Hotel as the guest of *Nouvel Observateur* for a four-day round-table discussion with writers and intellectuals. He stayed on a few days afterwards, moving to the cheaper Hotel Chomel, near Jean-Jacques Lebel's apartment. Just as he had nostalgically walked the streets and alleys of Tangier, he now showed Peter Hale the sites of his happy sojourn in Paris. They visited the old Beat Hotel at 9 rue Git le Coeur, now the Hotel de Vieille Paris, an expensive tourist hotel with every modern convenience. Allen went in and used the lobby bathroom, but did not introduce himself. (Now the hotel's website uses its Beat Generation connections as a major attraction.) They visited George Whitman at the Mistral bookshop, renamed Shakespeare and Company after Sylvia Beach's famous bookshop, and took a long walk through the Marais, along rue de Rosiers where Gregory and Peter used to change dollars to francs on the black market in Jewish grocery stores.

Allen had attended a teaching in 'Death Bardol Rebirth' just before his European trip; now he finished the year by going on a week's retreat with Gelek and one hundred students. He ruminated on an incident that occurred on Christmas Eve: 'Arriving here in dining hall, young Chinese lady embracing Rinpoche. I said, "Where are you from? Haven't seen you here before." She replied, "I've been here for years." And Rinpoche added, "She's a girl so he can't remember." . . . Last night sat up to read to whole Sangha, realised after that, despite applause, she saw I was selfish, closed off, timid. I should break the ice. New Year's Resolution.'

Since Trungpa's death, Allen had spent very little time meditating alone and in February he expressed his worries to Gelek at another Ann Arbor retreat. Gelek repeated that he shouldn't worry: 'You've done a lot and continue to do a lot for others, that's the important thing. It may be a matter of mental chemistry. Just keep your vow to be kind and compassionate at every moment, repeat all the mantras you've been given, as many as you can remember, forget about the sadhanas – you can do the short form Guru Yoga, then do that. And remember, if you pass away before I do – be sure I'm near,' he said. 'And if I pass away before you,' he hesitated. 'Good luck.'

Gelek had reason to be concerned; Allen's health was still in decline. In 1994 he had another liver biopsy, this time at Lenox Hill Hospital, but no cirrhosis was evident, so he concentrated on treating his heart failure and diabetes. With a specialist advisor, he created the recipe for a macrobiotic meal which was faxed to everyone who hired him for a reading. A month after his office instituted this regime he complained: 'Everywhere I go I get the same meal!' The office began to get complaints: 'We made this meal for him, then he ate off everybody else's plate.' With the aid of his macrobiotic diet, he was able to forestall insulin dependence for almost two years.

On 23 May 1995, Allen closed the purchase on a fifth floor loft at 304 East 13th Street which he bought for $299,000 from his old friend, the painter Larry Rivers. This was made possible by the 1994 sale of his archives, for one million dollars to Stanford University. They had been on deposit at Columbia University since the 1960s, but Columbia declined to buy them, even though they were the most used collection in the Butler Library. The money ended up being less than Allen had hoped: the Federal Government took thirty-eight per cent in taxes, the state twelve per cent, his agent took five per cent and he gave his archivist Bill Morgan one hundred thousand dollars for keeping track of everything for a decade. Allen was left with one third. Despite this, there was a tremendous self-righteous outcry in the press, accusing him of selling out and becoming a millionaire – much of it written by people who had been past recipients of Ginsberg largesse.

Throughout 1995, Ginsberg's journals reflected the continuing deterioration of his health: blood in faeces, short of breath, fainting spells, breathlessness, always tired, lack of sleep. He had become progressively more irritable, often losing his temper if someone disagreed with him. From the mid-1980s onwards: 'I got mad and yelled at the interviewer,' becomes a familiar journal entry. In many cases he later wrote regretfully of the incident, particularly if, as on one occasion, he lost his temper with a number of people in succession at a cocktail party. Most of the anger was directed at women. As usual, Allen continued to give a huge number of interviews and a comparison of those done with young men, and those done with women, is very revealing. If the women haven't done their homework, or ask a naive question, Allen lectures them irritably; young men are treated with the utmost care, every point explained. A male reporter from a college newspaper would leave Allen's apartment after a three-hour interview carrying a dozen books and several records, all for a one-page piece for a campus daily.

That August, Allen arranged to spend a day with Paul and Linda McCartney at their place on Long Island. The 10 a.m. Jitney was full so Allen hired a limo, and was aghast at the two-hundred-dollar fare. He arrived laiden with a Rolleiflex, one of his 1984 window photographs, photographs of Kerouac, and a new portrait of Robert Frank standing by a chainlink fence. He had books by Francesco Clemente, Peter Orlovsky, Andy Clausen (one of his students), paperbacks of *Howl* and *Journals Mid 50s*, Burroughs's CD *Dead City Radio* and some Naropa brochures.

They had lunch at Pierre Fresnay's home nearby in Springs, sitting on his deck overlooking Gardener Island and Block Island Sound under a clear blue sky. Cantaloupe soup with sherry and balls of cantaloupe was followed by an omelette with red and green peppers, chanterelles, small red potatoes and thinly sliced eggplant. Dessert was fresh figs and sliced orange in sweet syrup. In conversation, McCartney's daughter, Mary, told them that

Rossetti had liked twelve-year-old girls and had been shocked to discover that his wife had pubic hair. Back at the McCartney house, Allen phoned home for news of Peter. He had been living in a shelter, sharing a room with seven others. The news was not good: Peter was manic once more and had taxied uptown to sell letters and papers.

During the afternoon, Paul read Allen's new poem 'Ballad Of The Skeletons', while Allen signed photographs and books. Paul explained the origin of the Beatles' 'Lucy In The Sky With Diamonds' which was based on a drawing by John Lennon's four-year-old son, Julian. His nursery teacher had asked what the drawing was, and Julian said, 'Lucy in the sky with diamonds,' because the figure was of his friend Lucy. The teacher wrote the title on the top of the page. Lennon said, 'This is perfect, let's go upstairs, write a song.' Allen later noted: 'Lennon was credited as curious intellectual one but McCartney was there quietly visiting artists, going to Paris with Robert Fraser.' Paul played him 'Free As A Bird', the new Beatles song, recorded using an old Lennon vocal tape.

'That's past,' said Paul. 'The Beatles were and are no more.'

They all three worked on seventeen-syllable sentences, based on the haiku form in Allen's booklet, *Mind Writing Slogans*. The next day, Allen returned to New York by jitney after lunch. Peter was in the apartment causing chaos. Allen asked him for the keys; 'He gave them meekly.' Peter was given the choice of the Bellevue shelter or the VA ward.

Linda McCartney called to inquire after his return and recite a seventeen-syllable sentence she'd worked out, intrigued by his book of 'pastel sentences' based on the haiku form: 'Fear crawled into my open window and strangled me with my own hands.' Then Paul took the phone and added his own seventeen-syllable poem: 'Yellow sperm swim boldly across the surface of my eighth symphony.'

At the end of August, Allen went on a seven-day retreat with Gelek, and spent hours chanting the White Tara mantra. Gelek was clearly concerned about Allen's health and gave him a short form Vajrayogini mantra to work with, 'just in case of sudden death'. This was the culmination of Allen's study and he recorded: 'I was elated to receive near ultimate teachings, but many details were vague and I didn't understand all the categories and images, later to be supplied by Sura and Rinpoche on call.' Gelek humourously asked the traditional eighteen gold pieces for transmitting the teaching and Allen wrote him a check for $1,300. Back in New York, Allen yelled at a bus driver over change, and was immediately contrite at his own bad temper.

Allen had an October date at the Royal Albert Hall in London, and needed a guitar accompanist. He asked Paul McCartney for suggestions. Paul faxed a reply, suggesting a couple of his friends: Jeff Beck and Pink Floyd guitarist David Gilmour. He added that he would also be happy to do it, if Allen wanted. This was, of course, what Allen wanted all along. Paul suggested they get together before for rehearsal. His own office would handle security. Paul's participation was kept secret right up until Allen asked his accompanist to come on stage and the audience was astonished to see who it was.

Allen continued his trip, first to Amalfi, then by car with Francesco Clemente and his family to Rome, overnight train to Paris and a drive to Chateau Chenonceau for the opening of Clemente's '108 Pastels' show. Allen took part in a symposium at the Venice Biennale with Hiro Yamagata who was exhibiting a collection of painted automobiles. Allen had written a long preface to his catalogue – a project he put off until the very last minute, not knowing what to say – 'a kind of whorish deal in exchange for his kindness to Naropa, over a quarter million in the 12 month 1994 and another $120,000 in June 95. As well as his patronage of Gregory Corso $3–4,000 a month "for life" as Gregory says Hiro has promised him – oddly well received, the tent exhibition.'

On 28 May 1996, Steven Taylor called Allen from Boulder; he had just heard on the radio that Timothy Leary was near death. Allen had known of Leary's condition since the previous July and had been in weekly telephone contact with him ever since. There had been the usual media circus surrounding Leary's illness, the path of which was broadcast daily on his website. Allen remembered his last visit, with Hiro Yamagata in late January; how he was shocked to find Leary with a scotch and soda in one hand, a cigarette in the other, and a bacon sandwich on his lap. 'What are you doing?' Allen asked, incredulously.

'I'm living it up,' Leary told him. 'I'm still alive.'

Allen had spoken at length with him on the telephone ten days before, and was relieved – as were all Leary's friends – to hear that he'd given up the idea of organic brain freezing. They had discussed Leary's use of laughing gas and Allen described his own experience: of sound being the last sense to depart, 'like end of a symphony, no harm, no pain, chords of harmonious fading into silence, disembodied away', and mentioned his poem 'Laughing Gas'. Rosemary Wordruff – Leary's wife during the Millbrook period in the 1960s – called up later to ask how to get a copy. Allen sent him one – in the City Lights' *Kaddish* – and on a later call, Leary said it was amazing, longer than he expected; a delightful accurate description. Leary told him he was a wonderful friend, someone important in his life. Writing up his conversation, Allen recorded: 'I always suspected flattering and glib con but he persisted and I felt ashamed of joking, "Flattery will get you nowhere." '

At Steven's news Allen was sad, speculating how Leary's death would be received by his cynical critics, police, persecutors and prosecutors. Allen called Leary's home, and Rosemary said he was sinking fast; his attendants and son were waiting for him to let go. He was drifting in and out of consciousness, now beyond recognising anyone so it was no use his talking with him. Allen had earlier arranged for them to contact Gelek Rinpoche but they had not done so. Allen called him, and he said he hadn't been able to reach the Leary household. Allen arranged for Rosemary to call him right away, then called Burroughs who said he'd talked with Leary the day before. Leary had asked him, ambiguously, 'Is it true?' Burroughs, not sure if the reference was to himself on the telephone or to death approaching, had replied, 'Yes, it's true, it's William Burroughs here.'

Leary told him, 'I love you, Bill,' and Bill had echoed, 'I love you too.' The day before, Rosemary had quoted Leary saying earlier, 'This is for real!' perhaps astonished and acknowledging what was to come.

At two the next morning, a young woman called from Leary's household to say that Tim died at 12.29 a.m. (EST). Allen asked to speak with Rosemary. She said she had connected with Gelek Rinpoche. Leary wasn't conscious, she thought, but with the phone held to Leary's ear, Gelek had chanted for several minutes until a call-waiting signal interrupted. Gelek thought they'd been cut off but when he called back, he told Rosemary it was sufficient. He had told Leary to relax, to open up to empty space, and began *powtra* practice to help Leary to release from his body. He continued it after he heard of his death, completing it the next day.

Allen asked Rosemary if Leary wakened at all. She said yes, he'd opened his eyes near the end, indicated by a hand gesture that he wanted something. In a clogged voice, he asked, 'Why?' then looked at everybody in the room individually and, with a different intonation for each, asked 'Why not?' Allen repeated to her Trungpa Rinpoche's last adjuration on his father Louis' death: 'Please continue your celebration . . .' and they said goodnight. 'So he did well,' Allen wrote. 'His bravado in illness proved to be some kind of peaceful strength. She seemed prepared for the change and fortunately had reconciled with the late philosopher–criminal–hero, now "immortal" as I'd thought 24 hours before.'

Allen's poem 'The Ballad Of The Skeletons' was first published in the *Nation* in November 1995; his response to all the media hype about family values, contract with America, Newt Gingrich, Rush Limbaugh and all the right-wing talk-radio hosts.

He read it at a reading with Amiri Baraka in New York, accompanied by guitarist Mark Ribot, whom he had worked with previously on his *The Lion For Real* album. Allen was impressed by how much more dramatic the accompaniment made the poem. Then there was the Royal Albert Hall reading, with Paul McCartney as accompanist, and McCartney gave Allen a lot of ideas on how to set the poem to music. At a Tibet House benefit at Carnegie Hall, organised by Philip Glass, Allen was accompanied by guitarist David Mansfield, with whom he had also previously recorded. Lenny Kaye was at the benefit with singer Patti Smith, and Allen asked him if he would play bass with Mansfield. Allen's song was the big hit of the evening because it was the only rocker – everyone else did classical or quiet material.

At a reading in Princeton, film maker Gus Van Sant picked Allen up at the airport in a limousine; later, at the hotel, Van Sant pulled out a guitar. Allen asked if he would accompany him that night, after he had given his own lecture. Danny Goldberg, president of Mercury Records, had been in the audience at the Carnegie Hall reading, and called Allen's office, asking if he would like to record it. By this time Allen had a good idea of how the poem should sound when set to music, and was ready.

That May he got together Mark Ribot, Lenny Kaye and David Mansfield, and went in to the studio at Kampo Cultural Center, NY, with Kaye producing. The song lasted seven minutes forty-seven seconds; Allen recorded a version true to the text and a 'clean' version for American radio. A four-minute edited version was produced when the tracks were mixed.

The twenty-four-track master tape was sent overnight mail to Paul McCartney's studio in Sussex, for him to add whatever he wanted. Allen told him to take over, and ignore what was on tape already as it lacked dramatic musical structure. 'I'm glad to hear you say that,' McCartney said. 'It gives me licence.' Paul was disappointed when he received the tape. It was badly recorded, the sound was muddy and he couldn't do much with it. He later said, 'The sound was pretty awful. It should have started off in my studio.' It is normal recording practice to lay down the rhythm tracks first, but the tape lacked a drum track which Paul felt was essential for coherence. He recorded one, but the process was made difficult by the fact that Allen's vocal track was already done – normally it would be done last, except for solos and sweeteners which can be added later. Allen's timing was never perfect. Paul added maracas, and a swelling Hammond organ track, trying to sound like Al Kooper. He put on a strong guitar track, following Allen's voice, strengthening it and covering up Allen's mistakes. He worked all day, then shipped it back to Mercury Records.

Allen called from Boulder, and Kaye played him the first three minutes over the telephone; the studio speakers were perfectly audible. Allen wrote: 'As I heard the magical combination of instruments for the first time, I wept a little, realising the fruition of so many years' friendships, genius power and erotic and bodhissatvic and radical political aesthetic intelligent support that had come to pass in this popular delightful musicopoetic artwork that could pass on prophetic a mass section of human sangha in CD form.' Allen was happy all day and for many days after. He began to have fantasies of 'hitting the charts'. Philip Glass was in town when the tape arrived, and volunteered to add a piano track. Lenny Kaye was concerned that it was already a very full production, but Glass added sweeteners, very much in his repetitive style, which fitted perfectly.

Allen told Harvey Kubernik: 'Hal Wilner wound up mixing it and brought out McCartney's role and the structure that McCartney had given to it, because he gave it a very nice dramatic structure.' Hiro Yamagata designed a skull for the CD label while Robert Frank, Patti Hudson, Linda McCartney and Allen provided the photographs. Gus Van Sant was recruited to make the video, as all new records need a video to get televison airplay, and the project was complete. It was released in October to coincide with the publication of *Selected Poems '47–95'* by HarperCollins.

Other highlights of the year included a series of readings accompanying the Whitney Museum travelling Beat Generation exhibit, *Beat Culture and the New America 1950–1965*; a poetry–jazz telecast with Ornette Coleman for Canal+ in Paris; yet another tour of Czechoslovakia, this time with Philip Glass; and ten days with William Burroughs in Kansas to record an interview and take photographs of his old friend for the *Observer* newspaper in London. In August, he was the vocalist on 'Sunflower Sutra', at a concert of music by Philip Glass conducted by Yehudi Menuhin at Avery Fisher Hall, Lincoln Center, New York, and read before an audience of fourteen thousand at the San Francisco Cow Palace, on a bill with Orbital, Beck and Lemonheads. He spent the new year in a ten-day winter retreat with Gelek Rinpoche at Camp Copneconic, Michigan.

Around Christmas, Allen haunted all the Salvation Army stores in New York to furnish his new loft. He bought white leather settees and matching chairs and found to his delight that the SA had a plan that enabled someone to buy from four different stores and they would deliver everything at once for the one twenty-five-dollar delivery fee. Allen was still concerned with value for money.

His health was getting worse: he had experienced further heart trouble, and was suffering from fainting fits caused by sugar-lack from his diabetes. Since September he had felt weak and fatigued. His daily pill intake had risen to ten different pills for digitalis, diabetes, cramps, water retention and his heart, some of them taken twice a day. He had problems with overdosing on his blood pressure medicine, and the diabetes was making the heart medicine doses hard to stabilise. After a bad reaction to a new medication in February 1997, he decided to stop his regular trips to his cardiologist in Boston and develop a team of doctors close to home. He felt so weak prior to his last visit that Bob Rosenthal insisted on accompanying him on the shuttle.

Allen was now seventy. In designing the loft, he and Bob had made allowances for Allen's old age and ill health: there was wheelchair access and gripbars everywhere – congestive heart disease is a long, slow progressive disease. Bob had hired a housekeeper, so Allen didn't have to do his own shopping any more, and a car service, so he didn't have to hail a cab in winter. In Peter Hale and Bill Morgan, Bob now had the best office staff he had ever had. Everything was optimum, except Allen's health. In March, back in New York, Allen felt so unwell that Bob called Joel Gaidemak. When he described Allen's symptoms, he was told, 'Get him into hospital immediately.' Through a connection at Bob's synagogue, Bob arranged for Allen to have VIP treatment at Beth Israel Hospital. They hired a wheelchair for five dollars and got him to the emergency room. Once he was admitted, Allen felt a huge wave of relief, knowing something would finally be done.

Gaidemak said to try switching the medicines round, and suggested a liver biopsy. Allen had had hepatitis A and B and they suspected that he might have hepatitis C. He was taken off all his medicine to watch what would happen. Allen told Steven Taylor, 'I haven't felt this good in years.' He could see the windows of his new loft from his hospital bed.

The tests took several days. Bob Rosenthal brought in a bulging briefcase filled with Allen's medical files and mentioned to the doctor that Allen had had a messy appendectomy as a child. It was done by a relative, presumably as a favour, or for a reduced fee. Allen remembered walking around for several months with what he thought was his liver sticking out, a brown object projecting from the wound, until it finally dried up and fell off. He didn't tell anybody. Bob said, 'It always struck me, here was a poor boy, eight or nine years old, with no one to look at his body, not his father, not his mother.' The doctor examined Allen and said there had been a massive infection. Bob remembered: 'He turned to Allen, who was dozing in and out, and said: "So, Mr Ginsberg, you had this appendectomy when you were a child?" And Allen said, "Oh no, I wasn't a child. I must have been eight or nine." When did childhood stop? When did Allen ever have a childhood?' It was a heartbreaking reminder of the terrible events that shaped his life, and deprived him of a childhood.

The results came through; he had hepatitis C, but he also had cancer of the liver, described by his doctor as 'untreatable, incurable'. The cancer had metastasised everywhere. Allen was told he had from three to six months to live from onset, but they did not know when onset was. Allen said, 'That sounds too long.' It was the same disease that killed his father.

One of the long list of people he called when he returned from hospital was Miles, the author of this book: 'When they told me I felt a ripple of tranquility,' he said. 'I'm quite happy, unaccountably happy. In fact, ever since they told me I've been in this state. I always thought that if I heard I was gonna die I'd freak out, but I don't feel fear. I don't know why, I feel an immense calm.'

Back at Allen's new loft, everything was finally finished. Extra people had been hired, the furniture was installed, all the books were arranged on the bookshelves, labelled by category, every box finally unpacked. His staff were celebrating with a meal – Allen's favourite dish: whole flounder – when Allen called from the hospital. He told Bob the diagnosis on the phone, massive liver cancer, just weeks to live. Bob went to the office to order his thoughts, then summoned Peter Hale and Bill Morgan from the meal to tell them privately before going to the hospital.

Bob had organised an excellent medical plan for Allen, entitling him to a home hospice system which included free medicine, a twenty-four-hour medical hot-line, and home visits by doctors and 'glamourous cardiologists at my bedside', as Allen put it. A high hospital bed was installed and Peter took Allen's old bed, so there was always someone there. Over Bob's objections, Allen had insisted that Peter be his nurse. Peter had been clean for several years, but he was still unstable. Allen remembered how well Peter had nursed Louis, but as Bob pointed out, that was twenty years before.

When he returned home on the Wednesday, Allen was in good spirits. Bob's wife, Shelley, made him chicken soup and Allen took his last photograph – of Robert Frank, his photography teacher. Allen busied himself making plans and calling people. In the hospital he and Bob Rosenthal had written a list of about a hundred people, which he kept adding to as he thought of more friends, and tasks and details to clear up. He spoke with Amiri Baraka and told him: 'I'm dying, do you need any money?' He called Yuri Yamagata and extracted a promise that he would support Naropa. Allen was exaultant: 'It's great when you're dying, they can't say no to you.' He was unable to get through to financier George Soros, or Paul McCartney.

He told Miles: 'Gelek Rinpoche told me: "You people: Burroughs, you, Kerouac, will all go to heaven for introducing the dharma to this country." He didn't mean heaven, he meant dhakini heaven, for opening up the possibility of something other than monotheism, other ways of thought. "Just for that alone you'll go to heaven." It was great to hear that because the others have said it before, but he was the first one to publish it, to make a statement.'

He looked around the loft and said, 'It's fantastic, like heaven. It's beautiful now, all furnished. It's wonderful, I feel like I'm dying in heaven. Paintings on the wall, books on the shelves ... I'm dying in heaven.'

MTV had asked him to do an *Unplugged*, and he deeply regretted that he would not now be able to do it. He had assembled an all-star, though strangely matched, band. Everyone he asked had agreed: Beck, Dylan, Philip Glass, Ornette Coleman, Mark Ribot, Paul McCartney and Patti Smith. Johnny Depp said he would be the MC. It was going to be in July, because that was when McCartney was going to be in New York. 'That won't happen now, it's too late,' Allen said, ruefully. 'I was gonna do Ma Rainey's "C.C. Rider" because Dylan said I should do at least one cover.'

Not for Allen a quiet, peaceful death, tended by a few close friends and family members; he made 'megalomaniacal plans' for his remaining time on earth. He intended to get a twenty-four-track DAT recording system set up so that people like Dylan could lay down tracks when they visited, and McCartney could add tracks in Britain. He intended to get a piano, a real one, not an electric keyboard, and had arranged for Robert Frank to install video cameras to capture his deathbed scene. Allen had sat for three portraits by George Condo; the day Allen returned from hospital Condo delivered a huge painting of Allen as a pink harlequin to the loft. Allen told him: 'This is a great time for a deathbed portrait.'

Early on Thursday morning, Allen began telephoning old friends with the news, and trying to work on poems: 'I've been writing, Oh how I've been writing!' he told Miles. 'Fantastic poems, best things I've ever done! So many of them, they're pouring out of me, I'm scribbling them down. I'm trying to organise them, that's what I'm working on, when I can, when I've got the strength.' All but one of these was written in the hospital. Allen's staff ferried them back and forth, typing them up, printing them out and returning them to him for correction and revision. Allen only wrote one poem after his diagnosis, 'Things I'll Not Do (Nostalgias)'; the only one he didn't get to approve in transcript.

He didn't leave his bed except to visit the bathroom. One symptom of the liver cancer was that moving his bowels brought on waves of nausea; now it caused him to vomit for the first time. He was talking on the telephone to Italy, and it caught him by surprise: 'Funny, I've never done that before,' he commented. It was the middle of the afternoon and, as Bob helped him back into bed, he asked him, 'Are you going back to sleep Allen?' Allen turned to him and said, 'Oh, yes!' They were his last words.

That night Peter took over as Allen's nurse. His whole routine was written out, but Bob had his doubts that Peter was capable of administering it, particularly as the situation might continue for months. But that was Allen's wish. Bob went home, asking Peter to call him before ten o'clock. There was no phonecall and no answer to Bob's calls. At six in the morning, Bob awoke thinking something was wrong. He arrrived at the loft an hour later. Peter was not there. He tried to rouse Allen, to no avail. He called the hospital. The hospice doctor arrived and diagnosed a stroke; Allen's whole left side was paralysed, he was given hours to live. At this point Peter came in, leaving a bicycle in the hallway.

'I bought this bicycle for $400 on the street. You think I got a good deal?' he asked Bob.

'Well, Peter,' Bob said, 'a mountain bike like this costs about $400. But you bought it off the street, which means it was stolen. What's the karma of buying something you know to be stolen?'

'Well that's a really good question, Bob! I'll have to think about that!'

Bob did not tell him about Allen. 'He was so out of it, he hadn't been here, he was out buying things on the street, dealing God knows what.' The day nurse arrived to sit with Allen, and Bob got on the phone. He called Gelek Rinpoche who took the next plane from Michigan, bringing three Tibetan monks with him. Then he began calling Allen's friends and family.

The death watch continued all day. At one point there were seventy-five people in the loft. At first Bob bought food, then he realised that Allen could survive in a coma for days. Gelek Rinpoche and his monks chanted throughout, their prayers occasionally punctuated by bells. It was the tenth anniversary of the death of Trungpa, and that night, after a ceremony at the Shambala Center, many of the people came to see Allen. He lay in his narrow hospital bed, alongside the window overlooking 14th Street; the traffic and sirens of his beloved city resounding outside. His head leaned to one side, propped on two big striped pillows, with two small almost invisible tubes delivering oxygen to his nostrils from a small tank on the floor. He wore a Jewel Heart T-shirt, his thin white arms bare, bruised from the hospital blood tests. A medical chart of a human skeleton hung over the bed, placed there by Allen half as a joke, half as a reminder of human mortality. Joel Gaidemak doubted he would survive the night.

Around midnight people started to go home. Allen's brother Eugene leaned over, held Allen's hand, and whispered: 'Goodnight, little Allen. Goodbye, little Allen,' kissed him, and left. Gregory went home, Gelek retired to Philip Glass's house to sleep the night; a dozen or so people stayed on, including Rosebud Felieu, Allen's old friend from the 1960s, who sat stroking his feet. She wrote: 'Everyone was amazed at how beautiful he looked – all lines of stress and age smoothed – he looked patriarchal and strong. I had never seen him so handsome. The funny looking little boy had grown into this most wonderful looking man ... But so tiny! He seemed as fragile as a baby in his little T-shirt.'

At two o'clock everyone decided to get some rest. Bob Rosenthal and Joel Gaidemak lay on Allen's big bed, everyone else found settees, or chairs. Rosebud and her husband, the poet Simon Pettet, continued the vigil:

The loft was very quiet. Most were resting, half-asleep. Suddenly Allen began to shake, a small convulsion wracked his body. I called out, and Joel and Bob sat up and hurried over. I called louder, and everyone else came running. It was about 2:15. Joel examined him, pulse, etc., and said that his vital signs were considerably slower; he had had another seizure. The breathing went on, weaker ... Peter Orlovsky bent over and kissed his head, saying, 'Goodbye, Darling.'

Then a remarkable thing happened. A tremor went through him, and slowly, impossibly, he began to raise his head. He weakly rose until he was sitting almost upright, and his left arm lifted and extended. Then his eyes opened very slowly and very wide. The pupils were wildly delated. I thought I saw a look of confusion or bewilderment. His head began to turn very slowly and his eyes seemed to glance around him, gazing at each one of us in turn. His eyes were so deep, so dark, but Bob said they were empty of sight. His mouth opened, and we all heard as he seemed to struggle to say something, but only a soft low sound, a weak 'Aaah', came from him. Then his eyes began to close and he sank back onto the pillow. The eyes shut fully. He continued, then, to struggle through a few more gasping breaths, and his mouth fell open in an O. Joel said that these were the final moments, the O of the mouth the sign of approaching death.

At 2:39 a.m. on Saturday 5 April 1997, Joel Gaidemak checked once more for vital signs, and pronounced Allen dead. He pulled the thin blue sheet up to his chin. Peter Hale – a fellow Buddhist – took a small cup and spoon and touched Allen's lips with a few drops of dark liquid; the last food of the Buddhist ritual. Bob covered Allen's eyes and said the 'Sh'ma Israel'.

Afterword

Gelek Rinpoche and his monks arrived and began the appropriate chants. In Tibetan Buddhism the body should not be moved until the 'soul' or subconscious has finished meditating and left the body. With most people, this is supposed to take about thirty seconds, but the polite thing is to wait six to eight hours to make sure. Gelek continued to check for physical signs that Allen was ready to go. It took twenty hours. People stayed with Allen throughout the whole period. The stress was too much for Peter, who was telling people to take the books off the shelves because Rosenthal was going to send them all to Stanford. Stanford already owned them, and Peter was now the beneficiary. Some people humoured Peter, taking books and leaving them somewhere else in the apartment, but some things were stolen: books, shirts, small items. When Allen's body was deemed ready to leave, Bob sealed the loft and finally went to get some sleep.

At the funeral home Allen was given an Orthodox Jewish coffin – which corresponded to the Tibetan Buddhist ritual – with no metal and no nails so it decayed harmlessly. The following Monday, there was a Sukhavati ceremony at the Shambala Center on West 22nd Street with Gelek Rinpoche presiding. At Shambala the service was normally explained to the congregation, and some of it was conducted in English, but Gelek did everything in Tibetan which irritated some people; this however was the service that Allen wanted. Then Allen's body was taken to the crematorium.

His ashes were divided into three, with an equal amount going to Gelek Rinpoche, at the Jewel Heart Meditation Center, and to Shambala, where they mixed it into the foundation of a resting place at the Rocky Mountain Dharma Centre, where people stop on their climb up to the big stupa on the mountain side. The third portion was buried in the Ginsberg family plot in the B'nai Israel Cemetary, in Elizabeth, New Jersey, next to his father and Aunt Rose. Cremation is forbidden in Judaism, and ashes cannot not be buried in a Jewish cemetery, but this cemetery had lapsed into the ownership of the monument maker, who told Bob Rosenthal: 'I don't care what you bury as long as I get to make the stone.' Allen was buried in a prayer shawl, a *tallith*, that Zalmon Shacter Lubovitcher Rebbe – the 'hippie rabbi' – had given him several years before; Bob had to first remove the fringe.

Allen had told Bob what lines he would like on his gravestone: some words of Louis' and the last three lines of his own 'Father Death Blues':

Not to go to Father's funeral tomorrow morn?
Not to go back to Naropa teach Buddhist poetics all summer?
Not to be buried in the cemetery near Newark Airport some day?

The outpouring of emotion caused by Allen's death caught many people by surprise. No one had really realised how famous he was, or how many people's lives had been touched by him. There was an hour-long documentary on British television and *Rolling Stone* did a special tribute with statements from William Burroughs, Ken Kesey, Gregory Corso, Lou Reed, Yoko Ono, Norman Mailer, Philip Glass, Gary Snyder, Lawrence Ferlinghetti, Deborah Harry, John Cale, Kurt Vonnegut, Patti Smith, Bono and many others. He received long, considered obituaries in all the major newspapers, there were tribute concerts and events in New York, London, Los Angeles and other cities. His influence was debated on the radio. Allen would have been flattered, but he would also have enjoyed Roger Kimball's dissenting voice some four months later in the *Wall Street Journal*, under the headline 'The Death of Decency'. The managing editor of *New Criterion* attacked both Ginsberg and Burroughs – who died just three months after Allen – as 'drug abusing literary charlatans', and railed against their influence on contemporary American life: 'Anyone who read the obituaries these men received – especially Ginsberg, who got lavish front-page treatment almost everywhere – might be tricked into thinking that they might be important literary figures.' They were not completely assimilated into the establishment.

It must be left to history to determine Ginsberg's literary rank. Certainly he was pre-eminent among the poets of the post-war generations, their loudest and most influential voice. For Ginsberg, poetry, philosophy, political action and personal expression went hand in hand. His biggest battles were with society and with himself. His entire career, as lived in public and documented in his poetry and journals, was a struggle to explore and express his own awareness, and to protect the right of others to do the same. As he told the *Washington Post*: 'The condition of society is one of homogeneity and hyperindustrialism, so the individual perceptions of body and mind are not valued. Poetry is not an expression of the party line. It's that time of night, lying in bed, thinking what you really think, making the private world public, that's what the poet does.'

A number of major poets have noted their indebtedness to him: Robert Lowell declared that he changed his verse after hearing Allen read. He is known to have exerted considerable influence over John Berryman, and Stephen Spender broke his long-standing writer's block after reading 'Kaddish' in manuscript. Many younger poets have mentioned their obligation to him.

Since the publication of Don Allen's 1960 anthology *New American Poetry 1945–1960*, there has been a revolution in American poetry. The San Francisco Renaissance poets: Gary Snyder, Michael McClure, John Wieners, Lawrence Ferlinghetti, Philip Lamantia, Jack Spicer, Robert Duncan, Philip Whalen; the Black Mountain School: Robert Creeley, Ed Dorn, Charles Olson; the New York School: Frank O'Hara, Amiri Baraka (LeRoi Jones), Diane di Prima, John Ashbery, Kenneth Koch; the St Mark's Church group: Anne Waldman, Ted Berrigan, Ron Padgett, Ed Sanders, Jim Carroll, Gerard Malanga, Larry Fagin; and dozens more, have all taken their place in the pantheon of American letters. Thanks to the pioneer publishing of City Lights Books, Grove Press, Don Allen, Corinth Press, New Directions, and a multitude of small presses, open-form poetry has now been placed alongside 'establishment' verse. The reputations of William Carlos Williams, Basil Bunting, Charles Reznikoff, Denise Levertov, Louis Zukofsky, Lorine Niedecker and other open-form poets from an earlier generation have been secured, and a new post-Beat Generation of younger poets is emerging. Ginsberg's proselytising role in all this has been substantial, and aside from his own work, it is probably his biggest contribution to changing the direction of American culture.

Most countries have always had an artistic bohemia acting as the spearhead of new ideas and attitudes, and the Beat Generation continued this tradition in America. They shook up American life in ways other than literature. With their free-and-easy ways, their belief in love and visions and candour, they made the first cracks in the armour and gave America some breathing room after the claustrophobia of the post-war decade. Ginsberg has claimed that the Beat Generation influenced everything from gay liberation, black liberation and women's liberation to liberation of the word from censorship, the acceptance of marijuana as a harmless hallucinogenic, and the spread of ecological consciousness.

Some of these claims have been dismissed by critics. The Beats have no obvious connection with the civil rights movement, and most feminist historians are critical of the Beats for their misogyny – it would be ingenious to find the origins of the women's movement among Beat Generation literary activity, except perhaps as a reaction against it.

The gay movement, however, has clear roots in the kind of open-minded comradeship and male bonding found among the early Beats, particularly between Ginsberg and Kerouac, or Kerouac and Cassady. It was a kind of masculine tenderness out of Walt Whitman, virtually unknown in the late 1940s and early 1950s, which later became a prototype in the gay community, what Ginsberg called a 'co-operative tender heart'.

The bravery of Ginsberg's confessions in 'Howl' – 'America, I'm putting my queer shoulder to the wheel' or 'who let themselves be fucked in the ass by saintly motorcyclists, and screamed with joy' – revelations of homosexuality in the middle of the McCarthy period, made without guilt or shame, was inspirational to homosexuals across the country and heralded the beginnings of the gay liberation movement. Ginsberg held up his gay 'marriage' to Peter as exemplary, although he later worried about the harm that he may have caused to anyone copying him, and was later criticised by sectors of the movement for simply reproducing role stereotypes. He gave scores of benefits for gay causes and championed the cause in interviews and the media. In the history of the struggle to achieve acceptance for homosexuals in American society, Ginsberg was a central figure.

The Beats and their publishers, notably Barney Rosset at Grove Press, played an important role in ending literary censorship, through the trials of *Howl* and *Naked Lunch*. Ginsberg was always willing to put himself on the line, whether testifying on behalf of Jack Smith's film *Flaming Creatures*, which was seized as obscene, or opposing the 1988 FCC regulations that prohibited 'Howl' from being read aloud on the radio except after midnight. In later years, as a member of the PEN-American Center, Allen fought against censorship in Eastern Europe, Israel and Korea. Although Allen often claimed the Beat Generation as the genesis of the ideas of 1960s youth culture, in many instances, where some lasting influence on society can be shown, it was caused not by the Beat Generation, but by Ginsberg himself in his tireless campaigning for what he regarded as a better world.

The one continuous thread throughout his life was to fulfil the vow he made as a teenager, standing on the windswept prow of the Hoboken ferry on his way to take the Columbia University entrance examinations: to devote his life to helping mankind. He became the poet advocate of the underdog, and this has always been his greatest theme. To paraphrase Richard Ellmann on Oscar Wilde, Ginsberg's greatness as a writer is partly the result of the enlargement of sympathy that he demands for society's victims.

It was not an easy ride. Ginsberg's sincerity was doubted, his methods often criticised, his poetry ridiculed. For a time he was the most famous living poet on earth, one of America's best known cultural ambassadors, his poetry translated into virtually every language from Chinese to Serbo-Croat. He changed the world a little.

I'm famous,/ my poems have done some men good/ and a few women ill, perhaps the good/ outweighs the bad, I'll never know./ Still I feel guilty I haven't done more.

Chapter Notes

Abbreviations
AG: Allen Ginsberg; PO: Peter Orlovsky; LG: Louis Ginsberg; WSB: William Burroughs; JK: Jack Kerouac; GC: Gregory Corso; LC: Lucien Carr; HH: Herbert Huncke; EB: Eugene Brooks; LF: Lawrence Ferlinghetti; BM: Barry Miles.

Note: bibliographic details are only given if the book does not appear in the bibliography.

Chapter One: Childhood, Paterson.

The opening quote is from an unpublished mss.

AG describes the writing of 'Kaddish' in 'How Kaddish Happened' in Allen, Don and Tallman, Warren (Eds), *The Poetics of the New American Poetry*.

My interviews with Allen Ginsberg, 28 January 1971 and 15 August 1983, were principally about his family and childhood; also my interview with Allen Ginsberg's brother, Eugene Brooks, 11 February 1986, and his paternal aunt, Hannah Litzky, 19 January 1986. The Brooks and Litzky interviews provided material for the whole chapter. Other material comes from AG to BM: 20 February 1987 and conversations with AG 1983–1988.

I used the original mss of 'Kaddish' in the Fales Library, New York University; the 1964 'Kaddish' film script by AG and Robert Frank, and the dramatisation of 'Kaddish' by AG used by the Chelsea Theater Center, Brooklyn, NY in February 1972, as well as the published version.

The description of the CP meeting is from AG: 'America' [*Collected Poems, 1947–1980* version.]

His family background was established from notes and recordings of conversations between AG and his maternal aunt Edie Leegant. Also, Edie Leegant to AG: 26 March 1986; Gene Berlin to AG: 28 February 1987. AG's recorded conversation with Louis Ginsberg, 12 January 1976 [76D1/035] is about LG's youth, as was my interview with LG of 25 June 1970.

Details of Russia came from: Clarkson, Jesse D.: *A History Of Russia*,

Ran,dom House, New York, 1969; Greenberg, Louis: *The Jews In Russia: The Struggle For Emancipation* [2 vols], Yale University Press, New Haven, 1944 and 1951; Philipson, David: *Old European Jewries*, Jewish Publication Soc. of America, Philadelphia, 1894; Friedlander, Israel: *The Jews of Russia and Poland*, G.P. Putnams, New York, 1915; Alexander, Sidney: *Marc Chagall*, Cassell, London, 1979; Brym, Robert: *The Jewish Intelligentsia and Russian Marxism*, Macmillan, London, 1978; Dmytryshyn, Basil: *A History of Russia*, Prentice Hall, Englewood Cliffs, 1977; *Glavnoye Upravleniye Geodezii i Kartografii Atlas Belorusskoi Sovetskoi Sotzialisticheskoi Respubliki*, Moscow, 1958.

The Kay Boyle ref. is in McAlmon, Robert and Boyle, Kay: *Being Geniuses Together 1920–1930*, North Point Press, San Francisco, 1984, p. 18.

The Untermeyer and Wheelock quotes are from Ginsberg, Louis: *The Everlasting Minute*, Liveright, New York, 1937. See also Kreymborg, Alfred: *Troubadour, An Autobiography*, New York, Liveright, 1925.

AG's relationship with his parents comes from AG: unpublished journals and mss as well as Brooks, Eugene: 'Allen Ginsberg – Parents' Influence on Poetry and Politics'. nd (unpublished); Lester, Elenore: 'Allen Ginsberg Remembers Mama'. *New York Times*, 6 February 1972; AG's sexual relationship with LG dealt with in my interviews with AG of 15 August 1983 and 5 January 1988. Other material comes from conversations with LG in 1967 and 1970 onwards.

The episode with Morton is from AG: unpublished journals.

Fanny Hill: AG in *New York Times* Book Review, 6 June 1993.

Louis fainting: unpublished journals.

Marilyn Kass: unpublished journals.

AG's discovery of Whitman is described in 'The School Day I Remember Most', *Instructor Magazine*, May 1979, np [piece dated 21 September 1978].

'Genetic Origins of Schizophrenia', *Nature Genetics*, September 1992.

Episode taking Naomi to Lakewood is from 'Kaddish', poem and film script versions, plus my interview with AG of 15 August 1983.

Paul Roth: Roth, Paul to AG: 9 May 1943, AG: *Indian Journals*, p. 127, 173–4.

Chapter Two: A Columbia Education. The Origins of the Beat Generation.

My interview with AG of 6 June 1985 specifically covered AG's first spell at Columbia. This was augmented by my conversation with AG, 21 February 1984. AG: The LHBG lectures deal with this period in depth. The dialogue with Carr comes from AG: unpublished prose c.1944.

The description of Trilling is taken from my interviews with AG. Krupnick, Mark: *Lionel Trilling and the Fate of Cultural Criticism*, Northwestern University Press, Evanstan, Ill., 1986, and my conversation with AG, November 1983. Van Doren: my interviews with AG, also AG:

LHBG lectures. Hendrick, George, (Ed.) *The Selected Letters of Mark Van Doren*, Louisiana State University, Baton Rouge, 1987. Weaver: my interviews with AG. AG describes all three professors in the LHBG lectures.

Ginsberg's term papers, reading lists and journals were consulted at the Butler Library of Columbia University.

Lucien Carr: My interview with Lucien Carr, 9 March 1986, an unpublished transcription of a conversation between Lucien Carr, Barry Gifford, Lawrence Lee and James Grauerholz. JK: *Vanity of Duluoz*, AG: LHBG lectures.

Kammerer: My interview with AG. AG: LHBG lectures. Kammerer's room: from unpublished prose by AG and AG to JK, nd [September] 1944.

AG's meeting with WSB: The Shakespeare quote may originate from Henry V, Act 3, Scene 1: 'And sheathed their swords for lack of argument.' Howard Brookner's film: *William Burroughs*, *Current Biography*, v.32, No 10 (November 1971). WSB: interview *Paris Review* 35, Fall, 1965. My conversations with WSB, London 1973–4. AG: LHBG lectures. JK: *Vanity of Duluoz*.

Friendship with LC: My interview with AG, my interview with LC, 9 March 1986, which is used throughout this chapter.

West End: AG: 'West End Bar' unpublished prose [1944]. JK: *Visions of Cody*, JK: *Vanity of Duluoz*.

AG meeting with JK: JK: *Vanity of Duluoz*, JK: *Visions of Cody*, JK: interview: *Paris Review* 43, Summer 1968. AG to EB, Dec 1943. John Tytell interview with WSB in *The Beat Book*. Aaron Latham interview with AG, 1972, unpublished. AG: LHBG lectures deal with meeting in great detail.

Leaving Theological Seminary: My conversation with AG, March 1984 at the location. Aaron Latham interview with AG, 1972, unpublished. AG: LHBG lectures.

Visit to WSB: AG: 'Burroughs Memorabilia' unpublished prose. My interview. AG: LHBG lectures.

Death of Kammerer: LC to AG: 21 September 1944. LC to AG, 30 September 1944. LC to AG, 13 August 1944. Céline Young to JK, 1 October 1944. Céline Young to AG, 15 September 1944. Céline Young to JK, 8 October 1944. 4 undated letters: Céline Young to AG, 1944. JK to AG, 1944 [August?]. AG to EB, October 1944. AG: LHBG. AG to LG, nd [late 1944–early 1945]. AG to JK, August 1944. AG to JK, nd [September 1944]. AG to EB, September 1944. AG: unpublished prose. AG: unpublished journals. JK: *The Town and The City*, JK: *Vanity of Duluoz*.

Columbia: N.M. McKnight to AG, 13 November 1944. AG 'The Village Jade', unpublished prose [1944]; AG: 'Work In progress' unpublished prose [1944], AG: Journals and notebooks for the period.

AG as poet: Norton, Edward C.: 'Louis Ginsberg & Son, Poets', *Ave Maria* (Catholic Weekly, Notre Dame, Indiana), 6 September 1969.

WSB 'dangerous': LG to AG, nd [January 1945].

Columbia suspension: N.M. McKnight to LG, 2 January 1945. N.M. McKnight to LG, 17 March 1945. N.M. McKnight to LG, 30 March 1945. N.M. McKnight to AG, 17 March 1945. Céline, Louis-Ferdinand: *Journey To The End Of The Night*, Paris, 1932. AG: LHBG lectures. AG interview with Paul Geneson, 1974.

Chapter Three: A Street Education

My interview with AG of 6 June 1985 covers the period of this chapter. Bar lists are among Ginsberg's papers at Stanford.

WSB and HH: HH *The Evening Sky Turned Crimson*. WSB: *Junky*. JK: *Vanity of Duluoz*. *Town & the City*. AG: LHBG lectures. John Tytell interview with WSB in *The Beat Book*.

115th St: WSB in Howard Brookner film: *William Burroughs*. AG: LHBG lectures. My conversation with AG, 21 February 1984. JK to AG, 13 November 1945. EB to AG, 29 April 1945. My interview with AG, 6 June 1985. Feldman, Mitchell, interview with AG in *Red Hand* 3, Atlanta, Georgia, 20 January 1982.

AG sex life is from my interviews of 28 March 1985 and 5 January 1988. US Maritime service: LG to AG, 8 August 1945. LG to AG, 29 October 1945. AG to EB, 3 September 1945. AG to JK: nd, np [1945]. AG to JK: 12 August 1945. AG to JK: 22 August 1945. AG to JK: 4 September 1945. AG to JK, nd, np [September 1945]. AG to Lionel Trilling, 27 August 1945. JK to AG, 17 August 1945. JK to AG: 23 August 1945. JK to AG, 6 September 1945. Aaron Latham interview with AG: 1972, unpublished. WSB to JK, 24 July 1945. WSB to AG, 24 July 1945. Céline Young to AG, 3 August 1945. Four undated letters from Céline Young to AG [1945]. Background: Bates, Aaron: 'Eversoft At The Everard', *The Best of Gay*, 24 January 1972. AG: LHBG lectures.

Maritime service: US Coast Guard to AG: 23 May 1951.

WSB with Joan: Howard Brookner film: *William Burroughs*. JK: *Vanity of Duluoz*, JK: *The Town & The City*. JK: *Visions of Cody*. Ted Morgan papers at U of Arizona, Special Collections library (interviews with William Burroughs, Hal Chase and Edie Parker).

The Night of the Wolfeans: My interview with AG. AG: *Indian Journals*, p. 175. AG: unpublished journals. AG: LHBG lectures. Howard Brookner film: *William Burroughs*. JK: *Vanity of Duluoz*, AG: unpublished journals. My interview with AG.

The Herbert Huncke story is told in the special Huncke issue of *The Unspeakable Visions of the Individual*, v. 3, Nos 1–2, 1973. See also background in HH: *The Evening Sky Turned Crimson. Huncke's Journal. Guilty of Everything*.

Naomi in NYC from 'Kaddish'. Three undated letters from Naomi to AG. My interviews with AG. AG unpublished journals. 'Kaddish' film script, 1964. My interview with Eugene Brooks, 11 February 1986.

AG return to Columbia: My interview with AG, Columbia: N.M. McKnight to AG: 10 July 1946. Hans Wassing, MD to N.M. McKnight, 31 July 1946.

Joan's hearing: My interview with AG. My conversation with AG, 21 February 1984. Her use of amphetamine: HH interviewed in *Newave*, v. 1, No 5, New York, April, 1981.

WSB in Texas: WSB to AG, 1 September 1946. WSB to AG nd [late September 1946]. WSB to AG, 10 October 1946. HH to Joan Volmer, 8 October 1946. HH to AG, 23 September 1946. My conversation with AG, 21 February 1984. JK: *Vanity of Duluoz*, WSB: *Junky*. Three undated letters AG to JK [autumn, 1946].

First marijuana: AG narration for film *Fried Shoes, Cooked Diamonds*, February 1979. My interview with AG.

Naomi: 'Kaddish', my interview with EB, 11 February 1986. AG: unpublished journals.

AG and Neal Cassady: NC: *The First Third*. AG: 'Many Loves', JK: *The Town & The City*. JK: *Vanity of Duluoz*. JK: *On The Road*. John C. Holmes: *Go*. AG: LHBG lectures. AG: unpublished journals and *Journals*. The complete correspondence between Neal Cassady and AG is published in *As Ever*. I consulted the originals at the U of Texas, Austin, since there are minor errors of transcription in the published versions. LG to AG, 23 July 1948. LG to AG, 6 October 1948. Neal as 'sexual sadist', Carolyn Cassady interview by Gina Berriault, *Rolling Stone*, 12 October 1972.

Denver: Journals. LG to AG, July 1947. LG to AG, 13 August 1947. LG to AG, 18 August 1947. LG to AG, 15 September 1947. EB to AG, 4 September 1947. Becker, Drew interview with AG in the *Sunday Denver Post*, 12 August 1979.

Texas visit: HH to AG, 26 March 1947. AG to LG, 3 September 1947. AG to LG, 12 September 1947. AG: LHBG lectures. AG to JK, nd [fall, 1947]. AG to HH, October 1947 (from a notebook draft). WSB to AG, 19 February 1947. WSB to AG, nd [1947]. WSB to AG, 10 July 1947. JK to WSB, 14 July 1947. AG: 'The Green Automobile'. AG: 'The Monster Of Dakar', unpublished story. The bed: HH: *The Evening Sky Turned Crimson*, JK: *Visions of Cody*.

Naomi: 'Kaddish' poem and film script. My interview with AG.

AG to Wilhelm Reich, 11 March 1947.

Cézanne: AG interview, *Paris Review*, 37 (Spring, 1966). Paul Cézanne to Émile Bernard, 15 April 1904. Quoted in Émile Bernard, *Souvenirs sur Paul Cézanne* (Chez Michel, Paris, 1939). AG: Term paper on Cézanne in Columbia deposit.

NYC 1948–9: WSB to AG, 20 February 1948. WSB to AG, 3 March 1948. JK to AG, nd [April 1948]. JK to AG, 18 May 1948. WSB to AG, 5 June 1948. JK to AG, 23 May 1949.

The Blake Vision is described in great detail in Tom Clark's interview with AG in *Paris Review*, 37, Spring, 1966. The passage describing 'The Sick Rose' as following minutes after 'Ah! Sunflower' was annotated by AG in a copy of the first edition of this biography to read that 'The Sick Rose' was heard 'days later, on campus'. However, in the Clark interview AG is very specific that this was the second of three poems heard that first day. The Clark interview is twenty years earlier and more likely to be an accurate memory. See also Portugés, Paul: *The Visionary Poetics of Allen Ginsberg*. AG: *Journals*. Giacometti describes a similar experience in his essay 'The Dream, the Sphinx and the Death of T' (1946).

The episode of Huncke stealing Durgin's books was given fictional treatment in Holmes's *Go*, where Durgin appears as Verger, Huncke is Ancke and Ginsberg is Stofsky. WSB to AG, 14 October 1948. HH to AG, nd [February 1948?] The original mss of 'Howl' gives a list of Durgin's books. Description of 121 St: Gold, Herbert: 'My Last Two Thousand Years' in *Unspeakable Visions of the Individual*, v. 3, Nos 1–2, 1973.

Alan Ansen: Franan, Dorothy J: *Auden In Love*, Simon & Schuster, New York, 1984.

The story of Huncke, Little Jack and Vickie Russell is taken from AG's 'The Fall', a 147-page unpublished account of the entire period written in 1949 for his lawyer after his arrest. Holmes, John C.: *Nothing More To Declare*. Holmes: *Go*. AG: LHBG lectures. Fields, Rick interview AG in *Open Secret*, Naropa, Boulder, 1974. Sloman, Larry interview with AG in *High Times* 86, New York, 1982. 1973. AG: *Journals* and unpublished journals.

WSB in New Orleans: WSB to AG, 14 October 1948. WSB to AG, 4 November 1948. WSB to AG, 30 November 1948. WSB to JK, 30 November 1948. WSB to AG, 2 December 1948. NC: *As Ever*. WSB to AG, 10 January 1949. WSB to AG, 16 January 1949. WSB to AG, 17 January 1949. WSB to AG, 30 January 1949. WSB to JK, 15 March 1949. WSB to AG, 16 March 1949. WSB to AG, 26 March 1949. WSB to JK, 27 May 1949. WSB to AG, 16 April 1949. JK: *On The Road*. WSB to JK, 24 June 1949.

Other background: JK: 'The Origins of the Beat Generation' in *Playboy*, June 1959. JK to AG, 18 September 1948. JK to AG, 15 December 1948.

Arrest: *Daily Mirror*, 23 April 1949. *Herald Tribune*, 23 April 1949. *New York Times*, 23 April 1949. *Daily News*, 23 April 1949. Long account by AG in Kramer, Jane: *Allen Ginsberg In America*.

Chapter Four: The Subterraneans
Psychiatric Institute: A 1984 study conducted by UCLA at Oxford University between 1982 and 1983 concluded that artists, writers and poets are 35 times more likely to seek treatment for serious mood disorders than the average person, and of these three groups, poets suffered the severest forms of the disturbance. The poets in the study were limited only to those who had received the Queen's Gold Medal for poetry, a very conservative group compared to the less establishment poets of Ginsberg's milieu, yet even of these, nearly 20 per cent had suffered at least one episode of manic depression serious enough to require hospitalisation, and more than 50 per cent had received some form of medical treatment for mania or depression. Clearly Ginsberg was in a dangerous profession. Of American poets one thinks of Lowell, Roethke, Berryman,

Jarrell and Plath. Ginsberg's IQ test at the P.I. showed him to be near genius level.

P.I.: JK to AG, 10 June 1949. JK to AG: 5 July 1949. JK to AG, 26 July 1949. John C. Holmes to AG, 14 June 1949. John C. Holmes to AG, 6 July 1949. WSB to JK, 26 September 1949. WSB to AG, 13 October 1949. WSB to JK, 2 November 1949. WSB to AG, 8 November 1949. WSB to AG: 24 December 1949. AG to JK, 15 June 1949. AG to JK, 17 June 1949. JK to AG, 13 January 1950. WSB to JK, 1 January 1950. JK to AG, 13 January 1950. WSB to JK, 22 January 1950. WSB to JK, 28 January 1950. JK to AG, February 1950. WSB to JK, March 1950. WSB to AG, 1 May 1950. AG: LHBG lectures. AG to PO, 1 April 1958. AG unpublished journals. My interview with AG of 6 June 1986 covered the period of this chapter. AG's letters to NC in *As Ever* also cover the period. Solomon, Carl: *Mishaps Perhaps*. Interview with Carl Solomon in *The Beat Book*. AG: 'The Fall' mss. (unpublished).

William Carlos Williams reprinted most of the letter in part four of his poem 'Paterson'. See also Mariani, Paul: *William Carlos Williams, A New World Naked*, McGraw Hill, New York, 1981, p. 604 & 621.

San Remo: Landesman, Jay: *Rebel Without Applause*. Gruen, John: *The Party's Over Now*. McDarrah, Fred: *Kerouac & Friends*. Malina, Judith: *Diaries of Judith Malina 1947–1957*. AG: LHBG lectures. AG to JK, nd [March] 1950. WSB to AG, 1 May 1950. JK: *The Subterraneans*. Alan Ansen to AG, 5 June 1950. Alan Ansen to AG, 17 June 1950. JK to AG, June 1950. JK to AG, October 1950.

Helen Parker: AG: LHBG lectures. My interview with AG. WSB to JK, 18 September 1950. Helen Parker to AG, 7 July 1950, plus five undated letters from same period. WSB to AG, nd [summer 1950]. John C. Holmes to AG, 9 August 1950.

Ribbon Factory: AG: 'How Come He Got Canned At The Ribbon factory'.

Bill Cannastra: Harrington, Alan: *The Secret Swinger*, Alfred A Knopf, New York, 1966. Cannastra appears as Bill Genovese. In Holmes, John C.: *Get Home Free* and *Go* he appears as Bill Agatson. In JK: *Visions of Cody* he appears as Finistra. AG: LHBG lectures. Cannastra's death: *Herald Tribune*, 13 October 1950. *Daily News*, 13 October 1950. *Daily Mirror*, 13 October 1950.

Peyronie's Syndrome: conversation with AG. Rivers, Larry: *What Did I Do?* p. 153.

GC: *The Riverside Interviews 3*: GC gives family history. AG: LHBG lectures. Moraes, Dom: *My Son's Father*, Macmillan, New York, 1968, p. 202. My interview with AG. Interview in *The Beat Book*. Corso on Moreland: Naropa Kerouac conference, 1982.

WSB in Mexico: WSB to JK, 18 September 1950. WSB to JK, 26 December 1950. AG to JK, 15 May 1952.

Mexican Trip: My interview with LC of 9 March 1986. Howard Brookner's film, *William Burroughs*. My interview with AG, 28 March 1985.

Joan's death: *Daily News*, 8 September 1951. *New York Times*, 8 September 1951. *World Telegram & Sun*, 7 September 1951. *World Telegram & Sun*, 11 September 1951. *Journal American*, 9 September 1951. WSB to AG, 5 November 1951. Howard Brookner's film, *William Burroughs*. WSB: *Queer*.

Chapter Five: The Road To California

My interview with AG of 28 March 1985 covers the period in this chapter. AG was involved in a very heavy correspondence with Neal Cassady for most of the period, see *As Ever*. Burroughs, William: *Letters to Allen Ginsberg, 1953–1957*, also covers much of this period.

West 15th St: AG: unpublished journals and poems. WSB to AG, 1 January 1951. WSB to AG, 11 January 1951. WSB to LC, 5 March 1951. JK to AG nd [March 1951]. WSB to JK, 24 April 1951. AG to JK, nd [1951]. WSB to AG, 5 May 1951. JK to AG, July 1951. WSB to AG, November 1951. WSB to AG, 20 December 1951. AG: LHBG lectures. AG to JK, 15 February 1952.

AG writes about Dusty Moreland in his correspondence with Neal Cassady (*As Ever*). Also, GC: *Gregory Corso, The Riverside Interviews 3*, Binnacle Press, London, 1982. AG: unpublished journals.

Death of Phil 'The Sailor' White. AG to NC, 15 February 1952. WSB to AG, 19 January 1952.

Peyote: AG: *Journals*, AG: LHBG lectures.

Jan Kerouac: Kerouac, Jan: *Baby Driver*.

Pub of *Go*. Ts of Holmes's *Nothing More To Declare* in Ginsberg deposit at Stanford.

WSB in Mexico re *Junky*: WSB to JK, 26 March 1952. WSB to JK, nd [1952] JK: *On The Road*. WSB to AG, 20 February 1952. WSB to JK, 3 April 1952. WSB to AG, 20 March 1952. WSB to AG, 5 April 1952. WSB to AG, 9 April 1952. WSB to AG, 14 April 1952. WSB to AG, 26 April 1952. WSB to AG, 15 May 1952. WSB to AG, 4 June 1952. AG to WSB, 12 June 1952. WSB to AG, 15 June 1952. WSB to AG, 23 June 1952. WSB to AG, 27 June 1952. WSB to AG, 1 July 1952. WSB to AG, 6 July 1952. WSB to AG, 10 July 1952. WSB to AG, 13 July 1952. WSB to AG, 20 August 1952. WSB to AG, 6 October 1952. WSB to AG, November 1952. WSB to AG, 5 November 1952. WSB to AG, 6 November 1952. WSB to AG, 23 December 1952. WSB to AG, 24 December 1952. WSB to AG, 10 January 1953; 19 January 1953. [Goes to South America in search of yage]: WSB to AG, 25 January 1953. WSB to AG, 1 March 1953. WSB to AG, 12 April 1953. WSB to AG, 22 April 1953. WSB to AG, 30 April 1953. WSB to AG, 4 May 1953. WSB to AG, 5 May 1953. WSB to AG, 12 May 1953. WSB to AG, 15 May 1953. WSB to AG, 23 May 1953. WSB to AG, 30 May 1953. WSB to AG, 6 June 1953. WSB to AG, 8 June 1953. WSB to AG, 18 June 1953. WSB to AG, 8 July 1953. WSB to AG, 21 July 1953. WSB to AG, 17 August 1953.

AG: new 'sketching' style: transcript of AG talk at Warwick University,

6 November 1979. AG to JK and NC, February 1952. AG to JK, 8 March 1952. JK to AG, 12 March 1952. JK to AG, 15 March 1952. AG to JK and NC: February 1952. Aaron Latham interview, 31 August 1972, unpublished. AG to JK, 15 May 1952. JK to AG, 18 May 1952. JK to AG, 8 April 1952. WSB to JK, 8 April 1952. AG to Ezra Pound, 30 May 1952.

WCW: From AG: *Journals* and unpublished journals. WCW to AG, 27 February 1952. AG to JK, April 1952. AG: *Journals*, entry for 12 March 1952. AG to WCW, 9 March 1952. WSW to AG, 24 May 1952. AG to WCW, 6 June 1952. AG to WCW, 10 August 1952. AG interview in *Monmouth Letters*, Spring 1961. Wagner, Linda (Ed.), *Interviews With William Carlos Williams*, New Directions, New York, 1976.

JK in Mexico City: AG: LHBG lectures. AG to JK, 15 May 1952. JK to AG, 10 May 1952. JK to AG, 17 May 1952. JK to AG, 18 May 1952. AG to JK & WSB, 12 June 1952. JK to AG, 20 June 1952. JK to AG, 28 July 1952 (from Carolina).

AG and Dusty Moreland: His letters to NC (*As Ever*). JK to Dusty Moreland, nd [1952]. JK to AG, 1951.

JK's attack on his friends: 8 October 1952. JK to AG, 8 November 1952. JK to AG, 29 December 1952. JK's objection to name on *Junkie*: JK to AG, 21 February 1953. AG to JK, 24 February 1953. [friends again] JK to AG, 7 May 1953. AG to JK, May 1953. AG to JK, 13 July 1953.

Naomi: 'Kaddish': Naomi to AG, 5 January 1953. AG: unpublished journal, 18 January 1953. Naomi to EB, nd [1955].

Three Graces: AG: Annotated edition of *Howl*. My interview with AG. Elise Cowen: Johnson, Joyce: *Minor Characters*.

Ending to *Doctor Sax*: AG: LHBG lectures. JK to AG, 7 May 1953.

WSB in NYC: My interview with AG. AG: LHBG lectures. AG: unpublished journal gives transcriptions of long conversations. Wilson, Terry/Gysin, Brion: Here To Go: Planet R–101. WSB to JK, 14 December 1952. Howard Brookner film, *William Burroughs*.

Orgone Accumulator: device designed by Wilhelm Reich to gather orgone energy the natural life force in the atmosphere and concentrate it in a box. By sitting in the box, one became energised. See Reich, Wilhelm: *The Orgone Energy Accumulator, It's Scientific and Medical Uses*, Wilhelm Reich Insititute, Maine, 1951.

Mexico trip: AG: *Journals*, unpublished journals. AG to JK, NC and Carolyn Cassady, 9 January 1953. Shields, Karena: *The Changing Wind*, John Murray, London, 1960. The spelling of 'Xibalba' is taken from Shields. Ginsberg misspells it in his poem 'Siesta In Xbalba'. AG to LC, 18 January 1954. AG to LC, 18 February 1954. AG to LC [cable] 29 March 1954. AG to LC, 31 March 1954. AG to LC, 1 April 1954. WSB to JK, 22 April 1954. AG to LC, 21 May 1954. WSB to JK, 24 May 1954. AG to JK, 18 June 1954.

AG at the Cassady household: AG: unpublished journals. AG: LHBG lectures. Cassady, Carolyn: *Heartbeat*. Plummer, William: *Holy Goof*. JK to Carolyn Cassady, 17 May 1954. JK to AG, nd [May, 1954] JK to AG,

30 July 1954. AG to EB, 14 August 1954. JK to AG, 23 August 1954. Several undated letters from JK to AG.

Sheila Williams: AG to JK, 7 September 1954. AG to JK, 26 November 1954. NC to AG, 27 November 1954. AG to JK, 9 November 1954. AG: unpublished journals.

Kenneth Rexroth: Charters, Ann: *The Beats: Literary Bohemians in Postwar America – Part 2*. My conversations with Rexroth, 1966.

Robert Duncan: Fass, Ekbert: *Young Robert Duncan, Portrait of the Poet as Homosexual in Society*, Black Sparrow, Santa Barbara, 1983.

Life with Sheila: AG to JK, 7 September 1954. AG to JK, nd [October 1954]. AG to JK, 9 October 1954. AG to JK, 26 November 1954. AG to JK, 29 December 1954.

Problems with WSB: WSB to JK, 22 April 1954. WSB to JK, 4 May 1954. WSB to JK, 24 May 1954. WSB to JK, 17 July 1954. WSB to JK, nd [July? 1954] WSB to JK, 3 September 1954. JK to AG, 26 October 1954. JK to AG, 7 December 1954. WSB to JK, 7 December 1954. JK to AG, 7 December 1954.

Peter Orlovsky: Charters, Ann: *The Beats: Literary Bohemians in Postwar America – Part 2*. My conversations with PO, particularly Cherry Valley 1970–1. PO interview, *Gay Sunshine*. AG interview, *Gay Sunshine*. AG: unpublished journals.

City Lights Books: My interview with LF, 20 & 21 March 1986. My interview with Shigeyoshi Murao, 22 March 1986.

LF: Cherkovski, Neeli: *Ferlinghetti, A Biography*. Smith, Larry: *Lawrence Ferlinghetti, Poet-at-Large*.

Montgomery St: AG: unpublished journals. Photographs of interior in annotated edition of *Howl*. 'Howl' text from first draft mss. AG: LHBG lectures. WSB to AG, 6 January 1955. AG to JK, nd [January] 1955. WSB to AG, 9 January 1955. AG to JK, 12 January 1955. AG to JK, 14 January 1955. WSB to AG, 15 January 1955. JK to AG, 18–20, 1955. JK to AG, 10 February 1955. AG to JK, 11 February 1955. WSB to JK, 12 February 1955. JK to AG, 4 March 1955. AG to JK, 13 March 1955. AG to JK, 22 April 1955. AG to JK, 25 April 1955. AG to JK, 10 May 1955. JK to WSB nd [May 1955]. JK to AG, 11 May 1955. AG to JK, 27 May 1955. JK to AG, 27 May 1955. JK to AG, 1 June 1955. AG to JK, 1 June 1955. AG to JK, 5 June 1955. WSB to JK, 9 June 1955. JK to AG, 29 June 1955. AG to JK, nd [July 1955]. AG to JK, 5 July 1955. JK to AG, 14 July 1955. AG to LG, 28 July 1955. Bob LaVigne to AG, 6 August 1955. JK to AG, 7 August 1955.

Chapter Six: Howl and the San Francisco Renaissance
My interview with AG of 28 March 1985 covers this period. AG: LHBG lectures. AG: unpublished journals.

AG had given a number of full descriptions of writing 'Howl', the most detailed being in the annotated edition of *Howl*, and the liner notes to the album, reprinted in Parkinson, Thomas (Ed.) *Casebook On The Beat*. See also AG interview in *Paris Review*, 37, Spring, 1966. The quotes are from the first draft of the mss. and differ from the final version. JK to AG, 19 August 1955. AG to JK, 25 August 1955. AG to JK, 30 August 1955.

Montgomery St: Bob LaVigne to AG, 16 August 1955. AG to EB, 16 August 1955. AG to JK, nd [August 1955].

Berkeley Cottage: Bob LaVigne to AG, 6 September 1955. WSB to AG, 21 September 1955. Bob LaVigne to AG, 21 September 1955. AG to Bob LaVigne, 26 September 1955. WSB to AG, nd [October 1955]. LG to AG, 12 December 1955. AG to EB, 27 December 1955. AG to PO, 21 June 1958. AG to LC, 16 January 1956. AG to LG, 26 April 1956. AG to LG, nd [May, 1956]. AG to EB, 18 May 1956.

An anthology of articles about the Six Gallery Reading is in the annotated edition of *Howl*. See also McClure, Michael: *Scratching The Beat Surface*. Gary Snyder to AG, 24 February 1956.

Gary Snyder: JK: *The Dharma Bums*, Kherdian, David: *Six San Francisco Poets*. Kherdian, David: *A Biographical Sketch and Descriptive Checklist of Gary Snyder*. Almon, Bert: *Gary Snyder*. McNeil, Katherine: *Gary Snyder A Bibliography*. Snyder, Gary: *The Real Work, Interviews Talks, 1964–1979*. Philip Whalen: JK: *The Dharma Bums*, Kherdian, David: *Six San Francisco Poets*. Charters, Ann: *The Beats: Literary Bohemians in Postwar America – Part 2*.

Howl Part III: Smart, Christopher: *Selected Poems*, Carcanet, Manchester, 1979. Allen, Henry: 'The Poet's Poet: Stanley Kunitz at the Library of Congress'. The *Washington Post, Potomac magazine*, 5 January 1975.

'Yabyum': JK: *Dharma Bums*. DiPrima, Diane: *Memoirs of a Beatnik*.

Nudity: My interview with Philip Whalen of 16 March 1986. AG interviewed by Al Aronowitz in *New York Post*, twelve-part series, 'The Beat Generation', 9–22 March 1959.

Natalie's death: AG poem; unpublished.

San Francisco renaissance: My interview with Philip Whalen of 16 March 1986 covered this period as did my interview with Michael McClure of 19 March 1986, and my interview with Lawrence Ferlinghetti of 20–21 March 1986. LG to AG, 29 February 1956. AG to EB, 26 May 1956. LG to AG, 4 August 1956. LG to AG, 13 August 1956. GC to AG, 23 August 1956. LG to AG, 11 September 1956. AG to EB, 19 September 1956. Aaron Latham interview with AG, 31 August 1972, unpublished.

Naomi's death: AG: unpublished mss. Western Union telegram EB to AG, 9 June 1956. EB to AG, 11 June 1956. LG to AG, 20 June 1956. AG to Rebecca Ginsberg [Buba], 11 August 1956.

The Arctic Circle: AG: unpublished journals. AG to EB, 10 July 1956. AG to Hannah Litzky, 11 August 1956. AG to JK, 12 August 1956. AG to PO, 16 March 1956. AG to PO, nd [1956]. My interview with LF, 20–21 March 1986.

Publication of 'Howl'. AG to Richard Eberhart: 18 May 1956.

JK in Mexico: AG to JK, 10 March 1956. JK to AG, 26 September 1956. AG to JK, 10 October 1956.

WSB in Tangier: WSB to AG, 9 March 1956. Alan Ansen to AG, 18 June 1956. Alan Ansen to AG, 24 August 1956. WSB to AG, 16 September 1956. JK to AG, 26 September 1956. WSB to AG, 13 October 1956. WSB to AG, 29 October 1956. Ansen, Alan: 'William Burroughs, a Personal View' in *Review of Contemporary Fiction*, v. 4., No 1 (Spring 1984). Ansen, Alan: *William Burroughs*, Sudbury, Water Row, 1986.

Los Angeles visit: WSB to AG, 20 December 1956. AG to Anaïs Nin, nd [1956]. Lipton, Lawrence: *The Holy Barbarians*. Nin, Anaïs: *The Journals of Anaïs Nin, Volume Six*, Peter Owen, London, 1977. AG to LG, 31 October 1956.

Mexico: JK: *Desolation Angels*. AG to JK, 4 January 1957 [from NYC].

New York City: Diane DiPrima described the orgy with JK and AG in her book *Memoirs of a Beatnik*. AG on orgies: AG narration for film *Skeletons Rolling on the Noble Road*, Boulder, February 1979. Robert LaVigne to AG: 25 January 1957. Robert LaVigne to AG: 31 March 1957. Johnson, Joyce: *Minor Characters*. Breit, Harvey, 'En Garde', in the *New York Times*, 20 January 1957. Klausner, Howard: 'Paterson Man's Poems Draw Attention of Major Critics', the *Herald-News*, 25 February 1957. AG to Robert LaVigne, 15 January 1957. AG to Charles Olson, 18 February 1956. AG to LF, two undated letters [January–February 1957] AG to LF, 15 January 1957. AG to LF, 3 March 1957.

Dali: AG: unpublished journals.

WCW: AG: unpublished journals. Mariani, Paul: *William Carlos Williams, A New World Naked*, McGraw Hill, New York, 1981.

Chapter Seven: The Classic Stations of the Earth
My interview with AG of 28 March 1985 covers the period of this chapter.

WSB in Tangier: Bowles, Paul: 'Burroughs In Tangier' in *Big Table* 2, Chicago, summer 1959. WSB to AG, 18 August 1954. WSB to AG, 16 September 1956. WSB interviewed in *The Beat Diary*. Bowles on WSB quoted in Harold Norse interview in *Gay Sunshine*. WSB to AG, 14 February 1957. JK to AG, 21 January 1958.

JK in Tangier: JK: *Desolation Angels*. JK interview in *Paris Review*, 43, Summer 1968. JK to Alan Ansen, 20 August 1957 AG & PO in Tangier: AG: unpublished journals. JK: *Desolation Angels*. PO to Robert LaVigne, 3 May 1957. PO to Ron Lowenstein, 3 May 1957. PO to Robert LaVigne, 29 May 1957. PO to JK, 31 May 1957. Dillon, Millicent, *A Little Original Sin, The Life and Work of Jane Bowles*, New York, Holt Rinehart Winston, 1981, p. 347. Dillon, Millicent (Ed.) *Out In The World, Selected Letters of Jane Bowles*, Santa Barbara, Black Sparrow, 1985. AG to LF, 3 April 1957. AG to LC, 4 April 1957. AG to NC, 24 April 1957. William Carlos Williams to AG, 29 April 1957. AG to LF, 10 May 1957. AG to JK, 31 May 1957. AG to LC, nd [late May, 1957]. AG to LF, 31 May 1957. JK to AG & WSB, nd [June 1957]. JK to AG, 7 June 1957. AG to GC, 8 June 1957. AG to LG, June 1957. AG to William Carlos Williams, 22 August 1957. AG: unpublished journals.

AG & PO in Spain. PO to Robert LaVigne, 21 June 1957. AG to EB, 20 June 1957. PO to AG, 26 June 1958. AG: unpublished journals.

AG & PO in Venice: My conversation with AG and Alan Ansen, 1986. AG to LG, 26 June 1957. PO to AG, 10 February 1958. AG to LG, 9 July 1957. AG to LF, 10 July 1957. AG to EB, 15 July 1957. PO to Robert LaVigne, 25 July 1957. AG to EB, 10 August 1957. AG to LG, 10 August 1957. AG to JK, 13 August 1957. JK to Alan Ansen, 20 August 1957. AG to LF, 21 August 1957. LG to AG, 26 August 1957. AG to LF, 3 September 1957. PO to Henry Schlachler, 4 September 1957. AG to LG, 4 September 1957. AG to EB, 6 September 1957. WSB to AG, 6 September 1957. WSB to AG, 11 September 1957. AG to LG, September 1957. WSB to AG, 20 September 1957, WSB to AG, nd [September 1957] AG: unpublished journals.

'Howl' Trial: 'Statement of facts', City Lights Books, San Francisco, 11 April 1957. JK to AG, 7 June 1957. AG to LF, 10 June 1957.

Travels in Italy. AG to LG, 10 August 1957. AG to PO and Alan Ansen, 26 August 1957. AG to PO, 27 August 1957. AG to PO and Alan Ansen, 29 August 1957.

AG and Auden: Miller, Charles H.: *Auden, An American Friendship*, New York, Charles Scribner's Sons, 1983, p. 146. AG to LG, 1 September 1957.

AG & PO in Paris: My interview with Larry Fagin, 23 January 1986.

On The Road review: *New York Times*, 5 September 1957. AG to JK, September 1957. AG to JK, 9 October 1957. AG to JK, 16 October 1957.

'Howl' Trial. Ehrlich, J.W.: *Howl of the Censor, The Four Letter Word on Trial*, San Carlos, CA, Mourse, 1961. Cherkovski, Neeli: *Ferlinghetti, A Biography*. Podhoretz, Norman: 'A Howl of Protest in San Francisco' in the *New Republic*, 16 September 1957. Roberts, John: 'Juvenile Police Head Raids Bookshop in San Francisco' in *National Guardian*, 5 August 1957. Roberts, John: 'West Coast Censorship Trial Draws Big Audiences in Support of Poem' in *National Guardian*, 9 September 1957. [leader] *San Francisco Chronicle*, 7 October 1957. O'Gara, Francis: ' "Howl" Ruled Not Obscene; 2 Acquitted' in *San Francisco Examiner*, 4 October 1957. JK to AG, 18 October 1957.

Rue Git le Coeur: Zwerin, Michael: 'Brion Gysin , the Dreamer and His Dream Machine' in the *Paris Metro*, 16 August 1978. Feifer, Maxine: 'Times Past At The Beat Hotel' in the *Paris Metro*, 16 August 1978. WSB forward to *Beat Hotel* by Harold Norse. Norse, Harold: 'The Death of 9, rue Git le Coeur' in *City Lights Journal* 1, San Francisco, 1963. Chapman, Harold: *The Beat Hotel*. My conversations with Ian Sommerville, 1965–70. Wolff, Geoffrey: *Black Sun, The Brief Transit And Violent Eclipse Of Harry Crosby*, New York, Random House, 1976. Gysin, Brion: *Here To Go. Planet R–101*. AG to LG, 18 September 1957. AG to LF, 23 September 1957. AG to JK, 28 September 1957. AG to LG, 30 September 1957. JK to AG, 1 October 1957. AG to JK, 9 October 1957. AG to LF, 10 October 1957. WSB to AG, 14 October 1957. AG to JK, 16 October

1957. AG to LG, 19 October 1957. PO to Ron Lowenstein, 19 October 1957. WSB to AG, 19 October 1957. WSB to AG, 28 October 1957. WSB to AG, 31 October 1957. PO to Robert LaVigne, 2 November 1957. WSB to AG, 10 November 1957. AG to JK, 13 November 1957. WSB to AG, 26 November 1957. AG to LG, 30 November 1957. JK to AG, 30 November 1957. WSB to JK, 4 December 1957. WSB to AG, 4 December 1957. PO to JK, 5 December 1957. PO to Robert LaVigne, 7 December 1957. WSB to AG, 8 December 1957. JK to AG, PO & GC, 10 December 1957. AG to LC, 11 December 1957. AG to Edith Ginsberg, 15 December 1957. AG to JK, 4 January 1958. AG to LG, 14 January 1958. AG to JK, 11 January 1958. AG to LG, 14 January 1958. AG to PO, 20 January 1958. JK to AG, 21 January 1958. AG to EB, 23 January 1958. AG to LG, 23 January 1958. AG to PO, 23 January 1958. AG to PO, 28 January 1958. AG to LG, 2 February 1958. AG to PO, 3 February 1958. AG to PO, 15 February 1958. AG to PO, 24 February 1958. AG to LG, 2 March 1958. AG to EB, 12 March 1958. AG to LG, 15 March 1958. AG to PO, 16 March 1958. AG and WSB to JK, 29 March 1958.

AG begins 'Kaddish': AG to JK, 13 November 1957.

Breton, André: 'Free Union', first pub. 1931. See Jean Marcel (Ed.), *The Autobiography of Surrealism*, New York, Viking, 1980.

François: My interview with AG.

LeRoi Jones: AG to LG, Nov 30, 1957. Jones, LeRoi, *The Autobiography of LeRoi Jones/Amiri Baraka*.

PO returns to NYC: Johnson, Joyce: *Minor Characters* (p. 184–186.) Lafcadio Orlovsky to PO, 16 July 1957. PO to JK, 18 October 1957.

WSB in Paris. WSB to AG, 9 January 1958. WSB to AG, 13 January 1958. AG to LF, 18 January 1958. WSB to AG, 2 February 1958. AG to LF, 2 February 1958. WSB to AG, 10 February 1958. WSB to AG, 16 February 1958.

First UK trip: AG to LG, 2 February 1958. AG to PO, 3 February 1958. WSB to AG, 3 February 1957. GC to AG, 7 February 1957. AG to PO, 13 February 1958. AG to PO, 15 February 1958. WSB to AG, nd [1957]. AG to PO, 24 February 1958.

Spring in Paris: Buchwald, Art: 'Two Poets In Paris', in *New York Herald Tribune*, 26 June 1958. AG to PO, 1 April 1958. AG to PO, 9 April 1958. AG to LF, 15 April 1958. Philip Whalen to AG, 17 April 1957. AG to LF nd [April, 1958] Gary Snyder to AG, 22 April 1958. AG to LG, 24 May 1958. AG to LF, 24 May 1958. AG to Jack Micheline, 25 May 1958. AG to LC, 30 May 1958. AG to PO, 30 May 1958. AG to PO, 3 June 1958. AG to LG, 4 June 1958. AG to PO, 8 June 1958. AG to PO, 15 June 1958. AG to Hannah Litzky, 20 June 1958. AG to LF, 20 June 1958. AG to PO, 21 June 1958. AG to JK, 26 June 1958. JK to AG, 2 July 1958. AG to EB, nd [Spring, 1958]. AG to EB, 9 July 1958. AG to PO, 16 July 1958.

Second UK trip: Moraes, Dom, *My Son's Father*, Macmillan, New York, 1968. LG to AG, 5 March 1958. LG to AG, 10 April 1958. AG interview by David Widgery, *U* summer, 1965. AG to PO, 12 May 1958. AG to LG, 24 May 1958. AG to PO, 30 May 1958.

Edith Sitwell: 'The Only Rebellion Around', in *Life*, 30 November 1959. Letter from Edith Sitwell, *Life*, 8 February 1960. AG to PO, 30 May 1958. Salter, Elizabeth, *The Last Years Of A Rebel*, *A Memoir of Edith Sitwell*, Boston, Houghton Mifflin, 1967. Edith Sitwell to James Purdy, 25 July 1958, in Sitwell, Edith, *Selected Letters*, New York, Vanguard, 1970. Sitwell clearly believed that both Ginsberg and Corso were addicted to heroin.

Céline: My interview with AG. Conversation with WSB, February 1974. AG to PO, 11 July 1958. AG to NC, 7 July 1958.

Michaux. AG on Michaux for *Cahiers L'Herne*. Text written December 1965. GC to AG, 28 November 1958.

Chapter Eight: Kaddish
My interview with AG of 28 March 1985 covered this period.

NYC: AG to JK, 20 August 1958. AG to GC, 27 August 1958. AG to GC, November 1958. AG to JK, November 1958. AG to Robert LaVigne, 10 September 1958. AG to JK, 10 September 1958. Hyams, Joe, 'Good-bye to the Beatniks!', in *This Week Magazine*, 28 September 1958. Podhoretz, Norman, 'Where Is The Beat Generation Going?', in *Esquire*, December, 1958. Schleifer, Marc, 'Here To Save Us, But Not Sure From What', in *Village Voice*, 15 October 1958. [Review of] 'Beat Generation and the Angry Young Men', in *Time*, 9 June 1958. Nichols, Luther, 'Kerouac as the Savant of the Religious Beat', in *San Francisco Chronicle*, 5 October 1958. Schleifer, Marc, 'The Beat Debated – Is It or Is It Not?', in *Village Voice*, 19 November 1958. AG: 'The Dharma Bums', in *Village Voice*, 12 November 1958. Series of five undated letters. AG to LF, 6 March 1959. McDarrah, Fred, *Kerouac & Friends, a Beat Generation Album*.

JK's mother: JK to AG, 2 July 1958. Gabrielle Kerouac to AG, 13 July 1958. WSB to AG, 15 July 1958. WSB to AG, 24 July 1958. JK to AG, 11 August 1958.

Thelonius Monk: AG: unpublished journals. AG to JK, 16 September 1958.

JK's publishing career: AG to JK, 29 October 1958. AG to JK, 17 November 1958.

AG as agent: AG to LF, 20 August 1958. AG to LF, 4 September 1958. AG to LF, 10 September 1958. AG to LF, 30 September 1958. AG to LF, 23 January 1959. Gary Snyder to AG, 2 February 1959. AG to WSB, 27 August 1959 AG to WSB, 12 December 1959. AG to JK, 12 May 1959. AG to GC, May 1959.

Laughing Gas: AG to JK, nd [1958] also AG: unpublished journals.

Writing 'Kaddish': original mss in Fales Library, NYU. AG to Charles Olson, November 1958. AG to WCW, 23 January 1959. AG to LF, 19 March 1959. AG to WCW, 30 May 1959. AG: LHBG lectures.

PI patient: AG to Charles Olson, 26 November 1958.

'Pull My Daisy': JK: *Pull My Daisy*, Amram, David: *Vibrations*.

Chicago visit: AG, PO, GC to *Time* Magazine, 17 February 1959. AG to JK, 6 February 1959.

Columbia reading: AG to LF, 12 February 1959. Trilling, Diana: 'The Other Night At Columbia' in *Partisan Review*, Spring, 1959.

San Francisco: 'Poetry In The Bay Area', AG to SF Chronicle, in *San Francisco Chronicle*, 27 May 1959. AG to LG, 12 May 1959.

'Kaddish': AG to LG, 20 [May] 1959.

Beatitude magazine: Kelly, John, (Ed.) *Beatitude Anthology*. AG to LF, 15 August 1960.

Lower East Side: 'My conversations with Alexander Trocchi 1965–70'. AG: LHBG lectures.

Reading tours: [related] Dorfman, Elsa, *Elsa's Housebook, A Woman's Photojournal*, Boston: David R. Godine, 1974.

'Hairy Loss': AG, unpublished journals. AG, LHBG lectures.

Chapter Nine: Adventures in Psychedelia

Virtually all of the material in this chapter is taken from AG's unpublished South American journals. See also AG, 'Aether', 'Magic Psalm', and 'The Reply'. AG to LF, 14 March 1960; 6 April 1960. AG to EB, 2 June 1960. AG to WSB, 2 June 1960. AG to JK, 6 June 1960. AG to WSB, 10 June 1960. AG to LF, 15 August 1960.

WSB's search for Yage is detailed in AG with WSB, *The Yage Letters*. My interview with Burroughs of 28 May 1988.

Machu Picchu: 'The Might Of Machu Picchu' in *New York Times*, 9 June 1985.

NYC: AG, unpublished journals.

Completion of 'Kaddish': AG to LF, 5 July 1960; 16 September 1960. AG to JK, 19 September 1960. AG to LF, 5 October 1960; 11 October 1960; October 1960; 24 October 1960.

Cubans: Franqui, Carlos, *Family Portrait With Fidel*, New York, Random House, 1984. AG to GC, 25 September 1960.

Mailer: Manso, Peter, *Mailer*, New York: Simon & Schuster, 1985. Mills, Hilary, *Mailer, A Biography*, New York: Empire, 1982.

AG with Leary at Harvard: Leary, Timothy, *Flashbacks, An Autobiography*, Los Angeles, J.P. Tarcher, 1983; *High Priest*, New York, World, 1968; *The Politics of Ecstasy*, London, MacGibbon & Kee, 1970. Kerouac dialog: AG to GC, 8 December 1960. My interview with AG. My conversations with Leary 1967, 1969, 1983. Bryan, John, *Whatever Happened To Timothy Leary?* San Francisco, Renaissance, 1980. Whitmer, Peter, *Aquarius Revisited*.

Sessions with JK, Lowell: AG, unpublished journals. AG, 'Journal Night Thoughts.'

NYC: My interview with Lucien Carr.

Methadrine madness: AG, LHBG lectures.

Chapter Ten: Cut-Ups
My interview with AG of 28 March 1985, covers this period.
Departing NYC: AG to JK, 11 May 1962. AG, *Journals, Early Fifties, Early Sixties* p191. AG to LF, 30 January 1961; 17 February 1961.
Cut-ups: Gysin to the author, 13 February 1984. Gysin, *Planet R-101 Here To Go*. AG to Howard Schulman, October 1961. WSB, GC, Gysin, Beiles, *Minutes To Go*. WSB & Gysin, *The Exterminator, The Third Mind*.
Paris: PO unpublished journals, 22 April 1961–22 May 1961 [in U of Texas, Austin, collection]. AG, unpublished journals. AG to LF, nd [April 1961].
WSB's application of cut-ups to life: AG, LHBG lectures. AG to LeRoi Jones, 3 March 1961.
AG & PO in Tangier: [Note that Ginsberg always uses the French spelling, Tanger.] AG, unpublished mss, 'A wooden table on an Arab roof.' AG, *Journals, Early Fifties, Early Sixties*. Bowles, Paul, 'A Resumé' in The Beat Book, Without Stopping'. AG to Ted Wilentz, 12 June 1961.
Ian Sommerville: My talks with Sommerville 1965–70. My talks with Brion Gysin, 1964–84. AG, LHBG lectures.
Michael Portman: AG, LHBG lectures. AG to LC, 28 July 1961 [28 June].
Teasing PO: My talk with AG, 21 February 1984.
Conflict between PO and WSB: AG to Howard Schulman, October 1961. AG to LF, nd [October 1961] AG, LHBG lectures.
PO's transcriptions: Ernie Barry, 'A Conversation With Allen Ginsberg' in *City Lights Journal 2* (1964). 'Transcription #2' was made 12 July 1961. 'Transcription #3' was made 16 July 1961. AG and PO, *Straight Heart's Delight*.
PO leaves: PO to JK, 11 May 1961. AG to LF, nd [1961] AG to Howard Schulman, October 1961. AG to PO, 2 August 1961.
Tim Leary in Tangier: Leary, Timothy, *High Priest, Flashbacks*.
Greece: AG, *Journals, Early Fifties, Early Sixties*. AG to Hannah Litzky, 13 October 1961. AG to LF, nd [October 1961]. AG to Charles Olson, 14 August 1961. AG to GC, 30 August 1961; 31 August 1961. AG to LG, 12 November 1961.
Tel Aviv: GC to AG, 14 November 1961. AG to LF, 20 December 1961. AG to Diane diPrima, 30 November 1961. AG to LG, 2 November 1961; nd [November 1961]; 29 November 1961. AG to JK, 11 May 1962.
PO's family problems: EB to AG, 3 December 1961. AG to EB, 20 December 1961.
Martin Buber: AG, *Journals, Early Fifties, Early Sixties*, p191.

Chapter Eleven: India
Opening quote adapted from Snyder, Gary, *Passage Through India*, San Francisco, Grey Fox, 1983, p61.
India: AG, *Indian Journals*. Kyger, Joanne, *The Japan & India Journals, 1960–1964*, Bolinas, Tombouctu, 1981. Snyder, Gary, *Passage Through*

India. My interview with AG of 28 March 1985. My conversations with PO, particularly 1970. My conversations with Manjula Mitra, 1965–6. David Widgery, interview with AG in *U* magazine, (summer 1965). Alice Glaser, 'Back On The Open Road For Boys', *Esquire* v60 No 1 [356] (July 1963) AG, 'The Rain On Dasaswamedh', The *Illustrated Weekly of India* (4 March, 84.) Lafcadio O in trouble: PO to Kate & Marie Orlovsky, nd [1962].

Bombay & Calcutta: AG to LF, 25 February 1962. GC to AG, 9 March 1962. AG to GC, 19 April 1962. AG to Ted Wilentz, 24 April 1962. AG to LF, 24 April 1962. AG to JK, 11 May 1962. PO to LC, 29 May 1962. AG to PO, 6 June 1962. AG to Paul Bowles, 28 June 1962. AG to Robert LaVigne, 30 June 1962. AG to JK, 29 July 1962; 9 September 1962. AG to LC, 6 October 1962. AG to LG, 11 October 1962. AG to LF, nd [1962]. PO to Ted Wilentz, 25 October 1962. AG to LF, 2 November 1962. AG to Paul Bowles, nd [1962] AG to WCW, 19 November 1962.

Benares: AG, unpublished journals. AG to LG, 10 January 1963. AG to LF, 10 January 1963. AG to LC, nd [1963]. AG to LF, 1 February 1963. AG to Ted Wilentz, 2 March 1963. AG to Paul Bowles, nd [March 1963] AG to LF, 15 March 1963. AG to GC, 21 March 1963. AG to Ted Wilentz, 21 March 1963. AG to GC, 5 May 1963. AG to JK, 8 May 1963. AG to PO, 25 May 1963. AG to LG, 14 June 1963.

Chapter Twelve: The Change
My interview with AG of 28 March 1985 covers this chapter.

S.E. Asia: AG, unpublished journals. AG, 'The Change'. [original in journals]. Kyger, Joanne, *The Japan & India Journals*. AG interview *Paris Review* 37 (Spring, 1966). [AG in Saigon] 'Buddhists Find A Beatnik Spy' by David Halberstam, *New York Times* 6 June 1963. AG interview with Ernie Barry, *City Lights Journal* 2. San Francisco, 1964. JK to AG, 29 June 1963.

Bankok: AG to PO, 31 May 1963; 4 June 1963.

Thailand: AG to PO, 6 June 1963; 11 June 1963.

Japan: AG to LF, 14 June 1963. AG to PO, 16 June 1963; 27 June 1963; 28 June 1963; 1 July 1963; 9 July 1963; 14 July 1963.

Vancouver: AG, unpublished journals. AG to LF, 5 August 1963. AG to John Wieners, 16 August 1963. AG to LF, 19 August 1963. AG to LC, 19 August 1963.

San Francisco: AG, unpublished journals. Weil, Andrew T., 'The Strange Case of the Harvard Drug Scandal' in *Look*, 5 November, 1963. CIA memorandum dated 1 November 1963 concerning Richard Alpert and Tim Leary. AG, 'Statement to the Burning Bush', *Burning Bush II*, 1963. My interview with Lucien Carr of 9 March 1986. My interview with Lawrence Ferlinghetti of 20 March 1986. My interview with Michael McClure of 19 March 1986. My interview with Shig Murao of 22 March 1986. My interview with Philip Whalen of 16 March 1986. AG to PO, 17 August 1963; 29 August 1963; 18 September 1963 [cable]. AG to JK, 6

October 1963. AG to Charles Olson, 6 October 1963. AG to PO, 10 October 1963; 1 November 1963; 20 November 1963. AG to LC, 22 November 1963. AG to PO, 29 November 1963.

New York: Taylor Mead interview in *Gay Sunshine Interviews Vol 1*. AG intro to JK, *Visions of Cody*. Bob Dylan, sleeve 'Bringing It All Back Home'. Nat Freedland, 'Allen Ginsberg and The Law' in *New York Herald Tribune* 24 May 1964. AG to PO, 6 October 1963; 29 August 1963. Alan Ansen to AG, 1 October 1963. AG, unpublished journals. AG interview *New York Post* 5 March 1964. AG to LF, 14 March 1964. AG to LF, 4 April 1964. AG to LF, 10 August, 64. AG to LF, 12 August 1964; 30 September, 64. AG to Charles Olson, 21 October, 64.

Underground movies: AG, unpublished journals. Conversations with Gerard Malanga, 1984–6. AG to LF, 13 January, 64.

Kerista community: Rose Pettet: 'Thinking of Allen' in *Best Minds*.

Orgies: Conversations with Ann Buchanan, 1971–79. Conversations with Gerard Malanga, 1965–87. Conversations with Peter Orlovsky 1970–71. My interview with AG. AG interview with Bruce Kawin, October 1964 for WKCR-FM (Columbia University).

JK: AG to JK, nd [1964]; 26 February 1964; 10 June 1964. Problems with JK: AG to JK, April 1964; 20 June 1964.

LeMar: *New York Herald Tribune* 28 December 1984. My conversations with Michael Aldrich in 1969. *The Marijuana Review* 1–6. The *Marijuana Newsletter* 1–2.

Cambridge, Mass: AG to LF, 3 December 1964.

Chapter Thirteen: The King of May
Cuba: Virtually all material on Cuba comes from the three volumes of Ginsberg's unpublished Cuban journals. *El Mundo* 20 January 1965. *Bohemia* 5 February 1965. *El Mundo* 7 February 1965. *Hoy* 18 February 1965.

The El Puente group: No charges were brought against the boys but eight years later, on 23 August 1973, Manuel Ballagas was arrested and charged with writing poems and other literature critical of Cuba and of sending 'social information' to the US agent, Allen Ginsberg. They had maintained a correspondence over the years, some of which must have been intercepted. Ballagas was jailed for four years and eventually moved to the USA, paid for, in part, by Ginsberg. See 'When Police Took Poems, They Took His Heart, Too', *Miami Herald*, 16 August 1980. AG to LC, 17 January 1965. AG to LF, 18 January 1965. AG to PO, 4 February 1965; 5 February 1965; 15 February 1965. AG to Nicanor Parra, 20 August 1965.

Prague: My interview with Josef Skvorecky, 20 September 1984. Literarni Noviny 6 March 1965. Joseph Skvorecky entry, *Contemporary Authors Autobiography Series*, Volume 1. Igor Hajek to BM, nd. [October 1984]. AG to PO, 26 February 1965. AG to LF, nd. AG to PO, 1 March 1965; 12 March 1965.

Moscow: AG, unpublished journals. AG to PO, 17 March 1965; 27 March 1965. AG to Ed Sanders, 28 March 1965. AG to LC, 28 March 1965. AG to PO, 31 March 1965; 5 April 1965. AG to Charles Olson, 6 April 1965.

Prague [second visit]: AG to PO, 4 May 1965. AG, unpublished journals, 1994.

Chapter Fourteen: Into The Vortex

This period is covered by my interview with AG of 17 February 1986.

London: Tom McGrath, 'Ginsberg In London' in *Peace News*, 28 May 1965. AG to Nicanor Parra, 20 August 1965. GC to AG, nd. AG interview with David Widgery in *U* magazine, summer 1965. Pennebaker, D.A., Dylan, Bob, *Don't Look Back*, New York, Ballentine, 1968. My conversation with George Harrison, June, 1987. Kostelanetz, Richard, 'Ginsberg Makes The World Scene' in *New York Times* Magazine 11 July 1965. My notes made at the time. AG to PO, 25 May 1965; 10 June 1965; nd [p/c]. AG to the editor of *The Times* 19 June 1965.

Berkeley: The Berkeley Poetry Conference, 12–24 July, programme. AG, unpublished journals. 'Allen Ginsberg's suggestions for 20 November: Demonstration or Spectacle As Example, As Communication.' [unpublished document], Reynolds Frank,[with McClure, Michael], *Freewheelin' Frank*. Hell's Angels comment by Terry the Tramp quoted in Thompson, Hunter S., *Hell's Angels*, New York, Random House, 1966.

Dylan: *Les Crane Show*, February 1965. KQED-TV press conference, December 1965. My interview with Michael McClure of 19 March 1986. AG to PO, 18 August 1965. AG to BM, 20 August 1965. AG to PO, 28 August 1965; 1 September 1965. AG to GC nd. AG to PO, 9 September 1965; 10 September 1965. AG to GC, 29 September 1965.

Midwest: conversations with Ann Buchanan 1970–1977. 'Auto-poesy' tapes in Ginsberg archive.

New York: AG, LHBG lectures. Leary ad was in *New York Times*, 3 April 1966. The details of the Martin/Wilbourn case are in Little Caesar 9, Los Angeles 1979, p382–392. See also 'U.S. Plot to "Set Up" Ginsberg For Arrest Is Described To Jury' in *New York Times*, 14 April 1966 and Jay Levin, 'Jazzman Who Accused Feds Is Convicted' in *New York Post*, 15 April 1966.

LSD Hearings: The Narcotics Rehabilitation Act of 1966.

San Francisco: My interview with Larry Fagin of 23 January 1986. I have also referred to issues of *San Francisco Oracle*, and the *Berkeley Barb* for the period. AG, LHBG lectures. AG to BM, 29 September 1965. AG, NC, Carolyn Cassady, PO to JK, 1 October 1965. AG to Charles Olson, 26 October 1965. AG to LG: 6 November 1965. AG to Ted Wilentz, 23 November 1965. AG to LG, 29 November 1965. AG to HH, 5 December 1965. AG to LF, 24 December 1965. 'The Hippies, Philosophy of a Subculture', *Time*, 7 July 1967.

PO breakdown: AG to EB, 7 August 1967. AG to PO, 10 August 1967; 7 October 1967; 16 November 1967.

Ginsberg in London: Grogan, Emmett, *Ringolevio*. AG, unpublished journals. Sinclair, Iain, *The Kodak Mantra Diaries*. AG to PO, 12 July 1967; 18 July 1967; 26 July 1967.

Record pressing plant problems: Joe Berke to BM. 23 October 1968.

AG with Ezra Pound: AG, 'Encounters with Ezra Pound', Composed on the Tongue. Reck, Michael, *Ezra Pound: A Close Up*, New York, McGraw-Hill, 1973, pp150–159. Levy, Alan, *Ezra Pound: The Voice of Silence*, Sag Harbor, N.Y., Permanent Press, 1983. AG interview with Robert Kramer, for Antioch, 1967 (unpublished?). AG to LF, 29 September 1967. AG to PO, 25 October 1967; 2 November 1967. AG to LF, 11 November 1967; 26 November 1967. AG to BM, 19 December 1967.

Chapter Fifteen: Paterfamilias
I made much use of AG's unpublished journals for this period. The period is also covered by my interviews with AG of 28 March 1985, 17, 18 February 1986.

PO's Methadrine addiction: Notes made during visits to the farm in 1969 and when I moved there in 1970.

The meeting of AG and the Maharishi is taken from AG to BM, 13 October 1967. AG to BM, 29 December 1967. All dialogue from AG to BM, 24 January 1968.

Neal's death: Louis Cartwright, 'Message from Mexico', The *Beat Diary*. Note: The facts of this article are disputed by Ginsberg. I have used his own recollection of first hearing of the death of NC. See also AG: 'Elegy for Neal Cassady', *Collected Poems*. Notes from my conversations with Janice Brown, 1970.

Buying Cherry Valley farm: Gordon Ball to AG, 19 January 1969. 2 July 1968, given as date for downpayment in COP records. My interview with Gordon Ball, 26 November 1984. AG to BM, 31 August 1969. AG to LF, 9 September 1969.

Barbara Rubin: My interview with Gordon Ball, 26 November 1984. My interview with AG, 18 February 1986. See also Gordon Ball, '66 Frames.

Days of unrest: PO at Salem State College Symposium, April 1973.

Chicago 1968: List of delegates to National Peace Convention made by 113th Military Intelliegence Group, Fort Sheridan, Ill. (obtained by AG using the Freedom of Information Act). FBI memorandums of 27 September 1968; 30 September 1968; 1 October 1968; 1 October 1968, show how intense the FBI surveillance of AG was following the convention. AG interview in *Playboy*, April 1969. AG, Chicago Trial Testimony. AG, LHBG lectures. 'Scruffy Vagabonds Who Shook Up America', *National Observer*, 9 December 1968.

Kerouac's anti-Semitism: AG, LHBG lectures.

I observed AG composing the Blake songs while I stayed on the farm in 1969. See also AG interviewed by Alison Colbert and Anita Box, *West*

End 1, 1971. AG to BM, 19 November 1968. Charters, Ann, *Beats and Company*.

Car crash: AG to LF, 7 December 1969. AG to Charles Olson, 7 December 1969. AG to Shigeyoshi Murao, 7 December 1969. AG, unpublished journals.

I was the producer of *William Blake's Songs of Innocence and Experience*, Tuned by Allen Ginsberg, released on Verve FTS 3083. Reviewed in detail in *Blake Newsletter* 4, no 3 (Winter 1971).

Jack Kerouac's death: Ehrmann, Eric, and Davis, Stephen, 'There Really Is Nothing Inside', *Rolling Stone*, 29 November 1969. Holmes, John Clellon, 'Gone In October', *Cambridge Phoenix* 1, no 4 (30 October 1969). AG to Carolyn Cassady, 19 February 1970. Also described in all the biographies of JK. My conversations with AG on the farm, late 1969–70.

Chicago Trial: *The Chicago Trial Conspiracy vs. the Washington Kangaroos: Official Pogrom* (New York, Grove Press, 1969). Official trial transcript. *New York Times*, 12 December 1969. Nicholas von Hoffman, 'The Chicago Conspiracy Circus,' *Playboy*, December 1970.

Rubin's intentions are described in Abe Peck, Uncovering the Sixties. Also AG: LHBG lectures, AG unpublished journals.

I lived on the Cherry Valley farm March–October 1970, and the descriptions of Gregory Corso, Ray Bremser, Julius Orlovsky, PO's speed problem, etc., are taken from my journals. Also BM to WSB, 4 August 1970. PO on speed: AG, unpublished journals, 28 June 1970. Also AG archive tape 70D1/001 (20 June 1970). Ray Bremser to AG, 29 October 1969. AG to LF, 13 July 1970. AG to GC, 14 August 1970.

CIA smuggling drugs: See AG, *Allen Verbatim*. Levine, Steve, 'All of Us Have a Stake in Allen Ginsberg's Bet', *Denver Post*, 6 June 1971. Lewis, Flora, 'CIA and Drugs', *L.A. Times* Syndicate column, 6 May 1971. *New York Times*, 11 August 1971. Anderson, Jack, *Washington Post*, 22 March 1971.

Poem 'What Was The Vietnam War' from AG unpublished journals.

Chapter Sixteen: The Lion of Dharma

My interview with AG, 20 April 1986, covers this period.

Richard Howard: AG: *New York Times*, 4 April 1971.

Muktananda: My interview with AG, 20 April 1986.

Trungpa: Meeting Trungpa is covered in detail in an interview by James Harris, 21 August 1971 (unpublished? MS. in AG archives.) AG interviewed by Rick Fields, Boulder, 1971 (unpublished?). AG interviewed by Peter Chowka in *New Age Journal*, April 1976. AG interviewed by Irving Rosenthal in Kaliflower 3, no. 17 (26 August 1971).

AG shaves beard: AG, unpublished journals.

Homosexual rights: The Stonewall riot was 27 June 1969. 'Allen's Barb Ad' leaflet issued by *The Effeminist*, Berkeley, 1971.

John Lennon: AG unpublished journals. AG to BM, 13 October 1971.

Buddhist vows: My interview with AG. AG to George Dowden, 21 July 1972. AG to BM, 31 July 1972.

Bly, Snyder, Trungpa reading: Sanders, Ed, *The Party*. Clark, Tom, *The Great Naropa Poetry Wars*. My interview with Bob Rosenthal, 3 April 1986.

Kissinger: my interview with Gordon Ball, 26 November 1984.

Vietnam vets at Miami: AG, 'Television Address 1972', MS. See Rips, Geoffrey, *Unamerican Activities*, for details of the FBI Counterintelligence Programme against the New Left; see particularly the 12-point programme of 5 July 1968, recommending 'misinformation.'

Timothy Leary: AG to Leary's judge, telegram, 25 February 1970. Also AG, 'Declaration of Independence for Dr. Timothy Leary', 'Mock Sestina: The Conspiracy Against Dr. Tim Leary,' issued as a flier for Rallying Point, 16 May 1973.

Abbie Hoffman as cocaine dealer: AG letter to Liberation, September. 1973.

Meditation: PO to BM, 20 May 1972. 'Jackson Hole Meditation Sessions,' MS. AG to BM and Ann Buchanan, 24 September 1973. AG to BM, 14 September 1974.

CIA overthrows Allende: AG, unpublished journals.

W.H. Auden's death: AG, unpublished journals.

WSB and meditation: AG to BM, 14 February 1974.

Building house in California: Conversations with PO, 1977. AG, unpublished journals. My interview with AG.

Kerouac School: 42-page untitled transcript of an interview (c. 1975) with AG from AG archives gives detailed description of meeting Trungpa, starting Kerouac School, etc. 'General Practice of Kerouac School of Disembodied Poetics at Naropa Institute,' MS from AG archives.

'Ego Confession': AG, *Collected Poems*. Details in AG, unpublished journals.

Mugging: *New York Times*, 5 January 1975. And in AG, *Collected Poems*.

Details of the Columbia reading are from a transcript made by Victor Bockris.

Boulder: AG conversation with BM, summer 1983.

Rolling Thunder tour: *NME* (London), 6 December 1975. My interviews with Rob Stoner and Howie Wyeth, 1976 (for *NME*). On the road with Dylan: AG, unpublished journals. Cocaine: 'AG and Andrei Voznesensky in Conversation', *Paris Review* 78 (Summer 1980). Shepard, Sam, *Rolling Thunder Logbook*. Rolling Thunder dawn ceremony: Sloman, Larry, *On the Road With Bob Dylan*. All conversations with Dylan taken from AG, unpublished journals. Other details are from my conversations with Denise Mercedes and PO during and after the tour and from the Rolling Thunder tour daily newsletter. See the four-hour version of Bob Dylan's film *Renaldo and Clara* for AG reading 'Kaddish', sitting with Dylan at Kerouac's grave, and other scenes. AG to GC [1975]. AG to BM, 17 November 1975.

The assault on Merwin and Naone is taken from Sanders, Ed, *The Party*, and Clark, Tom, *The Great Naropa Poetry Wars*. AG and Jacqueline Gens both read through the sections of the MS on Trungpa and made various suggestions, correcting errors in Clark's book and clarifying certain points. I have used much of the new material provided by them. Material is also taken from my interviews with AG on 23 September 1988; 24 September 1988; 30 September 1988; 2 October 1988; 4 October 1988. Other details of Tibetan practices here and later are taken from my own library of Tibetan studies. The principal works consulted were: Dasgupta, Shashibhusan, *Obscure Religious Cults*, Calcutta, Mukhopadhyay, 1969; Ekvall, Robert, *Religious Observances in Tibet*, Chicago, University of Chicago, 1964; Anuruddha, R.P., *An Introduction to Lamaism*, Hoshiarpur, Vishveshvaranand Vedic Research Institution, 1959; Hoffman, Helmut, *The Religions of Tibet*, London, George Allen & Unwin, 1961; Carrasco, Pedro, *Land and Polity in Tibet*, Seattle, University of Washington, 1959; Norbu, Thubten Jigme and Turnbull, Colin, *Tibet, Its History, Religion and People*, London, Chatto & Windus, 1969. I also drew on conversation with Trungpa in the late sixties in London, 1970 in New York, and 1971 in Berkeley. I visited Tail of the Tiger and the Maitri Center with AG in 1973. AG interviewed by Peter Chowka for *New Age Journal*, April 1976. AG interviewed by Paul Portuges, July 1976, published in *Boston University Journal* 125, no. 1 (1977). Coe, Robert, 'Dharma Matter', *Village Voice*, 20 November 1978.

AG and John Lennon: AG, unpublished journals, and my interview with AG, 20 April 1986.

'Father Death Blues': AG, *Collected Poems*.

Louis Simpson review of *Journals*: *New York Times* Book Review, 23 October 1977.

Further details on Merwin affair from Sanders, Ed, *The Party* and Clark, Tom, *The Great Naropa Poetry Wars*. AG quote on Guyana from AG, unpublished journals. Wood, Robert [Tom Clark], 'Buddha Gate: Scandal and Cover-up at Naropa Revealed', *Berkeley Barb*, 29 March 1979.

Chapter Seventeen: Eminence Grise

My interviews with AG, 20 April 1986; 23 September 1988; 24 September 1988; 30 September 1988; 2 October 1988; 4 October 1988, cover this period. All quotes from Bob Rosenthal are my interview with him of 11 November 1999.

I am grateful to Victor Bockris, who provided me with a transcript of the National Book Awards ceremony. AG commented on the misspelling in a telephone call to the author a few weeks after the event.

Heritage Foundation and neoconservative reaction to Clark's book from my interview with AG, 20 April 1986, and from his extensive documentary files on the subject. The Republican attempt to withdraw NEA poetry funding was reported in the *New York Times*, 10 September 1985.

East European trip: My interview with Steven Taylor, 21 April 1986. Details of Barbara Rubin's death reported to me by Rosebud Pettet and AG in conversation at the time.

WSB Jr.'s death: AG, unpublished journals. AG, LHBG lectures. Morgan, Ted, *Literary Outlaw: The Life and Times of William Burroughs* details Billy's illness and death.

AG and The Clash: My interviews with AG. AG, unpublished journals. AG interviewed by Michael Schumacher, 11 March 1982; 23 March 1982 (unpublished?). AG interviewed by Katharyn Machan Aal at Cornell University, 20 June 1981 (transcript of a broadcast on college radio?). AG interview with Michael Feldman, 20 February 1982 for Red Hand 3. AG interview with Will Doherty, 8 March 1982, for Link 3.

AG's teaching methods: Explained to Nancy Bunge at Michigan State University, February 1981; published in *Washington Post*, 29 July 1984.

AG's meeting with Borges: AG, unpublished journals, and my interview with AG, 20 April 1986.

Peter's trip to Boulder: AG, unpublished journals.

Kerouac Conference: AG, unpublished journals. Allen, Henry, '25 Years Later', *Washington Post* 'Style', 2 August 1982. Schmidt, William, 'Beat Generation Elders Meet To Praise Kerouac', *New York Times*, 30 July 1982. Robertson, William, 'On the Road Again', *Miami Herald*, 24 October 1982. 'Celebrating the Beat Spirit', *Naropa Institute Bulletin*, February 1982. 'Beatnik Gurus Look Ahead and the Young Look Askance', *Philadelphia Inquirer* (date unknown).

Nicaragua: 'Ordinary Mind', AG interview with Jay Rubin, the *Sun 77*, March, 1982. 'Ginsberg On Ginsberg', *Up the Creek*, Denver, 28 May 1982. 'A Moveable Fiesta', AG interview with Ewan Courage, *SoHo Weekly News*, 16 February 1982. 'East Meets West Over a Bottle of Rum in Nicaragua', AG interview with Rod Norland, *San Francisco Examiner*, 13 February 1982. AG interview with S.K. Levin, *Colorado Daily*, 7 May 1982. AG interview with Jay Murphy and Mary Jane Ryals, *Red Bass 7*, 1984. AG interview with Leif Owen Klein, *Talking Heads 2* (Spring 1982). AG interview with Mark Kingsley, *Reporter*, 10 February 1984. AG interview, *Dartmouth Review*, 8 April 1984 (also discussed censorship).

Death of Oleg Orlovsky: AG, unpublished journals.

Scandinavian tour: AG, unpublished journals. My conversation with Simon Vinkenoog, Amsterdam, summer 1987 and London 1999.

USIA blacklist: Joel Brinkley, 'USIA's "Blacklist" ', *New York Times*, 15 March 1984.

'White Shroud', *New York Times* Magazine, 11 November 1984.

China: 'China Notebook' (unpublished). Salisbury, Harrison E., 'On the Literary Road: American Writers in China', *New York Times* Book Review, 20 January 1985. AG, 'China Through a Poet's Eyes', *San Jose Mercury News*, 20 February 1985 (released through UPI; appeared in a number of other papers, including *San Francisco Examiner*).

Collected Poems reviews: Rosenblatt, Roger, 'A Major Minor Poet', *New Republic*, 4 March 1985. Richman, Robert, 'Allen Ginsberg Then and Now', *Commentary 80*, no 1 (July 1985). *City Limits*, 24 May 1985. *Philadelphia Inquirer*, 15 March 1985. Maddox, Sam, 'Allen Ginsberg: Portrait of a Popular Poet', *Boulder Camera*, 14 April 1985. Remnick, David, 'The World & Allen Ginsberg', *Washington Post*, 17 March 1985. Abrams, Garry, 'Allen Ginsberg Still Controversial', *Los Angeles Times*, 18 April 1985. *Chicago Tribune*, 10 February 1985. *USA Today*, 4 January 1985. McCormack, Ed, 'A Real Howl', *N.Y. Daily News* Magazine, 19 May 1985. Cook, Bruce, 'Allen Ginsberg: The Beat Goes On', *Washington Post* Book World, 13 January 1985. Valeo, Tom, 'Ginsberg: He's Indignant As Ever and Proud of It', *Chicago Daily Herald*, 18 April 1985. *Los Angeles Times* Book Review, 20 January 1985. Tucker, Ken, 'Power of Babble', *Village Voice*, 29 January 1985. Sheppard, R.Z., 'Mainstreaming Allen Ginsberg', *Time*, 4 February 1985. Abrams, Alan, 'Still Making Poetic Waves', *Detroit Jewish News*, 1 March 1985. *Cherwell*, 10 May 1985. *Melody Maker*, 11 May 1985. *Detroit Free Press*, 13 February 1985. *Milwaukee Journal*, 4 March 1985. *New Musical Express*, 1 June 1985.

Chapter Eighteen: The Good Grey Poet
All references to journals are from the unpublished journals from this period in the AG archive in Stanford University. AG's photographic shows: *Washington Post*, 8 January 1985; 13 April 1985. *Miami Herald*, 2 February 1987. *Aperture 101* (winter, 1985). *Vanity Fair* 48 no 1 (January 1985).

William Gass: 'East vs. West in Lithuania: Rising Tempers at a Writers' Meeting' *New York Times* Book Review, 2 February 1986.

PO's breakdown: My interview with Bob Rosenthal of 11 November 1999. My interview with AG, 2 October 1988; 4 October 1988.

Charters, Ann, 'White Shroud', *Los Angeles Times*, 15 February 1987.

Death of Trungpa: My conversations with AG at the time. Goldman, Ari L., '2,000 Attend Buddhist Cremation Rite In Vermont', *New York Times*, 27 May 1987.

Pacifica Radio: 'Allen Ginsberg On Why He Can't Broadcast Howl', *Pacifica Radio*, press release, 31 December 1987.

AG in Israel: *New York Post*, 29 February 1988. *San Francisco Examiner*, 24 January 1988 (from AP and UPI wire services). Mitgang, Herbert, 'PEN Unit Chides Israel Over Censorship', *New York Times*, 25 June 1988.

Kerouac memorial: Podhoretz, Norman, 'Strange Honor for a False Prophet', *New York Post*, 6 January 1987. AG, 'I Sing of Norman P.,' in *Harpers* magazine, July 1987, reprinted from an interview in *New Letters*, Fall, 1987. *New Yorker*, 18 July 1988.

AG on Harry Smith and Gregory Corso, from unpublished journals and my conversations with AG 1988–9.

Osel Tendzin: Zaslowsky, Dyan, 'Buddhists in U.S. Agonize on AIDS Issue', *New York Times*, 21 February 1989. AG, unpublished journals.

PO breakdown, my interview with Bob Rosenthal, 11 November 1999. AG, unpublished journals. AG to BM in conversation. All following dialogue from AG unpublished journals, including conversations with President Havel. AG stayed with the author on the London segment of this trip.

Korea: AG, 'Seoul Notebooks', unpublished.

Gelek Rinpoche on friendship with AG; 'No More To Say, and Nothing To Weep For', An Elegy for Allen Ginsberg, 1926–1997, a one-hour documentary film by Colin Still, was screened on Channel Four (UK) 11 May 1997. It included footage by Jonas Mekas of AG on his death bed.

Visit with Dylan: AG, unpublished journals.

Alene Lee: AG, unpublished journals.

PO breakdown: AG, unpublished journals. My interview with Bob Rosenthal, 11 November 1999. The author was a witness to PO naked with the machete.

Harry Smith: AG, unpublished journals.

Arthur Russell: AG, unpublished journals.

Brooklyn College: AG, unpublished journals.

Carl Solomon: AG, unpublished journals.

Bono and U2: *International Herald Tribune*, 17 November 1993.

Paul Bowles: AG, unpublished journals.

Paul McCartney: the author took AG to visit McCartney, account taken from author's notes and from later conversations with McCartney.

Sale of archives: Bluenthal, Michael, 'Allen Ginsberg, Millionaire?' *New York Times*, 29 October 1994.

McCartney in Long Island: AG, unpublished journals.

Tim Leary: AG, unpublished journals.

'Dance of the Skeletons' CD: AG interviewed by Harvey Kubernik in *Hits*, 11 November 1996, and in *Los Angeles Times*, 7 April 1997. AG, unpublished journals. AG telephone conversation with the author. Author in conversation with Paul McCartney.

AG's death: AG telephone conversation with the author, 3 April 1997; 'No More To Say, and Nothing To Weep For', An Elegy for Allen Ginsberg, 1926–1997. James Grauerholz to BM, email April 5, 1997; Waldman, Anne, Brooks, Eugene, Taylor, Steven, Felieu-Pettet, Rosebud and di Prima, Diane: 'On Allen Ginsberg and William Burroughs' *Poetry Project Newsletter* 166, October/November 1997. Author interview with Bob Rosenthal, 11 November 1999, and my conversation with Peter Hale.

Afterword

My interview with Bob Rosenthal, 11 November 1999. *Rolling Stone* 761, (29 May 1997). Roger Kimball, 'The Death of Decency', *Wall Street Journal*, 12 August 1997.

Bibliography

Bibliography of books consulted. (This is not a complete bibliography of any of these writers.)

Books By Allen Ginsberg:
[With Cassady, Neal]: *As Ever, The Collected Correspondence* (Berkeley, Creative Arts, 1977)
[With Orlovsky, Peter]: *Straight Hearts' Delight, Love Poems & Selected Letters* (San Francisco, Gay Sunshine, 1980)
Airplane Dreams: Compositions From Journals (Toronto, Anansi, 1968)
Allen Ginsberg On Tour (Wuppertal, Lichtblick, 1983)
Allen Ginsberg: Photographs (Altadena, CA, Twelvetrees, 1991)
Allen Verbatim, Lectures On Poetry, Politics, Consciousness (NY, McGraw-Hill, 1974)
Ankor Wat (London, Fulcrum, 1968)
Bixby Canyon Ocean Path Word Breeze (NY, Gotham Book Mart, 1972)
Careless Love (Madison, Red Ozier, 1978)
Chicago Trial Testimony (San Francisco, City Lights, 1975)
Collected Poems 1947–1980 (NY, Harper & Row, 1985)
Composed on the Tongue (Bolinas, Grey Fox, 1980)
Cosmopolitan Greetings (NY, Harper & Row, 1994)
Death & Fame, Last Poems 1993–1997 (NY, HarperFlamingo, 1999)
Declaration of Independence for Dr Timothy Leary, July 4, 1971 (San Francisco, Hermes Free Press, 1971)
Documents On Police Bureaucracy's Conspiracy ... nd.np [self-published, NY, 1970]
Empty Mirror (NY, Totem/Corinth, 1961)
First Blues, Rags, Ballads & Harmonium Songs 1971–74 (NY, Full Court, 1975)
Fotografier 1947–87 (Arhus, Klim, 1987)
Gay Sunshine Interview With Allen Young (Bolinas, Grey Fox, 1974)
Honorable Courtship (np, Coffeehouse, 1993)

Howl and other Poems (San Francisco, City Lights, 1956)
Howl, Original Draft Facsimile (NY, Harper & Row, 1986)
Improvised Poetics (San Francisco, Anonym, 1972)
Indian Journals (San Francisco, City Lights, 1970)
Journals, Early Fifties, Early Sixties (NY, Grove, 1977)
Journals, Mid Fifties 1951–1958 (NY, HarperCollins, 1995)
Iron Horse (Toronto, Coach House, 1972)
Kaddish and Other Poems (San Francisco, City Lights, 1961)
Luminous Dreams (Gran Canaria, Zasterle, 1997)
Many Loves (NY, Pequod, 1984)
Mind Breaths (San Francisco, City Lights, 1978)
Mind Writing Slogans (Boise, Limberlost, 1994)
Mostly Sitting Haiku (Paterson, From Here, 1978)
Mystery in the Universe [Allen Ginsberg Interviewed by Edward Lucie-
    Smith] (London, Turret, 1965)
New Year Blues (NY, Phoenix Bookshop, 1972)
Old Love Story (NY, Lospecchio, 1986)
Poems All Over The Place, Mostly 'Seventies (Cherry Valley, NY, Cherry
    Valley, 1978)
Planet News (San Francisco, City Lights, 1968)
Plutonian Ode (San Francisco, City Lights, 1982)
Prose Contribution To Cuban Revolution (Detroit, Artists' Workshop,
    1966)
Reality Sandwiches (San Francisco, City Lights, 1963)
The Riverside Interviews 1: Allen Ginsberg (London, Binnacle, 1980)
Sad Dust Glories (Berkeley, Workingman's Press, 1975)
Scrap Leaves (Millbrook, NY, Poets' Press, 1968)
The Change (London, Writers' Forum, 1963)
The Fall of America. Poems On These States 1965–1971 (San Francisco,
    City Lights, 1972)
The Gates of Wrath (Bolinas, Grey Fox, 1972)
The Visions of the Great Rememberer (Amherst, Mulch, 1974)
To Eberhart From Ginsberg (Lincoln, Mass, Penmaen, 1976)
The Change (London, Writers' Forum, 1963)
Thieves Stole This Poem (Hull, Carnivorous, 1993)
TV Baby Poems (London, Cape-Goliard, 1967)
Visiting Father & Friends (Louisville, Thinker Review, 1993)
Wales, A Visitation (London, Cape Goliard, 1968)
White Shroud, Poems 1980–1985 (NY, Harper & Row, 1986)
Wichita Vortex Sutra (London, Peace News, 1966)
Your Reason and Blake's System (Madras, Hanuman, 1988)

Books by William S. Burroughs:
The Adding Machine, Collected Essays (London, John Calder, 1985)
The Burroughs File (San Francisco, City Lights, 1984)
The Job (NY, Grove 1972, 1974 [revised])

Junkie (NY, Ace, 1953)

Junky (NY, Penguin, 1977)

(Harris, Oliver [Ed]): *The Letters of William Burroughs 1945–1959* (London, Picador, 1993)

Letters to Allen Ginsberg (Genéve, Claude Givaudan, 1978)

The Naked Lunch (Paris, Olympia, 1959)

Queer (NY, Viking, 1985)

Roosevelt After Inauguration (NY, Fuck Press, 1964)

The Soft Machine (Paris, Olympia, 1960)

(Grauerholz, James [Ed]): *Word Virus, the William S. Burroughs Reader* (NY, Grove, 1999)

[W/Ginsberg, Allen]: *The Yage Letters* (San Francisco, 1960)

[W/Gysin, Brion]: *The Exterminator* (San Francisco, Auerhahn, 1960)

[W/Gysin, Brion]: *The Third Mind* (NY, Seaver, 1978)

[W/Corso, Gregory; Gysin, Brion; Beiles, Sinclair]: *Minutes To Go* (Paris, Two Cities, 1960)

Books by Jack Kerouac:

Big Sur (NY, Bantam, 1963)

Dear Carolyn, Letters to Carolyn Cassady (California, PA, Unspeakable Visions of the Individual, 1983)

Desolation Angels (London, Granada, 1972)

Doctor Sax (NY, Grove, 1959)

Heaven and Other Poems (San Francisco, Grey Fox, 1977)

Lonesome Traveller (London, André Deutsch, 1962)

Mexico City Blues (NY, Grove, 1959)

On The Road (Harmonsworth, Penguin, 1972)

Pull My Daisy (NY, Grove, 1960)

Satori in Paris (NY, Grove, 1966)

Scattered Poems (San Francisco, City Lights, 1971)

(Charters, Ann [Ed]): *Selected Letters 1940–1956* (NY, Viking, 1995)

(Charters, Ann [Ed]): *Selected Letters 1957–1969* (NY, Viking, 1999)

Some of the Dharma (NY, Viking, 1997)

The Book of Dreams (San Francisco, City Lights, 1961)

The Dharma Bums (London, Granada, 1972)

The Mexican Girl ([Brighton] Pacific Car Press, nd)

The Scripture Of The Golden Eternity (NY, Totem/Corinth, 1960)

The Subterraneans (London, André Deutsch, 1960)

The Town & The City (NY, Grosset & Dunlap, nd)

Tristessa (NY, Avon, 1960)

Vanity of Duluoz (NY, Paragon, 1979)

Visions of Cody (NY, McGraw-Hill, 1973)

Bohemia:

Easton, Malcolm: *Artists and Writers in Paris. The Bohemian Idea, 1803–1867.* (London, Edward Arnold, 1964)

Emile-Bayard, Jean: *Montmartre Past and Present* (NY, Brentano's, nd.)

Miller, Richard: *Bohemia, The Protoculture Then and Now* (Chicago, Nelson-Hall, 1977)

Murger, Henri: *The Bohemians of the Latin Quarter (Scènes de la Vie de Bohême)* (Paris, Société Des Beaux-Arts, 1915)

Parry, Alfred: *Garrets and Pretenders, a History of Bohemianism In America* (NY, Dover, Revised ed. 1960)

Richardson, Joanna: *The Bohemians* (South Brunswick, A.S. Barnes, 1971)

The Beats:

Allen, Donald & Butterick, George F. (Eds): *The Postmoderns* (NY, Grove, 1982)

Allen, Donald & Tallman, Warren (Eds): *The Poetics of the New American Poetry* (NY, Grove, 1973)

Allen, Donald (Ed.): *The New American Poetry, 1945–1960* (NY, Grove, 1960)

Bartlett, Lee: *The Beats, Essays In Criticism* (Jefferson, NC, McFarland, 1981)

Campbell, James: *Paris Interzone* (London, Secker & Warburg, 1994)

Charters, Ann: *Beats And Company* (Garden City, NY, Doubleday, 1986)

Charters, Ann: *The Beats: Literary Bohemians In Postwar America – Part 2. DLB 16.* (Gale Research, Ann Arbor, Michigan, 1983)

Charters, Ann: *Scenes Along The Road* (NY, Portents/Gotham Book Mart, 1970)

Cherkovski, Neeli: *Whitman's Wild Children* (San Francisco, Lapis, 1988)

Cook, Bruce: *The Beat Generation* (NY, Charles Scribners's Sons, 1971)

Clay, Mel: *Jazz-Jail and God, Bob Kaufman* (San Francisco, Androgyne, 1987)

Clay, Steven, and Phillips, Rodney: *A Secret Location on the Lower East Side* (NY, New York Public Library, 1998)

Davidson, Michael: *The San Francisco Renaissance* (Cambridge, Cambridge University Press, 1990)

de Grazia, Edward: *Girls Lean Back Everywhere. The Law of Obscenity and the Assault on Genius* (NY, Random House, 1992)

DiPrima, Diane & Jones, LeRoi: *The Floating Bear, A Newsletter 1–37* (La Jolla, CA, Laurence McGilvery, 1973)

DiPrima, Diane: *Memoirs of a Beatnik* (NY, Olympia, 1969)

Fass, Ekbert: *Towards A New American Poetics, Essays And Interviews* (Santa Barbara, Black Sparrow, 1979)

Feldman, Gene & Gartenberg, Max: *The Beat Generation and the Angry Young Men* (NY, Citadel, 1958)

Ferlinghetti, Lawrence & Peters, Nancy: *Literary San Francisco* (NY, Harper & Row, 1980)

Foster, Edward: *Understanding the Beats* (Columbia, U of South Carolina Press, 1992)

Girodias, Maurice (Ed.): *The Olympia Reader* (NY, Grove, 1965)

Gold, Herbert: *Bohemia* (NY, Simon & Schuster, 1993)

Hickey, Morgan: *The Bohemian Register: an Annotated Bibliography of the Beat Literary Movement* (Metuchen, NJ, Scarecrow, 1990)

Holmes, John C.: *Get Home Free* (NY, Dutton, 1964)

Holmes, John C.: *Go* (NY, New American Library, 1980)

Holmes, John C.: *Nothing More To Declare* (NY, Dutton, 1967)

Honan, Park (Ed.): *The Beats, An Anthology of 'Beat' Writing* (London, J.M. Dent, 1987)

Horemans, Rudi (Ed.): *Beat Indeed!* (Antwerp, EXA, 1985)

Huncke, Herbert: *Huncke's Journal* (NY, Poets Press, 1965)

Huncke, Herbert: *The Evening Sun Turned Crimson* (Cherry Valley, NY, Cherry Valley, 1980)

Huncke, Herbert: [Special Issue] *Unspeakable Visions of the Individual* (California, PA, 1973)

Johnson, Joyce: *Minor Characters* (London, Picador, 1983)

Jones, LeRoi: *The Autobiography of LeRoi Jones/Amiri Baraka* (NY, Freundlich, 1984)

Kelly, John (Ed.): *Beatitude Anthology* (San Francisco, City Lights, 1960)

Kherdian, David: *Beat Voices* (NY, Henry Holt, 1995)

Kherdian, David: *Six San Francisco Poets* (Fresno, Giligia, 1969)

Knight, Arthur & Kit (Eds): *Beat Angels* (California, PA, Unspeakable Visions of the Individual, 1982)

Knight, Arthur & Glee (Eds): *The Beat Book* (California, PA, Unspeakable Visions of the Individual, 1974)

Knight, Arthur & Kit (Eds): *The Beat Diary* (California, PA, Unspeakable Visions of the Individual, 1977)

Knight, Arthur & Kit (Eds): *The Beat Journey* (California, PA, Unspeakable Visions of the Individual, 1978)

Knight, Arthur & Kit (Eds): *The Beat Road* (California, PA, Unspeakable Visions of the Individual, 1984)

Knight, Arthur & Kit (Eds): *The Beat Vision* (NY, Paragon House, 1977)

Knight, Brenda: *Women of the Beat Generation* (Berkeley, CA, Conari, 1996)

Krim, Seymour: *Views Of A Nearsighted Cannoner* (London, Alan Ross, 1969)

Lee, Robert (Ed.): *The Beat Generation Writers* (London, Pluto, 1996)

Lipton, Lawrence: *The Holy Barbarians* (London, W.H. Allen, 1960)

Malina, Judith: *The Diaries of Judith Malina, 1947–1957* (NY, Grove, 1984)

McClure, Michael: *Scratching The Beat Surface* (San Francisco, North Point, 1982)

McDarrah, Fred: *Kerouac & Friends, A Beat Generation Album* (NY, William Morrow, 1985)

McDarrah, Fred & Gloria: *Beat Generation, Glory Days in Greenwich Village* (NY, Schirmer, 1996)

Norse, Harold: *Beat Hotel* (San Diego, Atticus, 1983)

608   Ginsberg

Nowinski, Ira: *Café Society, Photographs and Poetry from San Francisco's North Beach* (San Francisco, Carolyn Bean, 1978)

Ossman, David: *The Sullen Art* (NY, Corinth, 1963)

Parkinson, Thomas (Ed.): *Casebook On The Beat* (NY, Crowell, 1961)

Peabody, Richard (Ed.): *A Different Beat, Writings by Women of the Beat Generation* (London, High Risk, 1997)

Perloff, Marjorie: *Frank O'Hara, Poet Among Painters* (Austin, University of Texas, 1977)

Phillips, Lisa: *Beat Culture and the New America 1950–1965* (NY, Whitney Museum of American Art, 1996

Polsky, Ned: *Hustlers, Beats and Others* (NY, Anchor, 1969)

Rigney, Francis J. and Smith, L. Douglas: *The Real Bohemia* (NY, basic, 1961)

Rosset, Barney (Ed.): *The Evergreen Review Reader, 1957–1961* (NY, Grove, 1979)

Sargeant, Jack: *Naked Lens, Beat Cinema* (London, Creation, 1997)

Sawyer-Lauçanno, Christopher: *The Continual Pilgrimage, American Writers in Paris 1944–1960* (London, Bloomsbury, 1992)

Saroyan, Aram: *Genesis Angels. The Saga Of Lew Welch & The Beat Generation* (NY, William Morrow, 1979)

Seaver, Richard; Southern, Terry & Trocchi, Alexander (Eds): *Writers In Revolt, An Anthology* (NY, Frederick Fell, 1963)

Simpson, Louis: *A Revolution In Taste* (NY, Macmillan, 1978)

Snyder, Gary: *The Real Work, Interviews and Talks 1964–1979* (NY, New Directions, 1980)

Solomon, Carl: *Mishaps Perhaps* (San Francisco, Beach Books, Texts & Documents, 1966)

Solomon, Carl: *More Mishaps* (San Francisco, Beach Books, Texts & Documents, 1968)

Stephenson, Gregory: *The Daybreak Boys* (Carbondale, Southern Illinois U.P. 1990)

Tonkinson, Carole (Ed.): *Big Sky Mind: Buddhism and the Beat Generation* (NY, Riverhead, 1995)

Watson, Steven: *The Birth of the Beat Generation* (NY, Pantheon, 1995)

Waldman, Anne (Ed.): *The Beat Book* (Boston, Shambala, 1996)

Tytell, John: *Naked Angels* (NY, McGraw-Hill, 1976)

Watts, Alan W.: *Beat Zen Square Zen & Zen* (San Francisco, City Lights, 1959)

Whalen, Philip: *Off The Wall, Interviews With Philip Whalen* (Bolinas, Four Seasons, 1978)

Wilentz, Elias (Ed.): *The Beat Scene* (NY, Corinth, 1960)

The 1950s:

Amram, David: *Vibrations* (NY, Macmillan, 1968)

Broyard, Anatole: *Kafka Was the Rage, a Greenwich Village Memoir* (NY, Vintage, 1993)

Cassady, Carolyn: *Heart Beat. My Life With Jack & Neal* (Berkeley, Creative Arts, 1976)
Chapman, Howard: *The Beat Hotel* (Montpellier, Gris Banal, 1984)
Duberman, Martin: *Black Mountain, An Exploration In Community* (London, Wildwood, 1974)
Ebin, David (Ed.): *The Drug Experience* (NY, Orion, 1961)
Edinger, Claudio: *Chelsea Hotel* (NY, Abbeville, 1984)
Gruen, John: *The Party's Over Now* (NY, Viking, 1972)
Podhoretz, Norman: *Making It* (NY, Random House, 1967)
Podhoretz, Norman: *Ex-Friends* (NY, Free Press, 1999)
Rexroth, Kenneth: *An Autobiographical Novel* (Weybridge, Whittet, 1977)
Richards, Janet: *Common Soldiers* (San Francisco, Archer, 1979)
Rosenthal, Irving: *Sheeper* (NY, Grove, 1967)
Watts, Alan W.: *In My Own Way* (NY, Random House, 1972)
Wolf, Daniel & Fancher (Ed.): *The Village Voice Reader* (Garden City, NY, Doubleday, 1962)

The 1960s:
Alpert, Jane: *Growing Up Underground* (NY, William Morrow, 1983)
Anthony, Gene: *The Summer of Love, Haight-Ashbury At Its Highest* (Millbrae, Celestial Arts, 1980)
Benton, Ralph: *Psychedelic Sex* (Canoga Park, Viceroy, 1968)
Berke, Joseph (Ed.): *Counter Culture* (London, Peter Owen, 1968)
Bremser, Bonnie: *Troia, Mexican Memoirs* (NY, Croton, 1969)
Burroughs, William, Jr: *Kentucky Ham* (London, Picador, 1975)
Burroughs, William, Jr: *Speed* (NY, Olympia, 1970)
Clark, Tom: *Who Is Sylvia?* [novel] (Berkeley, Blue Wind, 1979)
[Congress of the US] *The Narcotics Rehabilitation Act of 1966. Hearings Before A Special Subcommittee of the Committee On The Judiciary United States Senate 89th Congress, Second Session* (Washington DC, 1966)
Davidson, Sara: *Loose Change* (NY, Doubleday, 1977)
Goldman, Albert: *Grass Roots* (NY, Harper & Row, 1979)
Goldman, Albert: *Freakshow* (NY, Atheneum, 1971)
Goodman, Mitchell: *The Movement Toward A New America* (NY, Alfred Knopf, 1970)
Gruen, John: *The New Bohemia* (NY, Shorecrest, 1966)
Gutman, Walter: *The Gutman letter* (NY, Something Else, 1969)
Hayes, Harold (Ed.): *Smiling Through The Apocalypse* (NY, McCall, 1970)
Hewison, Robert: *Too Much, Art & Society In The Sixties, 1960–1975* (London, Methuen, 1986)
Hoffman, Abbie and Anita: *To America With Love* (NY, Stonehill, 1976)
Hoffman, Abbie: *Revolution for the Hell of It* (NY, Dial, 1968)
Hoffman, Abbie: *Soon to be a Major Motion Picture* (NY, Putnam, 1980)

Hoffman, Abbie: *Steal This Book* (NY, Pirate, 1971)

Hoffman, Abbie; Rubin, Jerry; Sanders, Ed: *Vote!* (NY, Warner, 1972)

Hoffman, Abbie: [et al] *The Chicago 8 Speak Out! Conspiracy* (NY, Dell, 1969)

Hoffman, Abbie: *Woodstock Nation* (NY, Vintage, 1969)

Hoffman, Anita [as Fettamen, Ann]: *Trashing* (San Francisco, Straight Arrow, 1970)

Hollingshead, Michael: *The Man Who Turned On The World* (NY, Abelard-Schuman, 1973)

Holmquist, Anders: *The Free People* (NY, Outerbridge & Dienstfrey, 1969)

Hopkins, Jerry (Ed.): *The Hippie Papers* (NY, Signet, 1968)

Howard, Mel & Forcade, Thomas K. (Eds): *The Underground Reader* (NY, New American Library, 1972)

(Igliori, Paola [Ed]): *American Magus, Harry Smith* (NY, Inanout, 1996)

Jamer, Ronard: *Hippie Sex Communes* (LA. Impact, 1970)

Katzman, Allen (Ed.): *Our Time, Interviews From The East Village Other* (NY Dial, 1972)

Kerouac, Jan: *Baby Driver* (NY, Holt Rinehart & Winston, 1981)

Kerouac, Jan: *Trainsong* (NY, Henry Holt, 1988)

Kleps, Art: *Millbrook* (Oakland, Bench, 1977)

Kornbluth, Jesse (Ed.): *Notes From The New Underground* (NY, Viking, 1968)

Kostelanetz, Richard: *Master Minds* (NY, Macmillan, 1969)

Krasner, Paul: *How A Satirical Editor Became A Yippie Conspirator* (NY, Putnam, 1971)

Lee, Martin & Shlain, Bruce: *Acid Dreams* (NY, Grove, 1985)

Lennon, John: *Skywriting By Word Of Mouth* (NY, Harper & Row, 1986)

Lewis, Roger: *Outlaws Of America, The Underground Press and its Context* (London, Heinrich Hanau, 1972)

Leyland, Winston (Ed.): *Gay Sunshine Interviews, v. 1* (San Francisco, Gay Sunshine, 1978)

McNeill, Don: *Moving Through Here* (NY, Alfred Knopf, 1970)

McReynolds, David: *We Have Been Invaded By The 21st Century* (NY, Praeger, 1970)

Miles, Barry: *Paul McCartney: Many Years from Now* (London, Secker & Warburg, 1997)

Peck, Abe: *Uncovering The Sixties, Life and Times of the Underground Press* (NY, Pantheon, 1985)

Peppiatt, Michael: *Francis Bacon: Anatomy of an Enigma* (London, Weidenfeld & Nicholson, 1996)

Raskin, Jonah: *Out Of The Whale, An Autobiography* (NY, Links, 1974)

Rips, G.: *Unamerican Activities, The Campaign Against The Underground Press* (San Francisco, City Lights, 1981)

Rodman, Selden: *Tongues Of Fallen Angels, Conversations With Ginsberg [et al]* (NY, New Directions, 1974)

Rolling Stone (Editors): *The Age Of Paranoia. How The Sixties Ended* (NY, Pocket Books, 1972)

Roszak, Theodore: *The Making of a Counter Culture* (London, Faber, 1970)

Rubin, Jerry: *Do It!* (NY, Simon & Schuster, 1970)

Rubin, Jerry: *We Are Everywhere* (NY, Harper & Row, 1971)

Sanders, Ed: *Investigative Poetry* (San Francisco, City Lights, 1976)

Sanders, Ed: *Tales of Beatnik Glory* (NY, Stonehill, 1975)

Sanders, Ed: *Shards of God* (NY, Grove, 1970)

(Singh, Ravi [Ed.]): Smith, Harry: *Think of the Self Speaking, Selected Interviews* (Seattle, Elbow/Cityful,1999)

Snyder, Don: *Aquarian Odyssey* (NY, Liveright, 1979)

Solomon, David (Ed.): *The Marihuana Papers* (Indianapolis, Bobbs-Merrill, 1966)

Spitz, Robert: *Barefoot In Babylon, the Creation of the Woodstock Festival* (NY, Viking, 1979)

Stafford, Peter: *Psychedelic Baby Reaches Puberty* (NY, Praeger, 1971)

Stansill, Peter & Mairowitz, David: *Bamn, Outlaw Manifestos* (Harmondsworth, Penguin, 1971)

Taylor, Derek: *It Was 20 Years Ago Today* (London, Bantam, 1987)

Turner, Florence: *At The Chelsea* (London, Hamish Hamilton, 1986)

Warhol, Andy & Hackett, Pat: *POPism, the Warhol 60s* (NY, Harcourt Brace Jovanovich, 1980)

Whitehead, Peter: *Wholly Communion* (London, Lorrimer, 1965)

Whitmer, Peter: *Aquarius Revisited* (NY, Macmillan, 1987)

Willett, John (Ed.): *Astronauts of Inner-Space* (San Francisco, Stolen Paper, 1966)

Williams, Paul: *Pushing Upwards* (NY, Links, 1973)

Wolfe, Burton: *The Hippies* (NY, Signet, 1968)

Wolfe, Tom: *The Electric Cool Aid Acid Test* (NY, Farrar Straus and Giroux, 1968)

Youth International Party: *Blacklisted News, Secret History Chicago to 1984* (NY, Bleeker, 1983)

Zaroulis, Nancy & Sullivan, Gerald: *Who Spoke Up?* (NY, Holt Rinehart, 1984)

Biographies and Monographs:
William Seward Burroughs

Ansen, Alan: *William Burroughs* (Sudbury, Water Row, 1986)

Bockris, Victor: *With William Burroughs, A report From The Bunker* (NY, Seaver, 1981)

Caveney, Graham: *The 'Priest', They Called Him, The Life and Legacy of William S. Burroughs* (London, Bloomsbury, 1997)

Goodman, Michael: *Contemporary Literary Censorship, A Case History of Burroughs' Naked Lunch* (Metuchen, N.J., Scarecrow, 1981)

Goodman, Michael: *William S. Burroughs, An Annotated Bibliography* (NY, Garland, 1975)

Goodman, Michael (w/Coley, Lemuel): *William S. Burroughs. A Reference Guide* (NY, Garland, 1990)

Gysin, Brion: [w/Wilson, Terry] *Here To Go, Planet R–101* (San Francisco, Re/Search, 1982)

Gysin, Brion: *Brion Gysin Let The Mice In* (West Glover, VT, Something Else, 1973)

Loydell, Rupert (Ed.): *my kind of angel. i.m. william burroughs* (Exeter, Devon, Stride Conversation, 1998)

Lydenberg, Robin: *Word Cultures, Radical Theory And Practice In William S. Burroughs' Fiction* (Urbana, University of Illinois, 1987)

Maynard, Joe & Miles, Barry: *William S. Burroughs, A Bibliography 1953–1973* (Charlottesville, University of Virginia, 1978)

Mahoney, Denis; Martin, Richard; Whitehead, Ron (Eds): *A Burroughs Compendium* (Watch Hill, R.I., Ring Tarigh, 1998)

Miles, Barry: *A Catalogue of the William S. Burroughs Archive* (Ollon, Suisse and London, Covent Garden, 1973)

Miles, Barry: *William Burroughs, El Hombre Invisible* (London, Virgin, 1992)

Morgan, Ted: *Literary Outlaw, the Life and Times of William S. Burroughs* (NY, Henry Holt, 1988)

Mottram, Eric: *William Burroughs, The Algebra of Need* (London, Marion Boyars, 1977)

Murphy, Timothy: *Wising Up the Marks, the Amodern William Burroughs* (Berkeley, U of California, 1997)

Skerl, Jennie: *William S. Burroughs* (Boston, Twayne, 1985)

Sobieszek, Robert: *Ports of Entry: William S. Burroughs and the Arts* (Los Angeles, LA County Museum, 1996)

Neal Cassady

Cassady, Carolyn: *Neal In San Quentin* (Coventry, Beat Scene, nd.) Cassady, Neal: *The First Third* (San Francisco, City Lights, 1971, 1981 [expanded])

Cassady, Neal: *Grace Beats Karma, Letters From Prison 1958–1960* (NY, Blast, 1993)

Plummer, William: *The Holy Goof, A Biography of Neal Cassady* (Englewood Cliffs, NJ, Prentice-Hall, 1981)

Stephenson, Gregory: *Friendly & Flowing Savage* (Clarence Center, NY, Textile Bridge, 1987)

Gregory Corso

Skau, Michael: 'A Clown in a Grave', Complexities and Tensions in the Works of Gregory Corso* (Carbondale, Southern Illinois U.P., 1999)

Stephenson, Gregory: *Exiled Angel, a Study of the Work of Gregory Corso* (London, Hearing Eye, 1989)

Wilson, Robert: *A Bibliography of Works by Gregory Corso* (NY, Phoenix, 1966)

The Riverside Interviews: 3 Gregory Corso (London, Binnacle, 1983)

Lawrence Ferlinghetti

Cherkovski, Neeli: *Ferlinghetti, A Biography* (Garden City, Doubleday, 1979)

Silensky, Barry: *Ferlinghetti, the Artist in His Time* (NY, Warner, 1990)

Smith, Larry: *Lawrence Ferlinghetti, Poet At Large* (Carbondale, Southern Illinois University, 1983)

Allen Ginsberg

Dowden, George: *A Bibliography of Works by Allen Ginsberg, October, 1943 to July 1, 1967* (San Francisco, City Lights, 1971)

Hyde, Lewis (Ed.): *On The Poetry Of Allen Ginsberg* (Ann Arbor, University of Michigan Press, 1984)

Kramer, Jane: *Allen Ginsberg In America* (NY, Random House, 1969)

Kraus, Michelle P: *Allen Ginsberg, An Annotated Bibliography 1969–1977* (Metuchen, NJ, Scarecrow, 1980)

McBride, Dick: *Cometh With Clouds* (Memory: Allen Ginsberg) (Cherry Valley, NY, Cherry Valley, 1982)

Miles, Barry: *Ginsberg, A Biography* (NY, Simon & Schuster, 1989)

Miles, Barry: *Two Lectures on the Work of Allen Ginsberg* (London, Turret Papers, 1992)

Morgan, Bill & Rosenthal, Bob: *Best Minds, A Tribute to Allen Ginsberg* (NY, Lospecchio, 1986)

Morgan, Bill & Rosenthal, Bob: *Kanreki, A Tribute to Allen Ginsberg Part 2* (NY, Lospecchio, 1986)

Morgan, Bill: *The Response To Allen Ginsberg 1926–1994. A Bibliography of Secondary Sources* (Westport, CT, Greenwood, 1996)

Morgan, Bill: *The Works of Allen Ginsberg 1941–1994, A Descriptive Bibliography* (Westport, CT, Greenwood, 1995)

Mottram, Eric: *Allen Ginsberg in the Sixties* (Brighton, Unicorn, nd [1972])

Mottram, Eric: *The Wild Good and the Heart Ultimately: Ginsberg's Art Of Persuasion* (London, Spanner, 1978 [as *Spanner* v. 2 No. 5])

Portugés, Paul: *The Visionary Poetics of Allen Ginsberg* (Santa Barbara, Ross-Erikson, 1978)

Schumacher, Michael: *Dharma Lion, A Biography of Allen Ginsberg* (NY, St. Martins, 1992)

Sinclair, Iain: *The Kodak Mantra Diaries* (London, Albion Village, 1971)

Jack Kerouac

Amburn, Ellis: *Subterranean Kerouac* (NY, St Martins, 1998)

Beaulieu, Victor-Lévy: *Jack Kerouac, A Chicken Essay* (Toronto, Coach House, 1979)

Cassady, Carolyn: *Off the Road, Twenty Years With Cassady, Kerouac and Ginsberg* (London, Black Spring, 1990)

Challis, Chris: *Quest For Kerouac* (London, Faber & Faber, 1984)

Charters, Ann: *A Bibliography of Works By Jack Kerouac* (NY, Phoenix, 1967 and 1975 [revised])

Charters, Ann: *Kerouac* (NY, Warner, 1973 and 1974 [revised])

Christy, Jim: *The Long Slow Death of Jack Kerouac* (Toronto, ECW, 1998)

Clark, Tom: *Jack Kerouac* (NY, Harcourt Brace Jovanovich, 1984)

Eaton, V.J. (Ed.): *Catching Up With Kerouac* (Nesa, AZ, The Literary Denim, 1984)

Coolidge, Clark, et al: *Lowell Connector: Lines and Shots from Kerouac's Town* (West Stockbridge, MA, Hard, 1993)

Dorfner, John: *Kerouac: Visions of Lowell* (Raleigh, NC, Cooper Street, 1993)

Gifford, Barry & Lee, Lawrence: *Jack's Book* (NY, St Martin's, 1978)

Hipkiss, Robert A.: *Jack Kerouac, Prophet Of The New Romanticism* (Lawrence, Regents Press of Kansas, 1976)

Holmes, John C.: *Gone In October* (Hailey, IO, Limberlost, 1985)

Holmes, John C.: *Visitor: Jack Kerouac in Old Saybrook* (California, PA, Unspeakable Visions of the Individual, 1981)

Hunt, Tim: *Kerouac's Crooked Road* (Hamden, CT, Shoe String, 1981)

Jarvis, Charles E: *Visions of Kerouac* (Lowell, Mass, Ithica, 1973)

Knight, Arthur & Kit (Eds): *Kerouac and the Beats, A Primary Sourcebook* (NY, Paragon, 1988)

McDarrah, Fred: *Kerouac and Friends, A Beat Generation Album* (NY, William Morrow, 1985)

McNally, Dennis: *Desolate Angel, A Biography of Jack Kerouac* (NY, Random House, 1979)

Miles, Barry: *Jack Kerouac, King of the Beats* (London, Virgin, 1998)

Milewski, Robert: *Jack Kerouac: An Annotated Bibliography of Secondary Sources, 1944–1979* (Metuchen, NJ, Scarecrow, 1981)

Montgomery, John (Ed.): *Kerouac At The 'Wild Boar'* (San Anselmo, Fels & Firn, 1986)

Montgomery, John: *The Kerouac We Knew* (San Anselmo, CA, Fels & Firn, 1987)

Morton, J: *The Distance Instead . . . is the Feeling* (n.p. Dream of Jazz, 1986)

Nicosia, Gerald: *Memory Babe, A Critical Biography of Jack Kerouac* (NY, Grove, 1983)

Turner, Steve: *Jack Kerouac, Angelheaded Hipster* (London, Bloomsbury, 1996)

Weinreich, Regina: *The Spontaneous Poetics of Jack Kerouac* (Carbondale, Southern Illinois University, 1987)

Gary Snyder

Almon, Bert: *Gary Snyder* (Boise, Idaho, Boise State University, 1979)

Kherdian, David: *A Biographical Sketch and Descriptive Checklist of Gary Snyder* (Berkeley, Oyez, 1965)

McNeil, Katherine: *Gary Snyder, A Bibliography* (NY, Phoenix, 1983)

Acknowledgements

Beginning in 1982, in the course of my research for this book, I played back all the recordings I could find in Ginsberg's tape archives of conversations between Allen and his father, Louis. It came as a shock to find my own voice on a cassette from 1970, interviewing Louis about the Ginsberg family history in Newark before Allen was born. I was staying on Allen's farm in upstate New York, engaged in cataloguing his tape archives, when Louis, and Allen's stepmother, Edith, came for a vacation. It had seemed only natural to record Louis's memories. In a sense, then, I began researching this book three decades ago.

My acquaintance with Allen Ginsberg goes back even further. In 1965, he walked into the London bookshop I was managing. He needed a place to stay, so my wife and I put him up. Since then, he and I worked together on a number of projects. I produced spoken-word albums of two of his poetry readings in 1965, and published his Ankor Wat journals in *Long Hair* magazine – a literary magazine, named by Ginsberg, which I edited. Later in the 1960s, I produced his *William Blake's 'Songs of Innocence and Experience' Tuned by Allen Ginsberg*, which was released by MGM Records.

In 1970–71, I spent eighteen months cataloguing his tape archives and produced a sixteen-hour programme of the best available recording of each of his published poems. In the years I lived in New York City, I saw a lot of Allen, and later in the 1970s, he often stayed with me when he passed through London. During the winter of 1985–86, we worked together in New York, preparing the annotated edition of *Howl*, published by Harper & Row. Over the years I came to know many of his friends and members of his family. I therefore cannot claim complete impartiality, since I was present at many of the events I have written about in this book, and have been described in print as 'Ginsberg's advocate in Britain'. I tried to give as objective a view as possible of the events described, which meant, of course, that Allen and I did not always see eye to eye on what happened. The most contentious area was his involvement with Chogyam Trungpa, the subject of more than one argument.

Allen gave me complete access to his private papers and archives, and allowed me to interview him in depth. Allen was a pack-rat; he kept all the sixty-thousand plus letters he received throughout his life, and saved virtually all of his manuscripts, journals, notebooks, address books and doodles. For the last three decades he frequently tape-recorded his readings, lectures, his conversations with relatives and friends and, on occasion, his telephone conversations. His archive at Stanford includes faxes, photocopied for posterity, and floppy discs from the last period of his life. In addition to his voluminous correspondence over the years, from the mid-1960s onwards, he was one of the most interviewed men on earth.

Once I had established a rough draft of the book, Allen allowed me to begin questioning him about specifics that were unclear from his correspondence or from other people's recollections. He spent hours researching his own files to provide me with documents and photographs. He wrote to friends and relatives, answered questions in planes, taxicabs, buses, and on the Brooklyn Bridge, until at last he cried, 'I feel like I'm a robot being deprogrammed!' In a sense he was right; it was my prime intention to gather the facts for posterity. The main sources for this book, then, were threefold: Ginsberg's three hundred or so largely unpublished journals, his extensive correspondence with friends and family, and my interviews with Allen and his friends.

His criterion in authorising the book was that I could say what I wanted about him. He did, however, want to review my remarks about his friends for accuracy and in fear of invading their privacy, since much of my information about them was taken from his unpublished journals. I readily agreed to this. It was a tribute to his belief in the freedom of expression that he did not ask for a final veto over the book's contents. He read the final draft manuscript and made hundreds of suggestions. He corrected my chronology of his childhood, suggested new approaches to his relationship with his mother, disagreed violently with my interpretation of his visit to Cuba in 1965, and offered a great deal of new material on his relationship with Chogyam Trungpa. I used many of his suggestions, mostly as additions, and corrected the factual errors he identified. We agreed to differ over Cuba, and years later he wrote to me with an apology concerning one of our arguments over Tibet – he had found a new source of information which supported my argument.

When the book was published, he gave me an annotated copy, to use specifically in a future update 'when I'm dead'. He felt ambivalent about having a biography and a biographer. He enjoyed being able to telephone me to ask which year he worked in the Empire State Building, or the date his mother died, and took mischievous pleasure in being able to use me as a way of airing views he dared not speak himself for fear of upsetting old friends: 'Ho ho, Ferlinghetti's gonna be hopping mad when he reads this!' (It was a mild criticism of *City Lights*, which was struggling to avoid being swamped by Allen's ceaseless editorial suggestions.) On the down side, he was peeved at my attitude toward Trungpa, whom I knew from London, before he set up his kingdom in the States. He also thought I should give more credence to his political views, which I sometimes thought naive. In fact there was nowhere near enough space to deal with most of Allen's political campaigns, which have only just been touched upon here.

When I visited New York, we would have dinner, go to art shows or a movie. I continued to gather material on Allen's life, always intending to update the biography. I was privileged to be one of the people he telephoned the day before he went into his final coma. We talked for a long time, more than an hour, and much of the information he gave me then, I have used here.

In the five years it took to first write this book, an enormous number of people helped me by granting interviews, locating documents and photographs, extending hospitality, and suggesting ideas. I wish to thank: Richard Aaron, Simon Albury, Tsultrim Allioni, Jerry Aronson, Gordon Ball, Annabel Bartlett, Mary Beach, the late Julian Beck, Hazel Bennington, Ann Biderman, the late Peggy Biderman, Rick Blume, Eugene Brooks, Pete Brown, Michael Brownstein, the late William S. Burroughs, Lucien Carr, Carolyn Cassady, Simon Caulkin, Chris Challis, Ann Charters, Ira Cohen, Gregory Corso, Raymond Danowski, David Dawson, Ellie Dorfman, Valerie Estes, Larry Fagin, Mick Farren, Rosebud Felieu-Pettet, Lawrence Ferlinghetti, the late Rick Fields, James Fox, Raymond Foye, Robert Frank, Joseph Geraci, Edith Ginsberg, the late Louis Ginsberg, John Giorno, Jeff Goldberg, the late Albert Goldman, James Grauerholz, Theo Green, the late Brion Gysin, Igor Hajek, Peter Hale, Michael Henshaw, John Herman, Stellan Holm, Michael Horovitz, Jerry Howard, John Howe, Robert Jackson, Kathy John, Ted Jones, Terry Karten, Harvey Kubernik, Tony Lacey, Charles Landry, the late Harold Landry, Jay Landesman, the late Timothy Leary, Jean-Jacques Lebel, Edith Levy, Juanita Lieberman, Leo and Hannah Litzky, Colin McCabe, the late Linda McCartney, Paul McCartney, Patrick MacMullen, Gerard Malanga, Judith Malina, Mark and Anita Mannes, Pearce Marchbank, the late Felicity Mason, Steve Mass, Michael McClure, Legs McNeil, Susan Miles, Laury and Elizabeth Minard, Adrian Mitchell, Marko Modiano, Stuart Montgomery, Ted Morgan, the late Sterling Morrison, the late Eric Mottram, Shig Murao, Hank O'Neal, Julius Orlovsky, the late Edie Parker-Kerouac, Claude Pelieu, Jim Perrizo, Nancy Peters, Tom Pickard, Fernanda Pivano, Joyce Ravid, Randy Roark, Aram and Gailyn Saroyan, Michael Schumacher, Andrew Sclanders, Gavin Selerie, Joseph Skvorecky, the late Harry Smith, Gary Snyder, the late Carl Solomon, Vicki Stanbury, the late John Steinbeck, Jr., Bernard Stone, Steven Taylor, Lionel Tiger, Simon Vinkenoog, Jeffrey Vogel, Anne Waldman, Barry Wallenstein, Regina Weinreich, Philip Whalen, Damon Wise and Peter Wollen.

Ginsberg's correspondence has been preserved in rare book libraries across the United States. I would like to thank the following for their valuable assistance: Marilyn Wurzburger and her staff at the Special Collections dept of the Hayden Library, Arizona State University, Tempe;

Mary Angelotti at the Beinecke Rare Book and Manuscript Library of Yale University; Michael Davidson, Director of the Archive for New Poetry at the University of California, San Diego; James Davis, Rare Books Librarian, University of California, Los Angeles; Robert J. Bertholf, Curator, The Poetry/Rare Books Collection, State University of New York at Buffalo; Barbara A. Filipac, Manuscripts Division, Brown University Library; Timothy D. Murray, Curator of Manuscripts, Washington University In St Louis; Anthony S. Bliss, Rare Book Librarian, Bancroft Library, University of California at Berkeley; Robert A. Hull, Manuscripts Department, University of Virginia Library; Saundra Taylor, Curator of Manuscripts, Indiana University; J. Fraser Cocks, Curator, Special Collections, Miller Library, Colby College; Kevin F. McKelvey, Special Collections, Mugar Library, Boston University; George Butterick, Curator, Literary Archives, University of Connecticut; Alexandra Mason, Department of Special Collections, Kenneth Spencer Research Library, University of Kansas. Special thanks are due to the staff of the Fales Library of New York University, the staff of the Harry Ransom Humanities Research Center, University of Texas at Austin, and particularly to Kenneth A. Lohf, Director of Manuscripts and Rare Books, Bernard Crystal, Assistant Director and their staff at the Special Collections Divison, Butler Library, Columbia University. Since this book was first published, Ginsberg's archives have been sold to the Department of Special Collections, Green Library, Stanford University Libraries. I am greatly indebted to William McPheron, William Saroyan Curator for British and American Literature, and his staff, and also to Margaret Kimball, University Archivist, for their friendly assistance, and for making my stay in Palo Alto a pleasant one.

I owe an enormous debt to my friend Victor Bockris for his limitless hospitality; to Bobbie Bristol for her editorial suggestions and friendship; to Felix Dennis for being a stalwart friend; to Ginsberg's bibliographer, Bill Morgan, for his archive research and his many useful suggestions; to Peter Orlovsky for his helpful assistance over the years; to Ginsberg's secretary, Bob Rosenthal, for hours of valuable research and conversation; to my friend and agent, Andrew Wylie, for first suggesting the book and then seeing it through, and to the staff at the Wylie Agency, in particular Jeffrey Posternak and Rose Billington; to my editors at Simon and Schuster, Fred Hills and Burton Beals, and copy editor Marge Horvitz, who worked long hours over this book; to Humphrey Price, my editor at Virgin Books; to my wife, Rosemary Bailey, whose expert editorial eye read every draft, for her unstinting support throughout; and of course, to the late Allen Ginsberg, for agreeing to the project.

Index